# HARBRACE
# COLLEGE
# READER

*Fourth Edition*

**MARK SCHORER**
*University of California*
*Berkeley*

**PHILIP DURHAM**
*University of California*
*Los Angeles*

**EVERETT L. JONES**
*University of California*
*Los Angeles*

# HARBRACE COLLEGE READER

*Fourth Edition*

HARCOURT BRACE JOVANOVICH, INC.

*New York / Chicago*
*San Francisco / Atlanta*

© 1959, 1964, 1968, 1972 by Harcourt Brace Jovanovich, Inc.

All rights reserved. No part of this publication may be reproduced or transmitted in any form or by any means, electronic or mechanical, including photocopy, recording, or any information storage and retrieval system, without permission in writing from the publisher.

ISBN: 0-15-532411-X

Library of Congress Catalog Card Number: 76-188369
*Printed in the United States of America*

# PREFACE

The *Harbrace College Reader,* Fourth Edition, attempts to meet the needs of students in reading, rhetoric, and composition courses. Those elements of the previous editions that proved most successful in the classroom have been retained—the organization; the extensive, flexible program of exercises; the effective and durable selections.

Twenty-five selections are new to the fourth edition, which is somewhat longer than some of its predecessors. From first to last—from the bravura of Norman Mailer's visit to NASA's Manned Spacecraft Center to Abraham Kaplan's brilliant analysis of the popular arts—the new selections should interest and stimulate today's students, for this edition inevitably reflects many of their problems and attitudes. Thus, many of the new essays are inescapably contemporary in subject, stance, and diction and deal with students' primary concerns, including the recent continuing flux in moral and esthetic standards.

For both teachers and students, the *Harbrace College Reader* has a number of advantages:

*First,* it contains a wide range of material. Included are some familiar selections, classic and contemporary, that have proved peculiarly valuable for the purposes of English courses. The editors had no strong desire to be the first to lay the old aside. They have not hesitated, however, to be the first to try the new, and the book contains much that is fresh and timely, never before anthologized. Almost all the selections are expository; all have been chosen for their intrinsic interest, literary merit, or value as illustrations of a particular style, approach, or technique.

*Second,* this book can help students develop essential reading skills. The exercises are clearly labeled. Some test comprehension of vocabulary and content; others bring out the assumptions underlying each essay and the implications of what is said. The suggestions for class discussion and student writing encourage independent critical evaluation of the selections. Most important, the book contains good reading.

*Third,* this book can help students develop essential writing skills. Through the exercises, students come to recognize patterns of organization, types of paragraph development, the strength and complexity of many kinds of style, and the rich resources of the English language. The instructor can easily select those exercises that are most valuable for illustrating a particular principle or technique.

*Fourth,* it respects the ingenuity of the instructor. To him it offers a wealth of material together with complete freedom of selection. Although the essays are grouped in ways that many may find useful, they are completely independent of one another. All may be used for a program of extensive reading, or a few may be chosen for intensive analysis and discussion. The last may be first or the first last. Nothing in the book imposes a particular organization or emphasis upon the course. The exercises are so organized that the instructor can easily find and select only those that are directly relevant to what the class is studying. He may, for instance, choose only exercises that supplement class discussion of sentence structure or of paragraph development or rhetorical devices.

*Fifth,* this book respects and challenges the abilities of students. It recognizes that students who have undertaken college work have chosen, whether they fully realize it or not, to undertake the hard discipline of intelligent reading and careful writing. This book can help introduce them to both.

The preparation of this new edition has been a pleasant and instructive labor for the editors. We have been aided by suggestions from scores of teachers—more, unfortunately, than can be thanked individually. We also gratefully acknowledge the clerical assistance of Patti Hartman, Gloria Lester, Pauline Ward, and Patricia Yongue.

*Mark Schorer*

*Philip Durham*

*Everett L. Jones*

# SUGGESTIONS FOR USE
# OF THE EXERCISES

The exercises accompanying the essays in Parts 1 and 2 of this book can be used to encourage careful reading, to assist in the study of diction, sentence structure, and paragraph organization, and to provoke meaningful discussion and writing.

Part 1 contains models of narration, description, exposition, and argumentation, as well as examples of carefully prepared research papers. The exercises accompanying these essays are designed both to require intensive reading and to emphasize the peculiar problems and techniques of each kind of discourse.

But the exercises also permit an entirely different approach. Thus classes studying diction, usage, or use of the dictionary and other common reference tools may devote much of their time to exercises grouped under the heading *Words*. Classes studying problems of sentence structure as well as techniques of emphasis, coherence, and style may turn to exercises grouped under the heading *Sentences*. Classes studying organization and development of paragraphs and larger units of composition may most profitably use the exercises grouped under *Paragraphs* and *Content and Organization*.

Although these headings appear in every group of exercises, some essays are especially well suited to a particular kind of analysis or study. The following suggestions may be useful.

## WORDS

Among the exercises well suited for study of diction, etymology, and dictionary use are the following:

*meaning* "Life on the Mississippi 1970," p. 111; "The Unbanning of the Books," p. 123; "Langston Hughes's Jesse B. Semple: The Urban Negro as Wise Fool," p. 186; "Whose Country Is America?" p. 298; "Call This an Era?" p. 398.

*relationships*   "On Various Kinds of Thinking," p. 133.

*choice and exactness*   "The Block and Beyond," p. 84; "Call This an Era?" p. 398; "Brave Words for a Startling Occasion," p. 410.

*meaning, origin, and choice*   "Cocksure Women and Hensure Men," p. 160; "Stranger in the Village," p. 311; "On Privacy: The American Dream, What Happened to It?" p. 333.

Five essays are themselves discussions of different aspects of diction and usage:

*impact and connotation*   "Brave Words for a Startling Occasion," p. 410.

*choice and exactness*   "No Telling, No Summing Up," p. 401; "Politics and the English Language," p. 415.

*meaning and origin*   "Of Speech," p. 428.

*diction*   "Call This an Era?" p. 398.

## SENTENCES

Among the exercises well suited for study of sentence construction, rhetorical devices, and style are the following:

*style*   "The Ant War," p. 41; "When I Knew Stephen Crane," p. 77; "In Defense of Editing," p. 174.

*emphasis*   "In Defense of Editing," p. 174; "The Dark of the Moon," p. 387.

*rhetorical devices*   "The Cradle," p. 45; "The Unbanning of the Books," p. 123; "The Theory of Unconscious Creation," p. 200; "Whose Country Is America?" p. 298; "Population and Environment," p. 345; "Brave Words for a Startling Occasion," p. 410; "Looking Back on the Seventies," p. 451.

*style and rhetorical devices*   "Scott Fitzgerald," p. 14; "No Telling, No Summing Up," p. 401.

*parallelism*   "The Block and Beyond," p. 84; "Stranger in the Village," p. 311.

## PARAGRAPHS

Among the exercises well suited for study of paragraph coherence and development are the following:

*coherence*   "In Defense of Editing," p. 174; "A Valedictory," p. 241; "The Method of Scientific Investigation," p. 390; "Brave Words for a Startling Occasion," p. 410.

*unity, coherence, topic sentence, methods of development*   "The University Had Better Mind Its Own Business," p. 216; "No Telling, No Summing Up," p. 401.

## CONTENT AND ORGANIZATION

Among the exercises well suited for study of organization and development of themes and essays are the following:

*central ideas*   "A Valedictory," p. 241; "Why They Read Hesse," p. 435; "Looking Back on the Seventies," p. 451.

*organization*   "Los Angeles Notebook," p. 52; "The Spider and the Wasp," p. 88; "A Generation in Search of a Future," p. 164; "The Uniqueness of Man," p. 364.

*assumptions and implications*   "Of a Fire on the Moon," p. 2; "Scott Fitzgerald," p. 14; "Female Biology in a Male Culture," p. 151; "The Ecologist at Bay," p. 358.

For sophisticated discussion of the contents, problems, and organization of particular forms, six essays deserve special mention:

*criticism*   "Why They Read Hesse," p. 435; "Looking Back on the Seventies," p. 451.

*drama*   "Tragedy and the Common Man," p. 465.

*prose fiction*   "Preface to *The Spoils of Poynton*," p. 526.

*poetry*   "Robert Frost: The Way to a Poem," p. 470; "A Few Words of a Kind," p. 481.

## SUGGESTIONS FOR DISCUSSION

Every essay in the first two sections of the book is followed by *Suggestions for Discussion*, which vary widely in difficulty and challenge. Some are rather simple questions calling for straightforward reporting of experience and ideas. Others require reading and investigation. All, however, require thought and effort.

# TABLE OF
# CONTENTS

## part 1 READINGS FOR ANALYSIS

### Reporting What Happened

### Describing Persons, Places, and Things

### Explaining Facts and Ideas

### Persuading Other People

# RHETORICAL
# TABLE OF CONTENTS

The essays in Part 1 of this book are grouped by broad rhetorical genres—essentially narration, description, exposition, and argumentation. The essays in Part 2 are grouped by subject. Those in Part 3 are arranged in modified chronological order. These different arrangements have important advantages for certain kinds of discussion and for studies of the development of modern prose style.

This table of contents is included so that teachers have before them a rhetorical breakdown of the entire book. Since most authors employ many different techniques, the classification of these essays is necessarily arbitrary and frequently debatable. One essay, Francis Bacon's "Of Studies," is both so brief and so complex that it defies classification and is omitted from this analysis. Six essays incorporate such a variety of techniques that they are listed under *Explanation*. A few other essays are grouped under *Criticism and Interpretation,* an admittedly unusual heading for a rhetorical table of contents.

## Argument and Persuasion

## Satire and Humor

## Criticism and Interpretation

*part* 1
# READINGS
# FOR ANALYSIS

# Reporting What Happened

*To report what has happened or what might have happened is the purpose of much journalism, scholarship, and literature. But good reporting is more than the simple narration of events in time. Always it is informed by the writer's purpose—his desire to entertain, to move, to explain, to interpret, or to persuade.*

*The five essays that follow differ greatly from one another in subject matter, in purpose, in difficulty, and in effect. A well-known novelist engages in highly personal journalism, linking himself and his recent past to the nation's preparations to land men on the moon. Two of America's greatest writers meet for the first time, and one of them describes a strange trip in France; the other remembers the exultation of his first great success. Red and black ants fight a war near Walden Pond in Massachusetts, and a hunter makes his camp in Finnish Lapland. In some of these narratives the action is slight, but in all of them it has a larger significance. Sometimes that significance is explained; sometimes it is implicit in the narrative. Always it is made clear by a skillful writer.*

## Norman Mailer

## OF A FIRE ON THE MOON

1. Are we poised for a philosophical launch? There may be no way to do anything less. We will be trying after all to comprehend the astronauts. If we approach our subject via Aquarius, it is because he is a detective of sorts, and different in spirit from eight years ago. He has learned to live with questions. Of course, as always, he has little to do with the immediate spirit of the time. Which is why Norman on this occasion wonders if he may call himself Aquarius. Born January 31, he is entitled to the name, but he thinks it a fine irony that we now enter the Age of Aquarius since he has never had less sense of possessing the age. He feels in fact little more than

OF A FIRE ON THE MOON: Copyright © 1969, 1970 by Norman Mailer. From *Of a Fire on the Moon* by Norman Mailer, by permission of Little, Brown and Co.

a decent spirit, somewhat shunted to the side. It is the best possible position for detective work.

2.  Forgive him, then, if he takes mild pleasure in conjunction of dates. John F. Kennedy had made his declaration concerning the moon not six weeks before Hemingway was dead. The nation, Kennedy decided, "should commit itself to achieving the goal, before this decade is out, of landing a man on the moon and returning him safely to the earth. . . . This is a new ocean, and I believe the United States must sail upon it." Presumably, the moon was not listening, but if, in fact, she were the receiving and transmitting station of all lunacy, then she had not been ignoring the nation since. Four assassinations later; a war in Vietnam later; a burning of Black ghettos later; hippies, drugs and many student uprisings later; one Democratic Convention in Chicago seven years later; one New York school strike later; one sexual revolution later; yes, eight years of a dramatic, near-catastrophic, outright spooky decade later, we were ready to make the moon. It was a decade so unbalanced in relation to previous American history that Aquarius, who had begun it by stabbing his second wife in 1960, was to finish by running in a Democratic Primary for Mayor of New York during the hottest May and June he could ever recall. In sixty days he must have made three hundred speeches, he appeared on more radio and television than he could remember, walked streets, shook hands, sometimes two or three thousand hands a day, worked fourteen hours a day, often sixteen, went on four and five hours sleep, and awoke on many a morning with the clear and present certainty that he was going to win. Norman was lazy, and politics would make him work for sixteen hours a day the rest of his life. He was so guilty a man that he thought he would be elected as a fit and proper punishment for his sins. Still, he also wanted to win. He would never write again if he were Mayor (the job would doubtless strain his talent to extinction) but he would have his hand on the rump of history, and Norman was not without such lust.

3.  He came in fourth in a field of five, and politics was behind him. He had run, when he considered it, no very remarkable race. He had obviously not had any apocalyptic ability to rustle up huge numbers of votes. He had in fact been left with a huge boredom about himself. He was weary of his own voice, own face, person, persona, will, ideas, speeches, and general sense of importance. He felt not unhappy, mildly depressed, somewhat used up, wise, tolerant, sad, void of vanity, even had a hint of humility. Somewhat disembodied spirit. He burned something in his soul those eight

weeks of campaigning, but he was not certain just what he might have squandered. Nonetheless, he might be in superb shape to study the flight of Apollo 11 to the moon. For he was detached this season from the imperial demands of his ego; he could think about astronauts, space, space programs, and the moon, quite free of the fact that none of these heroes, presences, and forces were by any necessity friendly to him. No, he felt like a spirit of some just-consumed essence of the past, and so finally took the liberty to christen himself Aquarius. It was the perfect name for a man who would begin the study of rockets. The water-bearer traversed the earth and breathed the air: three elements were his medium, solid, liquid, and gas. That was kin to the rocket. Apollo 11 would leave the earth, travel on the combustion of its liquids, and traverse a space. What indeed was space but the final decompression of a gas? On such unscientific thoughts did Norman, sign of Aquarius, travel.

4. In the middle of his Mayoralty campaign, a story had appeared whose small headlines stated that he would receive a million dollars for doing a book about the astronauts. It was a peculiar story, because the sums listed in the journalistic details added up to $450,000, and this second figure, while certainly too generous, was not vastly inaccurate. Actually, Aquarius would be lucky if he were left with any real money at all, for he was in debt from having made three movies (for which he had put up the cash himself) and he calculated that with the restitution of consequent borrowings, and the payment of taxes, he would have enough to live and think for a year. Not so bad. He had only to write a book about the moon shot. Small matter. It would be as easy to go to the Amazon to study moon rocks as to write a book about these space matters, foreign to him, which everyone would agree is worth a million dollars. In fact everyone thought he was worth a million dollars already. Contributions for his campaign to the Mayoralty stopped on the instant the story appeared. He did not know whether to bless the gods, the *Times,* or somebody in the office of his agent.

5. Of course, he was not displeased that everyone thought a quick book by him—magazine, hard-cover, paperback, foreign rights, and syndication—was worth a million. While Aquarius had never been accorded the respect he thought he deserved as a novelist, he had been granted in compensation the highest praise as a journalist. People he had never met were forever declaring in print that he was the best journalist in America. He thought it was the superb irony of his professional life, for he knew he was not even a good jour-

nalist and possibly could not hold a top job if he had to turn in a story every day. He had known such journalists, and their work was demanding. They had first of all to have enormous curiosity, and therefore be unable to rest until they found out the secret behind even the smallest event. Since Aquarius had long built his philosophical world on the firm conviction that nothing was finally knowable (an exact and proper recompense to having spent his formative years and young manhood in searching for the true nature of women) he had almost no interest in the small secret behind a small event. (There was invariably another secret behind that.) He preferred to divine an event through his senses—since he was as nearsighted as he was vain, he tended to sniff out the center of a situation from a distance. So his mind often stayed out of contact with the workings of his brain for days at a time. When it was time, lo and behold, he seemed to have comprehended the event. That was one advantage of using the nose—technology had not yet succeeded in elaborating a science of smell.

6.    But calculate for yourself the small ails and woes which came upon Aquarius when he went to visit the NASA Manned Spacecraft Center in Houston two weeks after the conclusion of his Mayoralty campaign. The first and most unhappy truth was that there were no smells coming out of NASA. It was hardly the terrain for Aquarius.

7.    He had grown up in New York. He understood cities, particularly big cities, he had looked forward to getting to know a little of Houston—now, draw near to his vast pleasure in discovering that the Manned Spacecraft Center was not in Houston at all, but located about twenty-five miles south in the middle of that flat anonymous and near to tree-impoverished plain which runs in one undistinguished and not very green stretch from Houston to Galveston. Farther east as he would soon discover was Seabrook, Kemah, and Texas City south of that, then Galveston on the Gulf. Raunchy, sexy, hot and brooding, houses on stilts and old shacks—that was the Gulf of Mexico. He liked it. If he lived there, he too would write like Tennessee Williams. Tennessee, he discovered by this visit, was a natural and simple recorder of the elements.

8.    All that, however, was miles away. MSC (the Manned Spacecraft Center) was located on a tract of many acres, flat and dry as a parking lot, and at the moment of entering the gate past the guard, there was no way to determine whether one was approaching an industrial complex in which computers and electronic equipment were fashioned, or traveling into a marvelously up-to-date minimum-

security prison, not a clue to whether one was visiting the largest insurance and financing corporation which had ever decided to relocate itself in the flatlands behind a fence, or if this geometrically ordered arrangement of white modern buildings, severe, ascetic, without ornament, nearly all of two or three stories but for an Administration Building of eight stories, was indeed the newest and finest kind of hospital for radiological research. But, perhaps it was a college campus, one of those miserable brand-new college campuses with buildings white as toothpaste, windows set in aluminum casements, paths drawn by right angle or in carefully calculated zigzag to break the right angle, and a general air of studies in business administration, a college campus in short to replace the one which burned in the last revolution of the students.

9.   In fact, it was the Manned Spacecraft Center, MSC, the home of the astronauts, the place where they were given the bulk of their training in Mission Simulators and Docking Simulators, the Center from which Mission Control would direct and collaborate on their flights, the astronauts' brain on earth, to nail it thus crudely, when they were up in space. And if this assembly of buildings looked as we have said like the worst of future college campuses, all-but-treeless, milk-of-magnesia white, and composed of many windowless buildings and laboratories which seemed to house computers, and did! why the error was in fact natural. For when Lyndon Johnson, then Vice President, succeeded in getting the unmistakable plum of the new Manned Spacecraft Center located in Texas on land he just happened to know about south of Houston owned by some nice fellows named Humble (Humble Oil & Refining) and ready for the Federal Government to purchase reasonable—reasonable a word capable of being reasoned and expanded with upon occasion—why this purchase might even have a clause inserted that the buildings to be constructed must be capable, in the event of the demise of NASA and the Space Program, of being converted without difficulty into an adjunct of Rice University in Houston. Could it be a crypto-campus after all! Let no one say that Lyndon Johnson was not a super local patriot always working for TALC (Texas Association for the Advancement of Local Culture).

10.   Recognize then how much this Manned Spacecraft Center would honor Aquarius' sense of smell. Outside the Spacecraft Center, he could not say that his situation was improved. The immediate suburb, Nassau Bay, which housed many of the technicians, engineers, and executives in NASA, was situated on the other side of NASA Highway 1 from MSC, and was built around a body of water

called Clear Lake. Nassau Bay and adjoining suburbs like it were all new, their roads laid out in winding turns so absent of surprise that you could recognize they came off the French curve of the draftsman. If these homes were architecturally reasonable, built in sedate earth colors for the most part, charcoal browns, subdued clay-orange, stone-colored tans, houses which were modern but restrained adaptations for the most part of Swiss chalets, Tudor and Elizabethan, with hints of hacienda and ranch corral, they were nonetheless without flavor or odor. Aquarius was discovering that we cherish the sense of smell because it gives us our relation to time. We know how old something is by its odor; its youth, its becoming and its decay are subtly compounded to tell us at once— if we dare to contemplate mortality—how much time has been appropriated by such a life.

11. Nor were the people who worked for NASA bound to help him, since they were also by every evidence part of that vast convocation of Americans, probably a majority, whom one saw in New York only on television. They were, in short, Wasps, and it was part of the folklore of New York that Wasps were without odor. From the vantage point of New York, Wasps were already halfway to the moon, and devoted their efficiency to earning enough money to purchase large amounts of deodorant, depilatory, mouthwash, hair spray, and if they were ladies—Arrid. But these jokes are not very good. It would be tasteless to dwell on anybody's insulation from odor but for the fact that if this thesis is correct, if we honor or fear the presence of odors because they are a root to the past and an indication of the future, are indeed our very marriage to time and mortality, why then it is no accident that the Wasps were, in the view of Aquarius, the most Faustian, barbaric, draconian, progress-oriented, and root-destroying people on earth. They had divorced themselves from odor in order to dominate time, and thereby see if they were able to deliver themselves from death! No less! It is fiendish to get into such exaggeration so early, but think where Dr. Christiaan Barnard would be today if on the threshold of his first heart transplant, he had declared, "Nope, this organ ain't funky enough to make its new home happy!"

12. Obviously, then, if the great brain of NASA were attached to any particular sense, it was the eye. The eye was the collector of incontrovertible facts (which at MSC they called data-points). So the men who worked off NASA Highway 1 at the Manned Spacecraft Center were all clear-eyed and bullet-eyed and berry-eyed (pupils no larger than hard small acidic little berries) and they all

seemed to wear dark pants, short-sleeve button-down white shirts and somber narrow ties. They all had identification badges pinned to their shirt pockets and they wore them with pride. Practically all had straight hair, and most of them cut it close. Whether they were tall or short, they were rarely overweight, and the only distinction between them which enabled Aquarius to differentiate these engineers, technicians and young executives from one another was that many wore horn-rimmed glasses with dark frames, and these fellows were usually smaller, more sallow, and with that absolute lack of surface provocation, or idiosyncrasy of personality, which characterizes physicists, engineering students, statisticians, computer technicians, and many a young man of science. By accent, appearance, and manner they could have come from any part of America, although most, Aquarius judged, were from the Midwest.

13. The other category belonged in general to men who were taller, more athletic, meaner-looking, sunburned upon occasion—despite their hours of work in air-conditioned rooms—and had the contained anger and cool crisp manner of men who have domiciled their unruly and bust-out impulses: so they emit a sense of discipline, order, and unmistakably virile, if controlled, determination. Aquarius who, for all his forty-six years and wretched inability to lose weight, liked to keep a sense of his own virility—what more valuable possession had an artist?—was obliged somewhat ruefully to recognize that this second category of men were tough. They reminded him of the officers and enlisted men of the Texas outfit, the 112th Cavalry, in which he had served overseas during the war. So he took it for granted that these executives, athlete-engineers, hondos on Mission Control, aides or instructors for various astronaut training courses, and general troubleshooters were in the main from the Southwest. They had a lot of morale. They were so proud of NASA, the astronauts, the Command Module, Lem, the United States of America that their voices went husky a hint when they talked about such topics.

14. Yet both categories of men were absolutely helpful in every way. But in such a way that they were no help at all to Aquarius. There was a style at NASA he had begun to divine. Every question you asked was answered and the truth so far as he knew was always told. It was as if NASA, unlike other Government bureaus, had recognized why honesty is the best policy—it is simply because no intriguer will ever believe the truth which is presented to him, but will rather interpret it as a lie which only he can transform into the buried fact. The assumption is that honest men will come

to recognize your truth can make them strong. So everybody at NASA was courteous, helpful, generous of information, saintly at repeating the same information a hundred times, and subtly proud of their ability to serve interchangeably for one another, as if the real secret of their discipline and their strength and their sense of morale was that they had depersonalized themselves to the point where they were true Christians, gentle, helpful, replaceable, and serving on a messianic mission. The only flaw was that the conversation could only voyage through predetermined patterns. They would do their best to answer any technical question in the world, and voluminous mimeographings of NASA literature, often valuable enough to be classified, were available to all the Press. It was just that there was no way to suggest any philosophical meandering. Like real Americans, they always talked in code. It happened to be technological code. "The whole philosophy of power descent monitoring is that when the Pings [PGNCS] have degraded . . ." or "The bulk of Delta V is to kill his retrograde component." These were notes Aquarius picked out for himself after a half hour of talking to the Chief of Flight Operations Division, who would help to bring the Lem down to the surface of the moon, a hard green-eyed crew-cut man in his thirties named Gene Kranz who looked and talked like a professional football quarterback. And in fact his problems were not dissimilar. They arrived at the same rate of speed and were as massive. "During the first five minutes of descent," Kranz said, "the landing will be almost luxurious. But during the last three minutes, he'll be coming like Whistling Dixie." Behind Kranz as he spoke were the twenty-odd consoles and the forty-plus screens, the dull gray-green walls, the thirty-five square lights inset in the ceiling— the gray controlled environment of the Mission Control room. Kranz lived with phrases like Primary Guidance and Navigation Section and Abort Guidance Section (Pings and Ags), Service Modulator Controllers, Power Descent Information, Program Descent Rates, Sequential Events Control System, Time of Ephemeris Update, Transponder, he spoke of T Eff Em, and Reference Stable Member Matrix, of SMC, and PDI, SECST, the names and their related initials were used interchangeably—Kranz lived in a world of instruments and concepts which would take years for Aquarius to command well enough to make judgments on the other's character. Yes, real Americans always spoke in code. They encapsulated themselves into technological clans. Codes were like bloodlines. So they could be friendly and helpful and polite but they quietly separated themselves when their codes did not flourish. Aquarius was obliged to recognize that if the machine seemed a functional object to the artist, an instrument whose significance was that it was there to be used—as a typewriter was used for typing a manuscript—so to the engineer it was the communication itself which was functional. The machine was the art.

15. Perhaps for that reason, relations with these engineers reminded Aquarius of how he felt when he looked at the windowless walls of new buildings now sprouting all over the mean dry fields of the Space Center and the corporation developments outside the fence. These windowless buildings were as sinister to him as the arbitrary growth of ugly species of mushrooms in the middle of nowhere. These architectural fungoids were there to say: "Lo, we work in the electronics computeroid complex, and need no windows, for we are the architectural skull case for a new kind of brain."

16. Windowless, they also lack ears, so he cannot tell them, "My eyes are my windows."

17. "Recognize," the windowless walls say, "that something is taking over from you, kid."

18. He stayed in a motel surprising in its luxury on this Texas plain. He had two rooms, and one room had a private indoor pool four feet deep, seven feet long, and five feet wide, with a green light overhead. The other room had a full king-sized circular bed with a red velvet cover. He discovered on inquiry that the motel had been decorated by a new owner who hoped to attract honeymoon couples to memories of the deluxe in the middle of the flatlands. But the clientele continued to consist of engineers visiting MSC from corporations which did business with NASA. Aquarius had a picture of some of the engineers he had met, the ones with the lunar pallor, sleeping in the round red velvet-covered king-sized bed. As if to emphasize this conjunction of the two centuries, the red velvet of the Nineteenth and the gray transistors of the Twentieth, there was a club in the motel with two go-go girls and one of them walked off abruptly one night and went to the bar. When the bartender whispered to her, she went back to the platform, turned on the jukebox again, giggled and said to the technology-ridden air of her audience, "Shucks, I plumb forgot to take off my clothes."

19. She was a round sullen country girl. Aquarius saw her dance another night when she was full of relish for her work, slinging her breasts, undulating her belly on a river of cogitating promise— the voracity of her hip-sock suggested she was one real alligator, but then six of her friends were in from Houston and sitting in the center

seats, and they looked to have just gotten off their motorcycles. They were hardly from NASA.

20. There were exceptions to these uniform varieties of experience. He spent a night talking to Pete Conrad—Charles Conrad, Jr., the astronaut who would command Apollo 12 on the flight to the moon after Apollo 11—and it was not a bad night. Conrad was wiry, he was feisty, he could rap without too much of a look over his shoulder for the proprieties, and his wife Jane was sensationally attractive in a quiet way. They had four young and handsome sons, one of whom, Tommy, aged twelve, became famous forever in Aquarius' mind because he obliged a photographer by riding his bicycle off the slope of the garage roof right into the swimming pool. Norman was invited back to a party the Conrads gave for their neighbors, and he had a good time—it was a party like a night in Westchester, except that it was Texas, so he finally got into a bathing suit in order not to wrestle up and down the edge of the pool when enthusiasts were ready to throw him in. Agreeably drunk, he stood under the hot Texas night in the hot Texas pool, laughing with two Texas ladies—it was at least an approach to the sensate experience of the East. And the next day he remembered Conrad saying to him over the outdoor steak grill—"For six years I've been dreaming of going to the moon," and the moon—as a real and tangible companion of the mind—was suddenly there before him.

21. He saw Armstrong, Aldrin, and Collins through much of a long day they spent in press conferences with the newspapers, magazines, and the television networks, and he learned much. (In the absence of a sense of smell, the hairs in his nostrils began to quiver at clues.) He thought about astronauts often. He would probably be able to produce an interesting thought or two on the psychology of astronauts. He felt as if he had begun the study of a new world so mysterious to his detective's heart (all imaginative novelists, by this logic, are detectives) that he could only repeat what he had said on the day the assignment was first offered to him: it was that he hardly knew whether the Space Program was the noblest expression of the Twentieth Century or the quintessential statement of our fundamental insanity. It was after all the mark of insanity that its mode of operation was distinguished by its logic—insanity was often more logical than sanity when it came to attacking a problem.

22. Something of this question was in his mind when he talked to Dr. Gilruth, Robert R. Gilruth, Director of the Manned Spacecraft Center, but of course he did not pose the question directly and, if he had, would not have gotten an answer. Speculation was on no-

body's program at NASA. In any case, Gilruth was hardly one of the new technicians. A man in his late fifties, he had worked as a student under Piccard, the old balloonist, and had discovered the jet stream when a balloon built by his wife and himself was sent up in Minnesota and came down in Mississippi. This was the sort of story Gilruth had obviously told before to make an item in many a feature story, it was a way of keeping the interviewer away, and Aquarius recognized after a while that Dr. Gilruth was a man who had probably developed his official style in the Eisenhower period, in fact he looked like a mild version of Eisenhower in the mid-Fifties, he was half bald in about the same way, and had deep gentle sympathetic eyes which gave him almost a saintly appearance; he talked in a quiet voice in his large office high up in the Administration Building and therefore facing down on the rectilinear play of the campus walks and buildings. Aquarius looked for something charitable to say about the view, but that proved too hard to produce, so he tried to win Gilruth's confidence in other ways. But the good doctor was not particularly responsive to questions, which is to emphasize that he would take an ordinary question and go on at such length in his reply, rambling through such hesitancies—as if the act of speech were painful to him—that the next question was hardly spurred to appear. He was remarkably gentle and determinedly undistinguished, as if his deepest private view suggested that good administration and public communication were best kept apart. In this sense, he was certainly no proper representative of the NASA style, much rather like a Chinese mandarin—completely pleasant, altogether remote—it occurred that Eisenhower had also been a mandarin.

23. Just once did Aquarius reach him. He asked: "Are you ever worried, Dr. Gilruth, that landing on the moon may result in all sorts of psychic disturbances for us here on earth?" At the look of pain in Gilruth's eyes at the thought of mustering NASA-type answers for this sort of question, Aquarius went on quickly, "I mean, many people seem to react to the full moon, and there are tides of course."

24. He was not mistaken. As he stammered into silence, there was the breath of dread in the room. Just a hint, but his nostril quivered. Gilruth was feeling the same silence; he could swear to that. And Gilruth, when he answered, spoke gratefully of the tides and yes, they had an effect on geography and men's industry by the sea— no answer could have been more Eisenhooverian—but then as if the question held him also in its grip, Gilruth came out of this long

on to say that—*yes,* he had looked at some figures on the
and there seemed to be a higher incidence of hospital com-
reports of admission to mental institutions during the full
Dread in the room again, and a silence between the two
ich was exactly opposite to the silence of expectation when
ear, no, now it was the opposite, how rather to move off this
is continuing mounting silence. Who would be most implicated
king it? Now silence became the palpable appearance of the
that breath of the present which holds all ultimates in its
Iruth took responsibility by saying at last, "I expect the moon
things to many men. From Frank Borman's description on
8 we thought of it as rather a forbidding place"—he looked
in recollection—"whereas Stafford and Cernan and Young
give us the idea from Apollo 10 that the moon is agreeable, so to
speak, and not at all unpleasant but perhaps kind of a nice place to
be," and he smiled gently, hopefully, but perhaps a little regretfully
for filling his share of the silence. They nodded at one another.

## WORDS

*level of usage*   How would you characterize words like *spooky* (par. 2),
*raunchy* (par. 7), *funky* (par. 11), and *bust-out* (par. 13)? Are there
other examples of such words? What is their cumulative contribution to
the tone of the essay as a whole? In other words, what kind of voice
does the narrator assume? What manner of man is speaking?

*word origin*   *lunacy* (par. 2). Discuss the pun that Mailer is playing with.

*relationship*   Relate and discriminate between *person* and *persona* (par. 3).

*connotation*   What two presidents are suggested by the name *Eisenhooverian* (par. 24)? What quality of mind did these men share as suggested by Gilruth's answer? How does this answer differ from the narrator's implied expectations and the quality of *his* mind?

## SENTENCES

*rhetorical devices*   What figure of speech is in the last sentence of paragraph 2? In what terms is the narrator thinking of history? Why did he
choose this oblique if vivid way of letting us know about his ambitions?
In other words, what is the figure of speech meant to tell us about him
beside the fact that he is ambitious?

*variety*   With the second sentence of paragraph 19, the style suddenly
shifts. What is the author doing?

*style*   The final sentence of the essay is ironic understatement. What does
it *not* say?

*assumptions and implications* 1. In paragraph 5, the author distinguishes between his *mind* and his *brain*. How does he wish us to define each of these? He goes on to talk of *using the nose* instead of either *mind* or *brain*. What does that mean? Does it suggest that the senses are no part of either? From his metaphorical reference to *the nose,* the author goes into his more literal reflections on smells and odors. What is he trying to tell us about the world of modern technology, and with what other world is he implying a contrast? Does the single sentence of paragraph 17 help answer that last question? 2. Does the essay give any examples of that other world? What is the difference between the two worlds? 3. Paragraph 14 is given over largely to the matter of talking in what the author calls *code,* a manner of speech that he finds characteristic of technicians. Why is this depersonalized lingo appropriate to the Wasps as he describes them in paragraph 12?

## SUGGESTIONS FOR DISCUSSION

The use of acronyms has become very common in American discourse. It probably derives from the proliferation of bureaucratic agencies and the kind of jargon that characterizes bureaucratic style. It is well along the way to being that Newspeak that George Orwell describes in his novel about the ultimate bureaucracy, *1984.* Why is talking in code depressing, or don't you find it so? Do acronyms, for instance, have any linguistic virtue? Can you arrive at any generalizations about speech style and the nature of culture in general?

## *Ernest Hemingway*
# SCOTT FITZGERALD

*His talent was as natural as the pattern that was made by the dust on a butterfly's wings. At one time he understood it no more than the butterfly did and he did not know when it was brushed or marred. Later he became conscious of his damaged wings and of their construction and he learned to think and could not fly any more because the love of flight was gone and he could only remember when it had been effortless.*

SCOTT FITZGERALD is reprinted by permission of Charles Scribner's Sons from *A Moveable Feast* by Ernest Hemingway. Copyright © 1964 Ernest Hemingway, Ltd.

1. The first time I ever met Scott Fitzgerald a very strange thing happened. Many strange things happened with Scott but this one I was never able to forget. He had come into the Dingo bar in the rue Delambre where I was sitting with some completely worthless characters, had introduced himself and introduced a tall, pleasant man who was with him as Dunc Chaplin, the famous pitcher. I had not followed Princeton baseball and had never heard of Dunc Chaplin but he was extraordinarily nice, unworried, relaxed and friendly and I much preferred him to Scott.

2. Scott was a man then who looked like a boy with a face between handsome and pretty. He had very fair wavy hair, a high forehead, excited and friendly eyes and a delicate long-lipped Irish mouth that, on a girl, would have been the mouth of a beauty. His chin was well built and he had good ears and a handsome, almost beautiful, unmarked nose. This should not have added up to a pretty face, but that came from the coloring, the very fair hair and the mouth. The mouth worried you until you knew him and then it worried you more.

3. I was very curious to see him and I had been working very hard all day and it seemed quite wonderful that here should be Scott Fitzgerald and the great Dunc Chaplin whom I had never heard of but who was now my friend. Scott did not stop talking and since I was embarrassed by what he said—it was all about my writing and how great it was—I kept on looking at him closely and noticed instead of listening. We still went under the system, then, that praise to the face was open disgrace. Scott had ordered champagne and he and Dunc Chaplin and I drank it together with, I think, some of the worthless characters. I do not think that Dunc or I followed the speech very closely, for it was a speech and I kept on observing Scott. He was lightly built and did not look in awfully good shape, his face being faintly puffy. His Brooks Brothers clothes fitted him well and he wore a white shirt with a buttoned-down collar and a Guard's tie. I thought I ought to tell him about the tie, maybe, because they did have British in Paris and one might come into the Dingo—there were two there at the time—but then I thought the hell with it and I looked at him some more. It turned out later he had bought the tie in Rome.

4. I wasn't learning very much from looking at him now except that he had well shaped, capable-looking hands, not too small, and when he sat down on one of the bar stools I saw that he had very short legs. With normal legs he would have been perhaps two

inches taller. We had finished the first bottle of champagne and started on the second and the speech was beginning to run down.

5. Both Dunc and I were beginning to feel even better than we had felt before the champagne and it was nice to have the speech ending. Until then I had felt that what a great writer I was had been carefully kept secret between myself and my wife and only those people we knew well enough to speak to. I was glad Scott had come to the same happy conclusion as to this possible greatness, but I was also glad he was beginning to run out of the speech. But after the speech came the question period. You could study him and neglect to follow the speech, but the questions were inescapable. Scott, I was to find, believed that the novelist could find out what he needed to know by direct questioning of his friends and acquaintances. The interrogation was direct.

6. "Ernest," he said. "You don't mind if I call you Ernest, do you?"

7. "Ask Dunc," I said.

8. "Don't be silly. This is serious. Tell me, did you and your wife sleep together before you were married?"

9. "I don't know."

10. "What do you mean you don't know?"

11. "I don't remember."

12. "But how can you not remember something of such importance?"

13. "I don't know," I said. "It is odd, isn't it?"

14. "It's worse than odd," Scott said. "You must be able to remember."

15. "I'm sorry. It's a pity, isn't it?"

16. "Don't talk like some limey," he said. "Try to be serious and remember."

17. "Nope," I said. "It's hopeless."

18. "You could make an honest effort to remember."

19. The speech comes pretty high, I thought. I wondered if he gave everyone the speech, but I didn't think so because I had watched him sweat while he was making it. The sweat had come out on his long, perfect Irish upper lip in tiny drops, and that was when I had looked down away from his face and checked on the length of his legs, drawn up as he sat on the bar stool. Now I looked back at his face again and it was then that the strange thing happened.

20. As he sat there at the bar holding the glass of champagne the skin seemed to tighten over his face until all the puffiness was gone and then it drew tighter until the face was like a death's head.

The eyes sank and began to look dead and the lips were drawn tight and the color left the face so that it was the color of used candle wax. This was not my imagination. His face became a true death's head, or death mask, in front of my eyes.

21. "Scott," I said. "Are you all right?"

22. He did not answer and his face looked more drawn than ever.

23. "We'd better get him to a first aid station," I said to Dunc Chaplin.

24. "No. He's all right."

25. "He looks like he is dying."

26. "No. That's the way it takes him."

27. We got him into a taxi and I was very worried but Dunc said he was all right and not to worry about him. "He'll probably be all right by the time he gets home," he said.

28. He must have been because, when I met him at the Closerie des Lilas a few days later, I said that I was sorry the stuff had hit him that way and that maybe we had drunk it too fast while we were talking.

29. "What do you mean you are sorry? What stuff hit me what way? What are you talking about, Ernest?"

30. "I meant the other night at the Dingo."

31. "There was nothing wrong with me at the Dingo. I simply got tired of those absolutely bloody British you were with and went home."

32. "There weren't any British there when you were there. Only the bartender."

33. "Don't try to make a mystery of it. You know the ones I mean."

34. "Oh," I said. He had gone back to the Dingo later. Or he'd gone there another time. No, I remembered, there had been two British there. It was true. I remembered who they were. They had been there all right.

35. "Yes," I said. "Of course."

36. "That girl with the phony title who was so rude and that silly drunk with her. They said they were friends of yours."

37. "They are. And she *is* very rude sometimes."

38. "You see. There's no use to make mysteries simply because one has drunk a few glasses of wine. Why did you want to make the mysteries? It isn't the sort of thing I thought you would do."

39. "I don't know." I wanted to drop it. Then I thought of something. "Were they rude about your tie?" I asked.

40.   "Why should they have been rude about my tie? I was wearing a plain black knitted tie with a white polo shirt."

41.   I gave up then and he asked me why I liked this café and I told him about it in the old days and he began to try to like it too and we sat there, me liking it and he trying to like it, and he asked questions and told me about writers and publishers and agents and critics and George Horace Lorimer, and the gossip and economics of being a successful writer, and he was cynical and funny and very jolly and charming and endearing, even if you were careful about anyone becoming endearing. He spoke slightingly but without bitterness of everything he had written, and I knew his new book must be very good for him to speak, without bitterness, of the faults of past books. He wanted me to read the new book, *The Great Gatsby,* as soon as he could get his last and only copy back from someone he had loaned it to. To hear him talk of it, you would never know how very good it was, except that he had the shyness about it that all non-conceited writers have when they have done something very fine, and I hoped he would get the book quickly so that I might read it.

42.   Scott told me that he had heard from Maxwell Perkins that the book was not selling well but that it had very fine reviews. I do not remember whether it was that day, or much later, that he showed me a review by Gilbert Seldes that could not have been better. It could only have been better if Gilbert Seldes had been better. Scott was puzzled and hurt that the book was not selling well but, as I said, he was not at all bitter then and he was both shy and happy about the book's quality.

43.   On this day as we sat outside on the terrace of the Lilas and watched it get dusk and the people passing on the sidewalk and the grey light of the evening changing, there was no chemical change in him from the two whisky and sodas that we drank. I watched carefully for it, but it did not come and he asked no shameless questions, did nothing embarrassing, made no speeches, and acted as a normal, intelligent and charming person.

44.   He told me that he and Zelda, his wife, had been compelled to abandon their small Renault motor car in Lyon because of bad weather and he asked me if I would go down to Lyon with him on the train to pick up the car and drive up with him to Paris. The Fitzgeralds had rented a furnished flat at 14 rue de Tilsitt not far from the Etoile. It was late spring now and I thought the country would be at its best and we could have an excellent trip. Scott seemed so nice and so reasonable, and I had watched him drink two good

solid whiskies and nothing happened, and his charm and his seeming good sense made the other night at the Dingo seem like an unpleasant dream. So I said I would like to go down to Lyon with him and when did he want to leave.

45. We agreed to meet the next day and we then arranged to leave for Lyon on the express train that left in the morning. This train left at a convenient hour and was very fast. It made only one stop, as I recall, at Dijon. We planned to get into Lyon, have the car checked and in good shape, have an excellent dinner and get an early-morning start back toward Paris.

46. I was enthusiastic about the trip. I would have the company of an older and successful writer, and in the time we would have to talk in the car I would certainly learn much that it would be useful to know. It is strange now to remember thinking of Scott as an older writer, but at the time, since I had not yet read *The Great Gatsby,* I thought of him as a much older writer. I thought he wrote *Saturday Evening Post* stories that had been readable three years before but I never thought of him as a serious writer. He had told me at the Closerie des Lilas how he wrote what he thought were good stories, and which really were good stories for the *Post,* and then changed them for submission, knowing exactly how he must make the twists that made them into salable magazine stories. I had been shocked at this and I said I thought it was whoring. He said it was whoring but that he had to do it as he made his money from the magazines to have money ahead to write decent books. I said that I did not believe anyone could write any way except the very best he could write without destroying his talent. Since he wrote the real story first, he said, the destruction and changing of it that he did at the end did him no harm. I could not believe this and I wanted to argue him out of it but I needed a novel to back up my faith and to show him and convince him, and I had not yet written any such novel. Since I had started to break down all my writing and get rid of all facility and try to make instead of describe, writing had been wonderful to do. But it was very difficult, and I did not know how I would ever write anything as long as a novel. It often took me a full morning of work to write a paragraph.

47. My wife, Hadley, was happy for me to make the trip, though she did not take seriously the writing of Scott's that she had read. Her idea of a good writer was Henry James. But she thought it was a good idea for me to take a rest from work and make the trip, although we both wished that we had enough money to have a car and were making the trip ourselves. But that was something I

never had any idea would happen. I had received an advance of two hundred dollars from Boni and Liveright for a first book of short stories to be published in America that fall, and I was selling stories to the *Frankfurter Zeitung* and to *Der Querschnitt* in Berlin and to *This Quarter* and *The Transatlantic Review* in Paris and we were living with great economy and not spending any money except for necessities in order to save money to go down to the *feria* at Pamplona in July and to Madrid and to the *feria* in Valencia afterwards.

48. On the morning we were to leave from the Gare de Lyon I arrived in plenty of time and waited outside the train gates for Scott. He was bringing the tickets. When it got close to the time for the train to leave and he had not arrived, I bought an entry ticket to the track and walked along the side of the train looking for him. I did not see him and as the long train was about to pull out I got aboard and walked through the train hoping only that he would be aboard. It was a long train and he was not on it. I explained the situation to the conductor, paid for a ticket, second class— there was no third—and asked the conductor for the name of the best hotel in Lyon. There was nothing to do but wire Scott from Dijon giving him the address of the hotel where I would wait for him in Lyon. He would not get it before he left, but his wife would be presumed to wire it on to him. I had never heard, then, of a grown man missing a train; but on this trip I was to learn many new things.

49. In those days I had a very bad, quick temper, but by the time we were through Montereau it had quieted down and I was not too angry to watch and enjoy the countryside and at noon I had a good lunch in the dining car and drank a bottle of St.-Émilion and thought that even if I had been a damned fool to accept an invitation for a trip that was to be paid for by someone else, and was spending money on it that we needed to go to Spain, it was a good lesson for me. I had never before accepted an invitation to go on any trip that was paid for, instead of the cost split, and in this one I had insisted that we split the cost of the hotels and meals. But now I did not know whether Fitzgerald would even show up. While I had been angry I had demoted him from Scott to Fitzgerald. Later I was delighted that I had used up the anger at the start and gotten it over with. It was not a trip designed for a man easy to anger.

50. In Lyon I learned that Scott left Paris for Lyon but had left no word as to where he was staying. I confirmed my address there and the servant said she would let him know if he called. Madame was not well and was still sleeping. I called all the name

hotels and left messages but could not locate Scott and then I went out to a café to have an apéritif and read the papers. At the café I met a man who ate fire for a living and also bent coins which he held in his toothless jaws with his thumb and forefinger. His gums were sore but firm to the eye as he exhibited them and he said it was not a bad *métier*. I asked him to have a drink and he was pleased. He had a fine dark face that glowed and shone when he ate the fire. He said there was no money in eating fire nor in feats of strength with fingers and jaws in Lyon. False fire-eaters had ruined the *métier* and would continue to ruin it wherever they were allowed to practice. He had been eating fire all evening, he said, and did not have enough money on him to eat anything else that night. I asked him to have another drink, to wash away the petrol taste of the fire-eating, and said we could have dinner together if he knew a good place that was cheap enough. He said he knew an excellent place.

51. We ate very cheaply in an Algerian restaurant and I liked the food and the Algerian wine. The fire-eater was a nice man and it was interesting to see him eat, as he could chew with his gums as well as most people can with their teeth. He asked me what I did to make a living and I told him that I was starting in as a writer. He asked what sort of writing and I told him stories. He said he knew many stories, some of them more horrible and incredible than anything that had ever been written. He could tell them to me and I would write them and then if they made any money I would give him whatever I thought fair. Better still we could go to North Africa together and he would take me to the country of the Blue Sultan where I could get stories such as no man had ever heard.

52. I asked him what sort of stories and he said battles, executions, tortures, violations, fearful customs, unbelievable practices, debaucheries; anything I needed. It was getting time for me to get back to the hotel and check on Scott again, so I paid for the meal and said we would certainly be running into each other again. He said he was working down toward Marseilles and I said sooner or later we would meet somewhere and it was a pleasure to have dined together. I left him straightening out bent coins and stacking them on the table and walked back to the hotel.

53. Lyon was not a very cheerful town at night. It was a big, heavy, solid-money town, probably fine if you had money and liked that sort of town. For years I had heard about the wonderful chicken in the restaurants there, but we had eaten mutton instead. The mutton had been excellent.

54. There was no word from Scott at the hotel and I went to

bed in the unaccustomed luxury of the hotel and read a copy of the first volume of *A Sportsman's Sketches* by Turgenev that I had borrowed from Sylvia Beach's library. I had not been in the luxury of a big hotel for three years and I opened the windows wide and rolled up the pillows under my shoulders and head and was happy being with Turgenev in Russia until I was asleep while still reading. I was shaving in the morning getting ready to go out for breakfast when they called from the desk saying a gentleman was downstairs to see me.

55. "Ask him to come up, please," I said and went on shaving, listening to the town which had come heavily alive since early morning.

56. Scott did not come up and I met him down at the desk.

57. "I'm terribly sorry there was this mix-up," he said. "If I had only known what hotel you were going to it would have been simple."

58. "That's all right," I said. We were going to have a long ride and I was all for peace. "What train did you come down on?"

59. "One not long after the one you took. It was a very comfortable train and we might just as well have come down together."

60. "Have you had breakfast?"

61. "Not yet. I've been hunting all over the town for you."

62. "That's a shame," I said. "Didn't they tell you at home that I was here?"

63. "No. Zelda wasn't feeling well and I probably shouldn't have come. The whole trip has been disastrous so far."

64. "Let's get some breakfast and find the car and roll," I said.

65. "That's fine. Should we have breakfast here?"

66. "It would be quicker in a café."

67. "But we're sure to get a good breakfast here."

68. "All right."

69. It was a big American breakfast with ham and eggs and it was very good. But by the time we had ordered it, waited for it, eaten it, and waited to pay for it, close to an hour had been lost. It was not until the waiter came with the bill that Scott decided that we have the hotel make us a picnic lunch. I tried to argue him out of this as I was sure we could get a bottle of Mâcon in Mâcon and we could buy something to make sandwiches in a *charcuterie*. Or, if things were closed when we went through, there would be any number of restaurants where we could stop on our way. But he said I had told him that the chicken was wonderful in Lyon and that we

should certainly take one with us. So the hotel made us a lunch that could not have cost us very much more than four or five times what it would have cost us if we had bought it ourselves.

70. Scott had obviously been drinking before I met him and, as he looked as though he needed a drink, I asked him if he did not want one in the bar before we set out. He told me he was not a morning drinker and asked if I was. I told him it depended entirely on how I felt and what I had to do and he said that if I felt that I needed a drink, he would keep me company so I would not have to drink alone. So we had a whisky and Perrier in the bar while we waited for the lunch and both felt much better.

71. I paid for the hotel room and the bar, although Scott wanted to pay for everything. Since the start of the trip I had felt a little complicated about it emotionally and I found I felt much better the more things I could pay for. I was using up the money we had saved for Spain, but I knew I had good credit with Sylvia Beach and could borrow and repay whatever I was wasting now.

72. At the garage where Scott had left the car, I was astonished to find that the small Renault had no top. The top had been damaged in unloading the car in Marseilles, or it had been damaged in Marseilles in some manner and Zelda had ordered it cut away and refused to have it replaced. His wife hated car tops, Scott told me, and without the top they had driven as far as Lyon where they were halted by the rain. The car was in fair shape otherwise and Scott paid the bill after disputing several charges for washing, greasing, and for adding two liters of oil. The garage man explained to me that the car needed new piston rings and had evidently been run without sufficient oil and water. He showed me how it had heated up and burned the paint off the motor. He said if I could persuade Monsieur to have a ring job done in Paris, the car, which was a good little car, would be able to give the service it was built for.

73. "Monsieur would not let me replace the top."

74. "No?"

75. "One has an obligation to a vehicle."

76. "One has."

77. "You gentlemen have no waterproofs?"

78. "No," I said. "I did not know about the top."

79. "Try and make Monsieur be serious," he said pleadingly. "At least about the vehicle."

80. "Ah," I said.

81. We were halted by rain about an hour north of Lyon.

82. In that day we were halted by rain possibly ten times.

They were passing showers and some of them were longer than others. If we had waterproof coats it would have been pleasant enough to drive in that spring rain. As it was we sought the shelter of trees or halted at cafés alongside the road. We had a marvelous lunch from the hotel at Lyon, an excellent truffled roast chicken, delicious bread and white Mâcon wine and Scott was very happy when we drank the white Mâconnais at each of our stops. At Mâcon I had bought four more bottles of excellent wine which I uncorked as we needed them.

83. I am not sure Scott had ever drunk wine from a bottle before and it was exciting to him as though he were slumming or as a girl might be excited by going swimming for the first time without a bathing suit. But, by early afternoon, he had begun to worry about his health. He told me about two people who had died of congestion of the lungs recently. Both of them had died in Italy and he had been deeply impressed.

84. I told him that congestion of the lungs was an old-fashioned term for pneumonia, and he told me that I knew nothing about it and was absolutely wrong. Congestion of the lungs was a malady which was indigenous to Europe and I could not possibly know anything about it even if I had read my father's medical books, since they dealt with diseases that were strictly American. I said that my father had studied in Europe too. But Scott explained that congestion of the lungs had only appeared in Europe recently and that my father could not possibly have known anything about it. He also explained that diseases were different in different parts of America, and if my father had practiced medicine in New York instead of in the Middle West, he would have known an entirely different gamut of diseases. He used the word gamut.

85. I said that he had a good point in the prevalence of certain diseases in one part of the United States and their absence in others and cited the amount of leprosy in New Orleans and its low incidence, then, in Chicago. But I said that doctors had a system of exchange of knowledge and information among themselves and now that I remembered it after he had brought it up, I had read the authoritative article on congestion of the lungs in Europe in the *Journal of the American Medical Association* which traced its history back to Hippocrates himself. This held him for a while and I urged him to take another drink of Mâcon, since a good white wine, moderately full-bodied but with a low alcoholic content, was almost a specific against the disease.

86. Scott cheered a little after this but he began to fail again

shortly and asked me if we would make a big town before the onset of the fever and delirium by which, I had told him, the true congestion of the lungs, European, announced itself. I was now translating from an article which I had read in a French medical journal on the same malady while waiting at the American hospital in Neuilly to have my throat cauterized, I told him. A word like cauterized had a comforting effect on Scott. But he wanted to know when we would make the town. I said if we pushed on we should make it in twenty-five minutes to an hour.

87. Scott then asked me if I were afraid to die and I said more at some times than at others.

88. It now began to rain really heavily and we took refuge in the next village at a café. I cannot remember all the details of that afternoon but when we were finally in a hotel at what must have been Châlon-sur-Saône, it was so late that the drug stores were closed. Scott had undressed and gone to bed as soon as we reached the hotel. He did not mind dying of congestion of the lungs, he said. It was only the question of who was to look after Zelda and young Scotty. I did not see very well how I could look after them since I was having a healthily rough time looking after my wife Hadley and young son Bumby, but I said I would do my best and Scott thanked me. I must see that Zelda did not drink and that Scotty should have an English governess.

89. We had sent our clothes to be dried and were in our pajamas. It was still raining outside but it was cheerful in the room with the electric light on. Scott was lying in bed to conserve his strength for his battle against the disease. I had taken his pulse, which was seventy-two, and had felt his forehead, which was cool. I had listened to his chest and had him breathe deeply, and his chest sounded all right.

90. "Look, Scott," I said. "You're perfectly O.K. If you want to do the best thing to keep from catching cold, just stay in bed and I'll order us each a lemonade and a whisky and you take an aspirin with yours and you'll feel fine and won't even get a cold in your head."

91. "Those old wives' remedies," Scott said.

92. "You haven't any temperature. How the hell are you going to have congestion of the lungs without a temperature?"

93. "Don't swear at me," Scott said. "How do you know I haven't a temperature?"

94. "Your pulse is normal and you haven't any fever to the touch."

95. "To the touch," Scott said bitterly. "If you're a real friend, get me a thermometer."

96. "I'm in pajamas."

97. "Send for one."

98. I rang for the waiter. He didn't come and I rang again and then went down the hallway to look for him. Scott was lying with his eyes closed, breathing slowly and carefully and, with his waxy color and his perfect features, he looked like a little dead crusader. I was getting tired of the literary life, if this was the literary life that I was leading, and already I missed not working and I felt the death loneliness that comes at the end of every day that is wasted in your life. I was very tired of Scott and of this silly comedy, but I found the waiter and gave him money to buy a thermometer and a tube of aspirin, and ordered two *citron pressés* and two double whiskies. I tried to order a bottle of whisky but they would only sell it by the drink.

99. Back in the room Scott was still lying as though on his tomb, sculpted as a monument to himself, his eyes closed and breathing with exemplary dignity.

100. Hearing me come in the room, he spoke. "Did you get the thermometer?"

101. I went over and put my hand on his forehead. It was not as cold as the tomb. But it was cool and not clammy.

102. "Nope," I said.

103. "I thought you'd brought it."

104. "I sent out for it."

105. "It's not the same thing."

106. "No. It isn't, is it?"

107. You could not be angry with Scott any more than you could be angry with someone who was crazy, but I was getting angry with myself for having become involved in the whole silliness. He did have a point though, and I knew it very well. Most drunkards in those days died of pneumonia, a disease which has now been almost eliminated. But it was hard to accept him as a drunkard, since he was affected by such small quantities of alcohol.

108. In Europe then we thought of wine as something as healthy and normal as food and also as a great giver of happiness and well-being and delight. Drinking wine was not a snobbism nor a sign of sophistication nor a cult; it was as natural as eating and to me as necessary, and I would not have thought of eating a meal without drinking either wine or cider or beer. I loved all wines except sweet or sweetish wines and wines that were too heavy,

and it had never occurred to me that sharing a few bottles of fairly light, dry, white Mâcon could cause chemical changes in Scott that would turn him into a fool. There had been the whisky and Perrier in the morning but, in my ignorance of alcoholics then, I could not imagine one whisky harming anyone who was driving in an open car in the rain. The alcohol should have been oxidized in a very short time.

109. While waiting for the waiter to bring the various things I sat and read a paper and finished one of the bottles of Mâcon that had been uncorked at the last stop. There are always some splendid crimes in the newspapers that you follow from day to day, when you live in France. These crimes read like continued stories and it is necessary to have read the opening chapters, since there are no summaries provided as there are in American serial stories and, anyway, no serial is as good in an American periodical unless you have read the all-important first chapter. When you are traveling through France the papers are disappointing because you miss the continuity of the different *crimes, affaires,* or *scandales,* and you miss much of the pleasure to be derived from reading about them in a café. Tonight I would have much preferred to be in a café where I might read the morning editions of the Paris papers and watch the people and drink something a little more authoritative than the Mâcon in preparation for dinner. But I was riding herd on Scott so I enjoyed myself where I was.

110. When the waiter arrived with the two glasses with the pressed lemon juice and ice, the whiskies, and the bottle of Perrier water, he told me that the pharmacy was closed and he could not get a thermometer. He had borrowed some aspirin. I asked him to see if he could borrow a thermometer. Scott opened his eyes and gave a baleful Irish look at the waiter.

111. "Have you told him how serious it is?" he asked.

112. "I think he understands."

113. "Please try to make it clear."

114. I tried to make it clear and the waiter said, "I'll bring what I can."

115. "Did you tip him enough to do any good? They only work for tips."

116. "I didn't know that," I said. "I thought the hotel paid them something on the side."

117. "I mean they will only do something for you for a substantial tip. Most of them are rotten clean through."

118. I thought of Evan Shipman and I thought of the waiter

at the Closerie des Lilas who had been forced to cut his mustache when they made the American bar at the Closerie, and how Evan had been working out at his garden in Montrouge long before I had met Scott, and what good friends we all were and had been for a long time at the Lilas and of all of the moves that had been made and what they meant to all of us. I thought of telling Scott about this whole problem of the Lilas, although I had probably mentioned it to him before, but I knew he did not care about waiters nor their problems nor their great kindnesses and affections. At that time Scott hated the French, and since almost the only French he met with regularly were waiters whom he did not understand, taxi-drivers, garage employees and landlords, he had many opportunities to insult and abuse them.

119. He hated the Italians even more than the French and could not talk about them calmly even when he was sober. The English he often hated but he sometimes tolerated them and occasionally looked up to them. I do not know how he felt about the Germans and the Austrians. I do not know whether he had ever met any then or any Swiss.

120. On this evening in the hotel I was delighted that he was being so calm. I had mixed the lemonade and whisky and given it to him with two aspirins and he had swallowed the aspirins without protest and with admirable calm and was sipping his drink. His eyes were open now and were looking far away. I was reading the *crime* in the inside of the paper and was quite happy, too happy it seemed.

121. "You're a cold one, aren't you?" Scott asked and looking at him I saw that I had been wrong in my prescription, if not in my diagnosis, and that the whisky was working against us.

122. "How do you mean, Scott?"

123. "You can sit there and read that dirty French rag of a paper and it doesn't mean a thing to you that I am dying."

124. "Do you want me to call a doctor?"

125. "No. I don't want a dirty French provincial doctor."

126. "What do you want?"

127. "I want my temperature taken. Then I want my clothes dried and for us to get on an express train for Paris and to go to the American hospital at Neuilly."

128. "Our clothes won't be dry until morning and there aren't any express trains," I said. "Why don't you rest and have some dinner in bed?"

129. "I want my temperature taken."

130. After this went on for a long time the waiter brought a thermometer.

131. "Is this the only one you could get?" I asked. Scott had shut his eyes when the waiter came in and he did look at least as far gone as Camille. I have never seen a man who lost the blood from his face so fast and I wondered where it went.

132. "It is the only one in the hotel," the waiter said and handed me the thermometer. It was a bath thermometer with a wooden back and enough metal to sink it in the bath. I took a quick gulp of the whisky sour and opened the window a moment to look out at the rain. When I turned Scott was watching me.

133. I shook the thermometer down professionally and said, "You're lucky it's not a rectal thermometer."

134. "Where does this kind go?"

135. "Under the arm," I told him and tucked it under my arm.

136. "Don't upset the temperature," Scott said. I shook the thermometer again with a single sharp downward twitch and unbuttoned his pajama jacket and put the instrument under his armpit while I felt his cool forehead and then took his pulse again. He stared straight ahead. The pulse was seventy-two. I kept the thermometer in for four minutes.

137. "I thought they only kept them in for one minute," Scott said.

138. "This is a big thermometer," I explained. "You multiply by the square of the size of the thermometer. It's a centigrade thermometer."

139. Finally I took the thermometer out and carried it over by the reading light.

140. "What is it?"

141. "Thirty-seven and six-tenths."

142. "What's normal?"

143. "That's normal."

144. "Are you sure?"

145. "Sure."

146. "Try it on yourself. I have to be sure."

147. I shook the thermometer down and opened my pajamas and put the thermometer in my armpit and held it there while I watched the time. Then I looked at it.

148. "What is it?" I studied it.

149. "Exactly the same."

150. "How do you feel?"

151. "Splendid," I said. I was trying to remember whether

thirty-seven six was really normal or not. It did not matter, for the thermometer, unaffected, was steady at thirty.

152. Scott was a little suspicious so I asked if he wanted me to make another test.

153. "No," he said. "We can be happy it cleared up so quickly. I've always had great recuperative power."

154. "You're fine," I said. "But I think it would be just as well if you stayed in bed and had a light supper, and then we can start early in the morning." I had planned to buy us raincoats but I would have to borrow money from him for that and I did not want to start arguing about that now.

155. Scott did not want to stay in bed. He wanted to get up and get dressed and go downstairs and call Zelda so she would know he was all right.

156. "Why would she think you weren't all right?"

157. "This is the first night I have ever slept away from her since we were married and I have to talk to her. You can see what it means to us both, can't you?"

158. I could, but I could not see how he and Zelda could have slept together on the night just past; but it was nothing to argue about. Scott drank the whisky sour down very fast now and asked me to order another. I found the waiter and returned the thermometer and asked him how our clothes were coming along. He thought they might be dry in an hour or so. "Have the valet press them and that will dry them. It doesn't matter that they should be bone-dry."

159. The waiter brought the two drinks against catching cold and I sipped mine and urged Scott to sip his slowly. I was worried now he might catch cold and I could see by now that if he ever had anything as definitely bad as a cold he would probably have to be hospitalized. But the drink made him feel wonderful for a while and he was happy with the tragic implications of this being Zelda's and his first night of separation since their marriage. Finally he could not wait longer to call her and put on his dressing gown and went down to put the call through.

160. It would take some time for the call and shortly after he came up, the waiter appeared with two more double whisky sours. This was the most I had ever seen Scott drink until then, but they had no effect on him except to make him more animated and talkative, and he started to tell me the outline of his life with Zelda. He told me how he had first met her during the war and then lost her and won her back, and about their marriage and then about something tragic that had happened to them at St.-Raphael about a year ago.

This first version that he told me of Zelda and a French naval aviator falling in love was truly a sad story and I believe it was a true story. Later he told me other versions of it as though trying them for use in a novel, but none was as sad as this first one and I always believed the first one, although any of them might have been true. They were better told each time; but they never hurt you the same way the first one did.

161. Scott was very articulate and told a story well. He did not have to spell the words nor attempt to punctuate and you did not have the feeling of reading an illiterate that his letters gave you before they had been corrected. I knew him for two years before he could spell my name; but then it was a long name to spell and perhaps it became harder to spell all of the time, and I give him great credit for spelling it correctly finally. He learned to spell more important things and he tried to think straight about many more.

162. On this night though he wanted me to know and understand and appreciate what it was that had happened at St.-Raphael and I saw it so clearly that I could see the single seater seaplane buzzing the diving raft and the color of the sea and the shape of the pontoons and the shadow that they cast and Zelda's tan and Scott's tan and the dark blonde and the light blond of their hair and the darkly tanned face of the boy that was in love with Zelda. I could not ask the question that was in my mind, how, if this story was true and it had all happened, could Scott have slept each night in the same bed with Zelda? But maybe that was what had made it sadder than any story anyone had ever told me then, and, too, maybe he did not remember, as he did not remember last night.

163. Our clothes came before the call did and we dressed and went downstairs to have dinner. Scott was a little unsteady now and he looked at people out of the side of his eyes with a certain belligerency. We had very good snails, with a carafe of Fleury to start with and while we were about halfway through them Scott's call came. He was gone about an hour and I ate his snails finally, dipping up the butter, garlic and parsley sauce with broken bits of bread, and drank the carafe of Fleury. When he came back I said I would get him some more snails but he said he did not want any. He wanted something simple. He did not want a steak, nor liver and bacon, nor an omelette. He would take chicken. We had eaten very good cold chicken at noon but this was still famous chicken country, so we had *poularde de Bresse* and a bottle of Montagny, a light, pleasant white wine of the neighborhood. Scott ate very little and sipped at one glass of the wine. He passed out at the table with his

head on his hands. It was natural and there was no theater about it and it even looked as though he were careful not to spill nor break things. The waiter and I got him up to his room and laid him on the bed and I undressed him to his underwear, hung his clothes up, and then stripped the covers off the bed and spread them over him. I opened the window and saw it was clear outside and left the window open.

164.   Downstairs I finished my dinner and thought about Scott. It was obvious he should not drink anything and I had not been taking good care of him. Anything that he drank seemed to stimulate him too much and then to poison him and I planned on the next day to cut all drinking to the minimum. I would tell him that we were getting back to Paris now and that I had to train in order to write. This was not true. My training was never to drink after dinner nor before I wrote nor while I was writing. I went upstairs and opened all the windows wide and undressed and was asleep almost as soon as I was in bed.

165.   The next day we drove to Paris on a beautiful day up through the Côte d'Or with the air freshly washed and the hills and the fields and the vineyards all new, and Scott was very cheerful and happy and healthy and told me the plots of each and every one of Michael Arlen's books. Michael Arlen, he said, was the man you had to watch and he and I could both learn much from him. I said I could not read the books. He said I did not have to. He would tell me the plots and describe the characters. He gave me a sort of oral Ph.D. thesis on Michael Arlen.

166.   I asked him if he had a good connection on the phone when he talked to Zelda and he said that it was not bad and that they had many things to talk about. At meals I ordered one bottle of the lightest wine I could locate and told Scott he would do me a great favor if he would not let me order any more as I had to train before I wrote and should not under any circumstances drink more than half a bottle. He co-operated wonderfully and when he saw me looking nervous toward the end of a single bottle, gave me some of his share.

167.   When I had left him at his home and taken a taxi back to the sawmill, it was wonderful to see my wife and we went up to the Closerie des Lilas to have a drink. We were happy the way children are who have been separated and are together again and I told her about the trip.

168.   "But didn't you have any fun or learn anything, Tatie?" she asked.

169. "I learned about Michael Arlen, if I would have listened, and I learned things I haven't sorted out."

170. "Isn't Scott happy at all?"

171. "Maybe."

172. "Poor man."

173. "I learned one thing."

174. "What?"

175. "Never to go on trips with anyone you do not love."

176. "Isn't that fine?"

177. "Yes. And we're going to Spain."

178. "Yes. Now it's less than six weeks before we go. And this year we won't let anyone spoil it, will we?"

179. "No. And after Pamplona we'll go to Madrid and to Valencia."

180. "M-m-m-m," she said softly, like a cat.

181. "Poor Scott," I said.

182. "Poor everybody," Hadley said. "Rich feathercats with no money."

183. "We're awfully lucky."

184. "We'll have to be good and hold it."

185. We both touched wood on the café table and the waiter came to see what it was we wanted. But what we wanted not he, nor anyone else, nor knocking on wood or on marble, as this café table-top was, could ever bring us. But we did not know it that night and we were very happy.

186. A day or two after the trip Scott brought his book over. It had a garish dust jacket and I remember being embarrassed by the violence, bad taste and slippery look of it. It looked like the book jacket for a book of bad science fiction. Scott told me not to be put off by it, that it had to do with a billboard along a highway in Long Island that was important in the story. He said he had liked the jacket and now he didn't like it. I took it off to read the book.

187. When I had finished the book I knew that no matter what Scott did, nor how he behaved, I must know it was like a sickness and be of any help I could to him and try to be a good friend. He had many good, good friends, more than anyone I knew. But I enlisted as one more, whether I could be of any use to him or not. If he could write a book as fine as *The Great Gatsby* I was sure that he could write an even better one. I did not know Zelda yet, and so I did not know the terrible odds that were against him. But we were to find them out soon enough.

## WORDS

*meaning*  Define *métier* (par. 50), *charcuterie* (par. 69), and *citron pressés* (par. 98).

*word choice*  1. Is *system* in paragraph 3 defensible? Explain.  2. Why a *crusader* (par. 98)? Is the comparison developed later? Why is it particularly effective in this setting? How does it advance the characterization of Fitzgerald?

*level of usage*  1. What level does the first sentence of paragraph 19 indicate? Name some earlier clear examples of this level of usage. 2. What do the last two sentences of paragraph 84 show about Hemingway's preference in levels of usage? What do they imply about Fitzgerald's? Is this implication furthered in paragraph 86?

## SENTENCES

*style*  What devices of style does the author use in paragraphs 84–87 that let us know that this is all very funny? How does the device of indirect discourse assist?

*rhetorical devices*  1. Analyze the epigraph as an extended metaphor. Is it consistent? Are any ideas imposed on the metaphor that do not pertain to it?  2. Is the unexpected turn at the end of the last sentence in paragraph 2 an example of climax or anticlimax? Explain.  3. Is there an element of irony in the repetition of *good* in sentence 2 of paragraph 187? What is the implication of the entire sentence?

## PARAGRAPHS

*unity*  1. Considering the dialogue in paragraphs 29–40 as a single paragraph, you could diagram it like this: ⟋⟍ . What are the two high points? Do they give the exchange unity through a kind of parallelism? Explain.  2. Is paragraph 46 a unity or a miscellany? If the first, what subject contains the whole? If unity is there, are there internal devices that contribute to it?

*coherence*  Paragraph 54 is held together' by the first and last sentences, which concern the absence and presence of Fitzgerald. What is the function of the material between them?

## CONTENT AND ORGANIZATION

*assumptions and implications*  1. Hemingway's attitude toward Fitzgerald is not exactly pleasant. How early in the essay are you able to define it by tone alone? How would you define it?  2. How does paragraph 41 reveal the respective professional status of the two young writers? Who was George Horace Lorimer? Why is his name relevant here? 3. Paragraph 165 mentions Michael Arlen, who was a popular writer of pseudosophisticated novels in the 1920s. How do these references —and a later one in paragraph 169—contribute to Hemingway's characterization of Fitzgerald? 4. In that final reference, in a scene with Mrs. Hemingway, are you reminded of the earlier comment that she admires Henry James (par. 47)? If so, to what point? 5. What does paragraph 185 do to bring Hemingway himself into that circle of human frailty with which he has been so impatient throughout?

*organization* 1. Aside from the fact that he was probably there in actuality, what is the point in introducing Dunc Chaplin at the opening? He is not mentioned by name again after this scene. In what connection do we recall him at the end? 2. Is the meeting with the fire-eater (pars. 50–52) an intrusion, or does it contain details that contribute to the general subject? Does the figure of the fire-eater point up any more central figure or fact by contrast or analogy?

SUGGESTIONS FOR DISCUSSION

1. From such details as are given you about Zelda Fitzgerald (and their implications) write a brief characterization of her. 2. The essay implies two different views of the *literary life* (par. 98). Contrast the views. 3. Hemingway doesn't tell us explicitly about himself but implies a good deal through understatement, through the kind of details he observes (the shape of Fitzgerald's mouth, for example, and the length of his legs), and through his relationships, both casual and important, with other people. Can you write a character sketch of him from this essay alone, not including factual material that you may have gathered from other sources? 4. In what ways does Hemingway illustrate the old maxim "Style is the man"?


*F. Scott Fitzgerald*

## EARLY SUCCESS

*October, 1937*

1. Seventeen years ago this month I quit work or, if you prefer, I retired from business. I was through—let the Street Railway Advertising Company carry along under its own power. I retired, not

EARLY SUCCESS: F. Scott Fitzgerald, *The Crack-Up*. Copyright 1945 by New Directions Publishing Corporation. Reprinted by permission of New Directions Publishing Corporation.

on my profits, but on my liabilities, which included debts, despair, and a broken engagement, and crept home to St. Paul to "finish a novel."

2. That novel, begun in a training camp late in the war, was my ace in the hole. I had put it aside when I got a job in New York, but I was as constantly aware of it as of the shoe with cardboard in the sole, during all one desolate spring. It was like the fox and goose and the bag of beans. If I stopped working to finish the novel, I lost the girl.

3. So I struggled on in a business I detested and all the confidence I had garnered at Princeton and in a haughty career as the army's worst aide-de-camp melted gradually away. Lost and forgotten, I walked quickly from certain places—from the pawn shop where one left the field glasses, from prosperous friends whom one met when wearing the suit from before the war—from restaurants after tipping with the last nickel, from busy cheerful offices that were saving the jobs for their own boys from the war.

4. Even having a first story accepted had not proved very exciting. Dutch Mount and I sat across from each other in a carcard slogan advertising office, and the same mail brought each of us an acceptance from the same magazine—the old *Smart Set*.

5. "My check was thirty—how much was yours?"

6. "Thirty-five."

7. The real blight, however, was that my story had been written in college two years before, and a dozen new ones hadn't even drawn a personal letter. The implication was that I was on the down-grade at twenty-two. I spent the thirty dollars on a magenta feather fan for a girl in Alabama.

8. My friends who were not in love or who had waiting arrangements with "sensible" girls, braced themselves patiently for a long pull. Not I—I was in love with a whirlwind and I must spin a net big enough to catch it out of my head, a head full of trickling nickels and sliding dimes, the incessant music box of the poor. It couldn't be done like that, so when the girl threw me over I went home and finished my novel. And then, suddenly, everything changed, and this article is about that first wild wind of success and the delicious mist it brings with it. It is a short and precious time—for when the mist rises in a few weeks, or a few months, one finds that the very best is over.

9. It began to happen in the autumn of 1919 when I was an empty bucket, so mentally blunted with the summer's writing that I'd taken a job repairing car roofs at the Northern Pacific shops.

Then the postman rang, and that day I quit work and ran along the streets, stopping automobiles to tell friends and acquaintances about it—my novel *This Side of Paradise* was accepted for publication. That week the postman rang and rang, and I paid off my terrible small debts, bought a suit, and woke up every morning with a world of ineffable toploftiness and promise.

10.  While I waited for the novel to appear, the metamorphosis of amateur into professional began to take place—a sort of stitching together of your whole life into a pattern of work, so that the end of one job is automatically the beginning of another. I had been an amateur before; in October, when I strolled with a girl among the stones of a southern graveyard, I was a professional and my enchantment with certain things that she felt and said was already paced by an anxiety to set them down in a story—it was called *The Ice Palace* and it was published later. Similarly, during Christmas week in St. Paul, there was a night when I had stayed home from two dances to work on a story. Three friends called up during the evening to tell me I had missed some rare doings: a well-known man-about-town had disguised himself as a camel and, with a taxi-driver as the rear half, managed to attend the wrong party. Aghast with myself for not being there, I spent the next day trying to collect the fragments of the story.

11.  "Well, all I can say is it was funny when it happened." "No, I don't know where he got the taxi-man." "You'd have to know him well to understand how funny it was."

12.  In despair I said: "Well, I can't seem to find out exactly what happened but I'm going to write about it as if it was ten times funnier than anything you've said." So I wrote it, in twenty-two consecutive hours, and wrote it "funny," simply because I was so emphatically told it was funny. *The Camel's Back* was published and still crops up in the humorous anthologies.

13.  With the end of the winter set in another pleasant pumped-dry period, and, while I took a little time off, a fresh picture of life in America began to form before my eyes. The uncertainties of 1919 were over—there seemed little doubt about what was going to happen—America was going on the greatest, gaudiest spree in history and there was going to be plenty to tell about it. The whole golden boom was in the air—its splendid generosities, its outrageous corruptions and the tortuous death struggle of the old America in prohibition. All the stories that came into my head had a touch of disaster in them—the lovely young creatures in my novels went to ruin, the diamond mountains of my short stories blew up, my mil-

lionaires were as beautiful and damned as Thomas Hardy's peasants. In life these things hadn't happened yet, but I was pretty sure living wasn't the reckless, careless business these people thought—this generation just younger than me.

14. For my point of vantage was the dividing line between the two generations, and there I sat—somewhat self-consciously. When my first big mail came in—hundreds and hundreds of letters on a story about a girl who bobbed her hair—it seemed rather absurd that they should come to me about it. On the other hand, for a shy man it was nice to be somebody except oneself again: to be "the Author" as one had been "the Lieutenant." Of course one wasn't really an author any more than one had been an army officer, but nobody seemed to guess behind the false face.

15. All in three days I got married and the presses were pounding out *This Side of Paradise* like they pound out extras in the movies.

16. With its publication I had reached a stage of manic depressive insanity. Rage and bliss alternated hour by hour. A lot of people thought it was a fake, and perhaps it was, and a lot of others thought it was a lie, which it was not. In a daze I gave out an interview—I told what a great writer I was and how I'd achieved the heights. Heywood Broun, who was on my trail, simply quoted it with the comment that I seemed to be a very self-satisfied young man, and for some days I was notably poor company. I invited him to lunch and in a kindly way told him that it was too bad he had let his life slide away without accomplishing anything. He had just turned thirty and it was about then that I wrote a line which certain people will not let me forget: "She was a faded but still lovely woman of twenty-seven."

17. In a daze I told the Scribner Company that I didn't expect my novel to sell more than twenty thousand copies and when the laughter died away I was told that a sale of five thousand was excellent for a first novel. I think it was a week after publication that it passed the twenty thousand mark, but I took myself so seriously that I didn't even think it was funny.

18. These weeks in the clouds ended abruptly a week later when Princeton turned on the book—not undergraduate Princeton but the black mass of faculty and alumni. There was a kind but reproachful letter from President Hibben, and a room full of classmates who suddenly turned on me with condemnation. We had been part of a rather gay party staged conspicuously in Harvey Firestone's car of robin's-egg blue, and in the course of it I got an accidental

black eye trying to stop a fight. This was magnified into an orgy and in spite of a delegation of undergraduates who went to the board of Governors, I was suspended from my club for a couple of months. The *Alumni Weekly* got after my book and only Dean Gauss had a good word to say for me. The unctuousness and hypocrisy of the proceedings was exasperating and for seven years I didn't go to Princeton. Then a magazine asked me for an article about it and when I started to write it, I found I really loved the place and that the experience of one week was a small item in the total budget. But on that day in 1920 most of the joy went out of my success.

19. But one was now a professional—and the new world couldn't possibly be presented without bumping the old out of the way. One gradually developed a protective hardness against both praise and blame. Too often people liked your things for the wrong reasons or people liked them whose dislike would be a compliment. No decent career was ever founded on a public and one learned to go ahead without precedents and without· fear. Counting the bag, I found that in 1919 I had made $800 by writing, that in 1920 I had made $18,000, stories, picture rights, and book. My story price had gone from $30 to $1,000. That's a small price to what was paid later in the Boom, but what it sounded like to me couldn't be exaggerated.

20. The dream had been early realized and the realization carried with it a certain bonus and a certain burden. Premature success gives one an almost mystical conception of destiny as opposed to will power—at its worst the Napoleonic delusion. The man who arrives young believes that he exercises his will because his star is shining. The man who only asserts himself at thirty has a balanced idea of what will power and fate have each contributed, the one who gets there at forty is liable to put the emphasis on will alone. This comes out when the storms strike your craft.

21. The compensation of a very early success is a conviction that life is a romantic matter. In the best sense one stays young. When the primary objects of love and money could be taken for granted and a shaky eminence had lost its fascination, I had fair years to waste, years that I can't honestly regret, in seeking the eternal Carnival by the Sea. Once in the middle twenties I was driving along the High Corniche Road through the twilight with the whole French Riviera twinkling on the sea below. As far ahead as I could see was Monte Carlo, and though it was out of season and there were no Grand Dukes left to gamble and E. Phillips Oppenheim was a fat industrious man in my hotel, who lived in a bathrobe—

the very name was so incorrigibly enchanting that I could only stop
the car and like the Chinese whisper: "Ah me! Ah me!" It was not
Monte Carlo I was looking at. It was back into the mind of the
young man with cardboard soles who had walked the streets of New
York. I was him again—for an instant I had the good fortune to
share his dreams, I who had no more dreams of my own. And there
are still times when I creep up on him, surprise him on an autumn
morning in New York or a spring night in Carolina when it is so
quiet that you can hear a dog barking in the next county. But never
again as during that all too short period when he and I were one
person, when the fulfilled future and the wistful past were mingled
in a single gorgeous moment—when life was literally a dream.

## WORDS

*meaning* Define *ineffable* (par. 9), *metamorphosis* (par. 10), and
*unctuousness* (par. 18).

*exactness* 1. What is the force of the word *literally* in the last sentence
of paragraph 21? What is the difference in meaning between *literally* and
*figuratively?* 2. Clearly the word *professional* (pars. 10, 19) had an
important meaning for Fitzgerald, just as it did for Ernest Hemingway.
A professional earns money by practicing an art or taking part in a sport,
certainly, but how else does he differ from an amateur or dilettante?

*level of usage* This essay is written in an easy colloquial style. Why
would these locutions—"like they pound out extras in the movies" (par.
15) and "I was him again" (par. 21)—be unlikely in more formal writing?

## SENTENCES

*rhetorical devices* 1. Explain the allusions in these phrases: "as beautiful
and damned as Thomas Hardy's peasants" (par. 13); "at its worst the
Napoleonic delusion" (par. 20); and "E. Phillips Oppenheim was a fat
industrious man in my hotel" (par. 21). 2. Why are the last two sentences of paragraph 16 ironical? How did Fitzgerald's attitude toward his
youthful success change between 1920 and 1937, when this article was
written?

## PARAGRAPHS

*methods of development* Compare paragraphs 3, 18, and 20. Which two
of them are developed with details? Which is developed by comparison?

## CONTENT AND ORGANIZATION

*central ideas* 1. His Princeton experience was always important to Fitzgerald. Using the references to his college years in paragraphs 3, 7, and

18, define his attitude toward Princeton.   2. Many pieces of fiction and autobiography celebrate what critics have called an "epiphany"—a sudden insight into a spiritual truth or an instant understanding of the essence of an experience or state of being. What moment of epiphany is described in this narration?

*assumptions and implications*   1. How will a man who has "arrived" in his twenties differ in his reaction to later misfortunes from a man who has won success only in middle age (par. 20)?   2. What does Fitzgerald mean by saying that early success means that "in the best sense one stays young" (par. 21)?

SUGGESTIONS FOR DISCUSSION

1. Fitzgerald says that his article is "about that first wild wind of success and the delicious mist it brings with it" (par. 8). Describe the effects of sudden success as you have experienced it or observed its effects on another.   2. Fitzgerald was immensely successful in the twenties—"the Boom"—but personally troubled and professionally unsuccessful in the thirties. Describe someone—a college football hero who graduated, a businessman who retired, a politician who was not reelected—who outlived his fame or public esteem.   3. For a modern college student, the Jazz Age, the Boom, and the great depression are ancient history, but they have had lasting effects on contemporary government, social thought, and literature. Describe one of these effects.   4. Read *Tender Is the Night* or *The Great Gatsby* and compare the society it describes with the one you know.   5. If you have experienced a sudden moment of insight or heightened feeling comparable to Fitzgerald's feelings at twilight on the High Corniche Road, describe it and the circumstances surrounding it.

*Henry David Thoreau*

# THE ANT WAR

1.   One day when I went out to my woodpile, or rather my pile of stumps, I observed two large ants, the one red, the other much larger, nearly half an inch long, and black, fiercely contending with one another. Having once got hold they never let go, but struggled and wrestled and rolled on the chips incessantly. Looking farther, I was surprised to find that the chips were covered with such combatants, that it was not a *duellum,* but a *bellum,* a war between two

THE ANT WAR:   From *Walden* by Henry David Thoreau, 1854.

races of ants, the red always pitted against the black, and frequently two red ones to one black. The legions of these Myrmidons covered all the hills and vales in my woodyard, and the ground was already strewn with the dead and dying, both red and black. It was the only battle which I have ever witnessed, the only battlefield I ever trod while the battle was raging; internecine war; the red republicans on the one hand, and the black imperialists on the other. On every side they were engaged in deadly combat, yet without any noise that I could hear, and human soldiers never fought so resolutely. I watched a couple that were fast locked in each other's embraces, in a little sunny valley amid the chips, now at noonday prepared to fight till the sun went down, or life went out. The smaller red champion had fastened himself like a vice to his adversary's front, and through all the tumblings on that field never for an instant ceased to gnaw at one of his feelers near the root, having already caused the other to go by the board; while the stronger black one dashed him from side to side, and, as I saw on looking nearer, had already divested him of several of his members. They fought with more pertinacity than bulldogs. Neither manifested the least disposition to retreat. It was evident that their battle cry was "Conquer or die." In the meanwhile there came along a single red ant on the hillside of this valley, evidently full of excitement, who either had dispatched his foe, or had not yet taken part in the battle; probably the latter, for he had lost none of his limbs; whose mother had charged him to return with his shield or upon it. Or perchance he was some Achilles, who had nourished his wrath apart, and had now come to avenge or rescue his Patroclus. He saw this unequal combat from afar—for the blacks were nearly twice the size of the red—he drew near with rapid pace till he stood on his guard within half an inch of the combatants; then, watching his opportunity, he sprang upon the black warrior, and commenced his operations near the root of his right foreleg, leaving the foe to select among his own members; and so there were three united for life, as if a new kind of attraction had been invented which put all other locks and cements to shame. I should not have wondered by this time to find that they had their respective musical bands stationed on some eminent chip, and playing their national airs the while, to excite the slow and cheer the dying combatants. I was myself excited somewhat even as if they had been men. The more you think of it, the less the difference. And certainly there is not the fight recorded in Concord history, at least, if in the history of America, that will bear a moment's comparison with this, whether for the numbers engaged in it, or for the patriotism and heroism displayed. For numbers and for carnage it was an Austerlitz or Dresden. Concord Fight! Two killed on the patriots' side, and Luther Blanchard wounded! Why here every ant was a Buttrick—"Fire! for God's sake fire!"—and thousands shared the fate of Davis and Hosmer. There was not one hireling there. I have no doubt that it was a principle they fought for, as much as our ancestors, and not to avoid a three-penny tax on their tea; and the results of this battle will be as important and memorable to those whom it concerns as those of the battle of Bunker Hill, at least.

2. I took up the chip on which the three I have particularly described were struggling, carried it into my house, and placed it under a tumbler on my window sill, in order to see the issue. Holding a microscope to the first-mentioned red ant, I saw that, though he was assiduously gnawing at the near foreleg of his enemy, having severed his remaining feeler, his own breast was all torn away, exposing what vitals he had there to the jaws of the black warrior, whose breastplate was apparently too thick for him to pierce; and the dark carbuncles of the sufferer's eyes shone with ferocity such as war only could excite. They struggled half an hour longer under the tumbler, and when I looked again the black soldier had severed the heads of his foes from their bodies, and the still living heads were hanging on either side of him like ghastly trophies at his saddlebow, still apparently as firmly fastened as ever, and he was endeavoring with feeble struggles, being without feelers and with only the remnant of a leg, and I know not how many other wounds, to divest himself of them; which at length, after half an hour more, he accomplished. I raised the glass, and he went off over the window sill in that crippled state. Whether he finally survived that combat, and spent the remainder of his days in some Hôtel des Invalides, I do not know; but I thought that his industry would not be worth much thereafter. I never learned which party was victorious, nor the cause of the war; but I felt for the rest of that day as if I had had my feelings excited and harrowed by witnessing the struggle, the ferocity and carnage, of a human battle before my door.

WORDS

*meaning*  1. Thoreau often uses related words in pairs. Distinguish between *patriotism* and *heroism* (par. 1), *excited* and *harrowed* (par. 2), and *ferocity* and *carnage* (par. 2).  2. Note the consistent use of such battlefield words as *retreat, combatants,* and *operations.* Find others.

## SENTENCES

*style*  1. Thoreau is commonly thought of as one of America's outstanding prose stylists. Sentence variety is an aspect of style. Paragraph 1 has 24 sentences of 706 words, averaging 29.4 words a sentence, the shortest sentence having 2 words and the longest having 95. Were you aware of this variety in sentence length? Comment on the effectiveness of this variety.  2. In the middle of paragraph 1 the author has 3 sentences of 7, 7, and 11 words each, preceded by a sentence of 74 words and followed by one of 59. Do the three short sentences affect the tempo? Do they accentuate the scene? How do they lead into the transition that follows: "In the meanwhile"?  3. The shortest sentence, "Concord Fight!" is elliptical. Write it as a complete sentence, expressing what Thoreau means by referring to that fight.

*parallelism*  The long sentence (par. 1) beginning "He saw this unequal combat from afar" has parallel structure: "He saw," "he drew," "he stood," and "he sprang." Find two other sentences with this or other kinds of parallel structure.

*emphasis*  1. The sentence (par. 1) beginning "The smaller red champion" is balanced. In what ways is it balanced? Find another balanced sentence and name the balanced elements.  2. Is sentence 1 of paragraph 2 loose or periodic? Explain.

## PARAGRAPHS

*coherence*  Coherence is achieved by so interlinking sentences that the thought flows smoothly. Sentence arrangement, pronouns referring to preceding sentences, and repetition of words or ideas all aid in establishing coherent thought. Describe with illustrations the transitional devices in paragraph 2.

## CONTENT AND ORGANIZATION

*central idea*  Thoreau sets up an analogy between the ant war and human war. List the episodes and illustrations that caused the author to feel that he had been witnessing something like a human battle before his door.

*organization*  Are the analogies between ant and human warfare so central as, indeed, to provide the basic, organizing idea?

*assumptions and implications*  The author calls the red ants *republicans* and the black ones *imperialists,* thereby allying the two sides with two quite different forms of government. Why? Does this mean he sympathizes with the smaller, red ants?

1. Do you think that in the modern world there can be wars that are not internecine? Why or why not? 2. Why do you think Thoreau appears not to be interested in the cause of the ant war? Why does he not care to find out who won the war? Would you? 3. In your judgment, how important was the tea tax as a cause of the Revolution? Explain. Do you feel that the ants' "principle" was analogous to the tea tax? 4. Could you write a theme on either side of the question "Do wars have victors?" Or does one side seem to you indefensible?

## *Yrjö Kokko*

## THE CRADLE

1. Pietari Blank, a Lapp from the Tavgi tents that were pitched for the winter on the northern slopes of Jatunivaara, was driving his reindeer towards the ice-covered Muonio River. Behind him followed another sled drawn by a deer whose antlers still had bits of velvet clinging to them. Pietari's beast had lost its antlers. There was no one in the second sled, but the deer drawing it was on a leading-rein made fast to the back of Pietari's seat, which was strengthened by bands of copper curved like lilies.

2. The little string drove up on to a low, pine-covered hill. From here Pietari could see the course of the Muonio, and on it a long lead of open water that reflected the rays of the sun. It was as if molten silver had turned to oil and lay there glittering. He drove slowly down into a sheltered gully, pulled up, unharnessed the deer, and, wading through the snow, tethered each to a pine trunk by a long rein; then he returned to the sleds. He took off his cap— the *samikahpir*—that left a sharp line between the coppery tan caused by winter winds and the natural brown of his skin. The lower part of the *kahpir* was cone-shaped and bordered with white reindeer calf-skin. The rest of it was covered with red, green and yellow cloth over which were sewn brightly colored bands. The top was of dark blue cloth divided into four funnel-shaped folds adorned with similar bands in the form of a cross. Pietari threw it into the sled and unbuckled his broad Lapp belt of thick leather studded with

THE CRADLE: From *The Way of the Four Winds* by Yrjö Kokko, 1954. Reprinted by permission of G. P. Putnam's Sons.

silver, the holes of which were eyeleted with bone. From his belt hung the *leuku,* a knife as big as a billhook. Next he caught hold of the outer coat of brown deer-hide that reached to his knees and was bordered at the neck with red and yellow, and drew it off over his head like a nightshirt. He stood now in the heavy dark blue *kolt* of wadmal, with its short, pleated, bell-shaped skirt, over which he rebuckled his belt. This garment was very wide and made the top part of his body look broad and powerful, an impression enhanced by the colored bands sewn across shoulders and chest and reaching halfway down the sleeves. Three such stripes ran vertically down the back of the *kolt.* His breeches were of leather tanned yellow-brown, though the legs of them from the middle of the thigh downwards were made of the dark hide from the legs of deer. His shoes were also of deer-hide, and they turned up at the tips.

3. Pietari was not tall, but his striking, beautiful clothes, his coal-black hair and dark eyes—now deep as the *saivo,* the double-bottomed lake, now keen and mistrustful as those of a fox—his lithe movements and the coppery glow of his skin gave him an air of dignity. The gay colors of his dress did not jar against that snowy landscape, for spring sunshine bathed the drifts now in gold, now in rose-red, and threw shadows melting from pale violet into deep blue. The shadows of the gnarled birches twisted over the snow crust as if scribbled in ink by a child.

4. Pietari drew the *leuku* from its sheath, lopped twigs from the birches and kindled a fire. Shavings hacked from a fir made a cheerful blaze on the snow. From his haversack he took out a sooty little coffee-pot, over which he set a lump of snow impaled on a stick to melt in the warmth of the fire. Soon the pot was full of water and the coffee made. He ate his meal, and the deer too began to dig for reindeer moss beneath the snow.

5. He went down to the river bank where a little wooded promontory jutted into a stretch of open water below some falls. Close beside the water's edge in the shadow of a small pine tree he dug a hole in the snow, covered it with a thin layer of pine branches and swept the surrounding snow clear of tracks. He fetched a gun from his sled, and with haversack and outer coat over his arm he went back and hid himself in the hole.

6. The short spring day was ending. Shadows that had been blue turned to purple, then crimson, and lastly greyish blue before they disappeared. In the clear sky white clouds were gathering; they darkened in the middle while their edges turned red. The sky

became pale yellow and then green, and the clouds melted away. When dark night sank over the landscape and the stars came out, Northern Lights flared into the sky, their glow reflected in the rushing, singing falls until these looked like a cascade of light.

7. An animal was moving down by the snowy shore: at first it looked as big as a fox, but as it approached it seemed to shrink. It paused by the edge of the ice-hole, turned its round head and moved its trailing tail. The sleek coat gleamed in the aurora until the animal slipped into the water and dived among the eddies. The head appeared, then vanished again. Further downstream, where the surface was black and still, a point of light spread into a widening ring, in the middle of which the creature looked about with heady eyes. Now it began swimming against the current; for a moment its back appeared among the eddies of the falls, and suddenly it shot up at its starting-point on the edge of the ice.

8. "An otter," whispered Pietari, but he didn't shoot.

9. The otter seemed to be eating something, but soon ran with queer, bounding steps up the river bank.

10. Pietari pulled on his coat of deer-hide. He sat all that night in his hole, listening to the roar of the falls, peering into the darkness and picking up almost imperceptible sounds. Light returned; darkness slipped into the gold of morning that touched the hills with a rosy shimmer and made the snowdrifts glint as if alive. Day came quickly.

11. Pietari went back and moved the deer to fresh, undug pasture on the slope. He made coffee, ate, and lay down in the sled to sleep. The sun shone brightly and tits scrabbled on the trunks of the pines. An inquisitive Siberian jay flew over Pietari and winged his dreams.

12. It was afternoon when he woke. The deer lay chewing the cud. He lit another fire and put on the coffee-pot, and then, going to the second sled, he lifted the covers and came back with a strange-looking object under his arm. He sat down with it on his knees.

13. The thing he was holding was a sort of trough hollowed from a tree trunk, tapering at one end and cut off square at the other like a tiny boat. On the outside it was covered with tanned calf-skin, and the bows were hooded with the same material. The opening of the hood was hidden by a tiny flowered curtain, and from its upper edge to the stern of the little craft stretched colored, twisted cords. From one of these hung small silver bells like sleigh bells. One could have fancied that the boat was a fairy gondola in which one might sail to elfland. Was it a baby's sled, perhaps?

14. Pietari drew the curtain, peeped inside and loosened the thongs by which the leather side-flaps could be laced together like a shoe. Then he took out a tiny cap, but quickly put it back in the boat, glancing guiltily round as if afraid of being caught in an unlawful act. Standing up, he slipped the twisted cords over his shoulders so that the boat hung on his back, and shook it to make sure the cords would hold. Apparently pleased with the result, he slipped it off again, sat down and lit his pipe. As he smoked he rocked the boat on his knees as if he would lull it to sleep. Then he put it back in the sled, drank his coffee, slipped on the deer-hide coat and went down to the shore again with his gun, to hide in the hole as he had hidden the night before.

15. Afternoon turned to evening, but nothing happened. Pietari sat quietly in his hide, as befitted a Lapp, without impatience. Suddenly his face grew tense; he listened, and turned his keen gaze southwards. From the far distance came a sound as of a silver trumpet. Silence followed, and then the call was repeated, coming from high in the air and far away. At times it rang out clear and shrill, at others it was muffled. Then all was silent again. Pietari saw four white birds against the deepening blue of the southern sky. They sank lower and the setting sun lent them golden wings; they dropped to treetop level, followed the bank of the river, disappeared behind the woods at the bend, and then rose again. He saw their snow-white bodies, yellow beaks and black feet; he heard the rushing of their wings like the chime of distant bells, that died away as they crossed the patch of open water. He never shifted his gaze, but when the swans had passed he raised his gun and aimed at the pool.

16. The swans vanished into the far distance, then the sound of their cry returned, softly at first, but growing louder. They circled above the woods at Pietari's back, and soon he heard the sough of wings as the flock glided down over the lead—and at the instant when they held their wings outspread and motionless before folding them at the end of their flight, he fired, and the crack of the shot shattered the stillness.

17. For a fraction of a second nothing happened. Then the birds screamed and thrashed madly at the water with wings and feet, rushed along the surface, and rose high enough to clear the ice. Three were already hovering above it, but the fourth fell back upon the edge. It tried to rise, but could not, and tumbled with straggling wings into the water. The current carried it along as it struggled, but its movements grew feebler and ceased.

18. Its companions had flown away out of sight as the shot echoed to silence among the woods and hills. The swan floated on the quiet surface of the pool and stillness filled the landscape. Once again the bird lifted its head and uttered the sound that had heralded the approaching flock; once again the sound was repeated—more remotely, as it were—and turned to a broken chiming; then its beak sank again and the current bore the lifeless body slowly towards the edge of the ice.

19. Pietari jumped up from his hide, waded through the snow and on to the ice, and started creeping towards the edge. Just as he stretched out his hand to grasp the swan, he heard the rush of wings: one of the others had returned, and skimmed so low that he felt the wind of it as it passed over him. Quickly he grasped the body of the dead swan, hauled it on to the ice and hurried shoreward, dragging it after him by the neck. When he had regained the shelter of the wood, the dead swan's companion flew once more over the water, uttered its bell-like note and vanished beyond the treetops.

20. Pietari dragged the swan to his camping-place and lit a fire. When it was burning well, he drew his sheath-knife and slit the bird's throat lengthwise, removed the windpipe and thrust a stick of birch along inside it, then held it over the fire.

21. The evening grew darker, stars came out and Pietari threw more wood on the fire. From time to time he tested the windpipe with his thumbnail, and at last withdrew the stick. He then bent the tube into a ring, fitting the smaller end into the larger, and continued the drying process. When this was done he opened the ring, took from his breast pocket a round pellet of reindeer horn and slipped it into the tube, closing the ring once more. He shook it and it gave forth a resonant, silvery jingle. Now the rattle was stowed away in the tiny boat; Pietari threw more wood on the fire, broke pine branches and stacked them nearby before lying down to sleep.

22. The Northern Lights came out in unusual brilliance, to dance their noiseless, phantom dance.

WORDS

*meaning*  Define *gnarled* (par. 3), *promontory* (par. 5), and *aurora* (par. 7).

*level of usage*  Is the word *fetched* (par. 5) peculiar to a particular level of usage?

## SENTENCES

*rhetorical devices*   1. This selection abounds in similes (for example, "bands of copper curved like lilies," par. 1). List several.   2. There are also many metaphors (for example, "shadows melting," par. 3). List several.   3. "Winged his dreams" (par. 11) appears to be a metaphor of feeling rather than of specific meaning. Yet in relation to the whole essay it could have a meaning. What do you think it means?

## PARAGRAPHS

*methods of development*   1. Many paragraphs in this essay are developed by description. Name each thing described in the first eight paragraphs.   2. By what method does the author describe the changing of day into night (par. 6)?

## CONTENT AND ORGANIZATION

*central ideas*   1. The Lapps are believed to live very close to nature. What evidence in this story supports that belief?   2. In what manner is the sentence "Pietari sat quietly in his hide, as befitted a Lapp, without impatience" (par. 15) related to the central idea?

*organization*   1. How much time passes between the beginning and the end of the story? List the scenes into which the action is divided.   2. Although the reader has some clues, he does not know what Pietari is doing until the very end. Is this a common device of short-story writing? Is it effective here? Why or why not?   3. The story is called "The Cradle," yet the word *cradle* is not mentioned in it. An "object" is introduced in paragraph 12, but in which paragraph does the reader first realize that the object is a cradle?

*assumptions and implications*   1. Is the description of the cap (the *samikahpir*) in paragraph 2 clear enough to enable you to visualize the cap? Can you draw a picture of it?   2. As the book from which this selection was taken later makes clear, Pietari is making a rattle for his yet unborn child. What do his actions and the tone of the story do to show his attitude toward the child? to reveal other aspects of his character?   3. Is the characterization of Pietari complete? Do you believe, for instance, that a man with the kind of patience shown in this story could also have an explosive nature?

## SUGGESTIONS FOR DISCUSSION

1. Have you ever observed or been a part of an action or ceremony not familiar to most Americans? Describe it.   2. Describe a hunt, an experiment, or a social experience that required the qualities of patience and

endurance. 3. This story describes Pietari's method of getting a rattle for his child. Describe the actions and hardships of a modern American father trying to buy baby equipment in a department store the week before Christmas. 4. Do you think that qualities like patience and nobility are fostered by a life lived close to nature? What qualities, if any, are fostered by a job in a New York advertising agency, an apartment in Manhattan, and a life enriched by telephones, television sets, theaters, libraries, and taxicabs?

# Describing Persons, Places, and Things

*The following essays contain many kinds of description and exhibit a wide range of subjects, attitudes, and techniques. The first, by Joan Didion, is a delicately wrought evocation of a time and place; the last, by Alan Devoe, is a carefully written, precise description of animal hibernation. Between these extremes, four other essays display a great variety of tone, of rhetorical devices, and of writers' purposes. All merit careful analysis.*

## Joan Didion

### LOS ANGELES NOTEBOOK

1. There is something uneasy in the Los Angeles air this afternoon, some unnatural stillness, some tension. What it means is that tonight a Santa Ana will begin to blow, a hot wind from the northeast whining down through the Cajon and San Gorgonio Passes, blowing up sandstorms out along Route 66, drying the hills and the nerves to the flash point. For a few days now we will see smoke back in the canyons, and hear sirens in the night. I have neither heard nor read that a Santa Ana is due, but I know it, and almost everyone I have seen today knows it too. We know it because we feel it. The baby frets. The maid sulks. I rekindle a waning argument with the telephone company, then cut my losses and lie down, given over to whatever it is in the air. To live with the Santa Ana is to accept, consciously or unconsciously, a deeply mechanistic view of human behavior.

2. I recall being told, when I first moved to Los Angeles and was living on an isolated beach, that the Indians would throw themselves into the sea when the bad wind blew. I could see why. The Pacific turned ominously glossy during a Santa Ana period, and one woke in the night troubled not only by the peacocks screaming in the olive trees but by the eerie absence of surf. The heat was surreal. The sky had a yellow cast, the kind of light sometimes called "earth-

LOS ANGELES NOTEBOOK: Reprinted with the permission of Farrar, Straus & Giroux, Inc. from *Slouching Towards Bethlehem* by Joan Didion, copyright © 1961, 1964, 1965, 1966, 1967, 1968 by Joan Didion.

quake weather." My only neighbor would not come out of her house for days, and there were no lights at night, and her husband roamed the place with a machete. One day he would tell me that he had heard a trespasser, the next a rattlesnake.

3. "On nights like that," Raymond Chandler once wrote about the Santa Ana, "every booze party ends in a fight. Meek little wives feel the edge of the carving knife and study their husbands' necks. Anything can happen." That was the kind of wind it was. I did not know then that there was any basis for the effect it had on all of us, but it turns out to be another of those cases in which science bears out folk wisdom. The Santa Ana, which is named for one of the canyons it rushes through, is a *foehn* wind, like the *foehn* of Austria and Switzerland and the *hamsin* of Israel. There are a number of persistent malevolent winds, perhaps the best known of which are the mistral of France and the Mediterranean sirocco, but a *foehn* wind has distinct characteristics: it occurs on the leeward slope of a mountain range and, although the air begins as a cold mass, it is warmed as it comes down the mountain and appears finally as a hot dry wind. Whenever and wherever a *foehn* blows, doctors hear about headaches and nausea and allergies, about "nervousness," about "depression." In Los Angeles some teachers do not attempt to conduct formal classes during a Santa Ana, because the children become unmanageable. In Switzerland the suicide rate goes up during the *foehn,* and in the courts of some Swiss cantons the wind is considered a mitigating circumstance for crime. Surgeons are said to watch the wind, because blood does not clot normally during a *foehn.* A few years ago an Israeli physicist discovered that not only during such winds, but for the ten or twelve hours which precede them, the air carries an unusually high ratio of positive to negative ions. No one seems to know exactly why that should be; some talk about friction and others suggest solar disturbances. In any case the positive ions are there, and what an excess of positive ions does, in the simplest terms, is make people unhappy. One cannot get much more mechanistic than that.

4. Easterners commonly complain that there is no "weather" at all in Southern California, that the days and the seasons slip by relentlessly, numbingly bland. That is quite misleading. In fact the climate is characterized by infrequent but violent extremes: two periods of torrential subtropical rains which continue for weeks and wash out the hills and send subdivisions sliding toward the sea; about twenty scattered days a year of the Santa Ana, which, with its incendiary dryness, invariably means fire. At the first prediction of a

Santa Ana, the Forest Service flies men and equipment from northern California into the southern forests, and the Los Angeles Fire Department cancels its ordinary nonfirefighting routines. The Santa Ana caused Malibu to burn the way it did in 1956, and Bel Air in 1961, and Santa Barbara in 1964. In the winter of 1966–67 eleven men were killed fighting a Santa Ana fire that spread through the San Gabriel Mountains.

5. Just to watch the front-page news out of Los Angeles during a Santa Ana is to get very close to what it is about the place. The longest single Santa Ana period in recent years was in 1957, and it lasted not the usual three or four days but fourteen days, from November 21 until December 4. On the first day 25,000 acres of the San Gabriel Mountains were burning, with gusts reaching 100 miles an hour. In town, the wind reached Force 12, or hurricane force, on the Beaufort Scale; oil derricks were toppled and people ordered off the downtown streets to avoid injury from flying objects. On November 22 the fire in the San Gabriels was out of control. On November 24 six people were killed in automobile accidents, and by the end of the week the Los Angeles *Times* was keeping a box score of traffic deaths. On November 26 a prominent Pasadena attorney, depressed about money, shot and killed his wife, their two sons, and himself. On November 27 a South Gate divorcee, twenty-two, was murdered and thrown from a moving car. On November 30 the San Gabriel fire was still out of control, and the wind in town was blowing eighty miles an hour. On the first day of December four people died violently, and on the third the wind began to break.

6. It is hard for people who have not lived in Los Angeles to realize how radically the Santa Ana figures in the local imagination. The city burning is Los Angeles's deepest image of itself: Nathanael West perceived that, in *The Day of the Locust;* and at the time of the 1965 Watts riots what struck the imagination most indelibly were the fires. For days one could drive the Harbor Freeway and see the city on fire, just as we had always known it would be in the end. Los Angeles weather is the weather of catastrophe, of apocalypse, and, just as the reliably long and bitter winters of New England determine the way life is lived there, so the violence and the unpredictability of the Santa Ana affect the entire quality of life in Los Angeles, accentuate its impermanence, its unreliability. The wind shows us how close to the edge we are.

7. "Here's why I'm on the beeper, Ron," said the telephone voice on the all-night radio show. "I just want to say that this *Sex*

*for the Secretary* creature—whatever her name is—certainly isn't contributing anything to the morals in this country. It's pathetic. Statistics *show."*

8. "It's *Sex and the Office,* honey," the disc jockey said. "That's the title. By Helen Gurley Brown. Statistics show what?"

9. "I haven't got them right here at my fingertips, naturally. But they *show."*

10. "I'd be interested in hearing them. Be constructive, you Night Owls."

11. "All right, let's take *one* statistic," the voice said, truculent now. "Maybe I haven't read the book, but what's this business she recommends about *going out with married men for lunch?"*

12. So it went, from midnight until 5 A.M., interrupted by records and by occasional calls debating whether or not a rattlesnake can swim. Misinformation about rattlesnakes is a leitmotiv of the insomniac imagination in Los Angeles. Toward 2 A.M. a man from "out Tarzana way" called to protest. "The Night Owls who called earlier must have been thinking about, uh, *The Man in the Gray Flannel Suit* or some other book," he said, "because Helen's one of the few authors trying to tell us what's really going *on.* Hefner's another, and he's also controversial, working in, uh, another area."

13. An old man, after testifying that he "personally" had seen a swimming rattlesnake, in the Delta-Mendota Canal, urged "moderation" on the Helen Gurley Brown question. "We shouldn't get on the beeper to call things pornographic before we've read them," he complained, pronouncing it porn-ee-oh-graphic. "I say, get the book. Give it a chance." The original *provocateur* called back to agree that she would get the book. "And then I'll burn it," she added.

14. "Book burner, eh?" laughed the disc jockey good-naturedly.

15. "I wish they still burned witches," she hissed.

16. It is three o'clock on a Sunday afternoon and 105° and the air so thick with smog that the dusty palm trees loom up with a sudden and rather attractive mystery. I have been playing in the sprinklers with the baby and I get in the car and go to Ralph's Market on the corner of Sunset and Fuller wearing an old bikini bathing suit. That is not a very good thing to wear to the market but neither is it, at Ralph's on the corner of Sunset and Fuller, an unusual costume. Nonetheless a large woman in a cotton muumuu jams her cart into mine at the butcher counter. *"What a thing to wear to the market,"* she says in a loud but strangled voice. Everyone looks the other way and I study a plastic package of rib lamb chops and she

repeats it. She follows me all over the store, to the Junior Foods, to the Dairy Products, to the Mexican Delicacies, jamming my cart whenever she can. Her husband plucks at her sleeve. As I leave the check-out counter she raises her voice one last time: *"What a thing to wear to Ralph's,"* she says.

17. A party at someone's house in Beverly Hills: a pink tent, two orchestras, a couple of French Communist directors in Cardin evening jackets, chili and hamburgers from Chasen's. The wife of an English actor sits at a table alone; she visits California rarely although her husband works here a good deal. An American who knows her slightly comes over to the table.

18. "Marvelous to see you here," he says.

19. "Is it," she says.

20. "How long have you been here?"

21. "Too long."

22. She takes a fresh drink from a passing waiter and smiles at her husband, who is dancing.

23. The American tries again. He mentions her husband.

24. "I hear he's marvelous in this picture."

25. She looks at the American for the first time. When she finally speaks she enunciates every word very clearly. "He . . . is . . . also . . . a . . . fag," she says pleasantly.

26. The oral history of Los Angeles is written in piano bars. "Moon River," the piano player always plays, and "Mountain Greenery." "There's a Small Hotel" and "This Is Not the First Time." People talk to each other, tell each other about their first wives and last husbands. "Stay funny," they tell each other, and "This is to die over." A construction man talks to an unemployed screenwriter who is celebrating, alone, his tenth wedding anniversary. The construction man is on a job in Montecito: "Up in Montecito," he says, "they got one square mile with 135 millionaires."

27. "Putrescence," the writer says.

28. "That's all you got to say about it?"

29. "Don't read me wrong, I think Santa Barbara's one of the most—Christ, *the* most—beautiful places in the world, but it's a beautiful place that contains a . . . *putrescence*. They just live on their putrescent millions."

30. "So give me putrescent."

31. "No, no," the writer says. "I just happen to think millionaires have some sort of lacking in their . . . in their elasticity."

32. A drunk requests "The Sweetheart of Sigma Chi." The piano player says he doesn't know it. "Where'd you learn to play the piano?" the drunk asks. "I got two degrees," the piano player says. "One in musical education." I go to a coin telephone and call a friend in New York. "Where are you?" he says. "In a piano bar in Encino," I say. "Why?" he says. "Why not," I say.

## WORDS

*meaning* Define *flash point* (par. 1), *surreal* (par. 2), *apocalypse* (par. 6), *insomniac imagination* (par. 12), *oral history* (par. 26), *putrescence* (par. 27).

*exactness* 1. Which of the words under "meaning," above, is the author using with precision? 2. What word does the speaker possibly have in mind in paragraph 31 when he speaks of *elasticity?* Or if he really means *elasticity,* what does that mean?

## SENTENCES

*parallelism* 1. Does the conjunction of *hills* and *nerves* in paragraph 1 make sense? Does it help to explain the meaning of the final sentence of the paragraph? 2. Can you find another reference to a *mechanistic view* of human nature? Does this reference make the first any clearer?

## PARAGRAPHS

*topic sentence* What is the topic sentence of paragraph 5?

*methods of development* How is paragraph 5 developed?

*coherence* 1. What holds paragraph 26 together? 2. What is the point of the two illustrations (par. 26) of characteristic conversational phrases heard in Los Angeles bars?

## CONTENT AND ORGANIZATION

*organization* Since this is called a "Notebook," it is logical enough that the piece consists of a series of separate observations; yet taken together these are meant to give an overall impression of the quality of a place. The key observation seems to come in the last two sentences of paragraph 6. Isolate the words in these sentences that state the theme of the whole. Do the paragraphs that follow bear them out? What do the final five sentences of the piece tell about the author in relation to the general theme? Why does the author refer several times to her baby, and where is that baby in the final scene? Are we to assume that the Santa Ana wind is blowing throughout?

1. Paragraph 3 refers to a short story by Raymond Chandler called "Red Wind." Point out the similarities between this essay and "Red Wind." 2. The author refers (par. 6) to Nathanael West's novel about Los Angeles, *The Day of the Locust*. Read that novel and point out other thematic connections between the Didion piece and the book beyond their common concern with the burning of the city.

*David Bronsen*

## A CONVERSATION WITH
## HENRY ROTH

1. *When* Call It Sleep *appeared in 1934 critics were largely of one mind: Henry Roth's first novel, the story of the earliest years of a Jewish immigrant boy in New York, was a work of remarkable maturity and artistic command. With a narrative technique that still seems modern today and the acute perception of a major talent, the author had achieved a masterpiece that gave promise of being the first in a series of brilliant works. Maxwell Perkins of Scribner's, who read one hundred pages of what was intended to be Roth's second novel, predicted that that work would be "one of the outstanding books in contemporary American fiction." Yet that manuscript was destroyed before completion, and* Call It Sleep, *which soon went out of print, was destined for nearly three decades to become what Alfred Kazin has called "one of the underground classics of psychological fiction." In 1960 the book was rescued from limbo by an enterprising publisher and has since appeared in Dutch, French, Italian, Spanish, and British editions.*

2. *When I visited Henry Roth on his farm near Augusta, Maine, I had many questions in mind. What of himself had he poured into this novel? Why had he never published another book? Did the Jewish identity which permeates his novel cast any light on its author's arrested creativity? I soon discovered that Henry Roth was full of questions of his own. The author of* Call It Sleep *has accepted his*

A CONVERSATION WITH HENRY ROTH: © 1969 by Partisan Review. Reprinted by permission of the author and the Partisan Review. Minor revisions and additions have been made by the author.

*estrangement from literature and the isolation which has become a way of life for him, but has never stopped asking "why?"*

3. *There was an air of subdued animation in the deeply lined face and dark eyes of the slight man with whom I found myself confronted. A deliberate, ruminative quality seemed at various times in our day-long interview to be struggling with a spirited vitality, which by force of habit kept itself in check most of the time. The meeting did not turn out to be an interview between an interrogator and his subject, but rather a colloquy between a writer and his mind. This is a man who has been looking for answers for a long time, and the paths of his search are so well-defined, his process of discovery so evolved, that questions became mostly superfluous and direction on my part proved unnecessary.*

4. *Listening to Henry Roth recapitulating the facts of his life and the background of* Call It Sleep *was itself an experience. Marked by surprising candor, his personal remarks started out as quiet recollection and proceeded to run a gamut of emotions from anguish to exhilaration. In reliving his life by narrating it, he several times switched to the present tense. Although I have altered the tenses for the sake of grammatical consistency, these unconscious lapses pointed up the most poignant events in his life: his childhood in New York, the writing of* Call It Sleep, *the beating he took on the New York waterfront, and the deprivation that came with the loss of creativity.*

5. *Almost all of this man's conclusions, including the most assertive, give the impression of being hypotheses. Even his heated affirmations have an air of groping, of searching for signposts and certainties. He continues to hold his final judgment in abeyance, ready to reword, retract, rethink, as he has been doing for years. He remains a man for whom life has not ceased to be a mysterious and elusive puzzle, which is to say that he has not lost the novelist's turn of mind.*

6. *Henry Roth is obviously a person with an extraordinary need for self-expression, although his manner suggests that verbal communication has been a luxury for long periods of his life. At one point in the interview I remarked that he had never lost his command of language. He replied,* "That comes from having talked with myself for twenty-five years." *But by then he was well launched on his personal narrative.*

7. It's too bad I was not older when I was brought to America, so that I could recall the Old World and the original home of my

mother and father. I was born in Tysmenitsa, near Lemberg, Galicia, in 1906, and was only eighteen months old when my mother brought me to this country.

8.   My father had gone to New York and saved up enough money to bring my mother and me over in steerage. This is the material I used in the prologue of *Call It Sleep*. Since there was no birth certificate, there was some doubt about my age. My father said I was two and a half years old when I came, but my mother maintained I was a year younger. As proof she used to point out that my sister, who was conceived in America, was two years younger than I am, so I imagine that her version of my age is correct.

9.   My parents settled down in Brownsville at first, which corresponds to certain passages of the novel. Two years later we moved to Ninth Street on the Lower East Side of Manhattan. When we lived there in the years 1910 to 1914, the East Side represented a very secure enclave. Everyone in our building was Jewish, as were the neighbors to either side of us and the people across the street. Had I thought of it in those terms back then, I would have said that I was surrounded by a homogeneous environment and that I completely identified with it. In that atmosphere of devoutness and orthodoxy it would not have occurred to anyone to question the dietary regulations or the observance of holiday rituals. Those were the years when the huge influx of Eastern Jewish immigration was building the area up. The East Side was helpful, communicative, and highly interrelated—in short, a community. It was a place with the promise of opportunities and new horizons, where one could make a new start in life. And the Jew in those years was optimistic and dynamic, full of the feeling that nothing was holding him back.

10.   We lived in Ninth Street till I was eight years old, and then in the summer of 1914 we moved to Harlem. My mother's parents, along with several uncles and aunts, were brought over just before the outbreak of the First World War and settled by my maternal uncle in a steam-heated, hot-water apartment in Harlem. My mother wanted to be near her parents, which accounted for our moving there too. The move turned out to be crucial for me.

11.   We settled at 108 East 119th Street, near the trestle of the New York–New Haven Railroad. This part of the neighborhood, squeezed in between Little Italy to the east and the more prosperous and predominately Jewish area to the west, was considered the poorer part of Harlem. It was a mixture of Irish, Italians, and Jews, and a rough mixture. I was taken from a neighborhood that had been home for me and put in a highly hostile environment. That produced a

shock from which I have perhaps never recovered. Until then I had had a natural love of activity and enjoyed the companionship of other children. I had been a good student in school as well as in *cheder*. After the move to Harlem all that changed and I took to avoiding outside contact by staying in the house and near Mama as much as possible, so that I grew fat with the lack of activity. In fact, that is what the children used to call me—"fatty." For weeks I cried and had tantrums, begging to be taken back to Ninth Street. But no one paid any attention to me, nor was there any concern when I received C's for the first time on my report card. I got into fights at the new school for a while, but I soon learned to avoid any provocation. I retreated into myself and stayed out of people's way. Serious psychological damage had been brought about by this uprooting of a naturally conservative child, and it expressed itself after a while in my rejection of Jewish faith and customs, which until then had been a part of me. I felt no anguish over this at the time—I was throwing it all to the winds. My mother, who was the only source of security, did not understand what was going on, although I suppose her example was also influencing my behavior. She herself was reacting against the fanatical orthodoxy of her father, which had oppressed her as a child and a young woman. If her faith had not been tongue in cheek I might have been insulated against the influences of Harlem. But she did not seem to care if I became a Goy or not, and damn it, I became a Goy!

12. My father was also not particularly orthodox, he merely went through the motions. He did not fail to celebrate Seder and observe Yom Kippur, but at the core true devoutness no longer existed. My father had a pat phrase that he appended to every reference to God, which he continues to use till this day: *"op si doh a Gott"*—"if there is a God."

13. Looking at it in another way, I suppose my parents went through some of the same dislocation by coming to America that I experienced by moving to Harlem. That kind of change is much more of a trauma for the Eastern Jew than for the Westerner. The Jew coming out of his little Eastern European hamlet, with its insularity and stagnation, is likely to undergo a radical transformation when he gets caught up in the tumult and perpetual change of American life.

14. In any case, the move in 1914, the Goyish environment and the negative example of my parents threw me into a state of turmoil. I had gone to Harlem with a pronounced Jewish bent and proceeded to take on the conflicting characteristics of my new surroundings. It was as if two valences of the same element were at odds

with one another; at the time, of course, I could not intellectualize about the contradictions involved, but I did feel them emotionally, and my response took the form of rebelling against Judaism. I fought as hard as I could against going through with the Bar Mitzvah, even though my parents insisted on it and finally had their way. But only a year later, when I was fourteen, I firmly announced that I was an atheist.

15. *Call It Sleep* is set in the East Side, but it violates the truth about what the East Side was like back then. Ninth Street was only a fragmentary model for what I was doing. In reality, I took the violent environment of Harlem—where we lived from 1914 to 1928—and projected it back onto the East Side. It became a montage of milieus, in which I was taking elements of one neighborhood and grafting them onto another. This technique must have grown out of the rage I had been living with all those fourteen years. I was alienated —to use that old hack of a word—and my novel became a picture in metaphors of what had happened to me.

16. All the rancorous anti-Semitism which Hitler was beginning to epitomize was not limited to Germany alone. To a lesser degree it was being felt everywhere. It may be difficult to explain how such social forces affect the individual psyche, but it is clear that they have powerful behavioral effects. My own experience of being thrown into a neighborhood where anti-Semitism was growing provides an example, and the scene in *Call It Sleep* in which David Schearl lamely denies his being Jewish to the gang that is threatening him is an objectification of the same thing.

17. The characters in the novel have a cohesion of their own, but to really understand them you have to go through the characters and back to the author to find out what was motivating and disturbing him. I needed empirical reality for the sake of its plausibility, but I took off from it on a tangent. In other words, I was working with characters, situations, and events that had in part been taken from life, but which I molded to give expression to what was oppressing me. To a considerable extent I was drawing on the unconscious to give shape to remembered reality. Things which I could not fully understand but which filled me with apprehension played a critical role in determining the form of the novel. The father in the novel is a powerfully built, menacing person given to uncontrolled violence. My own father, who served as a model for this figure, was basically an impulsive little man with poor judgment, and perhaps a little unbalanced. He did not beat me often, but when he did he went crazy. Because I felt I could be overwhelmed at any time by forces

that were constantly threatening me, it became necessary to change this little man into someone capable of real destruction. Violence is associated as a rule with great strength, and to the mind of a child an adult seems to be seven feet tall.

18.   I worked with polarities in expressing the subjective reality of the little boy in the novel. I am referring to the personalities of the mother and father, as well as the characters of the mother and her sister. Actually, my own mother was the source of both of these contrasting female figures. I abstracted one side of my mother, rounded it out, and created an aunt who in most respects is the antithesis of David Schearl's mother. The presence of Aunt Bertha seemed to give an aesthetic justification to the character of the mother as well.

19.   My parents were hopelessly mismatched, and their life together was marked by furious quarreling. My mother, who felt profoundly cheated in her husband, could never bring herself to express the full force of her feelings against him until late in life, when an outbreak of paranoia tore down all her reserve. In her earlier years she turned all her attention to me. Since at that age I could hardly have any recourse to depth analysis, the Oedipal fixation that took hold of me was to keep me firmly in its grip.

20.   I made use of a number of incidents out of my childhood experiences, but recast them in a manner that is just as revealing of the author's frame of mind and his hindsight as it is of the character of the little boy. The critical episode in the novel of thrusting the milk dipper into the car track is an example. A couple of boys had enticed me into doing that for the sake of a prank. The author turned the incident into a personal statement: the impressionable boy living in hostile surroundings adopts as his own a destructive act to which he is instigated by outsiders to whom he has no personal relationship.

21.   After publication of *Call It Sleep* a number of critics pointed out what they thought were its social implications. My own feeling was that what I had written was far too private for me to have given much thought to specific social problems. My personal involvement had absorbed my entire consciousness, leaving no room to focus on anything else.

22.   When I force myself to be objective I realize that if I had not moved to Harlem I most likely would never have written the novel. But during the anxieties and hardships of the intervening years I have told myself that I would not hesitate to sacrifice *Call It Sleep* for a happy childhood, adolescence, and young manhood. Given the choice, I would have stayed on the East Side until I was at least eighteen years old. Then I would have gone forth.

23. Of course, I can see that moving to Harlem was a formative experience in its own right. It had the virtue of compelling an enlargement of vision and sympathy. I was presented at an impressionable age, when everything becomes emotionally charged, with the problem of trying to integrate in my mind a much greater diversity and many more contrasting forces than I would have known otherwise. If we had stayed on the East Side and I had gone on to write—two big ifs, because I wanted to become a biology teacher when I was a boy—it is possible that I might have written some honest portrayals of Jewish life on the East Side. Such writing would necessarily have reflected Jewish life *as* Jewish life, which is not the case with my novel; I do not regard *Call It Sleep* as primarily a novel of Jewish life. There is something positive in the writer striving for the broader awareness that enables him to interrelate many more disparate elements in an art form; such an aim, by its very nature, requires the consideration of a much wider world than the one I originally came from.

24. As an illustration you can take the case of Robert Frost. From my knowledge of his verse, Frost never broke through what might be called the bucolic curtain. Emotionally and ideologically he played it safe by never going out into the larger world to test his attitudes and views. Had I stayed on the Lower East Side I also would have been spared having to submit my feelings and beliefs to a wider experience and understanding.

25. During the years in which I devoted myself to writing *Call It Sleep* I came to regard myself as a disciplined writer who could turn his hand to whatever literary task he cut out for himself. I knew that the flow of creativity would not be uniform, and I had come to expect resistance from my material, but I felt that by working at it I could resolve all the difficulties I encountered. My self-confidence approached the point of arrogance in those years. I remember in a moment of introspection reviewing in my mind the authors and literary works that I considered important and that had personally affected me. At the same time, and with a good deal of pride, I felt that I was consciously fighting literary influences and going my own way.

26. T. S. Eliot, James Joyce, and Eugene O'Neill were the writers of major stature that interested me back then. Eliot's *Waste Land* had a devastating effect on me, I felt stunned by the vastness of its conception. I had been introduced to the work by Eda Lou Walton, a professor of literature at New York University. It was to her that I dedicated *Call It Sleep*. She was a woman twelve years older than I,

who was very devoted to me and who for a time supported and sponsored me. Our relationship had certain parallels to that of Thomas Wolfe and Aline Bernstein, although I do not stress the resemblance.

27. Some of the plays of Eugene O'Neill left a deep imprint. I went to see *The Great God Brown* with Eda Lou and came away feeling that I had been listening to the inner voice of a man.

28. I had already read Joyce as a freshman in college, and a copy of *Ulysses* which Eda Lou had brought me from France introduced me to an entirely new way of seeing things. I felt I could see doors swinging open on untried possibilities in literature.

29. But during the time I was writing the novel I was trying to establish a demarcation between myself and other authors. As far as I was concerned, no one could teach me anything and nothing was too big an undertaking.

30. I started writing *Call It Sleep* in 1929, worked on it for four years, and finished it in 1933, when I was twenty-seven. A substantial part of the book was written in Maine, in the small town of Norridgewock, in 1932. I learned of a farmhouse where an elderly widow, a woman of seventy, boarded the local schoolmistress; and since this was summer and the room vacant, she agreed to take me in as a boarder. For seven dollars a week I got room and board—and was fed royally. I had nothing to do but work on my novel, which I did from June till November. It was a happy stay, and years later, when I was casting about for a place in which to settle down, it must have been the memory of those satisfying months that made me decide on Maine.

31. The book was published in 1934 by Ballou and Company. I paid little attention to the contract at the time and just wondered how the publisher could possibly hope for any financial return on the book in the middle of the Depression. Viewed from today's vantage point, you would think Robert Ballou had a gold mine in his possession. Meyer Levin was one of his authors and John Steinbeck, who was just getting started, was another. But his firm was having difficulties, like so many others; one publisher after another was going on the rocks and selling his writers to the more affluent survivors. Owing to Ballou's rather desperate financial straits, he was relieved when David Mandel, a lawyer, put some money in the firm. That gave Mandel a share of the business and certain rights in deciding policy. Ballou was already favorably inclined to the book, and David Mandel, who subsequently married Eda Lou Walton, submitted to her urging to have the book published.

32. In later years people would say to me, "You haven't written because you were not given any recognition." That is not true; for

a first novel I was given a large measure of acclaim, enough to encourage any writer. And the fact is that I did write, for a time. . . .

33.   Even before the publication of *Call It Sleep* I was at work on a new book. I had met a colorful person around whom I was building my second novel. The man was a tough, second-generation German–American who had been raised on the streets of Cincinnati and relied on his fists and his physical stamina to cope with life. Being an illiterate, he had acquired almost everything he knew through his own experience. I was attracted to him because he always took pride in being able to defend himself, no matter what happened. His build and the way he carried himself made me think of a champion middleweight fighter, and as a matter of fact, he had trained with professionals. When he told me that he had never been beaten I was inclined to believe him. Then suddenly this man who had fought and brawled his way through life lost his right hand in an industrial accident. With that came the terrible shock and realization that he was no longer able to fight the world alone. His personal tragedy and the knowledge that he would have to turn to others for help were terrifying blows that hit him at the depth of the Depression and changed his whole outlook on life.

34.   Like many intellectuals during the Depression, I had become attracted to Marxism and felt the Communist Party to be its true expression. It was as a result of my contact with the Party that I met my German acquaintance and conceived the idea of basing a novel on him. The man and what I learned about him fitted in with what I thought the Party stood for. I carefully gathered the data of his life as well as my observations concerning him, and wrote about a hundred pages of manuscript. He had become an organizer for the Party, and several times I went along with him to distribute leaflets on the waterfront, where I used the Italian I had been studying on my own to make contacts with the longshoremen. There was no CIO at that time, and the Party was espousing the cause of industrial unions on the waterfront, in the same way that Harry Bridges had been doing on the West Coast.

35.   One day while I was accompanying him on his assignment, my "character," whose instincts for danger were better than mine, warned me, "Better stay close to me." With a hook for a hand he was still a man that no one was likely to cross. But I wandered away from him in the process of handing out the leaflets.

36.   The aims of the Communist Party had been coming into conflict with those of the AFL, which was well entrenched among the longshoremen. I was approached by one of the business agents of

the AFL, who asked me for a leaflet. When I held it out to him he belted me across the face, smashed my glasses, and proceeded to beat me up, all the time driving me across the highway as he pounded away at me. By the time my friend came running towards me the incident was over, but for a man of sensibility no further lesson was needed about the animosity and antagonism that arise from a struggle over vested interests.

37.  In the meantime, Ballou had gone bankrupt and sold Scribner's the rights to my second book. During the negotiations I had submitted the unfinished manuscript to Scribner's editor, Maxwell Perkins, who was so enthusiastic that he predicted the novel would be one of the outstanding books in contemporary American fiction. The poor man—he died without getting the rest of the manuscript. Once the contract was signed and Ballou was paid, I did not write another word. I had mapped out in detail the course I was to follow in each chapter of the book, but I seemed to have arrived at an utter impasse.

38.  Only after completing all the rest of *Call It Sleep* did I go back and write the prologue. But after doing the first hundred pages of the second book I changed directions and did the prologue as a pretext for not going on to Section II.

39.  My second book was supposed to be a short but substantial novel, that I was going to follow with a longer one, for which I had been saving myself. This work was to be far more ambitious and of greater scope; in it I would deal with the Jewish intellectual embracing many more elements of the social world. But my second novel was not getting anywhere. For a time I made all kinds of excuses to myself, then I decided I had made a mistake by limiting my perspective to the midwestern proletarian that was turning revolutionary. I wanted the words to come flowing out of me again, and I needed a fresh start; as a physical demonstration of this recognition I burned the manuscript I had shown Perkins and set to work on the next novel. I wrote the opening chapters, which dealt with autobiographical material from Harlem, but I felt I was not reaching the mark. My notes called for bringing together a great many disparate aspects of society and weaving them into an artistic whole. More than anything else I required a sense of unity in the work I did, a unity that could almost be reduced to a metaphor. I struggled with both the style and content, getting only so far before once again running up against immobility and total frustration.

40.  I found myself analyzing my views on progress and indulging for hours and days in mental excursions on the subject of moral

righteousness. To my surprise I found myself in sympathy with the South and its myths of tradition and languorous women. I carried on debates with myself in which my intellectual judgment and my sensuous orientation were at odds with each other. Common sense told me that my principles required that I side with the more enlightened North, that my phantasies were ignoring the disadvantaged Negro and the ugliness of racism. To my horror I caught myself musing about the Nazi cult of German brotherhood, and then I would shudder when I stopped to think what they were doing to the Jews in Germany.

41. I suppose all this was a revulsion from the emphasis on the struggle for social justice. The intellectual decision to identify myself with the proletariat had created a crisis which brought into sharp focus my dichotomy as a human being. I knew that justice was at stake, that Jews were involved, that one had to do something about poverty. But poverty is ugly and the proletarian bored me, with the result that the sensuousness in my nature was pulling me in the opposite direction. The artist in me had never gotten over the appeal of art for art's sake, which had flourished in the twenties. With this war going on inside of me I became immobilized to the point that I found myself incapable of making a narrative decision. All this is subjective evidence that something was knocking the props out from under me, that in spite of my tremendous creative urge something was working against me, stymieing me, preventing me from doing what I desired most. My efforts to get on with the novel petered out and the whole thing gradually shriveled and withered away, until finally I destroyed that manuscript as well. I regret that now. Had I kept the autobiographical material about Harlem it might have provided me at some later time with renewed motivation.

42. When a writer gives up what is most vital to him, the work in which he has placed his greatest hopes and which was going to be the object of his greatest efforts, he is undercutting his creative gifts and abilities. I was through. For a long time I thought that I was afflicted by some peculiar curse. But I have come to believe that there was something deeper and less personal in my misfortune, that what had happened to me was common to a whole generation of writers in the thirties. One author after another, whether he was Gentile or Jew, stopped writing, became repetitive, ran out of anything new to say or just plain died artistically. I came to this conclusion because I simply could not believe that anyone with as much discipline, creative drive, inbred feeling for the narrative and intense will to write as I had, could, after such rigorous efforts, still be balked.

43.   Looking about, I saw the same phenomenon manifesting itself in practically every writer I knew. They became barren. Daniel Fuchs decided after his third novel that he would write for Hollywood. He maintained that he had arrived at his decision clearly and rationally, but I do not believe that. James Farrell is another example. He had exhausted himself by the time he had written his third novel, and everything he wrote after that consisted of variations on played-out themes. Steinbeck is not radically different, as far as his real contribution is concerned; nothing else he ever wrote came up to *The Grapes of Wrath*. And Edward Dahlberg—what did he write after *Bottom Dogs* and *From Flushing to Calvary?* There was Hart Crane and Leonie Adams, both of whom ran into the stone wall of non-creativity. Crane committed suicide, and Nathanael West for his part conveniently died.

44.   I have to get a cigarette—this works me up! [*Mr. Roth lit his cigarette deliberately, abruptly changed the subject and bantered for several minutes before resuming his train of thought.*]

45.   How does one explain this peculiarity? It happened often enough that I began to reflect on it, and I have continued to reflect on it ever since. I do not have the training to make a scientific or sociological analysis, but it seems to me that World War II, which was already in the making, was a dividing line between an era which was coming to an end, namely ours, and another, which was coming into being. I think that we sensed a sharp turn in historic development. How do writers sense these things? We sense it in our prolonged malaise, and in our art—in the fact that, having been fruitful writers, we suddenly grow sterile. The causes are personal, but they are also bigger than any of us. When so many people are affected in the same way and each one is groping for his own diagnosis, you have to look for a broader explanation.

46.   To those of us who were committed to the Left, the Soviet Union was the cherished homeland; but that homeland had become an establishment which was interested in consolidating itself. In the Moscow trials the establishment was destroying the revolution, although at the time we were still loudly professing our allegiance. Events often do not become comprehensible until long after they have occurred.

47.   I am throwing out these ideas as possibilities. The scholar who some day will be making a formal study of the question will undoubtedly find other things to single out. One interesting facet he will have to investigate is the influence such historical factors exert on the artist. How do they get into the writer's bloodstream and affect his

creative sensibility? How are his potentialities inhibited? The world around him after all remains largely intact, but something inside of him has changed.

48. In 1938, when I was despairing of ever writing again, my relationship with Eda Lou Walton deteriorated. We separated, and almost immediately afterwards I met Muriel Parker at Yaddo, an artist's colony at Saratoga Springs. The following year we were married, but the only livelihood we had came from the WPA and relief. They had me working with pick and shovel laying sewer pipes as well as repairing and maintaining streets. In 1940 I wrote "Somebody Always Grabs the Purple," a story of a boy's visit to the public library, which was published in *The New Yorker*. When I notified the relief agency that I had received three hundred dollars for the publication I was reclassified as being no longer indigent, and promptly removed from the rolls.

49. Shortly after that I obtained a steady job as a substitute teacher at a high school in the Bronx. I decided that jobs offer security, that I would have to accept the obligations and compulsions that came my way and forget I had been a writer. When I discussed this with my wife we both agreed that I would never write again. I told myself I had done so many different things in the meantime that there would be no more suffering, yet there was some hidden reservation that lingered on and continued to crop up in moments of introspection.

50. By 1940 Europe was at war and the American economy was speeding up. I learned that people were being trained as craftsmen to turn out the immense volume of war material that was beginning to come off the assembly lines, and the thought of a skilled trade appealed to me. Although I had given up being a writer and accepted the idea that I would have to work for a living like everybody else, I still felt that anything remotely touching on my former interest—and that included advertising as well as clerical and office work—was repugnant to me. So I gravitated to machineshop work and became a precision grinder. That entailed doing the high precision finishing work on a variety of cutting tools, dies, fixtures, and jigs. The machinists who carried out the earlier parts of the operation left me only a few thousandths of an inch to take off. The ordinary machinist does not care for such slow and demanding work, but I had always been interested in mathematics, which was necessary for the required calculations, and I came to like the work. In time I was classified as A-1 on the basis of the skill I acquired.

51. For six years I plied that trade and regarded myself as a machinist. During those years, perhaps because it had been the scene

of my frustration, I developed a distaste for New York. I wanted to get away from anything that reminded me of my past as a writer. But leaving New York is a twofold undertaking for a New Yorker. First of all he has to decide to make the break, having always looked upon New York implicitly as the only place in which he could live. Then he has to decide where he is going. In 1945 I finally made the move and took the family to Boston.

52. Fifteen years passed before I was to return even briefly to New York. I discovered then that it was no longer my New York. I had been so versed in the city, I could see the little detail that spoke for the whole, and had developed an expertise in conning the place. I went back to visit Ninth Street and the East Side, the neighborhood I had known and identified with, and discovered the whole area had become Puerto Rican. The great spirit that had once vitalized that stack of bricks was gone. Nevertheless, I was moved by nostalgia the first time I went back there; perhaps there was a touch of symbolism in my "return." But now I would like to see everything there bulldozed down and some fit habitations erected. My response to prowling through Harlem was markedly different. You experience nostalgia if you are aware of a former identity which has been displaced or re-placed. I never had that kind of tie to Harlem, only the feeling that I did not belong.

53. After working in Boston during 1945 and 1946 I decided that was not the right place for me either. I found an inexpensive farm in Maine, not the one I am living on now, but in Montville, and the price of twelve hundred dollars included the house and barn. The one-hundred-ten acre farm described a ribbon a couple of hundred yards wide and a mile long. I bought the place in March, 1946, and two months later my wife and the two boys came out here to live. After continuing work for six more months in Boston I settled down with my family in Maine.

54. The years that followed were occupied with making a living and supporting the family. I started out by taking a job as a teacher at a school in which eight grades were all cooped up in one room. I never learned the knack of keeping them all busy; while I was teach-ing the eighth grade the first and second graders would get restless. I saw myself as a juggler trying to keep up an illusion of perpetual motion.

55. There followed a variety of odd jobs—from putting in heating insulation to fire fighting in the woods of Maine—whatever offered a livable wage. In 1949, the same year we moved to Augusta, I went to work as an attendant at the Augusta State Hospital and

later became a psychiatric aide, a position I held for four years. By then both of my boys were in school and my wife was able to start teaching. From that point on we managed fairly well, although our income never amounted to much. My wife was a wonderful sport and took the ups and downs in her stride. My own attitude was that there was no real meaning outside of writing, so it did not really matter what I did.

56.   Time passed, it became clear that the hospital job had no future, and I turned to something new. Since we were down in a hollow near a brook, I thought the farm would be a good place to raise waterfowl. With the help of my boys that is what I did for a number of years. I used to winter forty breeders each of ducks and geese in order to have fertile eggs in the spring. Then I would incubate the eggs and peddle the ducklings and goslings. I worked up a little trade in feathers too; goose feathers are worth two dollars a pound. When my sons came home from school they ran errands and did chores. That was a happy period for me; I found it wonderful to be working with my own boys.

57.   My life during those years revolved around the family. From time to time I used to wish I could take part in intellectual discussion, but it was pointless to attempt that with the neighbors. There was always my wife, however, and discussion was carried on at home. The area of contact between myself and the natives has been very slight, just as the overlapping of that which is vitally important for them and myself is minimal. The result is that my family and I have lived rather retired lives, to the point where I seem no longer to miss anything in the way of larger human contact. Being a Jew has not provided fellowship either—nor has it been a problem. The Jewish population in Maine is small and I doubt that most of the people I deal with know that I am Jewish.

58.   When my older boy got a scholarship to Phillips Exeter Academy and, a couple of years later, the other one went away to finish high school, my wife and I found ourselves alone. It became necessary to find something less taxing than raising waterfowl by myself, so I took to tutoring Latin and math.

59.   In the summer of 1959 Harold Ribalow, a critic of American–Jewish literature, came out here to talk with me about *Call It Sleep* and its possible republication. That was the first time it occurred to me that anyone might be interested in bringing out the book. I felt that from a business standpoint it would be a foolish venture and would not do any better than it had the first time. I was gratified, however, and hoped that it would result in some needed income.

Ribalow pointed out that my copyright was approaching the expiration date, after which the book would become public domain. My obliviousness to that fact shows how divorced I was from literature and writing. As a result of Ribalow's interest the book was brought out by Cooper Square Publishers in 1960, and then in 1964, thirty years after the first publication, it came out as a paperback with Avon Books. After all those years of being out of print the book had become accessible again.

60.    What I had perhaps overlooked is that one grows old and that a book like *Call It Sleep* can gain a certain value as an antiquity. At least I was still alive to see the revival of interest in the novel. I am sure that moving to Maine with its much slower pace of life, giving up the consuming attempt to keep writing at all costs, and the devotion of a steady and sensible wife account for my being alive today. Otherwise the republication of the book would have been a posthumous event. But as far as literature is concerned, I am in reality no longer alive. The renewed interest in *Call It Sleep* is being witnessed by a dead author who still happens to be ambulatory.

61.    But strangely enough, this dead author may be going through a resurrection. I started writing again in the summer of 1967, simultaneously with the outbreak and conclusion of the Israeli-Arab war. I was in Guadalajara, Mexico, at the time, where I had gone with my wife on the royalties of *Call It Sleep,* and where I followed the daily events of the war in the local newspapers with great avidity. I found myself identifying intensely with the Israelis in their military feats, which repudiated all the anti-Jewish accusations we had been living with in the Diaspora, and I was glorying in their establishment of themselves as a state through their own application and resources. An intellectual excitement seized hold of me that forced me to set down what was going through my mind, to record my thoughts about Israel and my new reservations regarding the Soviet Union. What I wrote seemed to reflect a peculiar adoption. Israel did not adopt me; I adopted my *ex post facto* native land. What seemed important was that I identified with Israel without being a Zionist and without having the least curiosity about Israel as a practical, political entity. Suddenly I had a place in the world and an origin. Having started to write, it seemed natural to go on from there, and I have been writing long hours every day since then. I am not yet sure what it is leading to, but it is necessary and is growing out of a new allegiance, an adhesion that comes from belonging.

62.    I had the need for us to be warriors; I had the need for us to be peasants and farmers, for us to exercise all the callings and

trades like any other people. I have become an extreme partisan of Israeli existence—for the first time I have a people. All this made me conscious of a latent conviction—that the individual *per se* disintegrates unless he associates himself with an institution of some sort, with a larger entity. I could not find that kind of bond in religion, and I do not think the Israelis do either. I found it in the existence of a nation. I have not been able to turn for that to America, which is presently committing the folly of destroying itself, so at least for the present I have adopted a people of my own, because they have made it possible for me to do so. And I am further indebted to Israel because I am able to write again.

63. If there is anything dramatic about all this, I suppose it can be explained as the way a fictioneer does things. Significant for me is that after his vast detour, the once-Orthodox Jewish boy has returned to his own Jewishness. I have reattached myself to part of what I had rejected in 1914. Even before the Israeli-Arab war I was beginning to feel that there might be some path that would lead me back to myself, although I realized there was no returning to the Jews of the East Side of more than a half-century ago. Then suddenly I discovered that I could align myself with a people that is forward-looking and engaged in the vital process of its own formation. And with the resumption of writing I find that I myself am reabsorbed into something that is immediately vital. One of the little—or big—projects I have undertaken is a work dealing with the artist responding to his world.

64. Being a Jew in the Diaspora is basically a state of mind, an attitude of not belonging. In that sense there are also Gentiles who are Jewish. Only two courses remain open to the Jew in America: he assimilates and disappears completely, while giving the best elements of himself to his native culture—and God knows that he has a lot to give; or he goes to Israel and does the same thing there. The emergence of Israel has proved to be the greatest threat to the continued survival of the Jew of the Diaspora. I do not think the Jew in America can exist much longer with a distinct identity, although he continues to make an attempt at it. I myself do not want the Diaspora. I am sick of it. Isn't it time we became a people again? Haven't we suffered enough?

65. *Abruptly the emotional pitch subsided, and an infinite weariness took its place, as Mr. Roth concluded,* "This has taken a lot out of me. I don't think I will be giving any more interviews."

66. *The impassioned note on which the long session had ended contrasted with the relaxed, good-natured mood which prevailed at the dinner table. Mrs. Roth had waited patiently until late evening and the conclusion of the interview, at which time this equable woman of Anglo-Saxon stock served us a superb meal consisting of well-known staples and delicacies of the Jewish cuisine. That in turn brought on reminiscences from Henry Roth about his childhood on the Lower East Side. At one point Mrs. Roth spoke of the travels abroad she and her husband have undertaken in the last few years and remarked with a touch of humor,* "Henry is a poor traveler. As soon as he gets somewhere he wants to settle down for good."*

67. *I went away thinking of a sentence by Simone Weil: "To be rooted is perhaps the most important and least recognized need of the human soul."*

## WORDS

*meaning* Define *enclave* (par. 9), *valences* (par. 14), *montage* and *milieus* (par. 15), *empirical* (par. 17), *disparate* (par. 39), *dichotomy* (par. 41), and *malaise* (par. 45).

*word choice* 1. How could the East Side be *highly interrelated* (par. 9)? 2. Where did New York's *Harlem* (par. 10) get its name? 3. What is an *Oedipal fixation* (par. 19)?

*exactness* Many people confuse *affect* (par. 16) and *effect*. Distinguish between them.

*level of usage* Because this interview is in a large part about Jews, it is necessary to understand certain terms. What is the meaning and significance of *cheder* and *Goy* (par. 11), *Seder* and *Yom Kippur* (par. 12), *Bar Mitzvah* (par. 14), and *Diaspora* (pars. 61, 64)?

## SENTENCES

*style* 1. Presumably the conversational style of an interview is different from other styles. Point out specific instances in which the style of Roth's conversation is different from that of, say, biography, fiction, or journalism. 2. If Robert Frost "never broke through what might be called the bucolic curtain" (par. 24), did this limitation affect his style adversely? Explain.

*variety* Discuss the characteristics of the third sentence in paragraph 37 and the first sentence of paragraph 44; then distinguish them in kind from the other sentences in those two paragraphs.

*rhetorical devices*   1. What is meant by "a picture in metaphors" (par. 15)?   2. How can a unity "almost be reduced to a metaphor" (par. 39)? 3. What do you think of the use of "In the meantime" (par. 37), which is an example of what is sometimes called the "meanwhile, back at the ranch" technique?

## PARAGRAPHS

*topic sentence*   Is the first sentence of paragraph 40 the topic sentence? If so, does the rest of the paragraph follow from it?

*coherence*   Comment on the effectiveness, or lack of it, of paragraphs 1, 44, 65, and 66. In what other kind of writing would this technique be useful?

## CONTENT AND ORGANIZATION

*central ideas*   Is this conversation primarily about Henry Roth, Jews, or *Call It Sleep?*

*organization*   1. Is this interview well organized? Explain your answer. 2. Does the comment "I found myself incapable of making a narrative decision" (par. 41) have anything to do with the organization? Why or why not?

*assumptions and implications*   1. Does Roth imply that had not *Call It Sleep* been reprinted there would have been no interview? Explain. 2. How is the last sentence of paragraph 63 related to the interview as a whole?

## SUGGESTIONS FOR DISCUSSION

1. What are the problems of the immigrant in New York City?   2. Would the ordinary immigrant be happier in a country town than in a big city? 3. Write a paper in which you compare the problems in Henry Roth's *Call It Sleep* with those in Abraham Cahan's *The Rise of David Levinsky.* 4. Write a paper in which you contrast the problems in Henry Roth's *Call It Sleep* with those in Philip Roth's *Portnoy's Complaint.*   5. Can you think of other novels that were "discovered" several years after the original publication? Why might this be?

# Willa Cather
# WHEN I KNEW STEPHEN CRANE

1. It was, I think, in the spring of '94 that a slender, narrow-chested fellow in a shabby gray suit, with a soft felt hat pulled low over his eyes, sauntered into the office of the managing editor of the *Nebraska State Journal* and introduced himself as Stephen Crane. He stated that he was going to Mexico to do some work for the Bacheller Syndicate and get rid of his cough, and that he would be stopping in Lincoln for a few days. Later he explained that he was out of money and would be compelled to wait until he got a check from the East before he went further. I was a junior at the Nebraska State University at the time, and was doing some work for the *State Journal* in my leisure time, and I happened to be in the managing editor's room when Mr. Crane introduced himself. I was just off the range; I knew a little Greek and something about cattle and a good horse when I saw one, and beyond horses and cattle I considered nothing of vital importance except good stories and the people who wrote them. This was the first man of letters I had ever met in the flesh, and when the young man announced who he was, I dropped into a chair behind the editor's desk where I could stare at him without being too much in evidence.

2. Only a very youthful enthusiasm and a large propensity for hero worship could have found anything impressive in the young man who stood before the managing editor's desk. He was thin to emaciation, his face was gaunt and unshaven, a thin dark moustache straggled on his upper lip, his black hair grew low on his forehead and was shaggy and unkempt. His gray clothes were much the worse for wear and fitted him so badly it seemed unlikely he had ever been measured for them. He wore a flannel shirt and a slovenly apology for a necktie, and his shoes were dusty and worn gray about the toes and were badly run over at the heel. I had seen many a tramp printer come up the *Journal* stairs to hunt a job, but never one who presented such a disreputable appearance as this storymaker man. He

WHEN I KNEW STEPHEN CRANE: Reprinted from *The World and the Parish: Willa Cather's Articles and Reviews, 1893–1902*, ed. by William Curtin, by permission of University of Nebraska Press. Copyright © 1970 by the University of Nebraska Press.

wore gloves, which seemed rather a contradiction to the general slovenliness of his attire, but when he took them off to search his pockets for his credentials, I noticed that his hands were singularly fine; long, white, and delicately shaped, with thin, nervous fingers. I have seen pictures of Aubrey Beardsley's hands that recalled Crane's very vividly.

3. At that time Crane was but twenty-four, and almost an unknown man. Hamlin Garland had seen some of his work and believed in him, and had introduced him to Mr. Howells, who recommended him to the Bacheller Syndicate. *The Red Badge of Courage* had been published in the *State Journal* that winter along with a lot of other syndicate matter, and the grammatical construction of the story was so faulty that the managing editor had several times called on me to edit the copy. In this way I had read it very carefully, and through the careless sentence structure I saw the wonder of that remarkable performance. But the grammar certainly was bad. I remember one of the reporters who had corrected the phrase "it don't" for the tenth time remarked savagely, "If I couldn't write better English than this, I'd quit."

4. Crane spent several days in the town, living from hand to mouth and waiting for his money. I think he borrowed a small amount from the managing editor. He lounged about the office most of the time, and I frequently encountered him going in and out of the cheap restaurants on Tenth Street. When he was at the office he talked a good deal in a wandering, absent-minded fashion, and his conversation was uniformly frivolous. If he could not evade a serious question by a joke, he bolted. I cut my classes to lie in wait for him, confident that in some unwary moment I could trap him into serious conversation, that if one burned incense long enough and ardently enough, the oracle would not be dumb. I was Maupassant-mad at the time, a malady particularly unattractive in a junior, and I made a frantic effort to get an expression of opinion from him on "Le Bonheur." "Oh, you're Moping, are you?" he remarked with a sarcastic grin, and went on reading a little volume of Poe that he carried in his pocket. At another time I cornered him in the Funny Man's room and succeeded in getting a little out of him. We were taught literature by an exceedingly analytical method at the university, and we probably distorted the method, and I was busy trying to find the least common multiple of *Hamlet* and the greatest common divisor of *Macbeth,* and I began asking him whether stories were constructed by cabalistic formulae. At length he sighed wearily and shook his drooping shoulders, remarking: "Where did you get all that rot?

Yarns aren't done by mathematics. You can't do it by rule any more than you can dance by rule. You have to have the itch of the thing in your fingers, and if you haven't—well, you're damned lucky, and you'll live long and prosper, that's all." And with that he yawned and went down the hall.

5. Crane was moody most of the time, his health was bad, and he seemed profoundly discouraged. Even his jokes were exceedingly drastic. He went about with the tense, preoccupied, self-centered air of a man who is brooding over some impending disaster, and I conjectured vainly as to what it might be. Though he was seemingly entirely idle during the few days I knew him, his manner indicated that he was in the throes of work that told terribly on his nerves. His eyes I remember as the finest I have ever seen, large and dark and full of luster and changing lights, but with a profound melancholy always lurking deep in them. They were eyes that seemed to be burning themselves out.

6. As he sat at the desk with his shoulders drooping forward, his head low, and his long, white fingers drumming on the sheets of copy paper, he was as nervous as a race horse fretting to be on the track. Always, as he came and went about the halls, he seemed like a man preparing for a sudden departure. Now that he is dead it occurs to me that all his life was a preparation for sudden departure. I remember once when he was writing a letter he stopped and asked me about the spelling of a word, saying carelessly, "I haven't time to learn to spell."

7. Then, glancing down at his attire, he added with an absent-minded smile, "I haven't time to dress either; it takes an awful slice out of a fellow's life."

8. He said he was poor, and he certainly looked it, but four years later when he was in Cuba, drawing the largest salary ever paid a newspaper correspondent, he clung to this same untidy manner of dress, and his ragged overalls and buttonless shirt were eyesores to the immaculate Mr. Davis, in his spotless linen and neat khaki uniform, with his Gibson chin always freshly shaven. When I first heard of his serious illness, his old throat trouble aggravated into consumption by his reckless exposure in Cuba, I recalled a passage from Maeterlinck's essay, "The Pre-Destined," on those doomed to early death: "As children, life seems nearer to them than to other children. They appear to know nothing, and yet there is in their eyes so profound a certainty that we feel they must know all. In all haste, but wisely and with minute care do they prepare themselves to live, and this very haste is a sign upon which mothers can scarce

bring themselves to look." I remembered, too, the young man's melancholy and his tenseness, his burning eyes, and his way of slurring over the less important things, as one whose time is short.

9. I have heard other people say how difficult it was to induce Crane to talk seriously about his work, and I suspect that he was particularly averse to discussions with literary men of wider education and better equipment than himself, yet he seemed to feel that this fuller culture was not for him. Perhaps the unreasoning instinct which lies deep in the roots of our lives, and which guides us all, told him that he had not time enough to acquire it.

10. Men will sometimes reveal themselves to children, or to people whom they think never to see again, more completely than they ever do to their confreres. From the wise we hold back alike our folly and our wisdom, and for the recipients of our deeper confidences we seldom select our equals. The soul has no message for the friends with whom we dine every week. It is silenced by custom and convention, and we play only in the shallows. It selects its listeners willfully, and seemingly delights to waste its best upon the chance wayfarer who meets us in the highway at a fated hour. There are moments too, when the tides run high or very low, when self-revelation is necessary to every man, if it be only to his valet or his gardener. At such a moment, I was with Mr. Crane.

11. The hoped-for revelation came unexpectedly enough. It was on the last night he spent in Lincoln. I had come back from the theater and was in the *Journal* office writing a notice of the play. It was eleven o'clock when Crane came in. He had expected his money to arrive on the night mail and it had not done so, and he was out of sorts and deeply despondent. He sat down on the ledge of the open window that faced on the street, and when I had finished my notice I went over and took a chair beside him. Quite without invitation on my part, Crane began to talk, began to curse his trade from the first throb of creative desire in a boy to the finished work of the master. The night was oppressively warm; one of those dry winds that are the curse of that country was blowing up from Kansas. The white, western moonlight threw sharp, blue shadows below us. The streets were silent at that hour, and we could hear the gurgle of the fountain in the Post Office square across the street, and the twang of banjos from the lower verandah of the Hotel Lincoln, where the colored waiters were serenading the guests. The drop lights in the office were dull under their green shades, and the telegraph sounder clicked faintly in the next room. In all his long tirade, Crane never

raised his voice; he spoke slowly and monotonously and even calmly, but I have never known so bitter a heart in any man as he revealed to me that night. It was an arraignment of the wages of life, an invocation to the ministers of hate.

12.    Incidentally he told me the sum he had received for *The Red Badge of Courage*, which I think was something like ninety dollars, and he repeated some lines from *The Black Riders*, which was then in preparation. He gave me to understand that he led a double literary life; writing in the first place the matter that pleased himself, and doing it very slowly; in the second place, any sort of stuff that would sell. And he remarked that his poor was just as bad as it could possibly be. He realized, he said, that his limitations were absolutely impassable. "What I can't do, I can't do at all, and I can't acquire it. I only hold one trump."

13.    He had no settled plans at all. He was going to Mexico wholly uncertain of being able to do any successful work there, and he seemed to feel very insecure about the financial end of his venture. The thing that most interested me was what he said about his slow method of composition. He declared that there was little money in storywriting at best, and practically none in it for him, because of the time it took him to work up his detail. Other men, he said, could sit down and write up an experience while the physical effect of it, so to speak, was still upon them, and yesterday's impressions made today's "copy." But when he came in from the streets to write up what he had seen there, his faculties were benumbed, and he sat twirling his pencil and hunting for words like a schoolboy.

14.    I mentioned *The Red Badge of Courage*, which was written in nine days, and he replied that, though the writing took very little time, he had been unconsciously working the detail of the story out through most of his boyhood. His ancestors had been soldiers, and he had been imagining war stories ever since he was out of knickerbockers, and in writing his first war story he had simply gone over his imaginary campaigns and selected his favorite imaginary experiences. He declared that his imagination was hidebound; it was there, but it pulled hard. After he got a notion for a story, months passed before he could get any sort of personal contact with it, or feel any potency to handle it. "The detail of a thing has to filter through my blood, and then it comes out like a native product, but it takes forever," he remarked. I distinctly remember the illustration, for it rather took hold of me.

15.    I have often been astonished since to hear Crane spoken of

as "the reporter in fiction," for the reportorial faculty of superficial reception and quick transference was what he conspicuously lacked. His first newspaper account of his shipwreck on the filibuster *Commodore* off the Florida coast was as lifeless as the "copy" of a police court reporter. It was many months afterwards that the literary product of his terrible experience appeared in that marvellous sea story "The Open Boat," unsurpassed in its vividness and constructive perfection.

16. At the close of our long conversation that night, when the copy boy came in to take me home, I suggested to Crane that in ten years he would probably laugh at all his temporary discomfort. Again his body took on that strenuous tension and he clenched his hands, saying, "I can't wait ten years, I haven't time."

17. The ten years are not up yet, and he has done his work and gathered his reward and gone. Was ever so much experience and achievement crowded into so short a space of time? A great man dead at twenty-nine! That would have puzzled the ancients. Edward Garnett wrote of him in the *Academy* of December 17, 1899: "I cannot remember a parallel in the literary history of fiction. Maupassant, Meredith, Henry James, Mr. Howells and Tolstoy, were all learning their expression at an age where Crane had achieved his and achieved it triumphantly." He had the precocity of those doomed to die in youth. I am convinced that when I met him he had a vague premonition of the shortness of his working day, and in the heart of the man there was that which said, "That thou doest, do quickly."

18. At twenty-one this son of an obscure New Jersey rector, with but a scant reading knowledge of French and no training, had rivaled in technique the foremost craftsmen of the Latin races. In the six years since I met him, a stranded reporter, he stood in the firing line during two wars, knew hairbreadth 'scapes on land and sea, and established himself as the first writer of his time in the picturing of episodic, fragmentary life. His friends have charged him with fickleness, but he was a man who was in the preoccupation of haste. He went from country to country, from man to man, absorbing all that was in them for him. He had no time to look backward. He had no leisure for *camaraderie*. He drank life to the lees, but at the banquet table where other men took their ease and jested over their wine, he stood a dark and silent figure, somber as Poe himself, not wishing to be understood; and he took his portion in haste, with his loins girded, and his shoes on his feet, and his staff in his hand, like one who must depart quickly.

## WORDS

*meaning*  Define *cabalistic* (par. 4), *tirade* (par. 11), *fickleness* and *camaraderie* (par. 18).

*word choice*  How do you account for such expressions as *eyes that seemed to be burning themselves out* (par. 5) and *all his life was preparation for sudden departure* (par. 6)?

*exactness*  1. Why did Willa Cather use *further* (par. 1) rather than *farther? confreres* (par. 10) rather than *friends* or *peers?*  2. How do you account for the word *knickerbockers* (par. 14)?

*level of usage*  Explain the use of *hairbreadth 'scapes* and *with his loins girded* (par. 18).

## SENTENCES

*style*  1. Willa Cather became one of our leading novelists, but this is a piece of journalism published in *Library,* in June 1900. To what extent is it journalistic? To what extent is it a eulogy (Crane had died on June 5, 1900)?  2. This essay has been described as "fictional in a number of details" (Crane had actually visited Lincoln, Nebraska, in February of 1895, rather than in the spring of 1894). Why did Miss Cather change the time for a piece of journalism?  3. Willa Cather edited (changed) the quote from Edward Garnett (par. 17). Is this good journalism?

*rhetorical devices*  No one seems to know what the "Funny Man's room" (par. 4) is. What do you think it might be? Would you use an allusion which might not be known outside your college? town? country?

## CONTENT AND ORGANIZATION

*central idea*  What most impressed Willa Cather about Stephen Crane?

*organization*  1. Is paragraph 1 a good introductory paragraph? Why or why not?  2. Is there a summary paragraph? More than one? Explain.

*assumptions and implications*  Is Willa Cather assuming that had Stephen Crane (1871–1900) lived longer he might have become a greater artist?

## SUGGESTIONS FOR DISCUSSION

1. What are the differences between journalism and fiction?  2. Are there times when the journalist can "create"?  3. Does such a sentence as "The white, western moonlight threw sharp, blue shadows below us" (par. 11) have a place in a journalistic account? Explain.  4. Many fiction writers have served apprenticeships as newspaper writers. Write an essay in which you argue that such experience is particularly good or

bad for the future fiction writer. 5. Should a writer of any kind take "time to learn to spell" (par. 6)? 6. Frequently when an artist knows or has a premonition that he is to have a short life, he doubles his activities. Should he slow down and take care of himself with the hope of extending his artistic life, or should he do all he can in the short time he believes is allocated to him?

## Alfred Kazin

## THE BLOCK AND BEYOND

1. The block: *my* block. It was on the Chester Street side of our house, between the grocery and the back wall of the old drugstore, that I was hammered into the shape of the streets. Everything beginning at Blake Avenue would always wear for me some delightful strangeness and mildness, simply because it was not of my block, *the* block where the clang of your head sounded against the pavement when you fell in a fist fight, and the rows of storelights on each side were pitiless, watching you. Anything away from the block was good: even a school you never went to, two blocks away; there were vegetable gardens in the park across the street. Returning from "New York," I would take the longest routes home from the subway, get off a station ahead of our own, only for the unexpectedness of walking through Betsy Head Park and hearing the gravel crunch under my feet as I went beyond the vegetable gardens, smelling the sweaty sweet dampness from the pool in summer and the dust on the leaves as I passed under the ailanthus trees. On the block itself everything rose up only to test me.

2. We worked every inch of it, from the cellars and the backyards to the sickening space between the roofs. Any wall, any stoop, any curving metal edge on a billboard sign made a place against which to knock a ball; any bottom rung of a fire escape ladder a goal in basketball; any sewer cover a base; any crack in the pavement a "net" for the tense sharp tennis that we played by beating a soft ball back and forth with our hands between the squares. Betsy Head Park two blocks away would always feel slightly foreign, for it belonged to the Amboys and the Bristols and the Hopkinsons as much as it did to us. *Our* life every day was fought out on the pavement and in the

THE BLOCK AND BEYOND: From *A Walker in the City*, copyright, 1951, by Alfred Kazin. Reprinted by permission of Harcourt Brace Jovanovich, Inc.

gutter, up against the walls of the houses and the glass fronts of the drugstore and the grocery, in and out of the fresh steaming piles of horse manure, the wheels of passing carts and automobiles, along the iron spikes of the stairway to the cellar, the jagged edge of the open garbage cans, the crumbly steps of the old farmhouses still left on one side of the street.

3. As I go back to the block now, and for a moment fold my body up again in its narrow arena—there, just there, between the black of the asphalt and the old women in their kerchiefs and flowered house dresses sitting on the tawny kitchen chairs—the back wall of the drugstore still rises up to test me. Every day we smashed a small black viciously hard regulation handball against it with fanatical cuts and drives and slams, beating and slashing at it almost in hatred for the blind strength of the wall itself. I was never good enough at handball, was always practicing some trick shot that might earn me esteem, and when I was weary of trying, would often bat a ball down Chester Street just to get myself to Blake Avenue. I have this memory of playing one-o'-cat by myself in the sleepy twilight, at a moment when everyone else had left the block. The sparrows floated down from the telephone wires to peck at every fresh pile of horse manure, and there was a smell of brine from the delicatessen store, of egg crates and of the milk scum left in the great metal cans outside the grocery, of the thick white paste oozing out from behind the fresh Hecker's Flour ad on the metal sign-board. I would throw the ball in the air, hit it with my bat, then with perfect satisfaction drop the bat to the ground and run to the next sewer cover. Over and over I did this, from sewer cover to sewer cover, until I had worked my way to Blake Avenue and could see the park.

4. With each clean triumphant ring of my bat against the gutter leading me on, I did the whole length of our block up and down, and never knew how happy I was just watching the asphalt rise and fall, the curve of the steps up to an old farmhouse. The farmhouses themselves were streaked red on one side, brown on the other, but the steps themselves were always gray. There was a tremor of pleasure at one place; I held my breath in nausea at another. As I ran after my ball with the bat heavy in my hand, the odd successiveness of things in myself almost choked me, the world was so full as I ran—past the cobblestoned yards into the old farmhouses, where stray chickens still waddled along the stones; past the little candy store where we went only if the big one on our side of the block was out of Eskimo Pies; past the three neighboring tenements where the last of the old women

sat on their kitchen chairs yawning before they went up to make supper. Then came Mrs. Rosenwasser's house, the place on the block I first identified with what was farthest from home, and strangest, because it was a "private" house; then the fences around the monument works, where black cranes rose up above the yard and you could see the smooth gray slabs that would be cut and carved into tombstones, some of them already engraved with the names and dates and family virtues of the dead.

5.  Beyond Blake Avenue was the pool parlor outside which we waited all through the tense September afternoons of the World's Series to hear the latest scores called off the ticker tape—and where as we waited, banging a ball against the bottom of the wall and drinking water out of empty coke bottles, I breathed the chalk off the cues and listened to the clocks ringing in the fire station across the street. There was an old warehouse next to the pool parlor; the oil on the barrels and the iron staves had the same rusty smell. A block away was the park, thick with the dusty gravel I liked to hear my shoes crunch in as I ran round and round the track; then a great open pavilion, the inside mysteriously dark, chill even in summer; there I would wait in the sweaty coolness before pushing on to the wading ring where they put up a shower on the hottest days.

6.  Beyond the park the "fields" began, all those still unused lots where we could still play hard ball in perfect peace—first shooing away the goats and then tearing up goldenrod before laying our bases. The smell and touch of those "fields," with their wild compost under the billboards of weeds, goldenrod, bricks, goat droppings, rusty cans, empty beer bottles, fresh new lumber, and damp cement, live in my mind as Brownsville's great open door, the wastes that took us through to the west. I used to go round them in summer with my cousins selling near-beer to the carpenters, but always in a daze, would stare so long at the fibrous stalks of the goldenrod as I felt their harshness in my hand that I would forget to make a sale, and usually go off sick on the beer I drank up myself. Beyond! Beyond! Only to see something new, to get away from each day's narrow battleground between the grocery and the back wall of the drugstore! Even the other end of our block, when you got to Mrs. Rosenwasser's house and the monument works, was dear to me for the contrast. On summer nights, when we played Indian trail, running away from each other on prearranged signals, the greatest moment came when I could plunge into the darkness down the block for myself and hide behind the slabs in the monument works. I remember the air whistling around me as I ran, the panicky thud of my bones in my sneak-

ers, and then the slabs rising in the light from the street lamps as I sped past the little candy store and crept under the fence.

7.   In the darkness you could never see where the crane began. We liked to trap the enemy between the slabs and sometimes jumped them from great mounds of rock just in from the quarry. A boy once fell to his death that way, and they put a watchman there to keep us out. This made the slabs all the more impressive to me, and I always aimed first for that yard whenever we played follow-the-leader. Day after day the monument works became oppressively more mysterious and remote, though it was only just down the block; I stood in front of it every afternoon on my way back from school, filling it with my fears. It was not death I felt there—the slabs were usually faceless. It was the darkness itself, and the wind howling around me whenever I stood poised on the edge of a high slab waiting to jump. Then I would take in, along with the fear, some amazement of joy that I had found my way out that far.

## WORDS

*word choice*   1. The author has re-created the neighborhood he knew as a boy not by systematic or enumerative description but through the evocation of smells, sounds, sights, and feelings of childhood. What feeling or experience is evoked by each of the following words and phrases (in its context): *sickening space* (par. 2), *blind strength* and *sleepy twilight* (par. 3), *choked* (par. 4), *crunch* (par. 5), *harshness* and *whistling* (par. 6), and *filling* (par. 7)?   2. What do such words as *smashed, viciously, fanatical, drives, slams, beating,* and *slashing* (par. 3) have to do with the writer's creation of a mood?

*exactness*   For each of the following words choose a more abstract or more literal substitute and then decide which word better communicates the author's feeling: *hammered, clang,* and *rose* (par. 1), *worked* and *fought* (par. 2), *fold, rises,* and *floated* (par. 3), *rise and fall* and *waddled* (par. 4), *panicky thud* and *rising* (par. 6), and *aimed* (par. 7).

## SENTENCES

*style*   The author has adopted a style to fit his floating memories. Rewrite the first sentences of paragraphs 2, 3, and 4 as if you were giving a literal description; then contrast your sentences with the original ones, noting the differences in sentence structure, diction, syntax, and punctuation.

*parallelism*   1. Pick out two sentences in paragraph 2 that make obvious use of parallel structure. List the parallel elements and, where they are missing, supply the implied words.   2. There is a well-balanced sentence in paragraph 4. Find it and comment on its effect.

*rhetorical devices*   1. Find metaphors in paragraphs 2, 4, 5, 6, and 7.
2. What is personification? Does the author use it? If so, find several
examples.

PARAGRAPHS

*topic sentences*   If paragraphs 4 and 7 have obvious topic sentences
indicate them. If not, write them.

*methods of development*   1. Choose what you believe is the most effective paragraph and explain the ways and means the author uses to describe
both an area and his feelings about it.   2. Pick out a paragraph that you
think is developed primarily by particulars and details. How are they
organized to give the paragraph coherence?

CONTENT AND ORGANIZATION

*assumptions and implications*   Can you infer from this selection that
if after many years the author caught a particular smell or heard a remembered sound he could call up a vision of his block? Why or why not?

SUGGESTIONS FOR DISCUSSION

1. Can you write about something with which you were familiar years
ago and communicate the feelings you had about it then?   2. To what
extent do you think the passage of time dims your remembrance of things
past?   3. When you returned to an old situation that you had long remembered, did you find it impossibly strange or did you "fold" back into it?
4. Would you argue with old men who say that neat playgrounds, swimming pools, and recreation halls are insipid substitutes for the open fields
and swimming holes of their youth?   5. Would the author's childhood
necessarily have been more healthy and stimulating if he had been reared
in an exclusive suburb?

*Alexander Petrunkevitch*

# THE SPIDER AND THE WASP

1.   In the feeding and safeguarding of their progeny insects and
spiders exhibit some interesting analogies to reasoning and some
crass examples of blind instinct. The case I propose to describe here

THE SPIDER AND THE WASP: From *Scientific American*, August 1952. Reprinted with permission. Copyright © 1952 by Scientific American, Inc. All
rights reserved.

is that of the tarantula spiders and their archenemy, the digger wasps of the genus Pepsis. It is a classic example of what looks like intelligence pitted against instinct—a strange situation in which the victim, though fully able to defend itself, submits unwittingly to its destruction.

2. Most tarantulas live in the tropics, but several species occur in the temperate zone and a few are common in the southern United States. Some varieties are large and have powerful fangs with which they can inflict a deep wound. These formidable looking spiders do not, however, attack man; you can hold one in your hand, if you are gentle, without being bitten. Their bite is dangerous only to insects and small mammals such as mice; for a man it is no worse than a hornet's sting.

3. Tarantulas customarily live in deep cylindrical burrows, from which they emerge at dusk and into which they retire at dawn. Mature males wander about after dark in search of females and occasionally stray into houses. After mating, the male dies in a few weeks, but a female lives much longer and can mate several years in succession. In a Paris museum is a tropical specimen which is said to have been living in captivity for 25 years.

4. A fertilized female tarantula lays from 200 to 400 eggs at a time; thus it is possible for a single tarantula to produce several thousand young. She takes no care of them beyond weaving a cocoon of silk to enclose the eggs. After they hatch, the young walk away, find convenient places in which to dig their burrows and spend the rest of their lives in solitude. The eyesight of tarantulas is poor, being limited to a sensing of change in the intensity of light and to the perception of moving objects. They apparently have little or no sense of hearing, for a hungry tarantula will pay no attention to a loudly chirping cricket placed in its cage unless the insect happens to touch one of its legs.

5. But all spiders, and especially hairy ones, have an extremely delicate sense of touch. Laboratory experiments prove that tarantulas can distinguish three types of touch: pressure against the body wall, stroking of the body hair and riffling of certain very fine hairs on the legs called trichobothria. Pressure against the body, by a finger or the end of a pencil, causes the tarantula to move off slowly for a short distance. The touch excites no defensive response unless the approach is from above where the spider can see the motion, in which case it rises on its hind legs, lifts its front legs, opens its fangs and holds this threatening posture as long as the object continues to move.

6. The entire body of a tarantula, especially its legs, is thickly clothed with hair. Some of it is short and woolly, some long and stiff.

Touching this body hair produces one of two distinct reactions. When the spider is hungry, it responds with an immediate and swift attack. At the touch of a cricket's antennae the tarantula seizes the insect so swiftly that a motion picture taken at the rate of 64 frames per second shows only the result and not the process of capture. But when the spider is not hungry, the stimulation of its hairs merely causes it to shake the touched limb. An insect can walk under its hairy belly unharmed.

7. The trichobothria, very fine hairs growing from disklike membranes on the legs, are sensitive only to air movement. A light breeze makes them vibrate slowly without disturbing the common hair. When one blows gently on the trichobothria, the tarantula reacts with a quick jerk of its four front legs. If the front and hind legs are stimulated at the same time, the spider makes a sudden jump. This reaction is quite independent of the state of its appetite.

8. These three tactile responses—to pressure on the body wall, to moving of the common hair and to flexing of the trichobothria— are so different from one another that there is no possibility of confusing them. They serve the tarantula adequately for most of its needs and enable it to avoid most annoyances and dangers. But they fail the spider completely when it meets its deadly enemy, the digger wasp Pepsis.

9. These solitary wasps are beautiful and formidable creatures. Most species are either a deep shiny blue all over, or deep blue with rusty wings. The largest have a wing span of about four inches. They live on nectar. When excited, they give off a pungent odor—a warning that they are ready to attack. The sting is much worse than that of a bee or common wasp, and the pain and swelling last longer. In the adult stage the wasp lives only a few months. The female produces but a few eggs, one at a time at intervals of two or three days. For each egg the mother must provide one adult tarantula, alive but paralyzed. The mother wasp attaches the egg to the paralyzed spider's abdomen. Upon hatching from the egg, the larva is many hundreds of times smaller than its living but helpless victim. It eats no other food and drinks no water. By the time it has finished its single gargantuan meal and become ready for wasphood, nothing remains of the tarantula but its indigestible chitinous skeleton.

10. The mother wasp goes tarantula-hunting when the egg in her ovary is almost ready to be laid. Flying low over the ground late on a sunny afternoon, the wasp looks for its victim or for the mouth of a tarantula burrow, a round hole edged by a bit of silk. The sex of the spider makes no difference, but the mother is highly

discriminating as to species. Each species of Pepsis requires a certain species of tarantula, and the wasp will not attack the wrong species. In a cage with a tarantula which is not its normal prey the wasp avoids the spider, and is usually killed by it in the night.

11. Yet when a wasp finds the correct species, it is the other way about. To identify the species the wasp apparently must explore the spider with her antennae. The tarantula shows an amazing tolerance to this exploration. The wasp crawls under it and walks over it without evoking any hostile response. The molestation is so great and so persistent that the tarantula often rises on all eight legs, as if it were on stilts. It may stand this way for several minutes. Meanwhile the wasp, having satisfied itself that the victim is of the right species, moves off a few inches to dig the spider's grave. Working vigorously with legs and jaws, it excavates a hole 8 to 10 inches deep with a diameter slightly larger than the spider's girth. Now and again the wasp pops out of the hole to make sure that the spider is still there.

12. When the grave is finished, the wasp returns to the tarantula to complete her ghastly enterprise. First she feels it all over once more with her antennae. Then her behavior becomes more aggressive. She bends her abdomen, protruding her sting, and searches for the soft membrane at the point where the spider's leg joins its body—the only spot where she can penetrate the horny skeleton. From time to time, as the exasperated spider slowly shifts ground, the wasp turns on her back and slides along with the aid of her wings, trying to get under the tarantula for a shot at the vital spot. During all this maneuvering, which can last for several minutes, the tarantula makes no move to save itself. Finally the wasp corners it against some obstruction and grasps one of its legs in her powerful jaws. Now at last the harassed spider tries a desperate but vain defense. The two contestants roll over and over on the ground. It is a terrifying sight and the outcome is always the same. The wasp finally manages to thrust her sting into the soft spot and holds it there for a few seconds while she pumps in the poison. Almost immediately the tarantula falls paralyzed on its back. Its legs stop twitching; its heart stops beating. Yet it is not dead, as is shown by the fact that if taken from the wasp it can be restored to some sensitivity by being kept in a moist chamber for several months.

13. After paralyzing the tarantula, the wasp cleans herself by dragging her body along the ground and rubbing her feet, sucks the drop of blood oozing from the wound in the spider's abdomen, then grabs a leg of the flabby, helpless animal in her jaws and drags it

down to the bottom of the grave. She stays there for many minutes, sometimes for several hours, and what she does all that time in the dark we do not know. Eventually she lays her egg and attaches it to the side of the spider's abdomen with a sticky secretion. Then she emerges, fills the grave with soil carried bit by bit in her jaws, and finally tramples the ground all around to hide any trace of the grave from prowlers. Then she flies away, leaving her descendant safely started in life.

14. In all this the behavior of the wasp evidently is qualitatively different from that of the spider. The wasp acts like an intelligent animal. This is not to say that instinct plays no part or that she reasons as man does. But her actions are to the point; they are not automatic and can be modified to fit the situation. We do not know for certain how she identifies the tarantula—probably it is by some olfactory or chemo-tactile sense—but she does it purposefully and does not blindly tackle a wrong species.

15. On the other hand, the tarantula's behavior shows only confusion. Evidently the wasp's pawing gives it no pleasure, for it tries to move away. That the wasp is not simulating sexual stimulation is certain, because male and female tarantulas react in the same way to its advances. That the spider is not anesthetized by some odorless secretion is easily shown by blowing lightly at the tarantula and making it jump suddenly. What, then, makes the tarantula behave as stupidly as it does?

16. No clear, simple answer is available. Possibly the stimulation by the wasp's antennae is masked by a heavier pressure on the spider's body, so that it reacts as when prodded by a pencil. But the explanation may be much more complex. Initiative in attack is not in the nature of tarantulas; most species fight only when cornered so that escape is impossible. Their inherited patterns of behavior apparently prompt them to avoid problems rather than attack them. For example, spiders always weave their webs in three dimensions, and when a spider finds that there is insufficient space to attach certain threads in the third dimension, it leaves the place and seeks another, instead of finishing the web in a single plane. This urge to escape seems to arise under all circumstances, in all phases of life, and to take the place of reasoning. For a spider to change the pattern of its web is as impossible as for an inexperienced man to build a bridge across a chasm obstructing his way.

17. In a way the instinctive urge to escape is not only easier but often more efficient than reasoning. The tarantula does exactly what is most efficient in all cases except in an encounter with a

ruthless and determined attacker dependent for the existence of her own species on killing as many tarantulas as she can lay eggs. Perhaps in this case the spider follows its usual pattern of trying to escape, instead of seizing and killing the wasp, because it is not aware of its danger. In any case, the survival of the tarantula species as a whole is protected by the fact that the spider is much more fertile than the wasp.

## WORDS

*meaning*  The author uses one scientific word, *trichobothria,* which he defines (par. 7). Why does he not define words like *chitinous* (par. 9) and *olfactory* and *chemo-tactile* (par. 14)? What do they mean?

*word choice*  In paragraph 12 the words *ghastly* and *terrifying* indicate the attitude of the author toward what he is describing. Would you expect to find these words in an engineering report? Why or why not?

## SENTENCES

*emphasis*  One way of achieving emphasis is by placing important words or phrases at the end of a sentence. Find examples of such words and phrases in paragraph 12.

*variety*  1. Paragraphs 1, 7, 13, and 16 all begin with simple sentences. How are subordinate ideas presented in these sentences?  2. Find in them (a) an appositive phrase, (b) an introductory modifier, and (c) a compound predicate.

## PARAGRAPHS

*unity*  Which one of paragraphs 4, 5, and 6 lacks obvious unity of subject? Why?

*topic sentences*  The first sentence of paragraph 14 states the idea developed in paragraphs 14 and 15. What is the topic sentence of paragraph 14? of paragraph 15?

*coherence*  1. The author links the sentences of paragraph 12 by using transitional expressions to indicate time. Point out these expressions. 2. This essay contains an obvious example of a transition paragraph. Which one is it? How does it do its job?

*methods of development*  1. Are paragraphs 5, 6, and 7 developed by a single example in each paragraph or by presentation of relevant details in each paragraph?  2. Are paragraphs 10 and 11 developed chronologically or logically?

*central idea*  1. What is the central idea of this essay?  2. How is it introduced in the first paragraph?  3. How is it explained in the concluding paragraphs?

*organization*  1. The tarantula is described in six paragraphs, from 2 through 7; the wasp is described in only one paragraph, 9. Why is the tarantula described in greater detail?  2. The wasp's actions are described in four paragraphs, 10–13; does this partially compensate for the one-paragraph description of the wasp?  3. How are the four final paragraphs developed as a conclusion?

*assumptions and implications*  1. What effect in this "scientific" account is gained by use of words ordinarily associated only with human life— words such as *grave* (par. 11)?  2. Think of the grave as a nest or incubator and consider how the essay might be written from the point of view of the wasp.  3. Does the author's description of the spider and its fate lead you to think of the spider as having a particular sex? Do you see any possible connection between the action described here and the "conflict" between men and women in modern life?

## SUGGESTIONS FOR DISCUSSION

1. How would you go about writing an equally terrifying essay with the title "Man and the Lamb"? "Man and the Trout"? or "The Cat and the Mouse"?  2. *Instinct* is a word difficult to define. Define it and give examples of its operation in man.  3. When is intelligent action clearly superior to instinctive action? Give examples.  4. It has been said that man is the most terrible animal in creation because only man systematically works to exterminate his own species. Agree or disagree and give your reasons.

*Alan Devoe*

# THE ANIMALS SLEEP

1.  Not many creatures of earth are visible now in the frozen woods and fields. A walker there can see only the few thick-furred gray squirrels and hares and deer that are pelted for cold weather, and can hear no livelier bird-music than the small call-notes of

THE ANIMALS SLEEP: Reprinted with the permission of Farrar, Straus & Giroux, Inc. from *Lives Around Us* by Alan Devoe, copyright 1942 by Alan Devoe, copyright renewed 1970 by Mary Devoe Guinn.

hardy nuthatches and chickadees. In December the populace of wild things has a meager look. But could a man see underneath the surface of the frozen earth and below the icy mud of brook-beds, he would be aware of the presence of a tremendous number of beasts. Only a very few of the denizens of outdoors removed to other climates when the autumn cold came. Some of the summer birds departed, to be sure, and some of the insects died. But innumerable animals only retired to hidden places and went to sleep. By thousands, when the first frosts were felt, they subsided into that lethargy called hibernation.

2.   Indians spoke of hibernation as the Long Sleep, but it is rather more than that. It is profound oblivion midway between sleep and death. It is an unknowing and unfeeling more deep and lasting than can be induced in man by the most powerful drugs, a suspension of life processes more thorough and protracted than even the "frozen slumber" which doctors have lately devised as a palliative of cancer. It is a phenomenon unique in nature, and though we are wiser about it than we were in those cradle-days of biology when Dr. Johnson thought that swallows passed the winter asleep in the mud at the bottom of the Thames, it remains a riddle still.

3.   The season of hibernating begins quite early for some of the creatures of outdoors. It is not alone the cold which causes it; there are a multiplicity of other factors—diminishing food supply; increased darkness as the fall days shorten; silence—frequently decisive. Any or all of these may be the signal for entrance into the Long Sleep, depending upon the habits and make-up of the particular creature. Among skunks, it is usually the coming of the cold that sends them, torpid, to their root-lined underground burrows; but many other mammals (for instance, ground squirrels) begin to grow drowsy when the fall sun is still warm on their furry backs and the food supply is not at all diminished. This ground-squirrel kind of hibernating, independent of the weather and the food supply, may be an old race habit, an instinctual behavior pattern like the unaccountable migrations of certain birds. Weather, food, inheritance, darkness—all of these obscurely play their parts in bringing on the annual subsidence into what one biologist has called "the little death." Investigation of the causes will need a good many years before they can be understood, for in captivity, where observation is more easy than in the wild, the hibernators often do not sleep at all.

4.   The preparations for hibernation begin in early fall, and they are various. The insects—such as survive the winters in adult form—make ready by a drastic dehydration. Their bodies lose the

moisture which they have in summer, and which would make them liable to fatal freezing, and become desiccated and brittle. Their reactions to the stimulus of light become, in most cases, the reverse of normal: beetles ordinarily attracted toward the light are violently repelled by it after dehydration. They creep to dark places. Some of them, like the May beetles, repair to deep subfrostline tunnels in the earth; some of them seek out crannies under the loose bark of trees and interstices in stumps. With all their body tissues radically dried, and all their responses to stimuli slowed and dulled, they lapse into immobility. Their bodies are stiff and straight, wings and legs held parallel. They are ready to remain unmoving and foodless until the spring thaws come. They are ready to undergo the experience, common enough among the surface-hibernating insects, of being chilled to well below 32 degrees Fahrenheit without suffering injury.

5. The frogs, in making ready, betake themselves to the deep, soft mud of the brook-bottoms and the shelter of flat underwater stones. The toads, their soft bodies equipped with curious many-fingered lumps of fat to serve as food supply, burrow on cool September days into sandy garden soil or into the banks of their breeding streams, and with arched backs and indrawn legs grow motionless. The snails cease feeding, bury themselves among the moss and leaves, and secrete a covering over the openings of their shells. The trout swim leisurely upstream and grow quiet and unhungry; the spiders that have not perished in the first cold weather withdraw into burrows or spin themselves cocoons.

6. Most striking is the Long Sleep of the mammals. Raccoons, chipmunks, bats, bears, woodchucks—all these make ready in the autumn for a greater or lesser period of dormancy. They are all animals with imprecisely regulated body temperatures, these mammalian hibernators; during normal summertime activity their temperatures often fluctuate by ten or fifteen degrees. They do not have a wholly static temperature, independent of the warmth of the outer air, as does a man or a wood mouse or a winter-active deer. They can survive the months of northern cold and snow only by lapsing into a quiescence hardly distinguishable from death. Some of them sleep more deeply than others, some for the whole winter and some for only a part of it. The commonest of them, the woodchuck, serves as a fair exemplar.

7. The woodchuck's hibernation usually starts about the middle of September. For weeks he has been foraging with increased appetite among the clover blossoms and has grown heavy and slow-moving. Now, with the coming of mid-September, apples and corn

and yarrow-tops have become less plentiful, and the nights are cool. The woodchuck moves with slower gait, and emerges less and less frequently for feeding-trips. Layers of fat have accumulated around his chest and shoulders, and there is thick fat in the axils of his legs. He has extended his summer burrow to a length of nearly thirty feet, and has fashioned a deep nest-chamber at the end of it, far below the level of the frost. He has carried in, usually, a little hay. He is ready for the Long Sleep.

8.    When the temperature of the September days falls below 50 degrees or so, the woodchuck becomes too drowsy to come forth from his burrow in the chilly dusk to forage. He remains in the deep nest-chamber, lethargic, hardly moving. Gradually, with the passing of hours or days, his coarse-furred body curls into a semi-circle, like a foetus, nose-tip touching tail. The small legs are tucked in, the hand-like clawed forefeet folded. The woodchuck has become a compact ball. Presently the temperature of his body begins to fall.

9.    In normal life the woodchuck's temperature, though fluctuant, averages about 97 degrees. Now, as he lies tight-curled in a ball with the winter sleep stealing over him, this body heat drops ten degrees, twenty degrees, thirty. Finally, by the time the snow is on the ground and the woodchuck's winter dormancy has become complete, his temperature is only 38 or 40. With the falling of the body heat there is a slowing of his heartbeat and his respiration. In normal life he breathes thirty or forty times each minute; when he is excited, as many as a hundred times. Now he breathes slower and slower—ten times a minute, five times a minute, once a minute, and at last only ten or twelve times in an hour. His heartbeat is a twentieth of normal. He has entered fully into the oblivion of hibernation.

10.    The Long Sleep lasts, on an average, about six months. For half a year the woodchuck remains unmoving, hardly breathing. His pituitary gland is inactive; his blood is so sluggishly circulated that there is an unequal distribution in the chilled body; his sensory awareness has wholly ceased. It is almost true to say that he has altered from a warm-blooded to a cold-blooded animal.

11.    Then, in the middle of March, he wakes. The waking is not a slow and gradual thing, as was the drifting into sleep, but takes place quickly, often in an hour. The body temperature ascends to normal, or rather higher for a while; glandular functions instantly resume; the respiration quickens and steadies at a normal rate. The woodchuck has become himself again, save only that he is a little thinner, and is ready at once to fare forth into the pale spring sunlight and look for grass and berries.

12. Such is the performance each fall and winter, with varying detail, of bats and worms and bears, and a hundred other kinds of creatures. It is a marvel less spectacular than the migration flight of hummingbirds or the flash of shooting stars, but it is not much less remarkable.

## WORDS

*meaning*  Define *palliative* (par. 2), *subsidence* (par. 3), *desiccated* and *interstices* (par. 4), *axils* (par. 7), and *foetus* (par. 8).

*connotation*  Express as precisely as you can what is suggested by the following phrases: *profound oblivion* and *cradle-days* (par. 2) and *the little death* (par. 3).

*word choice*  The following words are either themselves unusual or used in an unusual sense: *denizen* (par. 1), *repair* (par. 4), *betake* (par. 5), and *exemplar* (par. 6). What is the meaning of each in this essay? What advantage, if any, do these words have over possibly more familiar synonyms?

## SENTENCES

*style*  Devoe is an accomplished writer, one who uses many resources of language. In paragraphs 5 and 6, for example, find examples of sentence inversion, parallelism of phrases and of clauses, absolute constructions, and appositives.

*rhetorical devices*  Awkward employment of synonyms ("When John caught the football, he tucked the pigskin under his arm and carried the ovoid for more than twenty yards.") is sometimes called "elegant variation." How does Devoe introduce and employ synonyms for the word *hibernation?* List four of them. What do they contribute to the essay? How does Devoe's use of synonyms differ from "elegant variation"?

## PARAGRAPHS

*topic sentences*  Paragraph 5 has an implied topic sentence. Write a topic sentence for this paragraph.

*methods of development*  1. In what way and to what extent is paragraph 2 a paragraph of definition?  2. In the beginning of paragraph 3 the author gives four causes of hibernation, but in repeating the four causes later in the paragraph he substitutes a new cause for one previously mentioned. Which one has been replaced?  3. For two of the causes he gives examples. What are the examples?  4. Paragraph 9 uses comparison. Of what to what?  5. Chronological development is obviously used in five successive paragraphs. Which ones are they?

CONTENT AND ORGANIZATION

*central ideas*   1. Devoe gives a vivid account of hibernation. Then why is it that "it remains a riddle still" (par. 2)?   2. Why do you think that in captivity "the hibernators often do not sleep at all" (par. 3)?

*organization*   1. It takes the woodchuck four paragraphs to complete the process of hibernation. Which ones?   2. It takes him only one paragraph to awaken. Which one?   3. List some of the words or phrases that contribute to effective description of the woodchuck's going to sleep (for example, *slower gait,* par. 7, and *Gradually,* par. 8).   4. List a few of the words or phrases that dramatize his sudden awakening (for example, *quickens,* par. 11).

SUGGESTIONS FOR DISCUSSION

1. If a man living in Alabama said to you, "I am going into hibernation for a month," would you know what he meant? What would he mean?
2. It is said that people living in the far northern countries go into a kind of hibernation in the winter. Can you think of reasons why this might be so?   3. The author suggests that science, with its "frozen slumber" (par. 2), has only lately copied from nature. Can you think of other instances in which science has learned from nature?   4. Try to describe vividly and accurately some phenomenon with which you are familiar: spring fever among students, the preparations made before the Christmas season by a department store, the actions of athletes beginning training for strenuous sports.

# Explaining Facts and Ideas

*Definition, classification, enumeration, comparison, and analysis are some of the particular techniques of exposition. Although the essays that follow do not illustrate all these techniques, examples of them all can be found somewhere in this anthology. For this section the editors have chosen five selections that explain comparatively complex ideas or phenomena simply, completely, and clearly. This distinction makes these essays peculiarly valuable to students beginning an analysis of the problems of exposition.*

## Mary McCarthy

## AMERICA THE BEAUTIFUL

1. A visiting Existentialist wanted recently to be taken to dinner at a really American place. This proposal, natural enough in a tourist, disclosed a situation thoroughly unnatural. Unless the visiting lady's object was suffering, there was no way of satisfying her demand. Suki-yaki joints, chop suey joints, Italian table d'hôte places, French provincial restaurants with the menu written on a slate, Irish chophouses, and Jewish delicatessens came abundantly to mind, but these were not what the lady wanted. Schrafft's or the Automat would have answered, yet to take her there would have been to turn oneself into a tourist and to present America as a spectacle—a *New Yorker* cartoon or a savage drawing in the *New Masses*. It was the beginning of an evening of humiliations. The visitor was lively and eager; her mind lay open and orderly, like a notebook ready for impressions. It was not long, however, before she shut it up with a snap. We had no recommendations to make to her. With movies, plays, current books, it was the same story as with the restaurants. *Open City, Les Enfants du Paradis,* Oscar Wilde, a reprint of Henry James were *paté de maison* to this lady who wanted the definitive flapjack. She did not believe us when we said that there were no good Hollywood movies, no

AMERICA THE BEAUTIFUL:  Reprinted with the permission of Farrar, Straus & Giroux, Inc. from *On the Contrary* by Mary McCarthy, copyright © 1947, 1961 by Mary McCarthy.

good Broadway plays—only curios; she was merely confirmed in her impression that American intellectuals were "negative."

2.    Yet the irritating thing was that we did not feel negative. We admired and liked our country; we preferred it to that imaginary America, land of the *peaux rouges* of Caldwell and Steinbeck, dumb paradise of violence and the detective story, which had excited the sensibilities of our visitor and of the up-to-date French literary world. But to found our preference, to locate it materially in some admirable object or institution, such as Chartres, say, or French café life, was for us, that night at any rate, an impossible undertaking. We heard ourselves saying that the real America was elsewhere, in the white frame houses and church spires of New England; yet we knew that we talked foolishly—we were not Granville Hicks and we looked ludicrous in his opinions. The Elevated, half a block away, interrupting us every time a train passed, gave us the lie on schedule, every eight minutes. But if the elm-shaded village green was a false or at least an insufficient address for the *genius loci* we honored, where then was it to be found? Surveyed from the vantage point of Europe, this large continent seemed suddenly deficient in objects of virtue. The Grand Canyon, Yellowstone Park, Jim Hill's mansion in St. Paul, Jefferson's Monticello, the blast furnaces of Pittsburgh, Mount Rainier, the yellow observatory at Amherst, the little-theater movement in Cleveland, Ohio, a Greek revival house glimpsed from a car window in a lost river town in New Jersey—these things were too small for the size of the country. Each of them, when pointed to, diminished in interest with the lady's perspective of distance. There was no sight that in itself seemed to justify her crossing of the Atlantic.

3.    If she was interested in "conditions," that was a different matter. There are conditions everywhere; it takes no special genius to produce them. Yet would it be an act of hospitality to invite a visitor to a lynching? Unfortunately, nearly all the "sights" in America fall under the head of conditions. Hollywood, Reno, the sharecroppers' homes in the South, the mining towns of Pennsylvania, Coney Island, the Chicago stockyards, Macy's, the Dodgers, Harlem, even Congress, the forum of our liberties, are spectacles rather than sights, to use the term in the colloquial sense of "Didn't he make a holy spectacle of himself?" An Englishman of almost any political opinion can show a visitor through the Houses of Parliament with a sense of pride or at least of indulgence toward his national foibles and traditions. The American, if he has a spark of national feeling, will be humiliated by the very prospect of a foreigner's visit to Congress— these, for the most part, illiterate hacks whose fancy vests are spotted

with gravy, and whose speeches, hypocritical, unctuous, and slovenly, are spotted also with the gravy of political patronage, these persons are a reflection on the democratic process rather than of it; they expose it in its underwear. In European legislation, we are told, a great deal of shady business goes on in private, behind the scenes. In America, it is just the opposite, anything good, presumably, is accomplished *in camera,* in the committee rooms.

4.   It is so with all our institutions. For the visiting European, a trip through the United States has, almost inevitably, the character of an exposé, and the American, on his side, is tempted by love of his country to lock the inquiring tourist in his hotel room and throw away the key. His contention that the visible and material America is not the real or the only one is more difficult to sustain than was the presumption of the "other" Germany behind the Nazi steel.

5.   To some extent a citizen of any country will feel that the tourist's view of his homeland is a false one. The French will tell you that you have to go into their homes to see what the French people are really like. The intellectuals in the Left Bank cafés are not the real French intellectuals, etc., etc. In Italy, they complain that the tourist must not judge by the *ristorantes;* there one sees only black-market types. But in neither of these cases is the native really disturbed by the tourist's view of his country. If Versailles or Giotto's bell tower in Florence do not tell the whole story, they are still not incongruous with it; you do not hear a Frenchman or an Italian object when these things are noticed by a visitor. With the American, the contradiction is more serious. He must, if he is to defend his country, repudiate its visible aspect almost entirely. He must say that its parade of phenomenology, its billboards, super highways, even its skyscrapers, not only fail to represent the inner essence of his country but in fact contravene it. He may point, if he wishes, to certain beautiful objects, but here too he is in difficulties, for nearly everything that is beautiful and has not been produced by Nature belongs to the eighteenth century, to a past with which he has very little connection, and which his ancestors, in many or most cases, had no part in. Beacon Street and the Boston Common are very charming in the eighteenth-century manner, so are the sea captains' houses in the old Massachusetts ports, and the ruined plantations of Louisiana, but an American from Brooklyn or the Middle West or the Pacific Coast finds the style of life embodied in them as foreign as Europe; indeed, the first sensation of a Westerner, coming upon Beacon Hill and the gold dome of the State House, is to feel that at last he has traveled

"abroad." The American, if he is to speak the highest truth about his country, must refrain from pointing at all. The virtue of American civilization is that it is unmaterialistic.

6. This statement may strike a critic as whimsical or perverse. Everybody knows, it will be said, that America has the most materialistic civilization in the world, that Americans care only about money, they have no time or talent for living; look at radio, look at advertising, look at life insurance, look at the tired businessman, at the Frigidaires and the Fords. In answer, the reader is invited first to look instead into his own heart and inquire whether he personally feels himself to be represented by these things, or whether he does not, on the contrary, feel them to be irrelevant to him, a necessary evil, part of the conditions of life. Other people, he will assume, care about them very much: the man down the street, the entire population of Detroit or Scarsdale, the back-country farmer, the urban poor or the rich. But he himself accepts these objects as imposed on him by a collective "otherness" of desire, an otherness he has not met directly but whose existence he infers from the number of automobiles, Frigidaires, or television sets he sees around him. Stepping into his new Buick convertible, he knows that he would gladly do without it, but imagines that to his neighbor, who is just backing *his* out of the driveway, this car is the motor of life. More often, however, the otherness is projected farther afield, onto a different class or social group, remote and alien. Thus the rich, who would like nothing better, they think, than for life to be a perpetual fishing trip with the trout grilled by a native guide, look patronizingly upon the whole apparatus of American civilization as a cheap Christmas present to the poor, and city people see the radio and the washing machine as the farm wife's solace.

7. It can be argued, of course, that the subjective view is prevaricating possession of the Buick being nine-tenths of the social law. But who has ever met, outside of advertisements, a true parishioner of this church of Mammon? A man may take pride in a car, and a housewife in her new sink or wallpaper, but pleasure in new acquisitions is universal and eternal; an Italian man with a new gold tooth, a French bibliophile with a new edition, a woman with a new baby, a philosopher with a new thought, all these people are rejoicing in progress, in man's power to enlarge and improve. Before men showed off new cars, they showed off new horses; it is alleged against modern man that he as an individual craftsman did not make the car; but his grandfather did not make the horse either. What is imputed to Americans is something quite different, an abject dependence on

material possessions, an image of happiness as packaged by the manufacturer, content in a can. This view of American life is strongly urged by advertising agencies. We know the "others," of course, because we meet them every week in full force in *The New Yorker* or the *Saturday Evening Post,* those brightly colored families of dedicated consumers, waiting in unison on the porch for the dealer to deliver the new car, gobbling the new cereal ("Gee, Mom, is it good for you too?"), lining up to bank their paychecks, or fearfully anticipating the industrial accident and the insurance check that will "compensate" for it. We meet them also, more troll-like underground, in the subway placards, in the ferociously complacent One-A-Day family, and we hear their courtiers sing to them on the radio of Ivory or Supersuds. The thing, however, that repels us in these advertisements is their naive falsity to life. Who are these advertising men kidding, besides the European tourist? Between the tired, sad, gentle faces of the subway riders and the grinning Holy Families of the Ad-Mass, there exists no possibility of even a wishful identification. We take a vitamin pill with the hope of feeling (possibly) a little less tired, but the superstitution of buoyant health emblazoned in the bright, ugly pictures has no more power to move us than the blood of St. Januarius.

8.  Familiarity has perhaps bred contempt in us Americans: until you have had a washing machine, you cannot imagine how little difference it will make to you. Europeans still believe that money brings happiness, witness the bought journalist, the bought politician, the bought general, the whole venality of European literary life, inconceivable in this country of the dollar. It is true that America produces and consumes more cars, soap, and bathtubs than any other nation, but we live among these objects rather than by them. Americans build skyscrapers; Le Corbusier worships them. Ehrenburg, our Soviet critic, fell in love with the Check-O-Mat in American railway stations, writing home paragraphs of song to this gadget—while deploring American materialism. When an American heiress wants to buy a man, she at once crosses the Atlantic. The only really materialistic people I have ever met have been Europeans.

9.  The strongest argument for the unmaterialistic character of American life is the fact that we tolerate conditions that are, from a materialistic point of view, intolerable. What the foreigner finds most objectionable in American life is its lack of basic comfort. No nation with any sense of material well being would endure the food we eat, the cramped apartments we live in, the noise, the traffic, the crowded subways and buses. American life, in large cities, at any rate, is a

perpetual assault on the senses and the nerves; it is out of asceticism, out of unworldliness, precisely, that we bear it.

10. This republic was founded on an unworldly assumption, a denial of "the facts of life." It is manifestly untrue that all men are created equal; interpreted in worldly terms, this doctrine has resulted in a pseudo-equality, that is, in standardization, in an equality of things rather than of persons. The inalienable rights to life, liberty, and the pursuit of happiness appear, in practice, to have become the inalienable right to a bathtub, a flush toilet, and a can of Spam. Left-wing critics of America attribute this result to the intrusion of capitalism; right-wing critics see it as the logical dead end of democracy. Capitalism, certainly, now depends on mass production, which depends on large-scale distribution of uniform goods, till the consumer today is the victim of the manufacturer who launches on him a regiment of products for which he must make house-room in his soul. The buying impulse, in its original force and purity, was not nearly so crass, however, or so meanly acquisitive as many radical critics suppose. The purchase of a bathtub was the exercise of a spiritual right. The immigrant or the poor native American bought a bathtub, not because he wanted to take a bath, but because he wanted to be in a *position* to do so. This remains true in many fields today; possessions, when they are desired, are not wanted for their own sakes but as tokens of an ideal state of freedom, fraternity, and franchise. "Keeping up with the Joneses" is a vulgarization of Jefferson's concept, but it too is a declaration of the rights of man, and decidedly unfeasible and visionary. Where for a European, a fact is a fact, for us Americans, the real, if it is relevant at all, is simply symbolic appearance. We are a nation of twenty million bathrooms, with a humanist in every tub. One such humanist I used to hear of on Cape Cod had, on growing rich, installed two toilets side by side in his marble bathroom, on the model of the two-seater of his youth. He was a clear case of Americanism, hospitable, gregarious, and impractical, a theorist of perfection. Was his dream of the conquest of poverty a vulgar dream or a noble one, a material demand or a spiritual insistence? It is hard to think of him as a happy man, and in this too he is characteristically American, for the parity of the radio, the movies, and the washing machine has made Americans sad, reminding them of another parity of which these things were to be but emblems.

11. The American does not enjoy his possessions because sensory enjoyment was not his object, and he lives sparely and thinly among them, in the monastic discipline of Scarsdale or the barracks

of Stuyvesant Town. Only among certain groups where franchise, socially speaking, has not been achieved, do pleasure and material splendor constitute a life-object and an occupation. Among the outcasts—Jews, Negroes, Catholics, homosexuals—excluded from the communion of ascetics, the love of fabrics, gaudy show, and rich possessions still anachronistically flaunts itself. Once a norm has been reached, differing in the different classes, financial ambition itself seems to fade away. The self-made man finds, to his anger, his son uninterested in money; you have shirtsleeves to shirtsleeves in three generations. The great financial empires are a thing of the past. Some recent immigrants—movie magnates and gangsters particularly—retain their acquisitiveness, but how long is it since anyone in the general public has murmured, wonderingly, "as rich as Rockefeller"?

12.  If the dream of American fraternity had ended simply in this, the value of humanistic and egalitarian strivings would be seriously called into question. Jefferson, the Adamses, Franklin, Madison, would be in the position of Dostoevsky's Grand Inquisitor, who, desiring to make the Kingdom of God incarnate on earth, inaugurated the kingdom of the devil. If the nature of matter is such that the earthly paradise, once realized, becomes always the paradise of the earthly, and a spiritual conquest of matter becomes an enslavement of spirit, then the atomic bomb is, as has been argued, the logical result of the Enlightenment, and the land of opportunity is, precisely, the land of death. This position, however, is a strictly materialist one, for it asserts the Fact of the bomb as the one tremendous truth: subjective attitudes are irrelevant; it does not matter what we think or feel; possession again in this case is nine-tenths of the law.

13.  It must be admitted that there is a great similarity between the nation with its new bomb and the consumer with his new Buick. In both cases, there is a disinclination to use the product, stronger naturally in the case of the bomb, but somebody has manufactured the thing, and there seems to be no way *not* to use it, especially when everybody else will be doing so. Here again the argument of the "others" is invoked to justify our own procedures: if we had not invented the bomb, the Germans would have; the Soviet Union will have it in a year, etc., etc. This is keeping up with the Joneses indeed, our national propagandists playing the role of the advertising men in persuading us of the "others'" intentions.

14.  It seems likely at this moment that we will find no way of not using the bomb, yet those who argue theoretically that this machine is the true expression of our society leave us, in practice, with

no means of opposing it. We must differentiate ourselves from the bomb if we are to avoid using it, and in private thought we do, distinguishing the bomb sharply from our daily concerns and sentiments, feeling it as an otherness that waits outside to descend on us, an otherness already destructive of normal life, since it prevents us from planning or hoping by depriving us of a future. And this inner refusal of the bomb is also a legacy of our past; it is a denial of the given, of the power of circumstances to shape us in their mold. Unfortunately, the whole asceticism of our national character, our habit of living in but not through an environment, our alienation from objects, prepare us to endure the bomb but not to confront it.

15. Passivity and not aggressiveness is the dominant trait of the American character. The movies, the radio, the super highway have softened us up for the atom bomb; we have lived with them without pleasure, feeling them as a coercion on our natures, a coercion seemingly from nowhere and expressing nobody's will. The new coercion finds us without the habit of protest; we are dissident but apart.

16. The very "negativeness," then, of American intellectuals is not a mark of their separation from our society, but a true expression of its separation from itself. We too are dissident but inactive. Intransigent on paper, in "real life" we conform; yet we do not feel ourselves to be dishonest, for to us the real life is rustling paper and the mental life is flesh. And even in our mental life we are critical and rather unproductive; we leave it to the "others," the best-sellers, to create.

17. The fluctuating character of American life must, in part, have been responsible for this dissociated condition. Many an immigrant arrived in this country with the most materialistic expectations, hoping, not to escape from a world in which a man was the sum of his circumstances, but to become a new sum of circumstances himself. But this hope was self-defeating; the very ease with which new circumstances were acquired left insufficient time for a man to live into them: all along a great avenue in Minneapolis the huge stone chateaux used to be dark at night, save for a single light in each kitchen, where the family still sat, Swedish-style, about the stove. The pressure of democratic thought, moreover, forced a rising man often, unexpectedly, to recognize that he was *not* his position: a speeding ticket from a village constable could lay him low. Like the agitated United Nations delegates who got summonses on the Merritt Parkway, he might find the shock traumatic: a belief had been destroyed. The effect of these combined difficulties turned the new American into a

nomad, who camped out in his circumstances, as it were, and was never assimilated to them. And, for the native American, the great waves of internal migration had the same result. The homelessness of the American, migrant in geography and on the map of finance, is the whole subject of the American realists of our period. European readers see in these writers only violence and brutality. They miss not only the pathos but the nomadic virtues associated with it, generosity, hospitality, equity, directness, politeness, simplicity of relations—traits which, together with a certain gentle timidity (as of very *unpracticed* nomads), comprise the American character. Unobserved also is a peculiar nakedness, a look of being shorn of everything, that is very curiously American, corresponding to the spare wooden desolation of a frontier town and the bright thinness of the American light. The American character looks always as if it had just had a rather bad haircut, which gives it, in our eyes at any rate, a greater humanity than the European, which even among its beggars has an all too professional air.

18.  The openness of the American situation creates the pity and the terror; status is not protection; life for the European is a career; for the American, it is a hazard. Slaves and women, said Aristotle, are not fit subjects for tragedy, but kings, rather, and noble men, men, that is, not defined by circumstance but outside it and seemingly impervious. In America we have, subjectively speaking, no slaves and no women; the efforts of *PM* and the Stalinized playwrights to introduce, like the first step to servitude, a national psychology of the "little man" have been, so far, unrewarding. The little man is one who is embedded in status; things can be done for and to him generically by a central directive; his happiness flows from statistics. This conception mistakes the national passivity for abjection. Americans will not eat this humble pie; we are still nature's noblemen. Yet no tragedy results, though the protagonist is everywhere; dissociation takes the place of conflict, and the drama is mute.

19.  This humanity, this plain and heroic accessibility, was what we would have liked to point out to the visiting Existentialist as our national glory. Modesty perhaps forbade and a lack of concrete examples—how could we point to ourselves? Had we done so she would not have been interested. To a European, the humanity of an intellectual is of no particular moment; it is the barber pole that announces his profession and the hair oil dispensed inside. Europeans, moreover, have no curiosity about American intellectuals; we are insufficiently representative of the brute. Yet this anticipated and felt disparagement was not the whole cause of our reticence. We were

silent for another reason: we were waiting to be discovered. Columbus, however, passed on, and this, very likely, was the true source of our humiliation. But this experience also was peculiarly American. We all expect to be found in the murk of otherness; it looks to us very easy since *we* know we are there. Time after time, the explorers have failed to see us. We have been patient, for the happy ending is our national belief. Now, however, that the future has been shut off from us, it is necessary for us to declare ourselves, at least for the record.

20.   What it amounts to, in verity, is that we are the poor. This humanity we would claim for ourselves is the legacy, not only of the Enlightenment, but of the thousands and thousands of European peasants and poor townspeople who came here bringing their humanity and their sufferings with them. It is the absence of a stable upper class that is responsible for much of the vulgarity of the American scene. Should we blush before the visitor for this deficiency? The ugliness of American decoration, American entertainment, American literature—is not this the visible expression of the impoverishment of the European masses, a manifestation of all the backwardness, deprivation, and want that arrived here in boatloads from Europe? The immense popularity of American movies abroad demonstrates that Europe is the unfinished negative of which America is the proof. The European traveler, viewing with distaste a movie palace or a Motorola, is only looking into the terrible concavity of his continent of hunger inverted startlingly into the convex. Our civilization, deformed as it is outwardly, is still an accomplishment; all this had to come to light.

21.   America is indeed a revelation, though not quite the one that was planned. Given a clean slate, man, it was hoped, would write the future. Instead, he has written his past. This past, inscribed on billboards, ballparks, dance halls, is not seemly, yet its objectification is a kind of disburdenment. The past is at length outside. It does not disturb us as it does Europeans, for our relation with it is both more distant and more familar. We cannot hate it, for to hate it would be to hate poverty, our eager ancestors, and ourselves.

22.   If there were time, American civilization could be seen as a beginning, even a favorable one, for we have only to look around us to see what a lot of sensibility a little ease will accrue. The children surpass the fathers and Louis B. Mayer cannot be preserved intact in his descendants. . . . Unfortunately, as things seem now, posterity is not around the corner.

## WORDS

*meaning* Define *Existentialist* (par. 1), *foibles* and *unctuous* (par. 3), *phenomenology* (par. 5), *abject* (par. 7), *venality* (par. 8), *anachronistically* (par. 11), *egalitarian* (par. 12), *intransigent* (par. 16), and *generically* (par. 18).

*word choice* Account for the expression *the blood of St. Januarius* (par. 7).

*exactness* 1. What is a *definitive flapjack* (par. 1)? 2. In paragraph 6 Mary McCarthy uses *assume* and *infer*. Are they correctly used? Where would *imply* be correct?

*level of usage* Is *gobbling the new cereal* (par. 7) appropriate in this piece?

## SENTENCES

*style* 1. How would you describe the tone of this essay? Is it sophisticated? homey? flippant? 2. Discuss the appropriateness of such a statement as "We are a nation of twenty million bathrooms, with a humanist in every tub" (par. 10). 3. Mary McCarthy is thought to be an effective writer. What evidences of this do you find in this piece? What, if anything, do you not like about it?

*rhetorical devices* 1. Why is "Keeping up with the Joneses" a "vulgarization of Jefferson's concept" (par. 10)? 2. What is the effect of "as rich as Rockefeller" (par. 11)? 3. Why are "real life" and "others" (par. 16) in quotation marks?

## PARAGRAPHS

*topic sentence* Does paragraph 4 have a topic sentence or an implied one? If the latter, write it; if the former, quote it.

*coherence* What purpose is served by the last sentence of paragraph 5 and the first sentence of paragraph 6?

*methods of development* Choose a paragraph developed by example and defend your choice.

## CONTENT AND ORGANIZATION

*central idea* Is the author's thesis that "The virtue of American civilization is that it is unmaterialistic" (par. 5) or that the American "bought a bathtub, not because he wanted to take a bath, but because he wanted to be in a *position* to do so" (par. 10)? Choose one of these or a third possibility and explain why.

*organization* Is paragraph 22 an adequate summary paragraph? Why does Mary McCarthy conclude with "posterity is not around the corner"?

*assumptions and implications* 1. To what extent is this a pro-American essay? 2. How and where is there an implied criticism of America?

SUGGESTIONS FOR DISCUSSION

1. The Declaration of Independence states that "We hold these truths to be self-evident, that all men are created equal, that they are endowed by their Creator with certain unalienable Rights, that among these are Life, Liberty, and the pursuit of Happiness." Have these truths been continuously self-evident since this was written in 1776? 2. The final chapter of Thomas Wolfe's novel *You Can't Go Home Again* (1940) is called "Credo." One sentence of that creed is "I believe that we are lost here in America, but I believe we shall be found." Have we been lost, and how? Have we been or might we be found, and how? 3. Why might the people of one country have a greater reliance on symbols than the people of another country? 4. In paragraph 14 the author discusses "the bomb." Write a paper in which you compare and contrast Mary McCarthy's feelings about "the bomb" with those of William Faulkner.

*Peter Schrag*

# LIFE ON THE MISSISSIPPI 1970

1. If there was ever an American century, it was the nineteenth; if there was ever an American region, it was the Mississippi. The place and the moment coincided: time and rivers, people and beliefs flowing in upon themselves, fording at the narrows, spreading across the fields, overrunning the banks, down the Ohio from Pittsburgh, up the Missouri, down the Tennessee, spinning dreams and legends before the footprints had washed from the shores, creating eras that lasted no more than a generation, spawning literature —and the hardy clichés of tourism—that resist, even now, the depredations of the Pizza King, the Burger Chef, and the power plant.

2. The first time I crossed the river—Vicksburg in 1953, Highway 80 going west, sixty miles an hour in an old Studebaker—the misty darkness of the spring night obscured everything but hand-me-

LIFE ON THE MISSISSIPPI 1970:  Copyright 1970 Saturday Review, Inc. Reprinted by permission.

down memories: Down there Grant had erected his fortifications, down there his gunboats held the city under siege, down there 3,000 people retreated to the caves in the bluffs to sit out the bombardment.

3. *The cannon thunder rages, shells scream and crash overhead, the iron rain pours down, one hour, two hours, three, possibly six, then stops; silence follows, but the streets are still empty; the silence continues; by and by, a head projects here and there and yonder, and reconnoiters cautiously; the silence still continuing, bodies follow heads, and jaded, half-smothered creatures group themselves about, stretch their cramped limbs, draw in deep draughts of the grateful fresh air, gossip with the neighbors from the next cave; maybe struggle off home presently, or take a lounge through the town, if the stillness continues; and will scurry to the holes again, by and by, when the war tempest breaks forth once more.*

4. Not my private memory, not my words; all borrowed from Mister Mark Twain, who made them up and who, as much as anyone, invented this time and this place. Mister Twain and Tom and Huck and Jim; Mister Handy and the blues; Mister Huey Long getting hisself shot down there in Baton Rouge; Mister Mike Fink on his keelboat—the biggest screamer in the West, half-alligator, half-snapping turtle—can grin the bark off a tree and make the river itself stop dead in its tracks, *whoop, whoop,* gouging his way through river towns and frontier settlements; or, again, the Reverend Brigham Young assembling his Mormons at Nauvoo, Illinois, and then getting hisself run out of town by the scandalized citizens, just as he and his people had just been run out of Missouri and Ohio: polygamous freaks of another age searching for their commune. A cast of thousands—boatmen, planters, slaves, boys with rafts and fishing poles—some real, some only imagined (or should one say "only," since invention was often more important than fact and often outlived it?), spilling down those rivers, and then across, and producing along the way the singular American that once we all loved to celebrate. This, if anything, was The Country.

5. I came back again this fall to see if they were still there, to see, indeed, if the river itself still existed as a genuine presence or whether it flows deep only in the channels of wishful memory. Life on the Mississippi in 1970. The same 1,250,000 square miles draining into a river system, now dammed and leveed and diked, that can take a barge from Cincinnati to St. Paul or the Gulf, can take a man from Lake Itasca to New Orleans, can take thousands of barrels of oil or 70,000 tons of grain 1,500 miles with hardly a snag. Along the levee near Whitfield, Missouri, at Fort Defiance Park in Cairo,

and in a thousand other places, the fishing lines still go in every day, the hardier low-grade fish—catfish, carp, buffalo—still jump, defying effluents and pesticides, and the people, often as not, segregate themselves, black from white, with the barrier of a bridge or dike, or with invisible lines that demarcate the black man's fish from the white's. And in bypassed towns such as Louisiana, Missouri, or Clarksville or even Hannibal, which has turned Mark Twain into a tourist industry, the old men still amble down to the waterfront to watch the barges go by and to engage, as one of them said, in "talkin' and lyin', talkin' and lyin' "; while, from time to time, farm boys from Illinois or Tennessee or Mississippi still come to the river to sign on as hands with the barge lines—$27 a day or $330 a month with twenty days off for every thirty worked—shuttling with their cargoes from lock to lock, swapping stories with the lockmen, telling which skipper is a fool and which is a good man, asking about other tows, asking what happened to the *Bald Eagle* and her string of barges stuck against a bridge below the town or to a pilot or an engineer who used to work for Valley Barge above St. Louis. For many of them, however, the river has become a science, dredged, marked, and controlled, a thing to be judged by levels and distances, by locks and dams—is it rising or going down? What is the difference between water level in the pool, the reservoir behind the dam, and the tail below the huge gates that hold the water back to maintain a safe channel?—navigated now by radar and radio and map and only rarely by the reports of other pilots.

6. All along the river the men who work its tows, its locks, and its bridges live in a double realm in which the immediacy of electronic equipment, heavy engines, precise measurements, and reports on radio and television coexists with the ineffable mysteries of tradition and lore. The river itself is a ritual—always has been—but the ritual is relentlessly interrupted by reports from the loudspeaker and the tube. At a railroad bridge above Hannibal that must be opened and closed to allow traffic to pass, the bridge operator, his Corvette parked against the bank, sits beside his electronic gear, his teletype printer, his lights and whistles—alone for most of the eight hours of his working day—watching the St. Louis Cardinals beating the Washington Redskins in a televised football game, and casting a careful eye upstream after every play to check for the approach of tows coming down, a human rhythm exacted by the cycle of the game and the relentless demands of the stream.

7. And at Lock and Dam 22 just below Saverton, Missouri, a man named Jim Tutor, who shuttles between his job at the lock and

his eighty-acre dairy farm in nearby New London, talks without self-consciousness about his love of the river, about the changes in the water, and about the artifacts of time and place that the water brings into his life: "Now it's like a pond, but when the wind starts, the whitecaps are up in minutes. I can sit here and watch the sun come up—right now it comes up over there—that place on the Illinois shore, and with the colors on the leaves it's really something. In the winter there's the ice, and in spring the ice breaking up, always something new."

8. Jim Tutor, lean, open, easygoing, is the kind of person that visitors of the nineteenth century always regarded as the genuine American, and in the slow hours at the lock he will, without much prompting, tell you about his work, his family, his aspirations, and about the kinds of personal experience that form the roots of social belief and political behavior in America. He asks why kids are so dissatisfied, but he also understands that while his life seems to be right, life is not right for many others, that they do not have his sense of place, his opportunity to plan. For him it is the river that makes things right: "People just don't appreciate it. They don't know that without the river they wouldn't have any water, wouldn't have much of anything." On the back of his truck are two stickers. One is an appeal to stop polluting the river. The other says: AMERICA—LOVE IT OR LEAVE IT.

9. *People just don't appreciate it.* A century ago Mark Twain observed that "nearly all the river towns, big and little, have made up their minds that they must look mainly to railroads for wealth and upbuilding, henceforth. They are acting upon this idea. The signs are that the next twenty years will bring about some noteworthy changes in the valley, in the direction of increased population, and in the intellectual advancement and the liberalizing of opinion that go naturally with these. And yet, if one may judge by the past, the river towns will manage to find and use a chance, here and there, to cripple and retard their progress. They kept themselves back in the days of steamboating supremacy, by a system of wharfage dues so stupidly graded as to prohibit what may be called *retail* traffic in boats and passengers."

10. Mister Clemens hedged his bet, and so he came out right on both ends. The railroads came, bringing depots and repair shops and shipping points where grain, cotton, and lumber were loaded from boats to trains and shipped to the interior; the entrepreneurs of Hannibal thrived by floating lumber from Wisconsin down the river, cutting it up, and shipping it west on a locally owned rail-

road. At the same time, Cairo flourished at the confluence of the Ohio and the Mississippi, and at the conjunction of rail and river lines; in the Twenties, Cairo had a population of nearly 20,000 people and expected to grow indefinitely. And along with the railroads came industry—shoe and glove factories, lumber mills, and the retail establishments of the river front and the farmers' market. But even in that prosperity there was no permanence, and in the resulting "liberalizing of opinion" there was pigheadedness. Now the old factories are closing or have already closed, the trains and barges are passing the small towns by, and the river front, often as not, is populated by ghosts: abandoned warehouses and shops, gutted plants, and old men who remember better days. In the past decade, many of the smaller towns lost population and jobs: Hannibal dropped from 20,000 to 18,000; Quincy is down—from 44,000 to 42,000; and Cairo, which had shrunk to 9,200 by 1960, now has a population of 6,100 and has become a rundown, frightened city.

11.  Cairo: They call themselves the gateway to the South, and they advertise the fact that the town is farther south than Richmond, that the adjacent counties are the only regions in Illinois that grow cotton, and that the streets are graced by magnolias and mimosas. What the Chamber of Commerce does not say is that the city has become notorious for its racial violence, its economic decay, and its social desperation. Cairo is not representative of the South or of the river, but it illustrates what happens to time and place when the fantasies of riverfed prosperity inundate civic decency and economic sense. Cairo was facing south when it should have been facing north; it was, and is, facing the nineteenth century when it should have faced the twentieth. Here and in many other river towns Mark Twain's prophecy was borne out: To protect existing local industry, to hold down wages, or simply to preserve the river-washed somnambulance of the genteel life, the leading citizens actively discouraged new industry and resisted even the minimal standards of social justice that the rest of the country has tried to adopt. Textbook clichés of history and geography created a bemusement that bordered on paralysis. Inevitably, said the conventional wisdom, any community located at the confluence of two great rivers will enjoy a prosperous economic life; naturally, black people will settle for second-class citizenship; properly, social harmony in a community must be established according to the standards of the "better people."

12.  Cairo is becoming a ghost town, suffering not only the general economic decline of a place that is being passed by, but also a major boycott of downtown merchants by its own black commu-

nity, which represents about 32 percent of the population and which has been unable to secure even a minimum of decent jobs. As a consequence, the city has suffered a series of racial confrontations—shootings, marches, vigilantism, and, for a brief period, rule by martial law. The black people have heard the call of the twentieth century, but many whites have not. People like David Cain, the new publisher of the Cairo *Evening Citizen,* talk hopefully about the possibilities of economic revival, about the blessings of a new interstate highway that will pass near the city—when it is built, perhaps in five years—but they concede that many of their fellow citizens are still living in another age, waiting, maybe, for the boats to stop again, for the factories to come back, for the black community to return to its ante-bellum subservience. A few miles north of the city in a town called Thebes, a pre–Civil War courthouse stands on a bluff overlooking the Mississippi. After his escape from slavery and his recapture, Dred Scott was incarcerated there. The courthouse is now a museum, but on its door someone from the local poverty program has tacked a notice urging young men and women to join Operation Green Thumb, a project for high school dropouts conducted by the Neighborhood Youth Corps. And on the Ohio River levee at Cairo someone has painted a string of peace symbols and the slogan "Make Love Not War," but no one seemed to know who had done it. The river can be channeled and controlled. But the sentiments of an age, though underground, seem to be irresistible.

13. Sometimes it is hard to know where one is, and even harder to tell time. Where change is welcomed, it often defaces the symbols of the past; where it is not, it destroys them. The diners, the motels, the drive-ins snap at the heels of plantation houses and ante-bellum museums, and the news from Washington overwhelms the gossip of Water Street. The greatest calamity currently facing the cotton growers of the Delta—the Mississippi region that extends from Memphis to Vicksburg—is not the boll weevil or the declining market for cotton, but the possibility that the federal government will restrict its support payments to a maximum of $55,000 per grower. Men whose Congressional representatives like nothing so much as attacking handouts and celebrating the virtues of capitalism and economic independence are struggling to preserve their part of the action. Their plantations are mechanized; they no longer depend on the labor of black field hands (many of whom, having followed the shortest route north, are now in Chicago and St. Louis and Detroit), but they do depend on the protection and subsidies of that most contemptible of institutions, "the government in Washington." While the tourists go

through the old plantation homes, tripping over Spanish moss and Southern sentiment, the growers are wondering if they should start planting soybeans instead of cotton, wondering if their friends on the Agriculture Committee will come to the rescue, wondering if the legions of Congress will not be more devastating than the armies of Sherman and Grant.

14. Time and place: Obviously, the river has produced its own kind of high prosperity, and that prosperity has frequently enriched already attractive communities along the levee, but it is not the sort of success glorified by dream and legend. In its course from Minnesota to the Gulf, there are stretches where the Mississippi is lined with industry: oil refineries, grain elevators, fertilizer plants, barge terminals, and where the towns are surrounded by new shopping centers, libraries, and schools, but if they belong to any community, it is national or international, not local, and if they stimulate any corner of the imagination, it is technocratic rather than humanistic. What made the river such a powerfully integrating force was its ability to link the realms of "serious" adult endeavor—the riverboat, the plantation, the war to preserve the Union—with the play of childhood, with the process of growing up, and with the belief that rich, open land also promised rich, open lives. In some of the smaller cities, there are people who believe that all those dreams are still possible, that Hannibal, for example, is still a "good place to grow up in," and that in the increasing concern for the amenities of life and in the mounting disenchantment with large cities, the town that offers hunting and fishing and the apparent civilities of the small community will come back.

15. And yet, for the moment, the evidence does not support the hope. In Hannibal, the high school students all speak cheerfully about the blessings of their city and their river, about how "everyone knows everyone else," about the "great school spirit," about how "we're well brought up," but none of them have any intention of staying, or, eventually, of coming back. The kids are not radicals, and often they proudly explain that there are no freaks or hippies around, but anyone who talks to them long enough understands that "progress" can be as divisive as decay, that the kind of industry that means jobs and prosperity also separates men from their river and dictates activities in which the fantasies and passions of childhood have no place. Forty years ago being a boy on the Mississippi was probably not so different from what it was a century before, and there are still people who recall swimming across the stream and exploring the sandbars and islands and beaches on the other side.

They recall school outings on the steamboat to Keokuk and, later, excursion steamers with their big dance floors and their bands—"the best orchestras in the country." Now it is all gone. The dams and levees on the Upper River have destroyed many of the beaches, the cities and industries on its banks have polluted the water, and technology itself has brought other attractions. There are still kids who use the river, who fish from its banks or watch the barges going by, but the big sport requires a motorboat and a pair of water skis, and the big dream—in the few instances where a big dream exists—is not to sign on to a riverboat or take off for the romance of Memphis and New Orleans, but to hit the road—to go west or north—and, most of all, to get out.

16. In Hannibal, the superintendent of schools speaks proudly about his system's low dropout rate, about its modern facilities, about its with-it-ness, but he has no retort to the suggestion that Huck Finn, the most celebrated character of the Mississippi, was a dropout, too. The river is no longer an option.

17. Perhaps the differences are minor. Huck also wanted to hit the road, to light out for the territories, and *Life on the Mississippi* itself was written in Hartford, Connecticut. Perhaps indeed the whole romance of the river and of the lives around it was nothing but a fabrication of sentimental hindsight. Attempts to restore "history" result, almost inevitably, in a form of comstockery, in a cleaning-up that emphasizes the positive at the expense of the unpleasant. In Hannibal, they've turned the Laura Hawkins ("Becky Thatcher") House into a museum and bookstore displaying what I suppose is called Victorian charm (complete with a recorded girl's voice) but disregarding the more significant fact that in the 1840s life must have been something more than girl-boy romances and sunny afternoons with a fishing pole. (The restoration also ignores the fact that in the 1920s this house and many others in town were saloons and brothels serving the men who worked on the railroad.) Inevitably the official, advertised version of the past also disregards its victims—the sons of slaves, for example—and the practices that kept them in subjugation.

18. And yet, even if those things are recognized, it seems nonetheless true that there was a time when, for better or worse, the styles and sensibilities of this region grew on their own terms, when they flowed out to enrich the rest of the nation, and when the things that flowed in were adapted and transformed for local use. Sometimes the settlers fancied themselves Greeks and Romans, gave their towns classical names—Palmyra and Thebes, Cairo and Memphis—built

Greek-revival houses, and, when they could, tried to fashion or imitate a slave-supported elegance. But along with these manifestations there were also an indigenous architecture, an innate style of life, and a set of aspirations that valued enterprise and small-town decency in equal proportions, and that regarded technology not as an impersonal force but simply as a way of making man's labor less burdensome. The river had always mitigated provincialism, because, as someone in Quincy said, "You always knew there was something at the other end—north and south," and it always suggested that fortune and adventure, though they might be distant, were personally accessible, that they might, indeed, begin at the water's edge. The American dream was often an extension of the reveries of the river.

19. "Progress" has reversed the aspirations. Forty years ago the Mississippi was a presence, a monster that could flood cities, tear away bridges, and irrevocably alter individual lives. Living on the Missisippi was like living under a volcano. For some people in some places that fact hasn't changed. But for most, the great forces are now those that come from the outside: the factory that moves in or the company that moves away; wars in distant places; economic and social dislocations that may hit home but that originate not only in the distance but often in regions and forces that cannot even be conceived. "I grew up near here," said a forty-year-old factory worker in Quincy, "but I didn't know beans about anything until I got drafted into the Korean War." People in the offices of the Chamber of Commerce talk about employers coming in or moving out, and they proudly advertise the attractions of the area for settlers and tourists: summer tours of the river, a library, Mark Twain's restored home, a plantation house, the site of a Civil War battle, or a onetime stern-wheeler now converted into a museum and restaurant. At the same time, the economy and technology itself (or, on occasion, simple fear) seem to make it difficult to contemplate major local initiative, to consider the idea that local banks will promote local industry, improved local housing, or simply local amenities. There is endless rhetoric about free enterprise, about the virtues of work and community action, but there is, in place after place, overwhelming evidence that the things that matter are decided somewhere else, that the river, and much of America with it, has become an economic colony controlled by absentee owners.

20. Much of the river is unbelievably beautiful, twisting and changing with time and place; and yet, despite its fishermen, its water skiers, and its tourism, the Mississippi is the world's biggest industrial

canal. In St. Louis, near the arch that is supposed to be a memorial to Jefferson, there is an elegant modern apartment complex, said to be the only one of its kind along that part of the river. From its windows and balconies there is an expansive view of the Mississippi immediately to the east; on summer evenings, one can look out on the parking lot immediately below, at the yellow slicks emanating from the mills upstream, and at the belching plants of East St. Louis. The complex has its own swimming pools and a full schedule of social and cultural activities conducted on the premises, and the management insists on a thorough "security check" before renting to anyone. This, one might suppose, is also life on the Mississippi, but it is as antiseptic, as synthetic, and as air-conditioned as "modern" existence anywhere else. From the twenty-fifth floor, the river is an abstraction.

21.    Because the highways now take the traffic inland, around little towns and away from the old neighborhoods, the river often preserves its secrets, not only from the visitor but from the residents. Behind the railroad tracks of small cities, behind warehouses and factories no longer used, the shanty-towns survive with their unpaved streets, their acquiescent Negroes, and their angry children. If Hannibal, for example, is aware that it has a ghetto where black and white poor coexist uneasily side by side, few people will speak of it, and those who do are often ignored. It is hard to know how life is lived in "The Bottoms," but it is clear that if time has changed on the Mississippi, there are places it has left behind, that in the bayous of Louisiana and the dusty towns of the Delta the first steps of racial progress remain hesitant and uncertain, and economic growth a distant hope. "Progress" itself—the new road, the new plant, the new airport, the traffic on the river—is not merely creating prosperity but rendering the poverty and backwardness that remain invisible. All along the river there are ghost towns and ghost towns-to-be. Off Route 79 in Missouri the community of Monkey Run survives as a town of old people, most of them retired workers—at a cement plant that once employed several thousand and now has jobs for two hundred—cultivating gardens, raising chickens, and contemplating the old days when Monkey Run and the adjacent company town of Ilasco were thriving communities of groceries, flour mills, slaughterhouses, and saloons. Ilasco now consists of two churches, a store, and the cellar holes of the homes of its former inhabitants. It is dead, closed by order of the company.

22.    In talking to people along the river, it is difficult to resist the sentimental idea—which we all learned in childhood—that this is the mainstream of America, and harder still not to see a legend in every

stick that floats downstream, in every old house, and in every conversation on Commercial Street. In one city on the river, a young man from New York came to edit the local newspaper, because, as he put it, "here you still feel you can do something. Maybe you can still be a William Allen White running an *Emporia Gazette*." And yet it is even harder to argue away the feeling that the country is sorting itself out —has, indeed, already done so; that the nation's skill, talent, and energy do not represent the river or the small town but the ideas and institutions of national industries, national government, and the national media. People on the river rarely lived in isolation, but they created values and ideas on their own terms. Now they are confronted by the choice between, on the one hand, staying put and becoming outsiders in their own place or, on the other, packing their ideological bags and moving on. The river, once the greatest force between St. Paul and New Orleans, is now subject to forces from far beyond. The Mississippi is what we wanted to be, but it is not what we have become. Political rhetoric may—with varying degrees of honest confusion—still play to the sentiment of "Middle America." But this middle, at any rate, survives only as a major outpost of national industrial empires, of national television, and of music and ideas created somewhere else. Where life on the Mississippi tries to emulate the life of the past it dies. And where it lives it must, inevitably, become part of something else.

## WORDS

*meaning*   Define *effluents* and *demarcate* (par. 5), *ineffable* (par. 6), *artifacts* (par. 7), *entrepreneurs* (par. 10), *somnambulance* (par. 11), *technocratic* (par. 14), *indigenous* (par. 18), and *acquiescent* (par. 21).

*relationships*   1. What is meant by *hedged his bet* (par. 10)? What is meant on Wall Street by the term *hedge fund?*   2. What is meant by the term *ante-bellum* (pars. 12 and 13)? To what period of time does it refer in this essay?   3. What is the meaning of *comstockery* (par. 17), and what is the origin of the word?

*choice*   What rhetorical purpose is served by the use of phrases like "that most contemptible of institutions" and "tripping over Spanish moss and Southern sentiment"?

## SENTENCES

*rhetorical devices*   1. What is the meaning of the metaphor in the last sentence of paragraph 12?   2. What idea is supported by the allusions to Huck [Finn] and *Life on the Mississippi* (par. 17)?   3. What is a symbol?

Explain the symbolism in this sentence: "The Mississippi is what we wanted to be, but it is not what we have become." (par. 22).

## PARAGRAPHS

*methods of development* 1. Why does the author repeatedly use *hisself* —clearly not his ordinary diction—in developing the catalog of paragraph 4? 2. How does the author answer the two questions posed in the first sentence of paragraph 5? At what point in the paragraph does he begin to answer the second question? 3. What is the significance of the description (par. 20) of the apartment complex? What is the relationship of this description to the first sentence of the paragraph? To the last sentence?

## CONTENT AND ORGANIZATION

*central ideas* 1. The purpose of the essay is stated in the first sentence of paragraph 5. What is the author's final answer to his own questions (par. 22)? 2. How do paragraphs 10 to 12 illustrate the conclusion expressed in the last two sentences of the essay?

## SUGGESTIONS FOR DISCUSSION

1. Hannibal, Missouri, "has turned Mark Twain into a tourist industry." Describe another town (Dodge City, Kansas, or Deadwood City, South Dakota, for instance) that has turned its history into a tourist industry. 2. Every census shows that population continues to move from small towns to big cities. How will this movement end? 3. Should ending pollution of rivers like the Ohio and Mississippi be the responsibility of the polluters or of the federal and state government? Explain. 4. Peter Schrag maintains that the Mississippi Valley (and much of America) has become an economic colony controlled by absentee owners. Do you agree? Explain. 5. The big dream of young people in Hannibal, the author says, is "to get out." Is the dream the same in your own community? Why, or why not?

*Harry Levin*

# THE UNBANNING OF THE BOOKS

1.  When I was a freshman at Harvard, a Cambridge book-seller was jailed for selling a copy of Joyce's *Ulysses* to a customer who turned out to be an agent from the Watch and Ward Society of Massachusetts. The issue was brought home to some of us—if not to the court—when our most admired instructor, F. O. Matthiessen, testified in vain for the defense. Not that we had got as far as Harvard in innocence of the banned book. During a previous summer, like hundreds of other Americans, I had bought my own copy from the publisher, Sylvia Beach, at her little Paris bookshop on the Rue de l'Odéon. To pack it wrapped in laundry and smuggle it past the U.S. customs inspectors, thereby involving ourselves in what was called "booklegging," gave us an easy thrill of complicity with the embattled author and his courageous champions. It also widened our sense of a rift existing between true culture and the Establishment.

2.  Four years afterward, in 1933, soon after Prohibition had been repealed by the emergent New Deal, the ban on *Ulysses* was lifted. The critical decision, which opened the way for an American edition the following year, was handed down by Judge John M. Woolsey of the U.S. District Court for Southern New York. His incisive opinion acted as a great watershed, since it reversed the trend of earlier opinions and would be frequently cited in later ones. Specifically, books had been condemned on the basis of passages which sounded offensive when taken out of context and without concern for the author's design. Moreover, the determining question had been—in the reverberating phraseology of the so-called Hicklin Rule—whether the reading of such books would tend to "deprave and corrupt" those into whose hands they were likely to fall, regardless of—or rather, with special regard for—their immaturity.

3.  Some of the world's acknowledged classics could be adjudged obscene, and had been, by such procedures. The freedom to read had been abridged, for educated adults, because a mooted book might fall into the hands of children. Mr. Podsnap's cautionary prin-

THE UNBANNING OF THE BOOKS: From *Refractions: Essays in Comparative Literature* by Harry Levin. Copyright © 1966 by Harry Levin. Reprinted by permission of Oxford University Press, Inc., and the author.

ciple of Victorian morality had become a legal criterion: "Would it bring a blush into the cheek of a young person?" Instead of the *jeune fille* as final arbiter of the book's effect, Judge Woolsey proposed "what the French would call *l'homme moyen sensuel.*" The law now seems to recognize this concept of the normal adult reader, "a person with average sex instincts," as the counterpart to its "reasonable man" in matters of practical judgment. Curiously enough, the French expression—more correctly *l'homme sensuel moyen*—is never used in the sensual land of France. It seems to have been invented by Matthew Arnold, who, to be sure, was writing about George Sand.

4.    As for the dishing-up of salacious titbits carefully chosen to nauseate the courtroom, it is now general practice to consider a work of literature as a whole. Taking the trouble to master Joyce's demanding technique, Judge Woolsey found that *Ulysses* presented modern life in elaborate cross-section. Its round of daily activities included the library and concert-hall, as well as the bedroom and bathroom. Sexual and other bodily functions occupied no larger place than they might in ordinary lives. The same extenuation could scarcely be urged for *Lady Chatterley's Lover,* which is overwhelmingly preoccupied with sex. That may help to explain why it remained unpublishable in the United States until 1959 and in Great Britain until 1961, a generation after Lawrence's death. Nor could it be argued by his admirers that this intense last novel was his masterpiece, as *Ulysses* was Joyce's. Obviously, D. H. Lawrence was less the dispassionate artist than James Joyce.

5.    But Lawrence was a passionate moralist, who preached his unorthodox message with evangelical fervor, and therein lay the strength that could be rallied to his support when *Lady Chatterley's Lover* went on trial at the Old Bailey. The intervening years had seen drastic changes, if not in sexual habits or morals, then in the frankness and sincerity with which they could be publicly discussed. The voice in the wilderness had been amplified into a posthumous cause, while losing none of its militant solemnity. The very name of the case, *Regina v. Penguin,* suggesting as it does a chapter from *Alice in Wonderland,* aptly announced the procession of church dignitaries, lady dons, schoolmasters, librarians, editors, critics, and publicists who took the witness stand. Against those thirty-five respectable experts the prosecution could produce no adverse testimony, except for a fastidiously skeptical judgment by Katherine Anne Porter, which Lawrence's defenders promptly impugned.

6.    After a meticulous rereading, John Sparrow would contend

that Lady Chatterley's gamekeeper was not such a model of hetero-sexual normality as witnesses had claimed. But Penguin had already won its case, and was circulating 200,000 paperbacks at three shill-ings and sixpence apiece. In retrospect it seems particularly sig-nificant that, unlike other trials which have led to the unbanning of suppressed books, this one had been decided by a jury. The prose-cution, trying to extend the obsolete Hicklin Rule, had asked the jurymen: "Is it a book that you would even wish your wife or your servants to read?" And the defense had taken that point by remind-ing them that they lived in a democratic society, characterized by equal rights for women, the decline of the servant class, and the production of Penguin Books. The vindication of *Lady Chatterley's Lover* spoke, like the novel itself, for the social as well as the sexual revolution.

7. *Regina v. Penguin Books Limited* was the test case under the new Obscene Publications Act of 1959. Thus it rounded off a cycle, the century of the Hicklin Rule, which in turn had been based on Lord Campbell's Obscene Publications Act of 1857. By a coin-cidence which may be worth noting, that year likewise marked the interdiction of *Madame Bovary,* and it is certainly worth noting that Flaubert was acquitted. The idea of suppressing literature, on sus-picion of its demoralizing potentialities, is at least as old as Plato. Through the course of history, however, censorship has mainly been exerted against religious heresy or political subversion. The *Index Librorum Prohibitorum* was an instrument of the Church's Counter-Reformation. The censor as guardian of private morality is essen-tially a mid-Victorian figure. His period of dominance in Anglo-American culture was unconscionably prolonged, with such untoward results as can be read in the lives and works of Hardy, George Moore, and Shaw, or Whitman, Mark Twain, and Dreiser.

8. The brilliant writers of the early twentieth century grew up in an atmosphere of libertarian protest against what Lawrence called "the censor-morons"—whom we might recognize, under a courtlier phrase, as H. L. Mencken's *"virtuosi* of virtue." Joyce and Lawrence, each in his unique way, could realize their talents only through ex-patriation. Both *Ulysses* and *Lady Chatterley's Lover* could have been first published only in France, where tradition has been especially tolerant to books printed in English and destined for illegal export. The judicial decisions that naturalized these two novels into the body of English literature, all too belatedly, had to square them with pre-vailing moral standards. Judge Woolsey concluded his decision, with an epigrammatic flourish, by stating that the effect of *Ulysses,* while

somewhat emetic, was not aphrodisiac. *Lady Chatterley's Lover* could not be so easily exonerated from the charge of undue eroticism; but, given its preoccupation, it is clearly a tract for reform.

9. The volume that comes next on our shelf of literary contraband, though it has also been legitimatized by the courts, takes us into more problematic areas of discussion. *Tropic of Cancer* has not the high dedication of the two books we smuggled in before it. Indeed its utter laxity is a source of its appeal to a later generation which, perhaps, may feel more kinship with underground man than with the intransigent intellectual. Nor does the stature of Henry Miller begin to compare with that of Joyce or Lawrence; yet his critical reputation has profited from the confusions that have surrounded theirs. When compared with Joyce, as George Orwell pointed out in his farsighted essay "Inside the Whale," Miller hardly seems an artist at all. As a would-be moralist he stands at the opposite pole from Lawrence, who would have been more outraged than anyone else by the loveless fornications of *Tropic of Cancer*.

10. Insofar as there are degrees of vulnerability to attacks from more conventional moralists, this is a harder book to defend than its predecessors. Yet Miller has an undeniable talent, a kind of raffish gusto, as a braggart storyteller in the picaresque mode. While his monologue drifts along the gutters of Paris, it turns up some memorable flotsam. Unfortunately, and increasingly in his other work, this authentic vein of pungent humor is adulterated by messianic rhapsodies—*Leaves of Grass* gone to seed—which prove rather more embarrassing. Nevertheless, the seriousness of their intentions cannot be denied. Consequently in 1961, when the Attorney General of Massachusetts sought to ban the recent American edition of *Tropic of Cancer,* several critics were on hand to testify in its behalf. The case was heard in the Superior Court, where the judge decreed the book to be "obscene, indecent, and impure." That decree was subsequently reversed by the Supreme Judicial Court of the Commonwealth.

11. When I reread this decision, and see my testimony quoted, I must confess that my feelings are somewhat mixed. I had ventured to say—in effect—that the book's predominant mood was "one of sexual revulsion," and that its self-conscious morbidity reflected a sense of cultural decadence. Of course I stand by this view, and feel honored that some of the justices evidently concurred with it. But I cannot help wondering whether the book or I would have had their approval if the suggested line of interpretation had emphasized the joys of the flesh. The puritanical implication is that a writer may con-

cern himself with sex if he treats it as a bad thing, or so long as his treatment of it is emetic rather than aphrodisiac. As a matter of fact, my fellow witnesses found Miller's outlook healthier than I did. One of them even introduced a fascinating comparison between *Tropic of Cancer* and *Huckleberry Finn.*

12. My colleagues, whom I respect, may conceivably be right. In any case, as professors of literature, we are used to critical disagreements. I trust that the judges allow for this variance, and do not take our personal opinions for absolute verities simply because we are consulted as "experts" offering "evidence as to the literary, cultural, or educational character" of the writings in question. What surprised me, in the *Tropic of Cancer* affair, was that no evidence could be admitted from psychiatrists and social workers. Similarly, in *Regina v. Penguin,* where the court listened so patiently to schoolmistresses and theologians, the defense could get no hearing for doctors and "people who deal with those who are sexually depraved or corrupted." Granted that such expertise is hard to come by, that the behavioral sciences are far from exact in their application. We are all left in the dark on the crucial point: the actual impact of the alleged means of corruption.

13. With regard to obscenity, the law has modified itself so extensively in recent years that the interested layman is bewildered— and not less so when he finds himself suddenly called upon as an expert by the courts. Bewilderments are bound to arise from questions which lie open at both ends; and, though a book is an objective artifact, the intent of its author is subjective, and so is its effect upon the reader. As the Director of Public Prosecutions said, in discussing the Obscene Publications Bill, " 'Intent' is a difficult word." There is even a school of formalistic critics which would rule out "the intentional fallacy." Judge Woolsey supplied his colleagues on the bench with another epigram, which they have used to test the purity of a writer's motives, when he spoke of "dirt for dirt's sake." The late Justice Frankfurter, characteristically asking for more precision, suggested that the phrase be changed to "dirt for money's sake."

14. But to speak of dirt is to beg a subtle question. And if the practice of writing for money is generally approved, why should it be specially enjoined against when the subject matter happens to be the important matter of sex? Is it because of the possible effect? Then we shift our ground, and the lawyers begin to talk about provoking lustful thoughts or appealing to prurient interest. Ordinarily we praise a writer when, in dealing with any other subject, he man-

ages to convey sensations and stimulate reactions. Advertisers vie with one another, using a directly visual stimulus, to inject an erotic flavor into the most irrelevant situations. We cannot walk through our day without encountering dozens of random excitations which, if we are healthy, ought to arouse our susceptibilities. "A state of mind is not enough," Mr. Justice Douglas has written, "it is the relationship of that state of mind to overt action that would seem to be critical."

15. It is humbling to realize how little is known about the nature of that relationship, and how widely the trains of speculation diverge. Literature is full of stories that demonstrate—and possibly exaggerate—the influence of literature on behavior, such as Dante's poignant example of Paolo and Francesca, who became lovers after reading a romance together. Specialists in children's problems earnestly and endlessly debate over comic books: whether they are a major cause of juvenile delinquency or a valid inoculation against it. Classicists and psychoanalysts alike believe in catharsis, the notion that the mind can be purged of its antisocial tendencies by participating in vicarious passions. Tragedy has been exhibiting crimes on the stage for centuries, and its after-effects are usually regarded as elevating rather than conducive to further crime. Books that dwell on sexual episodes might be just as likely to relieve tensions as to incite lewd and lascivious conduct.

16. At all events, we must have broader experience, keener observation, and more systematic investigation before we can make confident assumptions as to how a given piece of reading-matter would affect an unforeseen variety of readers. It may be that the Kinsey Institute, which has assembled an impressive library of erotica, will carry its researches into this limbo and bring us back some antiseptic answers. In the meantime, the reading public has been enjoying an unprecedented latitude. The battles for Joyce (inclusion of sex as part of the all-round picture), Lawrence (emphasis on sex as a means of salvation), and Miller (obsession with sex as a nihilistic gesture) have opened the floodgates. After *Ulysses, Lady Chatterley's Lover,* and *Tropic of Cancer,* what then? Irreversibly the progression moves on, impelled by its own momentum, a sheer need for the next revelation to outstrip the last one. Having exploited the themes of normal sexuality, it seeks new disclosures by turning to perversion and inversion.

17. Censorship has backed down with less and less struggle, as Vladimir Nabokov's *Lolita* or William Burroughs' *Naked Lunch* has bridged the rapid transition from the Parisian bookleggers to a

New York imprimatur—and, what is more, to a *nihil obstat* in Boston. Nabokov would be an exception in any grouping, a displaced mandarin from a more elegant age, and his flirtation with vice is merely another whim of his idiosyncrasy. Burroughs continues Miller's sodden bohemianism well into its gangrenescent stage. He finds his material by wallowing deeper and deeper, and relies on drugs to give it an imaginative lift. Yet even *Naked Lunch* pays tribute to moralism in a preface and in an appended article written for *The British Journal of Addiction.* Therein Burroughs observes the convention of gallows literature, where the condemned man edifies the crowd by warning them against his particular fate. So Nabokov, tongue in cheek as usual, palms off *Lolita* as a psychiatric case-history.

18.  The quest for sensation has been approaching the line between serious literature and pornography, if indeed that borderline is still discernible. Joyce and Lawrence both drew it very sharply, since their artistic integrity depended upon it. "Genuine pornography is almost always underworld," Lawrence could write, "it doesn't come into the open." Manifestly, we live in another epoch. The notorious *Memoirs of a Woman of Pleasure,* which has won greater notoriety as *Fanny Hill,* earned John Cleland a reprimand from the Privy Council when he brought it out in the year of *Tom Jones.* Its transatlantic distribution led, in 1821, to the first American suppression for obscenity. Notwithstanding, it has gained and held a place in Anglo-American culture, quite properly a surreptitious place among bookdealers' *curiosa.* Lately it has been brought out from under the counter and commended to a waiting world by Nabokov's publisher, the reputable old firm that published Washington Irving and Herman Melville.

19.  In the light of these developments, we can appreciate the historic irony of the recent announcement by Maurice Girodias, head of the Olympia Press and original publisher of the once-prohibited books by Miller, Nabokov, and Burroughs. His remarkable list includes Samuel Beckett, Lawrence Durrell, and other English-writing luminaries of the current international twilight, along with certain titles which might still be classified somewhere as "hard-core pornography." M. Girodias has declared his intention of moving his operations from Paris to the United States, as soon as he can disentangle them from his present difficulties with the French government. We have come a long way from the days of Sylvia Beach; and so has France, presumably, in the other direction. M. Girodias has reason to envy the Grove Press of New York, which has been

so successful in domesticating many of the works that are giving him trouble, notably the English translation of Genet's *Notre-Dame des Fleurs.*

20. Jean Genet is a writer of unquestioned power, whose style alone would set his books apart from the pornographic confessions they often resemble, and from those American novels and stories which have recently been putting us into close touch with the homosexual *demimonde.* Yet it would be uncritical to think that Genet was not obscene, and his verbose apologist, Jean-Paul Sartre, argues the contrary: obscenity is the stance for Genet's virulent critique of modern society. In this respect, as in others, he is an heir to the Marquis de Sade, that pariah of the eighteenth century who has become a culture-hero today and whose most provocative writings have just been handsomely republished by the Grove Press. Since Mr. Justice Brennan has ruled in the Roth case of 1957 that "all ideas having even the slightest redeeming social importance" are entitled to constitutional protection, the needle's eye would seem to be large enough for the passage of such camels.

21. Not much room has been left for any working definition of pornography; its hard core has been softened, at any rate. Its etymological meaning, "writing about prostitution," should have some bearing on *Fanny Hill* (banned by the Massachusetts court that unbanned *Tropic of Cancer*), where every page invites what long ago Judge Woolsey called "the leer of the sensualist." But a book like *Candy* works both sides of the street by offering itself as a parody of the pornographic genre (pornography being itself a parody of more serious fiction). Rarities formerly locked in the librarians' Inferno are available in paperback, sometimes in competing editions where the sanctions of copyright fail to apply. It could be suspected that, whereas the old-fashioned censor-morons confounded art with pornography, we are now being invited to accept pornography as art. However, the old distinctions no longer serve. Those who might once have been stigmatized as purveyors of smut, "dirt for money's sake," are hailed as benefactors of civil liberties, *virtuosi* of virtue at a profit.

22. Established novelists do their best—and worst—to keep up with the subterranean movement, and to keep on the best-seller lists, by providing their characters with more detailed bedroom histories. Norman Mailer asserted in 1959 that sex was "perhaps the last remaining frontier of the novel which has not been exhausted by the nineteenth and early twentieth century novelists." One might have assumed that this territory was not altogether virgin before *An American Dream,* but Mailer is amply justified in his pioneering metaphor.

From its first emergence, with the breakthrough of the middle class into literature, the novel has been explicitly committed to the enlargement of human experience. Its great practitioners have all been realists, in the sense that they had to cut through conventions and fight against hypocrisies, while striving to capture some segment of reality which has hitherto gone unexpressed. Hence they scandalized the authorities of their day, who retorted with repressive tactics.

23. Flaubert, Dostoevsky, even the Brontës—no less than Lawrence, Joyce, and their successors—all arrived by *succès de scandale*. Invariably contemporaries are shocked by innovation in the arts, and commonly accuse the innovators of being sensation-mongers —which from time to time they must be. But the shock wears off with habituation, and what is no longer new can thereupon be judged by whether or not it seems true. It was shocking to see the forbidden monosyllables in print while *Ulysses* was proscribed, though they might not have offended in masculine conversation or in feminine stream of consciousness. Nowadays we have merely to ask ourselves whether or not they fit into the fictional contexts in which they so freely appear. The convention of using asterisks or dashes seems as quaint as Ernest Hemingway's substitution of the word "obscenity" for the Spanish oaths in *For Whom the Bell Tolls*. Profanity derives its peculiar force from the violation of a taboo; expletives become meaningless once the taboos lose their hold.

24. When the Berkeley students shouted dirty words from a public platform, they confirmed the proprieties against which they were protesting. If speech were completely free, no words would bring a blush to a young person's cheek or raise the eyebrows of an older one. As with the language, so with the contents of books. Descriptions of sexual intimacy, if we get used to reading them, ought to provoke no special titillation. We should be able to take them or leave them, depending on whether they carry honest conviction. When everything has been said, we can focus on how it is said. We may still need safeguards for the immature; but for adults so much is already permitted that not much can consistently be excluded. Our freedom to read, as guaranteed by the law, is virtually complete. Free speech and due process, the First and Fourteenth Amendments to the Constitution as reinterpreted by Justice Brennan, reaffirm the humanism of Terence: "I am a human being, and therefore consider nothing human alien to me."

25. Accordingly, when writers are allowed to write anything they please and publishers to put it in circulation, then the great responsibility for discrimination rests with the reader. Art in itself

may be neither moral nor immoral, as Oscar Wilde insisted; but, since we are potentially both, the courts stand ready to correct our overt immorality. Meanwhile it remains for us to determine the uses of art. If we abandon censorship, we depend all the more imperatively upon criticism. If we agree that books are neither dirty nor clean, we must be sure to remember that they are bad or good, and must not be distracted into ignoring that difference. After all, it has never been too difficult to tell a potboiler from a work of art, and it should be even simpler with potboilers that concentrate upon sex to the point of monotony. To criticize them is to discriminate between artistic imagination and autistic fantasy. One of the wholesome results of our hard-won candor is that it could end by driving the pornographers out of business.

## WORDS

*meaning* 1. Define *incisive* (par. 2), *mooted* (par. 3), *interdiction* and *unconscionably* (par. 7), *expatriation* (par. 8), *intransigent* (par. 9), *raffish* and *messianic* (par. 10), *verities* (par. 12), *prurient* (par. 14), *imprimatur* (par. 17), *pariah* (par. 20), *etymological* (par. 21), and *autistic* (par. 25). 2. What is the meaning of these common French phrases: *jeune fille* and *l'homme moyen sensuel* (par. 3) and *succès de scandale* (par. 23)?

*relationships* 1. How is *dispassionate* (par. 4) related to *disinterested?* Distinguish between *disinterested* and *uninterested.* 2. How are *concurred* (par. 11) and *concourse* related?

## SENTENCES

*style* What antithesis is used in both paragraph 8 and paragraph 11? Why is it "an epigrammatic flourish" (par. 8)?

*rhetorical devices* 1. This essay is rich in allusion. Why, for instance, does *Regina v. Penguin* remind the author of *Alice in Wonderland* (par. 5)? What is the nature and meaning of the allusion in "librarians' Inferno" (par. 21)? Who was Terence (par. 24)? 2. What is Norman Mailer's "pioneering metaphor" (par. 22)? Where do you find irony in the author's treatment of Mailer's work as a novelist?

## PARAGRAPHS

*topic sentence* The third sentence of paragraph 2 is a topic sentence for paragraphs 2, 3, and 4. What standards and methods of judicial consideration are contrasted in the three paragraphs?

*method of development* Is paragraph 15 developed by comparison, by definition, or by examples?

CONTENT AND ORGANIZATION

*central ideas* 1. How did the Woolsey decision reverse the trend of earlier decisions (pars. 2–4)? 2. Explain what the author means by saying, "When the Berkeley students shouted dirty words from a public platform, they confirmed the proprieties against which they were protesting" (par. 24). 3. Explain the distinction made in this sentence: "If we agree that books are neither dirty nor clean, we must be sure to remember that they are bad or good" (par. 25).

*assumptions and implications* Can the author's statement "We may still need safeguards for the immature" (par. 24) be reconciled with the idea in the concluding sentence, or is the author being self-contradictory?

SUGGESTIONS FOR DISCUSSION

1. Have you ever read a book that tended to corrupt or deprave you? Explain. 2. How can a reader "discriminate between artistic imagination and autistic fantasy" (par. 25)? 3. When and if you become a parent, what control will you exercise over your children's reading? 4. "Instead of fearing that my children will read bad books," said one parent, "I fear they may never learn to read any books." Comment. 5. "A writer may concern himself with sex if he treats it as a bad thing" (par. 11). Is this belief held by many Americans?

*James Harvey Robinson*

# ON VARIOUS KINDS OF THINKING

1. We do not think enough about thinking, and much of our confusion is the result of current illusions in regard to it. Let us forget for the moment any impressions we may have derived from the philosophers, and see what seems to happen in ourselves. The first thing that we notice is that our thought moves with such incredible rapidity that it is almost impossible to arrest any specimen of it long enough to have a look at it. When we are offered a penny for our thoughts we always find that we have recently had so many

ON VARIOUS KINDS OF THINKING: From *The Mind in the Making* by James Harvey Robinson. Copyright 1921 by Harper & Row, Publishers, Inc.; renewed 1949 by Bankers Trust Company.

things in mind that we can easily make a selection which will not compromise us too nakedly. On inspection we shall find that even if we are not downright ashamed of a great part of our spontaneous thinking it is far too intimate, personal, ignoble or trivial to permit us to reveal more than a small part of it. I believe this must be true of everyone. We do not, of course, know what goes on in other people's heads. They tell us very little and we tell them very little. The spigot of speech, rarely fully opened, could never emit more than driblets of the ever renewed hogshead of thought—*noch grösser wie's Heidelberger Fass*. We find it hard to believe that other people's thoughts are as silly as our own, but they probably are.

2.   We all appear to ourselves to be thinking all the time during our waking hours, and most of us are aware that we go on thinking while we are asleep, even more foolishly than when awake. When uninterrupted by some practical issue we are engaged in what is now known as a reverie. This is our spontaneous and favorite kind of thinking. We allow our ideas to take their own course and this course is determined by our hopes and fears, our spontaneous desires, their fulfillment or frustration; by our likes and dislikes, our loves and hates and resentments. There is nothing else anything like so interesting to ourselves as ourselves. All thought that is not more or less laboriously controlled and directed will inevitably circle about the beloved ego. It is amusing and pathetic to observe this tendency in ourselves and in others. We learn politely and generously to overlook this truth, but if we dare to think of it, it blazes forth like the noontide sun.

3.   The reverie or "free association of ideas" has of late become the subject of scientific research. While investigators are not yet agreed on the results, or at least on the proper interpretation to be given to them, there can be no doubt that our reveries form the chief index to our fundamental character. They are a reflection of our nature as modified by often hidden and forgotten experiences. We need not go into the matter further here, for it is only necessary to observe that the reverie is at all times a potent and in many cases an omnipotent rival to every other kind of thinking. It doubtless influences all our speculations in its persistent tendency to self-magnification and self-justification, which are its chief preoccupations, but it is the last thing to make directly or indirectly for honest increase of knowledge. Philosophers usually talk as if such thinking did not exist or were in some way negligible. This is what makes their speculations so unreal and often worthless.

4.   The reverie, as any of us can see for himself, is frequently

broken and interrupted by the necessity of a second kind of thinking. We have to make practical decisions. Shall we write a letter or no? Shall we take the subway or a bus? Shall we have dinner at seven or half past? Shall we buy U.S. Rubber or a Liberty Bond? Decisions are easily distinguishable from the free flow of the reverie. Sometimes they demand a good deal of careful pondering and the recollection of pertinent facts; often, however, they are made impulsively. They are a more difficult and laborious thing than the reverie, and we resent having to "make up our mind" when we are tired, or absorbed in a congenial reverie. Weighing a decision, it should be noted, does not necessarily add anything to our knowledge, although we may, of course, seek further information before making it.

5. A third kind of thinking is stimulated when anyone questions our beliefs and opinions. We sometimes find ourselves changing our minds without any resistance or heavy emotion, but if we are told that we are wrong we resent the imputation and harden our hearts. We are incredibly heedless in the formation of our beliefs, but find ourselves filled with an illicit passion for them when anyone proposes to rob us of their companionship. It is obviously not the ideas themselves that are dear to us, but our self-esteem, which is threatened. We are by nature stubbornly pledged to defend our own from attack, whether it be our person, our family, our property, or our opinion. A United States Senator once remarked to a friend of mine that God Almighty could not make him change his mind on our Latin-American policy. We may surrender, but rarely confess ourselves vanquished. In the intellectual world at least peace is without victory.

6. Few of us take the pains to study the origin of our cherished convictions; indeed, we have a natural repugnance to so doing. We like to continue to believe what we have been accustomed to accept as true, and the resentment aroused when doubt is cast upon any of our assumptions leads us to seek every manner of excuse for clinging to them. *The result is that most of our so-called reasoning consists in finding arguments for going on believing as we already do.*

7. I remember years ago attending a public dinner to which the Governor of the state was bidden. The chairman explained that His Excellency could not be present for certain "good" reasons; what the "real" reasons were the presiding officer said he would leave us to conjecture. This distinction between "good" and "real" reasons is one of the most clarifying and essential in the whole realm of thought. We can readily give what seem to us "good" reasons for being a Catholic or a Mason, a Republican or a Democrat, an ad-

herent or opponent of the League of Nations. But the "real" reasons are usually on quite a different plane. Of course the importance of this distinction is popularly, if somewhat obscurely, recognized. The Baptist missionary is ready enough to see that the Buddhist is not such because his doctrines would bear careful inspection, but because he happened to be born in a Buddhist family in Tokyo. But it would be treason to his faith to acknowledge that his own partiality for certain doctrines is due to the fact that his mother was a member of the First Baptist church of Oak Ridge. A savage can give all sorts of reasons for his belief that it is dangerous to step on a man's shadow, and a newspaper editor can advance plenty of arguments against the Bolsheviki. But neither of them may realize why he happens to be defending his particular opinion.

8.   The "real" reasons for our beliefs are concealed from ourselves as well as from others. As we grow up we simply adopt the ideas presented to us in regard to such matters as religion, family relations, property, business, our country, and the state. We unconsciously absorb them from our environment. They are persistently whispered in our ear by the group in which we happen to live. Moreover, as Mr. Trotter has pointed out, these judgments, being the product of suggestion and not of reasoning, have the quality of perfect obviousness, so that to question them

> . . . is to the believer to carry skepticism to an insane degree, and will be met by contempt, disapproval, or condemnation, according to the nature of the belief in question. When, therefore, we find ourselves entertaining an opinion about the basis of which there is a quality of feeling which tells us that to inquire into it would be absurd, obviously unnecessary, unprofitable, undesirable, bad form, or wicked, we may know that that opinion is a nonrational one, and probably, therefore, founded upon inadequate evidence.

9.   Opinions, on the other hand, which are the result of experience or of honest reasoning do not have this quality of "primary certitude." I remember when as a youth I heard a group of businessmen discussing the question of the immortality of the soul, I was outraged by the sentiment of doubt expressed by one of the party. As I look back now I see that I had at the time no interest in the matter, and certainly no least argument to urge in favor of the belief in which I had been reared. But neither my personal indifference to the issue, nor the fact that I had previously given it no attention, served to prevent an angry resentment when I heard *my* ideas questioned.

10.   This spontaneous and loyal support of our preconceptions

—this process of finding "good" reasons to justify our routine beliefs—is known to modern psychologists as "rationalizing"—clearly only a new name for a very ancient thing. Our "good" reasons ordinarily have no value in promoting honest enlightenment, because, no matter how solemnly they may be marshaled, they are at bottom the result of personal preference or prejudice, and not of an honest desire to seek or accept new knowledge.

11. In our reveries we are frequently engaged in self-justification, for we cannot bear to think ourselves wrong, and yet have constant illustrations of our weaknesses and mistakes. So we spend much time finding fault with circumstances and the conduct of others, and shifting on to them with great ingenuity the onus of our own failures and disappointments. *Rationalizing is the self-exculpation which occurs when we feel ourselves, or our group, accused of misapprehension or error.*

12. The little word *my* is the most important one in all human affairs, and properly to reckon with it is the beginning of wisdom. It has the same force whether it is *my* dinner, *my* dog, and *my* house, or *my* faith, *my* country, and *my* God. We not only resent the imputation that our watch is wrong, or our car shabby, but that our conception of the canals of Mars, the pronunciation of "Epictetus," the medicinal value of salicin, or the [birth] date of Sargon I, are subject to revision.

13. Philosophers, scholars, and men of science exhibit a common sensitiveness in all decisions in which their *amour propre* is involved. Thousands of argumentative works have been written to vent a grudge. However stately their reasoning, it may be nothing but rationalizing, stimulated by the most commonplace of all motives. A history of philosophy and theology could be written in terms of grouches, wounded pride, and aversions, and it would be far more instructive than the usual treatments of these themes. Sometimes, under Providence, the lowly impulse of resentment leads to great achievements. Milton wrote his treatise on divorce as a result of his troubles with his seventeen-year-old wife, and when he was accused of being the leading spirit in a new sect, the Divorcers, he wrote his noble *Areopagitica* to prove his right to say what he thought fit, and incidentally to establish the advantage of a free press in the promotion of Truth.

14. All mankind, high and low, thinks in all the ways which have been described. The reverie goes on all the time not only in the mind of the mill hand and the Broadway flapper, but equally in weighty judges and godly bishops. It has gone on in all the philoso-

phers, scientists, poets, and theologians that have ever lived. Aristotle's most abstruse speculations were doubtless tempered by highly irrelevant reflections. He is reported to have had very thin legs and small eyes, for which he doubtless had to find excuses, and he was wont to indulge in very conspicuous dress and rings and was accustomed to arrange his hair carefully. Diogenes the Cynic exhibited the impudence of a touchy soul. His tub was his distinction. Tennyson in beginning his "Maud" could not forget his chagrin over losing his patrimony years before as the result of an unhappy investment in the Patent Decorative Carving Company. These facts are not recalled here as a gratuitous disparagement of the truly great, but to insure a full realization of the tremendous competition which all really exacting thought has to face, even in the minds of the most highly endowed mortals.

15. And now the astonishing and perturbing suspicion emerges that perhaps almost all that had passed for social science, political economy, politics, and ethics in the past may be brushed aside by future generations as mainly rationalizing. John Dewey has already reached this conclusion in regard to philosophy. Veblen and other writers have revealed the various unperceived presuppositions of the traditional political economy, and now comes an Italian sociologist, Vilfredo Pareto, who, in his huge treatise on general sociology, devotes hundreds of pages to substantiating a similar thesis affecting all the social sciences. This conclusion may be ranked by students of a hundred years hence as one of the several great discoveries of our age. It is by no means fully worked out, and it is so opposed to nature that it will be very slowly accepted by the great mass of those who consider themselves thoughtful. As a historical student I am personally fully reconciled to this newer view. Indeed, it seems to me inevitable that just as the various sciences of nature were, before the opening of the seventeenth century, largely masses of rationalizations to suit the religious sentiments of the period, so the social sciences have continued even to our own day to be rationalizations of uncritically accepted beliefs and customs. *It will become apparent as we proceed that the fact that an idea is ancient and that it has been widely received is no argument in its favor, but should immediately suggest the necessity of carefully testing it as a probable instance of rationalization.*

16. This brings us to another kind of thought which can fairly easily be distinguished from the three kinds described above. It has not the usual qualities of the reverie, for it does not hover about our personal complacencies and humiliations. It is not made up of the

homely decisions forced upon us by everyday needs, when we review our little stock of existing information, consult our conventional preferences and obligations, and make a choice of action. It is not the defense of our own cherished beliefs and prejudices just because they are our own—mere plausible excuses for remaining of the same mind. On the contrary, it is that peculiar species of thought which leads us to *change* our mind.

17. It is this kind of thought that has raised man from his pristine, subsavage ignorance and squalor to the degree of knowledge and comfort which he now possesses. On his capacity to continue and greatly extend this kind of thinking depends his chance of groping his way out of the plight in which the most highly civilized peoples of the world now find themselves. In the past this type of thinking has been called Reason. But so many misapprehensions have grown up around the word that some of us have become very suspicious of it. I suggest, therefore, that we substitute a recent name and speak of "creative thought" rather than of Reason. *For this kind of meditation begets knowledge, and knowledge is really creative inasmuch as it makes things look different from what they seemed before and may indeed work for their reconstruction.*

18. In certain moods some of us realize that we are observing things or making reflections with a seeming disregard of our personal preoccupations. We are not preening or defending ourselves; we are not faced by the necessity of any practical decision, nor are we apologizing for believing this or that. We are just wondering and looking and mayhap seeing what we never perceived before.

19. Curiosity is as clear and definite as any of our urges. We wonder what is in a sealed telegram or in a letter in which someone else is absorbed, or what is being said in the telephone booth or in low conversation. This inquisitiveness is vastly stimulated by jealousy, suspicion, or any hint that we ourselves are directly or indirectly involved. But there appears to be a fair amount of personal interest in other people's affairs even when they do not concern us except as a mystery to be unraveled or a tale to be told. The reports of a divorce suit will have "news value" for many weeks. They constitute a story, like a novel or play or moving picture. This is not an example of pure curiosity, however, since we readily identify ourselves with others, and their joys and despair then become our own.

20. We also take note of, or "observe," as Sherlock Holmes says, things which have nothing to do with our personal interests and make no personal appeal either direct or by way of sympathy. This is what Veblen so well calls "idle curiosity." And it is usually idle

enough. Some of us when we face the line of people opposite us in a subway train impulsively consider them in detail and engage in rapid inferences and form theories in regard to them. On entering a room there are those who will perceive at a glance the degree of preciousness of the rugs, the character of the pictures, and the personality revealed by the books. But there are many, it would seem, who are so absorbed in their personal reverie or in some definite purpose that they have no bright-eyed energy for idle curiosity. The tendency to miscellaneous observation we come by honestly enough, for we note it in many of our animal relatives.

21.   Veblen, however, uses the term "idle curiosity" somewhat ironically, as is his wont. It is idle only to those who fail to realize that it may be a very rare and indispensable thing from which almost all distinguished human achievement proceeds, since it may lead to systematic examination and seeking for things hitherto undiscovered. For research is but diligent search which enjoys the high flavor of primitive hunting. Occasionally and fitfully idle curiosity thus leads to creative thought, which alters and broadens our own views and aspirations and may in turn, under highly favorable circumstances, affect the views and lives of others, even for generations to follow. An example or two will make this unique human process clear.

22.   Galileo was a thoughtful youth and doubtless carried on a rich and varied reverie. He had artistic ability and might have turned out to be a musician or painter. When he had dwelt among the monks at Valambrosa he had been tempted to lead the life of a religious. As a boy he busied himself with toy machines and he inherited a fondness for mathematics. All these facts are of record. We may safely assume also that, along with many other subjects of contemplation, the Pisan maidens found a vivid place in his thoughts.

23.   One day when seventeen years old, he wandered into the cathedral of his native town. In the midst of his reverie he looked up at the lamps hanging by long chains from the high ceiling of the church. Then something very difficult to explain occurred. He found himself no longer thinking of the building, worshipers, or the services; of his artistic or religious interests; of his reluctance to become a physician as his father wished. He forgot the question of a career and even the *graziosissime donne*. As he watched the swinging lamps he was suddenly wondering if mayhap their oscillations, whether long or short, did not occupy the same time. Then he tested this hypothesis by counting his pulse, for that was the only timepiece he had with him.

24.   This observation, however remarkable in itself, was not

enough to produce a really creative thought. Others may have noticed the same thing and yet nothing came of it. Most of our observations have no assignable results. Galileo may have seen that the warts on a peasant's face formed a perfect isosceles triangle, or he may have noticed with boyish glee that just as the officiating priest was uttering the solemn words, *ecce agnus Dei,* a fly lit on the end of his nose. To be really creative, ideas have to be worked up and then "put over," so that they become a part of man's social heritage. The highly accurate pendulum clock was one of the later results of Galileo's discovery. He himself was led to reconsider and successfully to refute the old notions of falling bodies. It remained for Newton to prove that the moon was falling, and presumably all the heavenly bodies. This quite upset all the consecrated views of the heavens as managed by angelic engineers. The universality of the laws of gravitation stimulated the attempt to seek other and equally important natural laws and cast grave doubts on the miracles in which mankind had hitherto believed. In short, those who dared to include in their thought the discoveries of Galileo and his successors found themselves in a new earth surrounded by new heavens.

25.   On the twenty-eighth of October, 1831, two hundred and fifty years after Galileo had noticed the isochronous vibrations of the lamps, creative thought and its currency had so far increased that Faraday was wondering what would happen if he mounted a disk of copper between the poles of a horseshoe magnet. As the disk revolved an electric current was produced. This would doubtless have seemed the idlest kind of an experiment to the stanch businessmen of the time, who, it happened, were just then denouncing the child-labor bills in their anxiety to avail themselves to the full of the results of earlier idle curiosity. But should the dynamos and motors which have come into being as the outcome of Faraday's experiment be stopped this evening, the businessman of today, agitated over labor troubles, might, as he trudged home past lines of "dead" cars, through dark streets to an unlighted house, engage in a little creative thought of his own and perceive that he and his laborers would have no modern factories and mines to quarrel about had it not been for the strange practical effects of the idle curiosity of scientists, inventors, and engineers.

26.   The examples of creative intelligence given above belong to the realm of modern scientific achievement, which furnishes the most striking instances of the effects of scrupulous, objective thinking. But there are, of course, other great realms in which the recording and embodiment of acute observation and insight have

wrought themselves into the higher life of man. The great poets and dramatists and our modern storytellers have found themselves engaged in productive reveries, noting and artistically presenting their discoveries for the delight and instruction of those who have the ability to appreciate them.

27. The process by which a fresh and original poem or drama comes into being is doubtless analogous to that which originates and elaborates so-called scientific discoveries; but there is clearly a temperamental difference. The genesis and advance of painting, sculpture, and music offer still other problems. We really as yet know shockingly little about these matters, and indeed very few people have the least curiosity about them. Nevertheless, creative intelligence in its various forms and activities is what makes man. Were it not for its slow, painful, and constantly discouraged operations through the ages man would be no more than a species of primate living on seeds, fruit, roots, and uncooked flesh, and wandering naked through the woods and over the plains like a chimpanzee.

28. The origin and progress and future promotion of civilization are ill understood and misconceived. These should be made the chief theme of education, but much hard work is necessary before we can reconstruct our ideas of man and his capacities and free ourselves from innumerable persistent misapprehensions. There have been obstructionists in all times, not merely the lethargic masses, but the moralists, the rationalizing theologians, and most of the philosophers, all busily if unconsciously engaged in ratifying existing ignorance and mistakes and discouraging creative thought. Naturally, those who reassure us seem worthy of honor and respect. Equally naturally those who puzzle us with disturbing criticisms and invite us to change our ways are objects of suspicion and readily discredited. Our personal discontent does not ordinarily extend to any critical questioning of the general situation in which we find ourselves. In every age the prevailing conditions of civilization have appeared quite natural and inevitable to those who grew up in them. The cow asks no questions as to how it happens to have a dry stall and a supply of hay. The kitten laps its warm milk from a china saucer, without knowing anything about porcelain; the dog nestles in the corner of a divan with no sense of obligation to the inventors of upholstery and the manufacturers of down pillows. So we humans accept our breakfasts, our trains and telephones and orchestras and movies, our national Constitution, our moral code and standards of manners, with the simplicity and innocence of a pet rabbit. We have absolutely inexhaustible capacities for appropriating what others do for us with no thought of

a "thank you." We do not feel called upon to make any least contributions to the merry game ourselves. Indeed, we are usually quite unaware that a game is being played at all.

## WORDS

*meaning*   Define *negligible* (par. 3), *pertinent* (par. 4), *illicit* (par. 5), *imputation* (par. 12), *abstruse* and *gratuitous* (par. 14), *pristine* (par. 17), *embodiment* (par. 26), and *lethargic* (par. 28).

*relationships*   1. Robinson uses the word *omnipotent* (par. 3). What does it mean? What does it have in common with words like *omniscient, omnibus, omnivorous?*   2. Robinson uses the word *isochronous* (par. 25). What does it mean? What does it have in common with the words *isosceles, isothermal, isobar?* What does it have in common with words like *chronology, chronometer, synchronous?*

## SENTENCES

*parallelism*   Paragraph 16 contains a series of four sentences used to define and to distinguish creative thought from other kinds of thought. How is the structure of these sentences parallel?

## PARAGRAPHS

*coherence*   1. In some paragraphs coherence is maintained by persistent use of the same subject and by parallel sentence structure. Explain how this is done in paragraphs 18 and 23.   2. In other paragraphs it is strengthened by the use of transitional words. What are the transitional words and phrases in paragraph 21?

*methods of development*   1. This essay contains uncomplicated examples of several different kinds of paragraph development. Paragraph 7 is developed by examples. What is its topic sentence?   2. Paragraph 16 is developed by elimination. What is its topic sentence?

## CONTENT AND ORGANIZATION

*central ideas*   1. In which paragraphs do you find the definitions for each of the four kinds of thinking? Paraphrase each definition.   2. Is rationalizing the process of finding "good" reasons or "real" reasons?   3. What is the value of "idle curiosity"?

*organization*   Why do the first three definitions come early in the essay and the fourth not until halfway through it?

*assumptions and implications*   1. If you were to write a short paper reporting a bit of reverie as faithfully as possible, would your paper have logical unity? 2. Why is decision-making "more difficult and laborious" (par. 4) than reverie? 3. Why are dynamos and electric motors "the outcome of Faraday's experiment" (par. 25)?

SUGGESTIONS FOR DISCUSSION

1. How have your reveries changed since (a) you first listened to or watched children's radio or television programs? (b) you first entered high school? (c) you chose the profession you wish to follow? 2. How are one's reveries "modified by often hidden and forgotten experiences" (par. 3)? 3. Write a paper in which you describe the process you followed in (a) making a difficult decision, (b) rationalizing an irrational decision, or (c) doing a piece of creative thinking or investigation. 4. Is there any difference between your "good" reasons and your "real" reasons for coming to college?

# J. B. S. Haldane
## ON BEING THE RIGHT SIZE

1. The most obvious differences between different animals are differences of size, but for some reason the zoologists have paid singularly little attention to them. In the large textbook of zoology before me I find no indication that the eagle is larger than the sparrow, or the hippopotamus bigger than the hare, though some grudging admissions are made in the case of the mouse and the whale. But yet it is easy to show that a hare could not be as large as a hippopotamus, or a whale as small as a herring. For every type of animal there is a most convenient size, and a large change in size inevitably carries with it a change of form.

2. Let us take the most obvious of possible cases, and consider a giant man sixty feet high—about the height of Giant Pope and Giant Pagan in the illustrated *Pilgrim's Progress* of my childhood. These monsters were not only ten times as high as Christian, but ten times as wide and ten times as thick, so that their total weight was a thousand times his, or about eighty to ninety tons. Unfortunately the cross sections of their bones were only a hundred times those of Christian, so that every square inch of giant bone had to support

ON BEING THE RIGHT SIZE: From *Possible Worlds* by J. B. S. Haldane. Copyright 1928 by Harper & Row, Publishers, Inc.; renewed 1956 by J. B. S. Haldane.

ten times the weight borne by a square inch of human bone. As the human thigh-bone breaks under about ten times the human weight, Pope and Pagan would have broken their thighs every time they took a step. This was doubtless why they were sitting down in the picture I remember. But it lessens one's respect for Christian and Jack the Giant Killer.

3. To turn to zoology, suppose that a gazelle, a graceful little creature with long thin legs, is to become large: it will break its bones unless it does one of two things. It may make its legs short and thick, like the rhinoceros, so that every pound of weight has still about the same area of bone to support it. Or it can compress its body and stretch out its legs obliquely to gain stability, like the giraffe. I mention these two beasts because they happen to belong to the same order as the gazelle, and both are quite successful mechanically, being remarkably fast runners.

4. Gravity, a mere nuisance to Christian, was a terror to Pope, Pagan, and Despair. To the mouse and any smaller animal it presents practically no dangers. You can drop a mouse down a thousand-yard mine shaft; and, on arriving at the bottom, it gets a slight shock and walks away, provided that the ground is fairly soft. A rat is killed, a man is broken, a horse splashes. For the resistance presented to movement by the air is proportional to the surface of the moving object. Divide an animal's length, breadth, and height each by ten; its weight is reduced to a thousandth, but its surface only to a hundredth. So the resistance to falling in the case of the small animal is relatively ten times greater than the driving force.

5. An insect, therefore, is not afraid of gravity; it can fall without danger, and can cling to the ceiling with remarkably little trouble. It can go in for elegant and fantastic forms of support like that of the daddy longlegs. But there is a force which is as formidable to an insect as gravitation to a mammal. This is surface tension. A man coming out of a bath carries with him a film of water of about one-fiftieth of an inch in thickness. This weighs roughly a pound. A wet mouse has to carry about its own weight of water. A wet fly has to lift many times its own weight and, as every one knows, a fly once wetted by water or any other liquid is in a very serious position indeed. An insect going for a drink is in as great danger as a man leaning out over a precipice in search of food. If it once falls into the grip of the surface tension of the water—that is to say, gets wet—it is likely to remain so until it drowns. A few insects, such as water beetles, contrive to be unwettable; the majority keep well away from their drink by means of a long proboscis.

6. Of course tall land animals have other difficulties. They have to pump their blood to greater heights than a man and, therefore, require a larger blood pressure and tougher blood-vessels. A great many men die from burst arteries, especially in the brain, and this danger is presumably still greater for an elephant or a giraffe. But animals of all kinds find difficulties in size for the following reason. A typical small animal, say a microscopic worm or rotifer, has a smooth skin through which all the oxygen it requires can soak in, a straight gut with sufficient surface to absorb its food, and a simple kidney. Increase its dimensions tenfold in every direction, and its weight is increased a thousand times, so that if it is to use its muscles as efficiently as its miniature counterpart, it will need a thousand times as much food and oxygen per day and will excrete a thousand times as much of waste products.

7. Now if its shape is unaltered, its surface will be increased only a hundredfold, and ten times as much oxygen must enter per minute through each square millimeter of skin, ten times as much food through each square millimeter of intestine. When a limit is reached to their absorptive powers, their surface has to be increased by some special device. For example, a part of the skin may be drawn out into tufts to make gills or pushed in to make lungs, thus increasing the oxygen-absorbing surface in proportion to the animal's bulk. A man, for example, has a hundred square yards of lung. Similarly, the gut, instead of being smooth and straight, becomes coiled and develops a velvety surface, and other organs increase in complication. The higher animals are not larger than the lower because they are more complicated. They are more complicated because they are larger. Just the same is true of plants. The simplest plants, such as the green algae growing in stagnant water or on the bark of trees, are mere round cells. The higher plants increase their surface by putting out leaves and roots. Comparative anatomy is largely the story of the struggle to increase surface in proportion to volume.

8. Some of the methods of increasing the surface are useful up to a point, but not capable of a very wide adaptation. For example, while vertebrates carry the oxygen from the gills or lungs all over the body in the blood, insects take air directly to every part of their body by tiny blind tubes called tracheae which open to the surface at many different points. Now, although by their breathing movements they can renew the air in the outer part of the tracheal system, the oxygen has to penetrate the finer branches by means of diffusion. Gases can diffuse easily through very small distances, not many times larger than the average length traveled by a gas molecule between

collisions with other molecules. But when such vast journeys—from the point of view of a molecule—as a quarter of an inch have to be made, the process becomes slow. So the portions of an insect's body more than a quarter of an inch from the air would always be short of oxygen. In consequence hardly any insects are much more than half an inch thick. Land crabs are built on the same general plan as insects, but are much clumsier. Yet like ourselves they carry oxygen around in their blood, and are therefore able to grow far larger than any insects. If the insects had hit on a plan for driving air through their tissues instead of letting it soak in, they might well have become as large as lobsters, though other considerations would have prevented them from becoming as large as man.

9.   Exactly the same difficulties attach to flying. It is an elementary principle of aeronautics that the minimum speed needed to keep an aeroplane of a given shape in the air varies as the square root of its length. If its linear dimensions are increased four times, it must fly twice as fast. Now the power needed for the minimum speed increases more rapidly than the weight of the machine. So the larger aeroplane which weighs sixty-four times as much as the smaller needs one hundred and twenty-eight times its horsepower to keep up. Applying the same principles to the birds, we find that the limit to their size is soon reached. An angel whose muscles developed no more power weight for weight than those of an eagle or a pigeon would require a breast projecting for about four feet to house the muscles engaged in working its wings, while to economize in weight, its legs would have to be reduced to mere stilts. Actually a large bird such as an eagle or kite does not keep in the air mainly by moving its wings. It is generally to be seen soaring, that is to say balanced on a rising column of air. And even soaring becomes more and more difficult with increasing size. Were this not the case eagles might be as large as tigers and as formidable to man as hostile aeroplanes.

10.   But it is time that we passed to some of the advantages of size. One of the most obvious is that it enables one to keep warm. All warm-blooded animals at rest lose the same amount of heat from a unit area of skin, for which purpose they need a food-supply proportional to their surface and not to their weight. Five thousand mice weigh as much as a man. Their combined surface and food or oxygen consumption are about seventeen times a man's. In fact a mouse eats about one quarter its own weight of food every day, which is mainly used in keeping warm. For the same reason small animals cannot live in cold countries. In the arctic regions there are no reptiles or amphibians, and no small mammals. The smallest mammal in Spitzbergen is

the fox. The small birds fly away in the winter, while the insects die, though their eggs can survive six months or more of frost. The most successful mammals are bears, seals, and walruses.

11.   Similarly, the eye is a rather inefficient organ until it reaches a large size. The back of the human eye on which an image of the outside world is thrown, and which corresponds to the film of a camera, is composed of a mosaic of "rods and cones" whose diameter is little more than a length of an average light wave. Each eye has about half a million, and for two objects to be distinguishable their images must fall on separate rods or cones. It is obvious that with fewer but larger rods and cones we should see less distinctly. If they were twice as broad two points would have to be twice as far apart before we could distinguish them at a given distance. But if their size were diminished and their number increased we should see no better. For it is impossible to form a definite image smaller than a wave length of light. Hence a mouse's eye is not a small-scale model of a human eye. Its rods and cones are not much smaller than ours, and therefore there are far fewer of them. A mouse could not distinguish one human face from another six feet away. In order that they should be of any use at all the eyes of small animals have to be much larger in proportion to their bodies than our own. Large animals on the other hand only require relatively small eyes, and those of the whale and elephant are little larger than our own.

12.   For rather more recondite reasons the same general principle holds true of the brain. If we compare the brain weights of a set of very similar animals such as the cat, cheetah, leopard, and tiger, we find that as we quadruple the body weight, the brain weight is only doubled. The larger animal with proportionately larger bones can economize on brain, eyes, and certain other organs.

13.   Such are a very few of the considerations which show that for every type of animal there is an optimum size. Yet although Galileo demonstrated the contrary more than three hundred years ago, people still believe that if a flea were as large as a man it could jump a thousand feet into the air. As a matter of fact the height to which an animal can jump is more nearly independent of its size than proportional to it. A flea can jump about two feet, a man about five. To jump a given height, if we neglect the resistance of the air, requires an expenditure of energy proportional to the jumper's weight. But if the jumping muscles form a constant fraction of the animal's body, the energy developed per ounce of muscle is independent of the size, provided it can be developed quickly enough in the small animal. As

a matter of fact an insect's muscles, although they can contract more quickly than our own, appear to be less efficient; as otherwise a flea or grasshopper could rise six feet into the air.

14. And just as there is a best size for every animal, so the same is true for every human institution. In the Greek type of democracy all the citizens could listen to a series of orators and vote directly on questions of legislation. Hence their philosophers held that a small city was the largest possible democratic state. The English invention of representative government made a democratic nation possible, and the possibility was first realized in the United States, and later elsewhere. With the development of broadcasting it has once more become possible for every citizen to listen to the political views of representative orators, and the future may perhaps see the return of the national state to the Greek form of democracy. Even the referendum has been made possible only by the institution of daily newspapers.

15. To the biologist the problem of socialism appears largely as a problem of size. The extreme socialists desire to run every nation as a single business concern. I do not suppose that Henry Ford would find much difficulty in running Andorra or Luxembourg on a socialistic basis. He has already more men on his payroll than their population. It is conceivable that a syndicate of Fords, if we could find them, would make Belgium Ltd. or Denmark Inc. pay their way. But while nationalization of certain industries is an obvious possibility in the largest of states, I find it no easier to picture a completely socialized British Empire or United States than an elephant turning somersaults or a hippopotamus jumping a hedge.

WORDS

*meaning* Define *formidable* and *proboscis* (par. 5) and *recondite* (par. 12).

*level of usage* This essay is an excellent example of the "plain style"— a style that avoids literary diction, slang or colloquialisms, and unnecessary technical terms or jargon, and that defines unusual words whenever they are used. Find examples of informal definition in paragraphs 5, 8, and 9.

SENTENCES

*parallelism* 1. How are three short parallel statements used in a single sentence (par. 4) to illustrate and dramatize a general statement? 2. How do parallelism and repetition in two general statements help to point an antithesis in paragraph 7?

*rhetorical devices*   Does the use of the hypothetical examples of the giants (par. 2) and the angel (par. 9) contribute more to Haldane's clarity and vividness than would literal examples? Why or why not?

## PARAGRAPHS

*coherence*   1. This selection contains many excellent examples of the use of transitional expressions to establish connections between paragraphs. What are these words or phrases in the first sentences of paragraphs 5, 6, 7, 11, and 13?   2. How is the repetition of words or ideas (backward reference) used in the first sentences of paragraphs 8, 9, 12, and 14?

*methods of development*   1. Find a paragraph developed by comparison. 2. Find a paragraph developed with particulars and details.

## CONTENT AND ORGANIZATION

*central idea*   The central idea of this essay is stated near the beginning in a single sentence. Which sentence?

*organization*   1. As the first sentence of paragraph 10 shows, most of this essay is the development of two related but separate ideas. What are these ideas?   2. Do paragraphs 14 and 15 make an effective conclusion for this essay? Have you seen other physical or natural scientists make applications of principles established in their own special fields of research to social or political theory?

*assumptions and implications*   Haldane, who is a physiologist, says that zoologists have paid little attention to differences of size (par. 1). Why should physiologists be more concerned with such differences?

## SUGGESTIONS FOR DISCUSSION

1. Can you write a similar essay on the size of buildings? What limits the height, for instance, of a Greek temple? of a Gothic cathedral? of a skyscraper?   2. How does an increase in size affect human institutions: small colleges that become large universities, small businesses that become large corporations, small towns that become large cities? Are they forced to change or modify their structure or organization?   3. In what ways has man learned to transcend some of the limitations imposed upon him by the structure of his body?   4. How does Haldane's discussion of flight (par. 9) help to explain the failure of all flying machines invented before 1900?

# Persuading Other People

*The writer who would persuade, who would change opinion or move to action, must be peculiarly aware of his audience—of its beliefs, its prejudices, and its ways of thinking. For that reason the essays that follow may profitably be analyzed for the ways in which the writers have approached their intended audiences. The first is an urbane argument, written for a general-circulation magazine, carefully establishing a moderate position in a sometimes heated controversy. The second is a satirical criticism of modern men and women, an extreme position made entertaining by the development of an extended metaphor. The third is a polemic originally given as a speech before a sympathetic and engaged audience. Another is a public defense of professional actions and decisions that have been publicly challenged; and the last is a sympathetic but critical personal letter written by an editor to an author. The presentation, and even the content, of each essay is influenced by the writer's awareness of his audience.*

## Diana Trilling

## FEMALE BIOLOGY IN A MALE CULTURE

1.  As a subject of conversation, women's liberation is certainly unequaled for putting everyone, women as well as men, in the happy state of mind that results from establishing one's superiority to whatever is benighted and ridiculous in human activity. In fact, I can think of only one other topic that matches it as a provoker of ignorant mirth among the presumably well-educated, and that is psychoanalysis—not psychiatry, which people have always recognized as a serious subject, but Freudian analysis.

2.  The parallel should not surprise us. In both situations the derisive response represents embarrassment at being caught in a decep-

FEMALE BIOLOGY IN A MALE CULTURE: From *Saturday Review*, October 10, 1970. Copyright 1970 Saturday Review, Inc.

tion, and a defense against being confronted with an unwanted truth. The amusement with which, even at this late date, the mention of psychoanalysis can be met is confirmation that we do indeed have a life of the unconscious that we are fearful of bringing to consciousness. And, just so, the ready mockery of women's liberation is confirmation that women are indeed regarded in our society as of a second order of being, and that we are afraid of having the falseness of this assumption revealed to us. By us, of course, I mean women no less than men.

3.  It is both appropriate and ironic that in undertaking to speak of the present movement for women's rights I bring it into such immediate conjunction with Freudian thought. The appropriateness lies in the fact that for many years my own view of the relation of the sexes was rather substantially shaped by Freud's perception of the differing biological natures of the sexes and of the consequent differences in their psychological lives and their social roles. Recently, this influence has been modified: I tend now to give more weight than I once did to the cultural, as opposed to the biological, determinism in sexual attitudes. For example, I am not as convinced as I might once have been that a woman's willingness to cede power to men necessarily represents a wholesome acceptance of her female role; now I might see it as a not very laudable cultural conformity or even an expediency or laziness. The irony of bringing Freud into immediaate connection with the subject of women's liberation lies in Freud's having had such an invidious view of the female sex. I am afraid that the man who sought to liberate the psyche from the hindrances imposed upon it in our human infancy was interested not at all in liberating women from the special handicaps imposed upon them in our society. Nowhere in his writings does Freud express sympathy for the problems that pertain to the female sex alone. On the contrary, his misogyny is now taken for granted even by his most admiring students.

4.  Freud's condescension toward women is rooted in his castration theory, which plays a vital part in his whole theory of neurosis. According to Freud, it is the male sexual organ that constitutes what might be called the natural, or ideal, endowment from which stems the genital envy particular to women and the anxiety shared by both sexes. And no doubt it is as an extension of this view of woman's basic biological inferiority that Freud makes his forthright statement in *Civilization and Its Discontents* that it is men who are the makers and carriers of culture. He adjures women not to interfere with man's life in culture.

5.  The adjuration could scarcely be more irritating, especially when we contemplate some of the activities that men regard as a

proper life in culture, like inventing hydrogen bombs or claiming the moon for their own country. Such being man's impulses in culture, one might have hoped that Freud would have encouraged women to tell their husbands to stay home and be sensible. On the other hand, there is nothing either in Freud's formulation of the castration fear or in his general statement of the different relation of men and women to culture that I would be prepared to fault or that people far more competent than I have succeeded in refuting. It would be pleasant, for instance, to accept the idea proposed by Dr. Karen Horney, the mother of Freudian revisionism, and so widely propagated by Margaret Mead, that womb-envy, man's envy of woman because she can have babies and he cannot, plays as much a part in the life of men as penis-envy plays in the life of women. Such an appealing reassignment of biological advantage is supported, however, neither by men's dreams nor their free associations during psychoanalytical treatment.

6.    As to the relative roles of men and women in culture, it would seem to be indisputable, at least historically, that for better or worse men have forged the ideas and provided the chief energies by which cultures develop, while women have devoted themselves to the conservation of what they have found valuable in the efforts of men. We may protest that there is no work in culture that is as valuable as woman's child-bearing and child-nurturing activities; that the ability to create and conserve the human race overshadows any other conceivable accomplishment in culture. But this, of course, begs the question of why women have not made even a small fraction of the intellectual, scientific, or artistic contributions to culture that men have made.

7.    Finally, we may protest that women's small contribution to culture is not an indication of their capacities but simply reflects the way that men have contrived things to be—that is, we can blame women's small place in culture *on* culture—except that this leaves unanswered the question of why it is that over the long years women have been willing that culture should follow the male dictate. It also leaves unanswered the even more fundamental question of why it is that in every society that has ever been studied—so Margaret Mead tells us—whatever it is that is the occupation of men has the greater prestige: If the men do the hunting and fighting, hunting and fighting are the status-giving occupations of that society; if the men do the weaving and baby-tending, then weaving and baby-tending are the superior activities. We may think of this value system as something that men impose upon women. But then we are forced to explain why it is that even where the women bear arms they have not imposed a different system of values.

8. The reference back to biology would seem to be unavoidable, and we are returned to Freud's use of the words "passivity" and "activity"—female passivity, male activity. The words themselves almost inevitably imply a judgment, especially in a culture like ours where passivity connotes unattractive attributes: inertness, laxness, the uncritical acceptance of whatever happens to be given. Even as a concept in the purely sexual relation of men and women it suggests that man is the seeker and that woman yields to man's importunities, a description of the sexual roles that is not particularly congruent with our modern sense of the sexual realities. But actually this distinction between the active and the passive sexual roles is an irrefutable fact in nature: The most active seduction or participation on the part of a woman cannot relieve the male partner of his primary physical responsibility in their sexual union. To put the matter at its crudest, the male has the biological capacity to rape; the female has not. We may, if we wish, accuse Freud of drawing too many, or mistaken, emotional and social inferences from this fundamental biological difference between the sexes, but to try to ignore the difference, as some of the women's liberation groups do, is to narrow rather than widen the prospects opened up to us in refusing the tyrannies of biology.

9. It is reported that Freud would be rather bitterly amused when accused of being dirty-minded because he wrote about infant sexuality; he would point out that it was not he who had created the condition, he had merely recognized it. And obviously he didn't create the different sexual endowments of men and women nor even the emotional consequences of the difference; he only recognized them, and attached these words "active" and "passive" to the differing sexual roles. After centuries of female subjugation, however, it was perhaps expectable that the essential lack of sympathy for women in orthodox psychoanalysis, and in particular its emphasis on women's envy of men with its implication of hostility, would be one of the aspects of Freud's thought that would be most readily received by our society. I think there is small doubt that Freudian doctrine, often scarcely understood or even misunderstood, has enormously powered the development in recent decades of what amounts to virtually an anti-female movement in American culture.

10. The informing sentiment of this movement is that women are out to destroy men: Women are the natural destroyers of the male species, at least in America. As statistics have been gathering on the appalling numbers of men who die from heart disease in this country, increasingly, the blame has been put on the American wife for the killing demands she makes upon her husband for houses, cars, wash-

ing machines, and clothes. She has been pictured as the ruthless exploiter of her male partner, a sort of prototypical domestic statement of the national imperialism. And as Freud's views on the childhood source of mental disorder have percolated into the culture, there has been mounted a growing campaign of mother-suspicion and mother-discreditation. From Sidney Howard's play *The Silver Cord,* in the mid-Twenties, to Philip Roth's still current *Portnoy's Complaint,* our literature has lent its traditional dignity to the idea that American women alternate a diet of husbands with a diet of sons.

11.  Nor is it solely on the ground of her inordinate appetites that the American mother is chivvied and mocked: If she cannot be blamed for devouring her young, she is blamed for rejecting them. For some fifty years now, it has been impossible for a woman, especially a mother, to be anything but wrong in our culture; and the more supposedly enlightened her community, the more varied and virulent the attacks, to the point where one often has the impression that the prestige of our best and most progressive private schools is built on the humiliations of young mothers. Moreover, this pernicious assault on women's minds and spirits comes not alone from men. Perhaps even more of the time, it comes from other women.

12.  Any adequate statement of woman's inhumanity to woman might perhaps suggest that what eventually is wrong with women is that there are other women in the world, and that women are to be condemned out of hand for their betrayals, overt and covert, of their own sex. But such harsh judgments of women minimize the range and subtlety of the difficulties by which they are beset. It may not be very edifying to contemplate the spectacle of women acceding in whatever is the form that the disparagement of their own sex may be at the moment be taking just so that men will be reassured that they deserve the status conferred upon them by their superior biological endowment, but if it is on a man's sexual confidence that a woman's sexual and maternal satisfactions depend, and if, too, the male in our society is willing to pay for his biological advantage by assuming the financial support of his wife and family, it is more than understandable, it is plainest reason, that a woman should place the male interest, whether real or only fancied, above that of other women.

13.  In particular it is understandable that women should come to feel that they are not defeated but fulfilled in accepting the passivity that is implied by acknowledging man's primary sexual-social role. For living by one's deference to the needs of those one loves is one of the pleasanter modes of existence—as well as, I might add, one of the most taxing. It is a grave fault of modern culture that it

trains us in the belief that whatever defers to others is an *in*action and therefore of only secondary social value.

14. And yet, even while we record the appeal on behalf of passivity, the question presses upon us whether our female-ists, who stress their satisfaction in devoting their lives to being good wives and mothers, would settle for this domestication of their capacities if they lived in a society where different requirements were made of women than are made in our culture. We are told that the women in the Israeli kibbutzim who serve side by side with their men in the army and in the fields and who give up the larger part of the rearing of their children to communal nurseries show no sign of being unfulfilled as women. Nor, apparently, are their men castrated by this sexual equality. It would also seem clear from Solzhenitsyn's remarkable novel *Cancer Ward* that, although a woman surgeon in the Soviet Union may return from a grueling day in the cancer hospital and, like working wives everywhere in our servantless world, still accept it as her job to do the marketing, cooking, cleaning, and laundry, it is not in her home and family but in her "real" work, her man's work if you will, that she invests her pride of being, including her peculiarly feminine pride of being. It is undoubtedly one of the significant revelations of this book that in a situation where the women carry equal responsibilities with men it is still the men who fill the top hospital posts; but no less fascinating is its revelation of the many wholly unself-conscious ways in which the women physicians manage to irradiate their grim hospital routines with a sexually distinguishing gentleness and delicacy. From evidences like these I think we must conclude that women are considerably more flexible in the matter of how they can derive their fulfillment than most American women are yet prepared to recognize, and that it is perhaps only because our culture prefers that its women find their best satisfaction in the activities of home and family that the women themselves obediently discover it there.

15. In other words, we are all of us, men and women both, the creatures of culture: We do and feel what our societies want us to do and feel, and the demands that they put upon us are not always either very consistent or very precisely correlated with biology. In wartime, for instance, when men are away and women not only take jobs in factories and on farms but make all the financial and practical decisions usually made by the male head of the family, no one thinks of accusing them of conduct unbecoming a woman. Or if a woman is forced through widowhood to earn her own living, no one is moved to put a brake on her competitiveness with men; she is thought a

castrating woman only if she now switches the dependence she once had on her husband to her grown children.

16.  And in a similar reversal of values, I can imagine a moment —and perhaps a not very distant moment—when the conserving instinct of women will become the most active force (and I emphasize the word "active") in the continuing life of society. I have in mind the active role that women may soon be called upon to play in rescuing the modern world from pollution; and when I say called upon, I mean called upon not by men but by themselves, by their own intelligence and appreciation of the extent of the emergency. Since so far it seems to be impossible for men to mobilize the energies they use for the conquest of other planets for the preservation of life on Earth, women may well have to take over the job. This is one kind of activity in culture, one form of competitiveness beyond the limits of home and family, in which the female sex would surely excel: the competition to perpetuate life. It is a program to which women's liberation could, and should, rally all women.

17.  But when I say that women are the creatures of culture, while I obviously mean the prevailing culture, I do not necessarily mean only the dominant culture of the society. It may well be that among those who most dramatically dissent from our dominant culture, and in particular among the young, there are being forged attitudes that will importantly alter the relation of the sexes in the dominant culture of the future.

18.  I suppose it is natural enough that in the matter of renovating the relations of men and women it is on the score of women's professional and legal rights that the voice of contemporary protest is making itself most readily heard. This is perhaps the area in which men are finally the least challenged; it is, of course, the area that is sanctioned by the historical efforts on behalf of sexual equality. It is nevertheless possible, I think, that the cause of women's professional rights—the demand that women receive equal pay for equal work and similar advancement for similar merit—may be becoming our newest middle-class liberal ritualism, to be embraced as a way of avoiding the need to look more closely at less crude but more troubling manifestations of the lack of parity between the sexes. I myself happen to think, for instance, that, although it will indeed be a great day for women when they are appointed to full professorships at our leading universities on the same basis as men, it will be an even greater day for women when right in their own living rooms they are given as much serious attention and credence as men now receive when they pass judgment, especially adverse judgment, on an idea or a person.

19.   It is not, however, the overt agitations on behalf of women that I actually have in mind when I speculate upon the possible effect our present-day dissent may eventually have upon the dominant culture. I am not closely enough acquainted with the dissident young to know exactly what decorousnesses, rules, and formalities pertain to their sexual relations, or what constitute their criteria of sexual worth and loyalty. What is nevertheless apparent even at my distance is the pervasive devaluation of those appurtenances of masculinity and femininity that our culture—by which I chiefly mean our competitive economy—sanctified for an earlier generation. I was myself of a generation in which any deviation from the specifications for female charm, as set down by Madison Avenue and the movies, was thought seriously to reduce a girl's sexual bargaining power. While intellectually we knew that the models by which we presumably were judged and by which we judged ourselves were the exceptions in any race of mortals, we suffered the private anguishes of living under the sexual dictates not of nature but of commerce. One recalls the father in Dostoevsky's *The Brothers Karamazov* who said there was no such thing as an ugly woman: The possibility that an opinion like this would one day infiltrate large sections of our society was beyond our wildest dreams, strained as we were by the demands for an ideal femininity put upon us by advertising and by Hollywood. This strain would happily seem to be gone, having disappeared in the radical effort to disavow the dominant capitalist culture. And as a woman, even though not a revolutionary, I can hope it is gone forever.

20.   And gone—or going—with it, through the same effort, is the social-sexual differentiation between men and women in terms of dress and hair style. While I confess to having no love for the shared slovenliness of so many young men and women, since I see in it a depreciation of their pride in themselves as persons, I welcome the unisexual appearance of the sexes if only for its criticism of a culture in which sexually differentiated styles of hair and dress, designed not by God but by man, were treated as if they were biological actualities. As I see it, or at least as I hope it, whatever reduces the false separations between men and women is bound to reduce their suspicions and hostilities, and thus permit them a fuller expression of their human potentiality. Free of the cultural detritus of our sexual differences, perhaps we can come to a sounder and happier knowledge of our distinctive maleness and femaleness than is now permitted us.

WORDS

*meaning* Define *benighted* (par. 1), *invidious* (par. 3), *adjuration* (par. 5), *prototypical* (par. 10), *credence* (par. 18), *appurtenances* (par. 19), and *detritus* (par. 20).

*relationships* 1. How is *misogyny* (par. 3) related to words like *gynecology, gynecocracy, misanthropy,* and *misogamy?* 2. How does *femaleist* (par. 14)—an unusual coinage—differ in meaning from the more usual *feminist?* 3. Compare the meaning of *adverse* (par. 18) with that of related words like *reverse, averse,* and *converse.*

PARAGRAPHS

*coherence* 1. What transitional words or phrases are used to link paragraphs 3, 6, 7, and 10 to the paragraphs that precede them? 2. How is repetition used to link paragraphs 5, 10, and 20 with the paragraphs that precede them? 3. What kind of transitional device introduces paragraphs 11, 14, 17, and 20?

*methods of development* How are the developments of paragraphs 10 and 14 similar?

CONTENT AND ORGANIZATION

*central ideas* 1. How are common attitudes toward Freudian analysis and women's liberation similar (pars. 1–2)? 2. What essential difference between the sexes is stressed in paragraph 8 and again referred to in paragraph 12? 3. What does the author consider to be "the cultural detritus of our sexual differences" (par. 20)?

*meaning and implication* 1. Do women themselves really believe that they are "of a second order" (par. 2)? If so, is this attitude culturally induced? If not, why might the author's avowed Freudian orientation lead her to a false assumption? 2. What is the significance of the qualification—"at least historically"—in paragraph 6? Is there any anthropological evidence for women's ascendency in prehistoric societies? 3. Why should a working Soviet woman surgeon "still accept it as her job to do the marketing, cooking, cleaning, and laundry" (par. 14)?

SUGGESTIONS FOR DISCUSSION

1. To what extent are common criticisms of women—that they are emotional, changeable, and illogical—comparable to stereotypes about Negroes or members of other cultural minorities in America? Explain. 2. Why should not women command passenger ships, commercial airliners, or even armies? 3. Are recent changes in hair styles and dress any indication of changing relations between the sexes in America? 4. What

similarities, if any, are there between women's suffrage movements at the beginning of this century and the contemporary women's liberation movement? 5. What is the attitude toward women expressed by one of the following authors: D. H. Lawrence, Henry Miller, Philip Roth, Norman Mailer?

## *D. H. Lawrence*

# COCKSURE WOMEN AND HENSURE MEN

1. It seems to me there are two aspects to women. There is the demure and the dauntless. Men have loved to dwell, in fiction at least, on the demure maiden whose inevitable reply is: Oh, yes, if you please, kind sir! The demure maiden, the demure spouse, the demure mother—this is still the ideal. A few maidens, mistresses and mothers *are* demure. A few pretend to be. But the vast majority are not. And they don't pretend to be. We don't expect a girl skilfully driving her car to be demure, we expect her to be dauntless. What good would demure and maidenly Members of Parliament be, inevitably responding: Oh, yes, if you please, kind sir!—Though of course there are masculine members of that kidney.—And a demure telephone girl? Or even a demure stenographer? Demureness, to be sure, is outwardly becoming, it is an outward mark of femininity, like bobbed hair. But it goes with inward dauntlessness. The girl who has got to make her way in life has got to be dauntless, and if she has a pretty, demure manner with it, then lucky girl. She kills two birds with two stones.

2. With the two kinds of femininity go two kinds of confidence: there are the women who are cocksure, and the women who are hensure. A really up-to-date woman is a cocksure woman. She doesn't have a doubt nor a qualm. She is the modern type. Whereas the old-fashioned demure woman was sure as a hen is sure, that is, without knowing anything about it. She went quietly and busily clucking around, laying the eggs and mothering the chickens in a kind of anxious dream that still was full of sureness. But not mental sureness.

COCKSURE WOMEN AND HENSURE MEN: From *Phoenix,* Vol. II, edited by Warren Roberts and Harry T. Moore. Copyright 1928 by Forum Publishing Company, © renewed 1956 by Frieda Lawrence Ravagli. Reprinted by permission of The Viking Press, Inc.

Her sureness was a physical condition, very soothing, but a condition out of which she could easily be startled or frightened.

3. It is quite amusing to see the two kinds of sureness in chickens. The cockerel is, naturally, cocksure. He crows because he is *certain* it is day. Then the hen peeps out from under her wing. He marches to the door of the hen-house and pokes out his head assertively: *Ah ha! daylight, of course, just as I said!*—and he majestically steps down the chicken ladder towards *terra firma,* knowing that the hens will step cautiously after him, drawn by his confidence. So after him, cautiously, step the hens. He crows again: *Ha-ha! here we are!* —It is indisputable, and the hens accept it entirely. He marches towards the house. From the house a person ought to appear, scattering corn. Why does the person not appear? The cock will see to it. He is cocksure. He gives a loud crow in the doorway, and the person appears. The hens are suitably impressed, but immediately devote all their henny consciousness to the scattered corn, pecking absorbedly, while the cock runs and fusses, cocksure that he is responsible for it all.

4. So the day goes on. The cock finds a tit-bit, and loudly calls the hens. They scuffle up in henny surety, and gobble the tit-bit. But when they find a juicy morsel for themselves, they devour it in silence, hensure. Unless, of course, there are little chicks, when they most anxiously call the brood. But in her own dim surety, the hen is really much surer than the cock, in a different way. She marches off to lay her egg, she secures obstinately the nest she wants, she lays her egg at last, then steps forth again with prancing confidence, and gives that most assured of all sounds, the hensure cackle of a bird who has laid her egg. The cock, who is never so sure about anything as the hen is about the egg she has laid, immediately starts to cackle like the female of his species. He is pining to be hensure, for hensure is so much surer than cocksure.

5. Nevertheless, cocksure is boss. When the chicken-hawk appears in the sky, loud are the cockerel's calls of alarm. Then the hens scuffle under the verandah, the cock ruffles his feathers on guard. The hens are numb with fear, they say: Alas, there is no health in us! How wonderful to be a cock so bold!—And they huddle, numbed. But their very numbness is hensurety.

6. Just as the cock can cackle, however, as if he had laid the egg, so can the hen bird crow. She can more or less assume his cocksureness. And yet she is never so easy, cocksure, as she used to be when she was hensure. Cocksure, she is cocksure, but uneasy. Hensure, she trembles, but is easy.

7.   It seems to me just the same in the vast human farmyard. Only nowadays all the cocks are cackling and pretending to lay eggs, and all the hens are crowing and pretending to call the sun out of bed. If women to-day are cocksure, men are hensure. Men are timid, tremulous, rather soft and submissive, easy in their very henlike tremulousness. They only want to be spoken to gently. So the women step forth with a good loud *cock-a-doodle-do!*

8.   The tragedy about cocksure women is that they are more cocky, in their assurance, than the cock himself. They never realise that when the cock gives his loud crow in the morning, he listens acutely afterwards, to hear if some other wretch of a cock dare crow defiance, challenge. To the cock, there is always defiance, challenge, danger and death on the clear air; or the possibility thereof.

9.   But alas, when the hen crows, she listens for no defiance or challenge. When she says *cock-a-doodle-do!* then it is unanswerable. The cock listens for an answer, alert. But the hen knows she is un-answerable. *Cock-a-doodle-do!* and there it is, take it or leave it!

10.   And it is this that makes the cocksureness of women so dangerous, so devastating. It is really out of scheme, it is not in rela-tion to the rest of things. So we have the tragedy of cocksure women. They find, so often, that instead of having laid an egg, they have laid a vote, or an empty ink-bottle, or some other absolutely unhatchable object, which means nothing to them.

11.   It is the tragedy of the modern woman. She becomes cock-sure, she puts all her passion and energy and years of her life into some effort or assertion, without ever listening for the denial which she ought to take into count. She is cocksure, but she is a hen all the time. Frightened of her own henny self, she rushes to mad lengths about votes, or welfare, or sports, or business: she is marvellous, out-manning the man. But alas, it is all fundamentally disconnected. It is all an attitude, and one day the attitude will become a weird cramp, a pain, and then it will collapse. And when it has collapsed, and she looks at the eggs she has laid, votes, or miles of typewriting, years of business efficiency—suddenly, because she is a hen and not a cock, all she has done will turn into pure nothingness to her. Suddenly it all falls out of relation to her basic henny self, and she realises she has lost her life. The lovely henny surety, the hensureness which is the real bliss of every female, has been denied her: she had never had it. Having lived her life with such utmost strenuousness and cock-sureness, she has missed her life altogether. Nothingness!

WORDS

*meaning*  Define *dauntless* (par. 1), *tremulous* (par. 7), and *devastating* (par. 10).

*relationships*  What connection does *confidence* (par. 2) have with *confide, confidant,* and *fiduciary?*

*word origin*  The word *cocksure* originally seems to have had only a denotative meaning, as in Shakespeare's use in *Henry IV,* Pt. One, II, i, 95: "We steale as in a Castle, cocksure." Here the word means "absolutely secure." Later associations with the rooster have given it the modern connotation that we have in Lawrence's use. What are the connotations of the word for you? Are there connotations of absurdity? Why? Are there such connotations in Lawrence's use of the word? Where?

*word choice*  Lawrence has made up some words that are not in the normal usage or even in the dictionary. Name them. Can you justify the inventions in terms of his general method and intention?

*level of usage*  Which of the following are colloquial and which standard English: *qualm* (par. 2), *cockerel* (par. 3), *gobble* (par. 4), *boss* and *verandah* (par. 5), and *cocky* (par. 8)?

SENTENCES

*style*  1. What is Lawrence's point in altering a familiar quotation in the final sentence of paragraph 1? 2. Through what devices of structure does Lawrence achieve the mildly jeering, satirical tone of paragraph 3? 3. Analyze paragraph 6 for repetition. What is the effect?

*variety*  In paragraph 1 find examples of declarative, exclamatory, and interrogative sentence structures.

PARAGRAPHS

*coherence*  This essay is extremely casual in its development, advancing through an association of ideas and images more than through clearly logical connections. Nevertheless, Lawrence links his paragraphs with transitions of one kind or another. Analyze each paragraph for its transitional device.

*methods of development*  Paragraph 3 advances chronologically. Does the series of little actions change anything or does the paragraph end where it began? What is the function of these little actions in the paragraph?

CONTENT AND ORGANIZATION

*central idea*  The mention of "masculine members" appears almost parenthetically in paragraph 1. What is the tone of this first remark? How does it suggest the view of men that the whole essay will take?

*organization* This whole little essay is an extended metaphor. What are the terms of the comparison? Where in paragraph 7 are they made explicit? Do they fail the author at any point (for example, do hens crow, as is asserted in paragraph 6)?

*assumptions and implications* 1. What is Lawrence's assumption about the natural roles of men and women? 2. Lawrence's essay assumes that today men and women have reversed their natural roles. Does he give any illustrations of this assumption in the case of women? in that of men?

SUGGESTIONS FOR DISCUSSION

1. Write a character sketch of a career woman you know. 2. Can you think of any profession today in which women do not take part? Can you think of any roles traditionally associated with women that are now shared by men? 3. It is commonly argued that our society is being transformed into a matriarchy. How does Lawrence's essay support this view? 4. What would Lawrence have to say about the phenomenon called Momism? How does it relate, if it does, to this essay?


*George Wald*

# A GENERATION IN SEARCH
# OF A FUTURE

1.    All of you know that in the last couple of years there has been student unrest breaking at times into violence in many parts of the world: in England, Germany, Italy, Spain, Mexico, and, needless to say, in many parts of this country. There has been a great deal of discussion as to what it all means. Perfectly clearly it means something different in Mexico from what it does in France, and something different in France from what it does in Tokyo, and something different in Tokyo from what it does in this country. Yet unless we are to assume that students have gone crazy all over the world, or that they have just decided that it's the thing to do, there must be some common meaning.

2.    I don't need to go so far afield to look for that meaning. I am a teacher, and at Harvard I have a class of about 350 students— men and women—most of them freshmen and sophomores. Over these past few years I have felt increasingly that something is terribly

A GENERATION IN SEARCH OF A FUTURE:   Reprinted by permission of the author.

wrong—and this year [1969] ever so much more than last. Something has gone sour, in teaching and in learning. It's almost as though there were a widespread feeling that education has become irrelevant.

3.  A lecture is much more of a dialogue than many of you probably appreciate. As you lecture, you keep watching the faces; and information keeps coming back to you all the time. I began to feel, particularly this year, that I was missing much of what was coming back. I tried asking the students, but they didn't or couldn't help me very much.

4.  But I think I know what's the matter, even a little better than they do. I think that this whole generation of students is beset with a profound uneasiness. I don't think that they have yet quite defined its source; I think I understand the reasons for their uneasiness even better than they do. What is more, I share their uneasiness.

5.  What's bothering those students? Some of them tell you it's the Vietnam War. I think the Vietnam War is the most shameful episode in the whole of American history. The concept of war crimes is an American invention. We've committed many war crimes in Vietnam; but I'll tell you something interesting about that. We were committing war crimes in World War II, even before the Nuremberg trials were held and the principle of war crimes started. The saturation bombing of German cities was a war crime. Dropping atom bombs on Hiroshima and Nagasaki was a war crime. If we had lost the war, some of our leaders might have had to answer for those actions.

6.  I've gone through all of that history lately, and I find that there's a gimmick in it. It isn't written out, but I think we established it by precedent. That gimmick is that if one can allege that one is repelling or retaliating for an aggression—after that everything goes. And you see we are living in a world in which all wars are wars of defense. All War Departments are now Defense Departments. This is all part of the double talk of our time. The aggressor is always on the other side. And I suppose this is why our ex-Secretary of State, Dean Rusk—a man in whom repetition takes the place of reason and stubbornness takes the place of character—went to such pains to insist, as he still insists, that in Vietnam we are repelling an aggression. And if that's what we are doing—so runs the doctrine—anything goes. If the concept of war crimes is ever to mean anything, they will have to be defined as categories of acts, regardless of alleged provocation. But that isn't so now.

7.  I think we've lost that war, as a lot of other people think, too. The Vietnamese have a secret weapon. It's their willingness to die, beyond our willingness to kill. In effect they've been saying, you can

kill us, but you'll have to kill a lot of us, you may have to kill all of us. And thank heavens, we are not yet ready to do that.

8. Yet we have come a long way—far enough to sicken many Americans, far enough even to sicken our fighting men. Far enough so that our national symbols have gone sour. How many of you can sing about "the rockets' red glare, bombs bursting in air" without thinking, those are *our* bombs and *our* rockets bursting over South Vietnamese villages? When those words were written, we were a people struggling for freedom against oppression. Now we are supporting real or thinly disguised military dictatorships all over the world, helping them to control and repress peoples struggling for their freedom.

9. But that Vietnam War, shameful and terrible as it is, seems to me only an immediate incident in a much larger and more stubborn situation.

10. Part of my trouble with students is that almost all the students I teach were born since World War II. Just after World War II, a series of new and abnormal procedures came into American life. We regarded them at the time as temporary aberrations. We thought we would get back to normal American life some day. But those procedures have stayed with us now for more than twenty years, and those students of mine have never known anything else. They think those things are normal. They think we've always had a Pentagon, that we have always had a big army, and that we always had a draft. But those are all new things in American life; and I think that they are incompatible with what America meant before.

11. How many of you realize that just before World War II the entire American army including the Air Force numbered 139,000 men? Then World War II started, but we weren't yet in it; and seeing that there was great trouble in the world, we doubled this army to 268,000 men. Then in World War II it got to be eight million. And then World War II came to an end, and we prepared to go back to a peacetime army somewhat as the American army had always been before. And indeed in 1950—you think about 1950, our international commitments, the Cold War, the Truman Doctrine, and all the rest of it—in 1950 we got down to 600,000 men.

12. Now we have 3.5 million men under arms: about 600,000 in Vietnam, about 300,000 more in "support areas" elsewhere in the Pacific, about 250,000 in Germany. And there are a lot at home. Some months ago we were told that 300,000 National Guardsmen and 200,000 reservists—half a million men—had been specially trained for riot duty in the cities.

13. I say the Vietnam War is just an immediate incident, be-

cause so long as we keep that big an army, it will always find things to do. If the Vietnam War stopped tomorrow, with that big a military establishment, the chances are that we would be in another such adventure abroad or at home before you knew it.

14. As for the draft: Don't reform the draft—get rid of it.

15. A peacetime draft is the most un-American thing I know. All the time I was growing up I was told about oppressive Central European countries and Russia, where young men were forced into the army; and I was told what they did about it. They chopped off a finger, or shot off a couple of toes; or better still, if they could manage it, they came to this country. And we understood that, and sympathized, and were glad to welcome them.

16. Now by present estimates four to six thousand Americans of draft age have left this country for Canada, another two or three thousand have gone to Europe, and it looks as though many more are preparing to emigrate.

17. A few months ago I received a letter from the Harvard Alumni Bulletin posing a series of questions that students might ask a professor involving what to do about the draft. I was asked to write what I would tell those students. All I had to say to those students was this: If any of them had decided to evade the draft and asked my help, I would help him in any way I could. I would feel as I suppose members of the underground railway felt in pre–Civil War days, helping runaway slaves to get to Canada. It wasn't altogether a popular position then; but what do you think of it now?

18. A bill to stop the draft was recently introduced in the Senate (S. 503), sponsored by a group of senators that ran the gamut from McGovern and Hatfield to Barry Goldwater. I hope it goes through; but any time I find that Barry Goldwater and I are in agreement, that makes me take another look.

19. And indeed there are choices in getting rid of the draft. I think that when we get rid of the draft, we must also cut back the size of the armed forces. It seems to me that in peacetime a total of one million men is surely enough. If there is an argument for American military forces of more than one million men in peacetime, I should like to hear that argument debated.

20. There is another thing being said closely connected with this: that to keep an adequate volunteer army, one would have to raise the pay considerably. That's said so positively and often that people believe it. I don't think it is true.

21. The great bulk of our present armed forces are genuine volunteers. Among first-term enlistments, 49 percent are true volun-

teers. Another 30 percent are so-called "reluctant volunteers," persons who volunteer under pressure of the draft. Only 21 percent are draftees. All reenlistments, of course, are true volunteers.

22. So the great majority of our present armed forces are true volunteers. Whole services are composed entirely of volunteers: the Air Force, for example, the Navy, almost all the Marines. That seems like proof to me that present pay rates are adequate. One must add that an Act of Congress in 1967 raised the base pay throughout the services in three installments, the third installment still to come, on April 1, 1969. So it is hard to understand why we are being told that to maintain adequate armed services on a volunteer basis will require large increases in pay; they will cost an extra $17 billion per year. It seems plain to me that we can get all the armed forces we need as volunteers, and at present rates of pay.

23. But there is something ever so much bigger and more important than the draft. That bigger thing, of course, is what ex-President Eisenhower warned us of, calling it the military-industrial complex. I am sad to say that we must begin to think of it now as the military-industrial-labor union complex. What happened under the plea of the Cold War was not alone that we built up the first big peacetime army in our history, but we institutionalized it. We built, I suppose, the biggest government building in our history to run it, and we institutionalized it.

24. I don't think we can live with the present military establishment and its $80 billion a year budget, and keep America anything like we have known it in the past. It is corrupting the life of the whole country. It is buying up everything in sight: industries, banks, investors, universities; and lately it seems also to have bought up the labor unions.

25. The Defense Department is always broke; but some of the things they do with that $80 billion a year would make Buck Rogers envious. For example: the Rocky Mountain Arsenal on the outskirts of Denver was manufacturing a deadly nerve poison on such a scale that there was a problem of waste disposal. Nothing daunted, they dug a tunnel two miles deep under Denver, into which they have injected so much poisoned water that beginning a couple of years ago Denver began to experience a series of earth tremors of increasing severity. Now there is a grave fear of a major earthquake. An interesting debate is in progress as to whether Denver will be safer if that lake of poisoned water is removed or left in place (New York *Times*, July 4, 1968; *Science*, Sept. 27, 1968).

26. Perhaps you have read also of those 6,000 sheep that

suddenly died in Skull Valley, Utah, killed by another nerve poison—a strange and, I believe, still unexplained accident, since the nearest testing seems to have been thirty miles away.

27. As for Vietnam, the expenditure of fire power has been frightening. Some of you may still remember Khe Sanh, a hamlet just south of the Demilitarized Zone, where a force of U.S. Marines was beleaguered for a time. During that period we dropped on the perimeter of Khe Sanh more explosives than fell on Japan throughout World War II, and more than fell on the whole of Europe during the years 1942 and 1943.

28. One of the officers there was quoted as having said afterward, "It looks like the world caught smallpox and died" (New York Times, Mar. 28, 1968).

29. The only point of government is to safeguard and foster life. Our government has become preoccupied with death, with the business of killing and being killed. So-called Defense now absorbs 60 percent of the national budget, and about 12 percent of the Gross National Product.

30. A lively debate is beginning again on whether or not we should deploy antiballistic missiles, the ABM. I don't have to talk about them, everyone else here is doing that. But I should like to mention a curious circumstance. In September 1967, or about one and a half years ago, we had a meeting of M.I.T. and Harvard people, including experts on these matters, to talk about whether anything could be done to block the Sentinel system, the deployment of ABM's. Everyone present thought them undesirable; but a few of the most knowledgeable persons took what seemed to be the practical view, "Why fight about a dead issue? It had been decided, the funds have been appropriated. Let's go on from there."

31. Well, fortunately, it's not a dead issue.

32. An ABM is a nuclear weapon. It takes a nuclear weapon to stop a nuclear weapon. And our concern must be with the whole issue of nuclear weapons.

33. There is an entire semantics ready to deal with the sort of thing I am about to say. It involves such phrases as "those are the facts of life." No—they are the facts of death. I don't accept them, and I advise you not to accept them. We are under repeated pressures to accept things that are presented to us as settled—decisions that have been made. Always there is the thought: let's go on from there! But this time we don't see how to go on. We will have to stick with those issues.

34. We are told that the United States and Russia between

them have by now stockpiled in nuclear weapons approximately the explosive power of fifteen tons of TNT for every man, woman, and child on earth. And now it is suggested that we must make more. All very regrettable, of course; but those are "the facts of life." We really would like to disarm; but our new Secretary of Defense has made the ingenious proposal that now is the time to greatly increase our nuclear armaments so that we can disarm from a position of strength.

35.   I think all of you know there is no adequate defense against massive nuclear attack. It is both easier and cheaper to circumvent any known nuclear defense system than to provide it. It's all pretty crazy. At the very moment we talk of deploying ABM's, we are also building the MIRV, the weapon to circumvent ABM's.

36.   So far as I know, the most conservative estimates of Americans killed in a major nuclear attack, with everything working as well as can be hoped and all foreseeable precautions taken, run to about 50 millions. We have become callous to gruesome statistics, and this seems at first to be only another gruesome statistic. You think, Bang!—and next morning, if you're still there, you read in the newspapers that 50 million people were killed.

37.   But that isn't the way it happens. When we killed close to 200,000 people with those first little, old-fashioned uranium bombs that we dropped on Hiroshima and Nagasaki, about the same number of persons was maimed, blinded, burned, poisoned, and otherwise doomed. A lot of them took a long time to die.

38.   That's the way it would be. Not a bang, and a certain number of corpses to bury; but a nation filled with millions of helpless, maimed, tortured, and doomed persons, and the survivors huddled with their families in shelters, with guns ready to fight off their neighbors, trying to get some uncontaminated food and water.

39.   A few months ago Senator Richard Russell of Georgia ended a speech in the Senate with the words: "If we have to start over again with another Adam and Eve, I want them to be Americans; and I want them on this continent and not in Europe." That was a United States senator holding a patriotic speech. Well, here is a Nobel Laureate who thinks that those words are criminally insane.

40.   How real is the threat of full-scale nuclear war? I have my own very inexpert idea, but realizing how little I know and fearful that I may be a little paranoid on this subject, I take every opportunity to ask reputed experts. I asked that question of a very distinguished professor of government at Harvard about a month ago. I asked him what sort of odds he would lay on the possibility of

full-scale nuclear war within the foreseeable future. "Oh," he said comfortably, "I think I can give you a pretty good answer to that question. I estimate the probability of full-scale nuclear war, provided that the situation remains about as it is now, at 2 percent per year." Anybody can do the simple calculation that shows that 2 percent per year means that the chance of having that full-scale nuclear war by 1990 is about one in three, and by 2000 it is about 50–50.

41. I think I know what is bothering the students. I think that what we are up against is a generation that is by no means sure that it has a future.

42. I am growing old, and my future so to speak is already behind me. But there are those students of mine who are in my mind always; and there are my children, two of them now seven and nine, whose future is infinitely more precious to me than my own. So it isn't just their generation; it's mine too. We're all in it together.

43. Are we to have a chance to live? We don't ask for prosperity, or security; only for a reasonable chance to live, to work out our destiny in peace and decency. Not to go down in history as the apocalyptic generation.

44. And it isn't only nuclear war. Another overwhelming threat is in the population explosion. That has not yet even begun to come under control. There is every indication that the world population will double before the year 2000; and there is a widespread expectation of famine on an unprecedented scale in many parts of the world. The experts tend to differ only in their estimates of when those famines will begin. Some think by 1980, others think they can be staved off until 1990, very few expect that they will not occur by the year 2000.

45. That is the problem. Unless we can be surer than we now are that this generation has a future, nothing else matters. It's not good enough to give it tender loving care, to supply it with breakfast foods, to buy it expensive educations. Those things don't mean anything unless this generation has a future. And we're not sure that it does.

46. I don't think that there are problems of youth, or student problems. All the real problems I know are grown-up problems.

47. Perhaps you will think me altogether absurd, or "academic," or hopelessly innocent—that is, until you think of the alternatives—if I say as I do to you now: we have to get rid of those nuclear weapons. There is nothing worth having that can be obtained by nuclear war: nothing material or ideological, no tradition

that it can defend. It is utterly self-defeating. Those atom bombs represent an unusable weapon. The only use for an atom bomb is to keep somebody else from using it. It can give us no protection, but only the doubtful satisfaction of retaliation. Nuclear weapons offer us nothing but a balance of terror; and a balance of terror is still terror.

48. We have to get rid of those atomic weapons, here and everywhere. We cannot live with them.

49. I think we've reached a point of great decision, not just for our nation, not only for all humanity, but for life upon the Earth. I tell my students, with a feeling of pride that I hope they will share, that the carbon, nitrogen, and oxygen that make up 99 percent of our living substance were cooked in the deep interiors of earlier generations of dying stars. Gathered up from the ends of the universe, over billions of years, eventually they came to form in part the substance of our sun, its planets, and ourselves. Three billion years ago life arose upon the Earth. It seems to be the only life in the solar system. Many a star has since been born and died.

50. About two million years ago, man appeared. He has become the dominant species on the Earth. All other living things, animal and plant, live by his sufferance. He is the custodian of life on Earth. It's a big responsibility.

51. The thought that we're in competition with Russians or with Chinese is all a mistake, and trivial. Only mutual destruction lies that way. We are one species, with a world to win. There's life all over this universe, but in all the universe we are the only men.

52. Our business is with life, not death. Our challenge is to give what account we can of what becomes of life in the solar system, this corner of the universe that is our home, and, most of all, what becomes of men—all men of all nations, colors, and creeds. It has become one world, a world for all men. It is only such a world that now can offer us life and the chance to go on.

WORDS

*meaning* 1. Identify or define the following: *Nuremberg trials* (par. 5), *categories of acts* (par. 6), *Cold War* and *Truman Doctrine* (par. 11), *Buck Rogers* (par. 25), *Gross National Product* (par. 29). 2. Define *gamut* (par. 18). How does this word illuminate the liberal author's humorous uneasiness when he finds himself in agreement with Barry Goldwater? 3. What does he mean in paragraph 23 when he says that we have *institutionalized* our military defenses, and what building represents the institution? 4. What is an *apocalyptic generation* (par. 43)?

*level of usage*  1. At what level would you place words and phrases like *crazy* (par. 1), *gimmick, double talk,* and *anything goes* (par. 6), *gone sour* (par. 8)?  2. Are there similar expressions in the paragraphs that follow? What tone do such expressions help to give the whole?

*connotation*  What more familiar expression does the author have in mind when he uses the phrase *balance of terror* (par. 47) and what rhetorical effect does he achieve through our almost automatic coupling of the two phrases?

## SENTENCES

*parallelism*  1. Analyze the structure of the writer's brief characterization of Dean Rusk in paragraph 6.  2. Analyze the last two sentences of paragraph 23 for their rhetorical effectiveness.

## CONTENT AND ORGANIZATION

*assumptions and implications*  1. Can you amplify the author's assertion in paragraph 6 that in our time "all wars are wars of defense"?  2. In paragraph 8 how does he contrast the character of such wars with an earlier one in our history?

*organization*  1. Can you see an ironic thematic connection between the author's reference to the "secret weapon" of the Vietnamese in paragraph 7 and his discussion of our weapons in paragraph 24 and following?  2. What discussion in the early part of the piece is recalled by the phrase "criminally insane" in paragraph 39?  3. "A Generation in Search of a Future" was an impromptu speech delivered without a written text, and, under these circumstances, one would expect from most speakers a rambling, loosely organized discourse. This speech, however, in spite of its informality of tone, its occasionally incomplete sentences, and its frequent very short paragraphs, all of which suggest the circumstances of its delivery, is tightly organized. The author promises at the outset to name the source of present unrest among the young throughout the world. Trace the steps by which he arrives at his goal.

## SUGGESTIONS FOR DISCUSSION

1. In paragraph 8, the author says that "our national symbols have gone sour," and gives us one example. Think of as many more examples as you can and consider how this situation in our national culture is reflected in the popular media of communication and in public conduct.  2. Is a war won or lost only when one side capitulates?  3. In *A Farewell to Arms,* Ernest Hemingway has a British major say that all the countries fighting the war were "cooked." But the "thing was not to realize it. The last

country to realize they were cooked would win the war." Write a paper accepting or rejecting the major's theory.  4. In what ways has the United States' position in Vietnam changed since this speech was delivered in 1969?

*Norman Podhoretz*

# IN DEFENSE OF EDITING

1.  It seems to have become the fashion lately for writers who have had difficulties with one magazine or another to complain in public about the terrible treatment they have received at the hands of insensitive editors. B. H. Haggin not long ago voiced such a complaint in *Partisan Review* against Robert Hatch of *The Nation;* more recently, in the *Hudson Review,* Hans J. Morgenthau had a go at me. As it happens, both Haggin and Morgenthau were speaking out of what might easily be regarded as personal pique, but the question they raised—Are editors necessary?—is nevertheless an interesting one, touching as it does on the general state of discourse in America and the whole issue of the maintenance of standards. To take up that question, one has to discuss aspects of the editorial process that were perhaps better kept private, but now that they are being made public from the point of view of the aggrieved author, they might just as well be talked about from the point of view of the working editor as well. And the only way for a working editor to begin talking honestly about them is to attempt an answer to the question as it was put in more positive form by John Fischer in the June *Harper's:* What do editors do?

2.  Most people, I imagine, if they think about it at all, think that the job of an editor is to pick and choose among finished pieces of work which have been submitted to him and deliver them to the printer; that is to say, he acts as a middleman between individual authors and an expectant public. In the six years that I have been editing *Commentary,* there have indeed been occasions when my job corresponded roughly to that conception of it. But the editorial process is usually far more complicated. Typically, between the receipt of a manuscript at the offices of almost any magazine and the dispatch

IN DEFENSE OF EDITING:   Copyright © 1965, by Minneapolis Star and Tribune Co., Inc. Reprinted from the October, 1965 issue of *Harper's Magazine* by permission of the author.

of a publishable article to the printer fall the shadows—of *doubt,* of *deliberation,* of *labor,* or *negotiation.*

3. *Doubt:* Every magazine that deserves the name has a character, a style, a point of view, a circumscribed area of concern, a conception of how discourse ought to be conducted; if it lacks these things, it is not a magazine but a periodical anthology of random writings. Obviously the editor's personality, his cast of mind, his biases, his interests are crucial to the formation of this character. Yet once it has been formed—if it has been truly formed—it takes on an independent existence of its own, resisting even the editor's efforts to change or qualify it. It is enormously important for him to fight his own magazine, to keep it from becoming hardened and predictable, to keep it open and mobile. Yet if he whores too avidly after strange gods, desiring this man's art and that man's scope, the magazine will avenge itself by refusing to assimilate the foreign substance. Instead of achieving surprise, he will achieve a tasteless incongruity, like a woman with the wrong hairdo; instead of looking more flexible and lively, his magazine will take on an uncertain and affected air. This is why phrases like "Not for us" or "Unsuitable" so often accompany rejected manuscripts. They are used partly to soothe the wounded feelings of authors, but there is a truth in them by which magazines live or die.

4. To understand that magazines have their own insistent characters is to understand why the vast majority of the articles they publish are likely to be commissioned. (The strictly literary magazines are an exception, for the obvious reason that poems and stories, unlike articles, are not as a rule written to order. But even a literary magazine can only become a real magazine—that is, acquire a character—by going after particular writers whom the editor values more highly than others; that, too, may perhaps be regarded as a form of commissioning.)

5. If an established writer or a regular contributor comes to a magazine with a proposal that the editor likes, he will naturally be told to go ahead. But before he is told to go ahead, the editor will indicate to him how he thinks the subject ought properly to be handled: "properly," of course, meaning the editor's conception of how the intrinsic demands of the subject can best be reconciled with the demands of the magazine's character.

6. The other, more common, form of commissioning follows not upon the writer's initiative but upon the editor's. The editor—or, mysteriously, the magazine itself—decides that an article is needed on a given subject and he looks for someone who can do it as far

as possible in the "right" way. This search for the right writer sets what is one of the editor's most interesting problems, but it can be exhausting; often the writer he wants is a busy man who must be cajoled, flattered, harassed, nagged. And even with cajolery, flattery, harassment, and nagging, the search ends half the time in failure, either because no one can be found, or because the person who eventually is found never delivers, or worse, turns out to be the wrong writer. With enough experience, however, an editor will know where to go, and with enough luck he will snare his man. Still, he has to be very lucky indeed or very inspired in his choice of the writer to get the piece *he* is dreaming of (and almost miraculously lucky to get it on the promised date). It happens once in a great while. But the typical conclusion to this phase of the editorial process is. the delivery of a manuscript which only faintly approximates the editor's ideal conception, or else differs radically from it. Thus *Doubt,* and then . . .

7. *Deliberation:* Is it right for *us?* Can it be made right for us? How? Will the author be willing to revise it? Can he revise it on time? Will he let *us* revise it? Are we willing to risk offending a valuable contributor by pushing very hard? Are we being unfair or too rigid? Should we perhaps publish the piece more or less as it is? Are we perhaps a little crazy?

8. Such are the questions that are struggled with at editorial conferences or via inter-office memos. Finally, when the manuscript may have gone the rounds of the editorial staff a second time (the conference having left everyone thoroughly uncertain) a decision, enthusiastic or grudging, is reached. A letter is written or a telephone conversation held or a lunch date arranged. "This is what we think still needs to be done. Will you do it?" If yes, the whole process is repeated when the revised version comes in. Or, if no: "Will you let us do it, then? Naturally you'll have an opportunity to check the edited version." If yes to that, the phase of deliberation gives way to . . .

9. *Labor:* One edits a manuscript by trying to correct the flaws that inevitably appear when it is subjected to the minutest scrutiny of which the editor is capable. In America (and indications are that this is beginning to happen in England, too), the overwhelming majority of the flaws to be corrected are either technical or minimally aesthetic: flaws of grammar, flaws of syntax, flaws of structure, flaws of rhetoric, flaws of taste.

10. But the deficiencies that tend to show up on a ruthlessly close study of a manuscript may be substantive too. Under the edi-

torial microscope things that were not visible to the naked eye—neither the editor's nor the author's—suddenly make an unexpected appearance. One sentence does not logically follow from the next; the paragraph on page 8 only makes sense if it is transposed to page 6 and stitched in with a clever transition to cover the seam; a point which seemed persuasive on a first reading turns out to need bolstering with more documentation (or the irrelevancies surrounding it have to be peeled away); an argument which looked reasonable before is now revealed as contradicting another argument elsewhere in the piece, or to have ignored or distorted the evidence on the other side of the case.

11. Some of these deficiencies—the logical and structural ones—can be remedied by the editor himself if he has acquired a truly inward grasp of what the author is trying to say and show and evoke. But it must be left to the author to fill in gaps, to add further information, to take up new questions that have arisen, to shore up weaknesses that have become evident. Accordingly the edited version of his article will be sent to him with a letter explaining what has been done to the manuscript and why, asking him to make sure that no inaccuracies have crept in through the editing, and requesting that he deal with the substantive problems which have emerged upon careful scrutiny. The phase of *Labor* has come to a close, and what remains is . . .

12. *Negotiation:* Seeing the edited manuscript, the author, as likely as not, is more than a little outraged. This is, after all, *his* article; he takes responsibility for it; it is to appear under his name. By what right does anyone presume to tamper with it? (On the other hand, some authors, curiously enough including many who write very well, are often grateful for editing.) When the outrage subsides, however, he will begin to wonder whether there might not perhaps be a certain justice in the criticisms reflected in the editing; not all, of course, but some. Adjustments will naturally have to be made here and there, but on the whole the edited version will do.

13. Just as the editor may have been worrying about the possibility of losing both article and author by pressing too hard on the manuscript, so on his side the author may be worried lest he lose his chance of publishing the piece and disaffect the editor. There is a clash of interests and vanities here which does not differ greatly in principle from the clash of opposing groups in politics, and it is ordinarily settled in much the same way as political struggles are—by negotiation. The author accepts most of the editing but insists on certain points (the restoration of a passage that has been cut or of a

formulation that has been changed), the editor agrees, and the piece is at long last sent to the printer.

14. Thus is the editorial process completed—so far as this one article is concerned. There may be as many as fifteen or twenty other pieces in the same issue. Not all of them will have involved so much effort. Two or three will have required only a little touching up or none at all; several others will have needed considerable editing but not in every sentence; still others will have needed more editing than the editor—knowing the author would object, and on balance wanting the piece even in an imperfect state—dared to do. (Reading such pieces in proof, or even in print, the editor can hardly control his pencil.)

15. It takes, then, a great deal of work, an enervating concentration on detail, and a fanatical concern with the bone and sinew of the English language to edit a manuscript—to improve an essentially well-written piece or to turn a clumsily written one into, at the very least, a readable and literate article, and, at the very most, a beautifully shaped and effectively expressed essay which remains true to the author's intention, which realizes that intention more fully than he himself was able to do. In addition to work, manuscript editing takes time—and time is critical to an enterprise that lives under the pressure of deadlines. And in addition to time, it takes a combination of sympathy—getting inside someone else's mind—and rigor—resistance to being swallowed up by that other mind, once inside—that is extremely difficult to maintain.

16. Is it all worth it? Over and over again one asks oneself that question, tempted as one is to hoard some of the energy that goes into editing for thinking one's own thoughts or doing one's own writing. One asks oneself whether anyone would know the difference if one simply sent all those pieces to the printer after a perfunctory reading. And one asks oneself whether anyone really cares about writing of this kind *as* writing. For all editors have had the experience of publishing inadequately edited pieces that were praised beyond their deserts, and articles they knew to be classics of their type that were scarcely noticed and certainly not valued at their proper worth. If such articles (which are not edited—one has no impulse to tamper with perfection) are not appreciated, what hope is there that lesser (edited) pieces will be?

17. In the end an editor is thrown back, as any man doing any job faithfully must be, on the fact that *he* cares and that he can therefore do no other. He cares about the English language; he cares about clarity of thought and grace of expression; he cares about

the traditions of discourse and of argument. It hardly needs to be said that even good editors will sometimes bungle a job and that bad editors invariably will, but it nevertheless remains true that the editorial process is a necessity if standards are to be preserved and if the intellectual life in America is not to become wholly compartmentalized and ultimately sterile in spirit.

18.  Apocalyptic as this may sound, I believe it to be an accurate statement of the case. It is no secret that the number of people in this country who can write an acceptable piece of exposition in literate English is astoundingly low. But if one goes beyond that minimal requirement and asks for a piece of exposition whose virtues include clarity, economy, coherence, and grace, one is hard put to find it even among professional journalists or professors of English, let alone professors of economics or sociology. (One is, however, rather more likely to find it among the professors of history, who as a class are for some reason the best writers in the academy today.) Whatever the causes of this sorry condition may be, the fact is that it exists, and until it is remedied the only alternative to (competent) editing must be a further debasement of our language and a further loosening of our already tenuous hold on the traditions of civilized public discourse.

19.  In our culture—I exaggerate only slightly—those who know cannot write, and those who can write do not know. An editor who wants an article on a given subject which seems important to him at a given time has very little trouble locating people with impeccable credentials and unquestionable authority. Since such people are rarely good writers, however, he has three choices as an editor: he can decide not to get a piece on the subject at all; he can resign himself to publishing one that is gratuitously unreadable and guilty of grave offenses against the art of exposition; or he can edit. To opt for the first choice is to lose opportunities; to opt for the second is to behave irresponsibly both toward the readers of his magazine and toward the standards of his profession; to opt for the third is to risk error and arrogance for the sake of creating the monthly illusion that we live in a world where a certain mode of serious discussion can still take place. What is today an illusion was once a reality; but without the illusion—that is, the sense of what is possible—before our eyes, how will we ever make it a reality again?

20.  Apart from standards, there is also the matter of American intellectual life itself. Once upon a time—or so it now seems—all educated men spoke the same language and therefore were able to communicate with one another. They strolled together in market-

places or ate together at High Table conversing all the while, wittily, on all manner of things. These educated men were all equally philosophers, equally theologians, equally scientists. But then one day, in the very midst of a conversation, they suddenly discovered that something strange had happened: they could no longer understand one another. They all wondered why they had been punished in this mysterious way by the multiplication of tongues (which soon came to be known as "disciplines"). Some blamed it on the growth of an idolatrous cult of Science among their fellows; others blamed it on the laziness and complacency of the *littérateurs*. The argument still rages today, but the "disciplines" are if anything further apart than they were in that far-off time when the common language was first shattered into a hundred isolated fragments.

21. In my view, the primary responsibility of the magazine editor is to participate in the struggle to reconstruct that shattered common language. There *must* be a language in which all but the most highly technical matters can be discussed without distortion or falsification or watering-down; there *must* be a language impartially free of all the various jargons through which the "disciplines" maintain their proud and debilitating isolation; there *must* be a language in which the kinship of these disciplines is expressed and revealed and reaffirmed.

22. A man who does not believe in the possibility of such a language cannot edit a magazine (though he may be able to edit a specialized journal of one kind or another). For from the belief in the possibility of such a language everything else that makes an editor follows: the conception of a culture as organic—as one and not many—and therefore accessible in all its modalities to the general intelligence; the correlative conviction that by the exercise of his general intelligence a man can determine what the important issues are even in areas in which he has no special training; the arrogance to assert that *this* is the relevant point rather than *that;* the nerve to tell others how to discuss things which they know more about than he does.

23. And so we come back to where we began: to manuscript editing. Mr. Fischer is right in stressing qualities like intuition, curiosity, and enthusiasm when he talks about the process by which an editor decides on subjects to be covered, problems to be investigated, issues to be raised. But it is manuscript editing and manuscript editing alone that makes it possible for these subjects to be covered properly, these problems to be investigated adequately, these issues to be raised incisively.

24. (I should add that the article you have just read was commissioned and deliberated upon, but not edited. Perhaps—I hope not—it should have been.)

## WORDS

*meaning* Define *pique* (par. 1), *intrinsic* (par. 5), *substantive* (par. 10), *disaffect* (par. 13), *debilitating* (par. 21), and *modalities* (par. 22).

*connotation* 1. What is the effect of this simile: "like a woman with the wrong hairdo" (par. 3)? 2. How can a magazine "take on an uncertain and affected air" (par. 3)?

## SENTENCES

*style* 1. Paragraph 7 is merely a series of ten questions. What unity does the paragraph have ? 2. What is meant by writing in *New Yorker* style? *Time* style? 3. Discuss and distinguish the *flaws* (par. 9) and the *deficiencies* (par. 10). How can flaws be *aesthetic?* And in what sense are deficiencies *substantive?* 4. How effective is the analogy in paragraph 13? 5. Is the statement "those who know cannot write, and those who can write do not know" (par. 19) an aphorism, proverb, adage, maxim, or epigram? Explain your choice.

*emphasis* 1. What does the author accomplish by using the series of participles "cajoled, flattered, harassed, nagged" (par. 6)? Why does he echo them with nouns in the following sentence? 2. What does the author achieve by repeating "To opt" (par. 19)? 3. What is accomplished by the repetition of *must* (par. 21), and why is the word italicized?

## PARAGRAPHS

*unity* What is the time of "Once upon a time" (par. 20)? Does this help unify the paragraph? Explain.

*coherence* 1. A writer once said he had an article returned with the editor's complaint that the beginning was not adequate. The writer interchanged the first two paragraphs, and the editor was happy. What does this indicate to you? Could you successfully interchange the first two paragraphs in this essay? Explain your answer. 2. What is meant by the first sentence of paragraph 21? Does the rest of the paragraph justify this initial sentence?

## CONTENT AND ORGANIZATION

*central idea* 1. Which of the first two paragraphs better suggests the central idea? 2. How successfully, and where specifically, does Podhoretz "defend" editing?

*organization* 1. An organizational plan is carefully spelled out at the end of paragraph 2, and it is worked out in paragraphs 3–15. What is the purpose of these paragraphs? What is the purpose of paragraphs 16–23? 2. How successful is paragraph 24 as an ending? In what sense is it ironic?

SUGGESTIONS FOR DISCUSSION

1. If you were the editor of a general-circulation magazine, would you accept this piece for publication? Why or why not? 2. Podhoretz is the editor of *Commentary*. Go through several issues of that magazine and then describe its character, style, and point of view (par. 3). 3. Read one or two issues each of *The Atlantic Monthly* and *Harper's Magazine*. Then write an essay in which you determine the extent to which an article from each could be identified by the "style" of the magazine (par. 3). 4. Would you be "outraged" if the editor of a magazine tried to "tamper" with an article of yours (par. 12)? 5. Do you see any relationship between an editor and a teacher? 6. Do you think "negotiation" is useful or valuable or worthwhile? 7. Do you agree that professors of history are "the best writers in the academy today" (par. 18)?

*Maxwell Perkins*

# LETTER TO MORLEY CALLAGHAN

*November 16, 1931*

DEAR CALLAGHAN:

1. I distrust the validity of the criticism I am about to make, but I can't shake off the feeling from which it arises. My suspicion of it comes from a fear that this feeling is derived from literary conventions—which both authors and editors should not be ruled by— but I'll give it to you tentatively for you to deal with.

2. In almost all your writing your characters were the common run of people—people who have not had the chance to develop much, intellectually or emotionally. This has led many readers, even some reviewers, to regard you as a "hard-boiled" writer. But there were reviewers, and some readers, not so utterly dumb; they saw

LETTER TO MORLEY CALLAGHAN: Reprinted with the permission of Charles Scribner's Sons from *Editor to Author: The Letters of Maxwell E. Perkins* edited by John Hall Wheelock. Copyright 1950 Charles Scribner's Sons.

that a very unusual delicacy of perception was one of your most marked and most distinguishing qualities, and that it was expressed with corresponding subtlety in your writing. They should have seen this even in your first book, about a bootlegger.

3.  But you were writing about a bootlegger and you naturally dealt in what I think is called realism. Many unpleasant details had a significance in that narrative and you put them in, and quite rightly. And this was true also in many, perhaps most, of the stories. Your very unusual delicacy in perception and expression did not generally get a fair show, alongside the mean and sordid details which belonged and were there.

4.  In this new story, this delicacy, or subtlety, or whatever, does get its first real show, and it is pervasive, and that is why I said this reveals your talent more fully and satisfyingly than anything you've done. But the mean and sordid details are still here and my feeling—which I can't feel sure is justified—is that they are not compatible with the glamor of this romance, or its tragical conclusion. The story is a tragic idyll, or could be. Sordid detail perhaps doesn't *belong*. And if it doesn't, perhaps you have brought it in because you have become accustomed to using it in stories where it does belong.

5.  All this is based on the assumption that when one writes a story he does not, of course, put everything in, but selects with a view to the motive of the story. Details he takes are those which are significant in the light of the motive. I question whether you have not, in turning to a new sort of story for you—and one which gives you a fine show—selected details partly under the influence of the writing you have done before.

6.  The fact is that in revising the story you have yourself tended to reduce those details which were unpleasant, presumably on this very account—because they were not suitable to the motive of this story. But even so, I think that that element of the rather sordid is still in the story to too great a degree, in the light of its essential character as an ideal.

7.  For instance, I think that perhaps the whole physical element of love is over-emphasized. Now, Peter takes up with the other girl only because he considers his love affair with Marion has concluded, and perhaps too much is made of his relations with the other girl, and he treats her too brutally at the end. Because this story is about the love between Marion and Peter, and it is a different kind of love from the merely physical, and should be so presented. And in the end of the story, where the idyllic qualities are more than ever marked, I do not think that the affair with the guide

need be gone into to the degree that it is. The only important thing about it is that it happened, and in circumstances which make it seem inevitable and excusable. In many places through the story there are almost naturalistic details, which do not seem to me to blend with the story's intent and motive. I would even question the incident of the false teeth. That was so horrible and unpleasant, and yet I recognize that it had a great value, too.

8. In fact, the whole difficulty with my position is that none of these things are false in the least, they are all true. But you are writing a story that is almost poetic, and the question is whether they belong. You know, it has been contended that when one writes tragedies the characters should be kings and queens, etc., because they are the most suitable material on account of their lofty position, their high obligations, etc. I don't agree to this, but what justice is in it serves to illustrate a point about the appropriateness of material to theme. A story of tragic love can be told, certainly, about people of any sort who are capable of love; but the few details selected from the thousands available should probably be those most significant in the light of the motive. Other details which would be significant in a plain story of commonplace reality should probably be discarded.

9. I don't advance this view with much confidence, but I can't shake off the feeling that there is a kind of sordidness in your story which could be in any story but seems to be inappropriate in this.

*Ever yours,*
MAXWELL PERKINS

WORDS

*meaning* 1. What are *literary conventions* in the sense in which Perkins uses the term (par. 1)? 2. Define *pervasive* and *sordid* (par. 4). 3. What is an *idyll* (par. 4)? 4. Is an *idyll* necessarily an *ideal* (par. 6)? 5. What are *naturalistic details* (par. 7)?

*word usage* Perkins uses the word *dumb* (par. 2) in a colloquial sense peculiarly American. What does he mean? How did the word come to have this meaning? (Consult the *Oxford English Dictionary* and its Supplement.)

SENTENCES

*emphasis* 1. In this letter, a sensitive and diplomatic editor is criticizing the work of an author. He is taking pains to be unemphatic, to qualify his statements, to avoid even the appearance of dogmatism or cocksureness. What is the effect of "distrust," "suspicion," and "tentatively" in the first paragraph? of "I don't advance this view with much confidence" in the last paragraph? 2. Why is this kind of humility likely to be more persuasive than unqualified statement?

## CONTENT AND ORGANIZATION

*central idea*   All qualification and explanation aside, what criticism does Perkins make of Callaghan's story?

*organization*   1. Perkins' whole career demonstrates that his humility was genuine and sincere ("Do not ever defer to my judgment," he wrote in a letter to F. Scott Fitzgerald). But this humility also serves an excellent rhetorical purpose. Notice that the first paragraph of this letter makes clear that a tentative, possibly mistaken, criticism follows; the second compliments the author for possession of delicacy of perception and subtlety of expression; the third speaks approvingly of other stories that properly contained unpleasant details. How do these paragraphs prepare the way for the criticism that is to follow? 2. What is the value, as effective persuasion, of Perkins' suggestion in the last sentences of paragraphs 4 and 5 of a possible reason for what he considers artistic flaws in the telling of the story? 3. What is the value, as persuasion, of the allusion in paragraph 6 to Callaghan's revision? 4. What is the value of deferring specific suggestions for revision of the story until paragraph 7? 5. The last paragraph begins with qualification. How does it end? Does it express Perkins' attitude clearly and forcefully?

## SUGGESTIONS FOR DISCUSSION

1. Discuss a story or novel you have read in which unpleasant—even sordid—details were necessary to the effective development of the story. 2. Discuss a story or novel you believe to have been flawed by the inclusion of unpleasant or sordid details. 3. Write a draft of a letter in which you criticize a good friend's attitude toward some current social, political, or campus problem. 4. Write an essay describing either the advantages or disadvantages of "low-pressure salesmanship." When is it effective? When is it ineffective?

# Presenting Results of Research

*All writing presents the results of the writer's experience or investigation. But the research paper parades what other kinds of writing may conceal—the sources of the writer's information.*

*Neither of the two essays that follow is a complete or formal research paper, but both are excellent models of some of the more common techniques of presenting the results of research in history or social science, and both illustrate a variety of commonly accepted procedures for acknowledging indebtedness and documenting or amplifying statements.*

## Lawrence E. Mintz

## LANGSTON HUGHES'S
## JESSE B. SEMPLE:
## THE URBAN NEGRO AS WISE FOOL

1. From the appearance of the comical servant Jonathan in Royall Tyler's play *The Contrast* (1787), through such figures as Seba Smith's "Major Jack Downing," Charles Farrar Browne's "Artemus Ward," Mark Twain, Finley Peter Dunne's "Mr. Dooley," and Will Rogers, the wise fool or common-sense, "crackerbox" philosopher has played a significant role in Amerian social and political satire.[1] The enormous American popularity of this archetypal character, whose literary history can be traced from the medieval *sottie* to the newspaper columns of such contemporary writers as Art Buchwald and Arthur Hoppe, is doubtlessly due to the considerable respect that Americans have had for "common sense" and "natural nobility"

---

[1] The wise-fool character in American literature has been discussed by Walter Blair, *Native American Humor* (New York, 1937), and *Horse Sense in American Humor* (New York, 1942), Constance Rourke, *American Humor* (New York, 1942), and Jennette Tandy, *Crackerbarrel Philosophers in American Humor and Satire* (New York, 1925).

LANGSTON HUGHES'S JESSE B. SEMPLE: From *Satire Newsletter,* fall, 1969. Reprinted by permission of the editor.

throughout our history. When Thomas Jefferson claimed, "State a moral case to a ploughman and a professor. The former will decide it as well, and often better than the latter, because he has not been led astray by artificial rules," he expressed the attitude that makes an untutored, "rustic," often comical *naif* an effective posture for the satirist.[2]

2. An interesting twentieth-century representative of this character type is Jesse B. Semple, or "Simple" as he is more frequently called, a creation of Langston Hughes. Hughes began the "Simple" sketches for the Negro newspaper *The Chicago Defender* in 1943 and continued them in *The New York Post* (after 1962). Many of these columns have been reprinted in five separate volumes.[3]

3. The place of Jesse B. Semple in the American wise-fool tradition has been noted by Hughes's bibliographer, Donald C. Dickinson: "His penetrating wit is in the high tradition of the so-called crackerbox philosophers, Josh Billings, Mr. Dooley, and Artemus Ward. If in Simple's case the crackerbox has been converted to a bar stool the total effect is pleasantly the same." [4] In *I Wonder As I Wander: An Autobiographical Journey* (New York, 1956), one of his two autobiographical volumes, Hughes indicates that Simple is part of an even older literary tradition: "One of the first things I did when I got to Mexico City was to get a tutor, a young woman friend of the Latinos, and began to read *Don Quixote* in the original, a great reading experience that possibly helped me to develop many years later, in my own books a character called Simple" (p. 291).

4. The "Simple" stories have been extremely popular both here and abroad. James Emanuel in his biography *Langston Hughes* (New York, 1967) points out that "After the third Simple book, a minimum of a hundred and twenty-nine reviews were available in periodicals and newspapers, forty-one of them foreign . . ." (p. 160). Donald C. Dickinson goes so far as to claim, "The world knows the American Negro best through Hughes's sketches of Jessie [sic] B. Semple" (p. 118). Although both Emanuel and Dickinson devote a few pages to the "Simple" material, and two articles treat it primarily from a sociological perspective, Emanuel is quite correct in noting, "A

---

[2] Quoted from John William Ward, *Andrew Jackson; Symbol for an Age* (New York, 1962), p. 49.

[3] The following abbreviations will be used for further references to this material: "Mind," *Simple Speaks His Mind* (New York, 1950), "Claim," *Simple Stakes a Claim* (New York, 1953), "Wife," *Simple Takes a Wife* (New York, 1953), "Sam," *Simple's Uncle Sam* (New York, 1965), and "Best," *The Best of Simple* (New York, 1961).

[4] *A Bio-bibliography of Langston Hughes* (Hamden, Connecticut, 1967), p. 98.

deeper analysis of the Simple books should be made" (p. 157).[5] Hughes's wise-fool writing is interesting for its humor, satiric style, and delightful characterization, as well as for its insights into the issues concerning the Negro in America.

5. Considering the gravity of these social issues, one well might ask why Langston Hughes chose a light, humorous approach in these stories.[6] Hughes answers this question with some comments on humor. To begin with, he notes that many features of the prejudices American whites have toward blacks are inherently funny. In an article entitled "White Folks Do the Funniest Things," Hughes writes, "Some incidents of Jim Crowism which I personally have experienced have amused me more than they have angered me—due as nearly as I can analyze them, to their very absurdity." [7] He goes on to tell about being served through a hole in the wall of a "segregated" lunch shack, and of his difficulty in leaving a whites-only waiting room when a law officer refused to let him *leave* through the front (and only) door. In the foreword to *Simple Stakes a Claim,* Hughes laments the absence of humor in the black magazines. "The serious colored magazines like the *Crisis* or *Phylon* do not publish humor even if given to them *free*. These magazines evidently think the race problem is too deep for comic relief. Such earnestness is contrary to mass Negro thinking. Colored people are always laughing at some wry Jim Crow incident or absurd nuance of the color line" (pp. 11–12).

6. In *The Book of Negro Humor* (New York, 1966) Hughes (its editor) says of humor: "Humor is laughing at what you haven't got when you ought to have it. Of course, you laugh by proxy. You're really laughing at the other guy's lacks, not your own. That's what makes it so funny. . . . Humor is your own unconscious therapy" (p. vii). This aspect of humor, "laughing to keep from crying," is an important feature of the "Simple" approach. It is humor touched with pathos, which leads Arthur P. Davis to say of Simple, "In this light Simple is no longer a comic character but a black Pagliacci. Underneath all of his gaiety and humor there is the basic tragedy of

---

[5] Emanuel, pp. 154–60, Dickinson, pp. 95–100. Arthur P. Davis, "Jesse B. Semple: Negro American," *Phylon,* XV (Spring 1954), 21–28, Heniz Rogge, "Die Figur des Simple im Werke von Langston Hughes," *Die Neueren Sprachen,* XII (1955), 555–66. The German article is virtually a restatement of Davis'.

[6] Of course it must be noted that Hughes's treatment of racial problems is not confined to the "Simple" sketches; the problems of the Negro in America pervade his more serious work. One discussion of Hughes's nonhumorous handling of racial matters is James Pressley, "The American Dream of Langston Hughes." *Southwest Review,* XLVIII (Autumn 1963), 380–86.

[7] *Common Ground,* IV (1944), 42.

the urban Negro and his circumscribed life" (p. 28). Simple expresses the therapeutic value of humor in the face of adversity, in his own amusing way, when he responds to the charge, "Nothing you say sounds funny to me," with "Laugh anyhow . . . if you do not laugh, you might get mad, that is no good for brotherhood" ("Claim," p. 173).

7. Also in the foreword to *Simple Stakes a Claim,* Hughes gives another reason for treating racial matters humorously. "Humor is a weapon, too, of no mean value against one's foes" (p. 12). Humor is used as a weapon in these stories in a variety of ways, from ridiculing the enemies of the black man to providing a gentle corrective to liberals and other well-meaning but unrealistic or insufficiently motivated friends of the Negro to criticizing blacks who either "disgrace the race" or are less militant and "race conscious" than Hughes would like them to be. Since Simple's humor also makes him likeable, his "message" is thus more readily accepted by a sympathetic audience.

8. In all of his writing, Langston Hughes concerned himself with a realistic approach to the daily life of his black brothers. He revolted against the romantic idealization of Negro "heroes" and the didactic "Horatio Algerish" works of some of his fellow black artists, and was often condemned by black as well as white critics for his militancy and his realistic treatment of "unsavory" aspects of Negro life.[8] Hughes is far from unfaithful to his belief in realism with his creation of Jesse B. Semple. Simple was born, Hughes tells us, as the result of a barroom encounter with a neighbor who worked in a war plant and made "cranks." Hughes inquired as to the function of those "cranks," and the following dialogue ensued:

> I said, "What kind of cranks?"
> He said, "Oh man, I don't know what kind of cranks."
> I said, "Well, do they crank cars, tanks, buses, planes, or what?"
> He said, "I don't know what them cranks crank."
> Whereupon his girl friend, a little put out at this ignorance of his job, said, "You've been working there long enough. Looks like by now you ought to know what them cranks crank."
> "Aw, Woman," he said, "You know white folks don't tell colored folks what cranks crank." ("Best," p. viii)

All of the characters in the "Simple" stories are based on the author's experiences in Harlem, and, as he notes ". . . it is impossible to live

[8] These themes, and the critical battles fought over them, are discussed in detail by Emanuel and Dickinson, and by Hughes in numerous articles, including "The Negro Artist and the Racial Mountain," *The Nation,* CXXII (June 13, 1926), 692–94.

in Harlem and not know at least a hundred Simples, fifty Joyces, twenty-five Zaritas, a number of Boyds, and several Cousin Minnies—or reasonable facsimiles thereof" ("Best," p. vii).

9.   The wise-fool character may be used by the satirist in one of two ways. He may be the subject of the ridicule, a negative "buffoon" who represents the opinion or attitude to be criticized by "innocent" emulation or "accidental" misunderstanding or misstating of it. Or he may adopt the posture of the common-sense critic, prefacing his remarks with "I don't know much . . . but . . . ." This dual perspective may sometimes create the problem often posed the reader of satire, of ascertaining whether the author is being critical of the central character or using him as his spokesman. Although Simple is often the clown (particularly in his domestic affairs), and occasionally the representative of a violent extremism that both he and Hughes ultimately reject, he is usually the common-sense philosopher, whose observations may be somewhat naive, but are meant to be taken as basically correct.

10.   Simple may be uneducated, but he is not stupid, and in the words of Donald C. Dickinson, "In his conversation Simple reveals an insight born of the streets, of low-paying, back-breaking jobs, of Saturday night parties, and Sunday prayer meetings" (p. 99). Simple appeals to his practical, experiential knowledge in his debates with his more educated drinking partner: "I do not care what you know out of a book, you also have to know a lots out of life" ("Wife," p. 161). Simple's "common sense" is sometimes so sophisticated that he is close to losing his mask as a wise fool, a problem encountered in many of the characters of this sort. For example, in one of his attacks on the slow pace of integration in the South, he delivers an analysis of international politics which asserts that "third world" forces of "Nasser, Nehru, and Chou" will ultimately force America to correct its treatment of black Americans, because of our need to protect our world image ("Claim," pp. 67–72). In the same manner he analyzes urban machine politics, feigning a belief that "politicianer" is a synonym for graft, but concluding with an astute observation of the relative importance of platform rather than results to a politician's future ("Claim," pp. 17–19). At times like these Simple's remarks, exclusive of the dialect, might easily be attributed to a well-educated journalist or political scientist.

11.   Above all Simple is a Negro. As Arthur P. Davis points out, "Our first impression of Mr. Jesse B. is that however unpredictable he may be in other things he is thoroughly consistent in one respect: first, last, and always, he is a 'race man'—a fourteen carat, one

hundred percent, dyed-in-the-wool race man" (p. 22). Accused of bringing race into every topic he discusses, Simple counters "I do . . . because that is what I am always coming face to face with—race" ("Claim," p. 58). A participant in the Harlem riots (of 1943), Simple is a militant advocate of civil rights who is essentially suspicious of, and hostile toward, whites. He is capable of praying that ". . . when Christ comes back this time . . . I hope he smites white folks down!" ("Mind," pp. 16–17). Yet when he is asked if he includes Mrs. Roosevelt in this blanket condemnation, he exempts her readily. Additionally he has kind words for some whites—a man who gave him a dime for ice cream when he was young, a white couple who stood up with him at his city-hall wedding, or an Irish cop who sided with a black cab driver in a dispute with a Southerner.

12. Unlike the nineteenth-century American wise-fool characters who were predominantly rural (like "Major Downing," "Orpheus C. Kerr," "Petroleum V. Nasby," or "Bill Arp"), Simple is thoroughly "urbanized." Born in Virginia ("I *would* be borned in a state named after a woman. From that day on, women never give me no peace" ["Mind," p. 4]), and though "country" in his taste for soul food and occasional nostalgia for boyhood serenity, Simple repeatedly reaffirms his love for Harlem and his unwillingness to leave the city: "I will not return to the country, North or South. No backwoods for me. I am a big-city man myself. My roots is here" ("Sam," p. 46). He rarely ventures beyond the borders of Harlem, and when he does the results are as often as not disastrous for him. A brief trip to New Jersey, for instance, ends in his losing a fight, catching cold, and being involved in an auto accident, to say nothing of the trouble it gets him into with his fiancée ("Wife," pp. 87–90). Simple feels comfortably at home in Harlem. He answers the query, "What is it you love about Harlem?" by claiming, "I feel like I got protection . . . from white folks. . . . Furthermore, I like Harlem because it belongs to me" ("Mind," p. 31).

13. The "Simple" sketches are in the form of dialogues, usually between Simple and a barroom companion who has been identified as Langston Hughes, but is called "Boyd" in the musical comedy that was based on the stories ("Simply Heavenly," 1957), and is twice referred to by that name in *Simple's Uncle Sam* (p. 72 and p. 152).[9]

9 Though the identification of Hughes as Simple's interviewer, made by both Dickinson (p. 97) and Davis (p. 21), is an obvious one—the interviewer shares Hughes's external description as to skin color, place of birth, education, etc.—it would be more accurate to use the name Boyd in discussing him, since he frequently expresses opinions inconsistent with positions adopted by Hughes

Boyd is described by Hughes in the character notes for "Simply Heavenly":

> Boyd: Boyd has probably been halfway through college before his army service in Europe. Serious-minded, pleasant-looking, trying to be a writer, perhaps taking courses at New York University on the last of his G.I. money. Almost every Harlem bar has such a fellow among its regular customers, who acts sometimes as a kind of arbiter when "intellectual" discussions come up. (New York, 1959, p. 4)

14. Though he is less militant and more "objective" on racial matters than Simple, Boyd is not really a "Tom," nor is he one of the members of the black bourgeoisie or corps of Negro "spokesmen" that Simple attacks frequently. Like his drinking buddy, Boyd is truly at home in the bars and on the streets of Harlem, where he may be found "observing life for literary purposes" ("Mind," pp. 18–19). Boyd has two functions in these stories. As an intellectual, a rationalist, and an objective observer, he provides a perspective different from Simple's, "correcting" the latter's excesses (it is he who brings up Mrs. Roosevelt when Simple condemns *all* whites). As a pedant fool, or foolish wise man, his function is reversed and he provides an opportunity for Simple to challenge unwarranted idealism or unrealistic assessments of the Negro's status in America.[10] When Boyd pontificates on the significance of cold climate to racial accomplishment, arguing that the American Negro has advanced beyond other blacks because "Cold weather makes you get up and go, gives you life, vim, vigor, vitality," Simple is set up to put this theory to rest by noting, "It does not give me anything but a cold" ("Wife," p. 198).

15. One technique that is common to most of the American wise-fool satirists is the employment of dialect.[11] The dialect, usually clearly indicative of lower-class status, identifies the character as the wise fool, as well as providing opportunities for humor and satiric

elsewhere in his writing. In fact in the "Simple" stories Simple more frequently speaks for Hughes, against "intellectual" objections from Boyd, who is, at times, the *target* of the criticism.

[10] As Arthur P. Davis assesses it, the Simple/Boyd relationship has more significant and subtle dimensions than that of a purely literary device of conflict-generating contrast. "The clash and interplay of these [Simple's "man-of-the-people" and Hughes's Negro intellectual] attitudes furnish much of the humor in Simple, but they also serve a deeper purpose; they point up and accentuate the two-level type of thinking which segregation tends to produce in all Negroes" (p. 22).

[11] Richard Bridgman, in his book *The Colloquial Style in America* (New York, 1966), provides some brief but useful comments concerning the use of dialect by nineteenth century wise-fool humorists (pp. 52–57).

comment.[12] In addition to its accuracy in reflecting the grammar and speech patterns of the lower class Harlemite, Simple's dialect is marked by puns, malapropisms, *double entendres,* and other types of wordplay. One of the better puns in Simple's canon is a double pun on the name "Butts," in a letter to a Negro "leader" of that name. The letter has been prompted by Dr. Butts's assertion that America is the best country in the world for blacks, and that things are getting better all the time. Simple responds: "Dr. Butts, I am glad to read that you writ an article in *The New York,* but also *sometime* I wish you would write one in the colored papers and let me know how to get out from behind all these *buts* that are staring me in the face. I know America is a great country *but*—and it is that but that has been keeping me where I is all these years" ("Wife," p. 227).

16. The malapropism is another convenient tool for Simple's work. He goes to "noteriety republicans" for legal aid ("Mind," p. 120), perhaps because of his habit of addressing judges as "Your Honery." When Boyd corrects Simple's reference to "Negro hysterians," Simple ignores the correction, and in his discussion of the subject makes the term appear appropriate ("Claim," p. 186). Simple continually capitalizes on words that sound alike, or can be distorted conveniently. When Boyd proclaims that white folks are currently "resolving to do better," Simple replies that "They have been *resolving* for two hundred years. I do not see how come they need to resolve any more. I say, they need to *solve*" ("Mind," p. 193). Similarly he answers the excuse that his poor treatment in a restaurant is the result of "untrained personnel" with the cynical comment, "person-hell!" ("Mind," p. 55). Another of his favorite tricks is to puncture the inflated posture of anyone who tries to badger him by using "ten dollar words." When his girlfriend Joyce tries to make him back down on his charge that she has been flirting with the barroom piano player by shouting "Don't insinuate," Simple responds, "Before you sin, *you* better wait" ("Mind," p. 80).

17. The wordplay in the "Simple" columns is both humorous and effective for the task of conveying Simple's point with no uncertainty. Boyd asks Simple if he intends to block the divorce action of his first wife, Isabel, by "cross-filing," and Simple answers, "I would not cross that wife of mine no kind of way, . . . with a file

[12] In addition to identifying Simple as a wise fool and providing opportunities for humor, Arthur P. Davis sees the dialect employed by Hughes as indicating a number of complex aspects of his personality, including his values, status, relationship to "in-group" thinking, and mood, or attitude toward a particular question (pp. 25–26).

nor otherwise" ("Mind," p. 228). As is often the case with "folk wisdom," the aphorism is employed by Simple to convey his message. His advice to young men concerning the dangers of romance is summed up as, "Mid-summer madness may bring winter sadness," and to young women, "If a chick wants to go straight, she shouldn't shake her tail gate." [13]

18.    In addition to dialect, Hughes employs vivid contrasts to illustrate his message. Often he contrasts Boyd's idealism with practical observations made by Simple. On several occasions Boyd generalizes concerning the improved status of the black man in America, and Simple replies by specifically describing his own status and lack of progress. *Boyd:* "How wonderful . . . that Negroes today are being rapidly integrated into every phase of American life from the Army and Navy to schools to industries—advancing, advancing." *Simple:* "I have not advanced one step. . . . Still the same old job, same old salary, same old kitchenette, same old Harlem and the same old color" ("Claim," p. 53).

19.    Another type of contrast juxtaposes a serious, tense point with a humorous punch line that eases the tension and helps make the argument less objectionable. After Simple lists the suffering to which whites would have to voluntarily subject themselves if they were to truly understand the plight of the Southern Negro, Boyd claims that if *he* were white he would never go so far in the cause of civil rights. Surprisingly Simple concurs, causing Boyd to triumph, "Then you would not be very good either." "No," said Simple, "but I would be white" ("Claim," pp. 31–32). A denunciation of the state of Mississippi in which the state's name is rendered acrostically as standing for such things as Murder, ignoramus, Satan, and other such harsh terms is softened when Simple gets to the last three letters: "After which I will double the P, as it is in the spelling. Excuse the expression, but right over Jackson, which is the state capital, I will P-P. . . . Now I come to the final letter which is I—I meaning *me*—who will spell as I fly, M-i-s-s-i-s-s—yes—I-P-P-i!" ("Claim," p. 166).

20.    If perhaps Simple tends to understate racial progress by insisting upon using his own status as the only yardstick (at that he overlooks his "progress" from boarding house to the kitchenette), he is as prone to overstate his woes in a most picturesque manner. The list of torments to which his feet have been subjected exhausts the reader almost as much as they must have Simple:

[13] These and others of Simple's sayings on women are collected in *The Book of Negro Humor*, p. 146.

These feet have stood on every rock from the Rock of Ages to 135th and Lenox. These feet have supported everything from a cotton bale to a hongry woman. These feet have walked ten thousand miles working for white folks and another ten thousand keeping up with colored. These feet have stood at altars, crap tables, free lunches, bars, graves, kitchen doors, betting windows, hospital clinics, WPA desks, social security railings, and in all kinds of lines from soup lines to the draft. If I just had four feet, I could have stood in more places longer. As it is I done wore out several hundred pairs of shoes, eighty-nine tennis shoes, twelve summer sandals, also six loafers. The socks that these feet have bought could build a knitting mill. The corns I've cut away would dull a German razor. The bunions I forgot would make you ache from now till Judgment Day. ("Mind," p. 5)

21.   Like his American predecessors in this mode, Hughes incorporates the tall tale into his wise fool's repertory. As James Emanuel notes, "The exaggerations of the tall tale, often heard in the animated exchanges in Negro barber shops and lounging places, seem a natural endowment of Simple's" (p. 159). Simple's flights into the realm of fantasy include imagining himself a Bunyanesque giant avenging segregation all over the world (South Africans are warned, "Apart your own hide!" ["Claim," p. 26]), a member of the Supreme Court, and a diplomat presiding over a summit meeting ("Sam," pp. 160–63). Simple conjures up a reversal of the traditional roles in the rural South, in which "Mammy Eastland" appeals to a paternalistic Simple for support of a "good" white church ("Sam," pp. 127–32). Perhaps the most intriguing of his fantastic schemes is a "pose-out" protest, in which Negroes all over the country will disrobe at the same prearranged time to shock Americans into a more decent treatment of its black citizens ("Sam," pp. 107–09). The plays on words, contrasts, and tall-tale situations are simultaneously entertaining and effective in Hughes's portrayal of the issues.

22.   There are two broad categories into which virtually all of the "Simple" sketches may be placed: race and women. Within these two categories Simple concerns himself with a number of topics including the pretensions of the Negro middle class, national political and economic policies, relationships between relatives, and the merits of urban life, among others; but he regularly relates his discourse on these matters to race or the battle of the sexes. A proud participant in the Harlem riots of 1943, Simple maintains a militant position toward questions of the injustices done to the black person in America. Boyd champions the N.A.A.C.P. approach of ". . . propaganda education, political action, and legal redress," but when Simple went

"looking for justice" he took two bricks ("Mind," pp. 167–68). In the "Simple" material, Hughes's position with regard to these two options appears to be that the former is preferable, but it is impossible to defeat the advocacy of the latter as long as one is unable to demonstrate the effectiveness of nonviolence.

23. One of Simple's frequently voiced complaints is that national politics, as reported in the press, is more concerned with international affairs than with the problems that he sees all around him in Harlem. He is also disturbed that naturalized citizens and second or third generation Americans are soon afforded full citizenship, whereas blacks whose ancestry is American from Colonial days are perpetually second-class citizens. Simple is skeptical of the sincerity of white liberals, and suspicious of Negroes who are less militant than he. He criticizes Boyd's inability to relate economic and political matters to the position of the black man in our society. For example Simple sees a parallel in the American bombing of Hiroshima and a beating he received from a white man as a boy in Virginia. Boyd considers this reasoning to be a *non sequitur,* but Simple argues that if you cannot see the connection "then you are not colored" ("Sam," pp. 121–23).

24. Simple also criticizes the conduct of "sassy" black clerks and waitresses, but he reserves most of the satire directed at members of his own race for Negro "Society" and Negro "Leaders." One of the pieces on this subject, "Banquet in Honor," is one of the best sustained examples of Hughes's satire writing ("Mind," pp. 83–90).[14] In this sketch Simple, at the insistence of his girlfriend Joyce, attends a dinner given by a Harlem club in honor of an aged black artist who was ignored by the Negro middle class when he needed, and was able to profit from, their support. Mrs. Sadie Maxwell-Reeves, the Harlem socialite that Hughes frequently uses to represent the pretensions of the black bourgeoisie, is the mistress of ceremony for the affair. She is described by Simple:

> She is built like a pyramid upside down anyhow. But her head was all done fresh and shining with a hair-rocker roached up high in front, and a advertised-in-*Ebony* snood down her back, also a small bunch of green feathers behind her ear and genuine diamonds on her hand. Man, she had bosom-glasses that pulled out and snapped back when she read her notes. But she did not need to read no notes, she were so full of her subject. (p. 86)

[14] One which closely rivals it is a non-"Simple" short story entitled "Professor," included in *Something in Common and Other Stories* (New York, 1963), pp. 136–43.

25. After such entertainment as the singing of "O Caro Nome" (which Simple reports as "O Carry Me Homey" and of which he remarks, "I don't see why culture can't be in English"), the speaker is introduced. His unusual banquet speech is Hughes's statement to the "genteel" Harlem critics who scored his treatment of "nitty gritty" literary subjects throughout his career:

> 'You think you are honoring me, ladies and gentlemen of the Athenyannis Arts Club, when you invited me here tonight? You are *not* honoring me a damn bit! I said, not a bit. . . . The way you could have honored me if you had wanted to, ladies and gentlemen, all these years, would have been to buy a piece of my music and play it, or a book of mine and read it, but you didn't. Else you could have booed off the screen a few of them Uncle Toms thereon and told the manager of the Hamilton you'd never come back to see another picture in his theatre until he put a story of mine in it, or some other decent hard-working Negro. But you didn't do no such thing. You didn't even buy one of my watercolors. You let me starve until I am mighty nigh blue-black in the face—and not one of you from Sugar Hill to Central Park ever offered me a pig's foot. (p. 87)

Naturally Simple is the only one at the banquet who appreciated this sort of speech, and his response of loud laughter embarrassed his fiancée terribly. He concludes his report of the evening by stating, "They wouldn't buy none of his Art when he could still enjoy the benefits. But me, I'd buy that old man a beer *any time*" (p. 90). Hughes also employs Simple to satirize the Negro slick magazines ("Claim," pp. 96–101), the move to the integrated suburbs of socially conscious blacks ("Claim," pp. 114–17), and similar aspects of the Negro middle class of which he disapproves.

26. Another popular target of Simple's wrath is Negro "leaders" who claim to speak for the black masses but who shun Harlem and similar ghettoes, and advise patience and hard work from their positions of prosperity, to the approval of white rather than black audiences. This is the theme of the above-mentioned "Letter to Dr. Butts," in which Simple tells the "spokesman," ". . . we have too many leaders now that nobody knows until they get from the white papers to the colored papers and from the colored papers to me who has never seen hair nor hide of you. Dear Dr. Butts, are you hiding from me—and leading me, too?" ("Wife," pp. 225–26). Simple accuses such leaders of being "Cellophane Bandannas," his term for "Uncle Toms" who mask their obsequious behavior behind a sophisticated, moderate facade ("Claim," pp. 126–30). He does, however, approve of Negro leaders who live among and truly represent their

constituencies. He says of Constance Baker Motley, then Borough President, "She looks like the Statue of Liberty to me" ("Sam," pp. 155–56).

27. Simple's relations with the opposite sex are complicated, amusing, and the subject of some of his more universal folk wisdom. "Women," he maintains, "is a sweet worriation." He qualifies his authority to make this observation by asserting

> I know womens. I've been married twice, and the sames as married more than once before, and between that. But from Isabel, my first, through Zarita, right on up to Joyce, I have never really won an argument yet. If a woman does not get the last word now, she will still be heard then. Oh, yes, a woman is not like a man. A man thinks the argument is over and done with. But no! A woman will not place a period.[15]

Some of the most entertaining of the Simple stories are those in which he matches wits with his shrewish landlady and her pampered dog, flirts with Zarita, a happy-go-lucky bar-girl, explains his way out of trouble with his exacting fiancée, Joyce, or retells the adventures of his troublesome cousin, Minnie.

28. In his autobiography, Mark Twain notes that many of the dialect humorists of the nineteenth century were forgotten soon after a brief span of popularity. He recalls ". . . a dozen other sparkling transients whose light shone for a time but has now, years ago, gone out." Twain's insight into this phenomenon is revealing:

> Why have they perished? Because they were merely humorists. Humorists of the "mere" sort cannot survive. Humor is only a fragrance, a decoration. Often it is merely an odd trick of speech and of spelling, as in the case of Ward and Billings and Nasby and the "Disbanded Volunteer," and presently the fashion passes and the fame along with it. There are those who say a novel should be a work of art solely and you must not preach in it, and you must not teach in it. That may be true as regards novels but it is not true as regards humor. Humor must not professedly teach, and it must not professedly preach, but it must do both if it would live forever. By forever I mean thirty years.[16]

By this criterion Langston Hughes's stories of Jesse B. Semple are good for their thirty years as humor, and perhaps even longer as poignant character studies. As sociological studies of Negro life they

---

[15] *The Book of Negro Humor*, pp. 137–38.
[16] Samuel L. Clemens, *The Autobiography of Mark Twain*, Charles Neider, ed. (New York, 1961), pp. 297–98.

are relevant, and as a part of the significant tradition of wise-fool social and political satire in America they are of interest to the student of literature. And they are still a source of amusement and insight to the general reader.

## WORDS

*meaning* 1. Define *sic* (par. 4), *nuance* (par. 5), *therapeutic* and *adversity* (par. 6), *didactic* (par. 8), *astute* (par. 10), *arbiter* (par. 13), *aphorism* (par. 17), *juxtaposes* and *acrostically* (par. 19), and *obsequious* (par. 26). 2. Explain the allusions to *Don Quixote* (par. 3), *Pagliacci* (par. 6), and *Bunyanesque giant* (par. 21).

*origin* 1. What is the relationship between *pontificates* (par. 14) and bridge building? 2. What is the origin of the word *malapropisms* (par. 15)?

## SENTENCES

*style* 1. One problem in research papers is the avoidance of unnecessary footnotes. How do the "short titles" of footnote 3 help to solve this problem? 2. How do quotations from *Thomas Jefferson* (par. 1) and from other critics (par. 4) help to explain and justify the content of this paper?

## PARAGRAPHS

*topic sentences* 1. What are the topic sentences of paragraphs 9 and 10? How is each of these paragraphs developed—by use of examples, by explanation, by comparison and contrast, or by extended definition? 2. How is the first sentence of paragraph 24 related to the last sentence of paragraph 25?

## CONTENT AND ORGANIZATION

*central ideas* 1. How does the author explain the seeming self-contradictions (oxymorons) of "wise fool" (par. 1) and "foolish wise man" (par. 14)? 2. Why is a malapropism "a convenient tool for Simple's work" (par. 16)? 3. List the subjects of Simple's criticisms (pars. 22–27). 4. What common assumptions of Simple's "folk wisdom" (par. 27) have been challenged by proponents of "women's liberation"?

## SUGGESTIONS FOR DISCUSSION

1. Read a book by Mark Twain and compare his humor with that of Langston Hughes. 2. Analyze the content and style of a humorous column or feature story from a newspaper. 3. Why is much humor con-

cerned with life's most serious concerns—sex, marriage, injustice, politics, and death?  4. Hughes sometimes uses Simple to satirize shortcomings of the Negro middle class. Write a paper ridiculing another social or occupational group that is guilty of thoughtlessness or hypocrisy. 5. Write a criticism of the depiction of a racial or cultural minority in television programs and motion pictures.

*Loren Eiseley*

# THE THEORY OF
# UNCONSCIOUS CREATION

1.  Two great geniuses of the nineteenth century, two men from widely distinct social worlds, yet of strangely similar cast of intelligence, have, by the vicissitudes of fortune, become posthumously involved in a stormy controversy among twentieth-century biologists. One was the poet, Samuel Taylor Coleridge, opium addict, creator of *The Rime of the Ancient Mariner* and the weird moonlit fragment *Christabel*. "For over a century," writes the critic Max Schulz, "the tradition has been that they [Coleridge's poems] defy analysis because the best of them are enchanted records of unearthly realms peopled by Mongol warriors, old navigators, albatrosses, and Lamia witchwomen. . . . " [1] Students of the subject have been until recently loth to perceive the conscious craftsman behind the dreamer. The tendency has been to accept "the sacred river," the sunless sea of dream as the primary source of Coleridge's inspiration. Out of these misty depths, according to entranced critics, were drawn in poetic ecstasy fragments of travelers' tales transmuted forever in the subconscious mind of the poet. The public appeal of this romantic interpretation of great poetry is tremendous. It flatters our imagination and our conception of the mysterious life of the literary artist.

2.  The other man, Charles Darwin, the equally noted discoverer of natural selection, has at first glance a different and scientific appearance. Yet his mind, too, was stuffed with the multitudinous lore of both incredibly wide reading and personal oceanic

---

[1] Max Schulz, *The Poetic Voices of Coleridge* (Detroit, 1963), p. 5.

THE THEORY OF UNCONSCIOUS CREATION:  Reprinted by permission from *Daedalus,* Journal of the American Academy of Arts and Sciences, Boston, Massachusetts, Volume 94, Number 3.

experience. He openly proclaimed himself a millionaire of odd and curious little facts. There floated in his vast memory the tortoises and lizards of islands under tropic suns. He had dug for fossil bones in Patagonia, and climbed Andean peaks in solitude. Navigators and albatrosses were part also of his experience. He, like Coleridge, had read insatiably.

3. But in his case the public imagination was, and is still, caught by the symbol of a great voyage, the voyage of the *Beagle*. After Darwin's book, *The Origin of Species,* was published in 1859 he wrote to the Reverend Baden Powell, "If I have taken anything from you, I assure you it has been unconsciously." [2] This was in response to a letter in which Powell had reproved Darwin for not referring to one of his works. Thus the legend of the unconscious, the role of the "sacred river," was destined to leave the realm of poetry and enter the field of science. The floating fragments from Darwin's sacred river need no longer be assigned place, name, or priority. They had become the property of genius, they had entered the dark domain of demonic creation. As it is in literature, where historic footnotes are not demanded of the poet, so now it was about to become in science. Charles Darwin was to be elevated beyond giving an account of even partial priority as that rule applied to other men.

4. Darwin's own excuse of the "unconscious" has been increasingly used in recent years by defenders of the great biologist in considering the problem of Darwin's meager attention to his predecessors. If Darwin "unconsciously" borrowed material without acknowledgment, some scholars imply that no blame can be attributed to him. Rather, they frown upon those historians of science who persist in probing beneath the insights of genius in order to seek the sources of their inspiration. Yet we must still ask, was the one man who should know where he got the idea of his famous theory unconscious of where he got it? Or did he consciously draw a veil over one predecessor in particular, rationalizing, perhaps, as he is known to have done on one occasion, when he implied that the man who successfully convinces the public of a new idea deserves all the credit which may accrue to him.[3]

5. The theory of the "unconscious" has been emphasized by Darwinian defenders particularly following the publication in 1959,

[2] Gavin de Beer, ed., "Some Unpublished Letters of Charles Darwin," *Notes and Records of the Royal Society of London,* Vol. 14, No. 1 (June 1959), p. 53.
[3] Nora Barlow, ed., *The Autobiography of Charles Darwin, 1809–1882* (London, 1958), p. 125.

in the *Proceedings of the American Philosophical Society,* of an article which explored the possible role played by Edward Blyth, a young British naturalist, in the formulation of the theory of natural selection.[4]

6. We now know that Blyth stated the basic tenets of the theory of natural selection in two articles in *The Magazine of Natural History* in the years 1835 and 1837.[5] We know also that Darwin footnoted Blyth copiously in his books on many subjects, but never on natural selection, although it is clear from the nature of his reading and interior evidence from his notebooks and early essays, as well as one letter, that he was familiar with the magazine containing these important articles. The recent publication of *Darwin's Notebooks on Transmutation of Species,*[6] in 1960, showed clearly that Darwin was aware of Blyth's writings on natural selection. In the *Second Notebook,*[7] never intended for publication, reference is made to the article of 1837 in which Blyth writes, after having earlier in 1835 described the conservative effects of natural selection: "May not, then, a large proportion of what are considered species have descended from a common parentage?"[8]

7. Several who are unwilling to credit Blyth with influencing Darwin refuse to quote this line of 1837—the very year that Darwin conceived of the role of natural selection in evolution. Sir Gavin de Beer, who edited the Notebooks, footnotes Blyth's article as mentioned by Darwin in the *Second Notebook,* but fails to point out its obvious import. In a brief discussion of Blyth in the Introduction to the *First Notebook* he at first remarks that Darwin probably owed nothing to Blyth so far as the construction of his theory is con-

[4] Loren Eiseley, "Charles Darwin, Edward Blyth, and the Theory of Natural Selection," *Proceedings of the American Philosophical Society,* Vol. 103, No. 1 (February 1959), pp. 94–158.

[5] Edward Blyth, "An Attempt to classify the 'Varieties' of Animals, with Observations on the marked Seasonal and other Changes which naturally take place in various British Species, and which do not constitute Varieties," *The Magazine of Natural History,* Vol. 8 (1835), pp. 40–53: Art. IV. "On the Psychological Distinctions between Man and all other Animals; and the consequent Diversity of Human Influence over the inferior Ranks of Creation, from any mutual and reciprocal Influence exercised among the Latter," *ibid.,* Vol. 1 (n.s.) (1837), pp. 1–9: Art. I; pp. 77–85: Art. IV; pp. 131–41: Art. VI.

[6] De Beer, ed., "Darwin's Notebooks on Transmutation of Species," *Bulletin of the British Museum (Natural History),* Historical Series, Vol. 2, Nos. 2–5 (1960).

[7] *Ibid., Second Notebook,* Part II, Vol. II, No. 3, p. 106.

[8] Blyth, "On Psychological Distinctions," etc. (1837), p. 147: Art. VI. All references to articles by Edward Blyth in this paper will refer to page numbers as reprinted in *Proceedings of the American Philosophical Society,* Vol. 103, No. 1 (February 1959).

cerned.[9] He confesses, however, in the same paragraph, that "there is nothing improbable in his [Darwin's] having copied some from Blyth." He then cautiously concedes that "Darwin (and others) may have been wrong in thinking that he owed him [Blyth] or them nothing on this score." Four years later, in 1964, in his biography of Darwin, de Beer has again retreated from a direct confrontation of the full nature of Blyth's speculations when he says that although Blyth "had been playing with the very tools that Darwin so successfully used, it is difficult to see that Darwin was indebted to him, for his conclusions were the exact negation of what Darwin was trying to prove." [10] Concerning this statement it is of interest to note that George Wald, writing on "Innovation in Biology," in the *Scientific American,* remarks that "all great ideas come in pairs, the one the negation of the other, and both containing elements of truth." [11] Edward Blyth, as we have seen, in a moment of insight glimpsed momentarily both faces of Natural Selection. It was enough to give an astute mind like Darwin's the clue that he was seeking. Today it is well recognized that this principle is composed of both creative and conservative aspects. In nature, natural selection maintains the species as well as promoting slow and tested change at the same time.

8. Theodosius Dobzhansky, who uses the "unconscious" theory to explain Darwin's failure to acknowledge his predecessors, accepts the fact that "the fundamental premises of the theory of natural selection are contained in Blyth's essays," [12] but maintains that Darwin might have been mistaken about the sources of some of his ideas, and his thinking process might not have been wholly free of subconscious components.[13] Dobzhansky's theory of the "subconscious components" as the probable cause of Darwin's omission of credit to Edward Blyth should be considered carefully because it gives us an opportunity to explore one interpretation of the creative processes of genius.[14]

[9] De Beer, Introduction to *First Notebook,* Part I, Vol. II, No. 2, p. 36.
[10] De Beer, *Charles Darwin: Evolution by Natural Selection* (New York, 1964), p. 102.
[11] George Wald, "Innovation in Biology," *Scientific American,* Vol. 199, No. 3 (September 1958), p. 100.
[12] Theodosius Dobzhansky, "Blyth, Darwin, and Natural Selection," *The American Naturalist,* Vol. 93, No. 870 (May–June 1959), p. 204.
[13] *Ibid.,* p. 205.
[14] When Dr. Dobzhansky proposed his theory in *The American Naturalist* he very graciously asked me if I would care to make a response. At the time, travel and administrative duties prevented me from accepting Dr. Dobzhansky's invitation. The present article exploring this subject was really stimulated by his generosity, and I am very glad to acknowledge this fact.

9.   "Is the origin of every idea which crosses our minds always clear to us?" [15] Dobzhansky asks. Nobody, he contends, has a perfect memory and is always aware of his thinking processes.

> Probably everyone is familiar with the feeling that an idea which arises in one's mind, or a phrase which emerges from one's pen, have been met with somewhere, but one cannot recall just where or when. This feeling is sometimes justified but perhaps more often illusory. Might not even Darwin have been mistaken about the sources of some of his ideas? [16]

10.   It is the mystery of the creative process in the mind of genius which the discovery of Edward Blyth forces us to face, argues Dobzhansky. In Darwin's defense, Dobzhansky cites John Livingston Lowes' well-known study of Coleridge, *The Road to Xanadu*. Dobzhansky feels, as did Lowes, that "it is not illegitimate to compare the creative processes of a poet, Coleridge, with those of a scientist, Darwin." [17] Since the creative work of a poet and of a scientist are not fundamentally different,[18] Dobzhansky maintains that Darwin had little more awareness of the soil in which his theories grew than did Coleridge of the sources of his poetry. Unfortunately for Dobzhansky's reliance upon Lowes' interpretation of Coleridge, however, later critics no longer see the great romantic poet as purely an inspired somnambulist. In the first volume of Kathleen Coburn's edition of Coleridge's notebooks, says Schulz, "the notations of ideas and images for future poems recorded in them reveal a mind knowing where it is going and moving purposefully toward that goal." [19]

11.   Could Darwin have been unaware of the fact that he had read and utilized the articles written by Edward Blyth on the subject which he was later to claim completely as his own discovery? Lowes has written:

> The "deep well of unconscious cerebration" underlies your consciousness and mine, but in the case of genius its waters are possessed of a peculiar potency. Images and impressions converge and blend even in the sleepy drench of our forgetful pools. But the inscrutable energy of genius which we call creative owes its secret virtue at least in part to the enhanced and almost incredible facility

[15] Dobzhansky, p. 205.
[16] *Ibid.*
[17] *Ibid.*, p. 206.
[18] There is a failure here, however, to distinguish between creativity in the arts and sciences and its traditional modes of expression. The poet is not called upon to footnote or to give the history of his ideas. The scientist by tradition honors and cites the significance of his precursors.
[19] Schulz, p. 7.

with which in the wonder-working depths of the unconscious the fragments which sink incessantly below the surface fuse and assimilate and coalesce. The depths are peopled to start out with (and this is fundamental) by conscious intellectual activity, keyed, it may be, as in Coleridge's intense and exigent reading, to the highest pitch. Moreover (and this crucially important consideration will occupy us in due time), it is again conscious energy, now of another and loftier type, which later drags the deeps for their submerged treasure, and moulds the bewildering chaos into unity. But interposed between consciousness and consciousness is the well. And therein resides the peculiar significance of such a phantasmagoria as lies before us in the [Coleridge's] Note Book, the seemingly meaningless jumble of which we have tried to grasp.[20]

12. In striking contrast to this view, however, Werner W Beyer, another Coleridge authority, emphasizes the role of the conscious and deliberate in the creative process. Writing in *The Enchanted Forest,* which the author says begins where *The Road to Xanadu* ended, Beyer states that Lowes' stress upon the importance of the unconscious "has given such wide currency to the concept of unconscious metamorphosis that its conscious counterpart has threatened to be ignored." [21] Beyer presents interesting evidence of Coleridge's use in his poetry of a crucial source until now undetected. This deals with the part C. M. Wieland's tale *Oberon,* translated by Coleridge around November 20, 1797, seems to have played in the genesis of *The Wanderings of Cain, The Rime of the Ancient Mariner, Christabel,* and *Kubla Khan.* Beyer has no doubt that Coleridge was aware of Wieland's poetry as a source of his own, since Coleridge translated the tale, and wrote this fact in a letter to Joseph Cottle.[22] Lowes, himself, in a letter of November 24, 1939, wrote to Beyer concerning this newly produced evidence:

> Why, in view of the fact that on p. 243 of *The Road to Xanadu* I referred to S.T.C.'s flat statement that he was translating *Oberon,* I didn't go farther, I can't, to save my soul, imagine! [23]

13. It was *conscious* judgment, Beyer insists, that led Coleridge to his discoveries of the potentialities of *Oberon.* More than Lowes suspected,

> . . . conscious and unconscious appear to have collaborated and interpenetrated in the genesis of the fabulous ballad [*Rime*]. *As*

[20] John Livingston Lowes, *The Road to Xanadu* (Boston, 1927), pp. 59–60.
[21] Werner W. Beyer, *The Enchanted Forest* (New York, 1963), p. 113.
[22] *Ibid.,* p. 49.
[23] *Ibid.,* p. 47.

*others have thought, the deliberate, purposive, and volitional appear
to have played a far greater role in the complex process of discovering and envisioning, assimulating and transforming the multifarious
stuff for its fabric and form. . . . Oberon makes it clear, I think,
that the genesis of the* Ancient Mariner, *which it generously abetted,
was not so largely a product of the subconscious as Lowes assumed.*[24]
(Italics mine, L. E.)

14. Beyer also cites another Coleridge authority, R. C. Bald,
who,

> . . . after a study of the later notebooks [of Coleridge], similarly
> stressed what Lowes had seemed to minimize; the *conscious* element
> in the creative process, the deliberateness of Coleridge's reading, for
> purposes of poetry, and the recency of some of it which therefore
> could not have been long submerged in the subconscious. . . .[25]

15. Since it has been noted that the creative processes of a
poet (Coleridge) may be compared to the creative processes of a
scientist (Darwin), it is impossible not to see the parallel between
these two geniuses in their working processes. *Oberon,* Beyer remarks, appears to have provided a scenario that Coleridge found

> . . . adaptable, kindling, and of high "symbolic potential." . . . It
> seems to have provided many materials, too, but, more important, to
> have served as a flexible form or matrix to help organize the richly
> diverse ingredients drawn from innumerable other sources and
> experience previously unrelated. And the conscious guidance it
> evidently afforded appears to put a somewhat different complexion
> on the story of the genesis of the great ballad, and at the same time
> to shed new light on various obscure passages.[26]

16. Coleridge once made the remark that men are caterpillars,
very few of whom succeed in successfully transmuting themselves into
butterflies. To introduce a bit of modern knowledge, one might observe that the caterpillar possesses glands in its head which at the
proper moment assist him to make that beautiful transformation. In
the case of men, even brilliant men, some outside incident, some
catalytic agent concealed in the environment, may be the initiator
of the transformation we call "creativity" or "genius." The man must
be receptive, his mind afloat perhaps with the random forms which
contain an unevolved future. It is then that the hidden key to the

---

[24] *Ibid.,* p. 113.
[25] *Ibid.,* p. 66, citing R. C. Bald, "Coleridge and *The Ancient Mariner,"
Nineteenth-century Studies* (Ithaca, N.Y., 1940).
[26] *Ibid.,* p. 75.

locked secret must be found. Otherwise the potential inspiration may drift past unrecognized into oblivion.

17. As *Oberon* was such a stimulus, a scenario for Coleridge's great poems, Blyth's articles on natural selection were conceivably Darwin's scenario, containing as they did the full series of stepping stones over which, as I have elsewhere pointed out, Darwin passed on his way into the new world of organic novelty. Lowes remarked as much of Coleridge:

> [In 1797] . . . a vast concourse of images was hovering in the background of Coleridge's brain, waiting for the formative conception which should strike through their confusion, and marshal them into clarity and order.[27]

18. In October or November, says Beyer, "the young poet-in-waiting discovered *Oberon,* and speedily began translating its teeming kaleidoscopic scenes—scenes which were *as if made for that service.*" [28] (Beyer's italics.) Coleridge may be compared to the young scientist Darwin, home from his voyage, freshly impressed with new lands and unknown creatures. Darwin suspected the reality of life's transformations, but he remained without a satisfactory mechanism to show how organisms were actually adapted to fit diverse environments.

19. Darwin wrote in his *Autobiography,* "Nor did I ever intermit collecting facts bearing on the origin of species; and I could sometimes do this when I could do nothing else from illness." [29] Then, said Darwin, he read by chance the work of Thomas Malthus in October 1838, and claimed to see in Malthus' work the key to natural selection in the animal world. It is, however, genuinely possible to conceive that it was the work of Blyth which Darwin, the scientist-in-waiting, read. Here was material which was, in the words of Beyer spoken in reference to Coleridge, "as if made for that service."

20. In the case of Coleridge, there exists a written admission that he was translating Wieland's *Oberon.* In the case of Charles Darwin, although he at no time mentioned Edward Blyth's ideas on natural selection,[30] interior evidence such as I produced in 1959 and which also appears in Darwin's *Second Notebook on Transmutation of Species* shows that he was fully aware of the papers which contained these ideas.

[27] Lowes, p. 228.
[28] Beyer, p. 186.
[29] Barlow, *Autobiography,* p. 99.
[30] He was able, however, to refer to everything else about Blyth's work in detail.

21. Fortunately Dr. Gerald Henderson of Brooklyn College has kindly allowed me to utilize additional evidence from his own recent unpublished investigations at the Cambridge University Library. Darwin's personal volume of *The Magazine of Natural History* of 1837 reveals annotations on Blyth's paper in Darwin's own hand. Moreover, a set of Darwin's page reminders which include Blyth's paper has been pinned to the inside of the back page. I will not encroach further upon Dr. Henderson's researches except to reiterate that Darwin knew and studied the 1837 paper he was never to mention in print. The volume at Cambridge is a presentation copy given to Darwin by Edward Charlesworth, its then editor.

22. Coleridge himself said: "Though [my mind] perceives the *difference* of things, yet [it] is eternally pursuing the likenesses, or, rather, that which is common [between them]." [31] The following lines were written concerning Coleridge. They could also have been written about Charles Darwin:

> We have to do, in a word, with one of the most extraordinary memories of which there is record, stored with the spoils of an omnivorous reading, and endowed into the bargain with an almost uncanny power of association.[32]

23. J. B. Beer adds:

> . . . from sources so widely separated in space and time, Coleridge had often elicited an image or a phrase which was infinitely richer than the sum of its source.[33]

24. Coleridge, far from defending the bathos of unconscious discovery, remarked with surprising practicality even in the midst of a commentary on sleep: "O then what visions have I had, what dreams—the Bark, the Sea . . . Stuff of Sleep & Dreams, & *yet my Reason at the Rudder*." [34] (Italics mine, L. E.) He lists sensations, items of interest in his notebooks, just as does Darwin, but this is the stuff of poetry, not poetry itself, just as Darwin's associations of ideas and lists of sources are the stuff of science but not the completed act of reason.

25. As Professor Schulz has indicated, Coleridge was not engaged in séance writing. Neither, we might add, was Darwin. In his *Biographia Literaria* Coleridge remarks of poetic endeavor that much

[31] S. T. Coleridge, *Anima Poetae,* ed. by E. H. Coleridge (London, 1895), pp. 87–88.
[32] Lowes, p. 43.
[33] J. B. Beer, *Coleridge the Visionary* (New York: Collier Books, 1962), p. 185.
[34] S. T. Coleridge, Notebook XVI, 6–13 December 1803.

may be gleaned from travels, books, natural history, and that all may be acquired as part of the writer's trade but that these cannot substitute for the ear of genius. He does not forget Lamb's dictum that "the true poet dreams being awake." [35] The artist dominates his subject.

26. Similarly it was from no "sunless sea" of memoryless dream that Darwin drew his own illumination. It was more like being led across the stepping stones of a brook into an enchanted land from which the first intruder, Edward Blyth, had leaped safely back to "reality." Darwin, by contrast, a genius like Coleridge with "Reason at the Rudder," grasped immediately that he had come upon the long sought magic which would bring order amongst all his idle facts and relate them in a rational pattern. He saw a vision for which he was prepared, but which he might never have glimpsed save for his perusal of Edward Blyth. The weary world traveler had had to come all the way back to London to find his secret in an unread magazine.

27. The widespread popularity of the "unconscious" theory concerning Charles Darwin can readily be explained by the fact that a cult of hero worship has developed about the great biologist, such as frequently happens to a prominent innovator in any field.[36] Darlington, the British geneticist, has commented ironically: "Among scientists there is a natural feeling that one of the greatest of our figures should not be dissected, at least by one of us." [37] In the face of evidence that Darwin made unacknowledged use of material from Blyth, the theory of the unconscious is the easiest, most polite way of evading the exploration of a delicate subject. Numerous naturalists who would never treat contemporaries so gently under similar circumstances are eager to make a "sleep walker" of a scientist whose letters and notes are models of persistent conscious inquiry upon a great range of subject matter.

28. George Gaylord Simpson, referring to Darwin's statement in his autobiography that he "never happened to come across a single one [naturalist] who seemed to doubt about the permanence of spe-

---

[35] Schulz, p. 104, citing Lamb.
[36] A parallel is seen in the case of Coleridge. A suggestion of plagiarism made by De Quincey concerning his friend Coleridge brought several critical replies. De Quincey, says John Metcalf, was accused of "bad taste, not to say treachery." One Coleridge enthusiast even declared that "One might as well . . . accuse the bee of theft for gathering treasures from many flowers." Sara Coleridge, while admitting her father's plagiarism, pleaded that "if he took, he gave." (See John Metcalf, *De Quincey: A Portrait* [New York, 1963], p. 115.)
[37] C. D. Darlington, *Darwin's Place in History* (Oxford, 1959), p. 57.

cies," [38] and Darwin's belief that he owed no debt to his predecessors, said: "These are extraordinary statements. They cannot be literally true, yet Darwin cannot be consciously lying, and he may therefore be judged unconsciously misleading, naive, forgetful, or all three." [39]

29. Nora Barlow has also used the "unconscious" theory to explain her grandfather's denial that the subject of evolution was in the air. Doubtless Darwin's isolation at Down kept him from being aware of opinions from workers in other fields than his own, said Lady Barlow, "so that he unconsciously overlooked indications that belief in the permanence of species was waning." [40] Nevertheless some of the very journals he consulted contained references to the evolutionary hypothesis.

30. As opposed to the theory of the unconscious, it strikes one that Darwin was, in general, a keenly alert, conscious thinker, and he was so characterized by his associate, Thomas Huxley.[41] It is strange that in Darwin's *The Descent of Man* and *Variation of Animals and Plants Under Domestication* [42] all factual material drawn from Blyth was carefully listed but the two papers of Blyth concerning natural selection should be quietly ignored. It is difficult to accept this as mere coincidence. In *Variation* a footnote refers to the same volume of *The Magazine of Natural History* of 1835 in which Blyth's first paper on natural selection appeared.[43] Also a footnote in *Variation* states: "Mr. Blyth has freely communicated to me his stores of knowledge on this and all other related subjects," [44] a somewhat cryptic and unenlightening statement. There is no possibility of doubt that Darwin used and studied *The Magazine of Natural History* in which Blyth's papers appeared.

31. Another odd circumstance has recently been brought to light by Gavin de Beer, even though he has refrained from any comment as to its potential significance. I refer to the recent disclosure that a number of pages are missing from Darwin's *First Notebook on*

[38] Barlow, *Autobiography*, p. 124.
[39] George Gaylord Simpson, review of *The Autobiography of Charles Darwin, 1809–1882*, ed. by Nora Barlow, *Scientific American*, Vol. 199, No. 2 (August 1958), p. 119.
[40] Barlow, *Autobiography*, p. 153.
[41] Leonard Huxley, ed., *Life and Letters of Thomas Henry Huxley* (2 vols.; New York, 1902), Vol. II, p. 42.
[42] Material for *Variation* was drawn from Darwin's original "big book" of the *Origin*.
[43] Charles Darwin, *Variation of Animals and Plants Under Domestication*, 1st authorized American edition, 2 vols. (New York, 1868), Vol. I, pp. 335–36, n. 8.
[44] *Ibid.*, Vol. I, p. 164, n. 1.

*Transmutation of Species.* The great importance of the *First Note-book* in tracing Darwin's early thought has been stressed by de Beer.[45] Yet fifty pages are missing from this *Notebook,* in which Darwin wrote on the first page: "All useful pages cut out. Dec. 7/1856/. (and again looked through April 21, 1873)."[46] Nothing was said about destroying the notes. As his son, Francis Darwin, pointed out in reminiscences of his father, Charles Darwin "felt the value of his notes, and had a horror of their destruction by fire. I remember, when some alarm of fire had happened, his begging me to be especially careful, adding very earnestly, that the rest of his life would be miserable if his notes and books were to be destroyed."[47]

32.   De Beer, who reported in 1960 on these missing pages, said they had been searched for unsuccessfully in the Cambridge University Library, at Down House and the Royal College of Surgeons, and in the British Museum of Natural History. "The nature of their contents can only be surmised after a close study of the two hundred and thirty pages that remain," de Beer remarked, "and an estimate can be made of what is missing from the information and the argument."[48] Although there are some pages missing from the other *Notebooks,* it is those from the *First Notebook* that would seem to have the most bearing upon the origin of Darwin's theory, since it was begun in July 1837, before the date when he said he received his inspiration from Malthus. To reiterate my own words, I believe it significant that "Darwin opened his first notebook on the 'species question' in 1837. In January of that year Edward Blyth ventured the beginning of a second paper in which there is comment upon the principle of natural selection."[49] This comment, as we have seen, goes considerably beyond Blyth's first statement of 1835. It introduces, if briefly, the possibility of organic change. The name and work of Edward Blyth are not noted in the existing portion of the *First Notebook,* although they do appear in the *Second.*

33.   "The idea of natural selection, so far as can be seen from the extant portions of the *Notebooks,* seems to have occurred to Darwin as a combination of the effects on him of the facts of variation, adaptation, and extinction,"[50] observed de Beer. Actually the missing fifty pages could have contained a great deal of information ex-

---

[45] De Beer, Introduction to *First Notebook,* p. 26.
[46] De Beer, *First Notebook,* p. 41.
[47] Francis Darwin, ed., *The Life and Letters of Charles Darwin,* 2 vols. (New York, 1959), Vol. I, p. 129.
[48] De Beer, Introduction, *First Notebook,* p. 26.
[49] Eiseley, p. 99.
[50] De Beer, Introduction to *Third Notebook,* Part III, Vol. II, No. 4, p. 126.

tending to Blyth's own views on these subjects. De Beer has avoided the suggestion that this fragmentary document may have contained more detailed references to Blyth's works. Since these pages compose the first part of the diary, their disappearance, taken with other evidence, cannot fail to hint of a genuinely "missing link" in the story of Natural Selection.

34. Much has been made by some of Darwin's defenders of his poor memory, though others have maintained it was prodigious. Huxley, who certainly knew him well, contended that Darwin had "a great memory." [51] Darwin himself remarked of his memory, that it "suffices to make me cautious by vaguely telling me that I have observed or read something opposed to the conclusion which I am drawing, or on the other hand in favour of it; *and after a time I can generally recollect where to search for my authority.*" [52] (Italics mine, L. E.)

35. It is also true, however, that Darwin did not have to depend upon memory, as he was a remarkably methodical man in his work. In discussing his work habits he mentioned the fact that since in several of his books he had used extensively facts observed by others, he kept

> from thirty to forty large portfolios, in cabinets with labelled shelves, into which I can at once put a detached reference or memorandum. I have bought many books, and at their ends I make an index of all the facts that concern my work; or, if the book is not my own, write out a separate abstract, and of such abstracts I have a large drawer full. Before beginning on any subject I look to all the short indexes and make a general and classified index, and by taking the one or more proper portfolios I have all the information collected during my life ready for use.[53]

36. One of Darwin's own statements, to which I have previously referred, strikes one as remarkably illuminating. In regard to an incidental matter of priority upon another biological matter which had occupied his attention briefly, he wrote in his autobiography: "It is clear that I failed to impress my readers; and he who succeeds in doing so deserves, in my opinion, all the credit." [54]

37. This statement is curiously revelatory to the perceptive student of character. There is involved in it a strange indifference to historical priority by a man in actuality highly sensitive on this score

[51] Huxley, Vol. II, p. 42.
[52] Darwin, *Life and Letters,* Vol. I, p. 82.
[53] *Ibid.,* p. 80.
[54] Barlow, *Autobiography,* p. 125.

so far as his own great generalization was concerned. Was Charles Darwin engaged in psychologically justifying a philosophy which permitted him to dismiss forerunners from whom he had drawn inspiration—men like his friend, "poor Blyth," [55] who "failed to impress" and therefore deserved no recognition from the world? One is forced to reflect upon this possibility, which has even been seized upon and brought forward by later writers as a justification of Darwin's attitude toward his predecessors.

38. There will always be an ineluctable mystery concerning the origin of the theory of Natural Selection, just as there will always be a shadowy web surrounding the real Charles Darwin, a web unseen but as real as the black cape in which we see him enveloped in a photograph taken of him on the verandah at Down at the age of seventy-two. One of Darwin's most ardent supporters, George Gaylord Simpson, states with perceptive acuteness:

> The mystery persists. The man is not really explained, his inner adventures are not fully revealed in his own autobiography, in the family biography by Francis Darwin, or in the many other biographical sketches and books. There will always be something hidden, as there is in every life. . . .[56]

39. It seems to be an inescapable conclusion that the mystery lies concealed in the remarkable similarity between Coleridge, the "library cormorant," as he chose to describe himself, and Darwin, a similar cormorant observer of nature and of nature recorded in books. Each man had his catalyzer and both were reticent enough that it has taken over a century to find the catalyzer.

WORDS

*meaning*   1. What is an *inspired somnambulist* (par. 10)?   2. Is the author using the word *scenario* (pars. 15 and 17) in our usual sense? If not, what does he mean by it?   3. Define *symbolic potential* (par. 15), *bathos* (par. 24), *séance writing* (par. 25), and *ineluctable* (par. 38).   4. Does the author use a synonym for *ineluctable* in his final paragraph?

*connotation*   1. In paragraph 1, the author speaks of Coleridge's *Christabel* as a *weird moonlit fragment.* How can a poem, finished or unfinished, be *moonlit*? Reading the poem may help with the answer.   2. How does the word *entranced* in paragraph 1 connect the critics it describes with the Coleridge they describe?

[55] Darwin, *Life and Letters,* Vol. II, p. 109.
[56] Simpson, p. 122.

## SENTENCES

*style*   What is a *cliché?* Find two *clichés* in the first sentence of this essay. Do they help interest you in what might otherwise seem rather grim subject matter, make you feel at home, as it were? Or is the author just being rather lazy?

*rhetorical devices*   1. What figure of speech is *sunless sea of dream* (par. 1)? Why *sunless?* Think of a similar figure to describe the opposite state of mind.   2. The phrase *dark domain of demonic creation* (par. 3) is heavily alliterative. What is alliteration? Although it is usually thought of as belonging to the province of poetry and poetic prose, here it is applied to Darwin. Why? Is it appropriate to scientific discourse?   3. What is a paradox? Is there one in the quotation from George Wald in paragraph 7? Explain.   4. In paragraph 16, there seems to be an implied metaphor in the word *afloat*. Is *afloat* consistent with the rest of the sentence? With the rest of the paragraph?   5. What is the rather elaborate figure of speech that constitutes the second sentence of paragraph 26 and is also referred to more briefly in paragraph 17? What is meant by *the new world of organic novelty,* also in paragraph 17?   6. Why is it ironic of the author to apply the phrase *"missing link"* at the end of paragraph 33 to the life of Charles Darwin? Why is it in quotation marks?

*variety*   The last two sentences of paragraph 25 state what is presumably the same idea in two ways. How do the statements differ? Do they in fact say the same thing? Discuss.

## CONTENT AND ORGANIZATION

*assumptions and implications*   The third sentence in paragraph 10 asserts that there is no fundamental difference between the work of a poet and of a scientist. Certainly there is a difference in the materials upon which the mind of each works. Describe the differences in these materials.

## SUGGESTIONS FOR DISCUSSION

1. This essay seems to imply that the only "fundamental" difference between the work of the poet and of the scientist is that the scientist is expected to document his sources and the poet is not (see footnote 18). Are there other and perhaps more important differences?   2. William Carlos Williams, one of the foremost American poets of the twentieth century, was also a practicing pediatrician during the fifty years in which he wrote his poetry. Discuss why a man of science and medicine, who has special knowledge of the biological "secrets" of life and death, might turn to poetry.

*part* **2**

# READINGS
# FOR DISCUSSION

# Criticism and Defense of Education

## Robert A. Nisbet

# THE UNIVERSITY HAD BETTER
# MIND ITS OWN BUSINESS

1.   The American university is in an exceedingly precarious position. The luster of even the most historic and distinguished of universities is fading rapidly. For the first time in the history of this country there is valid reason for wondering whether the university will survive. Alarmism may be the refuge of the timid, but any optimism at this time would be little more than euphoria. The university in America is in the most critical condition of its history.

2.   There are many reasons for this. Most of them arise directly from the university itself, especially from the profoundly dislocative changes during the past quarter century that have led to fragmentation of its authority in society and to near-dissolution of its internal dogma and community. No genuinely intellectual community can possibly exist save in terms of an aristocracy that consists of respect for the best ideas, scholars, and teachers, and the proper ranking of these in relation to ideas, teachers, and scholars of lesser worth. Nor can any genuinely intellectual community survive without a system of authority, a system made legitimate by its clearly perceived relation to the function or purpose around which community and aristocracy alike are built.

3.   The student-faculty insurrections of the 1960s did not break down academic authority. *It was the prior breakdown of authority that caused the insurrections.* This breakdown began in the 1950s, the result of profound economic and social changes that disrupted the

THE UNIVERSITY HAD BETTER MIND ITS OWN BUSINESS: Excerpted from *The Degradation of the Academic Dogma* by Robert Nisbet, © 1971 by Basic Books, Inc., Publishers, New York.

academic community and of a steadily rising internal politicization that fragmented traditional authority. In retrospect we can see that even if there had been no issues of Vietnam and of civil rights, no "malaise of student soul before technology," insurrections would surely have occurred in the 1960s. Everything we know about insurrectionary and delinquent behavior suggests that "reasons" can always be manufactured quickly by elites. What alone is sociologically crucial, however, is prior, extreme *liberalization and democratization of traditional authority.*

4.   Were it not for the degradation of the academic community there would be little cause for apprehension at the present time. The university has been under assault from the outside at other times in its history in America. Generally these assaults originated in politically conservative sectors of society, in American business, and in the fundamentalist parts of American religion. The university was under severe assault from the Right during the 1930s. Widespread economic misery sharpened these attacks. But then the university had a solid, tough core of resistance, formed by faculty members, administrators, students, and others who knew what the purpose of a university was, what it could rightly do.

5.   There was a general, if usually unstated, awareness by scholars of the privileged position of the university in American society; I say this with no desire to idealize that university and academic community. There was an awareness that the price for being able to engage in dispassionate scholarship and rigorous, honest teaching was a fairly high one.

6.   It was a kind of social contract. The academic community said in effect: if society will allow us the aristocratic pleasure of seeking knowledge for its own sake and then teaching this to our students, we will stay as far as possible out of politics, out of economic enterprise and, generally, out of the areas of society where partisan feelings are endemic and where passionate moralism is of the essence. And, allowing for occasional lapses, the social order generally agreed. The price was paid. To our shame it was the university that broke the contract beginning shortly after World War II.

7.   Our major weakness in the university at the moment is the nearly total lack of a sense of what the business of the university is, what its mission should be, what its distinctive contribution is to society. People will accept or put up with the variety of things the university does today just so long as there is some distinctive, motivating function that will seem uniquely important to its members, and

also to society in general Mere *number* of activities will not save the university from continuing degradation and eventual extinction.

8.   What is to be the university's future, assuming that there will be a future for the university after the present time of troubles has ended? Is it to be, as so many today announce, the capstone of the vast research establishment in the nation? This seems highly unlikely. Already there are dozens, even hundreds, of nonacademic organizations in existence, private and public, organized for the specific purpose of research and unhindered by any of the built-in liabilities along this line of the historic university. Is it to be superhumanitarian to society: dedicated at one and the same time to solving directly the ills of agriculture, labor, business, the urban complex, the ghetto, as well as foreign policy? The university's successes in such direct application of its resources in so many sectors of society at once have been far from notable. Is it to be benign therapist to the middle-class-sprung pains of youth and to youth's search for identity? After two decades of this life-adjustment type of education, especially in the liberal arts, youth on the campus would appear to be in worse position than it was before the rage of life adjustment began. Is it to be patron of all the arts? The best of the artists—today as in the times of Mozart, Beethoven, Marlowe, and Shakespeare—flourish in different contexts from those of academic curriculum and faculty. Is it to be the loyal revolutionary opposition, keeper of the moral conscience? Forget it.

9.   I suggest that the university's most feasible function, all things considered, is essentially what it has been for nearly a millennium now: *a setting for scholarly and scientific imagination continuously engaged in the joint labor of teaching and research in the learned disciplines.*

10.   No doubt such a conception will seem archaic, off the main line of history, even reactionary to many of those who hold other conceptions. But quite apart from the demonstrable infeasibility of these, why should the conception of the university as a setting for ideas, as a setting for both the discovery and the teaching of knowledge, seem any more archaic today than it did three or four decades ago? What, in a civilized society, could possibly be wrong with—or stagnant, archaic, or antiquarian about—the vision of an enclave in the social order whose principal purpose is to work creatively and critically with ideas through scholarship and teaching?

11.   Let us assume that the ideal of a community of ideas, undergirded by the primary functions of teaching and scholarship, is a worthy one for the university—probably the only worthy one. What then must be done to reestablish this academic community, to make it

once again as evocative and creative as we know it to have been at other times in its long history? I suggest the following:

12. *Repudiation of historicism.* This is vital, for already the air is full of proposals said to be rooted in the "clearly developing character of the contemporary university." No mistake can be greater than basing either proposal or analysis upon some imagined trajectory of development. The university's participation in politics, large-scale research, and humanitarianism is particularly pertinent here. Each of these involvements has a large number of advocates to whom it is "inevitable" or "inexorable." Failure to hook on to the locomotive of history results in being condemned to archaism, in being reactionary or nostalgic.

13. And of all dangers confronting the American university today the greatest is the assumption that some indwelling pattern of development exists and that planning for the university must be in accord with this pattern. Given this habit of mind, certain consequences follow. One sees the individual walking through university halls and saying: "This is traditional and must go; this is modern and must be lived with no matter how ugly; this is early future and must be built upon." The things found in a university are thus declared not simply good and bad, but inevitable or modern, on the one hand and, on the other, traditional or archaic. How preposterous!

14. One must indeed begin with existing realities. And clearly it is as fatuous to plan around something traditional *because* it is traditional as it is to plan around some figment of the imagination deemed to be the inevitable future. The first and indispensable step then in reform of the university is to abandon historicism. The sole objective of planning should be simply the highest possible combination of the desirable and the feasible.

15. *The restoration of authority.* Nothing else can be achieved until the university can create again a system of recognized authority such as it had until a decade or two ago. There was never anything perfect or puncture-proof in this authority. Universities are ever the scene of periodic eruptions of one kind or other. But the flouting of authority as supreme objective, the collapse of authority that we have seen for nearly ten years, is clearly insupportable from any point of view.

16. The first stage of this rehabilitation of legitimate authority lies in freeing the campus administration of the veto powers of faculty and students. During the past quarter of a century we have seen, as the result of such veto powers, the degradation of, first, department chairman, then dean, then president.

17. For a long time this was rationalized in terms of faculty participation in the university's system of authority. Granted, a good university is inconceivable apart from a substantial measure of reliance upon faculty judgment in those areas where it is uniquely informed and therefore vital. But faculty cannot create or run a university, and no great university has ever been established in this country without the leadership that flowed from strong administrators, particularly presidents.

18. It is not merely that Harvard, Berkeley, Chicago, Cornell, and other universities *became* distinguished under the leadership of strong presidents such as Charles William Eliot, Benjamin Ide Wheeler, William Rainey Harper, and Andrew Dickson White; it is that they succeeded in *remaining* great for long periods only as the result of this leadership. No administration can become effective if its every act is under the veto power of faculty committees.

19. There will be nothing easy in this restoration of authority to presidents and deans. On a score of grounds such restoration will be attacked as invasion of faculty and student democracy. But apart from such restoration I do not see how the university can do what it is supposed to do academically or how it can hope for the privileged enclave-like status that is the real structure of its freedom in society.

20. The faculty has the most to learn here. The wanton spreading of the view that the faculty must concern itself with every aspect of administrative life on the campus has led teachers and scholars into areas of governance and responsibility for which they are largely unfitted by temperament and by principal interest. One cannot devote himself effectively to teaching and scholarship if he must be forever sniffing out possible derelictions of those whose job it is to supervise plant and facilities, the social and moral behavior of students, athletics, relationships with trustees and alumni. Add to these the incessant rounds of faculty and committee meetings, not to mention conferences with students—whose capacity to be listened to is one of the great natural forces in the universe—and, all too clearly, the life of reason is made insecure at best.

21. Today the faculty's authority—in even those areas most vital to its and the university's existence—is at an all-time ebb, the result of its own mindless broadening into areas in which it has no qualification or competence.

22. Much nonsense is being spoken these days about student rights in governing the university. One even finds spokesmen for the view that students should sit on governing boards, faculty councils, the

committees concerned with appointment and promotion of faculty. All this is offered to a group that by its very nature is transitory in the university community. Students have a collective right to see their scholarly interests treated seriously; a right to make their views known to faculty and administration; a right to be spared the childhood-perpetuating restrictions and indignities that used to be heaped upon them *in loco parentis;* a right to speak out (even if not a divine right to be listened to incessantly); a right to participate as they see fit in activities outside the university. Above all, students have the right— I would say duty—to evaluate and assess as best they can, as effectively as they can, the quality of the teaching they are getting.

23. But it is utter nonsense to suppose that students should participate at high and crucial levels in the formal government of the university.

24. Without restoration of internal authority there is no possibility of arresting present encroachments upon the autonomy of the university by legislature, governor, Federal agency, and police. These encroachments are becoming as plain in the private universities as in the public ones. The chief consequence of breakdown of authority within an institution is invariably the rise of power, whether from within or outside. If members of the university faculty are unwilling to make a major distinction between the authority of president, dean, or department chairman on one hand, and the power of the legislature on the other, they are sure to get ever greater amounts of the latter.

25. *A clearing of the scene.* On a rough guess I should think at least 75 percent of all existing institutes, centers, bureaus, and projects in the academic sphere of the university should be phased out. There is no need to examine the toll taken by the higher capitalism in the university, or the results of the university's ill-advised effort to become adjunct government and superhumanitarian for American society. To these we must add the multitudinous faculty consultantships and other forms of moonlighting that augment high academic salaries. Despite a self-justifying myth to the contrary, these are rarely useful to scholarship and are almost always prejudicial to teaching.

26. It is not research, large or small, that should be phased out of the university. God forbid. Research, along with teaching, is what universities are all about. But it must be research-in-teaching and teaching-in-research of a scale that does not constantly threaten to dwarf the rest of the university. I am well aware that there is much research today that simply cannot be done except in vast, highly organized, bureaucratized centers. Very good. But let such research be done where it can be done more efficiently and without damage to the

academic community. And let those whose passions are directed toward this kind of research be free to move from the university.

27. Make no mistake about the powerful resistance that will be mobilized immediately against this clearing of the scene: by trustees, faculty, and graduate students, not to mention those in the great foundations, the Federal Government, and others whose vast funds have made the present jungle of institutes and projects possible. The cries of status pain, of income pain, of power pain will be awful to hear. It is inconceivable that the work of clearing the scene of the many forms of organized distraction could be done by any one university alone. My guess is that, given the very deep roots and very wide spread these organizations and activities have at the present time, only concerted action by the country's top twenty or thirty universities would bear substantial result. If this be conspiracy. . . .

28. *The depoliticization of the university.* The university today —private and public—is suffused by politics. The number of state and Federal laws and administrative regulations affecting university operation is at an all-time high. The campus has become a microcosm of the national and international scene in the number and intensity of ideological issues it has assimilated during the past two decades. And, finally, no one can miss the extent to which "participatory democracy" in university affairs has created a setting of instant and chronic politics that increasingly makes serious teaching and study impossible.

29. I have suggested that the earlier autonomy of the university in American society, its fairly substantial freedom to engage in teaching and research, was the consequence of a kind of social contract. Naturally, this social contract was never a perfect one. Threats to academic freedom existed from time to time. Both faculty and students participated in political, religious and other activities outside the university, though very moderately by present standards.

30. This did not imply that American professors were political eunuchs. Their isolation from politics has been grossly exaggerated by a present faculty generation that mistakes citizenship for unremitting political activism and that has shown itself willing to carry on this activism in the classroom, the learned-society meeting, and even in the pages of supposedly scholarly journals. From early times a sizable proportion of university faculty members and students engaged in politics and in humanitarian work. Still this social contract existed, and within it the university flourished.

31. Is it possible to resume such a contract today? Is depoliticization of the university possible? It is very hard to see much possibility of this. Once politicization becomes deeply ingrained, once Federal

and state governments are in the habit of penetrating any cultural or social sanctuary, once members of an organization begin to define their very constitutional status as citizens in terms of incessant political activism, and once the normal hierarchy of the academic community has been seriously weakened by spreading habits of participatory democracy, the likelihood of arresting these tendencies is not very great.

32. *The elevation of the function of teaching.* I should stress that I am referring to the *function* of teaching; that is, the activity itself. I do not refer to the largely futile efforts to persuade *individuals* —through annual awards, occasional salary increases, homilies, and such—that teaching is important when the entire weight of evidence in the contemporary university is that teaching is *not* important.

33. The function of teaching was degraded when the function of project- or grant- or institute-based research became the only genuinely valued function; when it became possible to win renown, high salary, and power in the university without more than a token appearance in the classroom and seminar. Of what avail is it today solemnly to remind young instructors of their "teaching obligations"; of what use is it for students to assess faculty performances? Of what incentive is it to offer annual teaching awards, when the evidence is so clear that through research alone one moves into the upper levels of success? Today the conspicuous abrogation of distinguished faculty members from the historic priority of teaching is without any question the chief source of both the bitterness among the students and the spreading cynicism about the purpose of the university among the nonacademic public.

34. How do we elevate the function of teaching to the point where it is at least as high as it was until World War II? Here again we are involved in special interests, accumulated privileges, and luxuries, as well as status values that make any thought of an easy answer absurd.

35. The first and most fundamental approach lies in what I called the clearing of the scene. There cannot be any honoring of teaching so long as the whole, vast structure of research-dominated institutes and centers towers above all else in the university. Add to this structure the diverse range of consulting, entrepreneurial, and humanitarian activities carried on by individual faculty members. Until this thick overgrowth is cleared it is difficult to see how the function of teaching can again become an honored one on the American campus.

36. The second requirement is the elevation once again of the

department—*in which teaching and research are joined indissolubly.* For, as recent history has demonstrated, once they are separated, invidious distinction is inevitable. The worst possible approach to the matter is the establishment of special schools or colleges in which "teaching, not research, will be made the sole function." Good students want to be where the intellectual action is. They do not want to be shunted off into areas that within a short time begin to resemble educationists' experiments at one extreme and an asylum for the retarded at the other.

37.   The third requirement is restoration of the kind of academic contract with faculty members that once was universal—one in which a full load of teaching is required irrespective of the research or professional status of the faculty member, a load that cannot be escaped through the easy outlets of joint appointments in institutes and centers, or through titles of "research professor," or through term or annual leaves of absence that so often make a mockery of allegedly continuing professorships.

38.   It may be—it will be—said that the effect of these measures can only be to diminish seriously the amount of research done in the university. I deny it. There is not a shred of evidence to support the view that this generation of scholars and scientists in the university is more creative, more productive in the valid sense of the term, than was the pre–World War II generation. At that time not all the research eminence imaginable freed a senior scholar from a load of teaching that was commonly three courses in the humanities and social sciences and two courses in the laboratory disciplines.

39.   One can live in an academic environment in which individual teaching takes its chances through the more or less normal processes of the free market. In an immense structure of tariffs, quotas, and monopolies in favor of research alone, teaching becomes degraded to the point where not all the individual awards, salary bonuses, and special asylums imaginable can be of any help.

40.   *A finite conception of the university.* This may well be the most difficult of all the requirements to meet, for somehow a nearly Faustian view of the university and its potential benefactions has developed in the American mind, academic and nonacademic. It is difficult to see how academic policy can operate any more effectively than foreign policy without some constraining sense of limits. It is no more possible for the university to serve all individual needs and tastes than it is possible for it to serve all social, economic, and political needs in society.

41.   The sound democratic conviction that all persons should

have reasonably equal access to the university has unfortunately become converted in recent decades to the dangerous conviction that the university must be incessantly reshaped to meet all possible interests and needs. This conviction is dangerous because of the inherent impossibility of ever fulfilling it.

42. If the limits of the university are to be as wide as those of modern society and culture then there is really no need for the university at all. The training necessary to fit individuals to jobs can be carried on within the precincts of occupation, profession, or social interest. So can the requisite search for knowledge that is necessary for technological survival.

43. It is simply impossible for the university to be anything and at the same time to be all things; to meet any personal needs and at the same time to meet all imaginable personal-psychological-social-cultural needs.

44. Can these requirements for the rehabilitation of the university be met during the next few years? Can any set of requirements designed to restore the university to the status it once had as an enclave for teaching and scholarship in the humanities and the sciences succeed? I hope so. Who could know?

45. Whether the university survives, how long it can survive—will be allowed to survive—in contemporary culture as the last vestige of medieval social organization, is impossible to foretell. I know only that while no society can do without knowledge and its diffusion to necessary groups and individuals—and this is, of course, notably the case in our technological age—it would be fatuous to assume that the university is indispensable. Great societies have existed before without universities in them; great sectors of contemporary society already show capacities for doing many of the things that only a few decades ago were done in the university alone.

46. There is no inherent, self-sustaining, irresistible majesty in the university; only the majesty that is conferred upon the university by a social order that, for whatever reason, has come to believe that there is something distinctive, something precious, something profoundly important in the university that is to be found nowhere else in society—not in factory, not in foundation, not in Government agency, not in the media, not in the church, not in mental-health clinic, nor anywhere else. And when this belief is allowed to erode, majesty erodes with it.

47. The greatness that is Harvard and the glory that is Berkeley can perish in but a few years, their presently celebrated degrees the objects of ridicule, their halls untenanted by any of the illustrious,

their mission degraded to the caring, the feeding, and the policing of the young. Not even the young, though, will long choose to stay at Harvard and Berkeley once the word gets around that history has passed the universities by, that what the universities have to offer is no longer valued deeply by either those inside the university or those outside. History is filled with degrees, titles, ranks, and diplomas that were once thought to be important but that became in due time—after their functional importance had disappeared—mere curiosities or relics.

48. For more than two decades now the leaders of the American university, from Berkeley to Harvard, have done their best to make the university "relevant" to society, nation, and world—through a calculated development of growths within the university for which the words "thicket" and "jungle" are at this moment scarcely extreme. And these same leaders—faculty and administrative—have somehow wound up having made the university seem more *irrelevant* at the present moment than it has ever seemed during the nearly ten centuries of its existence in the West. "Who needs it?" is a question one may confidently expect to hear in rising frequency from, not merely the students of the Left who shout it now, but from a great many members of American society. As the no doubt just, if cruel, punishment for having tried to be all things to all sectors of American society, the university has ended up ignominiously meaning little to anyone.

49. As matters now stand in the university we are like a religious monastery insisting upon all the affluence of a free-booting capitalism; an aristocracy masochistically tormenting itself with the slogans of revolutionary democracy; a community of pacifists insistent upon riding off in all directions at once to battle the enemy; an enclave of intellectual autonomy that is yet privileged to remake the entire social order through profligate humanitarianism or calculated revolution. We declare ourselves an intellectual elite, fully entitled to aristocratic tenure of status, and at the same time the microcosm of economic, political, social, and cultural activities that even the surrounding society often seems too small to contain. It is a lovely fantasy. So too must the feudal knight have once dreamed as he rode into the face of infantry and gunpowder. So, almost certainly, dreamed the guild master of the sixteenth century who was never more resplendent in his attire than just before his extinction.

50. If it be said that sheer volume of the capital represented by university plant and equipment should be sufficient to maintain

the university permanently in American society, I can only point to the equal volume of capital—relatively speaking—once expended on pyramids, coliseums, and cathedrals in the West, now gathering places for tourists and other sightseers. If it be said that surely *some* use will have to be found for the laboratories, classrooms, dormitories, faculty clubs, and student unions, I can only say that "some" use is not precisely what we are concerned with at the present time in discussions of the future of the American university. After all, there is no reason why all of these could not be used effectively, and at low-cost purchase, by business corporations, penological systems, the armed forces, and professional athletic teams. There is no easily seen end to the possibilities of use of plant and equipment in the contemporary university. They are not, however, what a university, or any form of cultural and intellectual community is about.

51. What the university *is* about, what its unique roles and statuses alone fit it for, what is alone the source of public respect and confidence, and continuing support, is *teaching and research in the learned disciplines:* teaching of a level that can be conducted only through an individual's continuing research; research of a scale that is combinable with continuing teaching. On this conception of the university alone have rested academic community and academic authority. Both of these will be regained only when the university regains its own identity.


WORDS

*meaning*  Define *euphoria* (par. 1), *politicization* and *malaise* (par. 3), *endemic* (par. 6), *benign* (par. 8), *enclave* (par. 10), *inexorable* (par. 12), *fatuous* (par. 14), and *wanton* (par. 20).

*exactness*  Are the following words used in their literal sense: *capstone* (par. 8), *derelictions* (par. 20), and *in loco parentis* (par. 22)? Choose a synonym for each and decide which word is the most effective—the original or your synonym.

*connotation*  1. Explain the meaning of the last sentence of paragraph 12.  2. What does the author mean by "a nearly Faustian view of the university" (par. 40)?

*word choice*  Would you use the phrase "middle-class-sprung pains of youth" (par. 8)? Why or why not?

*emphasis*  Does "or stagnant, archaic, or antiquarian" (par. 10) add emphasis? Explain.

## SENTENCES

*style*   1. Is this essay dogmatic, pontifical, hopeful, or pessimistic? If it is none of these, what would you call it?   2. What is the effect of such sentences as "Forget it" (par. 8), "How preposterous" (par. 13), "God forbid" and "Very Good" (par. 26)? Are any of them elliptical?   3. How do you react to such a statement as "But it is utter nonsense" (par. 23)?

*rhetorical devices*   What is being echoed in the statement "If this be conspiracy . . ." (par. 27)?

## PARAGRAPHS

*topic sentences and methods of development*   1. The author begins paragraphs 12, 15, 25, 28, 32, and 40 with comparable statements. Are they sentences? Do they serve as topic sentences? If they are topic sentences, do any serve for more than one paragraph? Are they parallel statements?   2. Paragraphs 35, 36, and 37 each make a separate point. What do these points have to do with the development of the essay?

## CONTENT AND ORGANIZATION

*central ideas*   1. Is the "American university . . . in an exceedingly precarious position" (par. 1)?   2. The author knows the "major weakness in the university" (par. 7). Do you agree? Do you think the university is weak? Explain.   3. Should the university remain as it always has been (par. 9)?

*organization*   Are each of the points made in paragraphs 12, 15, 25, 28, 32, and 40 of equal importance? Does Mr. Nisbet develop each of the six points more or less equally?

*assumptions and implications*   1. What does the author really believe to be the major problem in today's university?   2. Do you agree with some of the author's statements and disagree with others? Make a list of agreements and one of disagreements. What do you infer from these lists?

## SUGGESTIONS FOR DISCUSSION

1. The author was first a professor, then an administrator. Is his vantage point clear in this essay? What is it? How would you, as a student, write this?   2. Is there value in tradition?   3. Should the university retain some of the values of the medieval university, or should it reconstruct itself completely for the technological age?   4. Is the university indispensable? If it disappears, will it be replaced? By what?

*David J. O'Brien*

# POWER TO THE STUDENTS

1. A short time ago I was asked by a group of college students to participate in a symposium on the theme "The Great Man in History." Among the topics were Charlemagne, Marx, Mao Tse-tung, and "Students," the last assigned to me. I was at first puzzled by the inclusion of "Students" in the series but, with remarkable tolerance and infinite patience, the student leaders explained to me that what concerned them was the relationship between men and their times, whether, that is, the great man, or any man, makes history, or whether history makes him. Students, anxious to know personally and collectively, whether they can make history, naturally ask of themselves the question heretofore posed of individual great men. This is implicit in their concern with student power, for power is not simply, as the "realists" would have it, the influence of men over things or other men; rather power is the ability to act and not simply be acted upon. Do today's students have that ability to act? Can they, should they, make history?

2. On its most profound level the question is the old one of freedom and fate, of determination and free will. The presence of the students and myself in school, our common conviction that it is good for us to meet together, to exchange ideas, to argue and dispute, is by implication a commitment to an answer: that there is at least a narrow area of freedom open to us, and that our task is to broaden that area. Many of our contemporaries, in the deepest recesses of their beings, believe, in Tocqueville's words, "that men are not their own masters here below and that they obey . . . some insurmountable and unintelligent forces arising from anterior events." "These are false and cowardly doctrines," Tocqueville responded, "which can never produce anything but feeble men and craven nations. Providence didn't create mankind either entirely independent or completely in servitude. It traced, it is true, around every man a fatal circle that he cannot leave, but within that vast confine man is powerful and free, and so are nations."

3. Tocqueville's faith has never been more severely challenged

POWER TO THE STUDENTS: © 1969 Commonweal Publishing Co., Inc. Reprinted by permission.

than it is today. Most acutely the problem of human freedom is posed by the increasing importance of technology in the lives of men everywhere. If men lack understanding of themselves and their society and if they lack the will to make history, then history, in the form of technology and bureaucratic structures, will make them, and make them more directly and more completely than ever before seemed possible.

4. If this is an accurate assessment, then the most basic values which scholars and teachers must hold are severely threatened. Those of us who take seriously the life of the mind must believe in the possibilities of human reason and the potentiality of human freedom, for without freedom, reason cannot function, and without reason, education is absurd. These are values that must inform our work as scholars, as teachers, as men, and others have the right to insist that we stand behind those values, that we are not neutral on them, that we will fight to preserve and extend them. This commitment is intimately linked to our common sense of history. "Our interest in history," C. Wright Mills has written, "is not owing to any view that the future is inevitable, that the future is bounded by the past. . . . We study history to discern the alternatives within which human reason and human freedom can now make history." The making of history is the final justification of our work, and of the institutions we use—the universities—and the ability to make history is the true meaning of that word "power" which circulates so widely today.

5. Is student power possible? Should students have the ability to act or should their actions be carefully circumscribed? The beginning of an answer may be found in a story. In the 1830s when the moral question of the abolition of slavery was agitating the United States, a group of theological students at Lane Seminary demanded use of the chapel to discuss the slavery issue. The faculty opposed the discussion but did not forbid it, and for eighteen days the students debated the problem, concluding in the end for the abolitionist position. Their vigorous work among the black population of Cincinnati disturbed the Trustees who met the following summer and prohibited further discussion of slavery at Lane. The students upon their return protested and withdrew to Oberlin College, which became a training ground for abolitionist preachers who subsequently evangelized the Northwest, laying the groundwork for the repudiation of slavery which culminated in the Civil War.

6. The Lane Seminary rebels represented a recurrent theme in nineteenth-century American education. The colleges and universities, founded, like Harvard, to perpetuate the religious traditions of a dangerously mobile, independent, and rootless people, had also been

intended to produce prophets, men inspired to recall their fellows from worldly preoccupations to the insistent demands of a stern and righteous God. As the colleges, like the churches which fostered them, accommodated themselves to the demands of the new society, the prophetic tradition did not die out, but arose time and again to remind men of the original intention of extirpating sin, fulfilling the divine plan, and building the Kingdom of God here in this new land. The churches and the colleges, however much they departed from the ideals of their founders, could never entirely forget that they had been dedicated to shaping in America a new Zion.

7. Yet the prophetic dimension of American religion which was so intimately related to the birth of higher education could hardly withstand the pressures of material promise and social freedom. Democratization was difficult for the church but it was disastrous for the college. "As to the influence which the intellect of one man can have on that of another," Tocqueville noted in *Democracy in America*, "it must necessarily be very limited in a country where the citizens, placed on an equal footing, are all closely seen by each other; and where, as no signs of uncontestable greatness or superiority are perceived in any one of them, they are constantly brought back to their own reason as the most obvious and proximate source of truth. It is not only confidence in this or that man that is destroyed, but the disposition for trusting the authority of any man whatsoever."

8. Early American higher education suffered from this popular distrust of learning, and its emphasis on classical and religious instruction seemed to the public, and to many of the students, irrelevant to the real needs of the growing nation, a luxurious sport on the hectic, rough and tumble life of a raw, individualistic society. The colleges' design and rules reinforced the isolation of scholars and students. Heavy doses of prayer and sermons were supposed to curb the student's natural sinfulness, while the curriculum was geared to training his mental faculties by concentration on languages, scripture, and a hodge-podge of moral philosophy. Indeed some college teachers were truly anti-intellectual, like the President of Dartmouth who said in 1828: "The very cultivation of the intellect has frequently a tendency to impair the moral sensibilities, to induce the pride of conscious ability and variety of attainments which . . . are affections offensive to God."

9. This situation was transformed in the late nineteenth century by two major developments. The introduction of the elective system, "liberty in education," substituted for the rigid prescriptions the new breadth of course selection and a degree of specialization

which accorded well with business' new-found need for trained specialists and the student's own desire for economic mobility in an increasingly urbanized, industrialized society. German-style graduate education, complete with seminars, Ph.D.s, detailed scientific research, and the cult of scientific method and scholarly objectivity, fostered further specialization, brought new standards of intellectual excellence, raised the prestige, power, and status of professors, and eroded the moral and religious foundations of the collegiate model. Business and the state, and later the graduate school itself, set the standards and dictated the organization of undergraduate education. The distinctiveness and autonomy of undergraduate education were destroyed as the higher learning was reformed in accord with the needs of society and the aspirations of students.

10. To some extent these changes broadened the area of student freedom. Judged in the classroom on the basis of his academic performance rather than his deportment and decorum, free to pursue the program of his choosing, increasingly able to learn about the structure and operation of his own society, the student could, conceivably, achieve an education far superior to that available in the older colleges. On the other hand, the rapid expansion of many universities in the last half century led to the growth of professional student service departments staffed by deans and counselors who hoped to assist students in their adjustment to the demands of a sophisticated bureaucratic society.

11. Implicit in the growth of the para-academic establishment was a contempt for students that had deep roots in American higher education. It was Thomas Cooper of ante-bellum South Carolina College who exclaimed: "Republicanism is good but the idea of the rights of boys and girls is the offspring of democracy gone mad," while a Davidson professor remarked in 1855 that "the American student comes to college . . . with an undisciplined mind and an uncultivated heart, yet with exalted ideas of personal dignity, and a scowling contempt for all lawful authority and wholesome restraint. How is he to be controlled?"

12. A report presented a century later by two deans from the University of Minnesota indicated that such sentiments were far from dead. Students, they argued, "are the responsibility, you might even call them the wards of the institution. They have the freedom that the institution is willing to grant them."

13. No matter how liberal the benevolence of the university may be, the fact remains that freedom's limits for the students are almost always defined from the outside. "Most Americans," Henry

Steele Commager writes, "persist in thinking of college students as children who must be provided with intellectual, physical and moral guidance to fit them for just the kind of world they have come out of and will go back into, and who must be protected against ideas or associations which might make them discontented with that world and reluctant to conform to it."

14.    Always a bit behind, always seeking to accommodate traditional values of culture, religion, and learning to new demands within and without, the American university has been more passive than active, less a maker of history than the object of history-making forces in a dynamic and fluid country. As a result the student in the modern college or university is encompassed within a system which contains many cross-purposes and lacks a central unity. Told by his parents and secondary school teachers that entry into college is a high privilege and a great opportunity, that his years there will be the most crucial of his life, he discovers a reality far removed from the promise. He discovers that college carries no automatic guarantee of status or independence, that he is not necessarily admitted into an elite. As Martin Meyerson puts it, "The college student is no longer one of the happy few—he is one of the frustrated many. . . . He cannot afford not to go to college; college education is as necessary to him as secondary schooling, and has not much more standing than secondary schooling did a generation ago."

15.    While they are physically and emotionally adult, college students exist on the fringe of adult society. They are, as Kenneth Keniston points out, psychological adults and sociological adolescents, lacking the full integration into society's institutional structures which is characteristic of adult life. Despite the best efforts of Deans of Students, they are not even fully integrated into the university itself. And the university, while it serves as a processing medium for the integration of the student into society, still retains the archaism of academic freedom, providing areas of criticism and some commitment to values which run counter to those of the corporation and the individual state.

16.    It is just this conflict between outside pressures and independence from them that makes student radicalism, which is a function of nonintegration, possible. In responding to the pressures to integrate them into society, students quite naturally focus upon the university, which is the proximate vehicle for these pressures, and seldom recognize that their very ability and desire to resist largely depend upon that same university.

17.    The student entering the university is confronted with a

rhetoric of liberalism: he is "on his own"; he must "accept responsibility"; he must recognize the necessity to learn rather than wait to be taught. But the reality of large classes, bureaucratic controls, pressures of graduate admissions and course requirements, limit his freedom and his ability to accept responsibility even if he would. Once he has chosen a school, and a major, he has few meaningful educational choices left.

18. In the classroom, again quoting Meyerson, "whether the teacher shocks him, or ignores him, or bores him, or is friendly to him, the student is dependent on the teacher's mood and interest." Despite the realization of a generation of educational psychologies of the need to place greatest emphasis on learning by the student rather than on instruction by the teacher, the college, like the primary and secondary school, does everything possible to postpone the thrills of individual thinking and discovery until graduate school, until enough outdated information is transmitted or until the faculties have been disciplined.

19. Finally the entering student is presented, often for the first time, with a critical perspective on his own society from teachers and other students. In varying degrees he becomes conscious of wide gaps between accepted myths and dogmas and prevailing practice. In the process his religious faith, his confidence in his family, his sense of meaning and identity, are often severely shaken. For many this experience may be offset by fear of family rejection, of poverty, or of the shattering implications of what is dimly perceived, so that avoidance of the problem is easiest. The professional demands of vocational courses, the presence of many uncritical courses and programs, the work of student counselors, chaplains, and deans all help the student avoid the difficulties raised by consciousness of hypocrisy and dishonesty around him. The solidarity and community with which drugs, sex, and alcohol are discovered and enjoyed also help ease the pain and facilitate the transition. Student activism can serve a similar purpose, bringing together a number of young people in search of meaning and supplying the sense of identity and community missing elsewhere. Thus so frequently the movement seems more important than the goal, the euphoria of shared danger more significant than success or failure.

20. All these features of contemporary university life make it possible for revolt to take place within the university; particular issues serve to precipitate crises. Students who honestly wish to change the situation must recognize the historical dimension of their own experience and of the university itself. Today's university shares in the

contradictions of American society, but among its own contradictions is its occasional ability to act creatively and independently of society, to provide a haven for the critical intellect, to promote and defend democratic aspirations, and to represent a greater rationality at odds with the limited rationality of the technological society to which it has so substantially contributed.

21. Like the church, the university has often betrayed its true values, it has allowed itself to be used by the powers of this world, but it has also sometimes been true to its best ideals, and those ideals remain the basis for reform and reconstruction. It has sought to serve the people and has often served their masters; it has sought to find and speak the truth, and has sometimes shaped truth in its own interests; it has sought to make men free and has often forged for them new chains. Nevertheless it must continue to strive to serve, to find truth, and to make men free, and if it is to do so, all within the university must accept the task as their personal responsibility.

22. If the university is to do these things, its leaders must regain the faith that men can, indeed must, govern themselves, which is to say nothing more than that they can be their own men, that they can make decisions, and that they can join with others to solve common problems. Lacking any group or class within the university who can be depended upon to make correct decisions, they must stand with Thomas Jefferson, who rejected the whole ethos of the collegiate way with its stringent prescriptions and rules as early as 1823 in setting up the University of Virginia. "Our institution," Jefferson wrote, "will proceed on the principle of doing all the good it can without consulting its own pride or ambition; of letting everyone come and listen to whatever he thinks may improve the condition of his mind." As for student power, Jefferson had an answer that rings a timely note:

> The rock which I most dread is the discipline of the institution. . . . *The insubordination of our youth is now the greatest obstacle to their education.* We may lessen the difficulty perhaps by avoiding too much government, by requiring no useless observances, none which shall merely multiply occasions for dissatisfaction, disobedience and revolt, by referring to the more discreet of themselves the minor discipline, the graver to the civil magistrates.

23. The first requirement for the development of student power today is the formation of student identity and solidarity by means of a definition of student rights and freedoms and development of the organization to maintain and defend them. Students must think of

themselves first and foremost as students rather than as potential teachers, businessmen, or bureaucrats. Only when they are aware of being "intellectual workers" and not simply trainees will they be free to realize the dynamic potentiality of their situation.

24. To organize students as a force for change in the university and in society, the activist minority must combat the student's natural attention to present distractions and future success. Always alert to the dangers of complacency and apathy, they must use every means at their command to offset the pressures of the media and established authority to convince students that good will and cooperation will solve the world's problems. Like the union organizer, the student leader must insist that comfort granted by the paternalistic, benevolent powers that be is paid for in lost dignity and lost opportunity. In particular, change cannot be sought simply by incorporation into the present university structure, particularly if entry is seen as an expression of a natural campus community.

25. Instead the first goal must be the vindication through student action of student autonomy: recognition of their claim to be a distinctive group with their own interests and rights. They may find that the most promising avenue of mobilization of students is concentration on the need for freedom from arbitrary and undemocratic procedures within the university. The grading system, judicial procedures which vest student discipline in the hands of faculty and administration, and the student personnel bureaucracy must be fought, a statement of basic exemptions and rights must be adopted, it must not be subject to negotiation, and students must be ready to fight for it. To do so they must avoid division, resist being drawn into a false community of all in the university, and seek to find in their situation the basis for the kind of solidarity described by George Santayana. Students, he wrote, "are like passengers in a ship or fellow countrymen abroad; their sense of common interests and common emotions overwhelms all latent antipathies. They live in a sort of primitive brotherhood, with a ready enthusiasm for every good or bad project, and contagious good humor."

26. Student participation in university government should not be purchased at the cost of freedom or solidarity. Certain areas of student personal and academic freedom, like that of the faculty, must always remain outside the jurisdiction of the institution, and student associations, locally and nationally, exist to secure these freedoms for the individual student and the student body. The Senate, or any other structure which makes decisions, is a limited body in a limited institution. Its jurisdiction is not total, and it exists to serve its constituent

elements, faculty and students, in the promotion of their separate and joint objectives. This suggests that the university is not a miniature state, even a democratic one, but a system of separate levels which sometimes cooperate, sometimes ignore each other, and sometimes have to negotiate. If students are to share in this odd arrangement, they must do so not simply by having some of their number participate in the governing bodies but by developing their collective strength.

27. The students' role in policy-making should be proportionate to their interest in the decisions being made. Students and faculty have goals and concerns which are the same, goals and concerns which overlap, and goals and concerns which are different. Any government structured on the supposition that students and faculty are at war with one another, that the faculty is part of the racist power structure, or that the student is a "nigger," for example, will result in the fulfillment of the prophecy—it will lead to war. On the other hand the supposition of a community of scholars, the "Mister Chips" mystique, by denying very real functional and generational differences between teachers and students, will similarly bring disaster. Unnecessary and dishonest sources of division must be removed, but real differences will persist. This means that the grading system, which gives the professor enormous power over the students, must be radically revised, if not destroyed. On the other hand students must not demand the right to dictate hiring, firing, tenure grants, or the content of courses. They cannot substitute for the intimidation of the grade the blackmail of disruption, boycott, or violence.

28. On the top decision-making bodies, where common concerns and problems are resolved, students and faculty should have parity. Each has a vital interest in decisions on budget, priorities, buildings, and such matters, and each should have equal influence on decisions. In some areas student interests are predominant and faculty should have only a consultative voice: the choice of para-academic personnel like Deans of Students, financial aid officers, athletic and residence directors, together with policy for these officers. In other areas faculty interests predominate and students should have only a consultative role: disposition of research funds, choice of academic deans and department chairmen, hiring and firing of faculty, sabbaticals.

29. Where interests and concerns overlap, students and faculty should sometimes be equally represented, as on library and admissions committees. Elsewhere overlapping concerns should be negotiated through joint committees and collective bargaining procedures,

an approach particularly applicable on the departmental level. There the establishment of an atmosphere of mutual trust, flexibility, and openness on both sides will be best insured by maintaining autonomous, separate organizations recognizing the different age levels, professional and personal concerns of both sides. Each is protected by the ultimate weapon of the strike, while social and academic programs, open houses, and lounges can facilitate communication and good will.

30. Such an approach departs significantly from the mythology of the university as a community of scholars, and it brings the problems and processes of politics into the life of the university. The result will not be neat and it will mean permanent conflict and controversy. But in the end the life of the mind to which the university and all those within it are dedicated cannot bring comfort and security, but only alienation and anxiety.

31. If there is today a real university community which tripartite representation of faculty, students, and administration reflects, it is a community based on the domestication of the intellectual life. It means that university men have accepted society's definition of their role as service through education and research in useful things, that they do not feel they represent anything seriously at variance with society at large. Like the church before it the university has acquired influence and prestige at the cost of a vision of universal validity. The reign of reason and freedom, like the Kingdom of God, has been brought down to earth, where instead of standing in judgment on the world, it sanctifies men and nations obsessed with their own power and success.

32. In such a situation cooperation and good will alone will not bring significant change. The task is to rekindle commitment, and thus to reawaken, even to intensify, the conflicts which must beset those dedicated to the realization of high ideals in the world of structures and power. The quest for harmony expressed in the longed-for community of scholars is not only futile but unworthy, for it would suppress necessary conflict. Instead, by denying legitimacy to the university as it is and by insisting on the importance of what it might be, by challenging their teachers and their fellow students to take seriously the values they profess, the student activists may yet help us find the way to honesty, perhaps even to wisdom.

33. As for the rest of us, there are many other reasons for welcoming the drive for student power. The attainment of freedom from arbitrary control and manipulation is a necessary precondition for human dignity, for human development, and for education. There

are other reasons: the need to provide a model of a self-governing institution capable of reconciling its claim to serve men with the bureaucratic structures necessitated by democratic education; the need to break the vicious cycle of integration of men into an increasingly technologically determined society in order to insure a future in which free men will want to live; the need to learn democracy through its practice.

34. The challenges which confront this generation are as profound and crucial as any in history. We are, all of us, frightened, frightened of the future, frightened by our society, by many of our fellows, by the potential for evil we must recognize in ourselves. But, as Emerson said, "this time, like all times, is a very good time, if we but know what to do with it." And the university is where the times are being tested, where education and access to the life of the mind may be available for all, where men can gain the knowledge of themselves and their society by which is the basis for the power which belongs to those who can say "I am my own man." If the university, now in full flush of its first real wave of democracy, with students of all classes and races, sometimes seems to be a mess, remember the words of an early American college president: "We cannot be too often reminded that we are making an experiment untried in the progress of human society."

## WORDS

*meaning*   1. Define *decorum* (par. 10), *stringent* (par. 22), and *tripartite* (par. 31).   2. What is the geographical location of the *Northwest* (par. 5)?   3. What is the meaning of *hodge-podge of moral philosophy* (par. 8), *para-academic establishment* and *ante-bellum* (par. 11), *vest student discipline* (par. 25), *"Mister Chips" mystique* (par. 27), and *vision of universal validity* (par. 31)?

*level of usage*   What is a cliché? What is "a rhetoric of liberalism"? What is the author suggesting in paragraph 17?

## SENTENCES

*style*   1. Do the first sentences of paragraphs 3, 4, 5, 8, 9, and 10 serve as transitional sentences or topic sentences or both?   2. The kind of sentence which begins the essay is very common. What do you think of it? Is it effective here?   3. Do you accept the constant quoting of a person only, without specific references? Explain your answer.

*rhetorical devices*   The author frequently makes statements as unchallenged fact. Do you accept without question the first sentences of paragraphs 14, 16, 21, and 24?

*coherence* 1. A quick glance will show that the paragraphs are roughly the same length; i.e., there are no very short or very long ones. Does this help to hold the essay together? Or is it distracting and boring? 2. Are there paragraphs that could be combined for greater effectiveness?

*methods of development* 1. To what extent does the author rely on definition and example? Indicate paragraphs that use each. 2. Are most of the paragraphs developed logically or chronologically? Give several examples of the predominant method. 3. Many paragraphs are developed around ideas of individual men. Who are the following, what are their dates, and what do they have in common: Tocqueville (par. 2), Mills (par. 4), Commager (par. 13), Meyerson (par. 14), Keniston (par. 15), Jefferson (par. 22), Santayana (par. 25), and Emerson (par. 34)?

## CONTENT AND ORGANIZATION

*central ideas* 1. Is the central idea of this essay "power to the students"? Explain. 2. Could the essay be called "Beware of Student Power"? 3. Do you believe that the ability to make history is the true meaning of power? 4. How does early American higher education (par. 8) differ from contemporary American higher education?

*assumptions and implications* 1. Need important history be helpful to mankind? 2. Do you agree that "Democratization was difficult for the church but it was disastrous for the college" (par. 7)? 3. Is the Jefferson quote *"The insubordination of our youth is now the greatest obstacle to their education"* (par. 22) consistent with his earlier statement that the country needs frequent revolutions? Explain.

## SUGGESTIONS FOR DISCUSSION

1. Write a paper arguing for or against the thesis proposed in paragraph 3. 2. Would you participate in a symposium in which you had to maintain that "Students" are a great man (par. 1)? 3. What is the name of a professor at Lane Seminary (par. 5) whose wife wrote a very significant novel (1852)? Discuss the novel and decide what it has to do with "power."

## Lionel Trilling

# A VALEDICTORY

1. The valedictory address, as it has developed in American colleges and universities over the years, has become a very strict form, a literary *genre* which permits very little deviation. We all know what its procedure is. The chosen graduate begins with a conspectus of the world into which he and his classmates are now about to enter. His view of the world is not calculated to inspire cheer, it is usually pretty grim. He speaks of the disorder and violence that prevail in the world, perhaps even close to home. He speaks of the moral and intellectual inadequacy of society, of the dominance of personal self-interest, of indifference to the welfare of others and to all ideal considerations. This constitutes the first movement of the valedictory form.

2. In the second movement the speaker turns his attention to the graduating class in whose name he is saying farewell to their college. He remarks on the sheltered life which the members of the class have been privileged to enjoy for four years. He speaks of the intellectual and spiritual ideals which have been instilled into them and goes on to observe how these will be denied and assailed by that harsh world which is now to be the scene of their new endeavors. And then, in a concluding movement, the speaker urges his fellow graduates to hold fast to the virtues of the educated man and to try to exercise them in the hostile world which, in the degree that it opposes them, has need of them.

3. In short, the defining characteristic of the valedictory address is its statement of the opposition between the university on the one hand and the world on the other.

4. How well we know this opposition! For the academic person it may constitute a chief element of his sense of himself and of his position in society. It is charged with a most moving pathos from which the academic man may derive justification and courage. Surely no academic has ever failed to take heart from Matthew Arnold's famous apostrophe to his own university, of which the opposition is of the essence.

A VALEDICTORY: From *Tri-Quarterly Review,* No. 1 (Fall, 1964). Reprinted by permission of the author. All rights reserved.

5. "Adorable dreamer," says Arnold to Oxford—"adorable dreamer, whose heart has been so romantic! who has given thyself so prodigally, given thyself to sides and to heroes not mine, only never to the Philistine! home of lost causes, and forsaken beliefs, and unpopular names, and impossible loyalties! what example could ever so inspire us to keep down the Philistine in ourselves, what teacher could ever so save us from that bondage to which we are all prone . . . the bondage of"—and here Arnold quotes Goethe— "*'was uns alle bändigt,* DAS GEMEINE'": what binds us all, the narrow, the mundane, the merely practical.

6. This was, in point of fact, Arnold's actual valedictory to Oxford when he had concluded his term as Professor of Poetry at the university, and it contains the whole *mystique* of the valedictory: it gives ultimate expression to the idea of the opposition between the purity and gentle nobility of the university set over against the crassness of the world.

7. And what is a designated valedictorian to do if he finds that he cannot accept this established valedictory *mystique?* I am in just that situation. For some years now, it has seemed to me that the opposition between the university and the world, or at least half the world, is diminishing at a very rapid rate. Gone are the days when H. L. Mencken could laugh a book out of court by referring to its author as Professor, or Dr., or, worst of all, *Herr Professor Dr.* Gone are the days when middle-class fathers groaned and middle-class mothers wept when their sons announced their intention of making a career in the university—scholarship and teaching now appear to the parental mind as amounting to a profession like another, and throughout the land we hear the low purr of satisfaction that accompanies reference to "my son, the one who's abroad on a Fulbright," "my son, the one who's working on genes."

8. Perhaps there is no more striking fact in American social life today than the rapid upward social mobility of our academic personnel, the upward movement of the university itself in national esteem. If ever the university was the object of condescension as the place where abstraction consorted most happily with incompetence, it is now, perhaps more than any other American institution, an object of admiring interest and even of desire, as suggesting the possibility of a life of reason and order. I have the sense that the authority the university has over people's minds grows constantly. No less constant is the increase of the university's scope—it seems to be a chief characteristic of our American culture that virtually any aspect of human life can be thought of as an object of study, and

that eventually the intellectual discipline that develops around it seeks to find shelter in the university. Nothing is too mundane, nothing is too instinctual, nothing is too spiritual for the university to deal with.

9.   What is a valedictorian to do? How is he to evoke the appropriate valedictory pathos of the opposition that the world shows to the university when so much of the world is trying to crowd itself into the university? And he is the more debarred from the valedictory *mystique* and pathos if his own impression of the state of affairs is supplemented by a reading of Clark Kerr's recent book, *The Uses of the University*. Dr. Kerr is president of the University of California [1] and thus speaks with no small authority about university affairs. He tells us that we are witnessing a *rapprochement* of ever-increasing intimacy between the university and the world.

10.   But this puts it all too mildly. How far things have gone in this new direction is strikingly suggested by Dr. Kerr's statement—it is the statement not only of a university president but of a distinguished economist—that the university has become one of the decisive economic facts of our society. Dr. Kerr speaks of the university as being at the centre of what he calls "the knowledge industry," and he is not using a mere figure of speech when he makes that phrase. He does not mean that the university's activity and organisation may be thought of as in some ways analogous to the activity and organisation of a manufacturing or a processing industry. Nor does he mean that the knowledge that universities develop is a commodity which business men are eager to possess. He means that the existence of our universities bears a relation to the national economy that is materially comparable to those enterprises whose achievements are noted in the Dow-Jones averages. He tells us that "the production, distribution, and consumption of 'knowledge' in all forms is said to account for 29 per cent of gross national product . . . ; and knowledge production is growing at about twice the rate of the rest of the economy." And he goes on:

> What the railroads did for the second half of the last century and the automobile for the first half of this century may be done for the second half of this century by the knowledge industry: that is, to serve as the focal point of national growth. And the university is at the center of the knowledge process.

[1] This speech was delivered before the 1967 administration changes at the University of California.—EDITORS' NOTE.

11. *Adorable dreamer!*—is it this that you were dreaming about all these years: that some day you would "serve as the focal point of national growth"? That so much power could come into your hands?—for economic strength implies political power, and the end of your new economic strength is not yet in sight. Consider Dr. Kerr's plans for the new campus at La Jolla, where a new college to accommodate 2,500 students is to be organized and built every two years for the next twenty years: project these plans sufficiently far into the future and it becomes plain that the Governorship of California will be a mere honorary office, all real authority lying with the President of the University. Push the project yet a little further and we envisage the day when the President of the United States will call his cabinet together and will meet with the Dean of State, the Dean of Defense, the Dean of the Interior, when the Federal office commanding the greatest patronage will not be that of Postmaster General but that of Director of Admissions.

12. It is a splendid vision. We have always said that knowledge is power, and maybe this is going to turn out to be true. The idea of Philosopher-Kings has always haunted the academic mind and perhaps, on Dr. Kerr's showing, we are now on the point of ushering in their reign. And is it not characteristic of an American dream that Dr. Kerr, conceiving a city of the mind, should be so much more catholic, tolerant, and inclusive than Plato?—Dr. Kerr tells us that the fully developed university of the future, which he calls Ideopolis, so far from excluding the poets, as Plato did from his Republic, must find an honored place for all the creative arts. Dr. Kerr speaks of the creative arts as being "hitherto the ugly ducklings or Cinderellas of the academic world," but he is confident that this is a condition which is now to be changed.

> America [Dr. Kerr says] is bursting with creativity in painting, music, literature, the theatre, with a vigor equaled in few parts of the world today. Italy, France, Spain, Germany, Russia, England, the Low Countries have had great periods of cultural flowering. America is having one now. . . . The universities need to find ways . . . to accommodate pure creative effort if they are also to have places on stage as well as in the wings and in the audience in the great drama of cultural growth now playing on the American stage.

13. Let us not stop to question Dr. Kerr's belief that the university *should* be on-stage "in the great drama of cultural growth"— let us only investigate what the university must do to "accommodate

pure creative effort" in the arts, giving our fullest attention to literature. Let us appoint a Committee for the purpose, and endow it with
very considerable powers, of which one is that of choosing its personnel from among the illustrious dead if it wishes to do so, of which
another is that of considering the candidate at any point in his career
it elects.

14. And let us suppose the Committee to be a Committee of
the faculty of Northwestern University—then, without question, because of the superb biography by their colleague, Professor Richard
Ellman, the members will think first of James Joyce as an especially
impressive example of pure creative effort. The Committee considers
Mr. Joyce at that moment in his career when he has as yet published only *Dubliners* and *A Portrait of the Artist as a Young Man,*
but is on the point of bringing out *Ulysses.* The members are reassured by Mr. Joyce's academic attainments—he commands several
romance languages, has a working knowledge of the Scandinavian
tongues, and a strong interest in linguistics; he is adept in Scholastic
philosophy, gives signs of being a powerful theorist of aesthetics.
The Committee doesn't want to interfere with his writing, but it can't
help thinking that, in addition to carrying on his pure creative effort,
Mr. Joyce might well turn out to be useful in interdisciplinary
seminars.

15. But there are certain personal circumstances which raise
questions. One circumstance is that Mr. Joyce is not married to Mrs.
Joyce. Maybe in spirit but not in church and not in law. Then there is
the probability that Mrs. Joyce will not be happy in an academic
community—she is a lady (but not actually a *lady*) of very simple
education; so far from being of use to her husband in his work, like
a proper academic wife, she never reads what he writes. Mr. Joyce
makes inordinate demands on everyone around him, is never grateful
for what people do for him, believes that he is the object of treachery,
even of conspiracy. He drinks too much. It is an aspect of his pure
creative effort that he portrays actual people, including his literary
colleagues, usually satirically, and using their actual names. The
chances are that he will make no exception of his academic colleagues.
Is this good for faculty morale? The new book he is writing, the one
that is to be called *Ulysses,* is said to be a work of genius. But it is
full of indecent words and scatological and sexual details. It is going
to be prosecuted, condemned, burned. Early readers, even very intelligent ones, will find it harsh and cruel. To be sure, with the passing
decades, nobody will be troubled by its outspokenness, and the judgment of harshness and cruelty will yield to the opinion that this is a

sweet, kind, tender book, almost to the point of sentimentality. But does the university want to accommodate the decades of scandal it will cause?

16. With great reluctance the Committee decides against Mr. Joyce and turns its attention to another great creative personality. This one is also salient in Northwestern consciousness—it is Professor Erich Heller's "ironic German," Thomas Mann. He, too, is not only creative but learned—he is encyclopaedic in science, psychology, history, Egyptology, musicology. He is probably the world's leading authority on the work and personality of Thomas Mann—nothing would please him more than to give a course of lectures or a seminar on the development of this genius. His aptness for the academic life is suggested by his fondness for being known as *Dr.* Mann. It is pleasing to note that there can be no doubt that Dr. Mann is married to Frau Dr. Mann. No lives could be more orderly than theirs. In short, everything makes it clear that Dr. Mann should be recommended for appointment. The Committee moves fast, the Deans move fast, the President moves fast, the Trustees move fast—alas, to no avail: Harvard has got to him first. What is more, the University of California is after Dr. Mann, and is likely to snatch him from Harvard itself, for California plans to create a Mann-Goethe Institute which will be an exact replica of Weimar in 1775.

17. Disappointed but hopeful, the Committee turns to André Gide, an eventual Nobel Prize Winner. There can be no doubt about it: Monsieur Gide is married to Madame Gide. And yet—alas! . . . It is not that the Committee wishes to exclude sexual deviants from academic life; they have been there before. But Monsieur Gide insists on making a point of it, he defends it, he urges it. What is more, he represents the family as a malevolent institution. Who would deny his right to take these positions, yet should they be taken with the university as the forum? The parents of our students cannot be wholly left out of account.

18. But all these adverse considerations are in a sense irrelevant. For it turns out that Monsieur Gide would not accept the appointment even if it were offered him. For he conceives it to be of the essence of his existence as a writer that he startle and shock and dismay his readers. He cannot help entertaining the idea that the university is an institution, that it is by nature conservative, although not necessarily in any bad sense of that word, and respectable, in whatever sense may be attached to *that* word, and that if his writings were to issue from the university, they would seem certified as virtuous, they would lose much—perhaps all—of their shocking force.

19.   If not Gide, then certainly not Genet. Anyway, with his prison record he would have difficulty with the immigration authorities.

20.   What of Jean-Paul Sartre, not only eminent as a creative but as a speculative mind? We are large-minded enough to overlook his sometimes rather odd political positions and also *his* antagonism to respectable life. But Monsieur Sartre does not want to come to us. He likes to do his writing at a table in a café. Very well, this is one of the ways the university can accommodate creative effort—we will have a café; we need one anyway; we will engage Philip Johnson or Mies van der Rohe to build one as an annex to the student Union. Monsieur Sartre is touched, but still says no thank you. It isn't only the café, it is all of Paris: all that noise, all that distraction, all those political quarrels—how is a man to write without them?

21.   William Butler Yeats, when approached, returns something of the same answer. Ireland is wearing him out, tries his temper, frays his nerves. The Irish nation disgusts and infuriates him. How can he leave it? Not to mention the great houses, and the beautiful great ladies, and unforgivable England, and the language. How can the university possibly accommodate *these* necessities of Mr. Yeats' creative efforts? Rather to the relief of the Department of History, which was apprehensive that Mr. Yeats might wish to give a course on his theory of history as set forth in *A Vision,* a work which had been dictated to his wife by certain spirits whose academic background is quite vague, Mr. Yeats declines the offer.

22.   The Committee thinks that perhaps its century is wrong. It tries the nineteenth. Dostoevsky? A genius, but his political views are not easily accommodated by a liberal university. A genius, but an utterly impossible person. Count Leo Tolstoy? Without doubt he is married to the Countess, but he is just on the point of his religious conversion and there is trouble in the offing. Charles Dickens? Doesn't want to leave London and young Ellen Ternan.

23.   Perhaps, then, the art is wrong?—Cézanne stares when the Committee approaches him. Why, in the name of everything rational, should he want to leave these old hot southern rocks? As for apples, tablecloths, pitchers, he can find plenty here at home—what need for a university? What would he do there that he does not do here?— he paints and he paints and he paints: what else *is* there to do? Beethoven (a most deficient and maladjusted person—another *impossible* person) replies with a titanic stare, growl, and shrug. It occurs to both of them to ask, in a moment of terrifying geniality, what the Committee means by its talk of *pure creative effort.* "Pure,

pure; creative, creative," they say, "what *blague,* what *Quatsch* is this?—we are not making pure creative efforts: we are telling you God's truth." Sometimes, it appears, genius is touched with paranoia. Alas.

24. Our Committee retires to think things over. Like any Committee, ours will not admit that it has failed. It reports some strange, deeply ingrained resistance of the artists to the university, a resistance that is not to be in the least diminished by all that they are told about a new function the university has, which is that of serving as "the focal point of national growth." Like any Committee, ours looks to the future, to the time when the universities will have discovered the way to rear up a new generation of artists who will be trained to find it possible to accommodate themselves to the accommodation of pure creative effort in the arts that the university will devise.

### WORDS

*meaning* 1. Define *conspectus* (par. 1), *apostrophe* (par. 4), *Philistine* (par. 5), *catholic* (par. 12), *scatological* (par. 15), *salient* (par. 16), and *paranoia* (par. 23). 2. Account for the spelling of *endeavours* (par. 2) and *organisation* (par. 10). 3. Define the following and explain why they are italicized: *mystique* (par. 6), *rapprochement* (par. 9), and *blague* and *Quatsch* (par. 23).

*connotation* Why does Dr. Kerr call his future university Ideopolis (par. 12)? What commonly used words probably suggested this coinage?

### SENTENCES

*style* 1. What is the function of paragraph 3, a single simple sentence? 2. Does Trilling's translation (in the last sentence of par. 5) suggest a reason for Arnold's using Goethe's original German phrase? 3. Much of this essay is ironic. Choose two sentences from paragraphs 15 and 16 and show how each uses irony.

### PARAGRAPHS

*unity* Does paragraph 5 have a unity of its own? Could it just as well be an extension of paragraph 4?

*coherence* 1. The first three paragraphs clearly provide two "movements" and a summary. Describe the content and organization of paragraphs 4–6. 2. Point out a half-dozen paragraphs that begin with obvious transitions. To what extent do these transitions help the movement of the essay?

*methods of development* Why does Trilling quote passages from another person's book (pars. 10 and 12)? Is this more effective than paraphrasing? Explain.

CONTENT AND ORGANIZATION

*central idea* 1. What relationship does the title have to the central idea? 2. Does Trilling believe that the university can or should be at the center of "the knowledge industry" (par. 10)? 3. Does the first sentence of paragraph 13 imply that Trilling does not believe that the university *should* be on-stage "in the great drama of cultural growth"? 4. Does all the essay after paragraph 13 suggest that the university *cannot* be on-stage "in the great drama"?

*organization* 1. List the men of letters discussed in paragraphs 14–22. What do they have in common? Is the essay organized around these writers? Explain. 2. What is the relationship between paragraphs 1–3 and paragraph 24?

SUGGESTIONS FOR DISCUSSION

1. If Shakespeare were alive today, could he fit into the university? Would the administration and his colleagues tolerate him at age thirty? at age fifty? at all? Would you want him for a teacher? Why or why not? 2. Write an essay on some creative person who serves effectively both a university and an art. 3. Compare a contemporary university with a medieval one. 4. Does the "multiversity" (another of Dr. Clark Kerr's terms) have a necessary place in today's society? 5. To what extent do you believe that education is a part of our gross national product (par. 10)? 6. Do you believe that a state university would or could justify hiring a genius who used filthy language, drank too much, and lived with a woman not his wife? Explain.

*Randall Jarrell*

# THE SCHOOLS OF YESTERYEAR:
# A ONE-SIDED DIALOGUE

UNCLE WADSWORTH (*a deep, slightly grained or corrugated, comfortable-sounding voice, accompanied by an accordion*): School days, school days, dear old golden rule—

THE SCHOOLS OF YESTERYEAR: A ONE-SIDED DIALOGUE: From *A Sad Heart at the Supermarket* by Randall Jarrell. Copyright © 1956, 1962 by Randall Jarrell. Reprinted by permission of Atheneum Publishers.

ALVIN (*Alvin's voice is young*): Stop, Uncle Wadsworth!

UNCLE WADSWORTH: Why should I stop, Alvin boy?

ALVIN: Because it isn't *so,* Uncle Wadsworth. (*With scorn.*) Dear old golden rule days! That's just nostalgia, just sentimentality. The man that wrote that song was just too old to remember what it was really like. Why, kids hated school in those days—they used to play hookey all the time. It's different now. Children *like* to go to school now.

UNCLE WADSWORTH: Finished, Alvin boy?

ALVIN: Finished, Uncle Wadsworth.

UNCLE WADSWORTH: School days, school days, dear old golden rule days, Readin' and 'ritin' and 'rithmetic, Taught to—

ALVIN: Stop, Uncle Wadsworth!

UNCLE WADSWORTH: Why should I stop this time, Alvin boy?

ALVIN: Reading and writing and arithmetic! What a curriculum! Why, it sounds like it was invented by an illiterate. How could a curriculum like that prepare you for life? No civics, no social studies, no hygiene; no home economics, no manual training, no physical education! And extra-curricular activities—where were they?

UNCLE WADSWORTH: Where indeed? Where are the extra-curricular activities of yesteryear? Shall I go on, Alvin boy?

ALVIN: Go ahead, Uncle Wadsworth.

UNCLE WADSWORTH: School days, school days, dear old golden rule days, Readin' and 'ritin' and 'rithmetic, Taught to the tune of a hick'ry stick—

ALVIN: Stop! Stop! Stop, Uncle Wadsworth! (*He pants with emotion.*) Honestly, Uncle, I don't see how you can bear to say it. *Taught to the tune of a hickory stick!* . . . Imagine having to *beat* poor little children with a *stick!* Thank God those dark old days of ignorance and fear and compulsion are over, and we just appeal to the child's better nature, and get him to adjust, and try to make him see that what he likes to do is what we want him to do.

UNCLE WADSWORTH: Finished, Alvin boy?

ALVIN: Finished, Uncle Wadsworth.

UNCLE WADSWORTH: Well, so am I. I can't seem to get going in this song—every fifty yards I get a puncture and have to stop for air. You go on for a while and let me interrupt you. Go ahead, Alvin.

ALVIN: Go ahead where?

UNCLE WADSWORTH: Go ahead about those dark old days of ignorance and fear and compulsion. It makes my flesh creep—and I'm just like the fat boy, I *like* to have my flesh creep.

ALVIN: What fat boy?

UNCLE WADSWORTH: The one in *Pickwick Papers*. (*Silence from Alvin.*) You know, *Pickwick Papers*. (*Silence from Alvin.*) It's a book, son—a book by Charles Dickens. Ever read any Dickens?

ALVIN: Oh, sure, sure. I read *The Tale of Two Cities* in high school. And *Oliver Twist*—well, really I didn't read it exactly, I read it in *Illustrated Classics*. And I saw *Great Expectations* in the movies.

UNCLE WADSWORTH: Why, you and Dickens are old friends. But go on about the—the schools of yesteryear.

ALVIN: Well, I will, Uncle Wadsworth. After all, it's only because I was lucky enough to be born now that I didn't have to go to one of those schools myself. I can just see myself trudging to school barefooted in my overalls—because they didn't even have school buses then, you know—

UNCLE WADSWORTH: Not a one! If a school bus had come for me I'd have thought it was a patrol wagon someone had painted orange for Hallowe'en.

ALVIN: Well, there I am trudging along, and I'm not only trudging, I'm *limping*.

UNCLE WADSWORTH: Stub your toe?

ALVIN (*with bitter irony*): Stub my toe! I'm limping because I'm *sore*—sore all over, where the teacher beat me.

UNCLE WADSWORTH: All over isn't where the teacher beat you, Alvin boy—I know.

ALVIN: All right, all right! And when I get to the school is it the Consolidated School? Is there a lunch-room and a 'chute-the-'chute and a jungle-gym? Is it—is it like schools ought to be? Uh-*uh!* That school has one room, and it's *red*.

UNCLE WADSWORTH: You mean that even in those days the Communists—

ALVIN: No, no, not Red, *red!* Red like a barn. And when I get inside, the teacher is an old maid that looks like a broomstick, or else a man that looks like a—that looks like Ichabod Crane. And then this Crane-type teacher says to me, real stern: "Alvin McKinley, stand up! Are you aware, Alvin, that it is *three minutes past seven?*"

UNCLE WADSWORTH: Three minutes past seven! What on earth are you and Ichabod Crane doing in school at that ungodly hour?

ALVIN: That's when school starts then! Or six, maybe. . . . Then he says, pointing his finger at me in a terrible voice: "Three minutes tardy! And what, Alvin, what did I warn you would happen to you if you ever again were so much as one minute tardy? What did I tell you that I would do to you?" And I say in a little meek voice, because I'm scared, I say: "Whip me." And he says: "YES, WHIP YOU!" And I say—

UNCLE WADSWORTH: You say, "Oh, *don't* whip pore Uncle Tom, massa! If only you won't whip him he won't never—"

ALVIN: Oh, stop it, Uncle Wadsworth! That's not what I say at all, and you know it. How can I tell about the schools of yesteryear if you won't be serious? Well, anyway, he says to me: "Have you anything to say for yourself?" And I say, "Please, Mr. Crane, it was four miles, and I had the cows to milk, and Ma was sick and I had to help Sister cook the hoe-cakes—"

UNCLE WADSWORTH: Hoe-cakes! (*With slow relish.*) Hoe-cakes. . . . Why, I haven't had any hoe-cakes since. . . . How'd you hear about hoe-cakes, Alvin boy?

ALVIN: Uncle Wadsworth, if you keep interrupting me about irrevu— irrelevancies, how can I get anywhere?

UNCLE WADSWORTH: I apologize, Alvin; I am silent, Alvin.

ALVIN: Then he looks at me and he smiles like—like somebody in *Dick Tracy,* and he says: "Alvin, *spare your breath.*" And then he walks over to the corner next to the stove, and do you know what's in the corner?

UNCLE WADSWORTH: What's in the corner?

ALVIN: Sticks. Sticks of every size. Hundreds of sticks. And then he reaches down and takes the biggest one and—and—

UNCLE WADSWORTH: And—and—

ALVIN: And he *beats* me.

UNCLE WADSWORTH (*with a big sigh*): The Lord be praised! For a minute I was afraid he was going to burn you at the stake. But go ahead, Alvin.

ALVIN: Go ahead?

UNCLE WADSWORTH: It's still just ten minutes after seven. Tell me about your day—your school-day—your dear old golden rule day.

ALVIN: Well, then he says: "Take your Readers!" And I look around and everybody in the room, from little kids just six years old with their front teeth out to great big ones, grown men practically that look like they ought to be on the Chicago Bears—everybody in the room picks up the same book and they all start reading aloud out of the—*McGuffey Reader!* Ha-ha-ha! The McGuffey Reader!

UNCLE WADSWORTH: And why, Alvin, do you laugh?

ALVIN: Because it's funny, that's why! The McGuffey Reader!

UNCLE WADSWORTH: Have you ever seen a McGuffey Reader, Alvin?

ALVIN: How could I of, Uncle Wadsworth? I didn't go to school back in those days.

UNCLE WADSWORTH: Your account was so vivid that for a moment I forgot. . . . You've never seen such a Reader. Well, I have.

ALVIN: Oh, sure—you used one in school yourself, didn't you?

UNCLE WADSWORTH: No, Alvin—strange as it seems, I did not; nor did I ever shake the hand of Robert E. Lee, nor did I fight in the War of 1812, nor did I get to see Adam and Eve and the Serpent. My father used a McGuffey Reader; I did not.

ALVIN: I'm sorry, Uncle Wadsworth.

UNCLE WADSWORTH: No need, no need. . . . Alvin, if you will go over to the bookcase and reach into the right-hand corner of the top shelf, you will find a book—a faded, dusty, red-brown book.

ALVIN: Here it is. It's all worn, and there're gold letters on the back, and it says *Appletons' Fifth Reader*.

UNCLE WADSWORTH: Exactly. *Appletons' Fifth Reader*. Week before last, at an antique-dealer's over near Hillsboro, side by side with a glass brandy-flask bearing the features of the Father of our Country, George Washington, I found this Reader.

ALVIN: Look how yellow the paper is! And brown spots all over it. . . . Gee, they must have used it all over the country; it says New York, Boston, and Chicago, 1880, and it was printed in 1878 and 1879 too, and—look at the picture across from it, it's one of those old engravings. I guess they didn't have photographs in those days.

UNCLE WADSWORTH: Guess again, Alvin boy. And what is the subject of this old engraving?

ALVIN: A girl with a bucket, and back behind her somebody's plowing, and it's dawn. And there's some poetry underneath.

UNCLE WADSWORTH:

> While the plowman near at hand
> Whistles o'er the furrowed land
> And the milkmaid singeth blithe. . . .

ALVIN: That's right! You mean to say you *memorized* it?

UNCLE WADSWORTH: Fifty years ago, Alvin. Doesn't any of it have a—a familiar ring?

ALVIN: Well, to tell the truth, Uncle Wadsworth. . . .

UNCLE WADSWORTH: What does it say in small letters down at the right-hand corner of the page?

ALVIN: It says—"*L'Allegro,* page 420." *L'Allegro!* Sure! sure! Why, I read it in sophomore English. We spent two whole days on that poem and on—you know, that other one that goes with it. They're by John Milton.

UNCLE WADSWORTH: Yes, Milton. And in that same—

ALVIN: But Uncle Wadsworth, you don't mean to say they had Milton in a Fifth Reader! Why, we were sophomores in college, and there were two football players that were juniors, and believe me, it was all Dr. Taylor could do to get us through that poem. How could little kids in the fifth grade read Milton?

UNCLE WADSWORTH: Sit down, Alvin. Do you remember reading, at about the same time you read "L'Allegro," a poem called "Elegy Written in a Country Churchyard"?

ALVIN: Well—

UNCLE WADSWORTH: Gray's "Elegy"?

ALVIN: Say me some, Uncle Wadsworth.

UNCLE WADSWORTH:

> Full many a gem of purest ray serene
> The dark unfathom'd caves of ocean bear;
> Full many a flower is born to blush unseen
> And waste its sweetness on the desert air.

ALVIN: Sure, I remember that one. I liked that one.

UNCLE WADSWORTH: Well, Alvin, that very poem—

ALVIN: Oh *no,* Uncle Wadsworth! You're not going to tell me that that poem was in a Fifth Reader!

UNCLE WADSWORTH: No, Alvin, I am not. I want you to . . . to steel yourself. That poem was not in Appletons' Fifth Reader, that poem was in Appletons' Fourth Reader. (*Alvin groans in awe.*) And Wordsworth—you studied Wordsworth in your sophomore English?

ALVIN (*lifelessly*): Uh-huh.

UNCLE WADSWORTH: There are four of Wordsworth's poems in Appletons' Fourth Reader.

ALVIN: I guess in the Sixth Reader they were reading Einstein.

UNCLE WADSWORTH: No, but in the Fifth Reader—run your eye down the table of contents, Alvin—there are selections by Addison, Bishop Berkeley, Bunyan, Byron, Coleridge, Carlyle, Cervantes, Coleridge—the whole *Ancient Mariner,* Alvin—Defoe, De Quincey, Dickens, Emerson, Fielding, Hawthorne, George Herbert, Hazlitt, Jefferson, Dr. Johnson, Shakespeare, Shelley, Sterne, Swift, Tennyson, Thoreau, Mark Twain—

ALVIN: It's hard to believe.

UNCLE WADSWORTH: And there are also selections from simpler writers—

ALVIN: Yeah, simple ones—

UNCLE WADSWORTH: Simpler writers such as Scott, Burns, Longfellow, Cooper, Audubon, Poe, Oliver Wendell Holmes, Benjamin Franklin, Washington Irving. Alvin, have you ever—at college perhaps—ever read anything by Goethe?

ALVIN: I don't *believe* so.

UNCLE WADSWORTH: Well, Alvin boy, if after milking the cow and baking the hoe-cakes, you had limped four miles barefoot to that one-room red schoolhouse of yours, and had been beaten by that Ichabod Crane of a teacher, you would still have got to read, in your Appletons' Fifth Reader, one poem and five pages of prose from Goethe's immortal *Wilhelm Meister*. . . . As it is you don't limp, nobody beats you, and you read—whom *do* you read, Alvin? Tell me some of the writers you read in the fifth grade.

ALVIN: I don't exactly remember their *names*.

UNCLE WADSWORTH: There in the bookcase—that red and yellow and black book there—is the Fifth Reader of today. *Days and Deeds,* it is called; it is, I believe, the most popular Fifth Reader in the country. That's right, hand it over. Here on page 3 is its table of contents; come, Alvin, read out to me the names of the writers from whom the children of today get their knowledge of life and literature.

ALVIN: Well, the first one's Fletcher D. Slater, and then Nora Burglon, and Sterling North and Ruth G. Plowhead—

UNCLE WADSWORTH: Plowhead?

ALVIN: That's what it says. Then Ruth E. Kennell, Gertrude Robinson, Philip A. Rollins, J. Walker McSpadden, Merlin M.—

UNCLE WADSWORTH: You're sure you're not making up some of these names?

ALVIN: How could I? Merlin M. Taylor, Sanford Tousey, Gladys M. Wick, Marie Barton, Margaret Leighton, Edward C. James—no, Janes, Leonard K. Smith, P. L. Travers, Esther Shepherd, James C. Bowman, Dr. Seuss—

UNCLE WADSWORTH: Land! Land!

ALVIN: No, Seuss. Seuss.

UNCLE WADSWORTH: I speak figuratively. I mean that here, at last, is a name I recognize, the name of a well-known humorist and cartoonist.

ALVIN: Oh. Then there's Armstrong Sperry, Myra M. Dodds, Alden G. Stevens, Lavinia R. Davis, Lucy M. Crockett, Raymond Jannson, Hubert Evans, Ruth E. Tanner, Three Boy Scouts—

UNCLE WADSWORTH: Three Boy Scouts. An Indian, no doubt. . . . Never heard of him.

ALVIN: Heard of *them*. There're three of them.

UNCLE WADSWORTH: Three? Thirty! Three hundred! They're *all* Boy
Scouts! Alvin, these are names only a mother could love—names
only a mother would know. That they are honest names, respected
names, the names of worthy citizens, I have not the slightest doubt;
but when I reflect that it is *these* names that have replaced those of
Goethe, of Shakespeare, of Cervantes, of Dr. Johnson—of all the
other great and good writers of the Appleton Fifth Reader—when
I think of this, Alvin, I am confused, I am dismayed, I am *astounded.*

ALVIN: Uncle Wadsworth, you've got all red in the face.

UNCLE WADSWORTH: There are also in the Appleton Fifth Reader,
Alvin, elaborate analyses of the style, rhetoric, and organization of
the literary works included; penetrating discussions of their logic;
highly technical instructions for reading them aloud in the most
effective way; discussions of etymology, spelling, pronunciation, the
general development of the English language. And, Alvin, these are
*not* written in the insipid baby-talk thought appropriate for children
today. Here, in a paragraph about *Don Quixote,* is one of the Fifth
Reader's typical discussions of logic:

> The question here involved is the old sophism of Eubulides. . . .
> Is a man a liar who says that he tells lies? If he is, then he does
> not tell lies; and if he does not tell lies, is he a liar? If not, then is
> not his assertion a lie? . . . It will be noticed that the perplexity
> comes from the fact of self-relation: the one assertion relates to
> another assertion of the same person; and the one assertion being
> conditioned upon the other, the difficulty arises. It is the question
> of self-contradiction—of two mutually contradictory statements,
> one must be false. It is a sophism, but one that continually occurs
> among unsophisticated reasoners. It is also a practical sophism, for
> it is continually being acted in the world around us (e.g., a person
> seeks pleasure by such means that, while he enjoys himself, he un-
> dermines his health, or sins against his conscience, and thus draws
> inevitably on him physical suffering and an uneasy soul). It is
> therefore well worthy of study in its purely logical form. . . . All
> universal negative assertions (and a lie is a negation) are liable to
> involve the assertion itself in self-contradiction.

ALVIN: Ohhhhh. . . . *Ohhhhh.* . . . If I'd gone to school then, I'd
have known what that means in the *fifth grade?*

UNCLE WADSWORTH: You'd have known it or you never would have
got into the sixth grade.

ALVIN: Then I'd be the oldest settler in the fifth grade, because I'm
a junior in college and I still can't understand it.

UNCLE WADSWORTH: Yes, it's surprising what those fifth-graders were expected to know. The Reader contains a little essay called "Hidden Beauties of Classic Authors," by a writer named N. P. Willis.

ALVIN: N. P. Willis. . . . I guess he was Ruth G. Plowhead's grandpa.

UNCLE WADSWORTH: Yes, he isn't exactly a classic author himself. He tells you how he fell in love with Beaumont and Fletcher, and the *Faerie Queene,* and *Comus,* and *The Rape of the Lock;* he says that he knows

> no more exquisite sensation than this warming of the heart to an old author; and it seems to me that the most delicious portion of intellectual existence is the brief period in which, one by one, the great minds of old are admitted with all their time-mellowed worth to the affections.

Well, at the end of the essay there're some questions; what do you think is the first thing they ask those fifth-graders?

ALVIN: What?

UNCLE WADSWORTH: "Have you read Milton's *Comus?*—Pope's *Rape of the Lock?*"

ALVIN: Now Uncle Wadsworth, you've got to admit that that's a terrible thing to ask a little boy in the fifth grade.

UNCLE WADSWORTH: *I* think it's a terrible thing. But they didn't. As a matter of fact, *I* think it's a terrible thing to ask a big boy in his junior year in college. How about it, Alvin? Have *you* read Milton's *Comus?* Pope's *Rape of the Lock?*

ALVIN: Well, to tell you the truth, Uncle Wadsworth—

UNCLE WADSWORTH: Tell ahead.

ALVIN: Well, to—well—well, it just isn't the *sort* of question you can answer yes or no. I *may* have read Milton's *Comus;* it's the kind of thing we read hundreds of things like in our sophomore survey course; I guess the chances are ten to one I read it, and a year ago I could have told you for certain whether or not I read it, but right now all I can say is if I didn't read it, it would surprise me a lot.

UNCLE WADSWORTH: And *The Rape of the Lock?*

ALVIN: No.

UNCLE WADSWORTH: *No?* You mean you *know* you didn't read it?

ALVIN: Uh-huh.

UNCLE WADSWORTH: How do you know?

ALVIN: I—

UNCLE WADSWORTH: Go on, go on.

ALVIN: Well Uncle Wadsworth, it seems to me that a book with a title like that, if I'd read it I'd remember it.

UNCLE WADSWORTH: Alvin, if you weren't my own nephew I'd—I'd be proud to have invented you. . . . Here's another of those poems, the kind that *you* read in your sophomore year in college and that your great-grandfather read in the Fifth Reader. It's by George Herbert, the great religious poet George Herbert. Read it to me, Alvin; and when you've read it, tell me what it means.

ALVIN (*in careful singsong*): *Sunday.* By George Herbert.

> O Day most calm, most bright!
> The fruit of this, the next world's bud;
> The endorsement of supreme delight,
> Writ by a Friend, and with his blood;
> The couch of Time: Care's calm and bay:
> The week were dark but for thy light;
> Thy torch doth show the way.
>
> The other days and thou
> Make up one man, whose face thou art,
> Knocking at heaven with thy brow:
> The working-days are the back part;
> The burden of the week lies there;
> Making the whole to stoop and bow,
> Till thy release appear.
>
> Man had—man had—

Uncle Wadsworth, I'm all mixed up. I've *been* all mixed up. And if you ask me that fifth grade was mixed up too.

UNCLE WADSWORTH: Where did you first begin to feel confused?

ALVIN: I never did not feel confused.

UNCLE WADSWORTH: Surely the first line—

ALVIN: Yeah. Yeah. The first one was all right. *O Day most calm, most bright!* That means it's Sunday, and it's all calm and bright, the weather's all calm and bright. Then it says, *the fruit of this.* . . . *The fruit of this.* What's the fruit of this?

UNCLE WADSWORTH: *The fruit of this, the next world's bud. World* is understood.

ALVIN: Understood?

UNCLE WADSWORTH: Yes. The fruit of this world and the bud of the next world.

ALVIN: Oh. . . . *The endorsement of supreme delight.* (*Pauses.*) *The endorsement of supreme delight.* . . . Uncle Wadsworth, a line like that—you've got to admit a line like that's *obscure.*

UNCLE WADSWORTH: It means that—it *says* that Sunday is like the endorsement of a check or note; because of the endorsement this supreme delight, our salvation, is negotiable, we can cash it.

ALVIN: Oh. . . . Like endorsing a check. *Writ by a Friend—Friend's* got a capital *F.* . . . Oh! That means it was written by a Quaker. (*Uncle Wadsworth laughs.*) But that's what it does mean. We live on a road named the Friendly Road because it goes to a Quaker church. If *Friend* doesn't mean *Quaker* why's it got a capital *F?*

UNCLE WADSWORTH: *Writ by a Friend, and with his blood.* If you're talking about church and Sunday and the next world, and mention a Friend who has written something with his blood, who is that Friend, Alvin?

ALVIN: Oh. . . . *The couch of Time; Care's calm and bay.* . . . (*Pauses.*) Uncle Wadsworth, do we *have* to read poetry?

UNCLE WADSWORTH: Of course not, Alvin. Nobody else does, why should we? Let's get back to prose. Here's the way the Fifth Reader talks about climbing a mountain:

> Some part of the beholder, even some vital part, seems to escape through the loose grating of his ribs as he ascends. . . . He is more lone than you can imagine. There is less of substantial thought and fair understanding in him than in the plains where men inhabit. His reason is dispersed and shadowy, more thin and subtle, like the air. Vast, Titanic, inhuman Nature has got him at disadvantage, caught him alone, and pilfers him of some of his divine faculty. She does not smile on him as in the plains. She seems to say sternly, "Why come ye here before your time? . . . Why seek me where I have not called you, and then complain because you find me but a stepmother? Shouldst thou freeze, or starve, or shudder thy life away, here is no shrine, nor altar, nor any access to my ear. 'Chaos and ancient Night, I come no spy / With purpose to explore or to disturb / The secrets of your realm—' "

ALVIN: Uncle Wadsworth, if the prose is like that, I'd just as soon have stayed with the poetry. Didn't they have any plain American writers in that Fifth Reader?

UNCLE WADSWORTH: Plain American writers? That was Thoreau I was reading you. Well, if he's too hard, here's what the Fifth Reader has to say about him. It's talking about his account of the battle between the black ants and the red:

> The style of this piece is an imitation of the heroic style of Homer's "Iliad," and is properly a "mock-heroic." The intention of the author is two-fold: half-seriously endowing the incidents of every-

day life with epic dignity, in the belief that there is nothing mean and trivial to the poet and philosopher, and that it is the man that adds dignity to the occasion, and not the occasion that dignifies the man; half-satirically treating the human events alluded to as though they were non-heroic, and only fit to be applied to the events of animal life.

ALVIN (*wonderingly*): Why, it's just like old Taylor!

UNCLE WADSWORTH: Professor Taylor would lecture to you in that style?

ALVIN: He'd get going that way, but pretty soon he'd see we didn't know what he meant, and then he'd talk so we could understand him. . . . Well, if the Fifth Reader sounds like that about ants, I sure don't want to hear it about scansion and etymology!

UNCLE WADSWORTH: But Alvin, wouldn't you *like* to be able to understand it? Don't you wish you'd had it in the fifth grade and known what it was talking about?

ALVIN: Sure, sure! Would I have made old Taylor's eyes pop out! All we ever had in the fifth grade was Boy Scouts going on hikes, and kids going to see their grandmother for Thanksgiving; it was easy.

UNCLE WADSWORTH: And interesting?

ALVIN: Nah, it was corny—the same old stuff; how can you make stuff like that interesting?

UNCLE WADSWORTH: How indeed?

ALVIN: But how did things like Shakespeare and Milton and Dickens ever get in a Fifth Reader?

UNCLE WADSWORTH: Alvin, they've always *been* there. Yesterday, here in the United States, those things were in the Fifth Reader; today, everywhere else in the world, those things or their equivalent are in the Fifth Reader; it is only here in the United States, today, that the Fifth Reader consists of *Josie's Home Run,* by Ruth G. Plowhead, and *A Midnight Lion Hunt,* by Three Boy Scouts. I read, in a recent best-seller, this sentence: "For the first time in history Americans see their children getting less education than they got themselves." That may be; and for the first time in history Americans see a book on why their children can't read becoming a best-seller, being serialized in newspapers across the nation. Alvin, about school-buildings, health, lunches, civic responsibility, kindness, good humor, spontaneity, we have nothing to learn from the schools of the past; but about reading, with pleasure and understanding, the best that has been thought and said in the world—about *that* we have much to learn. The child who reads and understands the Appleton Fifth Reader is well on the way to becoming an educated, cultivated human being—and if he has to do it sitting in a one-room schoolhouse, if he has to do it sitting on a hollow log, he's better off than a boy sitting in the Pentagon reading *Days and Deeds*. There's a jug of cider in the ice-box, Alvin; you get it, I'll get the glasses; and let's drink a toast to—

ALVIN: To the Appleton Fifth Reader! long may she read! (*They drink.*)

UNCLE WADSWORTH: And now, Alvin, let us conclude the meeting with a song.

ALVIN: What song?

UNCLE WADSWORTH: What song? Alvin, can you ask? Start us off, Alvin!

ALVIN: School days, school days. . . .

BOTH: Dear old golden rule days. . . .

ALVIN: Louder, Uncle Wadsworth, louder!

BOTH: Reading' and 'ritin' and 'rithmetic
     Taught to the tune of a hick'ry stick. . . .

(*Alvin and Uncle Wadsworth and the accordion disappear into the distance.*)

## WORDS

*connotation*   What are the connotations of these names: Fletcher D. Slater, Nora Burglon, Sterling North, and Ruth G. Plowhead? and of these names: Goethe, Shakespeare, Cervantes, and Dr. Johnson? What effect is achieved by opposing two such lists?

## SENTENCES

*style*   1. What point does the author make by having Alvin fail to recognize Uncle Wadsworth's allusion to the fat boy in *Pickwick Papers?* by having him catch himself in a common mispronunciation of *irrelevant?* by having him make a serious allusion to *Dick Tracy?* by having him read poetry "in careful singsong"? by having him fail to remember or recognize poetry he has presumably studied?   2. Is Alvin's speech intended to show deficiencies in his education or in his intelligence?   3. How do the sentences in the dialogue differ from those in the other essays of this book? Why are they different?

## PARAGRAPHS

*unity*   In a dialogue such as this one, each speech is a paragraph, just as it would be if it were reported in a novel or short story. How do the paragraphs of this dialogue differ from those of most important essays? Are they longer or shorter? In what ways do they reproduce the rhythm and diction of informal conversation?

CONTENT AND ORGANIZATION

*central idea*   What single speech contains the central idea of the dialogue —the "message" of the author?

*organization*   1. The dialogue is one of the oldest literary forms. Find or recall a dialogue by Plato, Boethius, John Dryden, Walter Savage Landor, or Charles Erskine Scott Wood. What is its subject, and what advantages does its author gain from the dialogue form? 2. How does a dialogue differ from a play? from a closet drama?

*assumptions and implications*   1. The author shows that *Appletons' Fifth Reader* offered good and challenging literature to fifth-grade students. Does he also show that most students profited from this offering? 2. What evidence can be produced to show that the average American student is less well educated than his European counterpart? or than his American counterpart was seventy-five years ago?

SUGGESTIONS FOR DISCUSSION

1. Can you write a dialogue in which a stupid, bigoted, and ignorant oldster boasts to his nephew of the "old-time" education he received? 2. Do you believe that vulgarizations of our cultural inheritance—comic book condensations of Shakespeare, tin-pan-alley treatments of folk songs and classical themes, and "simplified" editions of great novels—do lasting damage either to the public or to the art itself? Explain.   3. Comment on Alvin's description of present educational practice: "we just appeal to the child's better nature, and get him to adjust, and try to make him see that what he likes to do is what we want him to do."   4. Defenders of modern education claim that many critics (like the author of this dialogue) have no realistic appreciation of the limitations of the average elementary-school student. Is their defense sound?   5. To what extent is Thoreau a "plain American writer"? What do you think of the account in the Fifth Reader of the Thoreau selection? (See "The Ant War," pp. 41–43.)

*Herbert Gold*

# A DOG IN BROOKLYN,
# A GIRL IN DETROIT:
# LIFE AMONG THE HUMANITIES

1.   What better career for a boy who seeks to unravel the meaning of our brief span on earth than that of philosopher? We all wonder darkly, in the forbidden hours of the night, punishing our parents and building a better world, with undefined terms. Soon, however, most of us learn to sleep soundly; or we take to pills or love-making; or we call ourselves insomniacs, not philosophers. A few attempt to define the terms.

2.   There is no code number for the career of philosophy in school, the Army, or out beyond in real life. The man with a peculiar combination of melancholic, nostalgic, and reforming instincts stands at three possibilities early in his youth. He can choose to be a hero, an artist, or a philosopher. In olden times, war, say, or the need to clean out the old west, might make up his mind for him. The old west had been pretty well cleaned up by the time I reached a man's estate, and Gary Cooper could finish the job. Heroism was an untimely option. With much bureaucratic confusion I tried a bit of heroic war, got stuck in the machine, and returned to the hectic, Quonset campus of the G.I. Bill, burning to Know, Understand, and Convert. After a season of ferocious burrowing in books, I was ready to be a Teacher, which seemed a stern neighbour thing to Artist and Philosopher. I took on degrees, a Fulbright fellowship, a wife, a child, a head crammed with foolish questions and dogmatic answers despite the English school of linguistic analysis. I learned to smile, pardner, when I asked questions of philosophers trained at Oxford or Cambridge, but I asked them nonetheless. I signed petitions against McCarthy, wrote a novel, went on a treasure hunt, returned to my roots in the Middle West and stood rooted there, discussed the menace of the mass media, and had another child.

A DOG IN BROOKLYN, A GIRL IN DETROIT: LIFE AMONG THE HUMANITIES:   Copyright © 1962 by Herbert Gold. From *The Age of Happy Problems* by Herbert Gold. Reprinted by permission of the publisher, The Dial Press.

3.  By stages not important here, I found myself teaching the Humanities at Wayne University in Detroit. I am now going to report a succession of classroom events which, retrospectively, seems to have determined my abandonment of formal dealing with this subject. The evidence does not, however, render any conclusion about education in the "Humanities" logically impregnable. It stands for a state of mind and is no substitute for formal argument. However, states of mind are important in this area of experience and meta-experience. However and however: it happens that most of the misty exaltation of the blessed vocation of the teacher issues from the offices of deans, editors, and college presidents. The encounter with classroom reality has caused many teachers, like Abelard meeting the relatives of Eloïse, to lose their bearings. Nevertheless this is a memoir, not a campaign, about a specific life in and out of the Humanities. Though I am not a great loss to the History of Everything in Culture, my own eagerness to teach is a loss to me.

4.  News item of a few years ago. A young girl and her date are walking along a street in Brooklyn, New York. The girl notices that they are being followed by an enormous Great Dane. The dog is behaving peculiarly, showing its teeth and making restless movements. A moment later, sure enough, the dog, apparently maddened, leaps slavering upon the girl, who is borne to earth beneath its weight. With only an instant's hesitation, the boy jumps on the dog. Its fangs sunk in one, then in the other, the dog causes the three of them to roll like beasts across the sidewalk.

5.  A crowd gathers at a safe distance to watch. No one interferes. They display the becalmed curiosity of teevee viewers.

6.  A few moments later a truckdriver, attracted by the crowd, pulls his vehicle over to the kerb. This brave man is the only human being stirred personally enough to leave the role of passive spectator. Instantaneously analysing the situation, he leaps into the struggle—*attacking and beating the boy*. He has naturally assumed that the dog must be protecting an innocent young lady from the unseemly actions of a juvenile delinquent.

7.  I recounted this anecdote in the classroom in order to introduce a course which attempted a summary experience of Humanities 610 for a monumental nine credits. There were a number of points to be made about the passivity of the crowd ("don't get involved," "not my business") and the stereotypical reaction of the truckdriver who had been raised to think of man's best friend as not another human being but a dog. In both cases, addicted to enter-

tainment and clichés, the crowd and the trucker could not recognise what was actually happening before their eyes; they responded irrelevantly to the suffering of strangers; they were not a part of the main. This led us to a discussion of the notion of "community." In a closely-knit society, the people on the street would have known the couple involved and felt a responsibility toward them. In a large city, everyone is a stranger. (Great art can give a sense of the brotherhood of men. Religion used to do this, too.) "Any questions?" I asked, expecting the authority of religion to be defended.

8. An eager hand shot up. Another. Another. Meditative bodies sprawled in their chairs. "Are all New Yorkers like that?" "Well, what can you do if there's a mad dog and you're not expecting it?" "Where does it say in what great book how you got to act in Brooklyn?"

9. I took note of humour in order to project humorousness. I found myself composing my face in the look of thought which teevee panellists use in order to project thinking. I discovered a serious point to elaborate—several. I mentioned consciousness and relevance and the undefined moral suggestion implied by the labour which produces any work of art or mind. A girl named Clotilda Adams asked me: "Why don't people try to get along better in this world?"

10. Somewhat digressively, we then discussed the nature of heroism, comparing the behaviour of the boy and the truckdriver. Both took extraordinary risks; why? We broke for cigarettes in the autumn air outside. Then, for fifty minutes more, we raised these interesting questions, referring forward to Plato, Aristotle, St. Thomas, Dostoevsky, Tolstoy, William James, and De Gaulle; and then boy, dog, girl, truckdriver and crowd were left with me and the crowned ghosts of history in the deserted room while my students went on to Phys Ed, Music Appreciation, Sosh, and their other concerns. Having been the chief speaker, both dramatist and analyst, I was exalted by the lofty ideas floated up into the air around me. I was a little let down to return to our real life in which dog-eat-dog is man's closest pal. Fact. Neither glory nor pleasure nor power, and certainly not wisdom, provided the goal of my students. Not even wealth was the aim of most of them. They sought to make out, to do all right, more prideful than amorous in love, more security-hungry than covetous in status. I saw my duty as a teacher: Through the Humanities, to awaken them to the dream of mastery over the facts of our lives. I saw my duty plain: Through the Humanities, to lead them toward the exaltation of knowledge and the calm of control. I had a whole

year in which to fulfil this obligation. It was a two-semester course.

11. Before she left the room, Clotilda Adams said, "You didn't answer my question." Fact.

12. Outside the university enclave of glass and grass, brick and trees, Detroit was agonising in its last big year with the big cars. Automation, dispersion of factories, and imported automobiles were eroding a precarious confidence. Fear was spreading; soon the landlords would offer to decorate apartments and suffer the pain. Detroit remembered the war years with nostalgia. Brave days, endless hours, a three-shift clock, insufficient housing, men sleeping in the all-night, triple-feature movies on Woodward and Grand River. Though the area around the Greyhound and Trailways stations was still clotted with the hopeful out of the hill country of the mid-south and the driven from the deep south—they strolled diagonally across the boulevards, entire families holding hands—some people suspected what was already on its way down the road: twenty per cent unemployment in Detroit.

13. The semester continued. We churned through the great books. One could classify my students in three general groups, intelligent, mediocre, and stupid, allowing for the confusions of three general factors—background, capacity, and interest. This was how we classified the Humanities, too: ancient, medieval, and modern. It made a lot of sense, and it made me itch, scratch, and tickle. Series of three form nice distinctions. According to Jung and other authorities, they have certain mythic significances. The course was for nine credits. All the arts were touched upon. We obeyed Protagoras; man, just man, was our study. When I cited him—"the proper study of man is Man"—Clotilda Adams stirred uneasily in her seat. "By which Protagoras no doubt meant woman, too," I assured her. She rested.

14. Now imagine the winter coming and enduring, with explosions of storm and exfoliations of gray slush, an engorged industrial sky overhead and sinus trouble all around. The air was full of acid and a purplish, spleeny winter mist. Most of Detroit, in Indian times before the first French trappers arrived, had been a swamp and below sea level. The swamp was still present, but invisible; city stretched out in all directions, crawling along the highways. Though Detroit was choked by a dense undergrowth of streets and buildings, irrigated only by super-highways, its work was done with frantic speed. The Rouge plant roared, deafened. The assembly lines clanked to the limit allowed by the UAW. The old Hudson factory lay empty, denuded, waiting to become a parking lot. Then the

new models were being introduced! Buick! Pontiac! Dodge! Ford and Chevrolet! Ford impudently purchased a huge billboard faced toward the General Motors Building on Grand Boulevard. General Motors retaliated by offering free ginger ale to all comers, and a whole bottle of Vernor's to take home if you would only consent to test-drive the new Oldsmobile, the car with the . . . I've forgotten what it had that year. All over town the automobile companies were holding revival meetings; hieratic salesmen preached to the converted and the hangers-back alike; lines at the loan companies stretched through the revolving doors and out on to the winter pavements. But many in those lines were trying to get additional financing on their last year's cars. The new models were an indifferent success despite all the uproar of display and Detroit's patriotic attention to it. Searchlights sliced up the heavens while the city lay under flu.

15. Teachers at Wayne University soon learn not to tease the American Automobile. *Lèse* Chrysler was a moral offence, an attack on the livelihood and the sanctity of the American garage. Detroit was a town in which men looked at hub caps as men elsewhere have sometimes looked at ankles. The small foreign car found itself treated with a violent Halloween kidding-on-the-square, scratched, battered, and smeared (another Jungian series of three!). A passionate and sullen town, Detroit had no doubts about its proper business. All it doubted was everything else.

16. I often failed at inspiring my students to do the assigned reading. Many of them had part-time jobs in the automobile industry or its annexes. Even a Philosopher found it difficult to top the argument, "I couldn't read the book this week, I have to *work*," with its implied reproach for a scholar's leisure. But alas, many of these stricken proletarians drove freshly-minted automobiles. They worked in order to keep up the payments, racing like laboratory mice around the cage of depreciation. Certain faculty deep thinkers, addicted to broad understanding of the problems of others, argued that these students were so poor they *had* to buy new cars in order to restore their confidence. The finance companies seemed to hear their most creative expressions, not me. Deep in that long Detroit winter, I had the task of going from the pre-Socratic mystics all the way to Sartre, for nine credits. Like an audio-visual monkey, I leapt from movie projector to records to slides, with concurrent deep labour in book and tablet. We read *The Brothers Karamazov,* but knowing the movie did not give credit. We studied *The Waste Land,* and reading the

footnotes did not suffice. We listened to Wanda Landowska play the harpsichord on records. We sat in the dark before a slide of Seurat's "La Grande Jatte" while I explained the importance of the measles of *pointillisme* to students who only wanted to see life clear and true, see it comfortably. Clotilda Adams said that this kind of painting hurt her eyes. She said that there was too much reading for one course—"piling it on. This isn't the only course we take." She said that she liked music, though. Moses only had to bring the Law down the mountain to the children of Israel; I had to bring it pleasingly.

17. We made exegeses. I flatly turned down the request of a dean that I take attendance. As a statesmanlike compromise, I tested regularly for content and understanding.

18. Then, on a certain morning, I handed back some quiz papers at the beginning of class. Out on the street, a main thoroughfare through town, it was snowing; this was one of those magical days of late winter snowfall—pale, cold, clean, and the entire city momentarily muffled by the silence of snow. The room hissed with steam heat; a smell of galoshes and mackinaws arose from the class. "Let us not discuss the test—let us rise above grades. Let us try to consider nihilism as a byproduct of the Romantic revival—" I had just begun my lecture when an odd clashing, lumping noise occurred on Cass Avenue. "Eliot's later work, including *The Four Quartets,* which we will not discuss here. . . ."

19. But I was interrupted by a deep sigh from the class. A product of nihilism and the romantic revival? No. It was that strange tragic sigh of horror and satisfaction. Out in the street, beyond the window against which I stood, a skidding truck had sideswiped a taxi. The truckdriver had parked and gone into a drugstore. The cab was smashed like a cruller. From the door, the driver had emerged, stumbling drunkenly on the icy road, holding his head. There was blood on his head. There was blood on his hands. He clutched his temples. The lines of two-way traffic, moving very slowly in the snow and ice, carefully avoided hitting him. There were streaks of perforated and patterned snow, frothed up by tyres. He was like an island around which the sea of traffic undulated in slow waves; but he was an island that moved in the sea and held hands to head. He slid and stumbled back and forth, around and about his cab in the middle of the wide street. He was in confusion, in shock. Even at this distance I could see blood on the new-fallen snow. Drivers turned their heads upon him like angry Halloween masks, but did not get involved. Snow spit at his feet.

20.  No one in the class moved. The large window through which we gazed was like a screen, with the volume turned down by habit, by snow, by a faulty tube. As the teacher, my authority took precedence. I ran out to lead the cab driver into the building. An elderly couple sat huddled in the car, staring at the smashed door, afraid to come out the other. They said they were unhurt.

21.  I laid the man down on the floor. He was bleeding from the head and his face was a peculiar purplish colour, with a stubble of beard like that of a dead man. There was a neat prick in his forehead where the union button in his cap had been driven into the skin. I sent a student to call for an ambulance. The cab driver's colour was like that of the bruised industrial sky. "You be okay till the ambulance—?"

22.  Foolish question. No alternative. No answer.

23.  We waited. The class was restless. When they weren't listening to me, or talking to themselves, or smudging blue books in an exam, they did not know what to do in this room devoted to the specialised absorption of ideas. Silence. Scraping of feet, crisping of paper. We watched the slow-motion traffic on the street outside.

24.  The cab driver moved once in a rush, turning over face down against the floor, with such force that I thought he might break his nose. Then slowly, painfully, as if in a dream, he turned back and lay staring at the ceiling. His woollen lumberjacket soaked up the blood trickling from one ear; the blood travelled up separated cilia of wool which drew it in with a will of their own. There was a swaying, osmotic movement like love-making in the eager little wisps of wool. An astounded ring of Humanities 610 students watched, some still holding their returned quiz papers. One girl in particular, Clotilda Adams, watched him and me with her eyes brilliant, wet, and bulging, and her fist crumpling the paper. I tried by imagining it to force the ambulance through the chilled and snowfallen city. I saw it weaving around the injured who strutted with shock over ice and drift, its single red Cyclop's eye turning, the orderlies hunched over on benches, chewing gum and cursing the driver. The ambulance did not arrive. Clotilda Adams' eye had a thick, impenetrable sheen over it. She watched from the cab driver to me as if we were in some way linked. When would the authorities get there? When the medics? There must have been many accidents in town, and heart attacks, and fires with cases of smoke inhalation.

25.  Before the ambulance arrived, the police were there. They came strolling into the classroom with their legs apart, as if they remembered ancestors who rode the plains. Their mouths were heavy

in thought. They had noses like salamis, red and mottled with fat. They were angry at the weather, at the school, at the crowd, at me, and especially at the prostrate man at our feet. He gave them a means to the creative expression of pique. (Everyone needs an outlet.)

26. Now Clotilda Adams took a step backward, and I recall thinking this odd. She had been treading hard near the pool of blood about the cab driver, but when the cops strolled up, she drifted toward the outer edge of the group of students, with a sly look of caution in her downcast, sideways-cast eyes. Her hand still crisped at the returned exam paper. This sly, lid-fallen look did not do her justice. She was a hard little girl of the sort often thought to be passionate—skinny but well-breasted, a high hard rump with a narrow curve, a nervous mouth.

27. The two policemen stood over the body of the cab driver. They stared at him in the classic pose—one cop with a hand resting lightly on the butt of his gun and the other on his butt, the younger cop with lips so pouted that his breath made a snuffling sound in his nose. They both had head colds. Their Ford was pulled up on the snow-covered lawn outside, with raw muddled marks of tread in the soft dirt. When the snow melted, there would be wounded streaks in the grass. The cab driver closed his eyes under the finicking, distasteful examination. At last one spoke: "See your driver's licence."

28. The cab driver made a clumsy gesture towards his pocket. The cop bent and went into the pocket. He flipped open the wallet, glanced briefly at the photographs and cash, glanced at me, and then began lip-reading the licence.

29. The cab driver was in a state of shock. There was a mixture of thin and thick blood on his clothes and messing the floor. "This man is badly hurt," I said. "Can't we get him to the hospital first?"

30. "This is only your *driver* licence," the cop said slowly, having carefully read through Colour of Hair: *Brn,* Colour of Eyes: *Brn,* and checked each item with a stare at the man on the floor. "Let me see your chauffeur licence."

31. "He's badly hurt," I said. "Get an ambulance."

32. "Teach'," said the older cop, "you know your business? We know ours."

33. "It's on the way," said the other. "Didn't you call it yourself?"

34. "No, one of the students. . . ." I said.

35. He grinned with his great victory. "So—don't you trust your pupils neither?"

36. Shame. I felt shame at this ridicule of my authority in the classroom. A professor is not a judge, a priest, or a sea captain; he does not have the right to perform marriages on the high seas of audio-visual aids and close reasoning. But he is more than an intercom between student and fact; he can be a stranger to love for his students, but not to a passion for his subject; he is a student himself; his pride is lively. The role partakes of a certain heft and control. There is power to make decisions, power to abstain, power to bewilder, promote, hold back, adjust, and give mercy; power, an investment of pride, a risk of shame.

37. Clotilda Adams, still clutching her exam, stared at me with loathing. She watched me bested by the police. She barely glanced, and only contemptuously, at the man bleeding from the head on the floor. She moved slightly forward again in order to participate fully in an action which apparently had some important meaning for her. She had lost her fear of the police when she saw how we all stood with them. The limits were established.

38. The police were going through the cab driver's pockets. They took out a folding pocketknife and cast significant looks at it and at each other. It had a marbled plastic hilt, like a resort souvenir. It was attached to a key ring.

39. "Hey!" one said to the half-conscious man. "What's this knife for?"

40. "Where'd you get them keys?" the other demanded, prodding the cabbie with his toe.

41. "A *skeleton* key. These cab companies," one of the cops decided to explain to Clotilda Adams, who was standing nearby, "they get the dregs. Hillbillies, you know?"

42. I said nothing, found nothing to say. I now think of Lord Acton's famous law, which is accepted as true the way it was uttered. The opposite is also true—the commoner's way: Having no power corrupts; having absolutely no power corrupts absolutely.

43. The bleeding seemed to have stopped. The cab driver sat up, looking no better, with his bluish, greenish, drained head hanging between his knees. His legs were crumpled stiffly. He propped himself on his hands. The police shot questions at him. He mumbled, mumbled, explained, explained.

44. "How long you been in Detroit? How come you come out of the mountains?"

45. "Why you pick up this fare?"

46. "What makes you think Cass is a one-way street?"

47. Mumbling and mumbling, explaining and explaining, the cab driver tried to satisfy them. He also said: "Hurt. Maybe you get me to the hospital, huh? Hurt real bad."

48. "Maybe," said one of the cops, "maybe we take you to the station house first. That boy you hit says reckless driving. I think personally you'd flunk the drunk test—what you think, Teach'?"

49. I sent one of the students to call for an ambulance again. In the infinitesimal pause between my suggestion and his action, an attentive reluctant expectant caesura, I put a dime in his hand for the call. One of the cops gave me that long look described by silent movie critics as the slow burn. "They drive careful," he finally said. "It's snowing. They got all that expensive equipment."

50. The snow had started again outside the window. The skid-marks on the lawn were covered. Though the sky was low and gray, the white sifting down gave a peaceful village glow to this industrial Detroit. Little gusts barely rattled the windows. With the class, the cops, and the driver, we were living deep within a snowy paper weight. I felt myself moving very slowly, swimming within thick glass, like the loosened plastic figure in a paper weight. The snow came down in large torn flakes, all over the buildings of Wayne University, grass, trees, and the pale radiance of a network of slow-motion super-highways beyond. Across the street a modern building— glass and aluminum strips—lay unfinished in this weather. Six months ago there had been a student boarding house on that spot, filled with the artists and the beat, the guitar-wielders and the modern dancers, with a tradition going all the way back to the Korean war. Now there were wheelbarrows full of frozen cement; there were intentions to build a Japanese garden, with Japanese proportions and imported goldfish.

51. My student returned from the telephone. He had reached a hospital.

52. The cab driver was fading away. Rootlets of shock hooded his eyes: the lid was closing shut. A cop asked him another question —what the button on his cap stood for—it was a union button—and then the man just went reclining on his elbow, he slipped slowly down, he lay in the little swamp of crusted blood on the floor. You know what happens when milk is boiled? The crust broke like the

crust of boiled milk when a spoon goes into coffee. The cop stood with a delicate, disgusted grimace on his face. What a business to be in, he seemed to be thinking. In approximately ten years, at age forty-two, he could retire and sit comfortable in an undershirt, with a non-returnable can of beer, before the colour teevee. He could relax. He could *start* to relax. But in the meantime—nag, nag, nag. Drunk cabbies, goddam hillbillies. The, reckless driver on the floor seemed to sleep. His lips moved. He was alive.

53. Then a puffing intern rushed into the room. I had not heard the ambulance. The policeman gave room and the intern kneeled. He undid his bag. The orderlies glanced at the floor and went back out for their stretcher.

54. I stood on one side of the body, the kneeling intern with his necklace of stethoscope, and the two meditative cops. On the other side was the group of students, and at their head, like a leader filled with wrath, risen in time of crisis, stood Clotilda Adams, still clutching her exam paper. There were tears in her eyes. She was in a fury. She had been thinking all this time, and now her thinking had issue: *rage.* Over the body she handed me a paper, crying out, "I don't think I deserved a *D* on that quiz. I answered all the questions. I can't get my credit for Philo of Ed without I get a *B* off you."

55. I must have looked at her with pure stupidity on my face. There is a Haitian proverb: Stupidity won't kill you, but it'll make you sweat a lot. She took the opportunity to make me sweat, took my silence for guilt, took my openmouthed gaze for weakness. She said: "If I was a white girl, you'd grade me easier."

56. Guilt, a hundred years, a thousand years of it; pity for the disaster of ignorance and fear, pity for ambition rising out of ignorance; adoration of desire; trancelike response to passion—passion which justifies itself because passionate. . . . I looked at her with mixed feelings. I could not simply put her down. In order to *put down,* your own mind must be made up, put down. She had beauty and dignity, stretched tall and wrathful, with teeth for biting and eyes for striking dead.

57. "But I know my rights," she said, *"mister.* My mother told me about your kind—lent my father money on his car and then hounded him out of town. He's been gone since fifty-three. But you can't keep us down forever, no sir, you can't always keep us down—"

58. She was talking and I was yelling. She was talking and yelling about injustice and I, under clamps, under ice, was yelling in a whisper about the sick man. She was blaming me for all her troubles, all the troubles she had seen, and I was blaming her for not

seeing what lay before her, and we were making an appointment to meet in my office and discuss this thing more calmly, Miss Adams. Okay. All right. Later.

59. The police, the doctor, the orderlies, and the injured cab driver were gone. The police car out front was gone and the snow was covering its traces. The janitor came in and swept up the bloodstains with green disinfectant powder. The frightened couple in the cab were released. They all disappeared silently into the great city, into the routine of disaster and recovery of a great city. I dismissed the class until tomorrow.

60. The next day I tried to explain to Miss Adams what I meant about her failing to respond adequately to the facts of our life together. Her mouth quivered. Yesterday rage; today a threat of tears. What did I mean she wasn't *adequate?* What did I know about adequate anyhow? Nothing. Just a word. Agreed, Miss Adams. I was trying to say that there were two questions at issue between us—her exam grade and her choice of occasion to dispute it. I would like to discuss each matter separately. I tried to explain why putting the two events together had disturbed me. I tried to explain the notions of empirical evidence and metaphor. Finally I urged her to have her exam looked at by the head of the department, but she refused because she knew in advance that he would support me. "White is Right," she said.

61. "Do you want to drop out of the class?"

62. "No. I'll stay," she said with a sudden patient, weary acceptance of her fate. "I'll do what I can."

63. "I'll do what I can too," I said.

64. She smiled hopefully at me. She was tuckered out by the continual alert for combat everywhere. She was willing to forgive and go easy. When she left my office, this smile, shy, pretty, and conventional, tried to tell me that she could be generous—a friend.

65. We had come to Thomas Hobbes and John Locke in our tour through time and the river of humanities. I pointed out that the English philosophers were noted for clarity and eloquence of style. I answered this question: The French? Isn't French noted for clarity? Yes, they too, but they were more abstract. On the whole. In general.

66. The class took notes on the truths we unfolded together. Spring came and the snow melted. There was that brief Detroit flowering of the new season—jasmine and hollyhocks—which, something like it, must have captivated the Frenchman Antoine de la

Mothe Cadillac when he paused on the straits of Detroit in 1701. University gardeners planted grass seed where the patrol car had parked on the lawn. The new models, all except the Cadillac, were going at mean discounts.

67. "The 'Humanities,' " wrote Clotilda Adams in her final essay, "are a necessary additive to any teacher's development worth her 'salt' in the perilous times of today. The West and the 'Free World' must stand up to the war of ideas against the 'Iron' Curtain." This was in answer to a question about Beethoven, Goethe, and German romanticism. She did not pass the course, but she was nevertheless admitted on probation to the student teacher programme because of the teacher shortage and the great need to educate our children in these perilous times. Of today.

68. Humanities 610 provided ballast for the ship of culture as it pitched and reeled in the heavy seas of real life; I lashed myself to the mast, but after hearing the siren song of grand course outlines, I cut myself free and leaned over the rail with the inside of my lip showing.

69. It would be oversimplifying to say that I left off teaching Humanities merely because of an experience. Such an argument is fit to be published under the title "I was a Teen-Age Humanities Professor." I also left for fitter jobs, more money, a different life. Still, what I remember of the formal study of Truth and Beauty, for advanced credit in education, is a great confusion of generalities, committees, conferences, audio-visual importunities, and poor contact. "Contact!" cried the desperate deans and chairmen, like radio operators in ancient war movies. And much, much discussion of how to get through to the students. How to get through? Miss Adams and Mr. Gold, cab driver and Thomas Hobbes, policemen and the faceless student who paused an instant for a dime for the telephone—we all have to discover how relevant we are to each other. Or do we *have* to? No, we can merely perish, shot down like mad dogs or diminished into time with no more than a glimpse of the light.

70. Words fade; our experience does not touch; we make do with babble and time-serving. We need to learn the meaning of words, the meaning of the reality those words refer to; we must clasp reality close. We cannot flirt forever, brown-nosing or browbeating. We must act and build out of our own spirits. How? How? We continually need new politics, new cities, new marriages and families, new ways of work and leisure. We also need the fine old

ways. For me, the primitive appeal to pleasure and pain of writing stories is a possible action, is the way in and out again, as teaching was not. As a teacher, I caught my students too late and only at the top of their heads, at the raw point of pride and ambition, and I had not enough love and pressure as a teacher to open the way through their intentions to the common humanity which remains locked within. As a writer, I could hope to hit them in their bodies and needs, where lusts and ideals are murkily nurtured together, calling to the prime fears and joys directly, rising with them from the truths of innocence into the truths of experience.

71. The peculiar combination of ignorance and jadedness built into most institutions is a desperate parody of personal innocence, personal experience. Nevertheless, education, which means a drawing out—even formal education, a formal drawing out—is a variety of experience, and experience is the only evidence we have. After evidence comes our thinking upon it. Do the scientists, secreting their honey in distant hives, hear the barking of the black dog which follows them? Will the politicians accept the lead of life, or will they insist on a grade of *B* in Power and Domination over a doomed race? We need to give proper answers to the proper questions.

72. Particular life is still the best map to truth. When we search our hearts and strip our pretences, we all know this. Particular life—we know only what we *know*. Therefore the policemen stay with me: I have learned to despise most authority. The cab driver remains in his sick bleeding: pity for the fallen and helpless. And I think of Clotilda Adams in her power and weakness; like the cops, she has an authority of stupidity; like the victim of an accident, she is fallen and helpless. But some place, since we persist in our cold joke against the ideal of democracy, the cops still have the right to push people around, Clotilda is leading children in the Pledge of Allegiance. We must find a way to teach better and to learn.

WORDS

*meaning* Define *nostalgic* (par. 2), *meta-experience* (par. 3), *enclave* (par. 12), *exfoliations* and *hieratic* (par. 14), *exegeses* (par. 17), *nihilism* (par. 18), *undulated* (par. 19), *cilia* (par. 24), *caesura* (par. 49), *grimace* (par. 52), and *jadedness* (par. 71).

*word choice* 1. How do the verb forms of paragraphs 4, 5, and 6 differ from those of the paragraphs preceding and following? What purpose does the author achieve by making this change? 2. What is the effect produced by the author's special use of capitalization in the following phrases of paragraphs 2 and 3: "burning to Know, Understand, and Convert," "ready to be a Teacher," and "History of Everything in Culture"?

## SENTENCES

*style*   1. One technique of this essay is ironic self-depreciation. Find a sentence in paragraph 2 that illustrates it. Find others in paragraphs 9 and 10.   2. Although the diction and sentence structure of this essay are frequently colloquial, capturing the movement and rhythm of educated speech, they are rich in allusion. What is the meaning of the allusion to Abelard and Eloïse in paragraph 3? of the statements "they were not a part of the main" (par. 7) and "He was like an island" (par. 19)?

*emphasis*   How are sentence fragments used in paragraphs 22 and 23? Would the essay be improved if they were rewritten so that they became parts of complete sentences? Why or why not?

## PARAGRAPHS

*unity*   What is the unifying idea or mood of paragraph 66?

*emphasis*   How do the two-word tags that end paragraphs 65 and 67 sum up and reinforce the ideas of these paragraphs?

*rhetorical devices*   Paragraph 68 is one extended metaphor. Is it also a mixed metaphor? Explain your answer.

## CONTENT AND ORGANIZATION

*central idea*   1. The central idea of this essay is expressed in one sentence of paragraph 69. Which sentence?   2. How do the descriptions of the injured cab driver and the harried cop in paragraph 52 combine to illustrate the central idea of the essay?

*organization*   1. The author uses a novelist's skill in showing, rather than describing, Miss Adams' personality. How does he show her inability to rise above clichés? her own prejudices?   2. What is the relevance to the theme of the essay of the repeated references to a particular unsuccessful year in the Detroit automobile industry? Why does the author indulge in what he calls *Lèse* Chrysler (par. 15)?   3. What is the truth illustrated by both the story of the dog in Brooklyn and the story of Clotilda Adams?

*assumptions and implications*   1. What did the author's students want from life (par. 10)? What is the author's expressed and implied criticism of their aspirations?   2. Is it one implication of this essay that Clotilda Adams was typical of all the author's students? Was he unable to reach and stir any of them?

## SUGGESTIONS FOR DISCUSSION

1. Have you ever watched an accident or fight and failed to help or intervene when you might have? Why? 2. Do you agree that a big city is different from a small community only because the city is a collection of many small communities? 3. Why do many "stricken proletarians [drive] freshly-minted automobiles" (par. 16)? 4. Why do many people walk past a man lying ill or unconscious on a sidewalk and yet flock to stand at the scene of a disaster where they can only cause confusion and create difficulties for police, firemen, and doctors?

# Freedom and Frustration
# in Modern Society

## Richard Poirier

## THE WAR AGAINST THE YOUNG

1. The social systems which organize and rationalize contemporary life have always been ingeniously armed for the day when youth would rebel against the essentially pastoral status assigned to it. Despite pamperings until recently unimaginable, despite economic briberies and various psychological coercions, the rebellion has broken out. Predictably, the response to it is a gradual escalation involving a more naked use of the tactics that were supposed to prevent, but which also helped to provoke, the crisis in the first place: patronizations, put-downs, and tongue-lashings, along with offers of a place in the governing system (if only the system is left intact) and promises that in any case the future itself holds the solution to whatever now seems to be the trouble. If this technique sounds familiar in its mixture of brutality and pacification, in its combination of aggression and absorption, noted by Edgar Freidenberg in his brilliant analysis of the adult treatment of the adolescent minority, if it sounds vaguely like methods used in other and related domestic and foreign conflicts, then the point is obvious: our society is unfortunately structured, in the prevalent forms of its language and thinking, in ways designed to suppress some of the most vital elements now struggling into consciousness and toward some awareness of their frustrated powers.

2. This struggle is essentially a cultural one, regardless of the efforts by older people to make political use of it or to place it, unflatteringly, within the terms of traditional politics, particularly cold-war politics. The intellectual weapons used in the war against youth

THE WAR AGAINST THE YOUNG: From *The Performing Self: Compositions and Decompositions in the Languages of Contemporary Life* by Richard Poirier. Copyright © 1971 by Oxford University Press, Inc. Reprinted by permission.

are from the same arsenal—and the young know this—from which war is being waged against other revolutionary movements, against Vietnam, against any effective justice, as distinguished from legislative melodrama, in matters of race and poverty. These weapons, as I've suggested, are by no means crude. They scarcely look at times like weapons at all, and many of the people most adroit in handling them, writers and teachers as well as politicians, aren't even aware that they are directing against youth arguments of a kind used also to rationalize other policies which they consider senseless and immoral. Aside from the political necessities of candidates, why is it that people who can be tough-mindedly idealistic in opposition to our actions in Vietnam or to our treatment of the powerless, talk about youth and think about the rebellion of youth in a manner implicit in the mentality that produces and excuses these other barbarities? The reason, I think, is that most people don't want to face the possibility that each of these troubles grows from the same root and can be traced back to the same habits of mind within each of us and within the social organisms to which we have lent ourselves. They prefer isolated and relatively visible sources for such difficulties, along with the illusion that each of them is susceptible to accredited forms of political or economic cleansing. By contrast, it is the conviction of the most militant young people, and of some older ones, that any solutions will require a radical change in the historical, philosophical, and psychological assumptions that are the foundations of any political or economic system. Some kind of cultural revolution is therefore the necessary prelude even to our capacity to think intelligently about political reformation.

3. Oddly enough, the young are proved right, in this supposition at least, by the nature of the attacks made against them. I don't mean attacks from the likes of Reagan and Wallace, but those coming from becalmed and sensible men, whose moderation is of a piece with their desire to increase the efficiency of the present system. At work in these attacks are the same tendencies of thought and language that shape the moderate, rationalizing analyses of the other nightmares I've mentioned.

4. Maybe the most prevalent of these tendencies is the insistence on a language that is intellectually "cool," a language aloof from militant or revolutionary vocabularies which in their exclusion sound excessive, exaggerated, and unserviceable. This cool language is not at all dull or plodding. On the contrary, it's full of social flair; it swings with big words, slang words, naughty words, leaping nimbly

from the "way out" to the "way in"—it really holds the world together, hips and squares alike. The best working example is the style of *Time* magazine, and it wasn't surprising to find there a piece full of compliments to what were called in the title "Anti-Revolutionaries." With the suave observation that writers like these "who prefer rationality to revolution are by no means conservative," they honored three distinguished commentators on youth and other scenes. One of the three, Benjamin DeMott, a professor of English at Amherst, diversely active as a novelist, critic, and educational innovator, had earlier written an essay in the Sunday *New York Times Magazine* on the style of what he called the "spirit of over-kill" among some of his fellow writers, especially those of the revolutionary fringe like Paul Goodman, Andrew Kopkind, and Susan Sontag.

5. According to DeMott, writing of the sixties in 1968, the verbal violence of this decade "was" (and I'll get to the significance of this past tense in a moment) "pressed not at new 'enemies' but at old ones already in tatters." Just at a glance one had to wonder why "enemies," new or old, were assigned the unreality of quotation marks. Had the semblance of negotiations made the war in Vietnam disappear as an "enemy"? Does he mean racial injustice? the horrors of urban life? the smothering effects of educational institutions of which he is himself one of the most astute critics? I'm afraid these enemies aren't so easily dispelled. The degree to which they press against DeMott's own "cool" dismissal of them is in fact made evident, with engaging innocence, in the very form of his essay. In order to find a requisite dispassion for his own style, as against what he mistakenly takes for the dominant style of this decade, he must project himself to the end of the century and then look back at us. Like other critics of our violence, he is himself already visiting the famous year 2000, programming for which, as we are cautioned by a number of distinguished economists, sociologists, and technicians, will only be disrupted by people who fail to remain politely soft-spoken amid the accumulating squalor, blood, and suffering of their lives.

6. This peculiar form of address, by which we are asked to hear our present as if it were our past, suggests yet another and more subtle method of repression—the futuristic—now especially popular in the social sciences. A notably unembarrassed practitioner, and yet another writer commended by the article in *Time* magazine, is Zbigniew Brzezinski, director of the Research Institute on Communist Affairs at Columbia, a sometime member of the Policy Planning Staff of the State Department, and head of Hubert Humphrey's "task force" on foreign affairs for the 1968 election. Also concerned be-

cause revolutionary loudmouths and their young adherents are incited by the past rather than the future—keep in mind that there is no present, in case you thought it was hurting someone—Brzezinski published two futuristic position papers in the *New Republic:* "The American Transition," and more recently, "Revolution and Counterrevolution (But Not Necessarily About Columbia!)." These were later incorporated into his book *Between Two Ages*. Happily bounding over invisible rainbows, Brzezinski lets us know that, like it or not, we are already becoming a "technetronic society," and any old-fashioned doctrinal or ideological habits—as if ideology wouldn't be inherent in his imagined social systems—will get us into real, permanent troubles instead of temporary ones. We'll fail to adapt, that is, to "the requirements of the metamorphic age," and thus miss the chance to create a "meritocratic democracy" in which "a community of organization-oriented, application-minded intellectuals [can relate] itself more effectively to the political system than their predecessors." We need only stay calm, and admittedly such language is not designed to excite us, since "improved governmental performance, and its increased sensitivity to social needs is being stimulated by the growing involvement in national affairs of what Kenneth Boulding has called the Educational and Scientific Establishment (EASE)."

7.  Deifications have of course always been announced by capitalization. As in religion, so in politics: an "excessive" concern for the present is a sure way of impairing your future. We are, remember, "between two ages." If, in the one case, you might as well surrender your will to God, in the other you might as well surrender it to EASE, or, getting gack to DeMott patiently waiting there at the turn of the century, to "the architects of the Great Disengagement," with "their determination to negotiate the defusing of The Words as well as of The Bombs." But I'm afraid it's merely symptomatic of how bad things are now that many of those who want the young and the rebellious to be more quiet follow the antique example of Hubert Humphrey: they speak to the young not about the past, not even about the present, but about some future, which, as prognosticators, they're already privileged to know. They are There; the revolutionists are living in the Past. And who is here and now, living, suffering, and impassioned in the present? Apparently no one, except maybe a few of what Brzezinski likes to call the "historical irrelevants."

8.  If the young are inarticulate, if, when they do try to expound their views, they sound foolish, are these, and other examples of adult thinking and writing which I'll get to presently, somehow

evidences of superior civilization, something to be emulated, the emanations of a system worth saving from revolution? Such arguments and such uses of language—almost wholly abstracted from the stuff of daily life as it is lived in this year, these months, this week— do not define but rather exemplify the cultural and linguistic crisis to which the young are responding with silence even more than with other demonstrations of their nearly helpless discontent. "Power, or the shadow cast by power, always ends in creating an axiological writing," as the French critic Roland Barth puts it, "in which the distance which usually separates fact from value disappears within the space of a word." To prefer "rationality" to "revolution" is good *Time* magazine language. It can't be faulted except by those who feel, as I do, that a revolution is probably necessary if rationality is to be restored to a society that thinks it has been operating rationally. If the young are "revolutionary," and if this is the reverse of "rational," what, then, is the nature of the rationality they're attacking? Quite aside from science fiction passing for history in the writings we've just looked at, are the practices of the United States government with regard to most issues of race, ecology, poverty, the war, the gun laws, or even the postal service rational? Is it rational to vote an increase of money for Vietnam, and on the same hot day in July cut appropriations for the summer employment of young Blacks and Puerto Ricans, thus helping to encourage a bloody summer at home while assuring one abroad?

9. These are all, as Brzezinski would point out, complex issues, and according to him, they will not be solved by "historical irrelevants," by those who, with revolutionary fervor, are yearning, as he would have it, for the simplicities of the past and who therefore "will have no role to play in the new technetronic society." But what has decided, since I know no people who have, that we want his "technetronic society," that it is desirable or inevitable? Who decides that it is necessary or even good for certain issues to be construed as complex and therefore susceptible only to the diagnosticians who would lead such a society? Why have certain issues become complex and who is served by this complexity? Why is the life we already lead, mysterious and frightening as it is, to be made even more so by the ridiculous shapes conjured up in Brzezinski's jaw-breaking terminologies? Some issues are not simple, which does not mean that some others are not unnecessarily complex. It is clear to everyone that Vietnam is "complex." But it is equally clear that it need not, for us, have become complex; that it might not even have existed as an issue,

except for those members of EASE who helped justify our continued presence there. Maybe the secret is that it is really "easy" to be complex.

10. The funniest and in a way the most innocent example of this kind of no-thinking passing in sound and cadence for responsible, grown-up good sense is offered by George Kennan. The third figure heralded for his rationality in the *Time* article, Kennan is a renowned historian, a former ambassador to the Soviet Union, and the author of yet another containment policy, this one for youth. Kennan's specialty is what might be called "the argument from experience," easily slipping into "the argument from original sin." "The decisive seat of evil in this world," he tells us in *Democracy and the Student Left,* a published debate between him and nearly forty students and teachers, "is not in social and political institutions, and not even, as a rule, in the ill-will or iniquities of statesmen, but simply in the weakness and imperfection of the human soul itself." No one can deny a proposition so general, but surely only someone who likes for other reasons to plead the inescapable complexity of issues could propose such an idea to people wondering how the hell we got into Vietnam or why millions of poor in a country so rich must go hungry every day, and why every summer New York becomes not Fun but Plague City.

11. Kennan has, of course, had direct experience with other revolutions and with other people who have ignored the imperfections of the human soul simply by denying its existence. No wonder it often sounds, then, as if the militant young are merely his chance at last to give a proper dressingdown to the kind of fellows who brought on the Russian Revolution, his historical analogies being to that extent, at least, more complimentary to the young than Brzezinski's evocation of Luddites and Chartists. "I have heard it freely confessed by members of the revolutionary student generation of Tsarist Russia," Kennan rather huffily reports, "that, proud as they were of the revolutionary exploits of their youth, they never really learned anything in their university years; they were too busy with politics." Earlier, from Woodrow Wilson at his prissiest, he describes an ideal "at the very center of our modern institutions of higher learning": it is a "free place," in Wilson's words, "itself a little world; but not perplexed, living with a singleness of aim not known without; the home of sagacious men."

12. It was such sagacious men, apparently, since it surely was not the rampaging students, who decided that this ideal place should also house ROTC units, defense projects, recruiters from Dow Chem-

ical, and agents of the CIA. An ideal institution freed of those per-plexities—which evidently do not bother Mr. Kennan—is precisely what the students have been agitating for. It is not possible to think about learning now without being, as he pejoratively puts it, "busy with politics." The university officials and the government have seen to that. But again, Kennan probably doesn't regard ROTC as a politi-cal presence on campus; students are "busy with politics" not in the precious hours wasted on drill and military science, but only while agitating against these activities, which are mostly useless even from a military point of view. Out of this mess of verbal and moral assump-tions, the finest and stiffest blossom is the phrase "freely confessed": imagine having the gall to tell someone outright that as a student you hadn't even done your assignments while trying to overthrow a cor-rupt and despotic government. Doubtless that government also pre-ferred its universities "not perplexed" by anything related to the conduct of public affairs.

13. Compared with the futuristic modes of Brzezinski and De-Mott, Kennan's mode of argument is at least honest about seeing the present only as if it were the past. In its rather ancient charm it isn't nearly so dangerously effective as still other less explicitly theological, less passionate, more academically systematized methods now in vogue for abridging youthful radicalism or transcendentalism. Consider for example what might be called the tight-contextual method. This is particularly useful in putting campus rioters in their place, their vio-lence always being in excess of any local cause (as if people of draft age or surrounded by a ghetto should care to be exacting about the precise sources of discontent) and in explaining why we cannot with-draw from Vietnam. That country gets reduced, in this form of argu-ment, to some thousands of vaguely identified friends whom we cannot desert, though their worth is even more difficult to locate than is their presence during combat operations.

14. Of course this kind of analysis works wonders on anything as worldwide and variously motivated as student or youth protest. Unanswerably the students at Columbia are not the students in Paris or Czechoslovakia or even Berkeley. Like the leaders in any genera-tion, the rebellious students are only a small minority of the young, a minority even of the student bodies they belong to. There are local, very special reasons not only for the motivations of each group but for each of the different acts of each group. What is astonishing, how-ever, is that they all do act, that they are all acting now, that the youth of the world almost on signal have found local causes—eco-nomic, social, political, academic ones—to fit an apparently general

need to rebel. So universal and simultaneous a response to scarcely new causes reveals in the young an imaginative largeness about the interconnection of issues, an awareness of their wider context, of a world in which what in former decades would have been a local war is now symptomatic, as is poverty and the quality of life in our cities, of where the dominant forms of thinking have taken us. Again, it can be said that the young are in effect rebelling against precisely the kinds of analysis that are inadequate to explain what the young are up to. More terrifying than the disorder in the streets is the disorder in our heads; the rebellion of youth, far from being a cause of disorder, is rather a reaction, a rebellion against the disorder we call order, against our failure to make sense of the way we live now and have lived since 1945.

15. Yet another form of restrictive or deflationary analysis . . . is a special favorite of literary critics and historians as well as politicians: the anti-apocalyptic. Implicit in some of the methods we've already looked at, this one dampens revolutionary enthusiasms with the information that history has recorded such efforts before and also recorded their failure—the Abolitionists, the young Bolsheviks, the Luddites. All claims to uniqueness are either tarnished by precedent or doomed to meaninglessness. We've been through it all, and are now doing the best we can, given—and here we're back at the borders of Original Sin—our imperfect state of being. In the treatment of militant groups, this type of argument is especially anxious to expose any elitist or fascist tinge in the young, with their stress on a chimerical "participatory democracy" or their infantile assumption that the worst must be allowed to happen—let us say the election of George Wallace—if ever the inherent horrors of the "System," and thus the necessities of revolution, are to become apparent to everyone. Some people do talk this way; some people always have. But only a minority of the articulate and protesting young lend themselves to anything so politically programmatic. Such arguments are wholly peripheral to the emergence of youth as a truly unique historical force for which there are no precedents.

16. Youth is an essentially nonpolitical force, a cultural force, that signals, while it can't by itself initiate, the probable beginnings of a new millennium, though hardly the one described in the Book of Revelation. If only because of its continuously fluid, continuously disappearing and emerging membership, it is incapable of organizing itself into shapes suitable to the political alliances that can be made by other, more stable minority groups like the blacks. It has no his-

tory; it may never have one, but it is that shared experience of all races which may come finally to dominate our imagination of what we are.

17.   What is happening to the youth of the world deserves the freest imagination, the freest attention that older people are capable of giving. It requires an enormously strenuous, and for most people, probably impossible, intellectual effort. Working within the verbal and conceptual frames—a sadly appropriate word—against which the rebellion of youth is in large part directed, we must try to invent quite different ways of seeing, imagining, and describing. So complicated is the task linguistically that it is possible to fail merely because of the vocabulary with which, from the best intentions, we decide to try. It is perhaps already irrelevant, for example, to discuss the so-called student revolt as if it were an expression of "youth." The revolt might more properly be taken as a repudiation by the young of what adults call "youth." It may be an attempt to cast aside the strangely exploitative and at once cloying, the protective and impotizing concept of "youth" which society foists on people who often want to consider themselves adults. Is it youth or is it the economic and sexual design of adult society that is being served by what Erik Erikson calls the "moratorium," the period when people under twenty-one are "allowed" to discover their identities without at the same time having to assume adult responsibilities? Quite painfully, the young have suddenly made us aware that the world we have been seeing isn't necessarily the world at all. Not only that France in the spring of 1968 didn't turn out to be the France anyone knew, but that even the young weren't necessarily that thing we call "young." It is no longer a matter of choice therefore: we must learn to know the world differently, including the young, or we may not know it until it explodes, thus showing forth its true nature, to follow the logic of Marx, only in the act and at the moment of breakdown.

18.   Before asking questions about the propriety and programs of young militants who occupy buildings, burn cars, and fight the police, let's first ask what kind of world surrounds these acts. Let's not conceive of the world as a place accidentally controlled by certain people whose wickedness or stupidity has been made evident by disaster, or as the scene of injustices whose existence was hidden from us. Because to do so implies that we are beguiled rather than responsible, responsible, I mean, even for specific things that we do not know are happening. We're in danger of becoming like the Germans before the war who afterward turned to their children with dismay, then

surprise, then amnesia. Such analogies to our present situation, and even more to an anticipated one, are not exact, but they are becoming increasingly less remote with each new crime bill contrived by the office of Attorney General Mitchell.

19. The world we now live in cannot get any better merely by changing its managers or improving some of its circumstances, however. It exists as it does because of the way we think about one another and because of our incapacity, so far at least, to learn to think differently. For those who fought in it and who are now the middle generation and parents of the young, World War II gave absolutely the worst kind of schooling. It trained us to think in extraordinarily simplistic terms about politics and history. One might even say that it made people my age strangely apolitical and ahistorical. We were convinced that evil resided in Nazism and Fascism, and that against these nothing less than total victory was acceptable. The very concept of total victory or unconditional surrender was part of a larger illusion that all wickedness was entrenched in certain groups, circumstances, and persons, and very subtly these were differentiated even from the people or the nations where they found hospitality. The Morgenthau plan had no chance of success, and not simply because it was economically unfeasible in proposing the creation of an agrarian state between the West and the East. It would have had the even more tactically dangerous effect of blaming a *people* for a war. Thereby two embarrassing questions would have been raised: either that the Germans were really a separate kind of people, or, if not, that they were like us, and must therefore have had some understandable provocation for acting as they did. And what could that provocation have been if not something for which we too had a responsibility? No —better just talk about the eradication of Nazism and warlords.

20. Like all wars, World War II blinded us to the conditions at home that required our attention, and so did the cold war that followed: for nearly twenty-five years we looked at foreign devils rather than domestic ills. The consequences were even worse in our thinking, however, or rather in our not thinking, about the true sources and locations of our trouble. They are within ourselves and within the mechanisms of our own society. One reason why those in the parental generation cannot understand the rebellion of the young is that our own "rebellion" was managed for us, while for the young now it is instinctive and invented and unprogrammed. Our protest movement was the war itself, the crusade against Nazism, Fascism, and Japanese imperialism. In many ways our youth didn't matter to the world. I

went into the infantry in 1943 at seventeen, fought in Germany, and came out in 1946 imagining that I'd helped cleanse the globe and could therefore proceed to make up for lost personal time at the university, where a grateful government paid my expenses.

21. If the war absorbed and homogenized the political feelings of the millions like me who are now the parents of people nearly old enough to be drafted for a quite different kind of war, the G.I. Bill of Rights gave us an experience of college and university life different from any before or since. The G.I. Bill was legislation of enormous political and social importance. It allowed the first huge influx into colleges, university, and later into the academic profession, of people who for financial and social reasons weren't before recognized as belonging to the group which represents youth as our society likes to imagine it—the students. But given their backgrounds, which made them poignantly anxious to take advantage of an opportunity they never thought available, much less a right, given their age, service experience, sexual maturity, and often marriage, this influx of a new kind of student had a stabilizing rather than a disrupting effect. We were maybe the first really serious mass of students who ever entered the academy, designed up till then, and still designed, to prolong immaturity until the ridiculous age of twenty-one or later.

22. If we were serious, it was in a bad sense, I'm afraid: we wanted so much to make it that we didn't much question the value of what we were doing. I'm not surprised that so few people my age are radical even in temperament. My fellow academicians who came through the process I've described have fitted all too nicely into the Anglophilic gentility of most areas of academic life, into the death-dealing social manners promoted by people who before the war could afford the long haul of graduate as well as undergraduate education. Much more than the reputed and exaggerated effect of television and other media in creating a self-conscious community of the young (effects shared, after all, by people in their thirties and forties), it is the peculiar nature of World War II and of subsequent schooling experience which separates the older from the younger but still contiguous groups.

23. In thinking about the so-called generation gap, then, I suggest that people my age think not so much about the strangeness of the young but about their own strangeness. Why is it "they" rather than "we" who are unique? By what astonishing arrogance do people my age propose to themselves the program described in the *New York Times* Sunday Book Review by a critic, John Simon, who wrote that during the summer he would support McCarthy and that "beyond

that, full-time opposition to radical or reactionary excesses in the arts and criticism strikes me as proper and sufficient activity for a critic. And political enough, too, in its ultimate implications." The ultimate implications are dead center. Dead because what can anyone mean now by an "excess," and from where does one measure it unless, like the person in question, he entertains, as do most of my contemporaries, the illusion that he has emerged a representative of True Nature?

24. Only when the adult world begins to think of itself as strange, as having a shape not entirely necessary, much less lovely, only when it begins to see that insofar as the world has been made visible to us in forms and institutions, a lot of it isn't *there,* maybe less than half of it—only then can we begin to meet the legitimate anguish of the young with something better than the cliché that they have no program. Revolutionaries seldom do. One can be sick and want health, jailed and want freedom, inwardly dying and want a second birth without a program. For what the radical youth want to do is to expose the mere contingency of facts which have been considered essential. That is a marvelous service, a necessary prelude to our being able, any of us, to think of a program which is more than merely the patching up of social systems that were never adequate to the people they were meant to serve.

25. Liberal reformers, no matter how tough, won't effect and might even forestall the necessary changes. In our universities, for example, there is no point in removing symptoms and leaving the germs. It is true, as the young have let us know with a zest that isn't always convenient even to sympathizers like myself, that our universities are too often run by fat cats, that renowned professors are bribed by no or little teaching, that a disproportionate amount of teaching is done by unselfish but miserably underpaid and distracted graduate assistants, that, as a consequence of this imbalance, research of the most exciting kind has very little immediate bearing on curriculum, which remains much as it has for the past fifty years, and that, as Martin Duberman eloquently shows in *The Uncompleted Past,* authoritarianism in curriculum and in teaching, not to be confused with being an authority in a subject, is so much a part of our educational system that university students arrive already crippled even for the freedom one is prepared to give them. These conditions exist in a pattern of idiotic requirements and childish, corrupting emoluments not simply because our universities are mismanaged. The mismanagement has itself a prior cause which is to be found in the way most

people think about scholarship and its relation to teaching—a question which is a kind of metaphor for the larger one of the relations between the generations: what conditions permit the most profitable engagements between an older mind that is trained and knowledgeable and a younger one anxious to discover itself but preconditioned by quite different cultural circumstances?

26. These circumstances have, of course, always differed between one generation and another, but never so radically as now. Never before have so many revered subjects, like literature itself, seemed obsolete in any strict compartmental form; never before have the divisions between such subjects as anthropology, sociology, and languages seemed more arbitrary and harmful to intelligent inquiry; and seldom in the history of modern civilization has there been a greater need felt by everyone for a new key to our mythologies, a key we nervously feel is about to be found. For if we are at a moment of terror we are also at a moment of great expectation and wonder, for which the young have a special appetite. To meet this challenge, the universities need to dismantle their entire academic structure, their systems of courses and requirements, their notion of what constitutes the proper fields and subjects of academic inquiry.

27. Most people who teach have in their heads some ideal university, and mine would be governed by a single rule: there is nothing that does not need to be studied in class, including, of course, the oddity of studying in a class. Everything and everybody, the more randomly selected the better, has to be subjected to questions, especially dumb questions, and to the elicitation of answers. The point is that nothing must be taken for other than "strange," nothing must be left alone. Study the morning paper, study the teacher, study the listless slouching of students—half-dead already at eighteen. But above all, those working in advanced research sponsored at any university would also let capable students study that research and ask questions about it. And if in fact some things cannot be taught, then that in itself should be the subject of inquiry.

28. The hierarchies that might evolve would be determined on a wholly pragmatic basis: for subjects, by the amount of effort and time needed to make something yield up the dimensions of its mystery; for any way of thinking, by the degree to which it raises a student to eye level with the potentialities of a subject, the degree to which it can tune his ears into it. Above all, the university would be a place where curricula are discovered anew perhaps every year or so. The argument that the demands of an existing student body cannot be allowed to determine policy for succeeding ones would mean the

reverse of what it now means: not that changes are difficult to effect, but that they would be effected year after year, if necessary, to meet the combined changes of interest in students and faculty. Given the sluggishness of most people, the results of such a policy would not be nearly as chaotic or exciting as one might imagine. Indeed, what would be hoped for is more disruption, and therefore more questioning and answering than one would ever get.

29. In confronting oppositions from youth as in other matters short of Vietnam, Lyndon Johnson was a genius in that his most decent impulses, and he had some, didn't merely serve, weren't merely synchronized with, but were indistinguishable from his often uncanny political instinct for pacifying any opposition, for castrating any force that threatened to move the system off the center track which carried him to power. While demonstrations at Columbia were making Hubert Humphrey sick "deep inside," and Nixon was reportedly saying that if there were a second Columbia uprising he wouldn't have to care whom he had to run against, LBJ was proposing that the vote be given to all people between eighteen and twenty-one. But the terrible price of the political logic he so masterfully handled is at once made evident if we ask what many of the young, and not simply the militant ones, will find to vote for. They are to join the electorate just when it is at last stagnating from our national satisfaction with the mere manipulation and redistribution of the poisons within us. So ingeniously is the center still in control of the manipulative forces, that there will not be a turn to the right within our political system (anyone who thinks Nixon is of the right is merely trying to jazz up our political life), and no one within the system represents the left. The danger sign will be abstention, political indifference, a decision not to care very much who wins, not to participate in a process that affords only negative choices.

30. When any large number of people demonstrate their indifference to the choices offered them, they tend to invent others that exist outside the going "democratic" process. They tend to gravitate toward some species of the "participatory democracy" for which the elitist young are most severely criticized. It was at least fortunate that Johnson's voting-age proposal couldn't be enacted in time for the young people of eighteen to twenty-one to enter a political imbroglio so contemptibly arranged as the 1968 election. It would only have further convinced them of the necessity for some kind of nondemocratic movement to replace the farce of democracy in which they'd have been asked to take part, and it would have allowed their critics to assign to them some blame for the consequences of the indifference

among the older electorate. The indifference grows on the momentum supplied not by the young but by the nature of our public life. The now not uncommon proposition that our problems are no longer manageable within existing political systems, and that we need an Authority empowered to decide what is best for us, cannot be ascribed merely to youth, Herbert Marcuse, Vietnam, race, violence, or any combination of these. The emerging failure of confidence in our way of managing ourselves and our interests in the world is the consequence of a political process now overwhelmed by the realities it has tried to hide.

31. Instinctively, the militant young are involved less in a political rebellion, where demands for their "program" would be relevant, than in an attack on the foundations of all of our current political programming. The issues they raise and the issues they personify are essentially anthropological, which brings us to the cultural rather than the political importance of the proposal to move the voting age back from twenty-one to eighteen. The importance can be dramatized, with no intention of melodrama, by predicting that within twenty years or so it will be necessary to propose, if not to pass, a voting age of sixteen. Like other mere changes of policy, changes in voting age should not be taken as a sign that we are suddenly to be governed by new or radical modes of thinking. Rather, such reforms signal the accumulated power of forces which our operative modes of thinking have before tried to ignore and which they will now try to make invisible by absorption.

32. But with the mass of youth (nearly half the population is now under twenty-five) our society is faced with an unprecedented difficulty in the application of this essentially social technique. For when it comes to the young, society is not simply absorbing a group which, like the Irish or labor, duplicates in its social organization each part of the dominant group. To give something like adult or historic identity to a mass that has up to now been relegated to the position of "youth" means a disruptive change in the concept of human identity, of when that identity is achieved, of what it properly should contribute to history.

33. The time scheme that governs our ideas of adolescence, youth, and maturity has changed many times in history since the sixteenth century—Juliet was fourteen, and early in the eighteenth century the age of consent was ten—but it was adjusted to the convenience of an extraordinarily small ruling minority which was in turn submissive to familial regulations. For the first time in history a change of this kind is being made on demand from a powerful mass

of young people freed of familial pieties, and never before has a society worked as strenuously as ours, through a mesh of mythologies, to hold these young people back, in an unmercifully prolonged state of adolescence and of what we call "youth." Especially in the United States, the representative and most talented young—the students—have for generations been forced not to take themselves seriously as men and women.

34. So far, the rebellion has accomplished at least one thing: it has succeeded in demoting "collegiate types" (and the sickly reminiscent values they injected into later life) from glamour to absurdity. The change is not complete, and it never will be. Whole campuses are holdouts, some quite distinguished ones, where the prep-school ethos remains dominant, while at others the overwhelming number of young clods makes it difficult for the few students who really are alive even to find one another, much less establish an *esprit* that can enliven more than a small circle. Still, recent agitations have confirmed some of the advances made by the earlier generation of students under the G.I. Bill and cleared still more room on American campuses for the kind of young person who does want to enter history at eighteen, and who is therefore contemptuous of society's cute and reassuring idea of the collegiate—with Lucille Ball as ideal House Mother. Such historical self-consciousness on the part of university students has been fairly common in Europe and in England, where, as shown by Peter Stansky and William Abrahams in *Journey to the Frontier,* students in the thirties could feel that the "journey" to the Spanish Civil War did not follow but rather began at Oxford and Cambridge. But the differences are obvious, and, again, relate to class and family: children of the English upper classes were educated to feel historical, and what distinguished them from lower-class boys was that from boyhood their "careers" meant something to the political and historical career of England. Only rarely, and almost exclusively at Harvard, does this phenomenon occur in American universities. Education in American universities has generally been a combination of utilitarian course work and play-acting, "getting ready" to be an adult, even if it meant still getting ready at twenty-two.

35. The shattering of this pattern has been the work of a complex of forces that include students within the larger power bloc of youth, with its enormous influence on dress and mores, and, perhaps above all, its success in the fields of entertainment. By force of numbers and energy alone, the young have created images which older people are now quite anxious to endow with a sexual-social signifi-

cance which they before refused to find in the activity of "kids." Put another way, youth has ceased to fufill the "literary" role which American society has been anxious to assign them. They no longer supply us with a pastoral, any more than the "darkies" do, and this is a serious, though to me a most satisfying cultural deprivation for which no replacement has yet been discovered.

36. Every civilization has to invent a pastoral for itself, and ours has been an idea of youth and of adolescence which has become socially and economically unprofitable, demographically unmanageable, and biologically comic. By a pastoral I mean any form of life which has, by common consent, been secured from the realities of time and history. Some form of pastoral is absolutely essential: it helps stabilize the cycles of individual lives and of civilizations. Its function is an idealizing, simplifying one: it secures certain elemental human attributes from the contaminations of time and of historical involvement. But if the logic of pastoral is to protect certain attributes, its ulterior motive is to keep the human embodiment of these attributes in their proper place, servants rather than participants in daily business where "real" men really face complex reality.

37. Insofar as America's imagination of itself can be inferred from literature, from popular entertainment, from fashions, conventions, and educational theory, it can be said that we have used youth as a revenge upon history, as the sacrificial expression of our self-contempt. Youth has been the hero of our civilization, but only so long as it has remained antagonistic to history, only so long as it has remained a literary or mythological metaphor.

38. War, the slaughter of youth at the apparent behest of history, is the ultimate expression of this feeling. The American hatred of history, of what it does to us, gets expressed in a preposterous and crippling idealization of youth as a state as yet untouched by history, except as a killer, and in a corresponding incapacity to understand the demand, now, by the best of the young, to be admitted into it. More hung up on youth than any nation on earth, we are also the more determined that youth is not to enter into history without paying the price of that adulteration we call adulthood. To justify what grown-ups have made of our young, virgin, uncontaminated land, it's as if we are compelled to show that what happened was necessary. Exceptions would prove our human culpability for what is otherwise ascribed to history, and so all that is best in our land must either be kept out of history or tarnished by it. Like our natural wonders, youth will be allowed to exist only on condition that it remain, like some

natural preserve, outside the processes that transform everything else into waste.

39. Surely the destination of our assets needn't be so bleak, so inexorable, so neurotically determined. It will now be seen whether or not we are to exhaust our youth, whether or not in its vulnerability, its continually evaporating and exposed condition, it can resist being made grist for the mill. Because youth is not a historically grounded pressure group, aware of its history, jealous of its progress, continuous and evolving. It is rather what we, all of us, sometimes are. I have avoided any precise definition of youth because it refers to the rare human condition of exuberance, expectation, impulsiveness, and, above all, of freedom from believing that all the so-called "necessities" of life and thought are in fact necessities. This condition exists most usefully, for the nation and the world, in people of a certain age, specifically in those who have attained the physical being that makes them wonderfully anxious to create life, to shape life, to enter into life rather than have it fed into them. It is the people of this age, members of what Freidenberg calls the "hot-blooded minority," who are in danger of obliteration as representatives of youth. It is impossible for them to remain youth, in any sense that would profit the rest of society, and also enter into history on the hateful terms now offered them by our political, economic, and technological system. Lyndon Johnson knew instinctively what he was up to when, calling for a vote for people of this age, he remarked that they deserved it because they are "adults in every sense."

40. Fine, if that means we now change our concept of adulthood to include an eighteen-year-old Bob Dylan rather than an eighteen-year-old Nixon, some creep valedictorian. But that isn't what he had in mind. LBJ hadn't changed his way of thinking about youth, adulthood, or anything else. He was merely responding to this fantastic cultural opportunity the way our leaders respond to any such opportunity for change: they merely make more room in the house with as little inconvenience as possible to the settled inhabitants. All the voting proposal means, and this will have some amusing as well as sad consequences, is that the term youth will be lifted from those who threatened us with it, and then held in reserve for the time, not far off, when it can be quietly left on the narrow shoulders of what we now call adolescents. Some tinkering will be necessary here and there, of course. The Adolescent Clinic at Children's Hospital in Boston chooses the ages thirteen to nineteen for its patients, but those who've seen some of the ten-to-twelve-year-olds who sneak in tell me that if the ranks of adolescence are to be depleted to fill the vacated

positions of youth, these in turn will be quickly occupied by Robert Coles's children of crisis. This will seem a facetious prediction to people who like to think they are reasonable.

41. So, what I'm saying is that if young people are freeing themselves from a repressive myth of youth only to be absorbed into a repressive, even though modified, myth of adulthood, then youth in its best and truest form, of rebellion and hope, will have been lost to us, and we will have at last wasted some of the very best of ourselves.

## WORDS

*meaning* Define *rationalize* (par. 2), *dispassion* (par. 5), *prognosticators* (par. 7), *emanations* and *axiological* (par. 8), *pejoratively* (par. 12), *apocalyptic* and *chimerical* (par. 15), *Anglophilic* (par. 22), and *culpability* (par. 38).

*relationships* How do *apolitical* and *ahistorical* (par. 19) differ from *unpolitical* and *unhistorical?* How does *amoral* differ from *immoral?*

*choice and exactness* 1. What does the author mean by "the *unreality* of quotation marks" (par. 5)? 2. Why does he consider *frames* a "sadly appropriate word" in paragraph 17?

## SENTENCES

*parallelism* Find one sentence in paragraph 26 and one in paragraph 27 in which repetition is used to strengthen and emphasize parallelism. Why is this technique a mark of the colloquial style, more common in speech than in formal writing?

*rhetorical devices* In paragraph 5, the author speaks of the "unreality of quotation marks." How does he himself utilize this "unreality" in paragraphs 8 and 9?

## PARAGRAPHS

*coherence* What transitional words or devices in the first sentences of paragraphs 4 through 10 serve to link each paragraph with the one before it?

*methods of development* How do the qualifications and concessions of paragraph 34—the "holdout" campuses and the "historical self-consciousness" of European students—affect the development of the paragraph's central idea?

## CONTENT AND ORGANIZATION

*organization* The first paragraph of this essay refers to "the essentially pastoral status" of youth, but the author does not explain his rather special use of the word *pastoral* until he comes to paragraph 36. Would the essay be improved if this explanation followed the first use of the word?

*assumptions and implications*　What basic assumption is implied clearly in paragraphs 2 and 19 and explicitly stated in paragraph 8?

SUGGESTIONS FOR DISCUSSION

1. Demanding or predicting "revolution" became almost fashionable among many intellectuals in the 1960s. But the word itself is ambiguous, ranging in reference from the violence of the French or Russian revolutions through the slower transformations in social and economic structure that followed the "industrial revolution." What kind of revolutions, if any, do you anticipate in your lifetime?　2. In literature, a pastoral is ordinarily an idealized portrayal of simple rural life in a remote time and place. Why do some critics consider the Western story to be an American form of pastoral?　3. In what ways have you faced problems or experienced difficulties because of the "generation gap"?　4. The author asks, "Are the practices of the United States government with regard to most issues of race, ecology, poverty, the war, the gun laws, or even the postal service rational?" What would you answer? Explain.

# Eric Hoffer

# WHOSE COUNTRY IS AMERICA?

1.　The conspicuous role played by the young in our society at present has prompted a widely held assumption that the young constitute a higher percentage of the population than they did in the past. Actually, in this country, the percentage of the under-25 age group has remained fairly constant through several decades—it hovers around 47 percent. The high-school and college age group—14 to 24 —has remained close to 15 percent. The nation as a whole has not been getting younger. The median age of all Americans in 1910 was 24. Today it is 27, and it is likely to go up since the birth rate right now is very low.

2.　The conspicuousness of the young is due to their greater

WHOSE COUNTRY IS AMERICA?　Adapted from Chapters 5 & 6 of *First Things, Last Things* by Eric Hoffer (originally appeared in New York Times Magazine, November 1970, under the title "Whose Country Is America?"). Copyright © 1970 by Eric Hoffer. Reprinted by permission of Harper & Row, Publishers, Inc.

visibility and audibility. They have become more flamboyant, more demanding, more violent, more knowledgeable, and more experienced. The general impression is that nowadays the young act like the spoiled children of the rich. We are discovering that there is such a thing as an "ordeal of affluence," that diffused affluence subjects the social order to greater strain and threatens social stability more than does diffused poverty. Order and discipline have up to now been attributes generated in the battle against want. Society itself originated in the vital need for a joint effort to wrest a livelihood from grudging nature. Not only our material but our moral and spiritual values are predicated on the immemorial curse: "In the sweat of thy face shalt thou eat bread." Thus diffused affluence unavoidably creates a climate of disintegrating values with its fallout of anarchy.

3. In the past, breakdowns of value affected mainly the older segment of the population. This was true of the breakdown of the Greco-Roman civilization, of the crisis that gave birth to the Reformation, and of the periods of social disintegration that preceded the French, the Russian, and the Nazi revolutions. That our present crisis particularly affects the young is due partly to the fact that widespread affluence is robbing a modern society of whatever it has left of puberty rites to routinize the attainment of manhood. Never before has the passage from boyhood to manhood been so difficult and explosive. Both the children of the well-to-do and of families on welfare are prevented from having a share in the world's work and of proving their manhood by doing a man's work and getting a man's pay. Crime in the streets and insolence on the campus are sick forms of adolescent self-assertion. The young account for an ever-increasing percentage of crimes against persons and property. The peak years for crimes of violence are 18 to 20, followed by the 21 to 24 age group.

4. Even under ideal conditions the integration of the young into the adult world is beset with strains and difficulties. We feel ill at ease when we have to adjust ourselves to fit in. The impulse is to change the world to fit us rather than the other way around. Only where there are, as in primitive societies, long-established rites of passage, or where the opportunities for individual self-assertion are fabulous, does growing up proceed without excessive growing pains.

5. Can a modern affluent society institute some form of puberty rites to ease the passage from boyhood to manhood? It is of interest in this connection that among the Bantu tribes in South Africa work is replacing the ritual related to puberty. It used to be that a young man had to kill a lion or an enemy to prove his manhood. Today many young natives do not feel they have become full-fledged adults

until they have put in a stint in the mines. Could not a ritual of work be introduced in this country? Every boy and girl on reaching 17, or on graduating from high school, would be given an opportunity to spend two years earning a living at good pay. There is an enormous backlog of work to be done both inside and outside the cities. Federal, state, and city governments, and also business and labor would pool their resources to supply the necessary jobs and training.

6.   The routinization of the passage from boyhood to manhood would contribute to the solution of many of our pressing problems. I cannot think of any other undertaking that would dovetail so many of our present difficulties into opportunities for growth.

7.   Though the percentage of the young, as pointed out, has remained constant through several decades, there has been a spectacular increase in the percentage of adolescents. At present, adolescence comprises a wider age range than it did in the past. Affluence is keeping persons in their late 20s in a state of delayed manhood, while television has lowered the threshold of adolescence. Nowadays, 10-year-olds have the style of life and the bearing of adolescents. Even children under 10 have an astounding familiarity with the intricacies and the mechanics of the adult world. By the time a child enters kindergarten, he has spent more hours learning about his world from television than the hours he will spend later in classrooms earning a college degree. It is a paradox that at a time when youths rioting in Chicago are called "mere kids," there are actually few genuine kids any more.

8.   The contemporary blurring of childhood is not unprecedented. During the Middle Ages, children were viewed and treated as miniature adults. Nothing in medieval dress distinguished the child from the adult. The moment children could walk and talk they entered the adult world, and took part in the world's work. In subsequent centuries, the concept of childhood became more clearly defined. Yet even as late as 1835 schoolbooks in this country made no concession to childhood in vocabulary or sophistication. Child labor, so widely practiced in the first half of the nineteenth century, and which we find abhorrent, was not totally anomalous in a society that did not have a vivid view of childhood as a sheltered, privileged age.

9.   To counteract an old man's tendency to snort at the self-important young, I keep reminding myself that until the middle of the nineteenth century the young acted effectively as members of political parties, creators of business enterprises, advocates of new philosophical doctrines, and leaders of armies. Most of the wars that figure in our history books were fought by teenagers. There were 14-year-old

lieutenants in Louis XIV's armies. In one of his armies the oldest soldier was under 18. The middle-aged came to the fore with the Industrial Revolution. The experience and capital necessary to make an industrialist required a long apprenticeship. One might say that from the middle of the nineteenth to the middle of the twentieth century the world was run by and for the middle-aged. The postindustrial age seems to be groping its way back to an immemorial situation interrupted by the Industrial Revolution.

10.    The middle-aged came to the fore with the Industrial Revolution. Another way of putting it is that the middle-aged came into their own with the full entrance of the middle class onto the stage of history. The present discomfiture of the middle-aged is a symptom of a downturn in the fortunes of the middle class.

11.    Adolescence as a clearly marked phase in the life of the individual, and the practice of keeping physically mature males in a state of delayed manhood are middle-class phenomena. The young of the working class and of the aristocracy come early in touch with the realities of life, and are not kept waiting in the wings. In neither the working class nor the aristocracy does age have the vital meaning it has in the middle class.

12.    Industrialization was the creation of the middle class. It is questionable whether the spectacular "mastery of things," the taming of nature on a global scale, could have been achieved by other human types. No other ruling class succeeded so well in energizing the masses, and infusing them with an automatic readiness to work. Aristocrats and intellectuals know how to generate in a population a readiness to fight and die, but they cannot induce an uncoerced, wholehearted participation of the masses in the world's work.

13.    Indeed, it is doubtful whether a nonmiddle-class society can be modern. Domination by aristocrats, intellectuals, workers, or soldiers results in a return to the past—to feudalism, the Middle Ages, or even the ancient river-valley civilizations. It is not as yet certain whether it is possible to have a free-wheeling science, literature, and art, or even a genuine machine age, without a middle class.

14.    Yet, despite its unprecedented achievements, the middle class is just now on the defensive, unsure of its footing. With the consummation of the Industrial Revolution and the approach of affluence the middle class seems to have nowhere to go. It no longer feels itself in possession of the true and only view possible for sensible people. One begins to wonder whether the unglamorous, hard-working middle class, so essential to the process of production in a climate of scarcity, is becoming anachronistic in an age of plenty where distribution is the

chief problem. Middle-class society is being strained to the breaking point not, as Marx predicted, by ever-increasing misery but by ever-increasing affluence. The coming of affluence has found the middle class unequipped and unprepared for a return to Eden.

15. Early in the nineteenth century, Saint-Simon characterized the coming of the industrial age as the passage "from the management of men to the administration of things." He did not foresee that once the industrial revolution had run its course there would have to come a reversion from the administration of things to the management of men. Up to quite recently, the middle class did not have to bother overmuch with the management of men since scarcity (unfulfilled needs), the factory, long working hours, etc., tamed and disciplined people automatically. Now, with affluence and leisure, people are no longer kept in line by circumstances. Discipline has to be implanted and order enforced from without. It is at this point that "men of words" and charismatic leaders—people who deal with magic—come into their own. The middle class, lacking magic, is bungling the job.

16. Thus, as the postindustrial age unfolds, we begin to suspect that what is waiting for us around the corner is not a novel future but an immemorial past. It begins to look as if the fabulous century of the middle class and the middle-aged has been a detour, a wild loop that turns upon itself, and ends where it began. We are returning to the rutted highway of history, which we left 100 years ago in a mad rush to tame a savage continent and turn it into a cornucopia of plenty. We see all around us the lineaments of a preindustrial pattern emerging in the postindustrial age. We are rejoining the ancient caravan, a caravan dominated by the myths and magic of elites, and powered by the young.

17. In this country, the coming of the postindustrial age may mean the loss of all that made America new—the only new thing in the world. America will no longer be the common man's continent. The common people of Europe eloped with history to America and have lived in common-law marriage with it, unhallowed by the incantations of "men of words." But the elites are finally catching up with us. We can hear the swish of leather as saddles are heaved on our backs. The intellectuals and the young, booted and spurred, feel themselves born to ride us.

18. The phenomenal increase of the student population is shaping the attitudes and aspirations of the young. There are now more students in America than farmers. For the first time in America, there is a chance that alienated intellectuals, who see our way of life as an instrument of debasement and dehumanization, might shape a

new generation in their own image. The young's sympathy for the Negro and the poor goes hand in hand with an elitist conceit that pits them against the egalitarian masses. They will fight for the Negro and the poor, but they have no use for common folk who work and moonlight to take care of their own. They see a free-wheeling democracy as a society stupefied by "the narcotic of mass culture." They reserve their wrath for the institutions in which common people are most represented: unions, Congress, the police, and the Army. Professor Edgar Z. Friedenberg thinks that "elitism is the great and distinctive contribution students are making to American society." Democracy is for the dropouts; for the elite, an aristocratic brotherhood.

19. Yet one cannot help but wonder how inevitable is the future that seemingly is waiting for us around the corner. Might not the common people, so cowed and silent at this moment, eventually kick up their heels, and trample would-be elitists in the dirt? There is no earthly reason why the common people who for more than a century have been doing things here that in other countries are reserved for elites, should not be capable of overcoming the present crisis.

20. Nowhere at present is there such a measureless loathing of educated people for their country as in America. An excellent historian thinks Americans are "the most frightening people in the world," and our foremost philologist sees America as "the most aggressive power in the world, the greatest threat to peace and to international cooperation." Others call America a "pig heaven," "a monster with 200 million heads," "a cancer on the body of mankind."

21. Novelists, playwrights, poets, essayists, and philosophers depict America as the land of the dead—a country where sensitive souls are starved and flayed, where nothing nourishes and everything hurts. Nowhere, they say, is there such a boring monotony: monotony of talk, monotony of ideas, monotony of aim, monotony of outlook on the world. One American writer says: "America is no place for an artist. A corn-fed hog enjoys a better life than a creative artist." One she-intellectual maintains that "the quality of American life is an insult to the possibilities of human growth."

22. It is hard to believe that this savage revulsion derives from specific experiences with persons and places. What is there in America that prevents an educated person from shaping his life, from making the most of his inborn endowments? With all its faults and blemishes, this country gives a man elbowroom to do what is nearest to his heart. It is incredible how easy it is here to cut oneself off from vulgarity, conformity, speciousness, and other corrupting influences

and infections. For those who want to be left alone to realize their capacities and talents, this is an ideal country.

23. The trouble is, of course, that the alienated intellectual does not want to be left alone. He wants to be listened to and be taken seriously. He wants to influence affairs, have a hand in making history, and feel important. He is free to speak and write as he pleases, and can probably make himself heard and read more easily than one who would defend America. But he can neither sway elections nor shape policy. Even when his excellence as a writer, artist, scholar, scientist, or educator is generally recognized and rewarded he does not feel himself part of the power structure. In no other country has there been so little liaison between men of words and the men of action who exercise power. The body of intellectuals in America has never been integrated with or congenial to the politicians and businessmen who make things happen. Indeed, the uniqueness of modern America derives in no small part from the fact that America has kept intellectuals away from power and paid little attention to their political views.

24. The nineteen-sixties have made it patent that much of the intellectual's dissent is fueled by a hunger for power. The appearance of potent allies—militant blacks and students—has emboldened the intellectual to come out into the open. He still feels homeless in America, but the spectacle of proud authority, in cities and on campuses, always surrendering before threats of violence, is to him a clear indication that middle-class society is about to fall apart, and he is all set to pick up the pieces.

25. There is no doubt that in our permissive society the intellectual has far more liberty than he can use; and the more his liberty and the less his capacity to make use of it, the louder his clamor for power—power to deprive other people of liberty.

26. The intellectual's allergy to America shows itself with particular clarity in what has happened to many foreign intellectuals who found asylum here during the Hitler decade. It is legitimate to assume that they had no anti-American preconceptions when they arrived. They were, on the contrary, predisposed to see what was best in their host country. Though no one has recorded what Herbert Marcuse said when he landed in New York in 1934, it is safe to assume that he did not see Americans as one-dimensional men, and did not equate our tolerance with oppression, our freedom with slavery, and our good nature with simple-mindedness.

27. We have a record of what some other foreign intellectuals said when they arrived in the nineteen-thirties. It is worth quoting in

full the words of Olga Schnitzler, the widow of Arthur Schnitzler: "So much is here to learn and to see. Everyone has been given an opportunity. Everyone who has not been completely worn out experiences here a kind of rebirth. Everyone feels what a grandiose, complex, and broad-minded country America is, how well and free one can live among these people without perfidy and malice. Yes, we have lost a homeland, but we have found a world."

28. Once they had settled down and found their place, many of these intellectuals began to feel constrained and stifled by the forwardness and the mores of the plebeian masses. They missed the aristocratic climate of the Old World. Inevitably, too, they became disdainful of our lowbrow, practical intelligence. They began to doubt whether Americans had the high-caliber intelligence to solve the problems of a complex, difficult age. Hardly one of them bethought himself that in Europe, when intellectuals of their kind had a hand in shaping and managing affairs, things had not gone too well. There was something that prevented them from sensing the unprecedented nature of the American experiment; that the rejected of Europe have come here together, tamed a savage continent in an incredibly short time, and, unguided by intellectuals, fashioned the finest society on a large scale the world has so far seen.

29. Scratch an intellectual and you find a would-be aristocrat who loathes the sight, the sound and the smell of common folk. Professor Marcuse has lived among us for more than 30 years and now, in old age, his disenchantment with this country is spilling over into book after book. He is offended by the intrusion of the vulgar, by the failure of egalitarian America to keep common people in their place. He is frightened by "the degree to which the population is allowed to break the peace where there is still peace and silence, to be ugly and uglify things, to ooze familiarity and to offend against good form." The vulgar invade "the small reserved sphere of existence" and compel exquisite Marcusian souls to partake of their sounds, sights, and smells.

30. To a shabby would-be aristocrat like Professor Marcuse there is something fundamentally wrong with a society in which the master and the worker, the typist and the boss's daughter do not live totally disparate lives. Everything good in America seems to him a sham and a fraud.

31. An interesting peculiarity of present-day dissenting intellectuals is their lack of animus toward the rich. They are against the Government, the Congress, the Army, and the police, and against corporations and unions, but hardly anything is being said or written

against "the money changers in the temple," "the economic royalists," "the malefactors of great wealth," and "the maniacs wild for gold" who were the butt of vituperation in the past. Indeed, there is nowadays a certain rapport between the rich and the would-be revolutionaries. The outlandish role the rich are playing in the affluent society is one of the surprises of our time. Though the logic of it seems now fairly evident, I doubt whether anyone had foreseen that affluence would radicalize the upper rich and the lowest poor and nudge them toward an alliance against those in the middle. Whatever we have of revolution just now is financed largely by the rich.

32. In order to feel rich, you have to have poor people around you. In an affluent society, riches lose their uniqueness—people no longer find fulfillment in being rich. And when the rich cannot feel rich they begin to have misgivings about success—not enough to give up the fruits of success, but enough to feel guilty, and emote soulfully about the grievances of the disadvantaged, and the sins of the status quo. It seems that every time a millionaire opens his mouth nowadays he confesses the sins of our society in public.

33. Now, it so happens that the rich do indeed have a lot to feel guilty about. They live in exclusive neighborhoods, send their children to private schools, and use every loophole to avoid paying taxes. But what they confess in public are not their private sins, but the sins of society, the sins of the rest of us, and it is our breasts they are beating into a pulp. They feel guilty and ashamed, they say, because the mass of people, who do most of the work and pay much of the taxes, are against integrated schools and housing, and do not tax themselves to the utmost to fight the evils that beset our cities. We are discovering that in an affluent society the rich have a monopoly of righteousness.

34. Moreover, the radicalized rich have radical children. There is no generation gap here. The most violent cliques of the New Left are made up of the children of the rich. The Weathermen, to whom workingmen are "honky bastards," have not a member with a workingman's background. The behavior of the extremist young makes sense when seen as the behavior of spoiled brats used to instant fulfillment who expect the solutions to life's problems to be there on demand. And just as in former days aristocratic sprigs horse-whipped peasants, so at present the children of the rich are riding roughshod over community sensibilities. The rich parents applaud and subsidize their revolutionary children, and probably brag about them at dinner parties.

35. As I said, the alienated rich are one of the surprises of our

time. It is not surprising to be told that America is a country where intellectuals are least at home. But it is startling to realize that the rich are not, and probably never have been, wholly at ease in this country. The fact that it is easy to get rich in America has not made it a rich man's country. The rich have always had it better elsewhere—better service, more deference, and more leisure and fun. In America, the rich have not known how to savor their riches, and many of them have not known how to behave and have come to a bad end.

36. There is a story about a British intellectual who traveled through this country toward the end of the last century. He was appalled by the monotony and unimaginativeness of the names of the towns he saw through the train window: Thomasville, Richardsville, Harrysville, Marysville, and so on. He had not an inkling of the import of what he was seeing: namely, that for the first time in history common people—any Tom, Dick, and Harry—could build a town and name it after his own or his wife's name. At one station, an old Irishwoman got on the train and sat next to him. When she heard his muttering and hissing she said: "This is a blessed country, sir. I think God made it for the poor." Crèvecœur, in the eighteenth century, saw America as an asylum where "the poor of Europe have by some means met together." The poor everywhere have looked on America as their El Dorado. They voted for it with their legs by coming over in their millions.

37. Yet during the nineteen-sixties, poverty became one of the chief problems that plague this country: one of several nagging problems—like race relations, violence, drugs, inflation—which defy solution. From being a land of opportunity for the poor, America has become a dead-end street for some 15 million unemployables—80 percent of them white, and most of them trapped in the cores of big cities. Money, better housing, and special schooling have little effect. Our society is showing itself unduly awkward in the attempt to turn the chronically poor into productive, useful citizens. Whereas, in the not too distant past, it was axiomatic that society lived at the expense of the poor, the present-day poor, like the Roman proletariat, live at the expense of society.

38. We have been transferred by affluence to a psychological age. Impersonal factors, including money, no longer play a decisive role in human affairs. It seems that, by mastering things, we have drained things of their potency to shape men's lives. It is remarkable that common people are aware of this fact. They know that at present money cannot cure crime, poverty, etc., whereas the social doctors

go on prescribing an injection of so many billions for every social ailment.

39. In the earliest cities, suburbs made their appearance as a refuge for dropouts who could not make the grade in the city. When eventually the cities decayed, the suburbs continued as the earliest villages. In our cities, the process has been reversed. The dropouts are stagnating in the cores of the cities, while people who are ideally suited for city life seek refuge in the suburbs. The indications are that we shall not have viable cities until we lure the chronically poor out of the cities and induce the exiled urbanites to return.

40. The diffusion of affluence has accelerated the absorption of the majority of workingmen into the middle class. The unemployable poor, left behind, feel isolated and exposed, and it is becoming evident that a middle-class society, which hugs the conviction that everyone can take care of himself, is singularly inept in helping those who cannot help themselves. If the rich cannot feel rich in an affluent society, the poor have never felt poorer.

41. Whose country, then, is America? It is the country of the common—the common men and women, a good 70 percent of the population—who do most of the work, pay much of the taxes, crave neither power nor importance, and want to be left alone to live pleasurable humdrum lives. "The founders of the United States," said Lord Charnwood, "did deliberately aspire to found a commonwealth in which common men and women should count for more than elsewhere."

42. Again and again, you come up against the mystery of what happens to common folk when they land on our shores. It is like a homecoming. They find here their natural habitat, their ideal milieu that brings their energies and capacities into full play.

43. Tasks that in other countries are reserved for a select minority, for a specially trained elite, are in this country performed by every Tom, Dick, and Harry. Not only did common Americans build and name towns, but they also founded states, propagated new faiths, commanded armies, wrote books, and ran for the highest office. It is this that has made America unprecedentedly new.

44. It tickled me no end that the astronauts who landed on the moon were not elite-conscious intellectuals but lowbrow ordinary Americans.* It has been the genius of common Americans to achieve

* Prof. Victor C. Ferkiss, author of "Technological Man," sees the astronauts as "thoroughly conventional and middle-class and essentially dull people who would make such nice neighbors and such unlikely friends." Could these, he

the momentous in an unmomentous matter-of-fact way. If space exploration remains in their keeping, they will soon make of it an everyday routine accessible to all.

45. The intellectuals call this giving access to the vulgar—vulgarization. The intellectuals' inclination is to complicate things, to make them so abstruse and difficult that they are accessible only to the initiated few. Where the intellectuals are in power, prosaic tasks become Promethean undertakings. I have yet to meet an intellectual who truly believes that common people can govern themselves and run things without outstanding leaders. In the longshoremen's union the intellectuals have a nervous breakdown anytime a common, barely literate longshoreman runs for office and gets elected.

46. To me it seems axiomatic that the common people everywhere are our natural allies, and that our chief contribution to the advancement of mankind should be the energizing and activation of common folk. We must learn how to impart to common people everywhere the technological, political, and social skills that would enable them to dispense with the tutorship of the upper classes and the intellectuals. We must deflate the pretensions of self-appointed elites. These elites will hate us no matter what we do, and it is legitimate for us to help dump them into the dustbin of history.

47. Our foreign aid to backward countries in Asia, Africa, and Latin America should be tailored to the needs of common people rather than of the elites. The elites hanker for the trappings of the twentieth century. They want steel mills, airlines, skyscrapers, etc. Let them get these trappings from elitist Russia. Our gift to the people in backward countries should be the capacity for self-help. We must show them how to get bread, human dignity, and strength by their own efforts. We must know how to stiffen their backbone so that they will insist on getting their full share of the good life and not allow themselves to be sacrificed to the Moloch of a mythical future.

48. There is an America hidden in the soil of every country and in the soul of every people. It is our task to help common people everywhere discover their America at home.

WORDS

*meaning* Define *flamboyant* (par. 2), anomalous (par. 8), *immemorial* (par. 9), *consummation* (par. 14), *charismatic* (par. 15), *unhallowed*

wonders, "be the supermen whom the race had struggled for a million years to produce"?

(par. 17), *egalitarian* (par. 18), *philologist* (par. 20), *speciousness* (par. 22), *patent* (par. 24), *perfidy* (par. 27), *animus* (par. 31), and *abstruse* (par. 45).

*word choice* The locution *cannot help but* (par. 19) is a redundancy—a compounding of *cannot help* and *cannot but*—that is avoided by most careful writers but still commonly used by many educated people. How can you account for this and other frequent redundancies in speech and writing?

## SENTENCES

*rhetorical devices* 1. The style of this essay employs many similes and metaphors, so many that some of them get tangled together in mixed metaphors. Thus paragraph 16 begins with the metaphor of the detour and then introduces other metaphors, one of them mixed. Find it. 2. What are the metaphors of paragraph 17? 3. Why is the first sentence of paragraph 24 a mixed metaphor? 4. Using standard reference dictionaries, explain the following allusions: *Saint-Simon* (par. 15), *Herbert Marcuse* (par. 26), *Arthur Schnitzler* (par. 27), *Promethean undertakings* (par. 45), and *Moloch* (par. 47).

## PARAGRAPHS

*topic sentences* What are the topic sentences of paragraphs 5, 20, and 21?

*methods of development* 1. How does the author explain the "paradox" of paragraph 7? 2. What generalization does the anecdote of paragraph 36 support? Explain.

## CONTENT AND ORGANIZATION

*central ideas* 1. What is the author's attitude toward student protestors and demonstrators (pars. 1–2)? 2. Why does he believe that the American middle class is "bungling the job" (par. 15)? 3. What is his criticism of intellectuals (pars. 20–30)? 4. Why are the rich "alienated" (par. 35)?

*assumptions and implications* How can the problems of the United States be solved by the 70 percent of the population "who do most of the work, pay much of the taxes, crave neither power nor importance, and want to be left alone to live pleasurable humdrum lives" (par. 41)?

## SUGGESTIONS FOR DISCUSSION

1. Eric Hoffer, who is widely known as "a longshoreman-philosopher," believes that American intellectuals are disaffected because they have been denied political power. Do you agree? Explain. 2. Studies of public

opinion have shown that most Americans believe that poverty is the fault of the poor—that it is caused by laziness, shiftlessness, and stupidity. Write a paper commenting on this point of view.  3. The status of "intellectuals" has never been so high in America as in Europe. Why not? 4. Eric Hoffer is a self-educated longshoreman who has gained a national reputation as a commentator on current social problems. Describe another self-educated man or woman whom you have known.  5. Comment on Hoffer's proposal that every high school graduate be given an opportunity to work for two years at good pay. What would be the advantages and disadvantages of such a government-sponsored program?

## James Baldwin

# STRANGER IN THE VILLAGE

1.   From all available evidence no black man had ever set foot in this tiny Swiss village before I came. I was told before arriving that I would probably be a "sight" for the village; I took this to mean that people of my complexion were rarely seen in Switzerland, and also that city people are always something of a "sight" outside of the city. It did not occur to me—possibly because I am an American—that there could be people anywhere who had never seen a Negro.

2.   It is a fact that cannot be explained on the basis of the inaccessibility of the village. The village is very high, but it is only four hours from Milan and three hours from Lausanne. It is true that it is virtually unknown. Few people making plans for a holiday would elect to come here. On the other hand, the villagers are able, presumably, to come and go as they please—which they do: to another town at the foot of the mountain, with a population of approximately five thousand, the nearest place to see a movie or go to the bank. In the village there is no movie house, no bank, no library, no theater; very few radios, one jeep, one station wagon; and, at the moment, one typewriter, mine, an invention which the woman next door to me here had never seen. There are about six hundred people living here, all Catholic—I conclude this from the fact that the Catholic church is open all year round, whereas the Protestant

STRANGER IN THE VILLAGE:   From *Notes of a Native Son* by James Baldwin. Reprinted by permission of the Beacon Press, copyright © 1953, 1955 by James Baldwin.

chapel, set off on a hill a little removed from the village, is open only in the summertime when the tourists arrive. There are four or five hotels, all closed now, and four or five *bistros,* of which, however, only two do any business during the winter. These two do not do a great deal, for life in the village seems to end around nine or ten o'clock. There are a few stores, butcher, baker, *épicerie,* a hardware store, and a money-changer—who cannot change travelers' checks, but must send them down to the bank, an operation which takes two or three days. There is something called the *Ballet Haus,* closed in the winter and used for God knows what, certainly not ballet, during the summer. There seems to be only one schoolhouse in the village, and this for the quite young children; I suppose this to mean that their older brothers and sisters at some point descend from these mountains in order to complete their education—possibly, again, to the town just below. The landscape is absolutely forbidding, mountains towering on all four sides, ice and snow as far as the eye can reach. In this white wilderness, men and women and children move all day, carrying washing, wood, buckets of milk or water, sometimes skiing on Sunday afternoons. All week long boys and young men are to be seen shoveling snow off the rooftops, or dragging wood down from the forest in sleds.

3. The village's only real attraction, which explains the tourist season, is the hot spring water. A disquietingly high proportion of these tourists are cripples, or semicripples, who come year after year —from other parts of Switzerland, usually—to take the waters. This lends the village, at the height of the season, a rather terrifying air of sanctity, as though it were a lesser Lourdes. There is often something beautiful, there is always something awful, in the spectacle of a person who has lost one of his faculties, a faculty he never questioned until it was gone, and who struggles to recover it. Yet people remain people, on crutches or indeed on deathbeds; and wherever I passed, the first summer I was here, among the native villagers or among the lame, a wind passed with me—of astonishment, curiosity, amusement, and outrage. That first summer I stayed two weeks and never intended to return. But I did return in the winter, to work; the village offers, obviously, no distractions whatever and has the further advantage of being extremely cheap. Now it is winter again, a year later, and I am here again. Everyone in the village knows my name, though they scarcely ever use it, knows that I come from America—though, this, apparently, they will never really believe: black men come from Africa—and everyone knows that I am the friend of the son of a woman who was born here, and that I am staying in their chalet. But

I remain as much a stranger today as I was the first day I arrived, and the children shout *Neger! Neger!* as I walk along the streets.

4. It must be admitted that in the beginning I was far too shocked to have any real reaction. In so far as I reacted at all, I reacted by trying to be pleasant—it being a great part of the American Negro's education (long before he goes to school) that he must make people "like" him. This smile-and-the-world-smiles-with-you routine worked about as well in this situation as it had in the situation for which it was designed, which is to say that it did not work at all. No one, after all, can be liked whose human weight and complexity cannot be, or has not been, admitted. My smile was simply another unheard-of phenomenon which allowed them to see my teeth—they did not, really, see my smile and I began to think that, should I take to snarling, no one would notice any difference. All of the physical characteristics of the Negro which had caused me, in America, a very different and almost forgotten pain were nothing less than miraculous —or infernal—in the eyes of the village people. Some thought my hair was the color of tar, that it had the texture of wire, or the texture of cotton. It was jocularly suggested that I might let it all grow long and make myself a winter coat. If I sat in the sun for more than five minutes some daring creature was certain to come along and gingerly put his fingers on my hair, as though he were afraid of an electric shock, or put his hand on my hand, astonished that the color did not rub off. In all of this, in which it must be conceded there was the charm of genuine wonder and in which there was certainly no element of intentional unkindness, there was yet no suggestion that I was human: I was simply a living wonder.

5. I knew that they did not mean to be unkind, and I know it now; it is necessary, nevertheless, for me to repeat this to myself each time that I walk out of the chalet. The children who shout *Neger!* have no way of knowing the echoes this sound raises in me. They are brimming with good humor and the more daring swell with pride when I stop to speak with them. Just the same, there are days when I cannot pause and smile, when I have no heart to play with them; when, indeed, I mutter sourly to myself, exactly as I muttered on the streets of a city these children have never seen, when I was no bigger than these children are now: *Your* mother *was a nigger.* Joyce is right about history being a nightmare—but it may be the nightmare from which no one *can* awaken. People are trapped in history and history is trapped in them.

6. There is a custom in the village—I am told it is repeated in many villages—of "buying" African natives for the purpose of

converting them to Christianity. There stands in the church all year round a small box with a slot for money, decorated with a black figurine, and into this box the villagers drop their francs. During the *carnaval* which precedes Lent, two village children have their faces blackened—out of which bloodless darkness their blue eyes shine like ice—and fantastic horsehair wigs are placed on their blond heads; thus disguised, they solicit among the villagers for money for the missionaries in Africa. Between the box in the church and the blackened children, the village "bought" last year six or eight African natives. This was reported to me with pride by the wife of one of the *bistro* owners and I was careful to express astonishment and pleasure at the solicitude shown by the village for the souls of black folk. The *bistro* owner's wife beamed with a pleasure far more genuine than my own and seemed to feel that I might now breathe more easily concerning the souls of at least six of my kinsmen.

7. I tried not to think of these so lately baptized kinsmen, of the price paid for them, or the peculiar price they themselves would pay, and said nothing about my father, who having taken his own conversion too literally never, at bottom, forgave the white world (which he described as heathen) for having saddled him with a Christ in whom, to judge at least from their treatment of him, they themselves no longer believed. I thought of white men arriving for the first time in an African village, strangers there, as I am a stranger here, and tried to imagine the astounded populace touching their hair and marveling at the color of their skin. But there is a great difference between being the first white man to be seen by Africans and being the first black man to be seen by whites. The white man takes the astonishment as tribute, for he arrives to conquer and to convert the natives, whose inferiority in relation to himself is not even to be questioned; whereas I, without a thought of conquest, find myself among a people whose culture controls me, has even, in a sense, created me, people who have cost me more in anguish and rage than they will ever know, who yet do not even know of my existence. The astonishment with which I might have greeted them, should they have stumbled into my African village a few hundred years ago, might have rejoiced their hearts. But the astonishment with which they greet me today can only poison mine.

8. And this is so despite everything I may do to feel differently, despite my friendly conversations with the *bistro* owner's wife, despite their three-year-old son who has at last become my friend, despite the *saluts* and *bonsoirs* which I exchange with people as I walk, despite the fact that I know that no individual can be taken to task

for what history is doing, or has done. I say that the culture of these people controls me—but they can scarcely be held responsible for European culture. America comes out of Europe, but these people have never seen America, nor have most of them seen more of Europe than the hamlet at the foot of their mountain. Yet they move with an authority which I shall never have; and they regard me, quite rightly, not only as a stranger in their village but as a suspect latecomer, bearing no credentials, to everything they have—however unconsciously—inherited.

9. For this village, even were it incomparably more remote and incredibly more primitive, is the West, the West onto which I have been so strangely grafted. These people cannot be, from the point of view of power, strangers anywhere in the world; they have made the modern world, in effect, even if they do not know it. The most illiterate among them is related, in a way that I am not, to Dante, Shakespeare, Michelangelo, Aeschylus, Da Vinci, Rembrandt, and Racine; the cathedral at Chartres says something to them which it cannot say to me, as indeed would New York's Empire State Building, should anyone here ever see it. Out of their hymns and dances come Beethoven and Bach. Go back a few centuries and they are in their full glory—but I am in Africa, watching the conquerors arrive.

10. The rage of the disesteemed is personally fruitless, but it is also absolutely inevitable; this rage, so generally discounted, so little understood even among the people whose daily bread it is, is one of the things that makes history. Rage can only with difficulty, and never entirely, be brought under the domination of the intelligence and is therefore not susceptible to any arguments whatever. This is a fact which ordinary representatives of the *Herrenvolk,* having never felt this rage and being unable to imagine it, quite fail to understand. Also, rage cannot be hidden, it can only be dissembled. This dissembling deludes the thoughtless, and strengthens rage and adds, to rage, contempt. There are, no doubt, as many ways of coping with the resulting complex of tensions as there are black men in the world, but no black man can hope ever to be entirely liberated from this internal warfare—rage, dissembling, and contempt having inevitably accompanied his first realization of the power of white men. What is crucial here is that, since white men represent in the black man's world so heavy a weight, white men have for black men a reality which is far from being reciprocal; and hence all black men have toward all white men an attitude which is designed, really, either to rob the white man of the jewel of his naïveté, or else to make it cost him dear.

11.   The black man insists, by whatever means he finds at his disposal, that the white man cease to regard him as an exotic rarity and recognize him as a human being. This is a very charged and difficult moment, for there is a great deal of will power involved in the white's man's naïveté. Most people are not naturally reflective any more than they are naturally malicious, and the white man prefers to keep the black man at a certain human remove because it is easier for him thus to preserve his simplicity and avoid being called to account for crimes committed by his forefathers, or his neighbors. He is inescapably aware, nevetheless, that he is in a better position in the world than black men are, nor can he quite put to death the suspicion that he is hated by black men therefore. He does not wish to be hated, neither does he wish to change places, and at this point in his uneasiness he can scarcely avoid having recourse to those legends which white men have created about black men, the most usual effect of which is that the white man finds himself enmeshed, so to speak, in his own language which describes hell, as well as the attributes which lead one to hell, as being as black as night.

12.   Every legend, moreover, contains its residuum of truth, and the root function of language is to control the universe by describing it. It is of quite considerable significance that black men remain, in the imagination, and in overwhelming numbers in fact, beyond the disciplines of salvation; and this despite the fact that the West has been "buying" African natives for centuries. There is, I should hazard, an instantaneous necessity to be divorced from this so visibly unsaved stranger, in whose heart, moreover, one cannot guess what dreams of vengeance are being nourished; and, at the same time, there are few things on earth more attractive than the idea of the unspeakable liberty which is allowed the unredeemed. When, beneath the black mask, a human being begins to make himself felt one cannot escape a certain awful wonder as to what kind of human being it is. What one's imagination makes of other people is dictated, of course, by the laws of one's own personality and it is one of the ironies of black-white relations that, by means of what the white man imagines the black man to be, the black man is enabled to know who the white man is.

13.   I have said, for example, that I am as much a stranger in this village today as I was the first summer I arrived, but this is not quite true. The villagers wonder less about the texture of my hair than they did then, and wonder rather more about me. And the fact that their wonder now exists on another level is reflected in their attitudes and in their eyes. There are the children who make those delightful, hilarious, sometimes astonishingly grave overtures of

friendship in the unpredictable fashion of children; other children, having been taught that that devil is a black man, scream in genuine anguish as I approach. Some of the older women never pass without a friendly greeting, never pass, indeed, if it seems that they will be able to engage me in conversation; other women look down or look away or rather contemptuously smirk. Some of the men drink with me and suggest that I learn how to ski—partly, I gather, because they cannot imagine what I would look like on skis—and want to know if I am married, and ask questions about my *métier*. But some of the men have accused *le sale nègre*—behind my back—of stealing wood and there is already in the eyes of some of them that peculiar, intent, paranoiac malevolence which one sometimes surprises in the eyes of American white men when, out walking with their Sunday girl, they see a Negro male approach.

14.    There is a dreadful abyss between the streets of this village and the streets of the city in which I was born, between the children who shout *Neger!* today and those who shouted *Nigger!* yesterday— the abyss is experience, the American experience. The syllable hurled behind me today expresses, above all, wonder: I am a stranger here. But I am not a stranger in America and the same syllable riding on the American air expresses the war my presence has occasioned in the American soul.

15.    For this village brings home to me this fact: that there was a day, and not really a very distant day, when Americans were scarcely Americans at all but discontented Europeans, facing a great unconquered continent and strolling, say, into a marketplace and seeing black men for the first time. The shock this spectacle afforded is suggested, surely, by the promptness with which they decided that these black men were not really men but cattle. It is true that the necessity on the part of the settlers of the New World of reconciling their moral assumptions with the fact—and the necessity—of slavery enhanced immensely the charm of this idea, and it is also true that this idea expresses, with a truly American bluntness, the attitude which to varying extents all masters have had toward all slaves.

16.    But between all former slaves and slave-owners and the drama which begins for Americans over three hundred years ago at Jamestown, there are at least two differences to be observed. The American Negro slave could not suppose, for one thing, as slaves in past epochs had supposed and often done, that he would ever be able to wrest the power from his master's hands. This was a supposition which the modern era, which was to bring about such vast changes in the aims and dimensions of power, put to death; it only begins, in

unprecedented fashion, and with dreadful implications, to be resurrected today. But even had this supposition persisted with undiminished force, the American Negro slave could not have used it to lend his condition dignity, for the reason that this supposition rests on another: that the slave in exile yet remains related to his past, has some means—if only in memory—of revering and sustaining the forms of his former life, is able, in short, to maintain his identity.

17. This was not the case with the American Negro slave. He is unique among the black men of the world in that his past was taken from him, almost literally, at one blow. One wonders what on earth the first slave found to say to the first dark child he bore. I am told that there are Haitians able to trace their ancestry back to African kings, but any American Negro wishing to go back so far will find his journey through time abruptly arrested by the signature on the bill of sale which served as the entrance paper for his ancestor. At the time —to say nothing of the circumstances—of the enslavement of the captive black man who was to become the American Negro, there was not the remotest possibility that he would ever take power from his master's hands. There was no reason to suppose that his situation would ever change, nor was there, shortly, anything to indicate that his situation had ever been different. It was his necessity, in the words of E. Franklin Frazier, to find a "motive for living under American culture or die." The identity of the American Negro comes out of this extreme situation, and the evolution of this identity was a source of the most intolerable anxiety in the minds and the lives of his masters.

18. For the history of the American Negro is unique also in this: that the question of his humanity, and of his rights therefore as a human being, became a burning one for several generations of Americans, so burning a question that it ultimately became one of those used to divide the nation. It is out of this argument that the venom of the epithet *Nigger!* is derived. It is an argument which Europe has never had, and hence Europe quite sincerely fails to understand how or why the argument arose in the first place, why its effects are so frequently disastrous and always so unpredictable, why it refuses until today to be entirely settled. Europe's black possessions remained—and do remain—in Europe's colonies, at which remove they represented no threat whatever to European identity. If they posed any problem at all for the European conscience, it was a problem which remained comfortingly abstract: in effect, the black man, *as a man,* did not exist for Europe. But in America, even as a slave, he was an inescapable part of the general social fabric and no American could escape having an attitude toward him. Americans attempt

until today to make an abstraction of the Negro, but the very nature of these abstractions reveals the tremendous effects the presence of the Negro has had on the American character.

19.  When one considers the history of the Negro in America it is of the greatest importance to recognize that the moral beliefs of a person, or a people, are never really as tenuous as life—which is not moral—very often causes them to appear; these create for them a frame of reference and a necessary hope, the hope being that when life has done its worst they will be enabled to rise above themselves and to triumph over life. Life would scarcely be bearable if this hope did not exist. Again, even when the worst has been said, to betray a belief is not by any means to have put oneself beyond its power; the betrayal of a belief is not the same thing as ceasing to believe. If this were not so there would be no moral standards in the world at all. Yet one must also recognize that morality is based on ideas and that all ideas are dangerous—dangerous because ideas can only lead to action and where the action leads no man can say. And dangerous in this respect: that confronted with the impossibility of remaining faithful to one's beliefs, and the equal impossibility of becoming free of them, one can be driven to the most inhuman excesses. The ideas on which American beliefs are based are not, though Americans often seem to think so, ideas which originated in America. They came out of Europe. And the establishment of democracy on the American continent was scarcely as radical a break with the past as was the necessity, which  Americans faced, of broadening this concept to include black men.

20.  This was, literally, a hard necessity. It was impossible, for one thing, for Americans to abandon their beliefs, not only because these beliefs alone seemed able to justify the sacrifices they had endured and the blood that they had spilled, but also because these beliefs afforded them their only bulwark against a moral chaos as absolute as the physical chaos of the continent it was their destiny to conquer. But in the situation in which Americans found themselves, these beliefs threatened an idea which, whether or not one likes to think so, is the very warp and woof of the heritage of the West, the idea of white supremacy.

21.  Americans have made themselves notorious by the shrillness and the brutality with which they have insisted on this idea, but they did not invent it; and it has escaped the world's notice that those very excesses of which Americans have been guilty imply a certain, unprecedented uneasiness over the idea's life and power, if not, indeed, the idea's validity. The idea of white supremacy rests simply

on the fact that white men are the creators of civilization (the present civilization, which is the only one that matters; all previous civilizations are simply "contributions" to our own) and are therefore civilization s guardians and defenders. Thus it was impossible for Americans to accept the black man as one of themselves, for to do so was to jeopardize their status as white men. But not so to accept him was to deny his human reality, his human weight and complexity, and the strain of denying the overwhelmingly undeniable forced Americans into rationalizations so fantastic that they approached the pathological.

22. At the root of the American Negro problem is the necessity of the American white man to find a way of living with the Negro in order to be able to live with himself. And the history of this problem can be reduced to the means used by Americans—lynch law and law, segregation and legal acceptance, terrorization and concession—either to come to terms with this necessity, or to find a way around it, or (most usually) to find a way of doing both these things at once. The resulting spectacle, at once foolish and dreadful, led someone to make the quite accurate observation that "the Negro-in-America is a form of insanity which overtakes white men."

23. In this long battle, a battle by no means finished, the unforeseeable effects of which will be felt by many future generations, the white man's motive was the protection of his identity; the black man was motivated by the need to establish an identity. And despite the terrorization which the Negro in America endured and endures sporadically until today, despite the cruel and totally inescapable ambivalence of his status in his country, the battle for his identity has long ago been won. He is not a visitor to the West, but a citizen there, an American; as American as the Americans who despise him, the Americans who fear him, the Americans who love him—the Americans who became less than themselves, or rose to be greater than themselves by virtue of the fact that the challenge he represented was inescapable. He is perhaps the only black man in the world whose relationship to white men is more terrible, more subtle, and more meaningful than the relationship of bitter possessed to uncertain possessor. His survival depended, and his development depends, on his ability to turn his peculiar status in the Western world to his own advantage and, it may be, to the very great advantage of that world. It remains for him to fashion out of his experience that which will give him sustenance, and a voice.

24. The cathedral at Chartres, I have said, says something to the people of this village which it cannot say to me; but it is important

to understand that this cathedral says something to me which it cannot say to them. Perhaps they are struck by the power of the spires, the glory of the windows; but they have known God, after all, longer than I have known him, and in a different way, and I am terrified by the slippery bottomless well to be found in the crypt, down which heretics were hurled to death, and by the obscene, inescapable gargoyles jutting out of the stone and seeming to say that God and the devil can never be divorced. I doubt that the villagers think of the devil when they face a cathedral because they have never been identified with the devil. But I must accept the status which myth, if nothing else, gives me in the West before I can hope to change the myth.

25. Yet, if the American Negro has arrived at his identity by virtue of the absoluteness of his estrangement from his past, American white men still nourish the illusion that there is some means of recovering the European innocence, of returning to a state in which black men do not exist. This is one of the greatest errors Americans can make. The identity they fought so hard to protect has, by virtue of that battle, undergone a change: Americans are as unlike any other white people in the world as it is possible to be. I do not think, for example, that it is too much to suggest that the American vision of the world—which allows so little reality, generally speaking, for any of the darker forces in human life, which tends until today to paint moral issues in glaring black and white—owes a great deal to the battle waged by Americans to maintain between themselves and black men a human separation which could not be bridged. It is only now beginning to be borne in on us—very faintly, it must be admitted, very slowly, and very much against our will—that this vision of the world is dangerously inaccurate, and perfectly useless. For it protects our moral high-mindedness at the terrible expense of weakening our grasp of reality. People who shut their eyes to reality simply invite their own destruction, and anyone who insists on remaining in a state of innocence long after that innocence is dead turns himself into a monster.

26. The time has come to realize that the interracial drama acted out on the American continent has not only created a new black man, it has created a new white man, too. No road whatever will lead Americans back to the simplicity of this European village where white men still have the luxury of looking on me as a stranger. I am not, really, a stranger any longer for any American alive. One of the things that distinguishes Americans from other people is that no other people has ever been so deeply involved in the lives of black men, and vice

versa. This fact faced, with all its implications, it can be seen that the history of the American Negro problem is not merely shameful, it is also something of an achievement. For even when the worst has been said, it must also be added that the perpetual challenge posed by this problem was always, somehow, perpetually met. It is precisely this black-white experience which may prove of indispensable value to us in the world we face today. This world is white no longer, and it will never be white again.

## WORDS

*meaning* 1. Define *forbidding* (par. 2), *human weight* (par. 4), *chalet* (par. 5), *residuum* (par. 12), *paranoiac* (par. 13), and *estrangement* (par. 25). 2. Identify *Lourdes* (par. 3), *Chartres* (par. 9), and *Herren-volk* (par. 10).

*word choice* 1. What can the author mean by the word *beautiful* (par. 3) as applied to maimed people? 2. *Routine* (par. 4) is used in a colloquial sense. What is its effect? Answer the same question for *saddled* (par. 7). 3. What is there about the phrase "the charm of this idea" (par. 15) that gives it special irony?

## SENTENCES

*style* 1. In paragraph 3, the author speaks of "a wind" that "passed with me." What does he mean by this figure of speech? Why *wind*? 2. What does he mean by speaking of *rage* (par. 10) as someone's "daily bread"? Whose "daily bread"? 3. What does he mean by "the jewel of his naïveté" (par. 10)? 4. Explain the paradox with which paragraph 12 ends.

*parallelism* 1. Which sentence in paragraph 8 is based on a series of parallel phrases? 2. Consider the first sentence of paragraph 10. What are the two large balanced elements that make up the sentence? What are the parallel elements within each part?

*variety* How does the author manage to vary the almost inevitable "there is . . ." and "there are . . ." constructions in his description of the village (par. 2)?

## PARAGRAPHS

*coherence* 1. What connects "The rage of the disesteemed" (opening of par. 10) with the preceding paragraph? 2. How does paragraph 17 connect with paragraph 16, which speaks of "at least two differences" but discusses only one of them? 3. In paragraph 5, the author begins to write about the Negro in America. How does the next paragraph, about a custom in the Swiss village, relate to that—and in which sentence?

CONTENT AND ORGANIZATION

*central idea*   The central idea of this essay seems to be stated in the first sentence of paragraph 23. Explain that idea.

*organization*   1. What sentence in the first paragraph is echoed in the last paragraph? Is this "frame" appropriate to the central idea? 2. How does the Swiss village where the author is an exotic stranger serve to dramatize his situation—and that of all Negroes—in the United States? 3. In which paragraph does the essay begin to point to the concluding sentence?

*assumptions and implications*   What does the author mean by calling the history of the American Negro problem "something of an achievement" (par. 26)? What is implied in the penultimate sentence of the essay?

SUGGESTIONS FOR DISCUSSION

1. What are some of the "legends" and "myths" that have been attached to the American Negro? 2. Have you, whether white or black, ever found yourself in an interracial situation that clarified some of your own attitudes? Can you analyze the motivations of these attitudes? 3. In answer to a question after an address, James Baldwin said in effect, "I have never asked anyone to help the Negro. I have asked you to help yourselves." In what ways does he want white people to help themselves?


*Daniel Bell*

# THE FORCES SHAPING THE CITY:
# THE FOUR FACES OF NEW YORK

1.   Cities differ for reasons of topography (regard only the superb site of San Francisco); of function (Washington as a political center, St. Louis as a commercial distribution center for the South, Detroit as an industrial center); and of social composition (behold

THE FORCES SHAPING THE CITY: THE FOUR FACES OF NEW YORK:   A paper presented at a symposium sponsored by the New York City Planning Commission, October 1964. Reprinted here from *New York* (the *New York Herald Tribune* Sunday magazine), November 15, 1964, by courtesy of *Scripps-Howard Newspapers*.

the extraordinary mixture of ethnic and native groups which is New York).[1] The different combinations provide different city-scapes, different rhythms and different attractions.

2. But for all these differences, there is an "essence" which is common to all cities, and which distinguishes it as a social form; the city is "man-made" and can be man-changed. The city is a center which draws people from surrounding environs and encourages movement and transiency. It is diverse, and therefore encourages choice.

3. The city is syncretistic. All modes and manners mingle, all creeds and cults jostle one another; inherited beliefs are challenged and the children depart from the paths of their fathers. Strange Gods make their rival claims. In the Rome of Constantine (as Jacob Burckhardt describes it), "On images of Fortuna there are to be seen, beside the oar and cornucopia which are appropriate to her, the breastplate of Minerva, the lotus of Isis, the thunderbolt of Jupiter; the fawn-skin of Bacchus, the cock of Aesculapius, and the like." And in present-day New York one finds the shrines of many faiths, whether they be the cathedrals of Rome, the churches of diverse Protestant creeds, the synagogues of orthodox, conservative and reform Jewry, the temples of B'Hai, the Vedic missions of Krishnamurti, the sects of Zen and Shin Buddhism, Sufi mysticism and Black Muslims, to the secular religions of the radical sects and the artistic and hallucinogenic cults.

4. New York is a palimpsest. Successive layers, never wholly erasing the earlier ones, have provided different outlines for the profiles of New York. And each of these profiles has given a different character to New York, providing at successive historical periods a distinctive face whose traces, etched deeply, remain visible.

5. New York was, first, a port city. The magnificent natural harbor—large, well-sheltered, deep enough for the largest ships, shallow enough for convenient anchorage—made New York the center for commerce as it became the primary transportation center for the exchange of raw materials from the West for the finished products of Europe and the eastern seaboard. Point-counterpoint followed with

---

[1] In 1960, the breakdown was roughly as follows: 25 per cent Jewish, 16 per cent Italian, 14 per cent Negro, 10 per cent Irish, 10 per cent German, and eight per cent Puerto Rican: the remaining 17 per cent were Poles, Russians, Ukrainians, Hungarians, Lithuanians, Greeks, Slovaks, Macedonians, Cypriots, Syrians, Lebanese, French, Dutch, Czech, Chinese, Japanese, Mexican and WASP. Equally important, 69 per cent had little more than the tie of one generation to the city: 19 per cent were foreign-born, 28 per cent are first-generation, and half of all Negroes above 20 years of age had come from the South.

economic logic. Frequent ship sailings, the rail-canal system to the West, the concentration of freight forwarders, insurance specialists, banks to facilitate credit, wholesalers to distribute imports—all these spurred the development of the port.

6. The port gave New York its 19th-century character, topographical and social. Downtown was the intense concentration of insurance, finance and wholesale sections. Along the rim of the port lay the dives and saloons and open brothels—along Water Street and Green Street—which gave the city its brawling character. Hordes of immigrants poured through the port, and many stayed here, providing not only a floating labor supply but the distinctive "foreign" sections which created an ecological mosaic of the city.

7. The second face of New York, emerging strongly at the turn of the century, was a manufacturing profile. New York today has 40,000 manufacturing establishments, with the largest factory work force (nearly a million industrial workers) and the largest manufacturing payroll (close to $3 billion a year) of any American city. The garment industry is the dominant one, but printing and publishing are also huge, providing one-fifth of all the printing and publishing in the U.S.

8. But this manufacturing is of a special character. It has not been transport savings or labor costs that have attracted industry, but "external economies," the availability of a pool of specialized facilities and skills that could be shared by firms without their having to carry these items as part of permanent overhead costs. Typically, this has meant that industries located in New York tend to be composed of small, fast-moving, risk-taking and highly competitive firms engaged in a rough-and-tumble race.

9. In essence, New York is a manufacturing bazaar in which speed, variety and specialization are the hallmarks of the services it offers. As Raymond Vernon points out in his *Metropolis/1985,* "Producers of made-to-order giant turbines and generators are not found in the region because they operate on production schedules which call for delivery three or four years after the placement of an order," and they require large, cheap industrial space for these plants. "But a high-style dress is sometimes conceived and executed in a fortnight; an advertising brochure may be only hours or days in the making; a lawyer's brief is often printed between midnight and morning." A dress house, therefore, will need to have immediately available a wide variety of buttons, buckles, embroidery, rhinestones or other trimmings, without wanting to carry full stocks of these items or machinery for making them; an advertising agency requires a large variety

of services, and specialized agencies—printing shops, photography establishments, model agencies—arise to service them.

10. This second face, which is identifiable largely with the development of the Jewish community, is the New York of the small enterpriser. (The archetypal novel of this period is Abraham Cahan's *The Rise of David Levinsky,* a novel about the class that moved from the sweatshops of the lower East Side to the lofts of Seventh Avenue.) But if the heart of this economic category has been the dress industry, the same problems turn up in an array of small-unit, single-plant firms—small companies engaged in printing, plastics, electronics and small-scale machine work. These industries are characterized by uncertainty, by the capacity to make quick-change production shifts, the search for an item or product that will be a sudden "hit." Each of these industries depends upon a whole range of auxiliary services. Each manufacturer being, so to speak, a retailer, has behind him a range of wholesalers who supply his needs. Because decisions have to be made swiftly there is scarcely an intra-firm hierarchy, little bureaucratization, and usually only a single establishment. The number of one-plant firms in New York, averaging about 25 employees each, is enormous. In 47 industries composed almost entirely of single-plant firms, 30 per cent of the total employment is concentrated in New York.

11. These factors make for an extraordinary reliance on financial institutions. Few of these firms have sufficient capital for expansion or, often enough, money to cover more than immediate operating costs. The commercial banks and factoring corporations advance short-term loans or take over accounts receivable as the way of supplying the small companies with cash. Thus, in a second way, the financial institutions of the city become enlarged, and constitute a decisive economic force.

12. The "moral" of all this is that the manufacturing base of New York is a fantastic variety of "non-rationalized" enterprises and services, relatively easy to break into because of low capital requirements, but in which survival and success depend upon ingenuity, quick initiative, often cutting the corner, and finding other ways to make the "fast buck." This is what has given New York a swift rhythm, a particular beat and distinctive character. It is now changing, but enough of this survives on the palimpsest, as does the port character, to be distinctively visible.

13. The "third face" of New York—the New York of the 1950s—is the New York of the corporate headquarters, a face displayed by the unbroken lines of the new glass houses on Park Ave-

nue to the towering high-rental apartment houses along the upper East Side. All this is quite remarkable. In the late 1940s, the talk in the business world was largely about the impossibility of New York as a business center and the need for decentralization. (General Foods moved out to Westchester. Time Inc., which owned the site of the Hotel Marguery, sold it and took an option on land in Rye.) Jean-Paul Sartre, a visitor here in 1950, commented sourly on the grid-shadowed streets of Midtown New York and predicted that no new skyscrapers would be built in the city.

14. Yet how wrong all that talk was. Since 1947, nearly 150 new large office buildings have been built in Manhattan. In all, 58 million square feet of office space—or nearly two-thirds as much as existed before 1947—has been added to Manhattan in the last 20 years. Today, more than 135 of the 500 largest industrial corporations in America have their headquarters in New York. And with this concentration of managerial personnel, the ancillary services of the white collar world—law firms, accounting houses, management consultants, advertising agencies (some 70 per cent of the national advertising agencies have their central offices here)—have expanded.

15. Why the large corporations have placed their headquarters here is not a question that economists can answer on the basis of their particular logic. In manufacturing, as Raymond Vernon points out, "An economic version of the Darwinian principle, feeble and dilute though its effects may be, operates to push industries towards the location which yields the largest return. [But] the central office of a large corporation produces no easily defined product whose costs can be 'priced out' at alternative locations."

16. There are, to be sure, some "external economies" available in New York to the mammoth corporation. Corporations with such diverse problems as taxes or advertising commercials can arrange for quick consultations with experts. Financial institutions, such as insurance companies, can draw upon economic and other experts for investment counsel. Yet in the age of the telephone conference, the closed circuit television and the private company airplane, distance is less of a barrier to communication than ever before.

17. What draws the rationalized corporate behemoths to New York is the ancient longing for display among one's own. New York is now a corporate bazaar with sleek symbols glorifying "Seagram" or "Pan Am" or "Lever Brothers" or "Pepsi-Cola"—the new doges of the central business district. New York is no longer the ethnic-dominated, nervously swift city of *I Can Get It for You Wholesale,*

but the place of the "executive suite." The horizontal axis has shifted from Seventh Avenue to Park Avenue.

18. Each of these "faces" has been symbolic of the multi-faceted nature of New York. Each, in its own way, has made or "remade" sections of the city. There is emerging now—its lineaments have always been present—a new, fourth face, a New York of the mid-'60s and '70s, with a set of new needs and a dominant style: the "cultural city."

19. New York has always been the publishing, music, art and drama center of the country. The United Nations has made it an international capital. It is a vast intellectual center, with more than 40 institutions of higher learning and one-fifth of all students in the United States doing post-graduate work concentrated here. Its score of museums give it the largest treasure trove of paintings in the world. Its several hundred art galleries and more than 2,000 art shows a year give it a centrality and excitement in the world of art. There are as many shows off-Broadway as there are on Broadway. And in the course of any week during the season one can find the greatest variety of opera, ballet, symphony concerts, experimental music and solo performance.

20. But several obvious elements conjoin to place a new emphasis on culture and learning as a new "face" of the coming decade. There is, first, the enormous expansion of higher education, undergraduate and graduate, which has given a new weight to the colleges and universities of the city. A new generation of younger businessmen and executives has brought a "culture-hungry" class to the fore, a class that has sought its own status symbols as well as desire for new taste, in the vast purchases of art and furnishings. The children of the immigrants, particularly the Jewish generation, with its own middle-class status, have vastly expanded the market for culture. It is in the creation of Lincoln Square as a new focal point of the city's performing arts, the expansion of Columbia University along Morningside Heights and the spread of New York University to engulf Washington Square, that we see the symbols of this new "fourth face" of the city.

21. Each of these developments has proceeded on its own with little or no social control or thought as to the consequences on other activities of the city. And yet, the central fact of life in the city is that the uncontrolled development of the several "faces" of New York life has levied vast "social costs" which are being paid now by the large majority of inhabitants in the traffic, conges-

tion, housing densities, air pollution and other blights which have befouled the city.

22. There are two major aspects to this failure to plan: one is the administrative failure of the City Planning Commission to exercise leadership for the city, and second is the lack of any mechanism which allows us to ascertain the real distribution of costs generated by decisions taken in the "market."

23. Under the 1938 Charter, a city planning commission was proposed which would have almost autonomous powers to do long-range planning for the city. The commission had three tasks: to prepare and maintain a "master plan of the city"; to prepare proposed zoning regulations for the Board of Estimate; and to prepare five-year capital programs.

24. More than 25 years later, there is still no comprehensive master plan as envisaged by the charter—and there is a good question, given the necessary regional integration which alone can move to meet many of the future needs of the metropolitan area, whether one is any longer possible.

25. Why the city has failed to adopt a master plan is a question far beyond the scope of this paper. One answer, suggested by Sayre and Kaufman in their comprehensive book of *Governing New York City*, suggests that it lies in the inability of the commission to mobilize a "stable constituency." Within the structure of city government, the commission comes into conflict with other offices, particularly that of the budget director and the Board of Estimate. Outside,

> The real estate interests, the building and construction industries, the transportation and utility groups . . . argue for minimum change in the settled patterns of bargaining and mutual concessions, for a public policy which leaves planning to the decisions of the market and to the ingenuity of its participants. The political party organizations hold aloof from the planning institution, relying mainly upon the Board of Estimate. The labor groups do not ordinarily feel involved in the planning process, intervening in *ad hoc* fashion but relying also mainly on the Board. In sum, then, the Planning Commission draws little strength and comfort from its constituency.

26. The 25-year plight of the City Planning Commission points up a necessary distinction between a "social decision" and the "sum total of individual decisions" (a distinction with a long history in utilitarian theory), which may cast light on the difficulty in planning. During the war, for example, a poll seeking to gauge the degree of

voluntary co-operation which might forestall rationing of cloth, asked: "Should manufacturers stop making civilian suits and use the limited amount of cloth for Army uniforms?" Most individuals, as patriots, answered, "Yes." But each individual, fingering his own threadbare coat, might say, "I need a suit," and go out and buy one. The public "as a whole" endorsed a social decision; yet the sum total of individual decisions, registered by the market, was very different indeed.

27. The major weight of "individual decisions" on New York, decisions affecting the physical layout of the city, rests in the hands largely of economic controllers—the large insurance companies and banks who, by granting or withholding mortgage money, by assessing any project necessarily in terms of cost-profit of the immediate site, have shaped the contours of New York. As I pointed out in an article more than three years ago (in the special New York issue of *Dissent*) Vincent Astor, shortly before his death, sought to put up a building with an open plaza on Park Avenue and 53d Street which, combined with the open space of Mies' Seagram Building, might have served as a focal point of city life. But he could not get the financing, and the National City Bank put up a squat building that covers the entire footage.

28. Erwin Wolfson, who put up the 60-story megalith behind Grand Central Station, remarked shortly before his death that the "only" valid argument he heard in opposition to his project was the idea of turning the three-and-a-half-acre site into a plaza. But this was impractical, he said. In terms of an economic calculus, yes. But is it impractical in terms of space and light, a haven for pedestrians, a resting place in the center, an enhancing of light and vista?

29. None of these decision makers are villains. Many probably protest the lack of amenities which their own decisions give rise to. But they are part of a system that assesses costs through a narrow economic calculus by individual decision units rather than in terms of social costs and gains.[2]

[2] One looks at the re-development of the Avenue of Americas from 50th Street to 59th and can only lament the lack of planning and the missed opportunity to create a vast new "plaza" for the city. In one of the rare instances of its kind, streets with small lots and nondescript buildings were torn down successively to make way for block-long buildings—Time-Life, Equitable, Sperry-Rand, C.B.S., the New York Hilton, and some apartment houses—which go for a half-mile to the edge of the Park. Yet if there had been some planning, one could envisage a second-story esplanade, 10 blocks long, "roofing" the avenue and uniting the buildings with a pedestrian mall, which would have allowed traffic to flow freely below and provided for a "galleria" of shops, stores and restaurants above leading into the Park that would have been one of the great "piazzas" of the world.

30.   To take the more mundane and less utopian question of traffic. The use of the midtown area city streets for private cars represents a subsidy to their owners of 20 feet of public space at a penalty of wasting time, enduring gas fumes and other social costs that must be borne by everyone else who works in the area, as well as a financial loss to the rapid-transit network whose revenues are thus reduced. Why not bar private cars from midtown? But even this "subsidy" pales compared with that made to the truckers and the industries they serve. Each morning and each evening midtown streets become all but impassable because of the large 40-foot trucks that crowd the streets and back up across the avenues, with the countless burdens of noise, harassment, lost time and other multiple indignities that such congestion creates. Why not compel all truck loadings to be undertaken before eight in the morning and after seven at night in the midtown district? This would be an added expense to the individual firm—one that could be offset by tax rebates and lower rents for the district—but a possible social gain to the rest of the community.

31.   Whether utopian or mundane, the point remains that few of these problems are ever explored from any cost calculus other than the individual economic unit—and often in this reckoning the city thinks of itself as one more such unit—with no conception of social costs or gains.

32.   To provide an "absurd" yet simple example: in recent years the city has decided, during the heavy snowfalls, not to hire additional trucks to remove the snow and dump it in the river, but to shovel the snow into the middle of the streets—including Fifth Avenue—where it is churned into slush by passing trucks, buses and cars, so that it can be hosed down into the sewers. Yet bystanders and pedestrians on the sidewalks find their clothes spattered by the slush churned up and it is likely that the cleaning bills of the individual citizens go up a total of a million dollars that week while the city can calmly say that it has "saved" money. In this instance, the "social decision" (applauded by taxpayer groups) results in an "irrational" cost which is placed on the unlucky bystander.

33.   But merely to blame the banks, real-estate lobbies, or powerful bureaucratic interests for the chaos of the city is too easy a game to play. Where politics is played only as a brokerage game, all groups defend private interests against a weakly defined social desideratum. Take, for example, the post-war decision to deal with slum clearance in Manhattan. Any wholesale uprooting in a city

where the vacancy ratio has diminished almost to zero could only result, as this operation did, in dumping the population in the housing slums, from one section of the city to another. Proposals for public housing in the open spaces of Staten Island, where garden-type developments would have been possible, or nearer the outskirts of the city, were decried: by property owners in those areas who didn't want Negroes; by politicians in Manhattan who feared the loss of their political base through dispersal; by liberals who felt it was wrong to penalize public housing residents by increasing the time they traveled to work. So high-rise, high-density barracks were built on the most expensive land in the world. Slum clearance as a reform slogan won the day—but it was a pyrrhic victory.

34. Clearly no effective plan for New York is possible in the next 25 years so long as the existing helter-skelter of 1,400 local governments, each with its own decision-making powers about taxes, traffic, schools, parks, housing, sewage, water, police, fire and other municipal services, continues to exist in the New York metropolitan region. The problems of New York obviously no longer make sense within the confines of the city. If the city's economy makes sense today only in regional terms, so must its polity. Without such dovetailing, none of the area's fundamental problems—transportation, housing, the port—can be solved.

### WORDS

*meaning*  Define *ethnic* (par. 1), *WASP* (fn. 1), *syncretistic* and *hallucinogenic* (par. 3), *palimpsest* (par. 4), *ecological* (par. 6), *behemoths* (par. 17), *ad hoc* (par. 25), *megalith* (par. 28), *desideratum* and *pyrrhic* (par. 33).

*word choice*  Is *doges* (par. 17), borrowed from the Renaissance Italian of Venice and Genoa, an apt choice here?

### SENTENCES

*style*  Experts on style used to maintain that one should never end a sentence with a preposition. Consider sentence 2 of paragraph 29. Would the sentence be more forceful if it read in either of these ways: "Many probably protest the lack of amenities to which their own decisions give rise," or "Many probably protest the lack of amenities which their own decisions decree"? Which of the three is best? Why?

*parallelism*  In paragraph 1, consider the "faulty" parallelism in the three parentheses. Is this a defect or a virtue of construction?

PARAGRAPHS

*development*  Paragraph 19 is developed by examples of an initial assertion. Does the paragraph move beyond the first assertion through these
examples to some point to be developed later?

CONTENT AND ORGANIZATION

*organization*  Summarize this essay. Having done so, did you find that
it falls into two main parts: (a) description of New York's "four faces"
and (b) criticism of the uncontrolled nature of the city's growth? Which
paragraph is the transition between the two parts?

SUGGESTIONS FOR DISCUSSION

1. Describe the growth of the town or city that you know best. If they
apply, use the kinds of economic or socio-cultural terms that Daniel Bell
uses. If they do not apply, what terms would you use to characterize the
history of this town?  2. Write an essay in which you define your sense of
yourself in relation to the environment, urban or rural, in which you grew
up.  3. "Where politics is played only as a brokerage game, all groups defend private interests against a weakly defined social desideratum" (par.
33). Explain the meaning of this quotation and discuss its application in
your own city to decisions concerning zoning, city planning, sanitation,
or parks and playgrounds.

*William Faulkner*

# ON PRIVACY:
# THE AMERICAN DREAM,
# WHAT HAPPENED TO IT?

1.  This was the American Dream: a sanctuary on the earth
for individual man: a condition in which he could be free not only
of the old established closed-corporation hierarchies of arbitrary
power which had oppressed him as a mass, but free of that mass into
which the hierarchies of church and state had compressed and held
him individually thralled and individually impotent.

ON PRIVACY: THE AMERICAN DREAM, WHAT HAPPENED TO IT?  Copyright © 1955
by William Faulkner. Reprinted from *Essays, Speeches and Public Letters of
William Faulkner,* edited by James B. Meriwether, by permission of Random
House, Inc.

2. A dream simultaneous among the separate individuals of men so asunder and scattered as to have no contact to match dreams and hopes among the old nations of the Old World which existed as nations not on citizenship but subjectship, which endured only on the premise of size and docility of the subject mass; the individual men and women who said as with one simultaneous voice: "We will establish a new land where man can assume that every individual man—not the mass of men but individual men—has the inalienable right to individual dignity and freedom within a fabric of individual courage and honorable work and mutual responsibility."

3. Not just an idea, but a condition: a living human condition designed to be coeval with the birth of America itself, engendered, created, and simultaneous with the very air and word *America,* which at that one stroke, one instant, should cover the whole earth with one simultaneous suspiration like air or light. And it was, it did: radiating outward to cover even the old weary repudiated still-thralled nations, until individual men everywhere, who had no more than heard the name, let alone knew where America was, could respond to it, lifting up not only their hearts but the hopes too which until now they did not know—or anyway dared not remember—that they possessed.

4. A condition in which every man would not only not be a king, he wouldn't even want to be one. He wouldn't even need to bother to need to be the equal of kings because now he was free of kings and all their similar congeries; free not only of the symbols but of the old arbitrary hierarchies themselves which the puppet-symbols represented—courts and cabinets and churches and schools —to which he had been valuable not as an individual but only as that integer, his value compounded in that immutable ratio to his sheer mindless numbers, that animal increase of his will-less and docile mass.

5. The dream, the hope, the condition which our forefathers did not bequeath to us, their heirs and assigns, but rather bequeathed us, their successors, to the dream and the hope. We were not even given the chance then to accept or decline the dream, for the reason that the dream already owned and possessed us at birth. It was not our heritage because we were its, we ourselves heired in our successive generations to the dream by the idea of the dream. And not only we, their sons born and bred in America, but men born and bred in the old alien repudiated lands, also felt that breath, that air, heard that promise, that proffer that there was such a thing as hope for individual man. And the old nations themselves, so old and so

long-fixed in the old concepts of man as to have thought themselves beyond all hope of change, making oblation to that new dream of that new concept of man by gifts of monuments and devices to mark the portals of that inalienable right and hope:

6.  "There is room for you here from about the earth, for all ye individually homeless, individually oppressed, individually un-individualized."

7.  A free gift left to us by those who had mutually travailed and individually endured to create it; we, their successors, did not even have to earn, deserve it, let alone win it. We did not even need to nourish and feed it. We needed only to remember that, living, it was therefore perishable and must be defended in its crises. Some of us, most of us perhaps, could not have proved by definition that we knew exactly what it was. But then, we didn't need to: who no more needed to define it than we needed to define that air we breathed or that word, which, the two of them, simply by existing simultaneously—the breathing of the American air which made America—together had engendered and created the dream on that first day of America as air and motion created temperature and climate on the first day of time.

8.  Because that dream was man's aspiration in the true meaning of the word *aspiration*. It was not merely the blind and voiceless hope of his heart: it was the actual inbreathe of his lungs, his lights, his living and unsleeping metabolism, so that we actually lived the Dream. We did not live *in* the dream: we lived the Dream itself, just as we do not merely live *in* air and climate, but we live Air and Climate; we ourselves individually representative of the Dream, the Dream itself actually audible in the strong uninhibited voices which were not afraid to speak clichés at the very top of them, giving to the cliché-avatars of "Give me liberty or give me death" or "This to be self-evident that all individual men were created equal in one mutual right to freedom" which had never lacked for truth anyway, assuming that hope and dignity and truth, a validity and immediacy absolving them even of cliché.

9.  That was the Dream: not man created equal in the sense that he was created black or white or brown or yellow and hence doomed irrevocably to that for the remainder of his days—or rather, not doomed with equality but blessed with equality, himself lifting no hand but instead lying curled and drowsing in the warm and airless bath of it like the yet-wombed embryo; but liberty in which to have an equal start at equality with all other men, and freedom in which to defend and preserve that equality by means of the individual

courage and the honorable work and the mutual responsibility. Then we lost it. It abandoned us, which had supported and protected and defended us while our new nation of new concepts of human existence got a firm enough foothold to stand erect among the nations of the earth, demanding nothing of us in return save to remember always that, being alive, it was therefore perishable and so must be held always in the unceasing responsibility and vigilance of courage and honor and pride and humility. It is gone now. We dozed, slept, and it abandoned us. And in that vacuum now there sound no longer the strong loud voices not merely unafraid but not even aware that fear existed, speaking in mutual unification of one mutual hope and will. Because now what we hear is a cacophony of terror and conciliation and compromise babbling only the mouth-sounds, the loud and empty words which we have emasculated of all meaning whatever—freedom, democracy, patriotism—with which, awakened at last, we try in desperation to hide from ourselves that loss.

10. Something happened to the Dream. Many things did. This, I think, is a symptom of one of them.

11. About ten years ago a well-known literary critic and essayist, a good friend of long standing, told me that a wealthy widely circulated weekly pictorial magazine had offered him a good price to write a piece about me—not about my work or works, but about me as a private citizen, an individual. I said No, and explained why: my belief that only a writer's works were in the public domain, to be discussed and investigated and written about, the writer himself having put them there by submitting them for publication and accepting money for them; and therefore he not only would but must accept whatever the public wished to say or do about them from praise to burning. But that, until the writer committed a crime or ran for public office, his private life was his own; and not only had he the right to defend his privacy, but the public had the duty to do so since one man's liberty must stop at exactly the point where the next one's begins; and that I believed that anyone of taste and responsibility would agree with me.

12. But the friend said No. He said: "You are wrong. If I do the piece, I will do it with taste and responsibility. But if you refuse me, sooner or later someone will do it who will not bother about taste or responsibility either, who will care nothing about you or your status as a writer, an artist, but only as a commodity: merchandise: to be sold, to increase circulation, to make a little money."

13. "I don't believe it," I said. "Until I commit a crime or an-

nounce for office, they can't invade my privacy after I ask them not to."

14. "They not only can," he said, "but once your European reputation gets back here and makes you financially worth it, they will. Wait and see."

15. I did. I did both. Two years ago, by mere chance during a talk with an editor in the house which publishes my books, I learned that the same magazine had already set on foot the same project which I had declined eight years before; I don't know whether the publishers were formally notified or if they just heard about it by chance too, as I did. I said No again, recapitulating the same reasons which I still believed were not even arguable by anyone possessing the power of the public press, since the qualities of taste and responsibility would have to be inherent in that power for it to be valid and allowed to endure. The editor interrupted.

16. "I agree with you," he said. "Besides, you don't need to give me reasons. The simple fact that you don't want it done is enough. Shall I attend to it for you?" So he did, or tried to. Because my critic friend was still right. Then I said:

17. "Try them again. Say 'I ask you: please don't.'" Then I submitted the same *I ask you: please don't* to the writer who was to do the piece. I don't know whether he was a staff writer designated to the job, or whether he volunteered for it, or perhaps himself sold his employers on the idea. Though my recollection is that his answer implied, "I've got to, if I refuse they will fire me," which is probably correct, since I got the same answer from a staff member of another magazine on the same subject.

18. And if that was so, if the writer, a member of the craft he served, was victim too of that same force of which I was victim— that irresponsible use which is therefore misuse and which in its turn is betrayal, of that power called Freedom of the Press which is one of the most potent and priceless of the defenders and pre-servers of human dignity and rights—then the only defense left me was to refuse to co-operate, have anything to do with the project at all. Though by now I knew that that would not save me, that nothing I could do would stop them.

19. Perhaps they—the writer and his employer—didn't be-lieve me, could not believe me. Perhaps they dared not believe me. Perhaps it is impossible now for any American to believe that anyone not hiding from the police could actually not want, as a free gift, his name and photograph in any printed organ, no matter how base or modest or circumscribed in circulation. Though perhaps the matter

never reached this point: that both of them—the publisher and the writer—knew from the first, whether I did or not, that the three of us, the two of them and their victim, were all three victims of that fault (in the sense that the geologist uses the term) in our American culture which is saying to us daily: "Beware!" the three of us faced as one not with an idea, a principle of choice between good and bad taste or responsibility or lack of it, but with a fact, a condition in our American life before which all three of us were (at that moment) helpless, at that moment doomed.

20. So the writer came with his group, force, crew, and got his material where and how he could and departed and published his article. But that's not the point. The writer is not to be blamed since, empty-handed, he would (if my recollection is right) have been fired from the job which deprived him of the right to choose between good and bad taste. Nor the employer either, since to hold his (the employer's) precarious own in a craft can compel even him, head and chief of one of its integral components, to serve the mores of the hour in order to survive among his rival ones.

21. It's not what the writer said, but that he said it. That he—they—published it, in a recognized organ which, to be and remain recognized, functions on the assumption of certain inflexible standards; published it not only over the subject's protests but with complete immunity to them; an immunity not merely assumed to itself by the organ but an immunity already granted in advance by the public to which it sold its wares for a profit. The terrifying (not shocking; we cannot be shocked by it since we permitted its birth and watched it grow and condoned and validated it and even use it individually for our own private ends at need) thing is that it could have happened at all under those conditions. That it could have happened at all with its subject not even notified in advance. And even when he, the victim, was warned by accident in advance, he was still completely helpless to prevent it. And even after it was done, the victim had no recourse whatever since, unlike sacrilege and obscenity, we have no laws against bad taste, perhaps because in a democracy the majority of the people who make the laws don't recognize bad taste when they see it, or perhaps because in our democracy bad taste has been converted into a marketable and therefore taxable and therefore lobbyable commodity by the merchandising federations which at the same simultaneous time create the market (not the appetite: that did not need creating: only pandering to) and the product to serve it, and bad taste by simple solvency was purified of bad taste and absolved. And even if there had been

grounds for recourse, the matter would still have remained on the black side of the ledger since the publisher could charge the judgment and costs to operating loss and the increased sales from the publicity to capital investment.

22. The point is that in America today any organization or group, simply by functioning under a phrase like Freedom of the Press or National Security or League Against Subversion, can postulate to itself complete immunity to violate the individualness—the individual privacy lacking which he cannot be an individual and lacking which individuality he is not anything at all worth the having or keepng—of anyone who is not himself a member of some organization or group numerous enough or rich enough to frighten them off. That organization will not be of writers, artists, of course; being individuals, not even two artists could ever confederate, let alone enough of them. Besides, artists in America don't have to have privacy because they don't need to be artists as far as America is concerned. America doesn't need artists because they don't count in America; artists have no more place in American life than the employers of the weekly pictorial magazine staff writers have in the private life of a Mississippi novelist.

23. But there are the other two occupations which are valuable to American life, which require, demand privacy in order to endure, live. These are science and the humanities, the scientists and the humanitarians: the pioneers in the science of endurance and mechanical craftsmanship and self-discipline and skill like Colonel Lindbergh who was compelled at last to repudiate it by the nation and culture one of whose mores was an inalienable right to violate his privacy instead of an inviolable duty to defend it, the nation which assumed an inalienable right to abrogate to itself the glory of his renown yet which had neither the power to protect his children nor the responsibility to shield his grief; the pioneers in the simple science of saving the nation like Dr. Oppenheimer who was harassed and impugned through those same mores until all privacy was stripped from him and there remained only the qualities of individualism whose possession we boast since they alone differ us from animals—gratitude for kindness, fidelity to friendship, chivalry toward women, and the capacity to love—before which even his officially vetted harassers were impotent, turning away themselves (one hopes) in shame, as though the whole business had had nothing whatever to do with loyalty or disloyalty or security or insecurity, but was simply to batter and strip him completely naked of the privacy lacking which he could never have become one of that handful of in-

dividuals capable of serving the nation at a moment when apparently nobody else was, and so reduce him at last to one more identityless integer in that identityless anonymous unprivacied mass which seems to be our goal.

24. And even that is only a point of departure. Because the sickness itself goes much further back. It goes back to that moment in our history when we decided that the old simple moral verities over which taste and responsibility were the arbiters and controls, were obsolete and to be discarded. It goes back to that moment when we repudiated the meaning which our fathers had stipulated for the words "liberty" and "freedom," on and by and to which they founded us as a nation and dedicated us as a people, ourselves in our time keeping only the mouth-sounds of them. It goes back to the moment when we substituted license in the place of liberty—license for any action which kept within the proscription of laws promulgated by confederations of the practitioners of the license and the harvesters of the material benefits. It goes back to that moment when in place of freedom we substituted immunity for any action to any recourse, provided merely that the act be performed beneath the aegis of the empty mouth-sound of freedom.

25. At which instant truth vanished too. We didn't abolish truth; even we couldn't do that. It simply quit us, turned its back on us, not in scorn nor even contempt nor even (let us hope) despair. It just simply quit us, to return perhaps when whatever it will be—suffering, national disaster, maybe even (if nothing else will serve) military defeat—will have taught us to prize truth and pay any price, accept any sacrifice (oh yes, we are brave and tough too; we just intend to put off having to be as long as possible) to regain and hold it again as we should never have let it go: on its own compromiseless terms of taste and responsibility. Truth—that long clean clear simple undeviable unchallengeable straight and shining line, on one side of which black is black and on the other white is white, has now become an angle, a point of view having nothing to do with truth nor even with fact, but depending solely on where you are standing when you look at it. Or rather—better—where you can contrive to have him standing whom you are trying to fool or obfuscate when he looks at it.

26. Across the board in fact, a parlay, a daily triple: truth and freedom and liberty. The American sky which was once the topless empyrean of freedom, the American air which was once the living breath of liberty, are now become one vast down-crowding

pressure to abolish them both, by destroying man's individuality as a man by (in that turn) destroying the last vestige of privacy without which man cannot be an individual. Our very architecture itself has warned us. Time was when you could see neither from inside nor from outside through the walls of our houses. Time is when you can see from inside out though still not from outside in through the walls. Time will be when you can do both. Then privacy will indeed be gone; he who is individual enough to want it even to change his shirt or bathe in, will be cursed by one universal American voice as subversive to the American way of life and the American flag.

27. If (by that time) walls themselves, opaque or not, can still stand before that furious blast, that force, that power rearing like a thunderclap into the American zenith, multiple-faced yet mutually conjunctived, bellowing the words and phrases which we have long since emasculated of any significance or meaning other than as tools, implements, for the further harassment of the private individual human spirit, by their furious and immunized high priests: "Security." "Subversion." "Anti-Communism." "Christianity." "Prosperity." "The American Way." "The Flag."

28. With odds at balance (plus a little fast footwork now and then of course) one individual can defend himself from another individual's liberty. But when powerful federations and organizations and amalgamations like publishing corporations and religious sects and political parties and legislative committees can absolve even one of their working units of the restrictions of moral responsibility by means of such catch-phrases as "Freedom" and "Salvation" and "Security" and "Democracy," beneath which blanket absolution the individual salaried practitioners are themselves freed of individual responsibility and restraint, then let us beware. Then even people like Dr. Oppenheimer and Colonel Lindbergh and me (the weekly magazine staff writer too if he really was compelled to choose between good taste and starvation) will have to confederate in our turn to preserve that privacy in which alone the artist and scientist and humanitarian can function.

29. Or to preserve life itself, breathing; not just artists and scientists and humanitarians, but the parents by law or biology of doctors of osteopathy too. I am thinking of course of the Cleveland doctor convicted recently of the brutal slaying of his wife, three of whose parents—his wife's father and his own father and mother— with one exception did not even outlive that trial regarding which the Press itself, which kept the sorry business on most of the na-

tion's front pages up to the very end, is now on record as declaring that it was overcovered far beyond its value and importance.

30. I am thinking of the three victims. Not the convicted man: he will doubtless live a long time yet; but of the three parents, two of whom died—one of them anyway—because, to quote the Press itself, "he was wearied of life," and the third one, the mother, by her own hand, as though she had said, *I can bear no more of this.*

31. Perhaps they died solely because of the crime, though one wonders why the coincidence of their deaths was not with the commission of the murder but with the publicity of the trial. And if it was not solely because of the tragedy itself that one of the victims was "wearied of life" and another obviously said, *I can bear no more* —if they had more than that one reason to relinquish and even repudiate life, and the man was guilty as the jury said he was, just what medieval witch-hunt did that power called Freedom of the Press, which in any civilized culture must be accepted as that dedicated paladin through whose inflexible rectitude truth shall prevail and justice and mercy be done, condone and abet that the criminal's very progenitors be eliminated from the earth in expiation of his crime? And if he was innocent as he said he was, what crime did that champion of the weak and the oppressed itself participate in? Or (to repeat) not the artist. America has not yet found any place for him who deals only in things of the human spirit except to use his notoriety to sell soap or cigarettes or fountain pens or to advertise automobiles and cruises and resort hotels, or (if he can be taught to contort fast enough to meet the standards) in radio or moving pictures where he can produce enough income tax to be worth attention. But the scientists and the humanitarian, yes: the humanitarian in science and the scientist in the humanity of man, who might yet save that civilization which the professionals at saving it—the publishers who condone their own battening on man's lust and folly, the politicians who condone their own trafficking in his stupidity and greed, and the churchmen who condone their own trading on his fear and superstition—seem to be proving that they can't.

WORDS

*meaning* Define *thralled* and *impotent* (par. 1), *coeval* and *suspiration* (par. 3), *congeries, integer,* and *docile* (par. 4), *oblation* (par. 5), *avatars* (par. 8), *cacophony* (par. 9), *pandering* (par. 21), *abrogate, impugned,* and *vetted* (par. 23), *aegis* (par. 24), *obfuscate* (par. 25), *parlay* and *empyrean* (par. 26), *opaque* and *conjunctived* (par. 27), and *paladin, rectitude, progenitors,* and *expiation* (par. 31).

*word origin*   1. What is the "true meaning of the word *aspiration*" (par. 8)?   2. What does the word *aspiration* have in common with the words *conspiracy, expiration, inspiration,* and *perspiration?*

*word choice*   1. Faulkner frequently uses the word *taste* (see pars. 11, 12, 15, 20, 21, 24, 25, 28, for example). What does it mean and why is understanding it important in understanding the essay?   2. In discussing "truth and freedom and liberty" (par. 26), the author uses three terms drawn from racing and meant, apparently, to be synonymous: "across the board," "a parlay," "a daily triple." Do they mean the same thing, and do they fit?   3. Faulkner once said that Hemingway had never been known to use a word that might cause a reader to check with a dictionary. Obviously, this was not Faulkner's own practice. Do you think this essay can be classified as "fine writing"? Write a paragraph explaining your answer. ("Fine writing," you may recall from an earlier exercise, is an ironic phrase meaning the unnecessary use of ornate words and expressions, a kind of writing in which words rather than ideas are emphasized.)

## SENTENCES

*style*   1. Take a Faulkner sentence containing more than 200 words— the last sentence of paragraph 23, for instance—and rewrite it as a series of shorter sentences. What is gained? What is lost?   2. Faulkner uses many fragments; in fact, the whole of paragraph 2 is a fragment. Pick out three fragments that begin paragraphs. Are they clear? Rewrite each as a complete sentence. Are your sentences an improvement? Explain.   3. How can a teacher of English justify, as he easily can, insisting that you try to obey "rules" of composition that Faulkner breaks?

*emphasis*   One characteristic of Faulkner's style is simply illustrated in the first sentence of paragraph 20: "So the writer came with his group, force, crew. . . ." What is the strength of this repetition, this seeming redundancy? What can be its weakness?

## PARAGRAPHS

*unity*   Paragraph 6 is a short "quotation." How does its brevity, together with the repetition of its key word, serve to emphasize the most important idea of all that has gone before?

*coherence*   What is the function of the brief paragraph 10?

## CONTENT AND ORGANIZATION

*central ideas*   1. In the first paragraph, Faulkner says that the American Dream was of freedom from two different kinds of oppression. With which kind of freedom is Faulkner most concerned in this essay?   2. How was the Dream lost (par. 9)? Did we abandon it intentionally?   3. In paragraphs 11 through 21, Faulkner relates a personal experience. What freedom was denied him? What freedom was denied the writer of the article? What freedom was denied the publisher of the magazine (par. 20)? 4. Faulkner's complaint against modern American life is stated in the first sentence of paragraph 22. How does his own experience help to substantiate this charge? What was similar in the experiences of Colonel Lindbergh and Dr. Oppenheimer (par. 23)? in the experience of the parents of the Cleveland doctor (par. 29)? 5. By whom may our lost freedom be regained (pars. 28–31)? How?

*assumptions and implications* 1. Why does Faulkner believe that public discussion of a writer's work is justifiable but public discussion of his life is not (par. 11)? Do you agree? 2. Faulkner says that privacy is not only a privilege but a condition indispensable to the achievement of the scientist, the artist, and the humanitarian (pars. 22 and 23). Do you agree? 3. What has happened to the architecture of our houses that Faulkner considers symbolic of what has happened to our right to privacy (par. 26)? 4. How does Faulkner believe that the word *Freedom* can be used to justify denial of freedom (par. 28)?

SUGGESTIONS FOR DISCUSSION

1. What obligation, if any, do newspapers and magazines have to their readers to report the private lives of famous authors, scientists, and other celebrities? 2. Do you believe that any legislative investigations have threatened or weakened American liberties? Do you believe that any legislative investigations have helped to defend American liberties? Explain your answers. 3. Do you agree with the man who said, "The trouble with my picture window is that it makes me a picture for my neighbors"? Explain. 4. Do you agree with the following statements: "Artists in America don't have to have privacy because they don't need to be artists as far as America is concerned. America doesn't need artists because they don't count in America . . ." (par. 22)? Why, or why not?

# Problems and Solutions in Science

## Paul R. Ehrlich

## POPULATION AND ENVIRONMENT

1.   The unhappy physical condition of our planet can be traced directly to the steady increase in the size of the human population. This population increase has been going on for a long time. So has environmental deterioration. For instance, large Middle Eastern and Mediterranean areas apparently lost much of their fertility before the time of Christ because of overgrazing and poor irrigation practices. Neither population growth nor environmental deterioration can continue for much longer. Indeed the world is in the midst of what may well be the final crisis for Homo sapiens.

2.   To find the origin of this crisis, it is necessary to go back to prehistory, to the start of the agricultural revolution, about 8,000 years ago. At that time some human groups changed from a nomadic food-gathering existence to a food-producing existence. It has been estimated that the human population of 6000 B.C. was about 5 million individuals. The population did not reach 500 million until about 1650 A.D., and it doubled to a billion people in about the next 200 years. It took only about 80 years for the next doubling—the population reached 2 billion around 1930. We now stand at around 3 billion, and our current doubling time seems to be about 37 years. The time for doubling to occur is still diminishing, pushing the rate of growth ever upward.

3.   Of course, this vast burgeoning of the human population has been made possible by technological advances in diverse areas such as agriculture, public health, and transportation. It has not been accompanied by equivalent advances in our understanding of such critical subjects as human social behavior and the subtle interactions between men and their physical and perceptual environments. Unfortunately the earth now is also largely under the control of a cul-

POPULATION AND ENVIRONMENT:   Chapter 5 of *Toward Century 21,* edited by C. S. Wallia, © 1970 by Basic Books, Inc., Publishers, New York.

ture that traditionally sees man's proper role as dominating nature, rather than living in harmony with it. It is a society that seems to equate "growth" and "progress" and considers both self-evidently desirable. It is this society that also is in the best position to take positive steps to avert catastrophe. Unhappily it still contains many "educated" individuals dedicated to nonsense concepts such as perpetually expanding economies and populations that can grow forever.

4. In Western society the quality of life for the average individual has improved over the last few centuries. It is ironic that the very forces that permitted this improvement are directly responsible for mankind's precarious position today. Rising populations in the West have been supported by continually increasing the level of manipulation and exploitation of the environment. In addition, the West has exported death control to other cultures, greatly accelerating their population explosions. Many people seem to feel that further technological effort can bring most of the comforts of the West to all mankind. The first point of technological attack would, of course, have to be an increase in the production of food, and the efficiency of its distribution.

5. At the moment it is shockingly apparent that the battle to feed humanity is being lost. In 1966 the population of the world increased by about 70 million individuals. No additional food was grown to feed them. This means that last year, on the average, each person on earth had 2 percent less to eat. The reduction is, of course, not uniformly distributed. Starvation already is a fact in many countries. Only 10 countries, including the United States, grew more food than they consumed—all other populous countries, including Russia, China, and India imported more than they exported. In 1966 the United States shipped one-quarter of its wheat crop, 9 million tons, to India. In spite of this aid, serious famines still threaten the Indian population. Our wheat reserves are now so low that they can no longer serve as antistarvation insurance for the Indian subcontinent. Every month about 1½ million more Indians are born. Should India's present population growth continue for another 10 years, it would take the entire grain production of the United States to relieve the Indian food shortage.

6. Agricultural experts state that a tripling of the world's food supply will be necessary between now and the beginning of the next century, if the 6 or 7 billion people who will be alive then are to be reasonably adequately fed. There is no question that, under ideal

conditions of research, development, and international cooperation, such an increase is possible. That is, it is possible if a massive effort commences immediately. Most experts, however, doubt whether even such ideal conditions will permit feeding 12 billion people in 2035, to say nothing of feeding about 24 billion in 2070, and so forth.

7. And what are the chances of immediately preparing to meet the food crisis? The United States has already virtually exhausted its surpluses while attempting to feed India. Although Russia has sent some grain to India, Russia herself is forced to import food. In short, the two most powerful countries in the world are not possessed of great surpluses. In addition, neither country shows any inclination to divert massive resources from other enterprises to push worldwide development of agricultural technology. As food gets shorter and shorter over the next few decades, can we expect massive international cooperation and self-sacrifice? A look at history does not give us much reason for encouragement.

8. Consider for a moment past attempts to deal cooperatively with the dwindling resources in the international whaling industry. The record of the International Whaling Commission up to now is largely one of failure of agreements and controls. The industry has not been able to regulate the size and composition of the catch. This has led to the virtual extermination of economically important whale species. Before 1940 there were an estimated 140,000 blue whales in Antarctic waters. In 1954 the total population was estimated to be between 10,000 and 14,000, and in 1963 the total was down to between 650 and 2,000. Capture of the blue whales has now been outlawed by the International Whaling Commission, and it remains to be seen whether the whales will make a comeback or continue to decrease to extinction. The result will depend in part on the whales and in part on the whalers. The outlook is not bright.

9. Many people are laboring under the delusion that the sea is an inexhaustible source of food. In fact, it might be possible, as C. M. Yonge has estimated, to double the present productivity of the sea. Is that likely to happen as the protein shortage becomes more extreme? As belt-tightening becomes worldwide, I suspect that incidents such as the invasion of our territorial waters by an occasional Russian trawler will escalate into a massive no-holds-barred race to harvest the sea. Careful cropping, that is, the harvesting of resources so that they are not depleted, seems even less likely than in the whaling industry. With technological concentration on efficiency of harvesting, it would not be surprising if the sea were made virtually lifeless in a few decades or less. Whether farming of marine microorganisms can then contribute

significantly to our food supply remains to be seen—the problems of sowing and reaping the ocean are colossal.

10. Attempts to steadily increase food production do not bode well for our surroundings. Plans for increasing food production invariably involve large-scale efforts at environmental modification. Land must be cleared of forests, water must be provided, fertilizers must enrich the soils, and pesticides must be used against organisms that compete with us by eating our crops. There seems to be little hope that we will suddenly have an upsurge in the level of responsibility or ecological sophistication of persons concerned with an emergency increase of agricultural output. Therefore, we can expect environmental deterioration to accelerate rapidly as the food crisis intensifies.

11. Poor land management, which led to the American dust bowl, is ruining soils today. One factor is the "mining" of the soil by grazing or single-crop farming. Minerals taken up by plants are not returned to the soil when cattle or crops are marketed. A second factor is careless irrigation, which permits salts to build up in the soil. Another unappreciated factor is the poisoning of the soil, which may well increase in importance since we can safely assume that the usage of synthetic pesticides, already massive, will increase. In spite of much publicity, the intimate relationship between pesticides on one hand, and the population crisis, food shortage, and environmental deterioration on the other, is not recognized.

12. One of the basic facts of population biology is that the simpler an ecological system (or ecosystem) is, the more unstable it is. A complex forest will persist year in and year out with no interference from man. A stand of one grass, such as a wheat field or a corn field, is subject to almost instant ruination if it is not guarded constantly. Man's activities generally tend to simplfy ecosystems, by destroying some organisms, and encouraging uniform populations of others. Synthetic pesticides are one of man's more potent simplifying tools. Not only do they reduce the diversity of life above ground, but long-term applications will almost certainly reduce the diversity in the soil. Remember, soil is not just crushed rock—it contains a rich fauna and flora that are critical to its fertility.

13. Other dangers of the massive use of synthetic pesticides are well known to biologists. Careful studies have been made on the effects of DDT, the best known and most widely used chlorinated hydrocarbon insecticide. Virtually all populations of animals throughout the world are contaminated with it. Concentrations of DDT in the fat bodies of Americans average 11 parts per million, and Israelis

have been found to have as much DDT as 19.2 parts per million. More significant in some ways has been the discovery of DDT residues in such unlikely places as the fat bodies of Eskimos, antarctic penguins, and antarctic seals. Pesticide pollution is truly a worldwide problem.

14. DDT breaks down only very slowly and will last for decades in soils. A recent study of a Long Island marsh that has been sprayed for 20 years for mosquito control revealed up to 32 pounds per acre of DDT in the upper layer of mud. Unhappily, the way DDT circulates in the ecosystem leads to a concentration of carnivores. The danger to life and the reproductive capacity of meat-eating birds may be approaching a critical point now, and the outlook for man if the current trends continue does not seem healthy. The day may soon be upon us when the obese people of the world must give up diets, since metabolizing their fat deposits will lead to DDT poisoning. But, on the brighter side, it is clear that fewer and fewer people in the future will be obese. We must remember that DDT has been in use for only about a quarter of a century. It is difficult to predict the results of another 50 years of the use of DDT and similar compounds, especially when those years will be filled with frantic attempts to feed more and more people. Of course, DDT is just one of many synthetic substances with which we are dosing our environment. Aside from the direct toxic threat to man, these compounds all have the effect of simplifying ecosystems and thus aggravate the instability created by man's agricultural and other activities.

15. Pest organisms ordinarily have large populations—that, indeed, is why they are pests. The large size of their populations makes them much more likely to have the kind of reserve genetic variability that most easily leads to the development of resistant strains. Therefore, extermination of a pest by the use of synthetic pesticides is unlikely—and, in fact, is almost unknown. The usual picture is one in which the pesticide decimates the natural enemies of the pest, while the pest develops resistant strains. Higher and higher dosages of pesticides are then necessary to achieve control.

16. These problems with pesticides are just one example of a seemingly inevitable trend as the human population expands. The more we manipulate our environment, the more we are required to manipulate it. The more we make use of synthetic pesticides, the less we can do without them. The more we deforest, the greater is the requirement for flood control dams. The more farmland we subdivide, the more we must artificially strain to increase the yield on the land that remains under cultivation. The more automobiles we build, the

more we must search for new sources of hydrocarbon fuels and for methods of altering the atmosphere to reduce smog hazards. It is critical that people be made aware of the relatively subtle and long-term deleterious effects of our technological programs. Then they will be able to weigh these effects against the obvious short-term advantages.

17. Perhaps more important than the changes in our physical environment are those in our psychic environment. Unhappily we cannot be sure of the importance of these latter changes—although riots and increased drug usage are hardly cheery signs. We cannot even be sure of how much of an individual's reaction to these environmental changes will be hereditarily conditioned and how much will be a function of his culture. The following is quoted from three biologists who have recently written on the subject.

> Unique as we think we are, we are nevertheless as likely to be genetically programmed to a natural habitat of clean air and a varied green landscape as any other mammal. To be relaxed and feel healthy usually means simply allowing our bodies to react in the way for which 100 millions of years of evolution has equipped us. Physically and genetically we appear best adapted to a tropical savanna, but as a cultural animal we utilize learned adaptations to cities and towns. For thousands of years we have tried in our houses to imitate not only the climate, but the setting of our evolutionary past: warm, humid air, green plants and even animal companions. Today, if we can afford it, we may even build a greenhouse or swimming pool next to our living room, buy a place in the country, or at least take our children vacationing on the seashore. The specific physiological reactions to natural beauty and diversity, to the shapes and colors of nature (especially to green), to the motions and sounds of other animals, such as birds, we as yet do not comprehend. But, it is evident that nature in our daily life should be thought of as part of the biological need. It cannot be neglected in the discussions of resource policy for man.

18. Man clearly has gone a long way toward adapting to urban environments and despoiled landscapes. We badly need to understand the effects of this adjustment, especially in terms of group behavior, and to be able to predict the effects of further changes in man's perceptual environment. It is important to note that our perceptual systems have evolved primarily to react to stimuli representing a sudden change in our environment—a lion's charge, a flaring fire, a child's cry. Long-term changes often are not noticed. We tend not to perceive a friend's aging, or the slowing of our reflexes. If the transition from the Los Angeles of 1928 to that of 1968 had occurred overnight

Angelenos would surely have rebelled. But a gradual 40-year transition has actually permitted southern Californians to convince themselves that the Los Angeles basin of 1968 is a suitable habitat for Homo sapiens.

19. I think that a severe depression in the quality of our surroundings has become obvious to all well-informed people. A moment's reflection, preferably in an airplane over the smog-blanketed bay, in the crowds watching the smoke and uproar in Yosemite Valley on a summer's evening, or while listening to a politician brag about how fast California's population is growing, brings one to the basic cause of this deterioration. There are simply too many people in this state and in the world in general. They are the reason San Francisco Bay is being filled. They are the reason we will soon have no primeval redwoods left. They are also a major reason why world peace seems like a hopeless dream.

20. People encouraging population growth in the hopes of keeping our economy expanding must realize the consequences of such advocacy. There may indeed be temporary economic benefits, and some men will accumulate substantial amounts of money to leave to their children. It is unfortunate that they are not looking beyond temporary gain to consider what kind of a world their children will inherit. Will they have created a massive unemployment problem for their children to solve? Will their children like wearing smog masks? Will they be satisfied with camping under vinyl trees planted in asphalt? Will they enjoy seaweed as a substitute for steak? Will they adapt easily to more regimentation and government control? Will they be ready to fight when we invade Canada to find *Lebensraum,* or defend our southern border against the Latin Americans? Above all, will there be a world for their heirs to inhabit?

21. Of course, ever since Malthus, people have been predicting an outstripping of food resources by growing populations. In spite of this, massive worldwide famines have been avoided—although the world as a whole has hardly been overnourished! Is there any more reason today to heed the doom criers than there was to heed them 150 years ago? Unfortunately there is. At essentially the same time as man instituted systematic death control, he also ran out of room for migration. Simultaneously he acquired exponentially greater power to alter his environment and to wage war. We know that sooner or later we must stabilize the world's population, if we are to survive. With the prospects of global war and famine looming large in the newspaper headlines, I doubt if there will ever be a more propitious time than the present to listen to the prophets of doom.

22. Even as a prophet of doom, I will not attempt to predict the size of future populations. Attempts to do this have proven consistently wrong, usually in the direction of underestimation. It is not, however, unreasonable to calculate physical limits, even though they may never be reached. J. H. Fremlin, a British physicist, has calculated that the physical problem of overheating will place a theoretical limit on terrestrial population size. People themselves, as well as their activities, convert other forms of energy into heat, which must be dissipated. Fremlin estimates that this limit would be reached if the population grows to $10^{16}$ to $18^{18}$ individuals—that is about 1 billion billion people. At near this figure there would be some 120 persons per square yard of the earth's surface, and they might be housed in a continuous 2,000-story building covering all of the land and the sea. The upper 1,000 stories would contain only the apparatus for running this gigantic warren, and ducting would occupy about half the lower stories. This would leave about 3 or 4 yards of floor space per person. I will leave to your imagination the physical details of existence in this ant heap, except to point out that all would not be black. Probably only a few hundred yards of travel would be possible because of the heat generated by movement. However, this would permit, as Fremlin says, each individual to choose his friends from among about 10 million people. In addition, entertainment on the worldwide television should be excellent, for at any time "one could expect some 10 million Shakespeares and rather more Beatles to be alive."

23. This happy state would be reached, if the doubling rate remains constant, in about 900 years. In other words, as far in the future as the Norman conquest is in the past. If the rate continues to increase, we might get there sooner.

24. Even without predicting exactly what will happen, some rather firm limiting statements about population growth can be made.

(1) The earth can sustain only a finite population, probably not more than one billion people.

(2) At any given time, at the current growth rate and given the technology to do so, it would take only about 50 years to populate Venus, Mercury, Mars, the moon, and the moons of Jupiter and Saturn to the same density as the earth. If we started shipping off our surplus people today, holding our population at its present level, in one half-century we would have spread today's degree of crowding throughout our planetary neighbors. We are, of course, not even close to having the technology necessary for transporting people to these planets and making these planets habitable.

(3) In the unlikely event that the fantastic problems of reach-

ing and colonizing the remaining planets of the solar system such as Jupiter and Uranus can be solved, it would take about 200 years to fill them earth-full.

(4) We can't ship our surplus to the stars. No serious scientist looks to interplanetary, let alone interstellar, transport of people for the solution of the population problem. Garrett Hardin, of the University of California at Santa Barbara, has dealt effectively with this fantasy. Using ridiculously optimistic assumptions, he has calculated that Americans, by cutting their standard of living down to 18 percent of its present level, could in one-year's time set aside enough capital to finance the exportation to the stars of one-day's increase in the population of the entire world.

25. The prospect of interstellar transport of surplus people is amusing. Since the ships would take generations to reach most stars, the only people who could be transported would be those willing to exercise strict birth control. Population explosions on space ships would be disastrous. Thus, we would have to export our responsible people, leaving the irresponsible at home on earth to breed.

26. The population explosion will come to an end—the only question is how and when? If emigration is not possible, a population will grow as long as its birthrate exceeds its death rate. The main factors contributing to the death rate in preexplosion human populations were three of the four apocalyptic horsemen—war, pestilence, and famine. Techonology temporarily has reduced the efficacy of pestilence and famine as population regulators in many areas. It has, however, also greatly augmented the potential value of war as a population-control device; indeed, it has given us the means for self-extermination.

27. No one, of course, seriously expects that the population will advance to the ultimate density predicted by Fremlin. Consideration of the problems of feeding the multiplying masses makes that clear. Increasing food production is treating a symptom, not the disease It is like using morphine as the sole treatment for an operable cancer. The disease of this planet is overpopulation. One of the symptoms is hunger, and it can be suppressed temporarily. The only possible cures are drastic reduction in the birthrate, or drastic increase in the death rate. Regardless of any improvement of food production, sooner or later we will have one cure or the other. Not that anyone impeding a reduction in the birthrate is automatically advocating increasing the death rate.

28. The goals of improved food production and distribution, and more efficient resource utilization are not necessarily undesirable

in themselves. Focusing on these goals, however, in the absence of a concentrated effort to stabilize or reduce world population is extremely dangerous. Further irreversible deterioration of our environment will inevitably attend a struggle to feed and house the increasing multitudes.

29. What can be done to attack the basic problem of overpopulation? Many biologists believe that some system must be developed that makes positive action necessary before reproduction is possible. This might be the addition of a temporary sterilant to staple food or to the water supply. An antidote would have to be taken to permit reproduction. Even with the antidote freely available, the result of such a program would be a drastic reduction in birthrates. If this reduction were not sufficient, the government could dole out the antidote in the proper quantities. If, for instance, we wished to stabilize the American population at its present level, each married couple could be permitted enough antidote to produce two offspring. Then each couple who wished could be given a chance in a lottery for enough antidote for a third child—the odds carefully computed to produce the desired constancy of population size. At the moment the chances of winning would have to be adjusted to about two out of five, assuming that all couples wanted to play the game!

30. An attempt to institute such a system is interesting to contemplate, especially when one considers the attitude of the general public toward fluoridation. I would not like to be the first elected official seriously to suggest that a sterility agent be added to Crystal Springs reservoir! Fortunately, we can start such a program by dosing the wheat we ship to India or fish meal we ship to South America. Or can we? As you doubtless realize, the solution does not lie in that direction. For one thing, saying that the population explosion is a problem of underdeveloped countries is like telling a fellow passenger "your end of the boat is sinking." For another, it is naive to think that Indians or Brazilians are any more anxious to be fed fertility-destroying chemicals with their daily bread than are Americans. Other people already are suspicious of our motives. Consider what their attitude would be toward an attempt to sterilize them en masse. It seems clear that any attempt by the United States to massively export birth control in any form will only stand a chance if we make clear our determination to limit our own population.

31. Most of us feel that governmental interference in our lives is already quite sufficient. Interference in our reproductive lives would seem like the "last straw." Unfortunately, as the population grows we are certain to have more erosion of our individual freedom and more

interference of government in our lives. There is now serious talk of limiting the number of gasoline-powered automobiles a family can own, further restricting the ownership and use of firearms, and further controlling the use of airspace by light planes. Tax collectors and police departments are beginning to depend on computers to keep track of the activities of our burgeoning population. Above all, there is a palpable increase in pressure toward governmental suppression of dissent. What do we gain from this eroding of our freedoms? Of what benefit are 6 billion people or more as compared with the 3 billion we now have? Should we not ask what people are for? Shall we consider large numbers of bodies to be more desirable than a limited number of men with the rights and attributes that most people consider "human"? We are already moving down the trail toward Fremlin's 2,000-story building, even though we won't complete the trip. And that's the bind—the cost of saving most of the remaining freedoms may be the giving up of our freedom to determine the size of our families.

32. Are there any alternatives to compulsory family regulation? Perhaps—at least we could try some. An obvious place to start is by changing some laws. Federal legislation should make illegal the passage of local laws limiting dissemination of birth control devices or information. The right of any woman to obtain legal abortions should also be protected by Federal statute. Our income tax system should be thoroughly revised, so that the people who impose the burden of excess children on society should pay for the privilege.

33. In addition to these measures, birth control instruction should be made mandatory in all public schools and birth control devices should be made available to all free of charge. By far, the most important step must be the initiation of a massive public reeducation program—a program to mobilize our citizens and get them behind the attempt to deal rationally with the population crisis. We must do away with attitudes and moral codes that evolved when it was advantageous for society to promote reproduction. A changing world has made these attitudes and codes obsolete, dangerous, and immoral.

34. Once we are fighting the battle at home, we can embark on a full-scale campaign to limit the population of the world. All our aid to countries with increasing populations can have strings attached. Every dollar's worth of food or aid would have to be paid for in an effort toward population control, and, eventually, in results. If people want our help, then they must act in a manner that will make it possible for us to help them. With the way populations are growing, most of our aid to the underdeveloped countries has simply been wasted.

To coordinate the efforts at home and overseas, it is imperative that we have a national policy-making committee concerned with population biology. It is imperative that a substantial portion of the funds that we now spend on research on death control be diverted to research on birth control and on related psychological and social problems. It is imperative also that we encourage the countries of the world, through the United Nations, to set up a world body to deal with what might be thought of as the most critical space problems. This planet is a spacecraft with a limited carrying capacity. It is time that we determine what the optimum crew size is for our ship, and start to design environmental systems to sustain that crew in an optimum state. Until the size of the crew is determined, there is no basis for rational planning of a quality environment.

35.  What can we do to decrease the heavy odds against mankind? One thing is to keep reminding ourselves and others that opposition to the Vietnam war, desirable as such opposition may be, is also basically a treatment of a symptom. Steadily increasing population pressures continue to deny man the breathing space he requires to alter his sociopolitical systems. Until such an opportunity can be provided, the chance of finding a sane solution to world problems seems nil. War in Vietnam will inevitably be followed by war elsewhere—perhaps in Thailand, the Philippines, Korea, or California. As serious as world tensions are today, consider what they will be like when almost everyone is hungry and nations are competing for increasingly scarce food resources. There is an old Chinese proverb that states "it is hard to tell the difference between right and wrong when the belly is empty." Indeed, the Chinese word for "peace," *ho-ping,* has a second meaning—"food for all." We must strive to prevent population pressures from building to gain the precious time needed to transform the way mankind thinks and behaves. Conservation, mental health programs, improving the condition of minority groups, striving for social justice, and so forth will rapidly be dead issues unless the most basic human problem is attacked.

WORDS

*meaning*   1. Define *Homo sapiens* (par. 1), *bode* (par. 10), *ecosystem* (par. 12), *carnivores* (par. 14), *deleterious* (par. 16), *savanna* (par. 17), and *exponentially* (par. 21).   2. What is the meaning of *decimate* (par. 15)? What was its original meaning, and why do you think that meaning is changing? Is it used correctly here?

*exactness*   Choose another way of saying "dosing our environment" (par. 14). Is your way as expressive or more effective?

SENTENCES

*style*  The author refers to himself as "a prophet of doom" (par 22). Is the tone of his article consistent with the necessity to heed "doom criers" (par. 21)? Explain.

*rhetorical devices*  1. "The outlook is not bright" for blue whales (par. 8). What is implied in this example? Find another instance where Ehrlich's pessimism finds "little hope." 2. What is the meaning of the fourth sentence of paragraph 4—the one about the West exporting death controls. Is this a simple statement or a device calculated to affect the reader? 3. Why is a politician's brag "a major reason why world peace seems like a hopeless dream" (par. 19)? 4. What is meant by "when we invade Canada to find *Lebensraum*" (par. 20)? 5. Do you find the "prospect of interstellar transport of surplus people" amusing (par. 25)? What device is the author using here? 6. In paragraph 26 the author gives you three of the four apocalyptic horsemen. What was the fourth?

PARAGRAPHS

*methods of development*  1. Does the author rely mostly on details or examples? Give evidence to support your answer. 2. Ehrlich develops his paragraphs both chronologically and logically. Give examples of each. Which method does he seem to prefer? 3. Do you find useful the point by point development of paragraph 24? Explain.

*topic sentence*  Assuming that the first sentence of paragraph 17 is the topic sentence, does the paragraph bear out the contention that the changes in our psychic environment are more important than those in our physical environment?

CONTENT AND ORGANIZATION

*central idea*  1. State the central idea of this piece. Is the statement in paragraph 27—"The disease of this planet is overpopulation"—too limiting? 2. Can Americans give up individual freedom for survival (par. 31)? Explain.

*organization*  As a broad outline, use paragraphs 1–3 as Rates of Population Growth; paragraphs 4–16 as Food Supply; paragraphs 22–25 as Physical Limits of Population; paragraphs 26–32 as Prospects for Century 21; and paragraphs 33–35 as Other Measures. Identify the substance of the individual paragraphs under each of these headings. Does your outline make sense? Can it be followed intelligently? What changes would you make?

*assumptions and implications*  1. Why did man feel he had to dominate nature in order to live in harmony with it (par. 3)? 2. Do you believe that our society seems to equate "growth" and "progress" (par. 3)? Explain.   3. Who was Malthus (par. 21)?   4. What is meant by man instituting "systematic death control" (par. 21)?

SUGGESTIONS FOR DISCUSSION

1. Compare this essay with "The Ecologist at Bay" (pp. 358–63) by Grahame J. C. Smith. Which is the more effective essay?   2. Can a prophet of doom change things? Can a folk hero?   3. What bothers you the most, the filth in the canals of Venice, Italy, or the pollution in a nearby stream? 4. Can one really be concerned about the state the world will be in 900 years from now?   5. Write an essay in which you accept or reject—for ecological reasons—the author's statement from the last paragraph: "War in Vietnam will inevitably be followed by war elsewhere."

## *Grahame J. C. Smith*

# THE ECOLOGIST AT BAY

1.   The ecologist has suddenly become a folk hero. He is cornered at cocktail parties by secretaries and faculty wives and on the streets by high school students and teachers, all of them looking to him for solutions to the environmental problems with which they are beset.

2.   The ecologist immediately recognizes that, by virtue of his training, he is better equipped than anyone else to consider these problems in their entirety. By definition, his field of study deals with the interactions of living organisms with each other and with their physical environment, and it is obvious that this is the only way to approach the problems of man in his total biological and physical surroundings. However, for practical purposes, the modern ecologist has not really been prepared to tackle the questions, much less to supply ready answers.

3.   First of all, ecologists weren't even called ecologists until quite recently. They were known as biologists or zoologists or by some other specialized name. Anyone who attempted to carry out research in the natural environment was viewed with scorn by the molecular-cellular biologists. From their precise and ordered view-

THE ECOLOGIST AT BAY:   From *Saturday Review,* January 2, 1971. Copyright 1970 by Saturday Review, Inc.

point, the ecologist was an anachronism, a dilettante in the specialized and exact world of biological research.

4. Attempting to become more quantitative and precise, and stimulated by an understandable desire to complete graduate research in a reasonable period of time, the budding ecologist was forced to select some facet of the total environment on which to carry out laboratory study. His research thus fragmented the world, but his theories overcame this by extrapolating from particular results into general concepts of environmental science.

5. Ecological theory was aimed at generality and was overwhelmingly academic. Every effort was made to avoid the attributes of applied science. One did not expect to hear any ecologist speaking out on the overall issue of man's relationship to his environment and the effects of new technological advances on the world in which we live.

6. Now that public interest has grown and a few ecologists have begun to speak openly of these global problems, all ecologists are being forced to consider man's relationship to his environment. In all probability most are being caught somewhat off guard. I know that I, when first confronted by an enthusiastic group of inquirers, was confused and unclear in my response. I could cite many instances of gruesome events ramifying from a clumsy and unintentional assault from some part of the planet, but I was at a loss to ascribe the whole effect to any one factor.

7. Most research in ecology over the past thirty years has been concerned with the growth of populations or, more specifically, with environmental factors that prevent unchecked growth of a population. Usually natural populations are under the control of various environmental factors such as weather, food supply, parasites, and predators, and so maintain an equilibrium. When this steady state is altered by a significant change in one factor, a population may increase to the point of catastrophe.

8. A classic example was provided on the Kaibab Plateau in Arizona. The area had been set aside as a game preserve, and to protect the deer population, their natural predators, mountain lions, wolves, and coyotes, were exterminated. The deer population increased beyond the carrying capacity of the environment, and an estimated 80,000 animals died of starvation. Even then the population continued to decline because forage plants had been damaged and could not regenerate quickly enough to support the remaining animals. With fewer plants to hold the soil, erosion took place, permanently damaging the area's productivity.

9. Since man has, to a large degree, removed the environmental limitation of disease, his population is increasing rapidly and environmental deterioration can superficially be linked to this overpopulation. Pollution, he will note, is an aspect of population density. The term refers not so much to particular substances as to the relative concentration of these substances. In most instances pollutants are elements or compounds that are useful resources in another context.

10. For example, lakes are considered polluted by sewage, which is only natural organic matter that has always been present in small amounts. It is the concentration of sewage to a degree such that the original fauna and flora are unable to persist that permits the definition of pollution.

11. This pollutant does not kill all life. Indeed, some organisms—such as many algae, fungi, and bacteria—grow much better in this situation. But many organisms native to the area cannot survive. It is easy in this case to asscribe a cause and to see a solution in the treatment of sewage.

12. Other major aspects of pollution are industrial and household wastes. Everyone is now aware that these have reached incredible proportions in the United States in recent years, and a consideration of this prompts the suggestion that it is not only population growth but also the disproportionate growth of technology that is producing the situation.

13. This country now uses 35 percent of all the minerals produced on Earth. At our current rate of growth we will gobble up all the mineral production of the non-Communist world by the year 2000. An efficient business should use resources fully and have very little waste. But industry in this country has had access to a limitless supply of air and water on which no one ever set a price, so production systems were devised by which these resources were used to remove waste products. It was cheaper to remove them in that way than to perfect production methods which produced less waste.

14. The business concern was not held responsible for the decrease in value of property along the stream, or for the cleaning bills for curtains and clothes, or for the ill health of employees who were forced to live in nearby areas. To this degree, technology is certainly responsible for the state of the world, and, in terms of the total pollution of the world, each American citizen must be fifty or more times as responsible as a Chinese or Indian citizen in his woefully overpopulated country. The decline in quality of this planet and the precarious aspect of continued existence of life on Earth are largely

results of this comfortable shell of consumer technology with which each American is surrounded.

15. Having outlined the problem to this degree the ecologist must ask what can be done. This question will confront him with the economists who will tell him that it simply does not pay to clean up beyond a certain point. To be sure, if we can document that the effects of dirty air cost each citizen $x$ dollars a year, we can then press for a cleanup. But we cannot expect to run our case on an argument of esthetics because we cannot put a dollar value on clean air and pure streams.

16. Furthermore, while legal channels are rapidly being set up to implement this cleanup, in each case of a complaint against a particular business we must present the court with solid evidence that a particular plant is responsible for particular damage amounting to $x$ dollars. This makes the battle to impose standards a long and expensive one, and only after the case has been proved can the company be forced to install a device that will lower the pollution somewhat— not completely, for that would be too expensive.

17. If all this takes three or four years and results in a decrease of 50 percent in the effluent, the improvement is only evanescent. By that time, a new factory will in all probability have been built in the same vicinity. Even if this factory should have built-in standards of emission at the new 50 percent level, the combined pollution would remain high.

18. Another aspect of the problem, the harassed ecologist now discovers, lies in the fragmented approach that we tend to take in seeking solutions. For example, the air pollution control agency may be very conscientious and active and force a factory to decrease emission by 50 percent. It is highly likely that the factory will comply with the instructions of the court by installing some sort of "scrubber," essentially a spray of water that removes particles of soot and some gases from the smokestack. The water containing these impurities may then be dumped in the nearby stream. Now the whole battle begins over again with the water control board trying to prove damages in a court of law.

19. This, the ecologist will point out exasperatedly, is exactly what the ecologists have been trying to overcome. They have tried to instill in people a feeling of the unity of the environment and a sense that all things are interrelated. An assault on one part of the environment should naturally be expected to have ramifications elsewhere.

20. A similar fragmentation exists at the level of municipal

government. In the tiny state of Rhode Island, there are thirty-nine municipalities, each of which jealously guards its local control, unwilling even to sit down and talk about a concerted effort to clean up the state.

21. Attempting to avoid political problems for the time, the ecologist turns to the question of what theoretically could be done to avoid the buildup of pollution as the population grows. Consider air pollution. It is now generally agreed that the automotive industry is responsible for at least 50 percent of the air pollution. A logical step, particularly in areas where the concentration of people and cars is greatest, would be to give up the automobile in favor of public transport, preferably in the form of electric trains. But public transit systems are not getting the financial support they need, while cities continue to issue bonds in order to build newer and bigger freeways. The highway bonds are bought by businessmen as a good investment, and these are the same men who will drive their cars on the freeway as they come to the city from their suburban homes.

22. When it comes to the acquisition of land on which to build the highway, the area chosen is always through the cheapest land, where the poorest people live. The residents of the ghetto receive the outpourings from the cars passing to and from the suburbs, and are subjected to the unquestioned hazards to health that these fumes constitute. A recent study in Buffalo, New York, showed that continued exposure to dense industrial pollution can double the death rate.

23. Even while being subjected to this insult, the poor people in city areas still have to ride the subway or bus, which is dirty and increasingly rundown. The suburbanite, of course, would rather bond a new highway than ride in that sort of public transit.

24. After these considerations, the ecologist is beginning to sweat a little. How did he get dragged from his considerations of theoretical populations into this confusing and alarming train of thought? He sees the wholeness of the environment. He understands the disturbances that can come from one careless act perpetrated against the intricate web of life on Earth. He knows the dangers of apathy and ignorance; DDT was used in vast quantities for more than twenty years with no monitoring before any objections were raised against it, and when Rachel Carson finally protested, industry dubbed her "a hysterical old maid." On top of this he knows that some 500 new chemicals of various sorts are being introduced to the environment each year, with absolutely no idea of what their effects might be. He sees the growth of industry outracing the piecemeal attempts at

regulation of effluents, and he takes a stand and begins to talk at public meetings, asking for a halt to this headlong industrial growth.

25. It is inevitable that at one of these meetings he will be confronted by another sort of reality. An auto worker asks, "If there is a slowdown of techology, what will become of me? It's all very well for you to stand up there and tell me that the fish will die, but without this industry the workers will be the first affected, and we will suffer. The executive will be affected but he's already at the safe end of the economic scale. We can't be expected to give up all this and live as sharecroppers or peasant farmers just for the sake of a few fish." The ecologist will have to grant that this man has a point, even though he knows that it is not just a few fish but perhaps all life on Earth that is threatened.

26. Having been forced to face these questions, the ecologist emerges with a new appreciation of the complexities of his man-made environment. He concludes that a real solution must involve a national or international planning board that will determine in which areas it would be safe to build a factory, and how that factory must be operated. This board would give consideration to the environment of the people who live near the factory, as well as the distant environment where the general manager may live. The ecologist sees the necessity for a slowdown in the consumption of the world's resources, perhaps through recycling of wastes or perhaps through a society that consumes less overall while safeguarding the rights of the poor as the transition takes place.

## WORDS

*meaning*   1. Define *extrapolating* (par. 4) and *effluent* and *evanescent* (par. 17).   2. What is the meaning of *harassed* (par. 18)? How do you pronounce it? What is the preferred pronunciation?   3. What is the meaning of *consumer technology* (par. 14)?

*word origin*   1. When did you first become aware of the word *ecology?* When did it first appear in the English language?   2. Why was the ecologist an *anachronism* (par. 3)?

*exactness*   Does *gobble up* (par. 13) fit the tone of this essay?

## SENTENCES

*rhetorical devices*   Why, when Rachel Carson finally protested, did industry dub her "a hysterical old maid" (par. 24)?

*coherence*   1. What key word is used in the first sentence of each of the first four paragraphs?   2. What similar word is used in the next three paragraphs?   3. What similar word is used in paragraphs 9 through 12?   4. The last three paragraphs refer to the ecologist as *he*. What effect does this give to the entire essay?

## CONTENT AND ORGANIZATION

*central idea*   1. Does this essay pretty thoroughly describe an ecologist? Try to define an ecologist in one sentence.   2. Why does the author consider himself "at bay"?

*assumptions and implications*   1. Why has the ecologist suddenly become a folk hero (par. 1)? Name some other folk heroes.   2. Why is it so "obvious" (par. 2) that there is only one way to approach the ecological problem?   3. What is more important to the ecologist, "technology" or "population growth"?   4. Was there a particular time in this country when we should have become aware of potential ecological problems? When?   5. Does ecology come closest to being a cause, a philosophy, a necessity, a theory, or an illusion?

## SUGGESTIONS FOR DISCUSSION

1. To solve ecological problems, is it necessary for everyone to become involved?   2. Do the most effective ecological leaders come from the academy, industry, or politics?   3. Describe a "classic example" (other than the one in paragraph 8) of how the ecological balance may be upset.   4. Write a theme suggesting the most effective manner of solving a major ecological problem.

## *Julian Huxley*

# THE UNIQUENESS OF MAN

1.   Man's opinion of his own position in relation to the rest of the animals has swung pendulum-wise between too great or too little a conceit of himself, fixing now too large a gap between himself and the animals, now too small. The gap, of course, can be diminished or

THE UNIQUENESS OF MAN:   From *Man Stands Alone* by Julian Huxley. Copyright 1939 by Julian S. Huxley. Reprinted by permission of Harper & Row, Publishers, Inc.

increased at either the animal or the human end. One can, like Descartes, make animals too mechanical, or, like most unsophisticated people, humanize them too much. Or one can work at the human end of the gap, and then either dehumanize one's own species into an animal species like any other, or superhumanize it into beings a little lower than the angels.

2. Primitive and savage man, the world over, not only accepts his obvious kinship with the animals but also projects into them many of his own attributes. So far as we can judge, he has very little pride in his own humanity. With the advent of settled civilization, economic stratification, and the development of an elaborate religion as the ideological mortar of a now class-ridden society, the pendulum began slowly to swing in the other direction. Animal divinities and various physiological functions such as fertility gradually lost their sacred importance. Gods became anthropomorphic and human psychological qualities pre-eminent. Man saw himself as a being set apart, and the rest of the animal kingdom created to serve his needs and pleasure, with no share in salvation, no position in eternity. In Western civilization this swing of the pendulum reached its limit in developed Christian theology and in the philosophy of Descartes: both alike inserted a qualitative and unbridgeable barrier between all men and any animals.

3. With Darwin, the reverse swing was started. Man was once again regarded as an animal, but now in the light of science rather than of unsophisticated sensibility. At the outset, the consequences of the changed outlook were not fully explored. The unconscious prejudices and attitudes of an earlier age survived, disguising many of the moral and philosophical implications of the new outlook. But gradually the pendulum reached the furthest point of its swing. What seemed the logical consequences of the Darwinian postulates were faced: man is an animal like any other; accordingly, his views as to the special meaning of human life and human ideals need merit no more consideration in the light of eternity (or of evolution) than those of a bacillus or a tapeworm. Survival is the only criterion of evolutionary success: therefore, all existing organisms are of equal value. The idea of progress is a mere anthropomorphism. Man happens to be the dominant type at the moment, but he might be replaced by the ant or the rat. And so on.

4. The gap between man and animal was here reduced not by exaggerating the human qualities of animals, but by minimizing the human qualities of men. Of late years, however, a new tendency has become apparent. It may be that this is due mainly to the mere in-

crease of knowledge and the extension of scientific analysis. It may be that it has been determined by social and psychological causes. Disillusionment with *laisser faire* in the human economic sphere may well have spread to the planetary system of *laisser faire* that we call natural selection. With the crash of old religious, ethical, and political systems, man's desperate need for some scheme of values and ideals may have prompted a more critical re-examination of his biological position. Whether this be so is a point that I must leave to the social historians. The fact remains that the pendulum is again on the swing, the man-animal gap again broadening. After Darwin, man could no longer avoid considering himself as an animal; but he is beginning to see himself as a very peculiar and in many ways a unique animal. The analysis of man's biological uniqueness is as yet incomplete. This essay is an attempt to review its present position.

5. The first and most obviously unique characteristic of man is his capacity for conceptual thought; if you prefer objective terms, you will say, his employment of true speech, but that is only another way of saying the same thing. True speech involves the use of verbal signs for objects, not merely for feelings. Plenty of animals can express the fact that they are hungry; but none except man can ask for an egg or a banana. And to have words for objects at once implies conceptual thought, since an object is always one of a class. No doubt, children and savages are as unaware of using conceptual thought as Monsieur Jourdain was unaware of speaking in prose; but they cannot avoid it. Words are tools which automatically carve concepts out of experience. The faculty of recognizing objects as members of a class provides the potential basis for the concept: the use of words at once actualizes the potentiality.

6. This basic human property has had many consequences. The most important was the development of a cumulative tradition. The beginnings of tradition, by which experience is transmitted from one generation to the next, are to be seen in many higher animals. But in no case is the tradition cumulative. Offspring learn from parents, but they learn the same kind and quantity of lessons as they, in turn, impart: the transmission of experience never bridges more than one generation. In man, however, tradition is an independent and potentially permanent activity, capable of indefinite improvement in quality and increase in quantity. It constitutes a new accessory process of heredity in evolution, running side by side with the biological process, a heredity of experience to supplement the universal heredity of living substance.

7. The existence of a cumulative tradition has as its chief con-

sequence—or if you prefer, its chief objective manifestation—the progressive improvement of human tools and machinery. Many animals employ tools; but they are always crude tools employed in a crude way. Elaborate tools and skilled technique can develop only with the aid of speech and tradition.

8. In the perspective of evolution, tradition and tools are the characters which have given man his dominant position among organisms. This biological dominance is, at present, another of man's unique properties. In each geological epoch of which we have knowledge, there have been types which must be styled biologically dominant: they multiply, they extinguish or reduce competing types, they extend their range, they radiate into new modes of life. Usually at any one time there is one such type—the placental mammals, for instance, in the Cenozoic period—but sometimes there is more than one. The Mesozoic is usually called the Age of Reptiles, but in reality the reptiles were then competing for dominance with the insects: in earlier periods we should be hard put to it to decide whether trilobites, nautiloids, or early fish were *the* dominant type. To-day, however, there is general agreement that man is the sole type meriting the title. Since the early Pleistocene, widespread extinction has diminished the previously dominant group of placental mammals, and man has not merely multiplied, but has evolved, extended his range, and increased the variety of his modes of life.

9. Biology thus reinstates man in a position analogous to that conferred on him as Lord of Creation by theology. There are, however, differences, and differences of some importance for our general outlook. In the biological view, the other animals have not been created to serve man's needs, but man has evolved in such a way that he has been able to eliminate some competing types, to enslave others by domestication, and to modify physical and biological conditions over the larger part of the earth's land area. The theological view was not true in detail or in many of its implications; but it had a solid biological basis.

10. Speech, tradition, and tools have led to many other unique properties of man. These are, for the most part, obvious and well known, and I propose to leave them aside until I have dealt with some less familiar human characteristics. For the human species, considered as a species, is unique in certain purely biological attributes; and these have not received the attention they deserve, either from the zoological or the sociological standpoint.

11. In the first place, man is by far the most variable wild species known. Domesticated species like dog, horse, or fowl may

rival or exceed him in this particular, but their variability has obvious reasons, and is irrelevant to our inquiry.

12. In correlation with his wide variability, man has a far wider range than any other animal species, with the possible exception of some of his parasites. Man is also unique as a dominant type. All other dominant types have evolved into many hundreds or thousands of separate species, grouped in numerous genera, families, and larger classificatory groups. The human type has maintained its dominance without splitting: man's variety has been achieved within the limits of a single species.

13. Finally, man is unique among higher animals in the method of his evolution. Whereas, in general, animal evolution is divergent, human evolution is reticulate. By this is meant that in animals, evolution occurs by the isolation of groups which then become progressively more different in their genetic characteristics, so that the course of evolution can be represented as a divergent radiation of separate lines, some of which become extinct, others continue unbranched, and still others divergently branch again. Whereas in man, after incipient divergence, the branches have come together again, and have generated new diversity from their Mendelian recombinations, this process being repeated until the course of human descent is like a network.

14. All these biological peculiarities are interconnected. They depend on man's migratory propensities, which themselves arise from his fundamental peculiarities, of speech, social life, and relative independence of environment. They depend again on his capacity, when choosing mates, for neglecting large differences of colour and appearance which would almost certainly be more than enough to deter more instinctive and less plastic animals. Thus divergence, though it appears to have gone quite a long way in early human evolution, generating the very distinct white, black, and yellow subspecies and perhaps others, was never permitted to attain its normal culmination. Mutually infertile groups were never produced: man remained a single species. Furthermore, crossing between distinct types, which is a rare and extraordinary phenomenon in other animals, in him became normal and of major importance. According to Mendelian laws, such crosses generate much excess variability by producing new recombinations. Man is thus more variable than other species for two reasons. First, because migration has recaptured for the single interbreeding group divergences of a magnitude that in animals would escape into the isolation of separate species; and secondly, because the resultant crossing has generated recombinations which both quantitatively and qualita-

tively are on a far bigger scale than is supplied by the internal variability of even the numerically most abundant animal species.

15. We may contrast this with the state of affairs among ants, the dominant insect group. The ant type is more varied than the human type; but it has achieved this variability by intense divergent evolution. Several thousand species of ants are known, and the number is being added to each year with the increase of biological exploration. Ways of life among ants are divided among different subtypes, each rigidly confined to its own methods. Thus even if ants were capable of accumulating experience, there could exist no single world-wide ant tradition. The fact that the human type comprises but one biological species is a consequence of his capacity for tradition, and also permits his exploitation of that unique capacity to the utmost.

16. Let us remind ourselves that superposed upon this purely biological or genetic variability is the even greater amount of variability due to differences of upbringing, profession, and personal tastes. The final result is a degree of variation that would be staggering if it were not so familiar. It would be fair to say that, in respect to mind and outlook, individual human beings are separated by differences as profound as those which distinguish the major groups of the animal kingdom. The difference between a somewhat subnormal member of a savage tribe and a Beethoven or a Newton is assuredly comparable in extent with that between a sponge and a higher mammal. Leaving aside such vertical differences, the lateral difference between the mind of, say, a distinguished general or engineer of extrovert type and of an introvert genius in mathematics or religious mysticism is no less than that between an insect and a vertebrate. This enormous range of individual variation in human minds often leads to misunderstanding and even mutual incomprehensibility; but it also provides the necessary basis for fruitful division of labour in human society.

17. Another biological peculiarity of man is the uniqueness of his evolutionary history. Writers have indulged their speculative fancy by imagining other organisms endowed with speech and conceptual thought—talking rats, rational ants, philosophic dogs, and the like. But closer analysis shows that these fantasies are impossible. A brain capable of conceptual thought could not have been developed elsewhere than in a human body.

18. The course followed by evolution appears to have been broadly as follows. From a generalized early type, various lines radiate out, exploiting the environment in various ways. Some of these comparatively soon reach a limit to their evolution, at least as regards major alteration. Thereafter they are limited to minor

changes such as the formation of new genera and species. Others, on the other hand, are so constructed that they can continue their career, generating new types which are successful in the struggle for existence because of their greater control over the environment and their greater independence of it. Such changes are legitimately called "progressive." The new type repeats the process. It radiates out into a number of lines, each specializing in a particular direction. The great majority of these come up against dead ends and can advance no further: specialization is one-sided progress, and after a longer or shorter time, reaches a biomechanical limit. The horse stock cannot reduce its digits below one; the elephants are near the limits of size for terrestrial animals; feathered flight cannot become more efficient than in existing birds, and so on.

19. Sometimes all the branches of a given stock have come up against their limit, and then either have become extinct or have persisted without major change. This happened, for instance, to the echinoderms, which with their sea-urchins, starfish, brittle-stars, sea-lilies, sea-cucumbers, and other types now extinct had pushed the life that was in them into a series of blind alleys: they have not advanced for perhaps a hundred million years, nor have they given rise to other major types.

20. In other cases, all but one or two of the lines suffer this fate, while the rest repeat the process. All reptilian lines were blind alleys save two—one which was transformed into the birds, and another which became the mammals. Of the bird stock, all lines came to a dead end; of the mammals, all but one—the one which became man.

21. Evolution is thus seen as an enormous number of blind alleys, with a very occasional path of progress. It is like a maze in which almost all turnings are wrong turnings. The goal of the evolutionary maze, however, is not a central chamber, but a road which will lead indefinitely onwards.

22. If now we look back upon the past history of life, we shall see that the avenues of progress have been steadily reduced in number, until by the Pleistocene period, or even earlier, only one was left. Let us remember that we can and must judge early progress in the light of its latest steps. The most recent step has been the acquisition of conceptual thought, which has enabled man to dethrone the non-human mammals from their previous position of dominance. It is biologically obvious that conceptual thought could never have arisen save in an animal, so that all plants, both green and otherwise, are at once eliminated. As regards animals, I need not

go through the early steps in their progressive evolution. Since some degree of bulk helps to confer independence of the forces of nature, it is obvious that the combination of many cells to form a large individual was one necessary step, thus eliminating all single-celled forms from such progress. Similarly, progress is barred to specialized animals with no blood-system, like planarian worms; to internal parasites like tapeworms; to animals with radial symmetry and consequently no head, like echinoderms.

23. Of the three highest animal groups—the molluscs, the arthropods, and the vertebrates—the molluscs advanced least far. One condition for the later steps in biological progress was land life. The demands made upon the organism by exposure to air and gravity called forth biological mechanisms, such as limbs, sense organs, protective skin, and sheltered development, which were necessary foundations for later advance. And the molluscs have never been able to produce efficient terrestrial forms: their culmination is in marine types like squid and octopus.

24. The arthropods, on the other hand, have scored their greatest successes on land, with the spiders and especially the insects. Yet the fossil record reveals a lack of all advance, even in the most successful types such as ants, for a long time back—certainly during the last thirty million years, probably during the whole of the Tertiary epoch. Even during the shorter of these periods, the mammals were still evolving rapidly, and man's rise is contained in a fraction of this time.

25. What was it that cut the insects off from progress? The answer appears to lie in their breathing mechanism. The land arthropods have adopted the method of air-tubes or tracheae, branching to microscopic size and conveying gases directly to and from the tissues, instead of using the dual mechanism of lungs and bloodstream. The laws of gaseous diffusion are such that respiration by tracheae is extremely efficient for very small animals, but becomes rapidly less efficient with increase of size, until it ceases to be of use at a bulk below that of a house mouse. It is for this reason that no insect has ever become, by vertebrate standards, even moderately large.

26. It is for the same reason that no insect has ever become even moderately intelligent. The fixed pathways of instinct, however elaborate, require far fewer nerve cells than the multiple switchboards that underlie intelligence. It appears to be impossible to build a brain mechanism for flexible behaviour with less than a quite large minimum of neurones; and no insect has reached a size to provide this minimum.

27. Thus only the land vertebrates are left. The reptiles shared biological dominance with the insects in the Mesozoic. But while the insects had reached the end of their blind alley, the reptiles showed themselves capable of further advance. Temperature regulation is a necessary basis for final progress, since without it the rate of bodily function could never be stabilized, and without such stabilization, higher mental processes could never become accurate and dependable.

28. Two reptilian lines achieved this next step, in the guise of the birds and the mammals. The birds soon, however, came to a dead end, chiefly because their forelimbs were entirely taken up in the specialization for flight. The subhuman mammals made another fundamental advance, in the shape of internal development, permitting the young animal to arrive at a much more advanced stage before it was called upon to face the world. They also (like the birds) developed true family life.

29. Most mammalian lines, however, cut themselves off from indefinite progress by one-sided evolution, turning their limbs and jaws into specialized and therefore limited instruments. And, for the most part, they relied mainly on the crude sense of smell, which cannot present as differentiated a pattern of detailed knowledge as can sight. Finally, the majority continued to produce their young several at a time, in litters. As J. B. S. Haldane has pointed out, this gives rise to an acute struggle for existence in the prenatal period, a considerable percentage of embryos being aborted or resorbed. Such intra-uterine selection will put a premium upon rapidity of growth and differentiation, since the devil takes the hindmost; and this rapidity of development will tend automatically to be carried on into postnatal growth.

30. As everyone knows, man is characterized by a rate of development which is abnormally slow as compared with that of any other mammal. The period from birth to the first onset of sexual maturity comprises nearly a quarter of the normal span of his life, instead of an eighth, a tenth or twelfth, as in some other animals. This again is in one sense a unique characteristic of man, although from the evolutionary point of view it represents merely the exaggeration of a tendency which is operative in other Primates. In any case, it is a necessary condition for the evolution and proper utilization of rational thought. If men and women were, like mice, confronted with the problems of adult life and parenthood after a few weeks, or even, like whales, after a couple of years, they could never

acquire the skills of body and mind that they now absorb from and contribute to the social heritage of the species.

31. This slowing (or "foetalization," as Bolk has called it, since it prolongs the foetal characteristics of earlier ancestral forms into postnatal development and even into adult life) has had other important by-products for man. Here I will mention but one—his nakedness. The distribution of hair on man is extremely similar to that on a late foetus of a chimpanzee, and there can be little doubt that it represents an extension of this temporary anthropoid phase into permanence. Hairlessness of body is not a unique biological characteristic of man; but it is unique among terrestrial mammals, save for a few desert creatures, and some others which have compensated for loss of hair by developing a pachydermatous skin. In any case, it has important biological consequences, since it must have encouraged the comparatively defenceless human creatures in their efforts to protect themselves against animal enemies and the elements, and so has been a spur to the improvement of intelligence.

32. Now, foetalization could never have occurred in a mammal producing many young at a time, since intra-uterine competition would have encouraged the opposing tendency. Thus we may conclude that conceptual thought could develop only in a mammalian stock which normally brings forth but one young at a birth. Such a stock is provided in the Primates—lemurs, monkeys, and apes.

33. The Primates also have another characteristic which was necessary for the ancestor of a rational animal—they are arboreal. It may seem curious that living in trees is a pre-requisite of conceptual thought. But Elliot Smith's analysis has abundantly shown that only in an arboreal mammal could the forelimb become a true hand, and sight become dominant over smell. Hands obtain an elaborate tactile pattern of what they handle, eyes an elaborate visual pattern of what they see. The combination of the two kinds of pattern, with the aid of binocular vision, in the higher centres of the brain allowed the Primate to acquire a wholly new richness of knowledge about objects, a wholly new possibility of manipulating them. Tree life laid the foundation both for the fuller definition of objects by conceptual thought and for the fuller control of them by tools and machines.

34. Higher Primates have yet another pre-requisite of human intelligence—they are all gregarious. Speech, it is obvious, could never have been evolved in a solitary type. And speech is as much the physical basis of conceptual thought as is protoplasm the physical basis of life.

35. For the passage, however, of the critical point between sub-

human and human, between the biological subordination and the biological primacy of intelligence, between a limited and a potentially unlimited tradition—for this it was necessary for the arboreal animal to descend to the ground again. Only in a terrestrial creature could fully erect posture be acquired; and this was essential for the final conversion of the arms from locomotor limbs into manipulative hands. Furthermore, just as land life, ages previously, had demanded and developed a greater variety of response than had been required in the water, so now it did the same in relation to what had been required in the trees. An arboreal animal could never have evolved the skill of the hunting savage, nor ever have proceeded to the domestication of other animals or to agriculture.

36. We are now in a position to define the uniqueness of human evolution. The essential character of man as a dominant organism is conceptual thought. And conceptual thought could have arisen only in a multicellular animal, an animal with bilateral symmetry, head and blood system, a vertebrate as against a mollusc or an arthropod, a land vertebrate among vertebrates, a mammal among land vertebrates. Finally, it could have arisen only in a mammalian line which was gregarious, which produced one young at a birth instead of several, and which had recently become terrestrial after a long period of arboreal life.

37. There is only one group of animals which fulfils these conditions—a terrestrial offshoot of the higher Primates. Thus not merely has conceptual thought been evolved only in man: it could not have been evolved except in man. There is but one path of unlimited progress through the evolutionary maze. The course of human evolution is as unique as its result. It is unique not in the trivial sense of being a different course from that of any other organism, but in the profounder sense of being the only path that could have achieved the essential characters of man. Conceptual thought on this planet is inevitably associated with a particular type of Primate body and Primate brain.

38. A further property of man in which he is unique among higher animals concerns his sexual life. Man is prepared to mate at any time: animals are not. To start with, most animals have a definite breeding season; only during this period are their reproductive organs fully developed and functional. In addition to this, higher animals have one or more sexual cycles within their breeding seasons, and only at one phase of the cycle are they prepared to mate. In general, either a sexual season or a sexual cycle, or both, operates to restrict mating.

39.   In man, however, neither of these factors is at work. There appear to be indications of a breeding season in some primitive peoples like the Eskimo, but even there they are but relics. Similarly, while there still exist physiological differences in sexual desire at different phases of the female sexual cycle, these are purely quantitative, and may readily be overridden by psychological factors. Man, to put it briefly, is continuously sexed: animals are discontinuously sexed. If we try to imagine what a human society would be like in which the sexes were interested in each other only during the summer, as in songbirds, or, as in female dogs, experienced sexual desire only once every few months, or even as in ants, only once in a lifetime, we can realize what this peculiarity has meant. In this, as in his slow growth and prolonged period of dependence, man is not abruptly marked off from all other animals, but represents the culmination of a process that can be clearly traced among other Primates. What the biological meaning of this evolutionary trend may be is difficult to understand. One suggestion is that it may be associated with the rise of mind to dominance. The bodily functions, in lower mammals rigidly determined by physiological mechanisms, come gradually under the more plastic control of the brain. But this, for what it is worth, is a mere speculation.

40.   Another of the purely biological characters in which man is unique is his reproductive variability. In a given species of animals, the maximum litter size may, on occasions, reach perhaps double the minimum, according to circumstances of food and temperature, or even perhaps threefold. But during a period of years, these variations will be largely equalized within a range of perhaps fifty per cent either way from the average, and the percentage of wholly infertile adults is very low. In man, on the other hand, the range of positive fertility is enormous—from one to over a dozen, and in exceptional cases to over twenty; and the number of wholly infertile adults is considerable. This fact, in addition to providing a great diversity of patterns of family life, has important bearings on evolution. It means that in the human species differential fertility is more important as a basis for selection than is differential mortality; and it provides the possibility of much more rapid selective change than that found in wild animal species. Such rapidity of evolution would, of course, be effectively realized only if the stocks with large families possessed a markedly different hereditary constitution from those with few children; but the high differential fertility of unskilled workers as against the professional classes in England, or of the French Canadians against the rest of the inhabitants of Canada,

demonstrates how rapidly populations may change by this means.

41. Still another point in which man is biologically unique is the length and relative importance of his period of what we may call "post-maturity." If we consider the female sex, in which the transition from reproductive maturity to non-reproductive post-maturity is more sharply defined than in the male, we find, in the first place, that in animals a comparatively small percentage of the population survives beyond the period of reproduction; in the second place, that such individuals rarely survive long, and so far as known never for a period equal to or greater than the period during which reproduction was possible; and thirdly, that such individuals are rarely of importance in the life of the species. The same is true of the male sex, provided we do not take the incapacity to produce fertile gametes as the criterion of post-maturity, but rather the appearance of signs of age, such as the beginnings of loss of vigour and weight, decreased sexual activity, or greying hair.

42. It is true that in some social mammals, notably among ruminants and Primates, an old male or old female is frequently found as leader of the herd. Such cases, however, provide the only examples of the special biological utility of post-mature individuals among animals; they are confined to a very small proportion of the population, and it is uncertain to what extent such individuals are post-mature in the sense we have defined. In any event, it is improbable that the period of post-maturity is anywhere near so long as that of maturity. In civilized man, on the other hand, the average expectation of life now includes over ten years of post-maturity, and about a quarter of the population enjoys a period of post-maturity almost as long as that of maturity. What is more, in all human societies above the lowest, a large proportion of the leaders of the community has always been post-mature.

43. This is truly a remarkable phenomenon. Through the new social mechanisms made possible by speech and tradition, man has been able to utilize for the benefit of the species a period of life which in almost all other creatures is a mere superfluity. We know that the dominance of the old can be over-emphasized; but it is equally obvious that society cannot do without the post-mature. To act on the slogan "Too old at forty"—or even at forty-five—would be to rob man of one of his unique characteristics, whereby he utilizes tradition to the best advantage.

44. We have now dealt in a broad way with the unique properties of man both from the comparative and the evolutionary point of view. Now we can return to the present and the particular

and discuss these properties and their consequences a little more in detail. First, let us remind ourselves that the gap between human and animal thought is much greater than is usually supposed. The tendency to project familiar human qualities into animals is very strong, and colours the ideas of nearly all people who have not special familiarity both with animal behaviour and scientific method.

45. Let us recall a few cases illustrating the unhuman characteristics of animal behaviour. Everyone is familiar with the rigidity of instinct in insects. Worker ants emerge from their pupal case equipped not with the instincts to care for ant grubs in general, but solely with those suitable to ant grubs of their own species. They will attempt to care for the grubs of other species, but appear incapable of learning new methods if their instincts kill their foster children. Or again, a worker wasp, without food for a hungry grub, has been known to bite off its charge's tail and present it to its head. But even in the fine flowers of vertebrate evolution, the birds and mammals, behaviour, though it may be more plastic than in the insects, is as essentially irrational. Birds, for instance, seem incapable of analysing unfamiliar situations. For them some element in the situation may act as its dominant symbol, the only stimulus to which they can react. At other times, it is the organization of the situation as a whole which is the stimulus: if the whole is interfered with, analysis fails to dissect out the essential element. A hen meadow-pipit feeds her young when it gapes and squeaks in the nest. But if it has been ejected by a young cuckoo, gaping and squeaking has no effect, and the rightful offspring is neglected and allowed to die, while the usurper in the nest is fed. The pipit normally cares for its own young, but not because it recognizes them as such.

46. Mammals are no better. A cow deprived of its calf will be quieted by the provision of a crudely stuffed calfskin. Even the Primates are no exception. Female baboons whose offspring have died will continue carrying the corpses until they have not merely putrefied but mummified. This appears to be due not to any profundity of grief, but to a contact stimulus: the mother will react similarly to any moderately small and furry object.

47. Birds and especially mammals are, of course, capable of a certain degree of analysis, but this is effected, in the main, by means of trial and error through concrete experience. A brain capable of conceptual thought appears to be the necessary basis for speedy and habitual analysis. Without it, the practice of splitting up situations into their components and assigning real degrees of significance to the various elements remains rudimentary and rare, whereas with

man, even when habit and trial and error are prevalent, conceptual thought is of major biological importance. The behaviour of animals is essentially arbitrary, in that it is fixed within narrow limits. In man it has become relatively free—free at the incoming and the outgoing ends alike. His capacity for acquiring knowledge has been largely released from arbitrary symbolism, his capacity for action, from arbitrary canalizations of instinct. He can thus rearrange the patterns of experience and action in a far greater variety, and can escape from the particular into the general.

48. Thus man is more intelligent than the animals because his brain mechanism is more plastic. This fact also gives him, of course, the opportunity of being more nonsensical and perverse: but its primary effects have been more analytical knowledge and more varied control. The essential fact, from my present standpoint, is that the change has been profound and in an evolutionary sense rapid. Although it has been brought about by the gradual quantitative enlargement of the association areas of the brain, the result has been almost as abrupt as the change (also brought about quantitatively) from solid ice to liquid water. We should remember that the machinery of the change has been an increase in plasticity and potential variety: it is by a natural selection of ideas and actions that the result has been greater rationality instead of greater irrationality.

49. This increase of flexibility has also had other psychological consequences which rational philosophers are apt to forget: and in some of these, too, man is unique. It has led, for instance, to the fact that man is the only organism normally and inevitably subject to psychological conflict. You can give a dog a neurosis as Pavlov did, by a complicated laboratory experiment: you can find cases of brief emotional conflict in the lives of wild birds and animals. But, for the most part, psychological conflict is shirked by the simple expedient of arranging that now one and now another instinct should dominate the animal's behaviour. I remember in Spitsbergen finding the nest of a Red-throated Diver on the shore of an inland pool. The sitting bird was remarkably bold. After leaving the nest for the water, she stayed very close. She did not, however, remain in a state of conflict between fear of intruders and desire to return to her brooding. She would gradually approach as if to land, but eventually fear became dominant, and when a few feet from the shore she suddenly dived, and emerged a good way farther out—only to repeat the process. Here the external circumstances were such as to encourage conflict, but even so what are the most serious features of human conflict were minimized by the outlet of alternate action.

50.  Those who take up bird-watching as a hobby tend at first to be surprised at the way in which a bird will turn, apparently without transition or hesitation, from one activity to another—from fighting to peaceable feeding, from courtship to uninterested preening, from panic flight to unconcern. However, all experienced naturalists or those habitually concerned with animals recognize such behaviour as characteristic of the subhuman level. It represents another aspect of the type of behaviour I have just been describing for the Red-throated Diver. In this case, the internal state of the bird changes, presumably owing to some form of physiological fatigue or to a diminution of intensity of a stimulus with time or distance; the type of behaviour which had been dominant ceases to have command over the machinery of action, and is replaced by another which just before had been subordinate and latent.

51.  As a matter of fact, the prevention of conflict between opposed modes of action is a very general phenomenon, of obvious biological utility, and it is only the peculiarities of the human mind which have forced its partial abandonment on man. It begins on the purely mechanical level with the nervous machinery controlling our muscles. The main muscles of a limb, for instance, are arranged in two antagonistic sets, the flexors bending and the extensors straightening it. It would obviously be futile to throw both sets into action at the same time, and economical when one set is in action to reduce to the minimum any resistance offered by the other. This has actually been provided for. The nervous connections in the spinal cord are so arranged that when a given muscle receives an impulse to contract, its antagonist receives an impulse causing it to lose some of its tone and thus, by relaxing below its normal level, to offer the least possible resistance to the action of the active muscle.

52.  Sherrington discovered that the same type of mechanism was operative in regard to the groups of muscles involved in whole reflexes. A dog, for instance, cannot very well walk and scratch itself at the same time. To avoid the waste involved in conflict between the walking and the scratching reflex, the spinal cord is constructed in such a way that throwing one reflex into action automatically inhibits the other. In both these cases, the machinery for preventing conflicts of activity resides in the spinal cord. Although the matter has not yet been analysed physiologically, it would appear that the normal lack of conflict between instincts which we have just been discussing is due to some similar type of nervous mechanism in the brain.

53.  When we reach the human level, there are new complications; for, as we have seen, one of the peculiarities of man is the

abandonment of any rigidity of instinct, and the provision of association-mechanisms by which any activity of the mind, whether in the spheres of knowing, feeling, or willing, can be brought into relation with any other. It is through this that man has acquired the possibility of a unified mental life. But, by the same token, the door is opened to the forces of disruption, which may destroy any such unity and even prevent him from enjoying the efficiency of behaviour attained by animals. For, as Sherrington has emphasized, the nervous system is like a funnel, with a much larger space for intake than for outflow. The intake cone of the funnel is represented by the receptor nerves, conveying impulses inward to the central nervous system from the sense organs: the outflow tube is, then, through the effector nerves, conveying impulses outwards to the muscles, and there are many more of the former than of the latter. If we like to look at the matter from a rather different standpoint, we may say that, since action can be effected only by muscles (strictly speaking, also by the glands, which are disregarded here for simplicity's sake), and since there are a limited number of muscles in the body, the only way for useful activity to be carried out is for the nervous system to impose a particular pattern of action on them, and for all other competing or opposing patterns to be cut out. Each pattern when it has seized control of the machinery of action, *should* be in supreme command, like the captain of a ship. Animals are, in many ways, like ships which are commanded by a number of captains in turn, each specializing in one kind of action, and popping up and down between the authority of the bridge and the obscurity of their private cabins according to the business on hand. Man is on the way to achieving permanent unity of command, but the captain has a disconcerting way of dissolving into a wrangling committee.

54. Even on the new basis, however, mechanisms exist for minimizing conflict. They are what are known by psychologists as suppression and repression. From our point of view, repression is the more interesting. It implies the forcible imprisonment of one of two conflicting impulses in the dungeons of the unconscious mind. The metaphor is, however, imperfect. For the prisoner in the mental dungeon can continue to influence the tyrant above in the daylight of consciousness. In addition to a general neurosis, compulsive thoughts and acts may be thrust upon the personality. Repression may thus be harmful; but it can also be regarded as a biological necessity for dealing with inevitable conflict in the early years of life, before rational judgment and control are possible. Better to have the capacity for more or less unimpeded action, even at the expense of possible neuro-

sis, than an organism constantly inactivated like the ass between the two bundles of hay, balanced in irresolution.

55. In repression, not only is the defeated impulse banished to the unconscious, but the very process of banishment is itself unconscious. The inhibitory mechanisms concerned in it must have been evolved to counteract the more obvious possibilities of conflict, especially in early life, which arose as by-products of the human type of mind.

56. In suppression, the banishment is conscious, so that neurosis is not likely to appear. Finally, in rational judgment, neither of the conflicting impulses is relegated to the unconscious, but they are balanced in the light of reason and experience, and control of action is consciously exercised.

57. I need not pursue the subject further. Here I am only concerned to show that the great biological advantages conferred on man by the unification of mind have inevitably brought with them certain counterbalancing defects. The freedom of association between all aspects and processes of the mind has provided the basis for conceptual thought and tradition; but it has also provided potential antagonists, which in lower organisms were carefully kept apart, with the opportunity of meeting face to face, and has thus made some degree of conflict unavoidable.

58. In rather similar fashion, man's upright posture has brought with it certain consequential disadvantages in regard to the functioning of his internal organs and his proneness to rupture. Thus man's unique characteristics are by no means all beneficial.

59. In close correlation with our subjection to conflict is our proneness to laughter. So characteristic of our species is laughter that man has been defined as the laughing animal. It is true that, like so much else of man's uniqueness, it has its roots among the animals, where it reveals itself as an expression of a certain kind of general pleasure—and thus in truth perhaps more of a smile than a laugh. And in a few animals—ravens, for example—there are traces of a malicious sense of humour. Laughter in man, however, is much more than this. There are many theories of laughter, most of them containing a partial truth. But biologically the important feature of human laughter seems to lie in its providing a release for conflict, a resolution of troublesome situations.

60. This and other functions of laughter can be exaggerated so that it becomes as the crackling of thorns under the pot, and prevents men from taking anything seriously; but in due proportion its value is very great as a lubricant against troublesome friction and a lightener

of the inevitable gravity and horror of life, which would otherwise become portentous and overshadowing. True laughter, like true speech, is a unique possession of man.

61. Those of man's unique characteristics which may better be called psychological and social than narrowly biological spring from one or other of three characteristics. The first is his capacity for abstract and general thought: the second is the relative unification of his mental processes, as against the much more rigid compartmentalization of animal mind and behaviour: the third is the existence of social units, such as tribe, nation, party, and church, with a continuity of their own, based on organized tradition and culture.

62. There are various by-products of the change from prehuman to the human type of mind which are, of course, also unique biologically. Let us enumerate a few: pure mathematics; musical gifts; artistic appreciation and creation; religion; romantic love.

63. Mathematical ability appears, almost inevitably, as something mysterious. Yet the attainment of speech, abstraction, and logical thought, bring it into potential being. It may remain in a very rudimentary state of development; but even the simplest arithmetical calculations are a manifestation of its existence. Like any other human activity, it requires proper tools and machinery. Arabic numerals, algebraic conventions, logarithms, the differential calculus, are such tools: each one unlocks new possibilities of mathematical achievement. But just as there is no essential difference between man's conscious use of a chipped flint as an implement and his design of the most elaborate machine, so there is none between such simple operations as numeration or addition and the comprehensive flights of higher mathematics. Again, some people are by nature more gifted than others in this field; yet no normal human being is unable to perform some mathematical operations. Thus the capacity for mathematics is, as I have said, a by-product of the human type of mind.

64. We have seen, however, that the human type of mind is distinguished by two somewhat opposed attributes. One is the capacity for abstraction, the other for synthesis. Mathematics is one of the extreme by-products of our capacity for abstraction. Arithmetic abstracts objects of all qualities save their enumerability; the symbol $\pi$ abstracts in a single Greek letter a complicated relation between the parts of all circles. Art, on the other hand, is an extreme by-product of our capacity for synthesis. In one unique production, the painter can bring together form, colour, arrangement, associations of memory, emotion, and idea. Dim adumbrations of art are to be found in a few creatures such as bower-birds; but nothing is found to which

the word can rightly be applied until man's mind gave the possibility of freely mingling observations, emotions, memories, and ideas, and subjecting the mixture to deliberate control.

65.   But it is not enough here to enumerate a few special activities. In point of fact, the great majority of man's activities and characteristics are by-products of his primary distinctive characteristics, and therefore, like them, biologically unique.

66.   On the one hand, conversation, organized games, education, sport, paid work, gardening, the theatre; on the other, conscience, duty, sin, humiliation, vice, penitence—these are all such unique by-products. The trouble, indeed, is to find any human activities which are not unique. Even the fundamental biological attributes such as eating, sleeping, and mating have been tricked out by man with all kinds of unique frills and peculiarities.

67.   There may be other by-products of man's basic uniqueness which have not yet been exploited. For let us remember that such by-products may remain almost wholly latent until demand stimulates invention and invention facilitates development. It is asserted that there exist human tribes who cannot count above two; certainly some savages stop at ten. Here the mathematical faculty is restricted to numeration, and stops short at a very rudimentary stage of this rudimentary process. Similarly, there are human societies in which art has never been developed beyond the stage of personal decoration. It is probable that during the first half of the Pleistocene period, none of the human race had developed either their mathematical or their artistic potentialities beyond such a rudimentary stage.

68.   It is perfectly possible that to-day man's so-called supernormal or extra-sensory faculties are in the same case as were his mathematical faculties during the first or second glaciations of the Ice Age—barely more than a potentiality, with no technique for eliciting and developing them, no tradition behind them to give them continuity and intellectual respectability. Even such simple performances as multiplying two three-figure numbers would have appeared entirely magical to early Stone Age men.

69.   Experiments such as those of Rhine and Salter on extra-sensory guessing, experiences like those of Gilbert Murray on thought transference, and the numerous sporadic records of telepathy and clairvoyance suggest that some people at least possess possibilities of knowing which are not confined within the ordinary channels of sense-perception. Salter's work is particularly interesting in this connection. As a result of an enormous number of trials with apparatus ingeniously designed to exclude all alternative explanation, he finds that

those best endowed with this extra-sensory gift can guess right about once in four times when once in five would be expected on chance alone. The results are definite, and significant in the statistical sense, yet the faculty is rudimentary: it does not permit its possessor to guess right all the time or even most of the time—merely to achieve a small rise in the percentage of right guessing. If, however, we could discover in what this faculty really consists, on what mechanism it depends, and by what conditions and agencies it can be influenced, it should be capable of development like any other human faculty. Man may thus be unique in more ways than he now suspects.

70. So far we have been considering the fact of human uniqueness. It remains to consider man's attitude to these unique qualities of his. Professor Everett, of the University of California, in an interesting paper bearing the same title as this essay, but dealing with the topic from the standpoint of the philosopher and the humanist rather than that of the biologist, has stressed man's fear of his own uniqueness. Man has often not been able to tolerate the feeling that he inhabits an alien world, whose laws do not make sense in the light of his intelligence, and in which the writ of his human values does not run. Faced with the prospect of such intellectual and moral loneliness, he has projected personality into the cosmic scheme. Here he has found a will, there a purpose; here a creative intelligence, and there a divine compassion. At one time, he has deified animals, or personified natural forces. At others, he has created a superhuman pantheon, a single tyrannical world ruler, a subtle and satisfying Trinity in Unity. Philosophers have postulated an Absolute of the same nature as mind.

71. It is only exceptionally that men have dared to uphold their uniqueness and to be proud of their human superiority to the impersonality and irrationality of the rest of the universe. It is time now, in the light of our knowledge, to be brave and face the fact and the consequences of our uniqueness. That is Dr. Everett's view as it was also that of T. H. Huxley in his famous Romanes lecture. I agree with them; but I would suggest that the antinomy between man and the universe is not quite so sharp as they have made out. Man represents the culmination of that process of organic evolution which has been proceeding on this planet for over a thousand million years. That process, however wasteful and cruel it may be, and into however many blind alleys it may have been diverted, is also in one respect progressive. Man has now become the sole representative of life in that progressive aspect and its sole trustee for any progress in the future.

72. Meanwhile it is true that the appearance of the human

type of mind, the latest step in evolutionary progress, has introduced both new methods and new standards. By means of his conscious reason and its chief offspring, science, man has the power of substituting less dilatory, less wasteful, and less cruel methods of effective progressive change than those of natural selection, which alone are available to lower organisms. And by means of his conscious purpose and his set of values, he has the power of substituting new and higher standards for change than those of mere survival and adaptation to immediate circumstances, which alone are inherent in pre-human evolution. To put the matter in another way, progress has hitherto been a rare and fitful by-product of evolution. Man has the possibility of making it the main feature of his own future evolution, and of guiding its course in relation to a deliberate aim.

73. But he must not be afraid of his uniqueness. There may be other beings in this vast universe endowed with reason, purpose, and aspiration: but we know nothing of them. So far as our knowledge goes, human mind and personality are unique and constitute the highest product yet achieved by the cosmos. Let us not put off our responsibilities onto the shoulders of mythical gods or philosophical absolutes, but shoulder them in the hopefulness of tempered pride. In the perspective of biology, our business in the world is seen to be the imposition of the best and most enduring of our human standards upon ourselves and our planet. The enjoyment of beauty and interest, the achievement of goodness and efficiency, the enchancement of life and its variety—these are the harvest which our human uniqueness should be called upon to yield.

## WORDS

*meaning* 1. Define *anthropomorphic* (par. 2), *reticulate* and *incipient* (par. 13), *propensities* (par. 14), *intra-uterine* (par. 29), *foetalization* (par. 31), *arboreal* (par. 33), *gregarious* (par. 34), and *antinomy* (par. 71). 2. What are *economic stratification* and *ideological mortar* (par. 2)? 3. What are *placental mammals* (par. 8)? What are *Mendelian recombinations* (par. 13)?

*level of usage* 1. Is such a usage as *pendulum-wise* (par. 1) consistent with the diction of the essay as a whole? 2. Is *pendulum-wise* comparable to the use of *class-ridden* (par. 2) and *man-animal* (par. 4)? Explain.

## SENTENCES

*style* 1. Reread the sentences in paragraph 2. Is there anything about these sentences that is peculiar to "scientific" writing? 2. Is there any relationship between the rhythm of these sentences and the metaphor of the slow swing of a pendulum?

*variety* The author makes frequent use of dashes. Why does he use them and how effective are they in paragraphs 7, 17, 20, 23, 24, 31, 32, 33, 34, 35, and 37?

*rhetorical devices* 1. Why is the metaphor in paragraph 54 an "imperfect" one? 2. What is meant by the allusion to "the ass between the two bundles of hay" (par. 54)?

## PARAGRAPHS

*methods of development* The author uses many different methods in developing his paragraphs: presentation of details, use of a single example, contrast, elimination, demonstration of cause and effect, analogy, description, definition, analysis, and classification. Determine the principal method used in each of the following paragraphs: 9, 13, 15, 16, 20, 23, 45, 46, 52, 61, 62, 63, and 68.

## CONTENT AND ORGANIZATION

*central ideas* 1. How did "Christian theology" and "the philosophy of Descartes" build a "barrier" between men and animals (par. 2)? 2. What relationship did Darwin have to the barrier (par. 3)? 3. How may man's uniqueness, a product of evolution, eventually affect the operation of the evolutionary process (pars. 71–73)?

*organization* 1. Which paragraphs combine to form the introduction? 2. Paragraph 10 probably performs several functions. What are they? 3. Paragraph 11 begins with "In the first place." If there is no "second place," is the organization adversely affected? or can you easily follow the essay? Explain. 4. What do you assume when you find a paragraph early in the essay (par. 13) beginning with *Finally?* What does it mean here? 5. What is the function of paragraph 36? 6. Does Huxley organize his essay by a logical, step-by-step method? Explain your answer by giving evidence to support it.

*assumptions and implications* 1. The author does not believe, apparently, that "The idea of progress is a mere anthropomorphism" (par. 3). But does he give any evidence to indicate that it is not? 2. "In the perspective of biology, our business in the world is seen to be the imposition of the best and most enduring of our human standards upon ourselves and our planet" (par. 73). If this idea is accepted, what is the future of revealed religion, the anopheles mosquito, the California condor, the hammerhead shark, and the surviving wilderness areas?

## SUGGESTIONS FOR DISCUSSION

1. List the things that man can neglect in choosing a mate (par. 14) that animals cannot neglect. Do most men neglect them? Why or why not? 2. A man can both scratch and walk at the same time, but a dog cannot (par. 52). Why is man therefore superior? 3. If the leader of a modern state (the United States, France, the U.S.S.R., or Japan) were given the authority to guide the direction of human evolution, what might be his goals? 4. Huxley says that "human mind and personality are unique and constitute the highest product yet achieved by the cosmos" (par. 73). Write a short essay proving that the same is true of the praying mantis, the whale, or the Siamese cat.

## Eric Sevareid

# THE DARK OF THE MOON

1.   This, thank goodness, is the first warm and balmy night of the year in these parts; the first frogs are singing. Altogether this is hardly the night for whispering sweet sentiments about the reciprocal trade act, the extension thereof. But since we are confined, by tradition, to the contemplation of public themes and issues, let us contemplate the moon. The lovely and luminous moon has become a public issue. For quite a few thousand years it was a private issue; it figured in purely bilateral negotiations between lovers, in the incantations of jungle witch doctors and Indian corn planters. Poets from attic windows issued the statements about the moon, and they made better reading than the Mimeographed handouts now being issued by assistant secretaries of defense.

2.   The moon was always measured in terms of hope and reassurance and the heart pangs of youth on such a night as this; it is now measured in terms of mileage and foot-pounds of rocket thrust. Children sent sharp, sweet wishes to the moon; now they dream of blunt-nosed missiles.

3.   There must come a time, in every generation, when those who are older secretly get off the train of progress, willing to walk back to where they came from, if they can find the way. We're afraid we're getting off now. Cheer, if you wish, the first general or Ph.D.

THE DARK OF THE MOON: From *The Reporter*, April 17, 1958. Copyright 1958 by Eric Sevareid. Reprinted by permission of the Harold Matson Company, Inc.

who splatters something on the kindly face of the moon. We shall grieve for him, for ourself, for the young lovers and poets and dreamers to come, because the ancient moon will never be the same again. Therefore, we suspect, the heart of man will never be the same.

4. We find it very easy to wait for the first photographs of the other side of the moon, for we have not yet seen the other side of Lake Louise or the Blue Ridge peak that shows through the cabin window.

5. We find ourself quite undisturbed about the front-page talk of "controlling the earth from the moon," because we do not believe it. If neither men nor gadgets nor both combined can control the earth from the earth, we fail to see how they will do so from the moon.

6. It is exciting talk, indeed, the talk of man's advance toward space. But one little step in man's advance toward man—that, we think, would be truly exciting. Let those who wish try to discover the composition of a lunar crater; we would settle for discovering the true mind of a Russian commissar or the inner heart of a delinquent child.

7. There is, after all, another side—a dark side—to the human spirit, too. Men have hardly begun to explore these regions; and it is going to be a very great pity if we advance upon the bright side of the moon with the dark side of ourselves, if the cargo in the first rockets to reach there consists of fear and chauvinism and suspicion. Surely we ought to have our credentials in order, our hands very clean and perhaps a prayer for forgiveness on our lips as we prepare to open the ancient vault of the shining moon.

## WORDS

*relationships*  1. The moon always has played an important part in man's life, and many terms are related to it. What is meant by the following words and phrases and what is their relationship to the moon: *lunacy, moon-struck, moonshine whiskey, moon-blind, moon-face, moon-gazing?* 2. In Greek and Roman mythology, who were Diana, Cynthia, and Artemis?  3. What is a lunar month? How long is it?  4. In what kind of songs and poems do you find allusions to the moon? Give some examples.

*exactness*  Why is *Mimeographed* (par. 1) capitalized?

## SENTENCES

*style*  This short essay was originally a radio broadcast. Why does Sevareid consistently use the pronoun *we?* Would this usage be appropriate in a student theme?

*emphasis* 1. One mark of effective writing is the use of concrete words with unblurred denotation and strong connotations. Why is "incantations of jungle witch doctors" (par. 1) superior to "magical rites of primitive men"? Why is "Children sent sharp, sweet wishes to the moon" (par. 2) more effective than "Children wished on the moon"? 2. What is the effect of the repetition of *and* in "fear and chauvinism and suspicion" (par. 7)? Why? 3. When identical or similar grammatical structures are used to express contrasted ideas, they are balanced. Analyze how this is done in paragraph 2. 4. Emphasis is secured by placing the most important ideas at the beginning and end of a paragraph. Explain how the use of a loose sentence at the beginning of paragraph 5, followed by a periodic sentence at the end, results in the emphatic placement of the most important ideas of the paragraph. 5. How is abrupt change in sentence length used to achieve emphasis and variety in paragraph 3?

## PARAGRAPHS

*methods of development* 1. Find three paragraphs in this essay that are developed by comparison or contrast. 2. How are the contrasts of paragraph 2 sharpened by the repetition of a word in the first sentence? by the use of antonyms in the second sentence?

## CONTENT AND ORGANIZATION

*central ideas* 1. What has brought about the change in the public attitude toward the moon (par. 2)? 2. Why is the writer getting off the train of progress (par. 3)? 3. Why, after someone lands on the moon, will the heart of man never be the same again (par. 3)? 4. What does not having seen the other side of Lake Louise have to do with waiting for photographs of the moon (par. 4)? 5. Why does Sevareid believe that "one little step in man's advance toward man" would be more exciting than man's advance toward space (par. 6)? 6. Why should we have a prayer for forgiveness on our lips as we approach the moon (par. 7)?

*assumptions and implications* 1. What will be lost, and why should Sevareid grieve over losing it, when something "splatters" on the moon (par. 3)? 2. What criticism of modern scientific advances does this essay make?

## SUGGESTIONS FOR DISCUSSION

1. Why is it more difficult for science to understand and control the heart of a child or a commissar than the trajectory of a rocket? 2. What possible practical advantages to the human race can be won by the development of space travel? 3. By what methods, scientific or non-scientific, is man attempting to explore and understand "the dark side" of the human spirit? 4. What do you believe should be the attitude of

our government toward the social sciences—anthropology, sociology, social psychology, and the like? Could we justify spending almost as much money on them as on physics, chemistry, and astronomy? Why or why not?  5. Look up Poe's "Sonnet—To Science," paraphrase it, and compare or contrast it, in meaning, to this essay.

*Thomas Henry Huxley*

# THE METHOD OF SCIENTIFIC INVESTIGATION

1.  The method of scientific investigation is nothing but the expression of the necessary mode of working of the human mind. It is simply the mode at which all phenomena are reasoned about, rendered precise and exact. There is no more difference, but there is just the same kind of difference, between the mental operations of a man of science and those of an ordinary person, as there is between the operations and methods of a baker or of a butcher weighing out his goods in common scales, and the operations of a chemist in performing a difficult and complex analysis by means of his balance and finely graduated weights. It is not that the action of the scales in the one case, and the balance in the other, differ in the principles of their construction or manner of working; but the beam of one is set on an infinitely finer axis than the other, and of course turns by the addition of a much smaller weight.

2.  You will understand this better, perhaps, if I give you some familiar example. You have all heard it repeated, I dare say, that men of science work by means of induction and deduction, and that by the help of these operations, they, in a sort of sense, wring from Nature certain other things, which are called natural laws, and causes, and that out of these, by some cunning skill of their own, they build up hypotheses and theories. And it is imagined by many, that the operations of the common mind can be by no means compared with these processes, and that they have to be acquired by a sort of special apprenticeship to the craft. To hear all these large words, you would think that the mind of a man of science must be constituted differently from that of his fellow men; but if you will not be frightened by terms,

THE METHOD OF SCIENTIFIC INVESTIGATION: From *Darwiniana* by Thomas Henry Huxley, 1896.

you will discover that you are quite wrong, and that all these terrible apparatus are being used by yourselves every day and every hour of your lives.

3.   There is a well-known incident in one of Molière's plays, where the author makes the hero express unbounded delight on being told that he had been talking prose during the whole of his life. In the same way, I trust, that you will take comfort, and be delighted with yourselves, on the discovery that you have been acting on the principles of inductive and deductive philosophy during the same period. Probably there is not one here who has not in the course of the day had occasion to set in motion a complex train of reasoning, of the very same kind, though differing of course in degree, as that which a scientific man goes through in tracing the causes of natural phenomena.

4.   A very trivial circumstance will serve to exemplify this. Suppose you go into a fruiterer's shop, wanting an apple—you take up one, and, on biting it, you find it is sour; you look at it, and see that it is hard and green. You take up another one, and that too is hard, green, and sour. The shopman offers you a third; but, before biting it, you examine it, and find that it is hard and green, and you immediately say that you will not have it, as it must be sour, like those that you have already tried.

5.   Nothing can be more simple than that, you think; but if you will take the trouble to analyse and trace out into its logical elements what has been done by the mind, you will be greatly surprised. In the first place, you have performed the operation of induction. You found that, in two experiences, hardness and greenness in apples went together with sourness. It was so in the first case, and it was confirmed by the second. True, it is a very small basis, but still it is enough to make an induction from; you generalise the facts, and you expect to find sourness in apples where you get hardness and greenness. You found upon that a general law, that all hard and green apples are sour; and that, so far as it goes, is a perfect induction. Well, having got your natural law in this way, when you are offered another apple which you find is hard and green, you say, "All hard and green apples are sour; this apple is hard and green, therefore this apple is sour." That train of reasoning is what logicians call a syllogism, and has all its various parts and terms—its major premiss, its minor premiss, and its conclusion. And, by the help of further reasoning, which, if drawn out, would have to be exhibited in two or three other syllogisms, you arrive at your final determination, "I will not have that apple." So that, you see, you have, in the first place, established a law by induction, and upon that you have founded a deduction, and reasoned out

the special conclusion of the particular case. Well now, suppose, having got your law, that at some time afterwards, you are discussing the qualities of apples with a friend: you will say to him, "It is a very curious thing, but I find that all hard and green apples are sour!" Your friend says to you, "But how do you know that?" You at once reply, "Oh, because I have tried them over and over again, and have always found them to be so." Well, if we were talking science instead of common sense, we should call that an experimental verification. And, if still opposed, you go further, and say, "I have heard from the people in Somersetshire and Devonshire, where a large number of apples are grown, that they have observed the same thing. It is also found to be the case in Normandy, and in North America. In short, I find it to be the universal experience of mankind wherever attention has been directed to the subject." Whereupon, your friend, unless he is a very unreasonable man, agrees with you, and is convinced that you are quite right in the conclusion you have drawn. He believes, although perhaps he does not know he believes it, that the more extensive verifications are—that the more frequently experiments have been made, and results of the same kind arrived at—that the more varied the conditions under which the same results are attained, the more certain is the ultimate conclusion, and he disputes the question no further. He sees that the experiment has been tried under all sorts of conditions, as to time, place, and people, with the same result; and he says with you, therefore, that the law you have laid down must be a good one, and he must believe it.

6.   In science we do the same thing; the philosopher exercises precisely the same faculties, though in a much more delicate manner. In scientific inquiry it becomes a matter of duty to expose a supposed law to every possible kind of verification, and to take care, moreover, that this is done intentionally, and not left to a mere accident, as in the case of the apples. And in science, as in common life, our confidence in a law is in exact proportion to the absence of variation in the result of our experimental verifications. For instance, if you let go your grasp of an article you may have in your hand, it will immediately fall to the ground. That is a very common verification of one of the best established laws of nature—that of gravitation. The method by which men of science establish the existence of that law is exactly the same as that by which we have established the trivial proposition about the sourness of hard and green apples. But we believe it in such an extensive, thorough, and unhesitating manner because the universal experience of mankind verifies it, and we can verify it ourselves at any

time; and that is the strongest possible foundation on which any natural law can rest.

7.   So much, then, by way of proof that the method of establishing laws in science is exactly the same as that pursued in common life. Let us now turn to another matter (though really it is but another phase of the same question), and that is, the method by which, from the relations of certain phenomena, we prove that some stand in the position of causes towards the others.

8.   I want to put the case clearly before you, and I will therefore show you what I mean by another familiar example. I will suppose that one of you, on coming down in the morning to the parlour of your house, finds that a teapot and some spoons which had been left in the room on the previous evening are gone —the window is open, and you observe the mark of a dirty hand on the window frame, and perhaps, in addition to that, you notice the impress of a hobnailed shoe on the gravel outside. All these phenomena have struck your attention instantly, and before two seconds have passed you say, "Oh, somebody has broken open the window, entered the room, and run off with the spoons and the teapot!" That speech is out of your mouth in a moment. And you will probably add, "I know he has; I am quite sure of it!" You mean to say exactly what you know; but in reality you are giving expression to what is, in all essential particulars, an hypothesis. You do not *know* it at all; it is nothing but an hypothesis rapidly framed in your own mind. And it is an hypothesis founded on a long train of inductions and deductions.

9.   What are those inductions and deductions, and how have you got at this hypothesis? You have observed, in the first place, that the window is open; but by a train of reasoning involving many inductions and deductions, you have probably arrived long before at the general law—and a very good one it is—that windows do not open of themselves; and you therefore conclude that something has opened the window. A second general law that you have arrived at in the same way is, that teapots and spoons do not go out of a window spontaneously, and you are satisfied that, as they are not now where you left them, they have been removed. In the third place, you look at the marks on the window sill, and the shoemarks outside, and you say that in all previous experience the former kind of mark has never been produced by anything else but the hand of a human being; and the same experience shows that no other animal but man at present wears shoes with hobnails in them such as would produce the marks in the gravel. I do not know, even if we could discover any of those "missing links" that are talked about, that they would help us to any

other conclusion! At any rate the law which states our present experience is strong enough for my present purpose. You next reach the conclusion that, as these kinds of marks have not been left by any other animal than man, nor are liable to be formed in any other way than by a man's hand and shoe, the marks in question have been formed by a man in that way. You have, further, a general law, founded on observation and experience, and that, too, is, I am sorry to say, a very universal and unimpeachable one—that some men are thieves; and you assume at once from all these premisses—and that is what constitutes your hypothesis—that the man who made the marks outside and on the window sill, opened the window, got into the room, and stole your teapot and spoons. You have now arrived at a *vera causa* [real cause]; you have assumed a cause which, it is plain, is competent to produce all the phenomena you have observed. You can explain all these phenomena only by the hypothesis of a thief. But that is a hypothetical conclusion, of the justice of which you have no absolute proof at all; it is only rendered highly probable by a series of inductive and deductive reasonings.

10. I suppose your first action, assuming that you are a man of ordinary common sense, and that you have established this hypothesis to your own satisfaction, will very likely be to go off for the police, and set them on the track of the burglar, with the view to the recovery of your property. But just as you are starting with this object, some person comes in, and on learning what you are about, says, "My good friend, you are going on a great deal too fast. How do you know that the man who really made the marks took the spoons? It might have been a monkey that took them, and the man may have merely looked in afterwards." You would probably reply, "Well, that is all very well, but you see it is contrary to all experience of the way teapots and spoons are abstracted; so that, at any rate, your hypothesis is less probable than mine." While you are talking the thing over in this way, another friend arrives, one of that good kind of people that I was talking of a little while ago. And he might say, "Oh, my dear sir, you are certainly going on a great deal too fast. You are most presumptuous. You admit that all these occurrences took place when you were fast asleep, at a time when you could not possibly have know anything about what was taking place. How do you know that the laws of Nature are not suspended during the night? It may be that there has been some kind of supernatural interference in this case." In point of fact, he declares that your hypothesis is one of which you cannot at all demonstrate the truth, and that you are by

no means sure that the laws of Nature are the same when you are asleep as when you are awake.

11. Well, now, you cannot at the moment answer that kind of reasoning. You feel that your worthy friend has you somewhat at a disadvantage. You will feel perfectly convinced in your own mind, however, that you are quite right, and you say to him, "My good friend, I can only be guided by the natural probabilities of the case, and if you will be kind enough to stand aside and permit me to pass, I will go and fetch the police." Well, we will suppose that your journey is successful, and that by good luck you meet with a policeman; that eventually the burglar is found with your property on his person, and the marks correspond to his hand and to his boots. Probably any jury would consider those facts a very good experimental verification of your hypothesis, touching the cause of the abnormal phenomena observed in your parlour, and would act accordingly.

12. Now, in this suppositious case, I have taken phenomena of a very common kind, in order that you might see what are the different steps in an ordinary process of reasoning, if you will only take the trouble to analyse it carefully. All the operations I have described, you will see, are involved in the mind of any man of sense in leading him to a conclusion as to the course he should take in order to make good a robbery and punish the offender. I say that you are led, in that case, to your conclusion by exactly the same train of reasoning as that which a man of science pursues when he is endeavouring to discover the origin and laws of the most occult phenomena. The process is, and always must be, the same; and precisely the same mode of reasoning was employed by Newton and Laplace in their endeavours to discover and define the causes of the movements of the heavenly bodies, as you, with your own common sense, would employ to detect a burglar. The only difference is, that the nature of the inquiry being more abstruse, every step has to be most carefully watched, so that there may not be a single crack or flaw in your hypothesis. A flaw or crack in many of the hypotheses of daily life may be of little or no moment as affecting the general correctness of the conclusions at which we may arrive; but, in a scientific inquiry, a fallacy, great or small, is always of importance, and is sure to be in the long run constantly productive of mischievous, if not fatal results.

13. Do not allow yourselves to be misled by the common notion that an hypothesis is untrustworthy simply because it is an hypothesis. It is often urged, in respect to some scientific conclusion, that, after all, it is only an hypothesis. But what more have we to guide us in nine-tenths of the most important affairs of daily life than hypotheses,

and often very ill-based ones? So that in science, where the evidence of an hypothesis is subjected to the most rigid examination, we may rightly pursue the same course. You may have hypotheses, and hypotheses. A man may say, if he likes, that the moon is made of green cheese: that is an hypothesis. But another man, who has devoted a great deal of time and attention to the subject, and availed himself of the most powerful telescopes and the results of the observations of others, declares that in his opinion it is probably composed of materials very similar to those of which our own earth is made up: and that is also only an hypothesis. But I need not tell you that there is an enormous difference in the value of the two hypotheses. That one which is based on sound scientific knowledge is sure to have a corresponding value; and that which is a mere hasty random guess is likely to have but little value. Every great step in our progress in discovering causes has been made in exactly the same way as that which I have detailed to you. A person observing the occurrence of certain facts and phenomena asks, naturally enough, what process, what kind of operation known to occur in Nature applied to the particular case, will unravel and explain the mystery? Hence you have the scientific hypothesis; and its value will be proportionate to the care and completeness with which its basis has been tested and verified. It is in these matters as in the commonest affairs of practical life: the guess of the fool will be folly, while the guess of the wise man will contain wisdom. In all cases, you see that the value of the result depends on the patience and faithfulness with which the investigator applies to his hypothesis every possible kind of verification.

WORDS

*meaning*  1. Define *induction* and *deduction* (par. 2).  2. Is the green-apple example (par. 4) deductive or inductive? Why?  3. Formal deduction employs *syllogisms* (par. 5). Give an example of a syllogism, indicating its major premise, minor premise, and conclusion.  4. What is the meaning of *natural phenomena* (par. 3) as distinct from *abnormal phenomena* (par. 11) and *occult phenomena* (par. 12)?  5. What is *experimental verification* (par. 5)?

*relationships*  1. What is a *hypothesis* (par. 8)? How does it differ from a law? from a theory?  2. How does *affecting* (par. 12) differ from *effecting?*

SENTENCES

*style*  1. This essay was written and delivered as a lecture to "working-men." Among the devices commonly used in manuscripts written to be read aloud are the frequent use of the second person (direct address to the listener) and the use of informal conversational tags such as *you see* and *well now*. Find examples of both in this essay. 2. Paragraph 7 begins with a fragment. Is it clear? Would the author be as likely to use a fragmentary sentence if this were not to be read aloud? Explain. 3. Find a rhetorical question in paragraph 13.

*rhetorical devices* The phrase "wring from Nature" (par. 2) is an example of which of the following devices: metonymy, alliteration, personification, or onomatopoeia?

## PARAGRAPHS

*coherence* 1. The author maintains coherence by starting many of his sentences with coordinating conjunctions. Find five of these sentences. Do you think that sentences of this kind would be more common in a speech than in an essay? Why or why not? 2. The author's paragraphs often begin with some kind of reference to the words or ideas of the preceding paragraphs. Find three paragraphs that do this. 3. What is the function of paragraph 7? 4. The author uses a variety of techniques to maintain coherence in paragraph 9. Point them out.

## CONTENT AND ORGANIZATION

*central ideas* 1. What is the central idea of this essay? Where is it stated? 2. In paragraph 12 the author remarks one difference between the hypotheses of science and those of everyday life. What is that difference?

*organization* Is this essay developed logically or chronologically? Why?

*assumptions and implications* The author says that we are guided by hypotheses in nine-tenths of daily life (par. 13). List two or more hypotheses that guide your own actions.

## SUGGESTIONS FOR DISCUSSION

1. On what hypotheses do you base your actions if you (a) lend a lawnmower to a friend? (b) buy a used car from "Madman Murdoch, the Workingman's Friend"? (c) refuse to associate with a person of another religion? (d) buy one pair of expensive shoes rather than two pairs of cheap shoes? 2. What is the danger of an induction made on the basis of inadequate evidence? Can you give examples of false conclusions arrived at in this way? 3. Analyze the processes you used to formulate a hypothesis to explain something that interested or puzzled you.

# Use and Abuse of Language

## Russell Baker

### CALL THIS AN ERA?

1.   "Using words that would have made no sense at all to our forebears and will, we hope, make even less to our posterity, please describe the era in which we live."

2.   "If I may rephrase your assignment so that it sounds more incomprehensible and, therefore, less alarming to our audience, you want me to implement an increased level of era-oriented awareness, wordwise, among our audience."

3.   "You have hit the nail squarely on your thumb."

4.   "Thank you, but if we are to get off on the right foot, I must point out that we live in an era when perceptive or agreeable statements no longer hit the nail squarely. Such statements are now simply right on."

5.   "Right on what?"

6.   "We live in an era when people who ask 'Right on what?' turn off millions of their fellow Americans. They turn off these millions because their question reveals that they are not tuned in."

7.   "Fascinating!"

8.   "We live in an era when mildly interesting phenomena are no longer fascinating but invariably fabulous."

9.   "Would you now proceed to fundamentals?"

10.   "Gladly. We live in an era when children can be radicalized, schools politicized, education conceptualized, the country polarized, and our war Vietnamized. And do you know why this is? It is because increasingly."

11.   "Increasingly?"

12.   "Increasingly sensitive, increasingly aware, increasingly perceptive, increasingly alienated, and increasingly so increasingly on."

CALL THIS AN ERA?   © 1970 by The New York Times Company. Reprinted by permission.

13. "Would you sketch a bit of the geography of the era in which we live?"

14. "We live in an era when everyone lives either in a ghetto or in the suburbs—everyone, that is, except the prototypical man of our era, who is, as you know, the forgotten man."

15. "If I may interrupt and recall your attention to the suburbs—isn't there a peculiar quality about those suburbs?"

16. "Yes, and thank you for reminding me. We live in an era when suburbs are lily-white. The forgotten man inhabits neither the ghetto nor the lily-white suburbs, however. He lives in middle America."

17. "With whom?"

18. "With the great silent majority."

19. "Would you discuss a few of the stranger things we do in the era in which we live, things that distinguish us from Americans who have lived in other eras?"

20. "Delighted. We initiate. We exacerbate. We relate. We increasingly alienate."

21. "I don't understand a single one of those stupid words."

22. "That is because you are not relating. You are exacerbating the situation by using strong rhetoric. You are increasingly alienating those who seek only to initiate a meaningful dialogue."

23. "Just a minute! Do you mean to say we live in an era when—?"

24. "Exactly! We live in an era when people speak both rhetoric and meaningful dialogue. An era, moreover, when people who do not engage in rhetoric and meaningful dialogue are not keeping silent, but maintaining a low profile."

25. "We live in an era when a buttoned lip can depress the profile?"

26. "We do."

27. "Fabulous!"

28. "In the era in which we live it is perfectly possible for radio stations to initiate new concepts of community-oriented communications policy. And to admit as much without shame."

29. "Are you suggesting that we live in an era when radio stations are not shame-oriented?"

30. "We live in an era when nobody is shame-oriented. Shame-oriented, in fact, may be the only -oriented that is out of style in the era in which we live. We live in an era in which everyone is new-concept-oriented. That is because new-concept-oriented rhetoric increasingly initiates implementation of growing levels of awareness that

are less likely to be counterproductive if a low-profile-oriented rhetoric image is carefully cultivated. Am I making any sense at all?"

31. "While I am sure the audience will not agree, it seems to me that you are speaking pure idiocy."

32. "You honor me, sir, by suggesting that I am the very model of the man of the era in which we live. Hardcore. Permissiveness. Radiclibs. Cooptation. Winning the peace. Disadvantaged elements . . ."

33. And to loud applause, the expert was led away babbling.

## WORDS

*meaning* 1. Is the author saying in paragraph 1 that many words used in this era have meaning only for those living now? Can one say, then, that there is a common meaning for those words? Do most people agree, for example, on the meaning of *alienate* (par. 12)? What does it mean to you? Does one have to be alienated *from* something? 2. Do all eras have words peculiar to them? 3. When does a word become archaic? 4. At what point does a new word get into dictionaries? 5. What does *wordwise* (par. 2) mean? *The American Heritage Dictionary of the English Language* (1969) says that the "practice of attaching -wise to nouns . . . is of dubious usage on any higher level." Do most of us speak or write on a "higher level"? Should we? Why might you resist using -wise words?

*relationships* Does *expatriate* have anything in common with *alienate*? Does *expatriate* mean the same thing today that it meant a generation ago? According to the dictionary, *expatriate* means one who has left his native land. What does the word mean to you? Was Hemingway correct by having Bill Gorton say (in *The Sun Also Rises,* 1926) to Jake Barnes, "You're an expatriate. You've lost touch with the soil"?

*word choice* 1. What is a cliché? Is *relating* (par. 22) a cliché? If not, why not? If so, why did it become one? 2. Why does the man speaking in paragraph 21 say he does not understand a single word spoken in paragraph 20? Do you understand them? What do they mean? Would your parents or grandparents understand them? 3. The author chooses particular words and phrases such as *right on* (par. 4), *fascinating* (par. 7), *increasingly* (par. 11), *exacerbate* (par. 20), and *fabulous* (par. 27). What do they mean, and why does he choose them?

*exactness* 1. Are the *-ized* words in paragraph 10 exact words? Explain. 2. Given the tone of this piece, what other words might the author have added? 3. Baker uses some contractions (pars. 15 and 21). Could he have used more? If so, why do you think he did not?

## SENTENCES

*style*  Paragraph 2 has one sentence of 34 words; paragraph 7 has one sentence with one word. What does this variation tell you about this piece?

## CONTENT AND ORGANIZATION

*central idea*  Does this dialogue come closest to parody, satire, travesty, or burlesque? Explain.

*assumptions and implications*  Compare this dialogue with "The Schools of Yesteryear: A One-Sided Dialogue" by Randall Jarrell. Comment.

## SUGGESTIONS FOR DISCUSSION

1. What is the author trying to do in this dialogue? Does he succeed? 2. Do you find the dialogue amusing? If so, why? If not, why not? 3. Before you look up the biographical note, try to determine Russell Baker's age. 4. How would you go about trying to change some aspect of society you did not like? 5. Describe slang, cant, or jargon that is overworked in campus conversation and the local college or university paper. Is its use a symptom of pretentiousness, laziness, or ignorance? Explain.

## Calvin Trillin

# NO TELLING, NO SUMMING UP

1.  Benjamin Nangle, a Yale English professor who has been one of the instructors of a fiction-writing course called Daily Themes since 1923, has read about so many young couples parting forever that he long ago lost count. Boys and girls have said goodbye at railroad stations, in dormitory rooms, in cars parked in the suburbs of Midwestern cities, in the booths of dingy restaurants—almost anyplace where the girl can walk slowly out of sight, or the boy can hang his head and listen to the retreating footsteps, or the girl can slam the door. "Boy-girl themes generally fall into two equally bad types," James Folsom, another Daily Themes instructor, once said in a speech. "The first of these deals with a boy—or occasionally a girl—innocent beyond belief, high-minded, studious, morally beyond reproach, who, for some reason which remains unfathomable, is treated

NO TELLING, NO SUMMING UP: From *The New Yorker*, June 11, 1966. Reprinted by permission; © 1966 The New Yorker Magazine, Inc.

with inhuman cruelty by someone of the opposite sex—someone cunningly disguised as a normal human being but in actuality heartless, vicious, sadistic, and corrupt. The second type details the fortunes of two young people who, through the malevolence of fate—or occasionally the malevolence of someone acting through incomprehensible motives of the purest evil—are separated from each other forever."

2. Undergraduates might be expected to consider experiences with girls important enough to write down; undergraduates taking Daily Themes, under pressure to produce a three-hundred-word piece of fiction every day for eight or nine weeks, eventually consider experiences with almost anyone important enough to write down. They begin to observe their roommates. Folsom considers the themes produced by roommate observation better, by and large, than those that result from recalling romances, though he admitted, in the same speech, "It is true that the general picture one gets of roommates when surveying the sizable field of roommate literature as a whole is that they are universally the most nasty, unwholesome, stupid, and despicable young men ever gathered together in one spot."

3. Yale English instructors have been reading daily themes for about sixty years—to the background music of countless writers saying that it is futile to try to teach something so obviously a matter of divine gift as writing, and of countless professors hinting that it is vaguely disreputable to try to teach something so obviously unscholarly as writing. From the start, a theme has been defined as "a part of a short story," a page or two long. "Daily" has always meant daily, or almost daily. "The title of the course is somewhat misleading," the lecturer often says at the first meeting of the class. "There are no themes due on either Saturday or Sunday, or on Thanksgiving. In other respects, however, the course title is not misleading. We mean that one theme is due every day. The first theme is due tomorrow." Undergraduates who are inclined to endure this regimen do not expect their burden to be lightened very often by praise from above. Daily Themes has always been one of the few courses in Yale College to use letter grades (later translated into the numerical grades used in Yale records), and the grade after D has always been W. Nobody is certain what W stands for, but most people believe it means "Worthless." An undergraduate on the way to his weekly conference with his instructor, where he receives marks and criticism on his last five themes, walks in the presence of W's. From the outset, it has been a tenet of Daily Themes that a student should not be permitted to leave a conference without a ray of hope—that somewhere in his five themes there must be at least one adjective that can be commended or one

phrase that is not as bad as all the others—but it is common for an instructor to leave the impression that a ray of hope was not easy to find.

4. To demonstrate what is *not* a daily theme, a lecturer sometimes reads to one of the early classes something called the Jawbone Theme—in which a man wanders through a ghost ship that has washed ashore, idly comes across a human jawbone, and suddenly realizes, to his distress, that he is holding the jawbone of his beloved. Trick endings are anathema to Daily Themes instructors, and telling an anecdote is a foolproof method of receiving a W. In fact, *telling* anything in Daily Themes is dangerous. Like most courses in writing, Daily Themes demands that its students "show, not tell"—show through dialogue and description, rather than tell by pronouncement or plot summary. "Telling" written in the margin of a daily theme is severe criticism, and so is "Summing up"—trying to explain what should have been revealed in the action by tacking on what is meant to be a pregnant last sentence. The most vivid event in the memory of one Daily Themes veteran is a lecture by Nangle that ended with the evils of "summing up." Nangle appealed to the class, almost poignantly, not to submit to him any more themes that ended with the sentence "He walked away in disgust." Wearily leaning over the lectern, he tried to make clear how many themes he had read over the years that ended that way, and how many he was likely to read in the future, no matter how many appeals he made. At that thought, he walked away in disgust.

5. Daily Themes instructors stress that what they consider a good theme is a scene—however mundane—that reveals something about the people in it. "We outlast them," Folsom says. "They run out of the experiences they had always thought they would 'write up someday,' and they have to look around." Looking around, undergraduates are never quite convinced that their daily lives are the stuff that fiction is made of. After the first week or so, most of them begin to find their supply of memorable adventures running thin, and then even mundane scenes seem to disappear from their lives. The world becomes a blank in the twenty-four hours between themes. The normal mood of Daily Themes students on a week night is desperation. They cull anecdotes (and W's) from their friends. They try to goad their roommates into behaving in nasty, unwholesome, stupid, or despicable ways. They probe their memories for goodbyes in high school or during summer vacations. They think of people they have disliked in the past. They strain their ears for overheard dialogue while waiting for green lights. When something out of the ordinary

happens on the campus, they feel delivered. For many years, Yale undergraduates were required to attend morning chapel, and they would all go from there to the post office to pick up their mail. An old vender with a horse and wagon was stationed between the two spots to catch the passing trade. One day, just after chapel was dismissed, the vender's aged horse fell to the pavement and, after a twenty-minute delay, died. Daily Themes instructors say that no horse's death has ever been more widely celebrated in fiction.

6. Normally, girls surpass horses as a subject of daily themes, but that triumph is fairly recent. For forty years—from 1909 to 1949—a collection of daily themes was produced in book form every year, each student contributing his favorite theme and his share of the printing bill. (The books were discontinued when printing costs got too high, and were resumed last year with the money from a recent bequest.) Richard Sewall, who taught Daily Themes for several years in the forties, once read through the hundred or so themes preserved from 1911, and he found only three girls—all of them pleasant and none of them saying goodbye. (One of them, a laundry-bill collector described as "one of those many old-faced little daughters of the poor," belonged to the small band of little old ladies, decrepit panhandlers, quaint Italians, and pathetic young girls who used to creep through the early themes as representatives of the lower classes.) Parents and their ilk appeared as rarely and as pleasantly. The one theme in the 1909 book that deals with generational relations is narrated by a young man who was reluctant to spend an evening with some friends of his parents but later concludes, "No small talk here of the belle of the ball, whose sheltered life furnished naught else; nor the crude accounts of the young men's coatroom, bred of an unbalanced outlook on life. That evening with experience-silvered heads—I would not give ten Proms for it."

7. A hero in last year's Daily Themes book found himself in a similar position:

> "Mother, will you please just leave me alone for a while?"
> "Can't you at least come down and say hello to them?"
> "No—they're your friends, not mine. I don't give a damn whether they ever come over. I don't care about them."
> "Well, they care about you. They want to see you."
> "Well, good for them. I don't want to see them—I don't want to see anyone right now."
> "I don't see how anyone can be so perverse. Is something bothering you?"
> "Yes, the whole damn world bothers me right now so I want

to be up here by myself and I especially don't feel like going down there and being hypocritically pleasant and civil to the Bayleys."

8. The early writers of daily themes had no precise substitutes for girls and parents, but they seemed to derive a lot of enjoyment from the look of the campus and the wonders of nature. A good number of burning logs crackled in cheerful campfires in those days, and a lot of snow was driven against the glistening windowpanes of rustic cabins. A typical nature lover of 1910 wrote, "Around the bend in the piney mountain trail where first the sapphire lake flashes into view I swing, just as the flaming sun sinks below the last azure hill of the intervale, flecking with pink and gold every fleecy August cloud." Going through most of the old Daily Themes books, Sewall found that the subject matter had not been greatly affected by the upheavals of the First World War and the Depression—both of which were pretty much ignored as subjects themselves. In the twenties and thirties, the language of the themes gradually lost some of its nineteenth-century flavor, but if the writers were having any serious confrontations with girls or parents or roommates, they were unwilling to write them down. The subject matter of the themes began to broaden at the time of the Second World War, but even today half the themes are still about college life. Some subjects are so common that instructors talk of the Mixer Theme, the Shoot Down (it is usually the boy who is shot down by the girl, occasionally at a mixer), the Lonely Theme (people are often lonely at mixers and after being shot down), and—a voice from the past—the Panhandler Theme. "There is also the Summer Job Theme and the Growing Up Theme," Folsom says. "And the theme about adventures in New York. There's a strong sub-genre of the New York Theme about being approached by a homosexual." Daily Themes writers are not known for their upbeat endings. Michael Cowan, who is one of the instructors of the course this year, says, "Although you can find happiness experiences, fulfillment experiences—sexual fulfillment or a guy getting elected to a club—the average story turns the other way. People laugh if someone reads a theme that implies any sort of easy happiness." There is some evidence, however, that today's undergraduates are not as far from musing on the beauties of azure hills as they seem. "Now we get the guy sitting on the beach musing about the girl he's slept with the night before," Folsom says. "Sometimes I think they've just replaced Swinburne romanticism with Hemingway romanticism."

9. Before the Daily Themes course was five years old, John Berdan, who taught it from 1907 until his retirement, in 1941, had

established the criteria governing the themes in the form of eight slogans, most of which lasted, without alteration, for more than fifty years. (But by the fifties the same slogans that had once brought forth flowery descriptions of nature and football were producing spare dialogues between surly boy and unwilling girl, or careful accounts of the most disgusting event of the weekend.) For the past several years, the slogans have not been used word for word as lecture topics, and teaching methods have become more varied now that the regular course has been supplemented by sophomore seminars at some of Yale's residential colleges. But Berdan's influence remains, even if modern students miss the opportunity of seeing him chalk a slogan in huge letters on the blackboard, turn to the class, and announce, "Individualize by Specific Detail!" Speaking before secondary-school English teachers at a conference sponsored by the Yale Master of Arts in Teaching Program, Sewall called "Individualize by Specific Detail" the eyeopener in Daily Themes' attempt to revive the sensitivity to detail that is often buried in secondary schools under the weight of parsed sentences and dull source themes— a "return to the vivid, honest, and direct observation of children." At a later conference, Nangle cited "A young, rather attractive girl stood on the street corner" as an example of the type of sentence that young, rather unsuspecting Daily Themes writers offer up for annihilation during the first week of the course. "Young?" Nangle asked. "How young? Two? Five? Twelve? Eighteen? Twenty-six? Attractive? What constitutes attraction? Color of hair, beauty of face or figure, mode of attire? Attractive to what instinct—the maternal, the sexual, the aesthetic, or some other? Can you see her?" After a conference or two, Daily Themes students who have been observing their roommates begin to observe them a bit more closely.

10. "Vivify by Range of Appeal!" Berdan would exhort after he had despaired of making any progress in persuading students to Individualize by Specific Detail. "Characterize by Speech and Gesture! Clarify by Point of View! Unify by a Single Impression! Combine Details for Coherence! Charge Words with Connotation! Choose Words for their Sounds!" In an effort to remind students that they had sound and odor as well as sight at their disposal (Vivify by Range of Appeal), Berdan would write a word like "garbage" or "perfume" on the board and wordlessly pass out paper. At the following lecture, with the reeking results in his hand, he would preach moderation in all things.

11. Today, the slogans have been replaced by "a kind of

brushfire approach," Folsom says—concentrating on whatever evils seem most widespread in the week's themes. There is never any shortage of horrible examples. Inevitably, some of the themes turned in during the first week of lectures are sensational tales of horrifying violence, and they are often followed by what Folsom calls Lost in the Jungle Week. Discouraged from the sensational ("Gentlemen, it is not necessary to kill off your grandmother for our benefit"), undergraduates often turn toward the scatological. The use of obscenity and swearing for effect is a fairly recent phenomenon. Looking through the themes of the Roaring Twenties, Sewall found "only a few 'damns,' one timid 'goddamn,' and one mild four-letter word." This and the fact that most of the themes seemed more romantic than roaring led him to conclude that Yale was suffering from a slight cultural lag. (The Class Book poll of seniors in 1925 showed their favorite novel to be *A Tale of Two Cities*.) By 1933, Daily Themes writers were catching up, with sentences like "When in hell would the damn music end?" For the past several years, Folsom has found it necessary to explain in an early lecture that realism cannot be obtained merely by sprinkling the page arbitrarily with obscenity. In a theme of only three hundred words or so, it is often not very difficult to see where the writer went wrong, and the clinker caused by an ill-chosen word can be deafening. (Nangle's favorite is a romantic description of a lovely girl that ends with the sun striking her "shiny blond pate.") The themes read in class remain anonymous, and some who have taken the course believe that the most important lesson it teaches an undergraduate is how to look as contemptuous as everyone else in the room while his own theme is being read.

12.   When Daily Themes advocates are told that writing courses belong in trade schools, they often answer that Daily Themes is the best course in literary criticism at Yale—that, as Folsom once said in a speech, it teaches "by example, rather than by precept, that the proper question to ask in the interpretation of literature is not 'What does the story mean?' but, rather, 'How does the story work?' " To those who say that writing cannot be taught, the instructors answer that it can at least be criticized, and that, to judge from the results, it can be improved by taking Daily Themes—although they don't pretend to know just what it is in the process that causes the improvement. "At least, it purges some of the nonsense from their style," says Sewall. "Sure, it may be rule of thumb, and a refined mind can find all kinds of philosophical arguments against it, but, damn it, it works. At the end of the semester, they write better than they did at the beginning."

13. Harry Berger, who once taught Daily Themes and is now chairman of the English Department of the University of California at Santa Cruz, says that the Daily Themes method is "fine as an exercise—a way of getting guys to do certain aspects of craft that they otherwise wouldn't do," but he adds, "The danger is that guys really think they're getting some kind of magic formula for being successful writers." Some students do fall into a formula. Attempting to avoid some of the more obvious means of getting a W, they tend to write in the flat dialogues that are associated with Hemingway or John O'Hara, and the dictum that they must show rather than tell can force them to put a character through some strenuous exercises in order to avoid telling the reader outright what is going on. But Daily Themes instructors say that after Thanksgiving, when the themes give way to weekly short stories, the undergraduates feel no special allegiance to the rules that haunted their autumn evenings.

14. Before that emancipation, most Daily Themes students accept the combination of daily grind and faint encouragement stoically, like Marine recruits who know they are voluntarily enduring consistent mistreatment. Occasionally, though, it all becomes too much to bear, and the student reacts (as he reacts to many of his daily difficulties) by writing a theme about it—purging himself of his anger and solving the problem of what to hand in the next morning. The exasperation of taking the course is one of the few theme subjects that have remained constant through the years. One piece of particularly angry interior dialogue that Nangle has saved was written by an undergraduate named Johnson in the early fifties. It begins, "By God he better understand this one. That old Wilder bastard better get *this* one. Ten themes of mine he's read now— ten themes and I don't think he's caught one thing I've said. Jesus, that guy must still be in the eighteenth century. Well, um, kaff, Mr. Jacobi, it's perfectly obvious that the girl here is in perfect control of the situation, um, kaff. No, Mr. Wilder, you blind old bastard, the girl is *not* in control of the situation, the girl is making an *ass* of herself, and if you had one-half an eye in your head you'd see that. . . . *I* get it. My *roommates* get it. My *friends* get it. . . . How did an old quack like you ever get to teach this course anyway?"

15. Johnson got a B for that one.


WORDS

*meaning*  Define *tenet* (par. 3), *anathema* (par. 4), *mundane* (par. 5), *scatological* and *pate* (par. 11), *dictum* (par. 13), and *stoically* (par. 14).

*word choice*  Why would a Yale instructor have referred to his students as *guys* (par. 13)? Does it have anything to do with their writing like Hemingway or O'Hara?

## SENTENCES

*style*  1. Trillin writes about the style of the student themes. How does his own style fit his subject?  2. There are only a few words under *meaning,* and you probably already knew most of them. Does this tell you anything about the author's style?  3. What does a vocabulary have to do with style?  4. What do you think is meant by "the flat dialogues that are associated with Hemingway or John O'Hara" (par. 13)?

*rhetorical devices*  1. The author relies on an abundance of examples. Choose any paragraph that uses examples and discuss their effectiveness. 2. Paragraph 7 uses an extended quoted example. How well does it serve the author's purpose? Would you use more or fewer examples of this kind? Explain.  3. To what extent does Trillin rely on similes? Choose one and point out how it is or is not successful.  4. What is wrong with writing about the death of a horse (par. 5)?  5. How do you account for the difference in style between the 1909 theme (par. 6) and the theme quoted in paragraph 7?

## PARAGRAPHS

*coherence*  Consider the transition between paragraphs 6 and 7. How are both paragraphs dealing with heroes in similar positions?

*topic sentences*  Review the first sentence of each paragraph. Approximately nine begin with instructors, four with students, and two with themes. How many of the paragraphs develop from the first sentences? Which sentences can be considered topic sentences?

## CONTENT AND ORGANIZATION

*central idea*  1. Is the central idea expressed in paragraph 4? If so, state it; if it is not there, where is it? What does paragraph 4 have to do with the title?  2. Explain the question "How does the story work?" (par. 12). How does Trillin's essay "work"?  3. What do you think John Ciardi was indicating by titling one of his books *How Does a Poem Mean?*

*organization*  1. What is Trillin's basic organizational plan? What part does chronology play in the development? Could the essay be organized around the types of themes such as *jawbone* (par. 4) or *mixer* (par. 8)? Could it be organized around the various men who taught the course? 2. If you were given these fifteen paragraphs, each as a separate piece of paper, not numbered, how would you outline the essay?

*assumptions and implications*  Did Johnson get a B because he railed against the instructor or because he wrote well (pars. 14–15)?

SUGGESTIONS FOR DISCUSSION

1. Is writing a daily theme desirable for today's student, or should this practice have been left in the nineteenth century? 2. Is writing a daily theme comparable to practicing the piano two hours a day? 3. Does the fact that "they write better than they did at the beginning" (par. 12) justify the method? 4. What part does discipline play in the learning process? 5. Considering the various kinds of modern communications, do you think writing is as important as it was once thought to be? 6. How many themes could you write each week and still "develop" as a writer?

*Ralph Ellison*

# BRAVE WORDS FOR
# A STARTLING OCCASION

1. First, as I express my gratitude for this honor which you have bestowed on me, let me say that I take it that you are rewarding my efforts rather than my not quite fully achieved attempt at a major novel. Indeed, if I were asked in all seriousness just what I considered to be the chief significance of *Invisible Man* as a fiction, I would reply: Its experimental attitude, and its attempt to return to the mood of personal moral responsibility for democracy which typified the best of our nineteenth-century fiction. That my first novel should win this most coveted prize must certainly indicate that there is a crisis in the American novel. You as critics have told us so, and current fiction sales would indicate that the reading public agrees. Certainly the younger novelists concur. The explosive nature of events mocks our brightest efforts. And the very "facts" which the naturalists assumed would make us free have lost the power to protect us from despair. Controversy now rages over just what aspects of American experience are suitable for novelistic treatment.

BRAVE WORDS FOR A STARTLING OCCASION:  Copyright © 1963, 1964 by Ralph Ellison. Reprinted from *Shadow and Act,* by Ralph Ellison by permission of Random House, Inc. First presented as a speech at the National Book Awards presentation ceremony, January 27, 1953.

The prestige of the theorists of the so-called novel of manners has been challenged. Thus after a long period of stability we find our assumptions concerning the novel being called into question. And though I was only vaguely aware, it was this growing crisis which shaped the writing of *Invisible Man.*

2. After the usual apprenticeship of imitation and seeking with delight to examine my experience through the discipline of the novel, I became gradually aware that the forms of so many of the works which impressed me were too restricted to contain the experience which I knew. The diversity of American life with its extreme fluidity and openness seemed too vital and alive to be caught for more than the briefest instant in the tight well-made Jamesian novel, which was, for all its artistic perfection, too concerned with "good taste" and stable areas. Nor could I safely use the forms of the "hard-boiled" novel, with its dedication to physical violence, social cynicism and understatement. Understatement depends, after all, upon commonly held assumptions and my minority status rendered all such assumptions questionable. There was also a problem of language, and even dialogue, which, with its hard-boiled stance and its monosyllabic utterance, is one of the shining achievements of twentieth-century American writing. For despite the notion that its rhythms were those of everyday speech, I found that when compared with the rich babel of idiomatic expression around me, a language full of imagery and gesture and rhetorical canniness, it was embarrassingly austere. Our speech I found resounding with an alive language swirling with over three hundred years of American living, a mixture of the folk, the Biblical, the scientific and the political. Slangy in one instance, academic in another, loaded poetically with imagery at one moment, mathematically bare of imagery in the next. As for the rather rigid concepts of reality which informed a number of the works which impressed me and to which I owe a great deal, I was forced to conclude that reality was far more mysterious and uncertain, and more exciting, and still, despite its raw violence and capriciousness, more promising. To attempt to express that American experience which has carried one back and forth and up and down the land and across, and across again the great river, from freight train to Pullman car, from contact with slavery to contact with a world of advanced scholarship, art and science, is simply to burst such neatly understated forms of the novel asunder.

3. A novel whose range was both broader and deeper was needed. And in my search I found myself turning to our classical nineteenth-century novelists. I felt that except for the work of William

Faulkner something vital had gone out of American prose after Mark Twain. I came to believe that the writers of that period took a much greater responsibility for the condition of democracy and, indeed, their works were imaginative projections of the conflicts within the human heart which arose when the sacred principles of the Constitution and the Bill of Rights clashed with the practical exigencies of human greed and fear, hate and love. Naturally I was attracted to these writers as a Negro. Whatever they thought of my people per se, in their imaginative economy the Negro symbolized both the man lowest down and the mysterious, underground aspect of human personality. In a sense the Negro was the gauge of the human condition as it waxed and waned in our democracy. These writers were willing to confront the broad complexities of American life and we are the richer for their having done so.

4. Thus to see America with an awareness of its rich diversity and its almost magical fluidity and freedom, I was forced to conceive of a novel unburdened by the narrow naturalism which has led, after so many triumphs, to the final and unrelieved despair which marks so much of our current fiction. I was to dream of a prose which was flexible, and swift as American change is swift, confronting the inequalities and brutalities of our society forthrightly, but yet thrusting forth its images of hope, human fraternity and individual self-realization. It would use the richness of our speech, the idiomatic expression and the rhetorical flourishes from past periods which are still alive among us. And despite my personal failures, there must be possible a fiction which, leaving sociology to the scientists, can arrive at the truth about the human condition, here and now, with all the bright magic of a fairy tale.

5. What has been missing from so much experimental writing has been the passionate will to dominate reality as well as the laws of art. This will is the true source of the experimental attitude. We who struggle with form and with America should remember Eidothea's advice to Menelaus when in the *Odyssey* he and his friends are seeking their way home. She tells him to seize her father, Proteus, and to hold him fast "however he may struggle and fight. He will turn into all sorts of shapes to try you," she says, "into all the creatures that live and move upon the earth, into water, into blazing fire; but you must hold him fast and press him all the harder. When he is himself, and questions you in the same shape that he was when you saw him in his bed, let the old man go; and then, sir, ask which god it is who is angry, and how you shall make your way homewards over the fish-giving sea."

6. For the novelist, Proteus stands for both America and the inheritance of illusion through which all men must fight to achieve reality; the offended god stands for our sins against those principles we all hold sacred. The way home we seek is that condition of man's being at home in the world, which is called love, and which we term democracy. Our task then is always to challenge the apparent forms of reality—that is, the fixed manners and values of the few, and to struggle with it until it reveals its mad, vari-implicated chaos, its false faces, and on until it surrenders its insight, its truth. We are fortunate as American writers in that with our variety of racial and national traditions, idioms and manners, we are yet one. On its profoundest level American experience is of a whole. Its truth lies in its diversity and swiftness of change. Through forging forms of the novel worthy of it, we achieve not only the promise of our lives, but we anticipate the resolution of those world problems of humanity which for a moment seem to those who are in awe of statistics completely insoluble.

7. Whenever we as Americans have faced serious crises we have returned to fundamentals; this, in brief, is what I have tried to do.

## WORDS

*connotation* 1. "A Startling Occasion," in the title, is clear enough, but why "Brave Words"? 2. What is implied by a *crisis* in the American novel (par. 1)? Is the author affecting a kind of humility? 3. How can the *hard-boiled* novel be dedicated to understatement (par. 2)? 4. What is a *hard-boiled stance* (par. 2)? 5. How can speech be *embarrassingly austere* (par. 2)?

*word choice* 1. How does Ellison's word choice illustrate "an alive language swirling" (par. 2)? 2. Contrast *slangy* and *academic* (par. 2). 3. How can speech be "mathematically bare of imagery" (par. 2)? 4. Why does Ellison use *passionate will* (par. 5) rather than, say, *determination?* 5. Account for the choice of the italicized words in the sentence "The way *home* we seek is that condition of man's being at *home* in the world, which is called *love,* and which we term *democracy"* (par. 6).

## SENTENCES

*emphasis* On at least one occasion (par. 2) Ellison uses a grammatically incomplete sentence. What effect does it have? Assuming that it creates a kind of force on the printed page, how would the audience have heard it?

*rhetorical devices* 1. The author piles word upon word and phrase upon phrase—"a language full of imagery and gesture and rhetorical canniness" (par. 2). Pick out a few more examples and discuss their rhetorical effect. Is this technique more appropriate to a speech than to a written piece? How do you imagine Ellison's audience reacted to this speech? 2. How successful is the allusion to the episode from the *Odyssey* (par. 5)? Would the audience have to be familiar with Homer's work, or is Ellison's version adequate by itself?

## PARAGRAPHS

*coherence* 1. The speech begins with the word *First*. Do you find a second, third, fourth? Why not? Are they necessary? Are they implied? If you had to go through the speech numbering the points, where would you put the numbers? 2. Could you consider paragraph 1 an introduction and paragraph 7 a summary? Explain. 3. To what extent do paragraphs 2–6 each contain single, unified ideas? 4. The name of the novel for which Ellison received his award is mentioned only in paragraph 1. Thereafter he does not discuss the novel *per se* but what he tried to do. What does his speech tell you about his novel?

## CONTENT AND ORGANIZATION

*central ideas* 1. What does paragraph 1 appear to promise? Is that promise fulfilled in the speech? 2. What "fundamentals" have Americans returned to (par. 7)?

*organization* Could you argue that his speech is organized around the single sentence "In a sense the Negro was the gauge of the human condition as it waxed and waned in our democracy" (par. 3)? If this sentence will not explain the organization, can you find another that will?

## SUGGESTIONS FOR DISCUSSION

1. In one of his essays, Ellison refers to *Huckleberry Finn* as having "a search for images of black and white fraternity." Do you think this "search" is what he is referring to when he says that except for the work of Faulkner "something vital had gone out of American prose after Mark Twain" (par. 3)? Do you agree with this thesis? Can you think of exceptions? 2. Write an essay in which you compare the "search" in *Huckleberry Finn* with a comparable "search" in a novel or story by William Faulkner. 3. Discuss an "American" prose (par. 4). 4. What kind of fiction would "arrive at the truth about the human condition" (par. 4)?

# George Orwell

# POLITICS AND THE
# ENGLISH LANGUAGE

1. Most people who bother with the matter at all would admit
that the English language is in a bad way, but it is generally assumed
that we cannot by conscious action do anything about it. Our civilization is decadent and our language—so the argument runs—must
inevitably share in the general collapse. It follows that any struggle
against the abuse of language is a sentimental archaism, like preferring candles to electric light or hansom cabs to aeroplanes. Underneath this lies the half-conscious belief that language is a natural
growth and not an instrument which we shape for our own purposes.

2. Now, it is clear that the decline of a language must ultimately have political and economic causes: it is not due simply to the
bad influence of this or that individual writer. But an effect can become a cause, reinforcing the original cause and producing the same
effect in an intensified form, and so on indefinitely. A man may take
to drink because he feels himself to be a failure, and then fail all the
more completely because he drinks. It is rather the same thing that is
happening to the English language. It becomes ugly and inaccurate because our thoughts are foolish, but the slovenliness of our language
makes it easier for us to have foolish thoughts. The point is that the
process is reversible. Modern English, especially written English, is
full of bad habits which spread by imitation and which can be avoided
if one is willing to take the necessary trouble. If one gets rid of these
habits one can think more clearly, and to think clearly is a necessary
first step towards political regeneration: so that the fight against bad
English is not frivolous and is not the exclusive concern of professional writers. I will come back to this presently, and I hope that by
that time the meaning of what I have said here will have become
clearer. Meanwhile, here are five specimens of the English language as
it is now habitually written.

3. These five passages have not been picked out because they
are especially bad—I could have quoted far worse if I had chosen—

POLITICS AND THE ENGLISH LANGUAGE: From *Shooting an Elephant and Other
Essays,* copyright, 1945, 1946, 1949, 1950, by Sonia Brownell Orwell. Reprinted by permission of Harcourt Brace Jovanovich, Inc.

but because they illustrate various of the mental vices from which we now suffer. They are a little below the average, but are fairly representative samples. I number them so that I can refer back to them when necessary:

(1) I am not, indeed, sure whether it is not true to say that the Milton who once seemed not unlike a seventeenth-century Shelley had not become, out of an experience ever more bitter in each year, more alien [*sic*] to the founder of that Jesuit sect which nothing could induce him to tolerate.

Professor Harold Laski
(Essay in *Freedom of Expression*)

(2) Above all, we cannot play ducks and drakes with a native battery of idioms which prescribes such egregious collocations of vocables as the Basic *put up with* for *tolerate* or *put at a loss* for *bewilder*.

Professor Lancelot Hogben (*Interglossa*)

(3) On the one side we have the free personality: by definition it is not neurotic, for it has neither conflict nor dream. Its desires, such as they are, are transparent, for they are just what institutional approval keeps in the forefront of consciousness; another institutional pattern would alter their number and intensity; there is little in them that is natural, irreducible, or culturally dangerous. But *on the other side*, the social bond itself is nothing but the mutual reflection of these self-secure integrities. Recall the definition of love. Is not this the very picture of a small academic? Where is there a place in this hall of mirrors for either personality or fraternity?

Essay on psychology in *Politics* (New York)

(4) All the "best people" from the gentlemen's clubs, and all the frantic fascist captains, united in common hatred of Socialism and bestial horror of the rising tide of the mass revolutionary movement, have turned to acts of provocation, to foul incendiarism, to medieval legends of poisoned wells, to legalize their own destruction of proletarian organizations, and rouse the agitated petty-bourgeoisie to chauvinistic fervour on behalf of the fight against the revolutionary way out of the crisis.

Communist pamphlet

(5) If a new spirit *is* to be infused into this old country, there is one thorny and contentious reform which must be tackled, and that is the humanization and galvanization of the B.B.C. Timidity here will bespeak canker and atrophy of the soul. The heart of Britain may be sound and of strong beat, for instance, but the British lion's roar at present is like that of Bottom in Shakespeare's *Midsummer Night's Dream*—as gentle as any sucking dove. A virile

new Britain cannot continue indefinitely to be traduced in the eyes or rather ears, of the world by the effete languors of Langham Place, brazenly masquerading as "standard English." When the Voice of Britain is heard at nine o'clock, better far and infinitely less ludicrous to hear aitches honestly dropped than the present priggish, inflated, inhibited, school-ma'amish arch braying of blameless bashful mewing maidens!

Letter in Tribune

4.   Each of these passages has faults of its own, but, quite apart from avoidable ugliness, two qualities are common to all of them. The first is staleness of imagery; the other is lack of precision. The writer either has a meaning and cannot express it, or he inadvertently says something else, or he is almost indifferent as to whether his words mean anything or not. This mixture of vagueness and sheer incompetence is the most marked characteristic of modern English prose, and especially of any kind of political writing. As soon as certain topics are raised, the concrete melts into the abstract and no one seems able to think of turns of speech that are not hackneyed: prose consists less and less of *words* chosen for the sake of their meaning, and more and more of *phrases* tacked together like the sections of a prefabricated hen-house. I list below, with notes and examples, various of the tricks by means of which the work of prose-construction is habitually dodged:

5.   *Dying metaphors.* A newly invented metaphor assists thought by evoking a visual image, while on the other hand a metaphor which is technically "dead" (e.g. *iron resolution*) has in effect reverted to being an ordinary word and can generally be used without loss of vividness. But in between these two classes there is a huge dump of worn-out metaphors which have lost all evocative power and are merely used because they save people the trouble of inventing phrases for themselves. Examples are: *Ring the changes on, take up the cudgels for, toe the line, ride roughshod over, stand shoulder to shoulder with, play into the hands of, no axe to grind, grist to the mill, fishing in troubled waters, on the order of the day, Achilles' heel, swan song, hotbed.* Many of these are used without knowledge of their meaning (what is a "rift," for instance?), and incompatible metaphors are frequently mixed, a sure sign that the writer is not interested in what he is saying. Some metaphors now current have been twisted out of their original meaning without those who use them even being aware of the fact. For example, *toe the line* is sometimes written *tow the line*. Another example is *the hammer and the anvil,* now always

used with the implication that the anvil gets the worst of it. In real life it is always the anvil that breaks the hammer, never the other way about: a writer who stopped to think what he was saying would be aware of this, and would avoid perverting the original phrase.

6. *Operators* or *verbal false limbs.* These save the trouble of picking out appropriate verbs and nouns, and at the same time pad each sentence with extra syllables which give it an appearance of symmetry. Characteristic phrases are *render inoperative, militate against, make contact with, be subjected to, give rise to, give grounds for, have the effect of, play a leading part* (*role*) *in, make itself felt, take effect, exhibit a tendency to, serve the purpose of,* etc., etc. The keynote is the elimination of simple verbs. Instead of being a single word, such as *break, stop, spoil, mend, kill,* a verb becomes a *phrase,* made up of a noun or adjective tacked on to some general-purposes verb such as *prove, serve, form, play, render.* In addition, the passive voice is wherever possible used in preference to the active, and noun constructions are used instead of gerunds (*by examination of* instead of *by examining*). The range of verbs is further cut down by means of the *-ize* and *de-* formations, and the banal statements are given an appearance of profundity by means of the *not un-* formation. Simple conjunctions and prepositions are replaced by such phrases as *with respect to, having regard to, the fact that, by dint of, in view of, in the interests of, on the hypothesis that;* and the ends of sentences are saved by anticlimax by such resounding common-places as *greatly to be desired, cannot be left out of account, a development to be expected in the near future, deserving of serious consideration, brought to a satisfactory conclusion,* and so on and so forth.

7. *Pretentious diction.* Words like *phenomenon, element, individual* (as noun), *objective, categorical, effective, virtual, basic, primary, promote, constitute, exhibit, exploit, utilize, eliminate, liquidate,* are used to dress up simple statements and give an air of scientific impartiality to biased judgments. Adjectives like *epoch-making, epic, historic, unforgettable, triumphant, age-old, inevitable, inexorable, veritable,* are used to dignify the sordid processes of international politics, while writing that aims at glorifying war usually takes on an archaic colour, its characteristic words being: *realm, throne, chariot, mailed fist, trident, sword, shield, buckler, banner, jackboot, clarion.* Foreign words and expressions such as *cul de sac, ancien régime, deus ex machina, mutatis mutandis, status quo, gleichschaltung, weltanschauung,* are used to give an air of culture and elegance. Except for

the useful abbreviations *i.e, e.g.,* and *etc.,* there is no real need for any of the hundreds of foreign phrases now current in English. Bad writers, and especially scientific, political and sociological writers, are nearly always haunted by the notion that Latin or Greek words are grander than Saxon ones, and unnecessary words like *expedite, ameliorate, predict, extraneous, deracinated, clandestine, subaqueous* and hundreds of others constantly gain ground from their Anglo-Saxon opposite numbers.[1] The jargon peculiar to Marxist writing (*hyena, hangman, cannibal, petty bourgeois, these gentry, lacquey, flunkey, mad dog, White Guard,* etc.) consists largely of words and phrases translated from Russian, German or French; but the normal way of coining a new word is to use a Latin or Greek root with the appropriate affix and, where necessary, the size formation. It is often easier to make up words of this kind (*deregionalize, impermissible, extramarital, non-fragmentary,* and so forth) than to think up the English words that will cover one's meaning. The result, in general, is an increase in slovenliness and vagueness.

8. *Meaningless words.* In certain kinds of writing, particularly in art criticism and literary criticism, it is normal to come across long passages which are almost completely lacking in meaning.[2] Words like *romantic, plastic, values, human, dead, sentimental, natural, vitality,* as used in art criticism, are strictly meaningless, in the sense that they not only do not point to any discoverable object, but are hardly ever expected to do so by the reader. When one critic writes, "The outstanding feature of Mr. X's work is its living quality," while another writes, "The immediately striking thing about Mr. X's work is its peculiar deadness," the reader accepts this as a simple difference of opinion. If words like *black* and *white* were involved, instead of the jargon words *dead* and *living,* he would see at once that language was being used in an improper way. Many political words are similarly abused.

[1] An interesting illustration of this is the way in which the English flower names which were in use till very recently are being ousted by Greek ones, *snapdragon* becoming *antirrhinum, forget-me-not* becoming *myosotis,* etc. It is hard to see any practical reason for this change of fashion: it is probably due to an instinctive turning-away from the more homely word and a vague feeling that the Greek word is scientific.

[2] Example: "Comfort's catholicity of perception and image, strangely Whitmanesque in range, almost the exact opposite in aesthetic compulsion, continues to evoke that trembling atmospheric accumulative hinting at a cruel, an inexorably serene timelessness. . . . Wrey Gardiner scores by aiming at simple bull's-eyes with precision. Only they are not so simple, and through this contented sadness runs more than the surface bitter-sweet of resignation." (*Poetry Quarterly.*)

The word *Fascism* has now no meaning except in so far as it signifies "something not desirable." The words *democracy, socialism, freedom, patriotic, realistic, justice,* have each of them several different meanings which cannot be reconciled with one another. In the case of a word like *democracy,* not only is there no agreed definition, but the attempt to make one is resisted from all sides. It is almost universally felt that when we call a country democratic we are praising it: consequently the defenders of every kind of régime claim that it is a democracy, and fear that they might have to stop using the word if it were tied down to any one meaning. Words of this kind are often used in a consciously dishonest way. That is, the person who uses them has his own private definition, but allows his hearer to think he means something quite different. Statements like *Marshal Pétain was a true patriot, The Soviet Press is the freest in the world, The Catholic Church is opposed to persecution,* are almost always made with intent to deceive. Other words used in variable meanings, in most cases more or less dishonestly, are: *class, totalitarian, science, progressive, reactionary, bourgeois, equality.*

9. Now that I have made this catalogue of swindles and perversions, let me give another example of the kind of writing that they lead to. This time it must of its nature be an imaginary one. I am going to translate a passage of good English into modern English of the worst sort. Here is a well-known verse from *Ecclesiastes:*

> I returned and saw under the sun, that the race is not to the swift, nor the battle to the strong, neither yet bread to the wise, nor yet riches to men of understanding, nor yet favour to men of skill; but time and chance happeneth to them all.

10. Here it is in modern English:

> Objective consideration of contemporary phenomena compels the conclusion that success or failure in competitive activities exhibits no tendency to be commensurate with innate capacity, but that a considerable element of the unpredictable must invariably be taken into account.

11. This is a parody, but not a very gross one. Exhibit (3), above, for instance, contains several patches of the same kind of English. It will be seen that I have not made a full translation. The beginning and ending of the sentence follow the original meaning fairly closely, but in the middle the concrete illustrations—race, battle, bread —dissolve into the vague phrase "success or failure in competitive activities." This had to be so, because no modern writer of the kind

I am discussing—no one capable of using phrases like "objective consideration of contemporary phenomena"—would ever tabulate his thoughts in that precise and detailed way. The whole tendency of modern prose is away from concreteness. Now analyse these two sentences a little more closely. The first contains forty-nine words but only sixty syllables, and all its words are those of everyday life. The second contains thirty-eight words of ninety syllables: eighteen of its words are from Latin roots, and one from Greek. The first sentence contains six vivid images, and only one phrase ("time and chance") that could be called vague. The second contains not a single fresh, arresting phrase, and in spite of its ninety syllables it gives only a shortened version of the meaning contained in the first. Yet without a doubt it is the second kind of sentence that is gaining ground in modern English. I do not want to exaggerate. This kind of writing is not yet universal, and outcrops of simplicity will occur here and there in the worst-written page. Still, if you or I were told to write a few lines on the uncertainty of human fortunes, we should probably come much nearer to my imaginary sentence than to the one from *Ecclesiastes*.

12.   As I have tried to show, modern writing at its worst does not consist in picking out words for the sake of their meaning and inventing images in order to make the meaning clearer. It consists in gumming together long strips of words which have already been set in order by someone else, and making the results presentable by sheer humbug. The attraction of this way of writing is that it is easy. It is easier—even quicker, once you have the habit—to say *In my opinion it is not an unjustifiable assumption that* than to say *I think*. If you use ready-made phrases, you not only don't have to hunt about for words; you also don't have to bother with the rhythms of your sentences, since these phrases are generally so arranged as to be more or less euphonious. When you are composing in a hurry—when you are dictating to a stenographer, for instance, or making a public speech—it is natural to fall into a pretentious, Latinized style. Tags like *a consideration which we should do well to bear in mind* or *a conclusion to which all of us would readily assent* will save many a sentence from coming down with a bump. By using stale metaphors, similes and idioms, you save much mental effort, at the cost of leaving your meaning vague, not only for your reader but for yourself. This is the significance of mixed metaphors. The sole aim of a metaphor is to call up a visual image. When these images clash—as in *The Fascist octopus has sung its swan song, the jackboot is thrown into the melting pot*—it can be taken as certain that the writer is not seeing a mental

image of the objects he is naming; in other words he is not really thinking. Look again at the examples I gave at the beginning of this essay. Professor Laski (1) uses five negatives in fifty-three words. One of these is superfluous, making nonsense of the whole passage, and in addition there is the slip *alien* for akin, making further nonsense, and several avoidable pieces of clumsiness which increase the general vagueness. Professor Hogben (2) plays ducks and drakes with a battery which is able to write prescriptions, and, while disapproving of the everyday phrase *put up with,* is unwilling to look *egregious* up in the dictionary and see what it means; (3), if one takes an uncharitable attitude towards it, is simply meaningless: probably one could work out its intended meaning by reading the whole of the article in which it occurs. In (4), the writer knows more or less what he wants to say, but an accumulation of stale phrases chokes him like tea leaves blocking a sink. In (5), words and meaning have almost parted company. People who write in this manner usually have a general emotional meaning—they dislike one thing and want to express solidarity with another—but they are not interested in the detail of what they are saying. A scrupulous writer, in every sentence that he writes, will ask himself at least four questions, thus: What am I trying to say? What words will express it? What image or idiom will make it clearer? Is this image fresh enough to have an effect? And he will probably ask himself two more: Could I put it more shortly? Have I said anything that is avoidably ugly? But you are not obliged to go to all this trouble. You can shirk it by simply throwing your mind open and letting the ready-made phrases come crowding in. They will construct your sentences for you—even think your thoughts for you, to a certain extent—and at need they will perform the important service of partially concealing your meaning even from yourself. It is at this point that the special connection between politics and the debasement of language becomes clear.

13. In our time it is broadly true that political writing is bad writing. Where it is not true, it will generally be found that the writer is some kind of rebel, expressing his private opinions and not a "party line." Orthodoxy, of whatever colour, seems to demand a lifeless, imitative style. The political dialects to be found in pamphlets, leading articles, manifestos, White Papers and the speeches of undersecretaries do, of course, vary from party to party, but they are all alike in that one almost never finds in them a fresh, vivid, homemade turn of speech. When one watches some tired hack on the platform mechanically repeating the familiar phrases—*bestial atrocities,*

*iron heel, bloodstained tyrannny, free peoples of the world, stand shoulder to shoulder*—one often has a curious feeling that one is not watching a live human being but some kind of dummy: a feeling which suddenly becomes stronger at moments when the light catches the speaker's spectacles and turns them into blank discs which seem to have no eyes behind them. And this is not altogether fanciful. A speaker who uses that kind of phraseology has gone some distance towards turning himself into a machine. The appropriate noises are coming out of his larynx, but his brain is not involved as it would be if he were choosing his words for himself. If the speech he is making is one that he is accustomed to make over and over again, he may be almost unconscious of what he is saying, as one is when one utters the responses in church. And this reduced state of consciousness, if not indispensable, is at any rate favorable to political conformity.

14. In our time, political speech and writing are largely the defence of the indefensible. Things like the continuance of British rule in India, the Russian purges and deportations, the dropping of the atom bombs on Japan, can indeed be defended, but only by arguments which are too brutal for most people to face, and which do not square with the professed aims of political parties. Thus political language has to consist largely of euphemism, question-begging and sheer cloudy vagueness. Defenceless villages are bombarded from the air, the inhabitants driven out into the countryside, the cattle machine-gunned, the huts set on fire with incendiary bullets: this is called *pacification*. Millions of peasants are robbed of their farms and sent trudging along the roads with no more than they can carry: this is called *transfer of population* or *rectification of frontiers*. People are imprisoned for years without trial, or shot in the back of the neck or sent to die of scurvy in Arctic lumber camps: this is called *elimination of unreliable elements*. Such phraseology is needed if one wants to name things without calling up mental pictures of them. Consider for instance some comfortable English professor defending Russian totalitarianism. He cannot say outright, "I believe in killing off your opponents when you can get good results by doing so." Probably, therefore, he will say something like this:

> While freely conceding that the Soviet régime exhibits certain features which the humanitarian may be inclined to deplore, we must, I think, agree that a certain curtailment of the right to political opposition is an unavoidable concomitant of transitional periods, and that the rigours which the Russian people have been called upon to undergo have been amply justified in the sphere of concrete achievement.

15.    The inflated style is itself a kind of euphemism. A mass of Latin words falls upon the facts like soft snow, blurring the outlines and covering up all the details. The great enemy of clear language is insincerity. When there is a gap between one's real and one's declared aims, one turns as it were instinctively to long words and exhausted idioms, like a cuttlefish squirting out ink. In our age there is no such thing as "keeping out of politics." All issues are political issues, and politics itself is a mass of lies, evasions, folly, hatred and schizophrenia. When the general atmosphere is bad, language must suffer. I should expect to find—this is a guess which I have not sufficient knowledge to verify—that the German, Russian and Italian languages have all deteriorated in the last ten or fifteen years, as a result of dictatorship.

16.    But if thought corrupts language, language can also corrupt thought. A bad usage can spread by tradition and imitation, even among people who should and do know better. The debased language that I have been discussing is in some ways very convenient. Phrases like *a not unjustifiable assumption, leaves much to be desired, would serve no good purpose, a consideration which we should do well to bear in mind,* are a continuous temptation, a packet of aspirins always at one's elbow. Look back through this essay, and for certain you will find that I have again and again committed the very faults I am protesting against. By this morning's post I have received a pamphlet dealing with conditions in Germany. The author tells me that he "felt impelled" to write it. I open it at random, and here is almost the first sentence that I see: "[The Allies] have an opportunity not only of achieving a radical transformation of Germany's social and political structure in such a way as to avoid a nationalistic reaction in Germany itself, but at the same time of laying the foundations of a co-operative and unified Europe." You see, he "feels impelled" to write—feels, presumably, that he has something new to say—and yet his words, like cavalry horses answering the bugle, group themselves automatically into the familiar dreary pattern. This invasion of one's mind by ready-made phrases (*lay the foundations, achieve a radical transformation*) can only be prevented if one is constantly on guard against them, and every such phrase anaesthetizes a portion of one's brain.

17.    I said earlier that the decadence of our language is probably curable. Those who deny this would argue, if they produced an argument at all, that language merely reflects existing social conditions, and that we cannot influence its development by any direct tinkering with words and constructions. So far as the general tone or spirit of a language goes, this may be true, but it is not true in

detail. Silly words and expressions have often disappeared, not through any evolutionary process but owing to the conscious action of a minority. Two recent examples were *explore every avenue* and *leave no stone unturned,* which were killed by the jeers of a few journalists. There is a long list of flyblown metaphors which could similarly be got rid of if enough people would interest themselves in the job; and it should also be possible to laugh the *not un-* formation out of existence,[3] to reduce the amount of Latin and Greek in the average sentence, to drive out foreign phrases and strayed scientific words, and, in general, to make pretentiousness unfashionable. But all these are minor points. The defence of the English language implies more than this, and perhaps it is best to start by saying what it does *not* imply.

18.   To begin with it has nothing to do with archaism, with the salvaging of obsolete words and turns of speech, or with the setting up of a "standard English" which must never be departed from. On the contrary, it is especially concerned with the scrapping of every word or idiom which has outworn its usefulness. It has nothing to do with correct grammar and syntax, which are of no importance so long as one makes one's meaning clear, or with the avoidance of Americanisms, or with having what is called a "good prose style." On the other hand it is not concerned with fake simplicity and the attempt to make written English colloquial. Nor does it even imply in every case preferring the Saxon word to the Latin one, though it does imply using the fewest and shortest words that will cover one's meaning. What is above all needed is to let the meaning choose the word, and not the other way about. In prose, the worst thing one can do with words is to surrender to them. When you think of a concrete object, you think wordlessly, and then, if you want to describe the thing you have been visualizing you probably hunt about till you find the exact words that seem to fit it. When you think of something abstract you are more inclined to use words from the start, and unless you make a conscious effort to prevent it, the existing dialect will come rushing in and do the job for you, at the expense of blurring or even changing your meaning. Probably it is better to put off using words as long as possible and get one's meaning as clear as one can through pictures or sensations. Afterwards one can choose—not simply *accept*—the phrases that will best cover the meaning, and then switch round and decide what impression one's words are likely to make on another person. This last effort of the mind cuts out all stale or mixed images,

[3] One can cure oneself of the *not un-* formation by memorizing this sentence: *A not unblack dog was chasing a not unsmall rabbit across a not ungreen field.*

all prefabricated phrases, needless repetitions, and humbug and vagueness generally. But one can often be in doubt about the effect of a word or a phrase, and one needs rules that one can rely on when instinct fails. I think the following rules will cover most cases:

(i) Never use a metaphor, simile or other figure of speech which you are used to seeing in print.

(ii) Never use a long word where a short one will do.

(iii) If it is possible to cut a word out, always cut it out.

(iv) Never use the passive where you can use the active.

(v) Never use a foreign phrase, a scientific word or a jargon word if you can think of an everyday English equivalent.

(vi) Break any of these rules sooner than say anything outright barbarous.

These rules sound elementary, and so they are, but they demand a deep change of attitude in anyone who has grown used to writing in the style now fashionable. One could keep all of them and still write bad English, but one could not write the kind of stuff that I quoted in those five specimens at the beginning of this article.

19.   I have not here been considering the literary use of language, but merely language as an instrument for expressing and not for concealing or preventing thought. Stuart Chase and others have come near to claiming that all abstract words are meaningless, and have used this as a pretext for advocating a kind of political quietism. Since you don't know what Fascism is, how can you struggle against Fascism? One need not swallow such absurdities as this, but one ought to recognize that the present political chaos is connected with the decay of language, and that one can probably bring about some improvement by starting at the verbal end. If you simplify your English, you are freed from the worst follies of orthodoxy. You cannot speak any of the necessary dialects, and when you make a stupid remark its stupidity will be obvious, even to yourself. Political language —and with variations this is true of all political parties, from Conservatives to Anarchists—is designed to make lies sound truthful and murder respectable, and to give an appearance of solidity to pure wind. One cannot change this all in a moment, but one can at least change one's own habits, and from time to time one can even, if one jeers loudly enough, send some worn-out and useless phrase—some *jackboot, Achilles' heel, hotbed, melting pot, acid test, veritable inferno* or other lump of verbal refuse—into the dustbin where it belongs.

WORDS

*meaning* Define *hackneyed* (par. 4), *banal* (par. 6), *euphonious* and *superfluous* (par. 12), *orthodoxy* (par. 13), *euphemism* (par. 14), and *quietism* (par. 19).

*relationships* 1. The author says that his translation of a verse from Ecclesiastes is a *parody* (par. 11). How does a parody differ from a travesty or a burlesque? 2. Is the comparison in "chokes him like tea leaves blocking a sink" (par. 12) a metaphor or a simile? In what ways is this figure of speech different from the ones Orwell is criticizing?

*exactness* 1. The author complains of mixed metaphors. What example of a mixed metaphor does he give in paragraph 12? Can you remember any other mixed metaphors you have read or heard? Give an example. 2. The author complains of the "decline of a language" (par. 2). What does he mean? Is English, like Latin, "declining" from some unspecified Augustan perfection? How exact is the denotation of the word *decline?*

SENTENCES

*rhetorical devices* 1. Although the author deplores the use of stale metaphors and similes, he uses a number of metaphors and similes himself. Are any of them stale? 2. What is the simile in paragraph 1? the analogy in paragraph 2? the simile in paragraph 4? the metaphor taken from geology in paragraph 11?

PARAGRAPHS

*emphasis* One characteristic of effective argument is modesty, real or false. In paragraph 16, for instance, the author says, "Look back through this essay, and for certain you will find that I have again and again committed the very faults I am protesting against." If you look back, do you find these faults? If you do, what are they? If you do not, why did the author accuse himself of them?

*topic sentences* What is the topic sentence of paragraph 14? How is it illustrated or proved—by comparison, by elimination, or by examples?

*methods of development* What idea do you find explained by elimination—by explanation of what it is not—in paragraphs 16, 17, or 18?

CONTENT AND ORGANIZATION

*assumptions and implications* 1. Do you agree that a "mixture of vagueness and sheer incompetence is the most marked characteristic of modern English prose, and especially of any kind of political writing" (par. 4)? 2. "In our time, political speech and writing are largely the defence of the indefensible" (par. 14). Does the author ever qualify this generalization?   3. What comment might the author make about the following lines from Wordsworth's *Prelude?* (See par. 17.)

> . . . though mean
> Our object and inglorious, yet the end
> Was not ignoble.

> . . . while far distant hills
> Into the tumult sent an alien sound
> Of melancholy not unnoticed.

> . . . I followed, not unseen,
> For oftentimes he cast a backward look,
> Grasping his twofold treasure.

> Not unresentful where self-justified;

4. "Probably it is better to put off using words as long as possible and get one's meaning as clear as one can through pictures or sensations" (par. 18). How useful is this advice for one who is thinking about political problems such as the stability of the dollar in the international monetary market, the comparative merits of manned aircraft and ballistic missiles, or the management of the national debt?

SUGGESTIONS FOR DISCUSSION

1. Do you agree that correct grammar and syntax have no importance so long as one makes one's meaning clear?   2. Complaints about ink-horn terms and Latinate words were common in Shakespeare's time. Is it possible to argue that none of the abuses of language cited by the author are signs of decline or decadence in language?   3. "If you simplify your English, you are freed from the worst follies of orthodoxy" (par. 19). Could it be said equally truthfully that if you simplify your English you may oversimplify your problems?   4. Choose a paragraph from a political speech and comment on the precision and effectiveness of its English.

## *Thomas Hobbes*

## OF SPEECH

1.   The invention of *printing,* though ingenious, compared with the invention of *letters,* is no great matter. But who was the first that found the use of letters, is not known. He that first brought them into

OF SPEECH:   From *The Leviathan* by Thomas Hobbes, 1651.

Greece, men say was Cadmus, the son of Agenor, king of Phœnicia. A profitable invention for continuing the memory of time passed, and the conjunction of mankind, dispersed into so many, and distant regions of the earth; and withal difficult, as proceeding from a watchful observation of the divers motions of the tongue, palate, lips, and other organs of speech; whereby to make as many differences of characters, to remember them. But the most noble and profitable invention of all other, was that of SPEECH, consisting of *names* or *appellations,* and their connexion; whereby men register their thoughts; recall them when they are past; and also declare them one to another for mutual utility and conversation; without which, there had been amongst men, neither commonwealth, nor society, nor contract, nor peace, no more than amongst lions, bears, and wolves. The first author of *speech* was God himself, that instructed Adam how to name such creatures as he presented to his sight; for the Scripture goeth no further in this matter. But this was sufficient to direct him to add more names, as the experience and use of the creatures should give him occasion; and to join them in such manner by degrees, as to make himself understood; and so by succession of time, so much language might be gotten, as he had found use for; though not so copious, as an orator or philosopher has need of: for I do not find anything in the Scripture, out of which, directly or by consequence, can be gathered, that Adam was taught the names of all figures, numbers, measures, colours, sounds, fancies, relations; much less the names of words and speech, as *general, special, affirmative, negative, interrogative, optative, infinitive,* all which are useful; and least of all, of *entity, intentionality, quiddity,* and other insignificant words of the school.

2.   But all this language gotten, and augmented by Adam and his posterity, was again lost at the Tower of Babel, when, by the hand of God, every man was stricken, for his rebellion, with an oblivion of his former language. And being hereby forced to disperse themselves into several parts of the world, it must needs be, that the diversity of tongues that now is, proceeded by degrees from them, in such manner, as need, the mother of all inventions, taught them; and in tract of time grew everywhere more copious.

3.   The general use of speech, is to transfer our mental discourse, into verbal; or the train of our thoughts, into a train of words; and that for two commodities, whereof one is the registering of the consequences of our thoughts; which being apt to slip out of our memory, and put us to a new labour, may again be recalled, by such words as they were marked by. So that the first use of names is to serve for *marks,* or *notes* of remembrance. Another is, when many

use the same words, to signify, by their connexion and order, one to another, what they conceive, or think of each matter; and also what they desire, fear, or have any other passion for. And for this use they are called *signs*. Special uses of speech are these: first, to register, what by cogitation, we find to be the cause of anything, present or past; and what we find things present or past may produce, or effect; which in sum, is acquiring of arts. Secondly, to show to others that knowledge which we have attained, which is, to counsel and teach one another. Thirdly, to make known to others our wills and purposes, that we may have the mutual help of one another. Fourthly, to please and delight ourselves and others, by playing with our words, for pleasure or ornament, innocently.

4. To these uses, there are also four correspondent abuses. First, when men register their thoughts wrong, by the inconstancy of the signification of their words; by which they register for their conception, that which they never conceived, and so deceive themselves. Secondly, when they use words metaphorically; that is, in other sense than that they are ordained for; and thereby deceive others. Thirdly, by words, when they declare that to be their will, which is not. Fourthly, when they use them to grieve one another; for seeing nature hath armed living creatures, some with teeth, some with horns, and some with hands, to grieve an enemy, it is but an abuse of speech, to grieve him with the tongue, unless it be one whom we are obliged to govern; and then it is not to grieve, but to correct and amend.

5. The manner how speech serveth to the remembrance of the consequence of causes and effects, consisteth in the imposing of *names,* and the *connexion* of them.

6. Of names, some are *proper,* and singular to one only thing, as *Peter, John, this man, this tree;* and some are *common* to many things, *man, horse, tree;* every of which, though but one name, is nevertheless the name of divers particular things; in respect of all which together, it is called an *universal;* there being nothing in the world universal but names; for the things named are every one of them individual and singular.

7. One universal name is imposed on many things, for their similitude in some quality, or other accident; and whereas a proper name bringeth to mind one thing only, universals recall any one of those many.

8. And of names universal, some are of more, and some of less extent; the larger comprehending the less large; and some again of equal extent, comprehending each other reciprocally. As for example: the name *body* is of larger signification than the word *man,*

and comprehendeth it; and the names *man* and *rational,* are of equal extent, comprehending mutually one another. But here we must take notice, that by a name is not always understood, as in grammar, one only word; but sometimes, by circumlocution, many words together. For all these words, *he that in his actions observeth the laws of his country,* make but one name, equivalent to this one word, *just.*

9. By this imposition of names, some of larger, some of stricter signification, we turn the reckoning of the consequences of things imagined in the mind, into a reckoning of the consequences of appellations. For example: a man that hath no use of speech at all, such as is born and remains perfectly deaf and dumb, if he set before his eyes a triangle, and by it two right angles, such as are the corners of a square figure, he may, by meditation, compare and find, that the three angles of that triangle, are equal to those two right angles that stand by it. But if another triangle be shown him, different in shape from the former, he cannot know, without a new labour, whether the three angles of that also be equal to the same. But he that hath the use of words, when he observes, that such quality was consequent, not to the length of the sides, nor to any other particular thing in his triangle; but only to this, that the sides were straight, and the angles three; and that that was all, for which he named it a triangle; will boldly conclude universally, that such equality of angles is in all triangles whatsoever; and register his invention in these general terms, *every triangle hath its three angles equal to two right angles.* And thus the consequence found in one particular, comes to be registered and remembered, as a universal rule, and discharges our mental reckoning, of time and place, and delivers us from all labour of the mind, saving the first, and makes that which was found true *here,* and *now,* to be true in *all times* and *places.*

10. But the use of words in registering our thoughts is in nothing so evident as in numbering. A natural fool that could never learn by heart the order of numeral words, as *one, two,* and *three,* may observe every stroke of the clock, and nod to it, or say *one, one, one,* but can never know what hour it strikes. And it seems, there was a time when those names of number were not in use; and men were fain to apply their fingers of one or both hands, to those things they desired to keep account of; and that thence it proceeded, that now our numeral words are but ten, in any nation, and in some but five; and then they begin again. And he that can tell ten, if he recite them out of order, will lose himself, and not know when he has done. Much less will he be able to add, and subtract, and perform all other operations of arithmetic. So that without words there is no possibility of reckoning

of numbers; much less of magnitudes, of swiftness, of force, and other things, the reckonings whereof are necessary to the being, or well-being of mankind.

11. When two names are joined together into a consequence, or affirmation, as thus, *a man is a living creature;* or thus, *if he be a man, he is a living creature;* if the latter name, *living creature,* signify all that the former name *man* signifieth, then the affirmation, or consequence, is *true;* otherwise *false.* For *true* and *false* are attributes of speech, not of things. And where speech is not, there is neither *truth* nor *falsehood; error* there may be, as when we expect that which shall not be, or suspect what has not been; but in neither case can a man be charged with untruth.

12. Seeing then that truth consisteth in the right ordering of names in our affirmations, a man that seeketh precise truth had need to remember what every name he uses stands for, and to place it accordingly, or else he will find himself entangled in words, as a bird in lime twigs, the more he struggles the more belimed. And therefore in geometry, which is the only science that it hath pleased God hitherto to bestow on mankind, men begin at settling the significations of their words; which settling of significations they call *definitions,* and place them in the beginning of their reckoning.

13. By this it appears how necessary it is for any man that aspires to true knowledge, to examine the definitions of former authors; and either to correct them, where they are negligently set down, or to make them himself. For the errors of definitions multiply themselves according as the reckoning proceeds, and lead men into absurdities, which at last they see, but cannot avoid, without reckoning anew from the beginning, in which lies the foundation of their errors. From whence it happens, that they which trust to books do as they that cast up many little sums into a greater, without considering whether those little sums were rightly cast up or not; and at last finding the error visible, and not mistrusting their first grounds, know not which way to clear themselves, but spend time in fluttering over their books; as birds that entering by the chimney, and finding themselves enclosed in a chamber, flutter at the false light of a glass window, for want of wit to consider which way they came in. So that in the right definition of names lies the first use of speech; which is the acquisition of science: and in wrong, or no definitions, lies the first abuse, from which proceed all false and senseless tenets; which make those men that take their instruction from the authority of books, and not from their own meditation, to be as much below the condition of ignorant men, as men endued with true science are above it. For between true

science and erroneous doctrines, ignorance is in the middle. Natural sense and imagination are not subject to absurdity. Nature itself cannot err; and as men abound in copiousness of language, so they become more wise, or more mad than ordinary. Nor is it possible without letters for any man to become either excellently wise, or, unless his memory be hurt by disease or ill constitution of organs, excellently foolish. For words are wise men's counters, they do but reckon by them; but they are the money of fools, that value them by the authority of an Aristotle, a Cicero, or a Thomas, or any other doctor whatsoever, if but a man.

## WORDS

*meaning*  1. In reading a philosopher such as Hobbes, who wrote in the seventeenth century, the reader must remember that the meanings of some words have changed since Hobbes used them. What, for instance, was the seventeenth-century meaning of *science* (par. 12)? In what century was the word *scientist* first used? (Consult the *Oxford English Dictionary* for the answers to these questions.)  2. Give the meanings that the following words have in this essay: *copious* (par. 1), *circumlocution* (par. 8), *tell* (par. 10), and *tenets* and *counters* (par. 13).

## SENTENCES

*style*  Why do so many of the author's sentences begin with *And, But,* and *For?* Is this usage peculiar to the author's style, or is it a necessary result of the kind of argument the author is conducting?

*rhetorical devices*  1. The author uses two different similes, both comparing men to birds, to illustrate dangers of the abuse of language (pars. 12 and 13). Are these similes used to show man's freedom or his helplessness? What is the difference between a metaphor and a simile?  2. The author cites the authority of Scripture. What is his opinion of those who argue from the authority of Aristotle, Cicero, or St. Thomas (par. 13)?

## PARAGRAPHS

*coherence*  1. One of the simplest ways of maintaining coherent paragraph development is used in the last half of paragraph 3 and throughout paragraph 4. What is it?  2. What is the word or phrase in each sentence in paragraph 8 that indicates its relationship to the statement preceding it?

## CONTENT AND ORGANIZATION

*central ideas*  1. What distinction does Hobbes make between *error* and *falsehood* (par. 11)? Which is inseparable from language?  2. What "schools" does Hobbes deride in the last sentences of paragraphs 1 and 12? 3. After reading paragraph 4, what do you believe Hobbes might say of each of the following statements: (a) The essence of oneness with the unknowable ultimate is true spirituality. (b) Two plus two is five. (c) The king is a dirty beast who lives in filth and slime.

SUGGESTIONS FOR DISCUSSION

1. What abuses of language do you find most objectionable in student arguments or in a particular newspaper or magazine? 2. Comment on the following statement: "Need is not the mother of all inventions; important inventions are conceived in leisure by disinterested curiosity." 3. Hobbes complains of the metaphorical use of words. What criticism might he make of a modern head of state who said, "We must lift our sword to defend our place in the sun and achieve our manifest destiny"? 4. Hobbes distinguishes between thought and its verbal expression. Is the distinction a valid one? 5. How do the diction, sentence structure, and punctuation of this passage written in seventeenth-century English differ from those of most of the other essays in this anthology? (This text has been less modernized than other classic essays in this book.)

# Creation and Criticism in Literature

## Kurt Vonnegut, Jr.

## WHY THEY READ HESSE

1.  Here are the bare bones of a tale that will always be popular with the young anywhere. A man travels a lot, is often alone. Money is not a serious problem. He seeks spiritual comfort, and avoids marriage and boring work. He is more intelligent than his parents and most of the people he meets. Women like him. So do poor people. So do wise old men. He experiments with sex, finds it nice but not tremendous. He encounters many queerly lovely hints that spiritual comfort really can be found. The world is beautiful. There is magic around.

2.  The story has everything but novelty. Chrétien de Troyes had success with it eight hundred years ago, in *Perceval le Gallois*. He had Perceval hunt for the Holy Grail, the cup Christ used at the Last Supper. Jack Kerouac and J. D. Salinger and Saul Bellow, among others, have been admired in recent times for their tales of quests.

3.  But the modern man who told them best was Hermann Hesse. He has been dead for eight years now. He was about my father's age. He was a German, and later a Swiss. He is deeply loved by those among the American young who are questing.

4.  His simplest, clearest, most innocent tale of seeking and finding is *Siddhartha* (1922). How popular is it? Nearly one million copies have been printed in America since 1957. One quarter of those were sold last year. This year is expected to be even better.

5.  Hesse is no black humorist. Black humorists' holy wanderers find nothing but junk and lies and idiocy wherever they go. A chewing-gum wrapper or a used condom is often the best they can do for a Holy Grail. Not so with the wanderers of Hesse; they always find something satisfying—holiness, wisdom, hope. Here are some Hesse endings to enjoy:

WHY THEY READ HESSE: © Copyright 1970 by American Heritage Publishing Co., Inc. Reprinted from *Horizon*, Spring 1970.

6.   "Perhaps . . . I will turn out to be a poet after all. This would mean as much, or perhaps more, to me than being a village councilor—or the builder of the stone dams. Yet it could never mean as much to me . . . as the memory of all those beloved people, from slender Rösi Girtanner to poor Boppi." (*Peter Camenzind*, 1904)

7.   "Govinda bowed low. Incontrollable tears trickled down his old face. He was overwhelmed by a feeling of great love, of the most humble veneration. He bowed low, right down to the ground, in front of the man sitting there motionless, whose smile reminded him of everything that he had ever loved in his life, of everything that had ever been of value and holy in his life." (*Siddhartha*)

8.   "I understood it all. I understood Pablo. I understood Mozart, and somewhere behind me I heard his ghastly laughter. I knew that all the hundred thousand pieces of life's game were in my pocket. A glimpse of its meaning had stirred my reason, and I was determined to begin the game afresh. . . . One day I would be a better hand at the game. One day I would learn how to laugh. Pablo was waiting for me, and Mozart, too." (*Steppenwolf*, 1927)

9.   "Dressing the wound hurt. Everything that has happened to me since has hurt. But sometimes when I find the key and climb deep into myself where the images of fate lie aslumber in the dark mirror, I need only bend over that dark mirror to behold my own image, now completely resembling him, my brother, my master." (*Demian*, 1925)

10.   Lovely. Hesse has had sensitive, truly bilingual English translators, by the way—Michael Roloff and Hilda Rosner and Ursule Molinaro among them.

11.   So an easy explanation of American youth's love for Hesse is this: he is clear and direct and well translated, and he offers hope and romance, which the young play hell finding anywhere else these days. And that is such a *sunny* explanation.

12.   But there are darker, deeper explanations to be found— and the clue that they exist is that the most important Hesse book to the American young, by their own account, is the wholly Germanic, hopelessly dated jumble called *Steppenwolf*.

13.   Students of the famous Generation Gap might ponder this: two of the leading characters in *Steppenwolf* are Johann Wolfgang von Goethe (1749–1832) and Wolfgang Amadeus Mozart (1756–91), who appear as ghosts in dreams.

14.   And here is a sample of dated dialogue, which the young do not choose to laugh at: The lonely hero, Harry Haller, has picked up a girl in a dance hall, and she says, "Now we'll go and give your

shoes and trousers a brush and then you'll dance the shimmy with me."

15. And he replies, "I can dance no shimmy, nor waltz, nor polka, nor any of the rest of them."

16. Twenty-three skiddoo!

17. The mere title *Steppenwolf* (a wolf of the steppes) has magic. I can see a lonesome freshman, coming from a gas-station community to a great university, can see him roaming the big bookstore for the first time. He leaves with a small paper bag containing the first serious book he has ever bought for himself: hey presto! *Steppenwolf!*

18. He has nice clothes and a little money, but he is depressed and leery of women. When he reads *Steppenwolf* in his dismal room, so far from home and mother, he will find that it is about a middle-aged man in a dismal room, far from home and mother. This man has nice clothes and a little money, but he is depressed and leery of women.

19. I recently asked a young drummer, a dropout from the University of Iowa and an admirer of *Steppenwolf,* why he thought the book was selling so well. I told him an astonishing fact: Bantam Books brought out a dollar-and-a-quarter edition of *Steppenwolf* in September of last year and sold 360,000 copies in thirty days.

20. The drummer said that most college people were experimenting with drugs and that *Steppenwolf* harmonized perfectly with their experiences.

21. "I thought the best part of the drug experience was that *everything* harmonized with it—everything but the police department," I said.

22. The drummer admitted this was so.

23. I suggested to him that America teemed with people who were homesick in bittersweet ways, and that *Steppenwolf* was the most profound book about homesickness ever written.

24. Characters in *Steppenwolf* do use drugs from time to time, it's true—a pinch of laudanum (tincture of opium) or a sniff of cocaine now and then to chase the blues. A jazz musician gives the hero a yellow cigarette that induces fantastic dreams. But the drugs are never adored, or feared either. They are simply medicines that friends pass around. Nobody is hooked, and nobody argues that drugs are the key to anything important.

25. Nor have I found Hesse to be tantalized by the drug experience in his other books. He is more concerned with alcohol.

Again and again, his holy wanderers love wine too much. They do something about it, too. They resolve to keep out of taverns, though they miss the uncritical companionship they've had there.

26. The politics espoused by the hero of *Steppenwolf* coincide with those of the American young, all right: he is against war. He hates armament manufacturers and super-patriots. No nations or political figures or historical events are investigated or praised or blamed. There are no daring schemes, no calls to action, nothing to make a radical's heart beat faster.

27. Hesse shocks and thrills the American young by taking them on a lunatic's tour of a splendid nightmare—down endless corridors, through halls of breaking mirrors, to costume balls, to empty theaters showing grotesque plays and films, to a wall with a thousand doors in it, and on and on. A sign appears once in an alley, fades forever. Sinister strangers hand the hero curious messages. And on and on.

28. A magic theater fantasy in which Harry Haller takes part proves, incidentally, that Hesse might have been one of the most screamingly funny men of his time. It may be that he was so anguished as he wrote *Steppenwolf* that his soul could get relief only by erupting into Charlie Chaplin comedy. The fantasy is about two men who climb a tree by a road. They have a rifle. They declare war on all automobiles and shoot them as they come by.

29. I laughed. There aren't many laughs in the works of Hermann Hesse. This is because romances work only if all the characters take life very seriously.

30. *Steppenwolf* is a Hesse freak for including a comedy—and a freak again for acknowledging modern technology and hating it, by and large. Most of his tales take place in villages and countrysides, often before the First World War. No internal-combustion engine ever shatters the silence. No telephone rings. No news comes from a radio. Messages are delivered by hand, or in the voices of a river or a wind.

31. Nobody in *Steppenwolf* has a telephone, although the cast is in a rich city after the war, doing the shimmy to jazz. The hero has no radio in his room, despite his swooning loneliness, but there are radios around, because he dreams of listening to one in the company of Mozart. The Concerto Grosso in F major, by Handel, is being broadcast from Munich. The hero says this about it, marvelously: "the devilish tin trumpet spat out, without more ado, a mixture of bronchial slime and chewed rubber; that noise that owners of gramophones and radios have agreed to call music."

32.  I have said that Hesse was about the same age as my father. My father wasn't a European, but part of his education took place in Strasbourg—before the First World War. And when I got to know him, when Hesse was writing *Steppenwolf,* my father, too, was cursing radios and films, was dreaming of Mozart and Goethe, was itching to pot shot automobiles.

33.  Curiously, Hesse, a man who spoke for my father's generation, is now heard loud and clear by my daughters and sons.

34.  And I say again: what my daughters and sons are responding to in *Steppenwolf* is the homesickness of the author. I do not mock homesickness as a silly affliction that is soon outgrown. I never outgrew it and neither did my father and neither did Hesse. I miss my Mommy and Daddy, and I always will—because they were so nice to me. Now and then, I would like to be a child again.

35.  And who am I when I spend a night alone in a motel outside, say, Erie, Pennsylvania? Who am I when I prowl that room, find only trash on television, when I search the phone book for nonexistent friends and relatives in Erie? Who am I when I think of going to a cocktail lounge for the easy comradeship there, when I imagine meeting a friendly woman out there and dread the kind of woman I would be likely to meet? I am Steppenwolf.

36.  The man who calls himself Steppenwolf, by the way, is one of the least carnivorous characters in fiction. He is a fool and a prig and a coward. He is a lamb.


37.  Hesse's German parents hoped, when he was a boy, that he would become a minister. But he suffered a severe religious crisis when he was fourteen. He ran away from the seminary, tried suicide by and by. In *Beneath the Wheel* (1906), the only Hesse book I've read that has a hopelessly unhappy ending, he shows himself as an abused schoolboy who gets drunk and drowns.

38.  He published his first book, *Peter Camenzind,* when he was twenty-seven. It was extremely popular in Germany. Hesse continued to prosper in his native land, and then, in 1912 when he was thirty-five, he left Germany forever. He eventually went to Switzerland.

39.  He removed himself from Kaiser Wilhelm's shrill militarism, Hitler, two lost world wars, the partitioning of Germany, and all that. And all that. While his former countrymen were dying and killing in the trenches, Hermann Hesse was being psychoanalyzed by Carl Jung in a multilingual peaceful little land. He published romantic novels and poetry, traveled to the Far East. He was married three times.

40. In 1946, one year after the death of Hitler, he received the Goethe Prize. He won a handsomely deserved Nobel Prize a year after that—not as a German but as a Swiss. He wasn't representing a German culture that was rising from the ashes. He was representing a culture that had cleared the hell out of Germany just before the holocaust began.

41. This is something a lot of young Americans are considering, too—clearing out before a holocaust begins. Much luck to them. Their problem is this: the next holocaust will leave this planet uninhabitable, and the Moon is no Switzerland. Neither is Venus. Neither is Mars. In all the rest of the solar system, there is nothing to breathe. Not only would *Steppenwolf* be homesick on some other planet. He would die.

## WORDS

*meaning*  Define *quests* (par. 2), *black,* as in "black humorist" (par. 5), *bilingual* and *multilingual* (pars. 10 and 39), and *holocaust* (par. 40).

*word choice*  1. What is the metaphor implied by the use of *espoused* in paragraph 26?  2. Why is *sunny* italicized in paragraph 11?  3. What is the rhetorical purpose of the two-word sentence that is the whole of paragraph 16?

## SENTENCES

*style*  1. In all of the first five paragraphs, there is only one compound or compound-complex sentence. Find it.  2. One reason for the comparative shortage of compound sentences in much modern journalism is the increasing tendency to display independent clauses as separate sentences. In this essay, for instance, even the first sentences of paragraphs frequently begin with coordinating conjunctions. Find five examples of this transitional device.

## PARAGRAPHS

*methods of development*  1. One seemingly simple paragraph in this essay is developed by a series of rhetorical questions followed by a brief answer. Find it.  2. How is the content of paragraph 27 reinforced by the style?

## CONTENT AND ORGANIZATION

*central ideas*  1. The central idea of this essay is implied in paragraphs 17 and 18, stated in paragraphs 23 and 34, and exemplified in paragraph 35. Restate it.  2. In what two ways is *Steppenwolf* different from Hesse's other work (pars. 28–31)?  3. How does Hesse agree with and how does he differ from many of modern youth in his attitude toward drugs, alcohol, politics, and technology (pars. 24–31)? 4. Why does Vonnegut consider modern American youth even more unfortunate than sensitive, cultured young men in pre-World War I Germany (par. 41)?

*organization* Can the seeming "aside" of paragraph 36 be interpreted as a comment on the life described in paragraphs 37 through 40?

### SUGGESTIONS FOR DISCUSSION

1. Kurt Vonnegut, Jr., says that a story of a quest has "everything but novelty." Can you think of *any* plot or kind of story that has novelty? 2. Have you ever experienced the kind of homesickness that Vonnegut describes in paragraph 18? Or that described in paragraph 35? 3. If you have lived as an expatriate in another country or as an immigrant in America, describe the rewards and the difficulties of the situation. 4. Do you share Vonnegut's pessimism about "the next holocaust" (par. 41)? Explain. 5. Vonnegut calls the novel *Steppenwolf* a "wholly Germanic, hopelessly dated jumble" (par. 12). What characteristics of any novel would you consider "wholly Germanic"? Explain.

## *Hermann Hesse*

# THE GREAT HUNT IN AUTOMOBILES

1. I realized that I was now left to myself and to the theater, and I went with curiosity from door to door and read on each its alluring invitation.

2. The inscription

JOLLY HUNTING

GREAT HUNT IN AUTOMOBILES

attracted me. I opened the narrow door and stepped in.

3. I was swept at once into a world of noise and excitement. Cars, some of them armored, were run through the streets chasing the pedestrians. They ran them down and either left them mangled on the ground or crushed them to death against the walls of the houses. I saw at once that it was the long-prepared, long-awaited, and long-feared war between men and machines, now at last broken

THE GREAT HUNT IN AUTOMOBILES: From *Steppenwolf* by Hermann Hesse. Copyright 1929, © 1957 by Holt, Rinehart and Winston, Inc. Reprinted by permission of Holt, Rinehart and Winston, Inc.

out. On all sides lay dead and decomposing bodies, and on all sides, too, smashed and distorted and half-burned cars. Airplanes circled above the frightful confusion and were being fired upon from many roofs and windows with rifles and machine guns. On every wall were wild and magnificently stirring placards, whose giant letters flamed like torches, summoning the nation to side with the men against the machines, to make an end at last of the fat and well-dressed and perfumed plutocrats who used machines to squeeze the fat from other men's bodies, of them and their huge fiendishly purring automobiles. Set factories afire at last! Make a little room on the crippled earth! Depopulate it so that the grass may grow again, and woods, meadows, heather, stream, and moor return to this world of dust and concrete. Other placards, on the other hand, in wonderful colors and magnificently phrased, warned all those who had a stake in the country and some share of prudence (in more moderate and less childish terms which testified to the remarkable cleverness and intellect of those who had composed them) against the rising tide of anarchy. They depicted in a truly impressive way the blessings of order and work and property and education and justice, and praised machinery as the last and most sublime invention of the human mind. With its aid, men would be equal to the gods. I studied these placards, both the red and the green, and reflected on them and marveled at them. The flaming eloquence affected me as powerfully as the compelling logic. They were right, and I stood as deeply convinced in front of one as in front of the other, a good deal disturbed all the time by the rather juicy firing that went on all round me. Well, the principal thing was clear. There was a war on, a violent, genuine, and highly sympathetic war where there was no concern for Kaiser or republic, for frontiers, flags, or colors and other equally decorative and theatrical matters, all nonsense at bottom; but a war in which every one who lacked air to breathe and no longer found life exactly pleasing gave emphatic expression to his displeasure and strove to prepare the way for a general destruction of this iron-cast civilization of ours. In every eye I saw the unconcealed spark of destruction and murder, and in mine too these wild red roses bloomed as rank and high, and sparkled as brightly. I joined the battle joyfully.

4. The best of all, however, was that my schoolfriend, Gustav, turned up close beside me. I had lost sight of him for dozens of years, the wildest, strongest, most eager and venturesome of the friends of my childhood. I laughed in my heart as I saw him blink at me with his bright blue eyes. He beckoned and at once I followed him joyfully.

5. "Good Lord, Gustav," I cried happily, "I haven't seen you in ages. Whatever has become of you?"

6. He gave a derisive snort, just as he used to do as a boy. "There you are again, you idiot, jabbering and asking questions. I'm a professor of theology if you want to know. But, the Lord be praised, there's no occasion for theology now, my boy. It's war. Come on!"

7. He shot the driver of a small car that came snorting towards us and, leaping into it as nimbly as a monkey, brought it to a standstill for me to get in. Then we drove like the devil between bullets and crashed cars out of town and suburbs.

8. "Are you on the side of the manufacturers?" I asked my friend.

9. "Oh, Lord, that's a matter of taste, so we can leave it out of account—though now you mention it, I rather think we might take the other side, since at bottom it's all the same, of course. I'm a theologian and my predecessor, Luther, took the side of the princes and plutocrats against the peasants. So now we'll establish the balance a little. This rotten car, I hope it'll hold out another mile or two."

10. Swift as the wind, that child of heaven, we rattled on, and reached a green and peaceful countryside many miles distant. We traversed a wide plain and then slowly climbed into the mountains. Here we made a halt on a smooth and glistening road that led in bold curves between the steep wall of rock and the low retaining wall. Far below shone the blue surface of a lake.

11. "Lovely view," said I.

12. "Very pretty. We'll call it the Axle Way. A good many axles of one sort or another are going to crash here, Harry, my boy. So watch out!"

13. A tall pine grew by the roadside, and among the tall branches we saw something like a little hut made of boards to serve as an outlook and point of vantage. Gustav smiled with a knowing twinkle in his blue eyes. We hurried out of the car, climbed up the trunk and, breathing hard, concealed ourselves in the outlook post, which pleased us much. We found rifles and revolvers there and boxes of ammunition. We had scarcely cooled down when we heard the hoarse imperious horn of a big luxury car from the next bend of the road. It came purring at top speed up the smooth road. Our rifles were ready in our hands. The excitement was intense.

14. "Aim at the chauffeur," commanded Gustav quickly just as the heavy car went by beneath us. I aimed, and fired at the chauffeur in his blue cap. The man fell in a heap. The car careened on,

charged the cliff face, rebounded, attacked the lower wall furiously with all its unwieldy weight like a great bumble bee, and, tumbling over, crashed with a brief and distant report into the depths below.

15. "Got him!" Gustav laughed. "My turn next."

16. Another came as he spoke. There were three or four occupants packed in the back seat. From the head of a woman a bright blue veil streamed out behind. It filled me with genuine remorse. Who could say how pretty a face it might adorn? Good God, though we did play the brigand we might at least emulate the illustrious and spare pretty women. Gustav, however, had already fired. The driver shuddered and collapsed. The car leaped against the perpendicular cliff, fell back and overturned, wheels uppermost. Its engine was still running and the wheels turned absurdly in the air; but suddenly with a frightful explosion it burst into flames.

17. "A Ford," said Gustav. "We must get down and clear the road."

18. We climbed down and watched the burning heap. It soon burned out. Meanwhile we made levers of green wood and hoisted it to the side of the road and over the wall into the abyss, where for a long time it went crashing through the undergrowth. Two of the dead bodies had fallen out as we turned the car over and lay on the road with their clothing partly burned. One wore a coat which was still in fairly good condition. I searched the pockets to see who he was and came across a leather portfolio with some cards in it. I took one and read: Tat Twam Asi.

19. "Very witty," said Gustav. "Though, as a matter of fact, it is all one what our victims are called. They're poor devils just as we are. Their names don't matter. This world is done for and so are we. The least painful solution would be to hold it under water for ten minutes. Now to work—"

20. We threw the bodies after the car. Already another one was tooting. We shot it down with a volley where we stood. It made a drunken swerve and reeled on for a stretch: then turned over and lay gasping. One passenger was still sitting inside, but a pretty young girl got out uninjured, though she was white and trembling violently. We greeted her politely and offered our assistance. She was too much shaken to speak and stared at us for a while quite dazed.

21. "Well, first let us look after the old boy," said Gustav and turned to the occupant of the car who still clung to his seat behind the chauffeur. He was a gentleman with short gray hair. His intelligent, clear gray eyes were open, but he seemed to be seriously

hurt; at least, blood flowed from his mouth and he held his neck askew and rigid.

22. "Allow me to introduce myself. My name is Gustav. We have taken the liberty of shooting your chauffeur. May we inquire whom we have the honor to address?"

23. The old man looked at us coolly and sadly out of his small gray eyes.

24. "I am Attorney-General Loering," he said slowly. "You have not only killed my poor chauffeur, but me too, I fancy. Why did you shoot on us?"

25. "For exceeding the speed limit."

26. "We were not traveling at more than normal speed."

27. "What was normal yesterday is no longer normal today, Mr. Attorney-General. We are of the opinion that whatever speed a motorcar travels is too great. We are destroying all cars and all other machines also."

28. "Your rifles too?"

29. "Their turn will come, granted we have the time. Presumably by tomorrow or the day after we shall all be done for. You know, of course, that this part of the world was shockingly over-populated. Well, now we are going to let in a little air."

30. "Are you shooting every one, without distinction?"

31. "Certainly. In many cases it may no doubt be a pity. I'm sorry, for example, about this charming young lady. Your daughter, I presume."

32. "No. She is my stenographer."

33. "So much the better. And now will you please get out, or let us carry you out, as the car is to be destroyed."

34. "I prefer to be destroyed with it."

35. "As you wish. But allow me to ask you one more question. You are a public prosecutor. I never could understand how a man could be a public prosecutor. You make your living by bringing other men, poor devils mostly, to trial and passing sentence on them. Isn't that so?"

36. "It is. I do my duty. It was my office. Exactly as it is the office of the hangman to hang those whom I condemn to death. You too have assumed a like office. You kill people also."

37. "Quite true. Only we do not kill from duty, but pleasure, or much more, rather, from displeasure and despair of the world. For this reason we find a certain amusement in killing people. Has it never amused you?"

38. "You bore me. Be so kind as to do your work. Since the conception of duty is unknown to you—"

39. He was silent and made a movement of his lips as though to spit. Only a little blood came, however, and clung to his chin.

40. "One moment!" said Gustav politely. "The conception of duty is certainly unknown to me—now. Formerly I had a great deal of official concern with it. I was a professor of theology. Besides that, I was a soldier and went through the war. What seemed to me to be duty and what the authorities and my superior officers from time to time enjoined upon me was not by any means good. I would rather have done the opposite. But granting that the conception of duty is no longer known to me, I still know the conception of guilt—perhaps they are the same thing. In so far as a mother bore me, I am guilty. I am condemned to live. I am obliged to belong to a state, to serve as a soldier, to kill, and to pay taxes for armaments. And now at this moment the guilt of life has brought me once more to the necessity of killing the people as it did in the war. And this time I have no repugnance. I am resigned to the guilt. I have no objection to this stupid congested world going to bits. I am glad to help and glad to perish with it."

41. The public prosecutor made an effort to smile a little with his lips on which the blood had coagulated. He did not succeed very well, though the good intention was manifest.

42. "Good," said he. "So we are colleagues. Well, as such, please do your duty."

43. The pretty girl had meanwhile sat down by the side of the road and fainted.

44. At this moment there was again the tooting of a car coming down the road at full speed. We drew the girl a little to one side and, standing close against the cliff, let the approaching car run into the ruins of the other. The brakes were applied violently and the car reared up in the air. It came to a standstill undamaged. We seized our rifles and quickly had the newcomers covered.

45. "Get out!" commanded Gustav. "Hands up!"

46. Three men got out of the car and obediently held up their hands.

47. "Is any one of you a doctor?" Gustav asked.

48. They shook their heads.

49. "Then be so good as to remove this gentleman. He is seriously hurt. Take him in your car to the nearest town. Forward, and get on with it."

50.   The old gentleman was soon lying in the other car. Gustav gave the word and off they went.

51.   The stenographer meanwhile had come to herself and had been watching these proceedings. I was glad we had made so fair a prize.

52.   "Madam," said Gustav, "you have lost your employer. I hope you were not bound to the old gentleman by other ties. You are now in my service. So be our good comrade. So much for that; and now time presses. It will be uncomfortable here before long. Can you climb, Madam? Yes? Then go ahead and we'll help you up between us."

53.   We all climbed up to our hut in the tree as fast as we could. The lady did not feel very well up there, but we gave her some brandy, and she was soon so much recovered that she was able to admire the wonderful view over lake and mountains and to tell us also that her name was Dora.

54.   Immediately after this, there was another car below us. It steered carefully past the overturned one without stopping and then gathered speed.

55.   "Poltroon!" laughed Gustav and shot the driver. The car zigzagged and dashing into the wall stove it in and hung suspended over the abyss.

56.   "Dora," I said, "can you use firearms?"

57.   She could not, but we taught her how to load. She was clumsy at first and hurt her finger and cried and wanted court-plaster. But Gustav told her it was war and that she must show her courage. Then it went better.

58.   "But what's going to become of us?" she asked.

59.   "Don't know," said Gustav. "My friend Harry is fond of pretty girls. He'll look after you."

60.   "But the police and the soldiers will come and kill us."

61.   "There aren't any police and such like any more. We can choose, Dora. Either we stay quietly up here and shoot down every car that tries to pass, or else we can take a car and drive off in it and let others shoot at us. It's all the same which side we take. I'm for staying here."

62.   And now there was the loud tooting of another car beneath us. It was soon accounted for and lay there wheels uppermost.

63.   Gustav smiled. "Yes, there are indeed too many men in the world. In earlier days it wasn't so noticeable. But now that everyone wants air to breathe, and a car to drive as well, one does notice it. Of course, what we are doing isn't rational. It's childishness, just

as war is childishness on a gigantic scale. In time, mankind will learn to keep its numbers in check by rational means. Meanwhile, we are meeting an intolerable situation in a rather irrational way. However, the principle's correct—we eliminate."

64. "Yes," said I, "what we are doing is probably mad, and probably it is good and necessary all the same. It is not a good thing when man overstrains his reason and tries to reduce to rational order matters that are not susceptible of rational treatment. Then there arise ideals such as those of the Americans or of the Bolsheviks. Both are extraordinarily rational, and both lead to a frightful oppression and impoverishment of life, because they simplify it so crudely. The likeness of man, once a high ideal, is in process of becoming a machine-made article. It is for madmen like us, perhaps, to ennoble it again."

65. With a laugh Gustav replied: "You talk like a book, my boy. It is a pleasure and a privilege to drink at such a fount of wisdom. And perhaps there is even something in what you say. But now kindly reload your piece. You are a little too dreamy for my taste. A couple of bucks can come dashing by here again any moment, and we can't kill them with philosophy. We must have ball in our barrels."

66. A car came and was dropped at once. The road was blocked. A survivor, a stout red-faced man, gesticulated wildly over the ruins. Then he stared up and down and, discovering our hiding place, came for us bellowing and shooting up at us with a revolver.

67. "Get off with you or I'll shoot," Gustav shouted down. The man took aim at him and fired again. Then we shot him.

68. After this two more came and were bagged. Then the road was silent and deserted. Apparently the news had got about that it was dangerous. We had time to enjoy the beauty of the view. On the far side of the lake a small town lay in the valley. Smoke rose from it and soon we saw fire leaping from roof to roof. Shooting could be heard. Dora cried a little and I stroked her wet cheeks.

69. "Have we all got to die then?" she asked. There was no reply. Meanwhile a man on foot went past below. He saw the smashed-up cars and began nosing round them. Leaning over into one of them he pulled out a gay parasol, a lady's handbag, and a bottle of wine. Then he sat down contentedly on the wall, took a drink from the bottle, and ate something wrapped in tinfoil out of the handbag. After emptying the bottle he went on, well pleased, with the parasol clasped under his arm; and I said to Gustav: "Could

you find it in you to shoot at this good fellow and make a hole in his head? God knows, I couldn't."

70. "You're not asked to," my friend growled. But he did not feel very comfortable either. We had no sooner caught sight of a man whose behavior was harmless and peaceable and childlike and who was still in a state of innocence than all our praiseworthy and most necessary activities became stupid and repulsive. Pah—all that blood! We were ashamed of ourselves. But in the war there must have been generals even who felt the same.

71. "Don't let us stay here any longer," Dora implored. "Let's go down. We are sure to find something to eat in the cars. Aren't you hungry, you Bolsheviks?"

72. Down in the burning town the bells began to peal with a wild terror. We set ourselves to climb down. As I helped Dora to climb over the breast work, I kissed her knee. She laughed aloud, and then the planks gave way and we both fell into vacancy—

73. Once more I stood in the round corridor, still excited by the hunting adventure. And everywhere on all the countless doors were the alluring inscriptions:

MUTABOR
TRANSFORMATION INTO ANY ANIMAL OR PLANT
YOU PLEASE

KAMASUTRAM
INSTRUCTION IN THE INDIAN ARTS OF LOVE
COURSE FOR BEGINNERS; FORTY-TWO DIFFERENT
METHODS AND PRACTICES

DELIGHTFUL SUICIDE
YOU LAUGH YOURSELF TO BITS

DO YOU WANT TO BE ALL SPIRIT?
THE WISDOM OF THE EAST.

DOWNFALL OF THE WEST
MODERATE PRICES. NEVER SURPASSED

COMPENDIUM OF ART
TRANSFORMATION FROM TIME INTO SPACE
BY MEANS OF MUSIC

LAUGHING TEARS
CABINET OF HUMOR

SOLITUDE MADE EASY
COMPLETE SUBSTITUTE FOR ALL FORMS OF
SOCIABILITY.

The series of inscriptions was endless. One was

GUIDANCE IN THE BUILDING UP OF THE
PERSONALITY. SUCCESS GUARANTEED

74. This seemed to me to be worth looking into and I went in
at this door.

## WORDS

*meaning*   Define *derisive* (par. 6), *imperious* (par. 13), *careened* (par.
14), *abyss* (par. 18), *enjoined* and *repugnance* (par. 40).

*connotation*   A few words used here were more common in 1927, when
the novel *Steppenwolf* was published, than they are now. What, for instance, are *plutocrats* (par. 3), and who were the *Bolsheviks* (par. 64)?
What emotional association does each of these words have?

## SENTENCES

*style*   1. How does the formal, polite dialogue between Gustav and the
wounded prosecutor (pars. 22–42) contribute to the dreamlike, surrealistic nature of the action?   2. How does the matter-of-fact exposition
of details in paragraph 3 help to make the incredible credible?

*rhetorical devices*   1. Why is Gustav's ordinary vocation as professor of
theology ironical in the context of the narrative?   2. What implied or
explicit parallels between the real world and the fantastic world of this
narrative can be found (pars. 3 and 63)?

## PARAGRAPHS

*coherence*   The dreamlike, surrealistic quality of the story is enhanced by
incoherence—by sudden juxtaposition of the beautiful and the horrible,
the serious and the trivial. How is this quality shown in paragraphs 53,
57, 68, and 69, for instance?

## CONTENT AND ORGANIZATION

*organization*   1. Compare the beginning and end of the "great hunt"
with the beginning and end of *Alice in Wonderland*. How are the two narratives similar?   2. How do the introductions of Gustav, a childhood
friend not seen for "dozens of years," and of Dora, the "stenographer,"
resemble the first view of characters in a dream?

*assumptions and implications*   What attitudes toward ecology, over-population, technology, and war are expressed in this narrative?

SUGGESTIONS FOR DISCUSSION

1. Gustav says, "Meanwhile, we are meeting an intolerable situation in a rather irrational way" (par. 63). Could any modern political or social groups make the same statement? Explain.   2. The narrator says that Americans are "extraordinarily rational" and consequently simplify life crudely (par. 64). What could be the justification of such a statement? 3. Dreams or visions have been the bases of poems, philosophies, and religions. Why have dreams always been important in men's lives? 4. Write a brief narrative in which you describe what might have happened after the narrator went in at the door inscribed GUIDANCE IN THE BUILDING UP OF THE PERSONALITY. SUCCESS GUARANTEED.   5. Is there a possibility that we can improve our civilization only by learning to use less power, less oil, coal, and metal, and far fewer machines? How could such "improvement" be achieved?   6. Does your reading of this selection from *Steppenwolf* help you to account for the great popularity of Hermann Hesse's works (described in Vonnegut's "Why They Read Hesse," p. 435)? Explain.

## *Benjamin DeMott*

# LOOKING BACK ON THE SEVENTIES

1.   Turning and turning, a puzzle no less to themselves than to their elders, the new youth were clearly contemptuous of old metaphors, had formed a habit actually of spitting at their pretensions, and could not be taught to stand still. "The rat race," "making it," "the bitch goddess," "the competitive way of life," success, failure, *The Rise of Silas Lapham, The Rise of David Levinsky,* at length (at midcentury) *The Man in the Gray Flannel Suit* Declining the Top Job—these icons and symbols, trivial or exotic to our ears, had been compelling figures for generations, holding fluidities of dailiness in a vessel of pseudo-understanding, providing evaluative measures for experience, determining the texture of imaginations, molding contours of hope. That the myths and figures mentioned were

LOOKING BACK ON THE SEVENTIES:   From the book *Surviving the 70's* by Benjamin DeMott. Copyright © 1971, 1970, 1969 by Benjamin DeMott. Published by E. P. Dutton & Co., Inc. and reprinted with their permission. This essay originally appeared in *The Atlantic* under a different title.

antihuman and perfunctory is demonstrable. Yet no less demonstrable is that their grip upon life (when God died *they* survived) was wonderfully intense. In a word, the moment of their own passing—we may safely date it after midcentury—was, for the elders of an entire culture, eerie, fearful, grave.

2.  For a time, inevitably, the decline in symbolic authority went unacknowledged: revolution is not ingested overnight. A debate raged, in magazines and books, on television and lecture platforms, and during election campaigns, whether major changes truly were in progress. What could be more probable, said some, than that exploiters and commercialists were attempting to create a "revolutionary youth" out of the void for vulgar purposes of profit? A pollster, Samuel Lubell, reported that "only 10 percent" of his interviewees saw the work-world differently from their parents. A California sociologist pronounced that in his area 400 out of 500 youngsters thought well of the elders. A psychologist at Michigan University, Joseph Adelson, argued that talk of a break in continuity was extravagant, and attributed its prevalence to "essays on youth" in quality magazines:

> Not too surprisingly perhaps [wrote Adelson, confidently] the most likely writer of these essays is an academic intellectual, teaching humanities or the social sciences in an elite university. Hence he is exposed, in his office, in his classes, to far more than the usual number of radical or hippyesque students. (And he will live in a neighborhood where many of the young adolescents are preparing themselves for such roles.) On top of this, he is, like the rest of us, subject to the common errors of social perception. . . .

But the comfort derived from such voices was of short duration, for those whose family lives had been touched by change demanded the right (in the contemporary phrase) to enter the dialogue. The magazine *Fortune* published a poll contradicting the conclusions of Lubell. The celebrated anthropologist Margaret Mead set her weight behind the thesis that the new youth were "like the first generation born in a new country," that they were in rebellion "all around the world, rebelling against whatever forms the governmental and educational systems take," and that the "deep, new, unprecedented, worldwide generation gap" was in no sense whatever fictive.

3.  Few forces were more influential in shortening the debate in question than the news media. Their attentiveness to the emergent sensibility was unrelenting; they soon put beyond doubt that a trans-

formation was occurring; their doggedness provided later generations with all that was to be known of The Early Ones, *Ur*-Metamorphics, whose example still speaks so tellingly.*

4. As every schoolboy knows, it was during Richard Nixon's first White House term, in the pages of a business paper, the *Wall Street Journal,* that the first reports of The Early Ones appeared. College-Trained Youth Shun the Professions for Free-Form Life, said the headline above an account of Primitive Metamorphic Life-style. A San Francisco Sextuple Darter named John Spitzer, in his twenties (cabdriver/bartender/magazine editor/Harvard *summa cum laude*/pianist/playwright), revealed that he was contemplating Septenary—a position as disc jockey. A second Early One, Clara Parkinson, proved to be a Fem Tyrowhirler. Clara had majored in government at Smith College, graduating in 1968, and thereafter taken up work as a letter carrier, because impelled to "get off the treadmill." "I've discovered," said the pioneer Tyrowhirler, in terms that may have stirred dread in contemporary readers' minds, "I've discovered a new sense of my physical strength from lifting mail sacks." And a third Early One was the Trimorph Chip Oliver (professional footballist/guru/cook), whose word for the press was that he had never felt "more together," and that he had lost a lot of weight ("50 pounds from his playing weight of 230").

5. To speak of one or another of The Early Ones as having "stirred dread" is, of course, speculative. (The present writer, a Dimorph whirled only recently from Playfiction to Playhistory, wishes to note here that he has already learned that few tasks are harder for the historian than that of imagining the familiar as it seemed to men when it was strange. More of this shortly.) But it does seem clear that attention wasn't long diverted from "the decline of the rat race." It seems equally clear that the first efforts to confront transformation were couched in moral vocabularies—assessments of the ethics of "dropping out." And it is no less certain that the preeminent moralists of the period were those of the Yale School.

6. Nervous, ill-informed, beamish, lacking in analytical foundation, the Yale School nevertheless played no small role—in collaboration with the media—in releasing the public from bondage to the fantasy that human nature would everywhere and always be the same. The chief spokesmen for the School were the novelist/youth-

* The term Metamorphic had interesting origins. The earliest recorded use we find occurs in a campaign speech delivered in 1976 by the last presidential candidate to run under the standard of the Republican political party—Spiro Agnew. The exact phrase was: "muddled meddling Metamorphics."

authority/undergraduate-counselor John Hersey, Charles Reich, a professor of law, and Kenneth Keniston, a psychologist. These writers laid it down that the rejection of "rat-racing," or competition, signified the advent of a higher moral consciousness, a new goodness, possibly the long-heralded perfection of the race. Hersey considered that the new youth had committed itself to a war on greed:

> Relating and helping are more important than making it. . . . "Relating" really means being able to give and take. The impulse to give, in a time when there is so much misery and pain at large, is very strong and takes many forms, from the handing out of oranges to total strangers at the Woodstock rock festival [a contemporary saturnalia], to the fevered, devoted work a Peace Corps volunteer may undertake. . . . Each young person in his way has had his urge to do *something* to make the world a better place. . . . The vast majority of young people believe that greed is at the root of most of the misery of the world, and that most businesses systematize greed. [*Letter to the Alumni,* 1970]

Reich concurred, attributing the movement toward moral self-improvement to nebulous (possibly nonexistent?) cultural and historical forces:

> Consciousness III [a name for New Youth] does not think much of fighting for change from the comfort of personal security and elegance. He feels that if he is to be true to himself he must respond *with* himself. . . . He may take a job teaching in a ghetto school, which offers neither prestige nor comfort but offers the satisfaction of personal contact with ghetto children. He does not assume that he can fight society while luxuriating in its benefits. He must take risks—the risk of economic loss, of discomfort, of physical injury, of a jail sentence. . . . Consciousness III is . . . seeking to replace the infantile and destructive self-seeking that we laud as "competition" by a new capacity for working and living together. [*The Greening of America,* 1970]

And Keniston claimed that young people were "taking the highest values" for their own, internalizing "these values and [identifying] them with their own best selves, [and struggling] to implement them."

7. As would be guessed, youth was not averse to learning of the achievement, by it, of moral distinction superior to that hitherto known. When, for example, the business paper quoted above asked Trimorph Chip Oliver about the moral dimensions of his dartings, this Early One slipped comfortably into self-congratulation:

> We're putting on a demonstration. . . . We're showing people a new way of life. We're showing people that as soon as you start

loving and relating to people you'll find those people loving and relating to you. [*Wall Street Journal,* June 24, 1970]

And it can be imagined that parents were heartened by his words: was not (if a small joke may be ventured), was not Chip off the old block?

8.   But dourer voices—knockers not boosters—demanded hearings. Reviewers and commentators took exception to Charles Reich's *The Greening of America,* objecting to the book's thesis that the young truly cared about others (an acerb New York *Times* writer named Lehmann-Haupt proposed the young were in love with their boots). The sociologist Edward Shils, writing in chilly tones in the English journal *Encounter,* doubted the *content* of the new morality: these children, said Shils, discover nothing but "the vacuum of the expanding and the contentless self." Bruno Bettelheim, the psychologist, spoke fiercely against children "fixated at the temper tantrum stage."

9.   Within months, furor about the Metamorphics' virtue (or lack of it) filled the press. An account of the moralized justifications, apologia, attacks, and counterattacks of the sixties and seventies—a survey of the Byzantine complications of casuistry on such matters as "arrogance" and "nihilism" versus "frankness" and "freshness"— is beyond the compass of a short monograph. We cannot begin to suggest the range of obsessions that seized those resolved in this period to be "fair to youth." Observer after observer—artists, social scientists, politicos—was waylaid by trivia, edged off from sustained, penetrating study of the new behavior by marginal, if furiously argued, considerations. There was—choosing one example at random—the Costume Issue. What was the meaning (so ran the momentous query) of the Metamorphics' dress code? The Yale School's Charles Reich found the clothes redolent of ethical significance:

> The new clothes express profoundly democratic values. There are no distinctions of wealth or status, no elitism; people confront each other shorn of these distinctions. . . . [The old clothes] spoke of competition, advantage, and disadvantage. The new clothes deny the importance of hierarchy, status, authority, position, and they reject competition. . . .

Others found the clothes merely redolent. The novelist Saul Bellow affirmed, in *Mr. Sammler's Planet* (1970), that the new costume constituted a descent into chaos and self-destruction:

> What one sees on Broadway while bound for the bus. All human types reproduced, the barbarian, Redskin, or Fiji, the dandy, the

buffalo hunter, the desperado, the queer, the sexual fantasist, the squaw, bluestocking, princess, poet, painter, prospector, troubador, guerrilla, Che Guevara, the new Thomas Becket. . . . Just look [at this] imitative anarchy of the streets—these Chinese revolutionary tunics, these babes in unisex toyland, these surrealist warchiefs, Western stagecoach drivers—Ph.D.'s in philosophy, some of them. . . . They sought originality. They were obviously derivative. And of what—of Paiutes, of Fidel Castro? No, of Hollywood extras. Acting mythic. Casting themselves into chaos. . . .

The critic John Aldridge construed the costume as a badge of banality:

> . . . the U.S. army tunics of World War I . . . the broad-brimmed hats and plunging sideburns of the Western plainsman . . . the headband of Comanche braves . . . Edwardian suits, the smocks of French Bohemian painters, or the gaudy saris of guruland. . . . The young need to have something to do with their banality. . . . [*In the Country of the Young*, 1970]

Scores of other opinions were sternly set down.

10.  Or consider the battle about sexuality. Did the Metamorphics intend to banish Masculinity? Would Matriarchy come again? A sleuth known for probes of homosexuality in classic American fiction, Leslie Fiedler, looked warily at "The New Mutants" (1965) for evidence of the feminization of culture. A psychologist, Karl Stern, took up cudgels on the other side, in a work called *The Flight from Woman* (1965), hinting that any weakening of competitive energies might mean a coming-to-terms at last with the long-suppressed femininity of the male psyche itself: all hail an imminent reign of tenderness. Everywhere, as it seemed, intellect drove itself toward the peripheral, the inessential, the sensational, the reductive, with the result that, as at many an earlier moment in human history when breath was departing a ruling myth, and the path ahead was darkness, confusion and distraction mounted.

11.  And at length were overcome. That latter part of our story, the brilliant *fin-de-siècle* effort at reconstruction, has been well told elsewhere. Heroic names and achievements have been recorded; the classic texts have had their scrupulous exegetes; minor technical problems alone remain. One further word may be said here, though, toward the end of dispelling the impression, rather widespread just now, that the age we survey was in every intellectual quarter inane. Granted, a backward glance over those troops of self-important, preening "youth authorities," pundits, moralists, social science "experts,"

cynical political revivifiers (on the right) of a dying superego—granted that such a backward glance gives small encouragement to the belief that the age knew any growing points save the Early Metamorphics themselves. Granted too that, with the quality of the general mind of the day firmly before us, it seems likely that The Early Ones' refusal to articulate a program, their preference for doing it rather than saying it, was at bottom a response to the lambent dullness roundabout.

12.    Amid so much muck, madness, nonsense, and false piety, who could possibly have grasped the truth?

13.    Yet while impatience with the age is understandable, it is not altogether just. The language we now speak, the conceptual schemes on which we now rest, were, true enough, little dreamed of then. Dartings, whirlings, substitute lateral gratification, possibilitarianism, the movement from Tyrowhirler to Septenary and on across the band toward Life-Exhaustion—few could have comprehended the bearings of these terms. Our commonplaces: awareness that life-meaning resides wholly in the exploration of human possibility, in the process of multiple self-creation, not in any goals, results, or consequences; our commitment to the maintenance of open-mindedness and universal Playwork Participation in all public and private roles—these commonplaces of our times have no precise counterparts in late-twentieth-century thought.

14.    Yet from this it does not follow that the period must be dismissed out of hand as a blank. Calling the roll of the insightful of those times is saddening: some voices have been lost, and none that survives achieved life-contact with The Early Ones themselves. Still, a few of these minds matter. One notable, if abstract, formulation of proteanism appeared in the mid-sixties, for instance, in a foundation-supported journal called *Daedalus*. The formulator was a young political scientist, G. Kateb by name, who wrote as follows:

> We have . . . referred to the utopian possibility of making life as a whole "more plastic." What we mean to suggest by these phrases is the allowance for a greater relaxation in the definitions of self, role, vocation, than the world customarily allows. Proteus could become the symbol of the tone of utopian life. The aim would be to encourage self-expression to the point where the traditional boundaries between fantasy and reality would become more blurred, to allow individuals to assume various "personae" without fear of social penalty, to allow groups to come together and affect diverse communal relations and then disband, to allow for the greatest possible accumulation of vicarious, mimetic, or semi-genuine experience, to

strive to have each self be able to say, in the words of Walt Whitman's "Song of Myself," "I am large, I contain multitudes," and, finally, in the name of heightened consciousness and amplitude of being to diminish the force of the duality of male and female. And for this "playing at life" to take worthwhile forms and conclude in splendid enrichment of character, the mind and feelings must be cultivated, the capacity to experience the higher pleasures must be developed, the higher faculties must be in control. Otherwise the playing at life would remain just that, and not be, instead, an instrument of self-transcendence. [*Utopia and the Good Life,* Spring, 1965]

15. The strongest work of the period, however, was that of the still-remembered Henry S. Kariel. It was Kariel who, in *The Promise of Politics* (1966), drew attention to metamorphic, self-exploratory, nonauthoritarian dimensions of "such disparate personalities as Socrates, Diogenes, Montaigne, Voltaire, Franklin, Henry Adams, Brecht, and Kennedy, and . . . Don Quixote and Huck Finn," and who delivered, in a remarkable chapter which is entitled "Man in Process," a virtual prophecy of the present age:

In this . . . newly framed picture, man may be seen as an elusive, incomplete being forever in the process of self-discovery and self-development. He is pre-eminently an innovating creature. In the concise terms of Christian Bay, he is "free to the extent that he has the *capacity,* the *opportunity,* and the *incentive* to give expression to what is in him and to develop his potentialities." There is no effort here to fill in what he is to be free *for.* He is simply free from those self-mutilating traits that produce the mindless fanatic, enthusiast, or nihilist, that keep him from acknowledging and developing himself. In the language of Marx, he is free "to do one thing today and another tomorrow, to hunt in the morning, fish in the afternoon, rear cattle in the evening, criticize after dinner." He is free to play these roles, Marx significantly added, "without ever *becoming* hunter, fisherman, shepherd, or critic. . . ." He is a probing, experimenting being, always in motion, attaching and detaching values, inflating and deflating alternatives, unsure of his place in the order of things, skeptical and above all, aware of his skepticism.

16. Kariel moved on from these themes to the greater issues, in *Open Systems: Arenas for Political Action* (1968), even coming to face the question that has preoccupied our own century: "How open an area for protean action can we contemplate?" In a most moving preface to the latter work, he speaks of the gulf separating him from The Early Ones, both Primitive Metamorphics like Clara and Chip and John, and the Great Early One, Jerry Rubin himself:

. . . I also know there are roles I *could* play [Kariel writes wanly].
. . . There are a great many . . . roles I can conceive of myself
playing. And yet, it is obvious to me, I fail to play them. I do not
travel readily or lightly. Not for me Ishmael's voyage. I am tenured,
committed, identified, defined. I still have various options—not
playing Ahab, to be sure, but possibly Ishmael. Yet I fail to exercise
them. I am aware not only of being limited (which no longer de-
presses me) but of being *needlessly* limited. I *could* without damage
to myself test more possibilities and be at least somewhat more
playful. I could play more parts, participate more. Nevertheless,
here I am, voluntarily limited and enclosed.

17. Who among us, reading these sentences, can fail to be
touched by the pathos of this address, and by the implicit difficulty of
the struggle in those years to Break Free? And who among us can be
unmoved by the tale of Kariel's neglect in his own time? His pioneering essays rationalizing the Metamorphics as "proto-types of the open-
ended personality system" were printed in literary reviews with sub-
scription lists of a few thousand. None of the great university
presses or trade publishers of the period undertook to bring out his
pioneering volumes on enlarging experiential range, or those works
contending that men "must test the degree of *tolerable* disruption,"
that politics must be injected into all closed systems, that men must
*pry open* their personality systems, their science and knowledge systems, their social systems, and that the aim of life is to *disrupt imposed
experiences.* (The seminal volume, *Open Systems,* was brought out in
a tiny unnoticed edition by Loyola University Press.) Kariel held no
honored chair in his teaching lifetime (much of his career was spent
at the University of Hawaii!), and the bibliographies of that age, which
show endless special issues and festschrifts for the likes of "Herman
Marcuse," "Norbert O. Brown," "N. Mailer," and other unidentifiables, reveal no interest in his name. Even within his own profession,
when his themes were glancingly touched upon—process orientation,
for instance, or the protean psychological style (see an essay published in 1967 called "Protean Man" by a professor named Robert
Lifton)—Kariel's name went unmentioned. The clear case is that the
quest for the new gospel began in his pages, and the story of his neglect is truly depressing.

18. Were there others? A few. None of their writing has the
force of the classic texts, to be sure. None matches, say, those extraordinary paeans to self-disorientation found in Jerry's touchstone parable
of the Yippies freaking the college newspaper editors:

The room echoed with hysterical screams. "Stop it! Stop it! Stop it!" A voice boomed over a bullhorn: "Attention! This is Sergeant Haggerty of the Washington Police. These films were smuggled illegally into the country from North Vietnam. We have confiscated them and arrested the people who are responsible. Now clear this room! Anyone still here in two minutes will be arrested!"

The editors fell over themselves rushing for the door. People were trampled. Noses bloodied. Clothes ripped to shreds. . . . A husky crewcut cat, in suit and tie . . . climbed up on a chair and yelled, "I've just come back from Vietnam. My brothers died in my arms. The fools in the White House are going to kill us all. We are college editors. We have power. We must be brave!"

Is this guy real? Or part of the Washington Theater group? I didn't know. But did it make any difference? Everything was *real and unreal*. The editors were stunned. Chaos and anarchy reigned. . . . "You will have to decide for yourself whether the police are real or not. . . ." People broke down, crying. . . . They began talking to one another. . . . It was an emotional breakthrough. Through theater they learned something about themselves.

Such words do not abide our question.

19. Yet on occasion, the cause of disorientation, and of movement through roles, was articulated, even this early, in terms of specific changes in public servants and public policy. An urban planner, Richard Sennett, argued, in a work called *The Uses of Disorder* (1970), that people of his profession victimized themselves and others by overrigid self-definitions. Sennett compared the city planners to certain overprotective young doctors:

. . . these young doctors have . . . a peculiar kind of strength— a power to cut themselves off from the world around them, to make themselves distant, and perhaps lonely, by defining themselves in a rigid way. This fixed self-definition gives them a strong weapon against the outside world. . . . The threat of being overwhelmed by difficult social interactions is dealt with by fixing a self-image *in advance,* by making oneself a fixed object rather than an open person liable to be touched by a social situation.

Sennett argued that the same rigidity afflicted planners, and that it must be overcome, for, as he declared:

This attitude is a way of denying the idea of history, i.e., that a society will come to be different than it expected to be in the past. In this way, a planner at his desk can steel himself against the unknown outside world in the same way that a young doctor steels himself against his fear about the experience of dealing with his patients. . . .

20.   And in 1970 a striking paper was read to the Committee on Social Stratification and Social Mobility of the Seventh World Congress of Sociology at Varna, Bulgaria. Entitled "Strategies for Social Mobility," it was the work of two scholars, S. M. Miller of New York University and Pamela Roby of George Washington University, who acknowledged uncompromisingly that the metaphor of the rise had lost substance for the commonality. Better henceforth, they proposed, to imagine mobility as a progress through various kinds of work, not as linear upward movement in a particular organization. "Higher and lower positions are not so much the issue," they opined; the crux is movement, change, variety, freshness. Theirs was, admittedly, a primitive effort. There was no hint of relish of Self-Whirl or Self-Explore in this paper. The motive was merely to patch up programs of compensatory education originally aimed at guaranteeing "upward mobility" to what were called "the disadvantaged." Yet, studied in its own context, it stands as a landmark.

21.   And, as may as well be added, something of the same landmark quality attaches to the early commune-meditation centers. For invariably these institutes stressed role-variousness in their programs —witness an advertisement for a center called CUMBRES, founded in 1970 at Dublin, New Hampshire:

> All permanent members of the staff share all the work. There is physical labor in gardening, maintaining the grounds, cleaning, preparing and serving food. There are creative and intellectual efforts in conducting seminars, leading groups, writing and designing brochures, coordinating programs, etc. There is spiritual work in study groups and in meditation. A member of the staff may be found preparing breakfast for the community in the morning, answering correspondence in the afternoon and leading a discussion group in the evening.

22.   But subtly, almost imperceptibly, the act of drawing together such documents teases us out of proportioned perception. We yield to the supposition that these documents were widely studied, that men "must have learned" from them the true character of the age struggling to birth. (Surely they knew as much by the beginning of the century's eighth decade—how else explain the quantity of evidence, as attested by our clusters of citations, bearing the date 1970?) Altogether easy for us to riffle through the museum of the past, collecting the prefiguring texts that have touched us, fashioned our being—great

early works like Emerson's "Circles," key apothegms from "Self Reliance":

> When good is near you, when you have life in yourself, it is not by any known or accustomed way . . .—the way, the thought, the good shall be wholly strange and new.

> Power ceases in the moment of repose, it resides in the moment of transition from a past to a new state, in the shooting of the gulf, in the darting to an aim.

How could process-orientation have remained a mystery?

23. But our question is, in the end, inadmissible. Best to speak flatly: what is obvious to us now—our way of reading the great texts, Marx, Sorel, Dewey, Bergson, Pirandello, and the rest—was not obvious to them. Those who struggled, those who perceived the future and did not bog down in puerile squabbles about clothes or feminization or moral improvement or stabilization of egos, those who refused to meet the challenge of a dying age by scrambling back into the political rejuvenation of Superego—to these we owe full respect. They are our fathers, indeed, our very selves.

24. But that such minds breathed—and were met with opprobrium or laughter—must not muffle our compassion for the others: even for the mockers themselves, the wholly blind. The historical hour they passed through had been transversed before. Serious disturbances had been known by their great-grandfathers, in the mid-nineteenth century, when the continuity of man and nature was disclosed, and again, two centuries earlier, when the planets were set in motion and poets shuddered:

> Moving of th' earth brings harmes and feares,
> Men reckon what it did and meant—

But the human fact is that the birth of the new is not made easier by memory of earlier births. The coming of an age when self too would "move," would seek endlessly, richly, appetitively the experience of transformation and metamorphosis: this was an eruption of terror like the quaking of planets. It cannot too often be repeated that for generations men had told each other the meaning of life lay not in the afterlife, not in the service of divinity, but in *work itself,* the struggle upward. "We must work!" cried Vershinin in Chekhov's *Three Sisters.* "There is nothing for us but work, all of us must work!"

25. And then all at once, as we have seen, work turned meaningless. Children shrugged, smiled condescendingly to their

fathers. A university president of the period, Martin Meyerson, appears often to have repeated, in public speeches, the words of one of his students: "I know one thing, though. I know work isn't my thing. I do know work isn't my thing." Seemingly his tone was bemused—troubled but not hysterical. He doubtless hoped to allay fears of parents as he repeated the phrases, surrounding them with hopeful easing words. But it cannot have been easy for those listening then to hear life-values lightly mocked. —My children won't work. . . . But what then will they do? Who will discharge their obligations? How can society's labor be performed? How can human civilization be preserved? Are men to be orgiasts for life, grooving endlessly down the ringing grooves of change? People gazed into each other's eyes, frowning, looked away in fear. Old Scripture promised that "thy children shall return to thy borders"; but Old Scripture had no authority, and New Scripture was as yet unimaginable. Dismay, a steadily deepening sense of uselessness, worthlessness, purposelessness—the death of meaning. This was the experience, these were the torments.

26. For us, thinking backward, penetrating the period imaginatively, perceiving the emotional excess of its depressions, reflecting on the ingenuity of our own open structures, our devices for nonviolent testings of freedom, our marvelously flexible patterns of disruption, above all our opportunities for exhilarating lifetimes of self-whirling—for us the temptation is strong to consider that there is no lesson here save that of our superiority, our huge distance from their mean level of achievement. But here as elsewhere, as always for men, the truest lesson is the most compassionate. There is but one meaning in these years of quest and seeming defeat now far gone from living memory, that of human resiliency: the superb, *trustable* permanence of men's power—no matter what blankness oppresses our days—forever to renew and reconceive ourselves.

## WORDS

*meaning*   1. Define *Ur-Metamorphics* (par. 3). What is the point of the footnote to the sentence in which the word appears? 2. Define *Sextuple Darter* and *Fem Tyrowhirler* (par. 4), *saturnalia* (par. 6), and *Byzantine* (par. 9). 3. What is meant by *cynical political revivifiers* (*on the right*) *of a dying superego* (par. 11)?

*connotation*   What is the author trying to suggest by his expression *Playwork Participation* (par. 13)?

*relationship*   The word *redolent* is used in two different ways in paragraph 9. How do these two meanings connect?

## SENTENCES

*rhetorical devices*   1. Can you translate into literal terms the series of metaphors beginning with *holding fluidities* in paragraph 1?   2. The author is given to putting ironical comments into parentheses. What is the irony of the parenthesis (*in the contemporary phrase*) near the end of paragraph 2? Could he with equal point have put that parenthesis behind another word in the same sentence?   3. What is ironical about the parenthesis (*possibly non-existent*) in paragraph 6?   4. The quotation from Saul Bellow in paragraph 9 ends with a number of ironical figures of speech. Analyze them for their logic.   5. Who are the *unidentifiables* to whom the author refers in paragraph 17 and what point is his irony trying to score?

## CONTENT AND ORGANIZATION

*assumptions and implications*   1. The author assumes that his readers have considerable knowledge of literature and other matters. Identify the titles in his opening paragraph.   2. What is the meaning of the references to *Ishmael* and *Ahab* in paragraph 16?   3. What are the accomplishments of the three men mentioned in paragraph 8?   4. What are the great discoveries referred to in paragraph 23?

*organization*   Work out the time scheme on which this essay is based.

*central ideas*   1. The opening words of the essay, *Turning and turning,* echo the opening of William B. Yeats's famous poem, "The Second Coming,"

> Turning and turning in the widening gyre
> The falcon cannot hear the falconer;
> Things fall apart; the centre cannot hold . . .

Point to specific places in the essay where the author plays with the idea of *turning*. The Yeats poem is about the end of one great phase of civilization and the beginning of a new and rather frightening one. Does this general theme have relevance to the essay as a whole?   2. In paragraph 25, the author seems to be echoing a line from Tennyson's famous poem of praise for an age of technological progress, "Locksley Hall,"

> Not in vain the distance beckons. Forward, forward
>      let us range,
> Let the great world spin for ever down the ringing
>      grooves of change.

To what use does he put these lines? Why might one say that the allusion has inverted relevance to the essayist's theme and general attitude?

## SUGGESTIONS FOR DISCUSSION

1. At about what date would you say the author is pretending to write? The author speaks of a whole new age, of the sixties and seventies as nearly forgotten. Consider paragraph 13, with its references to "the

language we now speak, the conceptual schemes on which we now rest,"
etc. Now consider paragraph 11, especially sentence 3: What kind of
language is he using there? Is it radically new or is it in fact all too
familiar in the present? Is the language in general radically different from
the language now? If so, can you find examples? Does he give us a clear
idea of the new "conceptual schemes" to which he refers? If so, summarize them.  2. Read Edward Bellamy's *Looking Backward* (1888), and
then write an essay in which you define what is meant by *utopia* and by
*dystopia*. Or discuss the value of utopian (or dystopian) literature as a
means of prevention and/or remedy of contemporary "ills."


*Arthur Miller*

# TRAGEDY AND THE COMMON MAN

1.  In this age few tragedies are written. It has often been held
that the lack is due to a paucity of heroes among us, or else that
modern man has had the blood drawn out of his organs of belief by
the skepticism of science, and the heroic attack on life cannot feed on
an attitude of reserve and circumspection. For one reason or another,
we are often held to be below tragedy—or tragedy above us. The
inevitable conclusion is, of course, that the tragic mode is archaic, fit
only for the very highly placed, the kings or the kingly, and where
this admission is not made in so many words it is most often implied.

2.  I believe that the common man is as apt a subject for tragedy
in its highest sense as kings were. On the face of it this ought to be
obvious in the light of modern psychiatry, which bases its analysis
upon classific formulations, such as the Oedipus and Orestes com-
plexes, for instance, which were enacted by royal beings, but which
apply to everyone in similar emotional situations.

3.  More simply, when the question of tragedy in art is not at
issue, we never hesitate to attribute to the well-placed and the exalted
the very same mental processes as the lowly. And finally, if the exaltation of tragic action were truly a property of the high-bred character
alone, it is inconceivable that the mass of mankind should cherish
tragedy above all other forms, let alone be capable of understanding it.

4.  As a general rule, to which there may be exceptions un-

TRAGEDY AND THE COMMON MAN:  From *The New York Times,* February 17,
1949. Reprinted by permission of International Famous Agency. Copyright ©
1949 by The New York Times for Arthur Miller.

known to me, I think the tragic feeling is evoked in us when we are in the presence of a character who is ready to lay down his life, if need be, to secure one thing—his sense of personal dignity. From Orestes to Hamlet, Medea to Macbeth, the underlying struggle is that of the individual attempting to gain his "rightful" position in his society.

5.   Sometimes he is one who has been displaced from it, sometimes one who seeks to attain it for the first time, but the fateful wound from which the inevitable events spiral is the wound of indignity, and its dominant force is indignation. Tragedy, then, is the consequence of a man's total compulsion to evaluate himself justly.

6.   In the sense of having been initiated by the hero himself, the tale always reveals what has been called his "tragic flaw," a failing that is not peculiar to grand or elevated characters. Nor is it necessarily a weakness. The flaw, or crack in the character, is really nothing—and need be nothing—but his inherent unwillingness to remain passive in the face of what he conceives to be a challenge to his dignity, his image of his rightful status. Only the passive, only those who accept their lot without active retaliation, are "flawless." Most of us are in that category.

7.   But there are among us today, as there always have been, those who act against the scheme of things that degrades them, and in the process of action everything we have accepted out of fear or insensitivity or ignorance is shaken before us and examined, and from this total onslaught by an individual against the seemingly stable cosmos surrounding us—from this total examination of the "unchangeable" environment—comes the terror and the fear that is classically associated with tragedy.

8.   More important, from this total questioning of what has previously been unquestioned, we learn. And such a process is not beyond the common man. In revolutions around the world, these past thirty years, he has demonstrated again and again this inner dynamic of all tragedy.

9.   Insistence upon the rank of the tragic hero, or the so-called nobility of his character, is really but a clinging to the outward forms of tragedy. If rank or nobility of character was indispensable, then it would follow that the problems of those with rank were the particular problems of tragedy. But surely the right of one monarch to capture the domain from another no longer raises our passions, nor are our concepts of justice what they were to the mind of an Elizabethan king.

10.   The quality in such plays that does shake us, however, de-

rives from the underlying fear of being displaced, the disaster inherent in being torn away from our chosen image of what and who we are in this world. Among us today this fear is as strong as, and perhaps stronger than, it ever was. In fact, it is the common man who knows this fear best.

11.   Now, if it is true that tragedy is the consequence of a man's total compulsion to evaluate himself justly, his destruction in the attempt posits a wrong or an evil in his environment. And this is precisely the morality of tragedy and its lesson. The discovery of the moral law, which is what the enlightenment of tragedy consists of, is not the discovery of some abstract or metaphysical quantity.

12.   The tragic right is a condition of life, a condition in which the human personality is able to flower and realize itself. The wrong is the condition which supresses man, perverts the flowing out of his love and creative instinct. Tragedy enlightens—and it must, in that it points the heroic finger at the enemy of man's freedom. The thrust for freedom is the quality in tragedy which exalts. The revolutionary questioning of the stable environment is what terrifies. In no way is the common man debarred from such thoughts or such actions.

13.   Seen in this light, our lack of tragedy may be partially accounted for by the turn which modern literature has taken toward the purely psychiatric view of life, or the purely sociological. If all our miseries, our indignities, are born and bred within our minds, then all action, let alone the heroic action, is obviously impossible.

14.   And if society alone is responsible for the cramping of our lives, then the protagonist must needs be so pure and faultless as to force us to deny his validity as a character. From neither of these views can tragedy derive, simply because neither represents a balanced concept of life. Above all else, tragedy requires the finest appreciation by the writer of cause and effect.

15.   No tragedy can therefore come about when its author fears to question absolutely everything, when he regards any institution, habit or custom as being either everlasting, immutable or inevitable. In the tragic view the need of man to wholly realize himself is the only fixed star, and whatever it is that hedges his nature and lowers it is ripe for attack and examination. Which is not to say that tragedy must preach revolution.

16.   The Greeks could probe the very heavenly origin of their ways and return to confirm the rightness of laws. And Job could face God in anger, demanding his right, and end in submission. But for a moment everything is in suspension, nothing is accepted, and in this stretching and tearing apart of the cosmos, in the very action of so

doing, the character gains "size," the tragic stature which is spuriously attached to the royal or the highborn in our minds. The commonest of men may take on that stature to the extent of willingness to throw all he has into the contest, the battle to secure his rightful place in his world.

17. There is a misconception of tragedy with which I have been struck in review after review, and in many conversations with writers and readers alike. It is the idea that tragedy is of necessity allied to pessimism. Even the dictionary says nothing more about the word than that it means a story with a sad or unhappy ending. This impression is so firmly fixed that I almost hesitate to claim that in truth tragedy implies more optimism in its author than does comedy, and that its final result ought to be the reinforcement of the onlooker's brightest opinions of the human animal.

18. For, if it is true to say that in essence the tragic hero is intent upon claiming his whole due as a personality, and if this struggle must be total and without reservation, then it automatically demonstrates the indestructible will of man to achieve his humanity.

19. The possibility of victory must be there in tragedy. Where pathos rules, where pathos is finally derived, a character has fought a battle he could not possibly have won. The pathetic is achieved when the protagonist is, by virtue of his witlessness, his insensitivity, or the very air he gives off, incapable of grappling with a much superior force.

20. Pathos truly is the mode for the pessimist. But tragedy requires a nicer balance between what is possible and what is impossible. And it is curious, although edifying, that the plays we revere, century after century, are the tragedies. In them, and in them alone, lies the belief—optimistic, if you will—in the perfectibility of man.

21. It is time, I think, that we who are without kings, took up this bright thread of our history and followed it to the only place it can possibly lead in our time—the heart and spirit of the average man.

WORDS

*meaning* Define *paucity* and *archaic* (par. 1), *dynamic* (par. 8), *immutable* (par. 15), *spuriously* (par. 16), *protagonist* (par. 19), and *perfectibility* (par. 20).

*connotation* The following phrases cannot be defined in the strict way that is possible with the words listed under *meaning*. What, then, is the meaning of "the heroic attack on life" (par. 1), "total compulsion to evaluate himself justly" (par. 5), and "the very air he gives off" (par. 19)?

*relationships*  What is the connection of *posits* (par. 11) with *impose,*
*repository,* and *posture?*

## SENTENCES

*parallelism*  1. In the opening sentence of paragraph 15, find two parallel
series of words.  2. In paragraph 12, find the two nearly parallel sentences. Rewrite one of the sentences in order to make its structure exactly
parallel with the other. Is this exact parallelism more or less effective
than the original version? Why?

*rhetorical devices*  1. What quality do the following figures of speech
share: "the heroic attack on life" (par. 1), "act against the scheme of
things" (par. 7), and "points the heroic finger at the enemy" and "The
thrust for freedom" (par. 12)?  2. How completely does this common
quality of these figures of speech also represent the essence of tragedy in
the author's argument?  3. List as many other such figures as you can
find in the essay. Do you find any that do not share in the quality observed
in the group listed above? Taking together the qualities you can abstract
from this figurative language, can you characterize the author's sense of
what is valuable in human experience or his assumptions about the nature
of man?

## PARAGRAPHS

*unity*  Newspaper editors do not like long paragraphs. Would paragraphs
4 and 5 have greater or less unity if they were simply run together?

*topic sentences*  1. Which is the topic sentence of paragraph 2?  2. Do
you think that this sentence can fairly be said to state the topic of the
whole essay, or is there material in the essay that does not in some way
develop or refer to this sentence?

## CONTENT AND ORGANIZATION

*central ideas*  1. Every man must meet the same basic situations in life.
What are they (par. 10)? Today, the "common man" is made even more
aware of them than is the extraordinary man. Does the author illustrate
this assertion with examples? Can you?  2. The tragic hero challenges
things as they are on behalf of his individual dignity. The challenge gives
him his heroic stature. What makes him tragic?

*organization*  Does paragraph 13 contradict paragraph 2, or are they
making quite different statements on the same general topic?

*assumptions and implications*  1. The author says that the tragic hero can
be the common man. Who is the common man?  2. "Most of us" pas-
sively accept things as they are (par. 6). Is there a contradiction between
assumptions 1 and 2? Explain.

1. Is Miller's own well-known play *Death of a Salesman* a tragedy by the definition in this essay? Or does it fall into the category of "the pathetic" (pars. 19–20)? 2. It may well be true that the great tragedies are among the most treasured works in the world's literature, but do you believe that it follows that "the mass of mankind" cherishes "tragedy above all other forms" (par. 3)? In your experience of the mass audience in modern America, is tragedy highly regarded? Does the film industry think that it is? 3. Can you summarize one or two actual situations in which a man or woman of your acquaintance made "the heroic attack on life" (par. 1) in defense of "his sense of personal dignity" (par. 4) and suffered catastrophe as a result? 4. Could you argue that, by the author's own reasoning, tragedy demonstrates the absurdity (rather than the validity) of the idea of "the perfectibility of man" (par. 20)?

*John Ciardi*

# ROBERT FROST:
# THE WAY TO THE POEM

### STOPPING BY WOODS ON A SNOWY EVENING

Whose woods these are I think I know.
His house is in the village though;
He will not see me stopping here
To watch his woods fill up with snow.

My little horse must think it queer
To stop without a farmhouse near
Between the wood and frozen lake
The darkest evening of the year.

He gives his harness bells a shake
To ask if there is some mistake.
The only other sound's the sweep
Of easy wind and downy flake.

ROBERT FROST: THE WAY TO THE POEM: From the *Saturday Review*, April 12, 1958. Reprinted by permission of the *Saturday Review*.

"Stopping by Woods on a Snowy Evening": From *The Poetry of Robert Frost* edited by Edward Connery Lathem. Copyright 1923 by Holt, Rinehart and Winston, Inc. Copyright 1951 by Robert Frost. Reprinted by permission of Holt, Rinehart and Winston, Inc.

The woods are lovely, dark and deep.
But I have promises to keep,
And miles to go before I sleep,
And miles to go before I sleep.

1.   The School System has much to say these days of the virtue of reading widely, and not enough about the virtues of reading less but in depth. There are any number of reading lists for poetry, but there is not enough talk about individual poems. Poetry, finally, is one poem at a time. To read any one poem carefully is the ideal preparation for reading another. Only a poem can illustrate how poetry works.

2.   Above, therefore, is a poem—one of the master lyrics of the English language, and almost certainly the best-known poem by an American poet. What happens in it?—which is to say, not *what does* it mean, but *how* does it mean? How does it go about being a human reenactment of a human experience? The author—perhaps the thousandth reader would need to be told—is Robert Frost.

3.   Even the TV audience can see that this poem begins as a seemingly simple narration of a seemingly simple incident but ends by suggesting meanings far beyond anything specifically referred to in the narrative. And even readers with only the most casual interest in poetry might be made to note the additional fact that, though the poem suggests those larger meanings, it is very careful never to abandon its pretense to being simple narration. There is duplicity at work. The poet pretends to be talking about one thing, and all the while he is talking about many others.

4.   Many readers are forever unable to accept the poet's essential duplicity. It is almost safe to say that a poem is never about what it seems to be about. As much could be said of the proverb. The bird in the hand, the rolling stone, the stitch in time never (except by an artful double-deception) intend any sort of statement about birds, stones, or sewing. The incident of this poem, one must conclude, is at root a metaphor.

5.   Duplicity aside, this poem's movement from the specific to the general illustrates one of the basic formulas of all poetry. Such a grand poem as Arnold's "Dover Beach" and such lesser, though unfortunately better known, poems as Longfellow's "The Village Blacksmith" and Holmes's "The Chambered Nautilus" are built on the same progression. In these three poems, however, the generalization is markedly set apart from the specific narration, and even seems additional to the telling rather than intrinsic to it. It is this sense of division one has in mind in speaking of "a tacked-on moral."

6.   There is nothing wrong-in-itself with a tacked-on moral.

Frost, in fact, makes excellent use of the device at times. In this poem, however, Frost is careful to let the whatever-the-moral-is grow out of the poem itself. When the action ends the poem ends. There is no epilogue and no explanation. Everything pretends to be about the narrated incident. And that pretense sets the basic tone of the poem's performance of itself.

7.   The dramatic force of that performance is best observable, I believe, as a progression in three scenes.

8.   In scene one, which coincides with stanza one, a man—a New England man—is driving his sleigh somewhere at night. It is snowing, and as the man passes a dark patch of woods he stops to watch the snow descend into the darkness. We know, moreover, that the man is familiar with these parts (he knows who owns the woods and where the owner lives), and we know that no one has seen him stop. As scene one forms itself in the theater of the mind's eye, therefore, it serves to establish some as yet unspecified relation between the man and the woods.

9.   It is necessary, however, to stop here for a long parenthesis: Even so simple an opening statement raises any number of questions. It is impossible to address all the questions that rise from the poem stanza by stanza, but two that arise from stanza one illustrate the sort of thing one might well ask of the poem detail by detail.

10.   Why, for example, does the man not say what errand he is on? What is the force of leaving the errand generalized? He might just as well have told us that he was going to the general store, or returning from it with a jug of molasses he had promised to bring Aunt Harriet and two suits of long underwear he had promised to bring the hired man. Frost, moreover, can handle homely detail to great effect. He preferred to leave his motive generalized. Why?

11.   And why, on the other hand, does he say so much about knowing the absent owner of the woods and where he lives? Is it simply that one set of details happened-in whereas another did not? To speak of things "happening-in" is to assault the integrity of a poem. Poetry cannot be discussed meaningfully unless one can assume that everything in the poem—every last comma and variant spelling —is in it by the poet's specific act of choice. Only bad poets allow into their poems what is haphazard or cheaply chosen.

12.   The errand, I will venture a bit brashly for lack of space, is left generalized in order the more aptly to suggest *any* errand in life and, therefore, life itself. The owner is there because he is one of the forces of the poem. Let it do to say that the force he represents is the village of mankind (that village at the edge of winter)

from which the poet finds himself separated (has separated himself?) in his moment by the woods (and to which, he recalls finally, he has promises to keep). The owner is he-who-lives-in-his-village-house, thereby locked away from the poet's awareness of the-time-the-snow-tells as it engulfs and obliterates the world the village man allows himself to believe he "owns." Thus, the owner is a representative of an order of reality from which the poet has divided himself for the moment, though to a certain extent he ends by reuniting with it. Scene one, therefore, establishes not only a relation between the man and the woods, but the fact that the man's relation begins with his separation (though momentarily) from mankind.

13. End parenthesis one, begin parenthesis two.

14. Still considering the first scene as a kind of dramatic performance of forces, one must note that the poet has meticulously matched the simplicity of his language to the pretended simplicity of the narrative. Clearly, the man stopped because the beauty of the scene moved him, but he neither tells us that the scene is beautiful nor that he is moved. A bad writer, always ready to overdo, might have written: "The vastness gripped me, filling my spirit with the slow steady sinking of the snow's crystalline perfection into the glimmerless profundities of the hushed primeval wood." Frost's avoidance of such a spate illustrates two principles of good writing. The first, he has stated himself in "The Mowing": "Anything *more* than the truth would have seemed too weak" (italics mine). Understatement is one of the basic sources of power in English poetry. The second principle is to let the action speak for itself. A good novelist does not tell us that a given character is good or bad (at least not since the passing of the Dickens tradition): he shows us the character in action and then, watching him, we know. Poetry, too, has fictional obligations: even when the characters are ideas and metaphors rather than people, they must be *characterized in action*. A poem does not *talk about* ideas; it *enacts* them. The force of the poem's performance, in fact, is precisely to act out (and thereby to make us act out empathically, that is, to *feel out,* that is, to *identify with*) the speaker and why he stopped. The man is the principal actor in this little "drama of why" and in scene one he is the only character, though as noted, he is somehow related to the absent owner.

15. End second parenthesis.

16. In scene two (stanzas two and three) a *foil* is introduced. In fiction and drama, a foil is a character who "plays against" a more important character. By presenting a different point of view or an opposed set of motives, the foil moves the more important character to

react in ways that might not have found expression without such opposition. The more important character is thus more fully revealed —to the reader and to himself. The foil here is the horse.

17.   The horse forces the question. Why did the man stop? Until it occurs to him that his "little horse must think it queer" he had not asked himself for reasons. He had simply stopped. But the man finds himself faced with the question he imagines the horse to be asking: what *is* there to stop for out there in the cold, away from bin and stall (house and village and mankind?) and all that any self-respecting beast could value on such a night? In sensing that other view, the man is forced to examine his own more deeply.

18.   In stanza two the question arises only as a feeling within the man. In stanza three, however (still scene two), the horse acts. He gives his harness bells a shake. "What's wrong?" he seems to say. "What are we waiting for?"

19.   By now, obviously, the horse—without losing its identity as horse—has also become a symbol. A symbol is something that stands for something else. Whatever that something else may be, it certainly begins as that order of life that does not understand why a man stops in the wintry middle of nowhere to watch the snow come down. (Can one fail to sense by now that the dark and the snowfall symbolize a death-wish, however momentary, *i.e.,* that hunger for final rest and surrender that a man may feel, but not a beast?)

20.   So by the end of scene two the performance has given dramatic force to three elements that work upon the man. There is his relation to the world of the owner. There is his relation to the brute world of the horse. And there is that third presence of the unownable world, the movement of the all-engulfing snow across all the orders of life, the man's, the owner's, and the horse's—with the difference that the man knows of that second dark-within-the-dark of which the horse cannot, and the owner will not, know.

21.   The man ends scene two with all these forces working upon him simultaneously. He feels himself moved to a decision. And he feels a last call from the darkness: "the sweep / Of easy wind and downy flake." It would be so easy and so downy to go into the woods and let himself be covered over.

22.   But scene three (stanza four) produces a fourth force. This fourth force can be given many names. It is certainly better, in fact, to give it many names than to attempt to limit it to one. It is social obligation, or personal commitment, or duty, or just the realization that a man cannot indulge a mood forever. All of these and more. But, finally, he has a simple decision to make. He may go into the

woods and let the darkness and the snow swallow him from the world of beast and man. Or he must move on. And unless he is going to stop here forever, it is time to remember that he has a long way to go and that he had best be getting there. (So there is something to be said for the horse, too.)

23.    Then and only then, his question driven more and more deeply into himself by these cross-forces, does the man venture a comment on what attracted him: "The woods are lovely, dark and deep." His mood lingers over the thought of that lovely dark-and-deep (as do the very syllables in which he phrases the thought), but the final decision is to put off the mood and move on. He has his man's way to go and his man's obligations to tend to before he can yield. He has miles to go before his sleep. He repeats that thought and the performance ends.

24.    But why the repetition? The first time Frost says "And miles to go before I sleep," there can be little doubt that the primary meaning is: "I have a long way to go before I get to bed tonight." The second time he says it, however, "miles to go" and "sleep" are suddenly transformed into symbols. What are those "something-elses" the symbols stand for? Hundreds of people have tried to ask Mr. Frost that question and he has always turned it away. He has turned it away *because he cannot answer it*. He could answer some part of it. But some part is not enough.

25.    For a symbol is like a rock dropped into a pool: it sends out ripples in all directions, and the ripples are in motion. Who can say where the last ripple disappears? One may have a sense that he knows the approximate center point of the ripples, the point at which the stone struck the water. Yet even then he has trouble marking it surely. How does one make a mark on water? Oh, very well—the center point of that second "miles to go" is probably approximately in the neighborhood of being close to meaning, perhaps, "the road of life"; and the second "before I sleep" is maybe that close to meaning "before I take my final rest," the rest in darkness that seemed so temptingly dark-and-deep for the moment of the mood. But the ripples continue to move and the light to change on the water, and the longer one watches the more changes he sees. Such shifting-and-being-at-the-same-instant is of the very sparkle and life of poetry. One experiences it as one experiences life, for every time he looks at an experience he sees something new, and sees it change as he watches it. And that sense of continuity in fluidity is one of the primary kinds of knowledge, one of man's basic ways of knowing, and one that only the arts can teach, poetry foremost among them.

26.    Frost himself certainly did not ask what that repeated last line meant. It came to him and he received it. He "felt right" about it. And what he "felt right" about was in no sense a "meaning" that, say, an essay could apprehend, but an act of experience that could be fully presented only by the dramatic enactment of forces which is the performance of the poem.

27.    Now look at the poem in another way. Did Frost know what he was going to do when he began? Considering the poem simply as an act of skill, as a piece of juggling, one cannot fail to respond to the magnificent turn at the end where, with one flip, seven of the simplest words in the language suddenly dazzle full of never-ending waves of thought and feeling. Or, more precisely, of felt-thought. Certainly an equivalent stunt by a juggler—could there be an equivalent—would bring the house down. Was it to cap his performance with that grand stunt that Frost wrote the poem?

28.    Far from it. The obvious fact is that *Frost could not have known he was going to write those lines until he wrote them.* Then a second fact must be registered: *he wrote them because, for the fun of it, he had got himself into trouble.*

29.    Frost, like every good poet, began by playing a game with himself. The most usual way of writing a four line stanza with four feet to the line is to rhyme the third line with the first, and the fourth line with the second. Even that much rhyme is so difficult in English that many poets and almost all of the anonymous ballad makers do not bother to rhyme the first and third lines at all, settling for two rhymes in four lines as good enough. For English is a rhyme-poor language. In Italian and in French, for example, so many words end with the same sounds that rhyming is relatively easy—so easy that many modern French and Italian poets do not bother to rhyme at all. English, being a more agglomerate language, has far more final sounds, hence fewer of them rhyme. When an Italian poet writes a line ending with "vita" (life) he has literally hundreds of rhyme choices available. When an English poet writes "life" at the end of a line he can summon "strife, wife, knife, fife, rife," and then he is in trouble. Now "life-strife" and "life-rife" and "life-wife" seem to offer a combination of possible ideas that can be related by more than just the rhyme. Inevitably, therefore, the poets have had to work and rework these combinations until the sparkle has gone out of them. The reader is normally tired of such rhyme-led associations. When he encounters "life-strife" he is certainly entitled to suspect that the poet did not really want to say "strife"—that had there been in English such a word as, say, "hife," meaning "infinite peace and harmony," the poet would as

gladly have used that word instead of "strife." Thus, the reader feels that the writing is haphazard, that the rhyme is making the poet say things he does not really feel, and which therefore the reader does not feel except as boredom. One likes to see the rhymes fall into place, but he must end with the belief that it is the poet who is deciding what is said and not the rhyme scheme that is forcing the saying.

30.  So rhyme is a kind of game, and an especially difficult one in English. As in every game, the fun of the rhyme is to set one's difficulties high and then to meet them skillfully. As Frost himself once defined freedom, it consists of "moving easy in harness."

31.  In "Stopping by Woods on a Snowy Evening" Frost took a long chance. He decided to rhyme not two lines in each stanza, but three. Not even Frost could have sustained that much rhyme in a long poem (as Dante, for example, with the advantage of writing in Italian, sustained triple rhyme for thousands of lines in "The Divine Comedy"). Frost would have known instantly, therefore, when he took the original chance, that he was going to write a short poem. He would have had that much foretaste of it.

32.  So the first stanza emerged rhymed a-a-b-a. And with the sure sense that this was to be a short poem, Frost decided to take an additional chance and to redouble: in English three rhymes in four lines is more than enough; there is no need to rhyme the fourth line. For the fun of it, however, Frost set himself to pick up that loose rhyme and to weave it into the pattern, thereby accepting the all but impossible burden of quadruple rhyme.

33.  The miracle is that it worked. Despite the enormous freight of rhyme, the poem not only came out as a neat pattern, but managed to do so with no sense of strain. Every word and every rhyme falls into place as naturally and as inevitably as if there were no rhyme restricting the poet's choices.

34.  That ease-in-difficulty is certainly inseparable from the success of the poem's performance. One watches the skill-man juggle three balls, then four, then five, and every addition makes the trick more wonderful. But unless he makes the hard trick seem as easy as an easy trick, then all is lost.

35.  The real point, however, is not only that Frost took on a hard rhyme-trick and made it seem easy. It is rather as if the juggler, carried away, had tossed up one more ball than he could really handle, and then amazed himself by actually handling it. So with the real triumph of this poem. Frost could not have known what a stunning effect his repetition of the last line was going to produce. He could not even know he was going to repeat the line. He simply found himself

up against a difficulty he almost certainly had not foreseen and he had to improvise to meet it. For in picking up the rhyme from the third line of stanza one and carrying it over into stanza two, he had created an endless chain-link form within which each stanza left a hook sticking out for the next stanza to hang on. So by stanza four, feeling the poem rounding to its end, Frost had to do something about that extra rhyme.

36.   He might have tucked it back into a third line rhyming with the *know-though-snow* of stanza one. He could thus have rounded the poem out to the mathematical symmetry of using each rhyme four times. But though such a device might be defensible in theory, a rhyme repeated after eleven lines is so far from its original rhyme sound that its feeling as rhyme must certainly be lost. And what good is theory if the reader is not moved by the writing?

37.   It must have been in some such quandary that the final repetition suggested itself—a suggestion born of the very difficulties the poet had let himself in for. So there is that point beyond mere ease in handling a hard thing, the point at which the very difficulty offers the poet the opportunity to do better than he knew he could. What, aside from having that happen to oneself, could be more self-delighting than to participate in its happening by one's reader-identification with the poem?

38.   And by now a further point will have suggested itself: that the human insight of the poem and the technicalities of its poetic artifice are inseparable. Each feeds the other. That interplay is the poem's meaning, a matter not of WHAT DOES IT MEAN, for no one can ever say entirely what a good poem means, but of HOW DOES IT MEAN, a process one can come much closer to discussing.

39.   There is a necessary epilogue. Mr. Frost has often discussed this poem on the platform, or more usually in the course of a long-evening-after a talk. Time and again I have heard him say that he just wrote it off, that it just came to him, and that he set it down as it came.

40.   Once at Bread Loaf, however, I heard him add one very essential piece to the discussion of how it "just came." One night, he said, he had sat down after supper to work at a long piece of blank verse. The piece never worked out, but Mr. Frost found himself so absorbed in it that, when next he looked up, dawn was at his window. He rose, crossed to the window, stood looking out for a few minutes, and *then* it was that "Stopping by Woods" suddenly "just came," so that all he had to do was cross the room and write it down.

41.   Robert Frost is the sort of artist who hides his traces. I

know of no Frost worksheets anywhere. If someone has raided his wastebasket in secret, it is possible that such worksheets exist somewhere, but Frost would not willingly allow anything but the finished product to leave him. Almost certainly, therefore, no one will ever know what was in that piece of unsuccessful blank verse he had been working at with such concentration, but I for one would stake my life that could that worksheet be uncovered, it would be found to contain the germinal stuff of "Stopping by Woods"; that what was a-simmer in him all night without finding its proper form, suddenly, when he let his still-occupied mind look away, came at him from a different direction, offered itself in a different form, and that finding that form exactly right the impulse proceeded to marry itself to the new shape in one of the most miraculous performances of English lyricism.

42. And that, too—whether or not one can accept so hypothetical a discussion—is part of HOW the poem means. It means that marriage to the perfect form, the poem's shaped declaration of itself, its moment's monument fixed beyond all possibility of change. And thus, finally, in every truly good poem, "How does it mean?" must always be answered "Triumphantly." Whatever the poem "is about," *how* it means is always how Genesis means: the word become a form, and the form become a thing, and—when the becoming is true—the thing become a part of the knowledge and experience of the race forever.

---

### POSTSCRIPT

Mr. Ciardi published the following letter in the *Saturday Review* three weeks after "Robert Frost: The Way to the Poem."

In my article on Robert Frost (*SR* Apr. 12) I said I did not know of any Frost worksheets in existence and that no one knows what long blank-verse poem it was that Frost had been working on just before writing "Stopping by Woods."

Since publication of the article my good friend John Holmes, poet, critic, and scholar of Frost, has written to tell me that some Frost worksheets do exist and that it was his understanding from Mr. Frost that the long poem in question is "New Hampshire." I am happy to add this information to the record. If the long poem is indeed "New Hampshire," my guess that it must have contained the germinal stuff of "Stopping by Woods" becomes questionable.

JOHN CIARDI

*New York, N.Y.*

---

POSTSCRIPT: From Letters to the Editor, *Saturday Review,* May 3, 1958.

WORDS

*meaning*   Define *duplicity* (par. 3), *spate* (par. 14), *agglomerate* (par. 29), *quandary* (par. 37), and *germinal* (par. 41).

*connotation*   1. In the phrase "that hunger for final rest and surrender that a man may feel" (par. 19), consider the word *surrender*. What does it suggest that life is? Who or what is to surrender to whom or what?   2. Notice that the author takes a very businesslike view of poetry: it is an art, yes, but it is not some vague and mysterious thing that can be explained only by words such as *inspiration* (does the author ever use that word?). Its art depends upon its craft, and its craft can be discussed, analyzed, taken apart. How does the use of the word *works* (par. 1) support this view?

SENTENCES

*style*   1. In paragraph 14, the author invents an example of what he obviously regards as bad writing. Is it clear? What is bad about it?   2. Does the author's own style at any point approach such writing?

*variety*   Paragraphs 13 and 15 consist of single nonsentences and are different from any other sentences in the essay. What is the effect of this variation? Is the variation justified by the function of these sentences?

*rhetorical devices*   1. In paragraph 4 the author asserts that this whole poem is at root a metaphor. What does he mean? Has he himself just used a metaphor?   2. Throughout this essay the author employs an implied metaphor for the poet. It begins in paragraph 3, is continued in paragraphs 4 and 6, and then appears, with variations, throughout. What is it basically? What are the variations? Trace it through the essay.   3. What are the metaphorical implications the author finds in apparently simple words such as *errand, owner, village,* and *winter* (par. 12)?   4. In paragraph 14, the author discusses the rhetorical device of *understatement*. Find examples other than the one he cites in the poem. Can you find any in the author's own writing?

PARAGRAPHS

*methods of development*   1. Paragraph 20, which begins with the loosely linking word *So,* is developed by recapitulation. What does this mean? What is the function of the paragraph in the whole? Does it carry the analysis forward at all?   2. The thought in paragraph 25 is developed through an extended simile, which is stated in the opening five sentences. What is this simile? Why, in the next sentence, does the author break in with "Oh, very well"? How does this interruption alter the progress of the paragraph, and with what is the remainder of the paragraph concerned?

*central idea*   The author tells us that we will be concerned not with *what* the poem means but with *how* it means. What is this distinction? Consider exactly what the author talks about, what elements of the poem he discusses. Is the distinction clarified by Archibald MacLeish's famous statement "A poem should not mean, but be"?

*assumptions and implications*   1. Do the assertions in paragraph 26 contradict those in paragraph 11? 2. The author assumes and argues that this poem is dramatic. What elements does it share with the techniques of the stage play?

*organization*   1. The author calls paragraphs 9–12 and paragraphs 14–15 parentheses. Why? Do they provide the reader with material that assists him in understanding what follows? 2. Paragraph 27 clearly announces that the author is turning to a new portion of his whole thought. Can you find other examples of paragraphs that mark a turn in the thought of the essay?

SUGGESTIONS FOR DISCUSSION

1. Write an essay in which you treat the woods, "lovely, dark and deep," not as the world of death but as the world of imagination—still in distinction to the owner's world of social obligation and the horse's world of brute impulse. If you could do this successfully, would you be demonstrating that the author's conception of *symbol* is right or wrong? 2. Take another short poem of Frost's and try to break it down into dramatic scenes. 3. Symbols, like metaphors, can become clichés. In motion pictures, for instance, the camera pans away from a love scene to a storm outside or from a deathbed to an open window with the curtains blowing out. Can you describe other clichés of movie-making? 4. When this essay was first published, many readers complained that detailed analysis harmed the poem and destroyed their pleasure in it. One reader said that the author was "pulling the wings off a butterfly." Do you agree? Explain.

*Dylan Thomas*

## A FEW WORDS OF A KIND

1.   I am going to read aloud from the works of some modern British poets, and also read a few poems of my own. My own ones include some early ones, some fairly hurly-burly ones, very recent

A FEW WORDS OF A KIND:   From "On Reading His Poetry," *Mademoiselle,* July 1956. Copyright © 1956 by Street and Smith Publications Inc. Reprinted by permission of Harold Ober Associates Inc.

ones, reasoned, decent ones, lamenting ones and lamentable ones, together with a few comments whenever they may or may not be necessary.

2. I wondered what kind of words I should put down to introduce these laboriously churning poems of mine. Indeed, I thought, they want from me no introduction at all. Let them stand on their own feet, the little lyrical cripples. But I felt, too, that there must be a few words of a kind before or between the ranting of the poems. A whole hour of loud and unrelieved verse-speaking is, I imagine, hell to anyone except some brash antiseptic forty-two-toothed smilingly ardent young hunters of culture with net, notebook, poison bottle, pin and label, or to the dowager hunters of small seedy lions, stalking the metropolitan bush with legs and rifles cocked, or to the infernal androgynous literary ladies with three names who produce a kind of verbal ectoplasm to order as a waiter dishes up spaghetti. But to an ordinary audience—not that there's any such thing but only, like yourselves, bushes of eccentrics—there must be a hush between poems. And how was I going to fill that hush with harmless words until the next poem came woodenly booming along like a carved bee?

3. I couldn't, I knew, say much if anything about what the poems might mean. In a few cases, of course, I didn't anyway know myself—though that is true, I hope, only of certain of my earliest published poems, explosive bloodbursts of a boily boy in love with the shape and sound of words, death, unknown love and the shadows on his pillow. And for the rest of the poems, they are what they mean, however obscure, unsuccessful, sentimental, pretentious, ludicrous, rhetorical, wretched, ecstatic, plain bad. Or could I shove in autobiographical snippets saying where I lived and how, when I wrote this or that, indicating how I felt in heart and head at that particular time?

4. I could, for instance, talk about my education, which critics say I have not got. And that's true enough. But I do wish I had learned some other languages apart from English, BBC Third Program and saloon. Then perhaps I could understand what some people mean when they say I have been influenced by Rimbaud.

5. My education was the liberty I had to read indiscriminately and all the time, with my eyes hanging out. I never could have dreamed there were such goings-on, such do's and argie-bargies, such ice blasts of words, such love and sense and terror and humbug, such and so many blinding bright lights breaking across the just awaking wits and splashing all over the pages, as they can never quite do

again after the first revelation. In a million bits and pieces, all of which were words, words, words, and each of which seemed alive forever in its own delight and glory and right.

6. It was then, in my father's brown study before homework, usually the first botched scribblings of gauche and gawky heart-choked poems about black-bloomered nymphs, the jussive grave and the tall, improbable loves of the sardine-packed sky, poems never to be shown to anyone except on pain of death, that I began to know one kind of writing from another, one kind of badness, one kind of goodness. I wrote endless imitations, though I never at the time of writing thought them to be imitations but rather colossally original, things unheard of, like eggs laid by tigers, imitations of whatever I happened to be golloping then, Thomas Browne, Robert W. Service, Stevenson, De Quincey, Eskimo Nell, Newbolt, Blake, Marlowe, the Imagists, the boy's own paper, Keats, Poe, Burns, Dostoevsky, Anon. and Shakespeare. I tried my little trotters at every poetical form. How could I know the tricks of this trade unless I tried to do them myself? For the poets wouldn't soar from the grave and show me how their poems were done by mirrors, and I couldn't trust the critics then—or now. I learned that the bad tricks come easy and the good tricks, which help you to say what you think you wish to say in the most meaningful, moving way, naturally I am still learning—though in earnest company I must call these tricks by other, technical names. Nothing in those days was too much for me to try. If *Paradise Lost* had not already been written, I would have had a shot at it.

7. My early days, dear God! I never thought that one day I might be here or anywhere filling up time before, I'm afraid, a drone of poems by talking about my early days, just as though I were a man of letters. I used to think that once a writer became a man of letters, if only for ten minutes, he was done for. But I feel all right. I suppose I am suffering from one of the first pleasant injections of insidious corruption. "My early days" seems to me to suggest that I am responsible and established, that all the old doubts and worries are over. Now I need bother my head about nothing except birth, death, sex, money, politics and religion, that, jowled and wigged, aloof and branded as a bloodhound, sober as a judge in my bit of vermin, I can summon my juvenile literary delinquence before me and give it a long periodic sentence. For me to think of prefacing my poems by talking about my early days is to invite myself to indulge myself with a hundred tongue-picked, chopped and chiseled evocative shock phrases in a flamboyant rememoration of past and

almost entirely fictitious peccadilloes of interest to nobody but me and my guardian angel, who was, I believe, an unsuccessful psychoanalyst in this life and who is lolloping above me now, casebook in claw, a little seedy and down at wing and heel, in the guttural consulting room of space. I am the kind of human dredger that digs up the wordy mud of his own Dead Sea, a kind of pig that roots for unconsidered truffles in the reeky wood of his past.

8. But still I gladly accept the fact that I first saw the light and screamed at it in a loud lump of Wales. I'm only human, as the man says who deep inside him refuses to believe it, and of course my writing would not be what it is—always experimental and always completely unsatisfactory—if it had not been for the immortal fry of the town in which I simmered up. Naturally, my early poems and stories, two sides of an unresolved argument, came out of a person who came willy-nilly out of one particular atmosphere and environment, and are part and parcel, park and castle, lark and sea shell, dark and school bell, muck and entrail, cock, rock and bubble, accent and sea-lap, root and rhythm of them. And that, so far as I am concerned, is all there is to it. If I had been born and brought up in an igloo and lived on whales, not in it, about the same would be true, except that then it would have been extremely unlikely had I become a writer. And "Goody!" cry my justified detractors.

9. Or I could preface this small reading by talking about poets. I think they're pretty dull. It's a common failing to underestimate the sheer ordinariness of the lives and characters of many dead poets, and to overestimate that of living poets whom one might come across. Indeed it is not unusual for people, after they have met a more or less living poet, to wonder with hardly concealed amazement how he could ever have produced the work he has. I except certain oldish poets alive today who are made solemn and unapproachable, not so much by their poetry or their strict religious observance as by their judicial positions on the boards of eminent publishers who may even then at one's time of meeting, be considering one's own first experimental novel of innocence lost and wisdom catastrophically gained by the age of nineteen. The same kind of amazement, the idol destroyed ("How *could* such a man have written such marvelous devotional poetry, I saw him fall downstairs yesterday in his suspenders!"), might well have occurred to us had we met many of the poets now dead. I think it was Logan Pearsall Smith who remembered how, as a small boy, he saw of all people Matthew Arnold in a restaurant, and Matthew Arnold talked and laughed much too loud.

10. I couldn't talk about poets, but I do wish that I were read-

ing only the work of other modern poets now, and not my own at all. That is, I wish I were reading the work of modern poets I like, for I like to read only the poets I like. This means, of course, that I have to read a lot of poems I don't like before I find the ones I do, but when I do find the ones I do, then all I can say is, "Here they are," and read them aloud to myself or to anyone, like yourselves, voluntarily cornered. And when I read aloud the poems of modern poets I like very much, I try to make them alive from inside. I try to get across what I feel, however wrongly, to be the original impetus of the poem. I am a practicing interpreter, however much of a flannel-tongued one-night-stander.

11.    But in my own poems I've had my say, and when I read them aloud I can only repeat it. When I read, for instance, my earliest poems aloud, my interpretation of them—though that's far too weighty a word just for reading them aloud—can't be considered as the final or original interpretation, performance or blare. I do not remember now the first impulse that pumped and drove those lines along, and that which is in them is for you more than for me, for you or for anyone, or of course for no one, to make what you or he will of them. In these poems I've had my say; now I'm only saying it again.

12.    But what does it matter? Poetry is what in a poem makes you laugh, cry, prickle, be silent, makes your toenails twinkle, makes you want to do this or that or nothing, makes you know that you are alone and not alone in the unknown world, that your bliss and suffering is forever shared and forever all your own. All that matters about poetry is the enjoyment of it, however tragic it may be. All that matters is the eternal movement behind it, the great undercurrent of human grief, folly, pretension, exultation, and ignorance, however unlofty the intention of the poem.

13.    Now I'm going to read some poems straight, without hindrance, for this isn't a lecture at all. It isn't about trends and impacts and the influence of someone on someone else. It isn't trying to prove anything by quotations, to groove one hypothetical school of poetry oilily into another, to jigsaw all the pieces that are poems into one improbable picture and then say, "Here it is, this is modern poetry." I am no gray and tepid don smelling of water biscuits. Only posterity can see the picture of the poetry of today as a whole, and the function of posterity is to look after itself. You can tear a poem apart to see what makes it technically tick, and say to yourself when the works are laid out before you, the vowels, the consonants, the rhymes and rhythms, Yes, this is it, this is why the poem moves me so. It is because of the craftsmanship. But you're back again where

you began. The best craftsmanship always leaves holes and gaps in the works of the poem so that something that is not in the poem can creep, crawl, flash or thunder in. "Everything," Yeats said, though he was talking of the highest moments of the most exalted art, "everything happens in a blaze of light." Only the printed page or the interior monologue or the private discussion can give to each separate poem the full concentrated time that the poem is justified in asking for the assessment of its success or failure to demonstrate its own hypothesis. In public all I think that can be presented is the poem itself, and all that can be experienced in public is the realization of the immediacy or lack of immediacy through which the hypothesis, the central motive of the poem, affects the reader through his ear. The printed page is the place in which to examine the works of a poem, and the platform the place on which to give the poem the works.

14. You won't ask me any questions afterward, will you? I don't mind answering a bit, only I can't. Even to such simple questions as, "What is the relationship of the poet to society in a hydrogenous age?" I can only cough and stammer. And some of the questions I remember from the nightmare past—"Tell me, are the young English intellectuals really psychological?" "Is it absolutely essential, do you think, to be homosexual to write love poems to women?" "I always carry Kierkegaard in my pocket. What do you carry?"

WORDS

*connotation* Affix simple denotative meanings to as many of the following words as you can: *boily* (par. 3), *do's* and *argie-bargies* (par. 5), *jussive* and *golloping* (par. 6), *lolloping* (par. 7), and *prickle* (par. 12). Write out your notion of the connotative sense of the remaining words and state your reasons.

*meaning* Which word in the second quoted question in paragraph 14 makes the question ridiculous? Why?

*relationships* What is the meaning of *androgynous* (par. 2)? of *hydrogenous* (par. 14)? Do the two words have any relationship? How do one or the other or both of these two words relate to the following words: *generic, genealogy, misogynist, gynecology, generous, polyandry, androgen*?

*word choice* Why does the author refer to his audience as "bushes of eccentrics" (par. 2) and to himself as "a flannel-tongued one-nightstander" (par. 10)? Why would the audience be enchanted—as they were—by this kind of derogation of themselves and of the person they paid money to hear?

## SENTENCES

*style* 1. The first sentence of paragraph 1 is a down-to-earth statement of the author's intention. How does the second sentence differ from the first? What might you expect will follow, stylistically, when the author says "My own ones" instead of "My own"? 2. How do you think the audience felt after hearing this opening?

*variety* The general tone of this piece is sometimes flippant, sometimes rhapsodic, and sometimes even ranting. But can you find several sentences in which the poet seriously attempts clear exposition of rather complex ideas?

*rhetorical devices* 1. In what various ways do the following examples of metaphor challenge the attention: "laboriously churning poems of mine"; "the little lyrical cripples"; "forty-two-toothed smilingly ardent young hunters of culture with net, notebook, poison bottle, pin and label"; "verbal ectoplasm"; "the next poem came woodenly booming along like a carved bee" (par. 2)? 2. Is the apostrophe with which paragraph 7 opens effective or foolish? Explain. 3. The sixth sentence in paragraph 7 is an extended metaphor about mature judgment on youthful folly. Do the phrases in the following sentence, "branded as a bloodhound," "in my bit of vermin," and "give it a long periodic sentence," enrich the metaphor or confuse it (note especially that word *vermin*)?

## PARAGRAPHS

*methods of development* Does paragraph 7 "develop" at all? In other words, has an initial statement, relatively bare, grown into a larger or clearer statement by the end of the paragraph? What more, in fact, do you know at the end of the paragraph than you knew at the beginning?

*coherence* Many of the paragraphs in this essay begin with the first person: *I am, I wondered, I couldn't, I could,* etc. Does this strike you as self-important? Do the author's situation and his opening paragraph justify such loosely associated transitions? Do they overlay a basic logic in the progression of ideas?

## CONTENT AND ORGANIZATION

*central ideas* 1. "I am no gray and tepid don smelling of water biscuits," says the poet (par. 13). To what degree does this feeling about himself determine what he has to say and his manner of saying it? 2. From what qualities in human nature and society is he trying to rescue poetry and the reading of poetry?

## SUGGESTIONS FOR DISCUSSION

1. Much of this essay insults its audience, by implication if not directly. When is an insult a compliment? 2. The author says that he was not "educated" (par. 4). What kind of essay would he have written if he had been? 3. If you had only one volume to carry in your pocket (see par. 14), would it be *The Collected Works of Dylan Thomas* or Kierkegaard? 4. Have you ever known a student, writer, minister, or teacher who seemed to affect the "mucker pose"—who tried to talk and act "tougher" than you thought he really was? Describe him. How did his talk and action affect you? Why does anyone make great effort to disguise idealism, sensitivity, or honest feeling?

*part* **3**

# READINGS
# FOR EVALUATION

## Francis Bacon

# OF STUDIES

Studies serve for delight, for ornament, and for ability. Their chief use for delight is in privateness and retiring; for ornament, is in discourse; and for ability, is in the judgment and disposition of business; for expert men can execute, and perhaps judge of particulars, one by one; but the general counsels, and the plots and marshalling of affairs come best from those that are learned. To spend too much time in studies is sloth; to use them too much for ornament is affectation; to make judgment wholly by their rules is the humour of a scholar. They perfect nature, and are perfected by experience; for natural abilities are like natural plants, that need pruning by study; and studies themselves do give forth directions too much at large, except they be bounded in by experience. Crafty men contemn studies, simple men admire them, and wise men use them; for they teach not their own use; but that is a wisdom without them and above them, won by observation. Read not to contradict and confute, nor to believe and take for granted, nor to find talk and discourse, but to weigh and consider. Some books are to be tasted, others to be swallowed, and some few to be chewed and digested; that is, some books are to be read only in parts; others to be read but not curiously; and some few to be read wholly, and with diligence and attention. Some books also may be read by deputy, and extracts made of them by others; but that would be only in the less important arguments and the meaner sort of books; else distilled books are, like common distilled waters, flashy things. Reading maketh a full man; conference a ready man; and writing an exact man. And, therefore, if a man write little, he had need have a great memory; if he confer little, he had need have a present wit; and if he read little, he had need have much cunning, to seem to know that he doth not. Histories make men wise; poets, witty; the mathematics, subtile; natural philosophy, deep; moral, grave; logic and rhetoric, able to contend: *Abeunt studia in mores!* [Studies become habits!] Nay, there is no stand or impediment in the wit but may be wrought out by fit studies; like as diseases of the body may have appropriate exercises. Bowling

OF STUDIES: From *Essays or Counsels, Civil and Moral* by Francis Bacon, 1597.

is good for the stone and reins [gonads and kidneys], shooting for the lungs and breast, gentle walking for the stomach, riding for the head, and the like. So if a man's wit be wandering, let him study the mathematics; for in demonstrations, if his wit be called away never so little, he must begin again. If his wit be not apt to distinguish or find differences, let him study the school-men; for they are *cymini sectores* [hair-splitters]! If he be not apt to beat over matters, and to call up one thing to prove and illustrate another, let him study the lawyers' cases. So every defect of the mind may have a special receipt.

*Jonathan Swift*

## A MODEST PROPOSAL

For Preventing the Children of Poor People in Ireland from Being a Burden to Their Parents or Country, and for Making Them Beneficial to the Public

It is a melancholy object to those who walk through this great town, or travel in the country, when they see the streets, the roads, and cabin-doors, crowded with beggars of the female sex, followed by three, four, or six children, all in rags, and importuning every passenger for an alms. These mothers, instead of being able to work for their honest livelihood, are forced to employ all their time in strolling to beg sustenance for their helpless infants; who, as they grow up, either turn thieves for want of work, or leave their dear native country to fight for the Pretender in Spain, or sell themselves to the Barbadoes.

I think it is agreed by all parties, that this prodigious number of children in the arms, or on the backs, or at the heels of their mothers, and frequently of their fathers, is, in the present deplorable state of the kingdom, a very great additional grievance; and, therefore, whoever could find out a fair, cheap, and easy method of making these children sound, useful members of the commonwealth, would deserve so well of the public, as to have his statue set up for a preserver of the nation.

But my intention is very far from being confined to provide only for the children of professed beggars; it is of a much greater extent,

A MODEST PROPOSAL: 1729.

and shall take in the whole number of infants at a certain age, who are born of parents in effect as little able to support them, as those who demand our charity in the streets.

As to my own part, having turned my thoughts for many years upon this important subject, and maturely weighed the several schemes of our projectors, I have always found them grossly mistaken in their computation. It is true, a child, just dropped from its dam, may be supported by her milk for a solar year, with little other nourishment; at most, not above the value of two shillings, which the mother may certainly get, or the value in scraps, by her lawful occupation of begging; and it is exactly at one year old that I propose to provide for them in such a manner, as, instead of being a charge upon their parents, or the parish, or wanting food and raiment for the rest of their lives, they shall, on the contrary, contribute to the feeding and partly to the clothing, of many thousands.

There is likewise another great advantage in my scheme, that it will prevent those voluntary abortions, and that horrid practice of women murdering their bastard children, alas, too frequent among us! sacrificing the poor innocent babes, I doubt more to avoid the expense than the shame, which would move tears and pity in the most savage and inhuman breast.

The number of souls in this kingdom being usually reckoned one million and a half, of these I calculate there may be about two hundred thousand couple whose wives are breeders; from which number I subtract thirty thousand couple, who are able to maintain their own children (although I apprehend there cannot be so many, under the present distresses of the kingdom); but this being granted, there will remain a hundred and seventy thousand breeders. I again subtract fifty thousand, for those women who miscarry, or whose children die by accident or disease within the year. There only remain a hundred and twenty thousand children of poor parents annually born. The question therefore is, How this number shall be reared and provided for? which, as I have already said, under the present situation of affairs, is utterly impossible by all the methods hitherto proposed. For we can neither employ them in handicraft or agriculture; we neither build houses (I mean in the country), nor cultivate land: they can very seldom pick up a livelihood by stealing, till they arrive at six years old, except where they are of towardly parts; although I confess they learn the rudiments much earlier; during which time they can, however, be properly looked upon only as probationers; as I have been informed by a principal gentleman in the county of Cavan, who protested to me, that he never knew above one or two instances under the age of six, even in a part of the kingdom so renowned for the quickest proficiency in that art.

I am assured by our merchants, that a boy or a girl before twelve years old is no saleable commodity; and even when they come to this age they will not yield above three pounds, or three pounds and half-a-crown at most, on the exchange; which cannot turn to account either to the parents or kingdom, the charge of nutriment and rags having been at least four times that value.

I shall now, therefore, humbly propose my own thoughts, which I hope will not be liable to the least objection.

I have been assured by a very knowing American of my acquaintance in London, that a young healthy child, well nursed, is, at a year old, a most delicious, nourishing, and wholesome food, whether stewed, roasted, baked, or boiled; and I make no doubt that it will equally serve in a fricassee or a ragout.

I do therefore humbly offer it to public consideration, that of the hundred and twenty thousand children already computed, twenty thousand may be reserved for breed, whereof only one-fourth part to be males; which is more than we allow to sheep, black-cattle, or swine; and my reason is, that these children are seldom the fruits of marriage, a circumstance not much regarded by our savages, therefore one male will be sufficient to serve four females. That the remaining hundred thousand may, at a year old, be offered in sale to the persons of quality and fortune through the kingdom; always advising the mother to let them suck plentifully in the last month, so as to render them plump and fat for a good table. A child will make two dishes at an entertainment for friends; and when the family dines alone, the fore or hind quarter will make a reasonable dish, and, seasoned with a little pepper or salt, will be very good boiled on the fourth day, especially in winter.

I have reckoned, upon a medium, that a child just born will weigh twelve pounds, and in a solar year, if tolerably nursed, will increase to twenty-eight pounds.

I grant this food will be somewhat dear, and therefore very proper for landlords, who, as they have already devoured most of the parents, seem to have the best title to the children.

Infants' flesh will be in season throughout the year, but more plentifully in March, and a little before and after: for we are told by a grave author, an eminent French physician, that fish being a prolific diet, there are more children born in Roman Catholic countries about nine months after Lent, than at any other season; therefore, reckoning a year after Lent, the markets will be more glutted than usual, because the number of Popish infants is at least three to one in this kingdom; and therefore it will have one other collateral advantage, by lessening the number of Papists among us.

I have already computed the charge of nursing a beggar's child (in which list I reckon all cottagers, labourers, and four-fifths of the farmers) to be about two shillings per annum, rags included; and I believe no gentleman would repine to give ten shillings for the carcass of a good fat child, which, as I have said, will make four dishes of excellent nutritive meat, when he has only some particular friend, or his own family, to dine with him. Thus the squire will learn to be a good landlord, and grow popular among his tenants; the mother will have eight shillings net profit, and be fit for work till she produces another child.

Those who are more thrifty (as I must confess the times require) may flay the carcass; the skin of which, artificially dressed, will make admirable gloves for ladies, and summer-boots for fine gentlemen.

As to our city of Dublin, shambles may be appointed for this purpose in the most convenient parts of it, and butchers, we may be assured, will not be wanting; although I rather recommend buying the children alive, then dressing them hot from the knife, as we do roasting pigs.

A very worthy person, a true lover of his country, and whose virtues I highly esteem, was lately pleased, in discoursing on this matter, to offer a refinement upon my scheme. He said, that many gentlemen of this kingdom, having of late destroyed their deer, he conceived that the want of venison might be well supplied by the bodies of young lads and maidens, not exceeding fourteen years of age, nor under twelve; so great a number of both sexes in every country being now ready to starve for want of work and service; and these to be disposed of by their parents, if alive, or otherwise by their nearest relations. But, with due deference to so excellent a friend, and so deserving a patriot, I cannot be altogether in his sentiments; for as to the males, my American acquaintance assured me, from frequent experience, that their flesh was generally tough and lean, like that of our schoolboys, by continual exercise, and their taste disagreeable; and to fatten them would not answer the charge. Then as to the females, it would, I think, with humble submission, be a loss to the public, because they soon would become breeders themselves: and besides, it is not improbable that some scrupulous people might be apt to censure such a practice (although indeed very unjustly), as a little bordering upon cruelty; which, I confess, has always been with me the strongest objection against any project, how well soever intended.

But in order to justify my friend, he confessed that this expedient was put into his head by the famous Psalmanazar, a native of the island Formosa, who came from thence to London above twenty years ago; and in conversation told my friend, that in his country, when any young person happened to be put to death, the executioner sold the carcass to persons of quality as a prime dainty; and that in his time the body of a plump girl of fifteen, who was crucified for an attempt to poison the emperor, was sold to his imperial majesty's prime minister of state, and other great mandarins of the court, in joints from the gibbet, at four hundred crowns. Neither indeed can I deny, that, if the same use were made of several plump young girls in this town, who, without one single groat to their fortunes, cannot stir abroad without a chair, and appear at playhouse and assemblies in foreign fineries which they never will pay for, the kingdom would not be the worse.

Some persons of a desponding spirit are in great concern about that vast number of poor people, who are aged, diseased, or maimed; and I have been desired to employ my thoughts, what course may be taken to ease the nation of so grievous an encumbrance. But I am not in the least pain upon that matter, because it is very well known, that they are every day dying, and rotting, by cold and famine, and filth and vermin, as fast as can be reasonably expected. And as to the young labourers, they are now in almost as hopeful a condition: they cannot get work, and consequently pine away for want of nourishment, to a degree, that if at any time they are accidentally hired to common labour, they have not strength to perform it; and thus the country and themselves are happily delivered from the evils to come.

I have too long digressed, and therefore shall return to my subject. I think the advantages by the proposal which I have made are obvious and many, as well as of the highest importance.

For first, as I have already observed, it would greatly lessen the number of Papists, with whom we are yearly over-run, being the principal breeders of the nation, as well as our most dangerous enemies; and who stay at home on purpose to deliver the kingdom to the Pretender, hoping to take their advantage by the absence of so many good Protestants, who have chosen rather to leave their country than stay at home and pay tithes against their conscience to an Episcopal curate.

Secondly, The poorer tenants will have something valuable of their own, which by law may be made liable to distress, and help to pay their landlord's rent; their corn and cattle being already seized, and money a thing unknown.

Thirdly, Whereas the maintenance of a hundred thousand children, from two years old and upward, cannot be computed at less than ten shillings a piece per annum, the nation's stock will be thereby increased fifty thousand pounds per annum, beside the profit of a new dish introduced to the tables of all gentlemen of fortune in the kingdom, who have any refinement in taste. And the money will circulate among ourselves, the goods being entirely of our own growth and manufacture.

Fourthly, The constant breeders, beside the gain of eight shillings sterling per annum by the sale of their children, will be rid of the charge of maintaining them after the first year.

Fifthly, This food would likewise bring great custom to taverns; where the vintners will certainly be so prudent as to procure the best receipts for dressing it to perfection, and, consequently, have their houses frequented by all the fine gentlemen, who justly value themselves upon their knowledge in good eating: and a skilful cook, who understands how to oblige his guests, will contrive to make it as expensive as they please.

Sixthly, This would be a great inducement to marriage, which all wise nations have either encouraged by rewards, or enforced by laws and penalties. It would increase the care and tenderness of mothers toward their children, when they were sure of a settlement for life to the poor babes, provided in some sort by the public, to their annual profit or expense. We should see an honest emulation among the married women, which of them could bring the fattest child to the market. Men would become as fond of their wives during the time of their pregnancy as they are now of their mares in foal, their cows in calf, their sows when they are ready to farrow; nor offer to beat or kick them (as is too frequent a practice) for fear of a miscarriage.

Many other advantages might be enumerated. For instance, the addition of some thousand carcasses in our exportation of barrelled beef; the propagation of swine's flesh, and improvement in the art of making good bacon, so much wanted among us by the great destruction of pigs, too frequent at our table; which are no way comparable in taste or magnificence to a well-grown, fat, yearling child, which, roasted whole, will make a considerable figure at a lord mayor's feast, or any other public entertainment. But this, and many others, I omit, being studious of brevity.

Supposing that one thousand families in this city would be constant customers for infants' flesh, beside others who might have it at merry-meetings, particularly at weddings and christenings, I compute that Dublin would take off annually about twenty thousand carcasses; and the rest of the kingdom (where probably they will be sold somewhat cheaper) the remaining eighty thousand.

I can think of no one objection, that will possibly be raised against this proposal, unless it should be urged, that the number of people will be thereby much lessened in the kingdom. This I freely own, and it was indeed one principal design in offering it to the world. I desire the reader will observe, that I calculate my remedy for this one individual kingdom of Ireland, and for no other that ever was, is, or I think ever can be, upon earth. Therefore let no man talk to me of other expedients: of taxing our absentees at five shillings a pound: of using neither clothes, nor household furniture, except what is our own growth and manufacture: of utterly rejecting the materials and instruments that promote foreign luxury: of curing the expensiveness of pride, vanity, idleness, and gaming in our women: of introducing a vein of parsimony, prudence, and temperance: of learning to love our country, in the want of which we differ even from LAPLANDERS, and the inhabitants of TOPINAMBOO: of quitting our animosities and factions, nor acting any longer like the Jews, who were murdering one another at the very moment their city was taken: of being a little cautious not to sell our country and conscience for nothing: of teaching landlords to have at least one degree of mercy toward their tenants: lastly, of putting a spirit of honesty, industry, and skill into our shopkeepers; who, if a resolution could now be taken to buy only our native goods, would immediately unite to cheat and exact upon us in the price, the measure, and the goodness, nor could ever yet be brought to make one fair proposal of just dealing, though often and earnestly invited to it.

Therefore I repeat, let no man talk to me of these and the like expedients, till he has at least some glimpse of hope, that there will be ever some hearty and sincere attempt to put them in practice.

But, as to myself, having been wearied out for many years with offering vain, idle, visionary thoughts, and at length utterly despairing of success, I fortunately fell upon this proposal; which, as it is wholly new, so it has something solid and real, of no expense and little trouble, full in our own power, and whereby we can incur no danger in disobliging ENGLAND. For this kind of commodity will not bear exportation, the flesh being of too tender a consistence to admit a long continuance in salt, although perhaps I could name a country, which would be glad to eat up our whole nation without it.

After all, I am not so violently bent upon my own opinion as to reject any offer proposed by wise men, which shall be found equally innocent, cheap, easy and effectual. But before something of that kind shall be advanced in contradiction to my scheme, and offering a better, I desire the author, or authors, will be pleased maturely to consider two points. First, as things now stand, how they will be able to find food and raiment for a hundred thousand useless mouths and backs. And, secondly, there being a round million of creatures in human figure throughout this kingdom, whose whole subsistence put into a common stock would leave them in debt two millions of pounds sterling, adding those who are beggars by profession, to the bulk of farmers, cottagers, and labourers, with the wives and children who are beggars in effect; I desire those politicians who dislike my overture, and may perhaps be so bold as to attempt an answer, that they will first ask the parents of these mortals, whether they would not at this day think it a great happiness to have been sold for food at a year old, in the manner I prescribe, and thereby have avoided such a perpetual scene of misfortunes, as they have since gone through, by the oppression of landlords, the impossibility of paying rent without money or trade, the want of common sustenance, with neither house nor clothes to cover them from the inclemencies of the weather, and the most inevitable prospect of entailing the like, or greater miseries, upon their breed for ever.

I profess, in the sincerity of my heart, that I have not the least personal interest in endeavouring to promote this necessary work, having no other motive than the public good of my country, by advancing our trade, providing for infants, relieving the poor, and giving some pleasure to the rich. I have no children by which I can propose to get a single penny; the youngest being nine years old, and my wife past child-bearing.

*Thomas De Quincey*

# LITERATURE OF KNOWLEDGE
# AND LITERATURE OF POWER

What is it that we mean by *literature?* Popularly, and amongst the thoughtless, it is held to include everything that is printed in a book. Little logic is required to disturb *that* definition; the most thoughtless person is easily made aware that in the idea of *literature* one essential element is—some relation to a general and common interest of man, so that what applies only to a local—or professional —or merely personal interest, even though presenting itself in the shape of a book, will not belong to literature. So far the definition is easily narrowed; and it is as easily expanded. For not only is much that takes a station in books not literature; but inversely, much that really *is* literature never reaches a station in books. The weekly sermons of Christendom, that vast pulpit literature which acts so extensively upon the popular mind—to warn, to uphold, to renew, to comfort, to alarm, does not attain the sanctuary of libraries in the ten thousandth part of its extent. The drama again, as, for instance, the finest of Shakspere's plays in England, and all leading Athenian plays in the noontide of the Attic stage, operated as a literature on the public mind, and were (according to the strictest letter of that term) *published* through the audiences that witnessed [1] their representation some time before they were published as things to be read; and they were published in this scenical mode of publication with much more effect than they could have had as books, during ages of costly copying or of costly printing.

Books, therefore, do not suggest an idea co-extensive and inter-changeable with the idea of literature; since much literature, scenic, forensic, or didactic (as from lecturers and public orators), may never come into books; and much that *does* come into books, may

[1] Charles I, for example, when Prince of Wales, and many others in his father's court, gained their known familiarity with Shakspere—not through the original quartos, so slenderly diffused, nor through the first folio of 1623, but through the court representations of his chief dramas at Whitehall.

LITERATURE OF KNOWLEDGE AND LITERATURE OF POWER: From a review of *The Works of Alexander Pope,* edited by W. Roscoe, 1847; the review was published in 1848.

connect itself with no literary interest. But a far more important correction, applicable to the common vague idea of literature, is to be sought—not so much in a better definition of literature, as in a sharper distinction of the two functions which it fulfils. In that great social organ, which collectively we call literature, there may be distinguished two separate offices that may blend and often *do* so, but capable severally of a severe insulation, and naturally fitted for reciprocal repulsion. There is first the literature of *knowledge,* and secondly, the literature of *power.* The function of the first is—to *teach;* the function of the second is—to *move:* the first is a rudder, the second an oar or a sail. The first speaks to the *mere* discursive understanding; the second speaks ultimately it may happen to the higher understanding or reason, but always *through* affections of pleasure and sympathy. Remotely, it may travel towards an object seated in what Lord Bacon calls *dry* light; but proximately it does and must operate, else it ceases to be a literature of *power,* on and through that *humid* light which clothes itself in the mists and glittering *iris* of human passions, desires, and genial emotions. Men have so little reflected on the higher functions of literature, as to find it a paradox if one should describe it as a mean or subordinate purpose of books to give information. But this is a paradox only in the sense which makes it honourable to be paradoxical. Whenever we talk in ordinary language of seeking information or gaining knowledge, we understand the words as connected with something of absolute novelty. But it is the grandeur of all truth which *can* occupy a very high place in human interests, that it is never absolutely novel to the meanest of minds: it exists eternally by way of germ or latent principle in the lowest as in the highest, needing to be developed but never to be planted. To be capable of transplantation is the immediate criterion of a truth that ranges on a lower scale. Besides which, there is a rarer thing than truth, namely, *power* or deep sympathy with truth. What is the effect, for instance, upon society—of children? By the pity, by the tenderness, and by the peculiar modes of admiration, which connect themselves with the helplessness, with the innocence, and with the simplicity of children, not only are the primal affections strengthened and continually renewed, but the qualities which are dearest in the sight of heaven—the frailty for instance, which appeals to forbearance, the innocence which symbolizes the heavenly, and the simplicity which is most alien from the worldly, are kept up in perpetual remembrance, and their ideals are continually refreshed. A purpose of the same nature is answered by the higher literature, viz. the literature of power. What do you learn from Paradise Lost? Nothing at all. What do you learn from a cookery-book? Something new, something that you did not know before, in every paragraph. But would you therefore put the wretched cookery-book on a higher level of estimation than the divine poem? What you owe to Milton is not any knowledge, of which a million separate items are still but a million of advancing steps on the same earthly level; what you owe—is *power,* that is, exercise and expansion to your own latent capacity of sympathy with the infinite, where every pulse and each separate influx is a step upwards—a step ascending as upon a Jacob's ladder from earth to mysterious altitudes above the earth. *All* the steps of knowledge, from first to last, carry you farther on the same plane, but could never raise you one foot above your ancient level of earth: whereas, the very *first* step in power is a flight—is an ascending into another element where earth is forgotten.

Were it not that human sensibilities are ventilated and con-tinually called out into exercise by the great phenomena of infancy, or of real life as it moves through chance and change, or of literature as it recombines these elements in the mimicries of poetry, romance, &c., it is certain that, like any animal power or muscular energy fall-ing into disuse, all such sensibilities would gradually droop and dwindle. It is in relation to these great *moral* capacities of man that the litera-ture of power, as contradistinguished from that of knowledge, lives and has its field of action. It is concerned with what is highest in man: for the Scriptures themselves never condescend to deal by suggestion or co-operation, with the mere discursive understanding: when speak-ing of man in his intellectual capacity, the Scriptures speak not of the understanding, but of *"the understanding heart"*—making the heart, *i.e.,* the great *intuitive* (or non-discursive) organ, to be the inter-changeable formula for man in his highest state of capacity for the infinite. Tragedy, romance, fairy-tale, or epopee, all alike restore to man's mind the ideals of justice, of hope, of truth, of mercy, of retribu-tion, which else (left to the support of daily life in its realities) would languish for want of sufficient illustration. What is meant for instance by *poetic justice?* It does not mean a justice that differs by its object from the ordinary justice of human jurisprudence; for then it must be confessedly a very bad kind of justice; but it means a justice that differs from common forensic justice by the degree in which it *attains* its object, a justice that is more omnipotent over its own ends, as dealing—not with the refractory elements of earthly life—but with elements of its own creation, and with materials flexible to its own purest preconceptions. It is certain that, were it not for the literature of power, these ideals would often remain amongst us as mere arid notional forms; whereas, by the creative forces of man put forth in literature, they gain a vernal life of restoration, and germinate into vital activities. The commonest novel, by moving in alliance with human fears and hopes, with human instincts of wrong and right, sustains and quickens those affections. Calling them into action, it rescues them from torpor. And hence the pre-eminency over all authors that merely *teach,* of the meanest that *moves;* or that teaches, if at all, indirectly *by* moving. The very highest work that has ever existed in the literature of knowledge, is but a *provisional* work: a book upon trial and sufferance, and *quamdiu bene se gesserit* [as long as it conducted itself well]. Let its teaching be even partially revised, let it be but expanded, nay, even let its teaching be but placed in a better order, and instantly it is superseded. Whereas the feeblest works in the literature of power, surviving at all, survive as finished and unalterable amongst men. For instance, the *Principia* of Sir Isaac Newton was a book *militant* on earth from the first. In all stages of its progress it would have to fight for its existence: 1*st,* as regards absolute truth; 2*dly,* when that combat is over, as regards its form or mode of presenting the truth. And as soon as a La Place, or anybody else, builds higher upon the foundations laid by this book, effectually he throws it out of the sunshine into decay and darkness; by weapons won from this book he superannuates and destroys this book, so that soon the name of Newton remains, as a mere *nominis umbra* [shadow of a name], but his book, as a living power, has transmigrated into other forms. Now, on the contrary, the Iliad, the Prometheus of Æschylus, the Othello or King Lear, the Hamlet or Macbeth, and the Paradise Lost, are not militant but triumphant for ever as long as the languages exist in which they speak or can be taught to speak. They never *can* transmigrate into new incarnations. To reproduce *these* in new forms, or variations, even if in some things they should be improved, would be to plagiarize. A good steam-engine is properly superseded by a better. But one lovely pastoral valley is not superseded by another, nor a statue of Praxiteles by a statue of Michael Angelo. These things are not separated by imparity, but by disparity. They are not thought of as unequal under the same standard, but as differing in *kind,* and as equal under a different standard. Human works of immortal beauty and works of nature in one respect stand on the same footing: they never absolutely repeat each other: never approach so near as not to differ; and they differ not as better and worse, or simply by more and less: they differ by undecipherable and incommunicable differences, that cannot be caught by mimicries, nor be reflected in the mirror of copies, nor become ponderable in the scales of vulgar comparison.

Applying these principles to Pope, as a representative of fine literature in general, we would wish to remark the claim which he has, or which any equal writer has, to the attention and jealous winnowing of those critics in particular who watch over public morals. Clergymen, and all the organs of public criticism put in motion by clergymen, are more especially concerned in the just appreciation of such writers, if the two canons are remembered, which we have endeavoured to illustrate, viz., that all works in this class, as opposed to those in the literature of knowledge, 1*st,* work by far deeper agencies; and, 2*dly,* are more permanent; in the strictest sense they are κτηματα ἐς ἀει [possessions forever]: and what evil they do, or what good they do, is commensurate with the national language, sometimes long after the nation has departed. At this hour, 500 years since their creation, the tales of Chaucer,[2] never equalled on this earth for tenderness, and for life of picturesqueness, are read familiarly by many in the charming language of their natal day, and by others in the modernizations of Dryden, of Pope, and Wordsworth. At this hour, 1800 years since their creation, the Pagan tales of Ovid, never equalled on this earth for the gaiety of their movement and the capricious graces of their narrative, are read by all Christendom. This man's people and their monuments are dust: but *he* is alive: he has survived them, as he told us that he had it in his commission to do, by a thousand years; "and *shall* a thousand more."

All the literature of knowledge builds only ground-nests, that are swept away by floods, or confounded by the plough; but the literature of power builds nests in aerial altitudes of temples sacred from violation, or of forests inaccessible to fraud. *This* is a great prerogative of the *power* literature: and it is a greater which lies in the mode of its influence. The *knowledge* literature, like the fashion of this world, passeth away. An Encyclopædia is its abstract; and, in this respect, it may be taken for its speaking symbol—that, before one generation has passed, an Encyclopædia is superannuated; for it speaks through the dead memory and unimpassioned understanding, which have not the *rest* of higher faculties, but are continually enlarging and varying their phylacteries. But all literature, properly so called—literature κατ' ἐξοχην [great literature], for the very same reason that it is so much more durable than the literature of knowledge, is (and by the very

---

[2] The Canterbury Tales were not made public until 1380 or thereabouts: but the composition must have cost 30 or more years; not to mention that the work had probably been finished for some years before it was divulged.

same proportion it is) more intense and electrically searching in its impressions. The directions in which the tragedy of this planet has trained our human feelings to play, and the combinations into which the poetry of this planet has thrown our human passions of love and hatred, of admiration and contempt, exercises a power bad or good over human life, that cannot be contemplated when seen stretching through many generations, without a sentiment allied to awe.[3] And of this let every one be assured—that he owes to the impassioned books which he has read, many a thousand more of emotions than he can consciously trace back to them. Dim by their origination, these emotions yet arise in him, and mould him through life like the forgotten incidents of childhood.

[3] The reason why the broad distinctions between the two literatures of power and knowledge so little fix the attention, lies in the fact, that a vast proportion of books—history, biography, travels, miscellaneous essays, &c., lying in a middle zone, confound these distinctions by interblending them. All that we call "amusement" or "entertainment" is a diluted form of the power belonging to passion, and also a mixed form; and where threads of direct *instruction* intermingle in the texture with these threads of *power,* this absorption of the duality into one representative *nuance* neutralises the separate perception of either. Fused into a *tertium quid,* or neutral state, they disappear to the popular eye as the repelling forces, which in fact they are.

## *John Stuart Mill*

# ON LIBERTY

The subject of this Essay is not the so-called Liberty of the Will, so unfortunately opposed to the misnamed doctrine of Philosophical Necessity; but Civil, or Social Liberty: the nature and limits of the power which can be legitimately exercised by society over the individual. A question seldom stated, and hardly ever discussed, in general terms, but which profoundly influences the practical controversies of the age by its latent presence, and is likely soon to make itself recognized as the vital question of the future. It is so far from being new, that, in a certain sense, it has divided mankind, almost from the remotest ages; but in the stage of progress into which the more civilized portions of the species have now entered, it presents itself under new conditions, and requires a different and more fundamental treatment.

ON LIBERTY: From *On Liberty; and Thoughts on Parliamentary Reform* by John Stuart Mill, 1859.

The struggle between Liberty and Authority is the most conspicuous feature in the portions of history with which we are earliest familiar, particularly in that of Greece, Rome, and England. But in old times this contest was between subjects, or some classes of subjects, and the Government. By liberty, was meant protection against the tyranny of the political rulers. The rulers were conceived (except in some of the popular governments of Greece) as in a necessarily antagonistic position to the people whom they ruled. They consisted of a governing One, or a governing tribe or caste, who derived their authority from inheritance or conquest, who, at all events, did not hold it at the pleasure of the governed, and whose supremacy men did not venture, perhaps did not desire, to contest, whatever precautions might be taken against its oppressive exercise. Their power was regarded as necessary, but also as highly dangerous; as a weapon which they would attempt to use against their subjects, no less than against external enemies. To prevent the weaker members of the community from being preyed upon by innumerable vultures, it was needful that there should be an animal of prey stronger than the rest, commissioned to keep them down. But as the king of the vultures would be no less bent upon preying on the flock than any of the minor harpies, it was indispensable to be in a perpetual attitude of defence against his beak and claws. The aim, therefore, of patriots was to set limits to the power which the ruler should be suffered to exercise over the community; and this limitation was what they meant by liberty. It was attempted in two ways. First, by obtaining a recognition of certain immunities, called political liberties or rights, which it was to be regarded as a breach of duty in the ruler to infringe, and which, if he did infringe, specific resistance, or general rebellion, was held to be justifiable. A second, and generally a later expedient, was the establishment of constitutional checks, by which the consent of the community, or of a body of some sort, supposed to represent its interests, was made a necessary condition to some of the more important acts of the governing power. To the first of these modes of limitation, the ruling power, in most European countries, was compelled, more or less, to submit. It was not so with the second; and, to attain this, or when already in some degree possessed, to attain it more completely, became everywhere the principal object of the lovers of liberty. And so long as mankind were content to combat one enemy by another, and to be ruled by a master, on condition of being guaranteed more or less efficaciously against his tyranny, they did not carry their aspirations beyond this point.

A time, however, came, in the progress of human affairs, when men ceased to think it a necessity of nature that their governors should be an independent power, opposed in interest to themselves. It appeared to them much better that the various magistrates of the State should be their tenants or delegates, revocable at their pleasure. In that way alone, it seemed, could they have complete security that the powers of government would never be abused to their disadvantage. By degrees this new demand for elective and temporary rulers became the prominent object of the exertions of the popular party, wherever any such party existed; and superseded, to a considerable extent, the previous efforts to limit the power of rulers. As the struggle proceeded for making the ruling power emanate from the periodical choice of the ruled, some persons began to think that too much importance had been attached to the limitation of the power itself. *That* (it might seem) was a resource against rulers whose interests were habitually opposed to those of the people. What was now wanted was, that the rulers should be identified with the people; that their interest and will should be the interest and will of the nation. The nation did not need to be protected against its own will. There was no fear of its tyrannizing over itself. Let the rulers be effectually responsible to it, promptly removable by it, and it could afford to trust them with power of which it could itself dictate the use to be made. Their power was but the nation's own power, concentrated, and in a form convenient for exercise. This mode of thought, or rather perhaps of feeling, was common among the last generation of European liberalism, in the Continental section of which it still apparently predominates. Those who admit any limit to what a government may do, except in the case of such governments as they think ought not to exist, stand out as brilliant exceptions among the political thinkers of the Continent. A similar tone of sentiment might by this time have been prevalent in our own country, if the circumstances which for a time encouraged it, had continued unaltered.

But, in political and philosophical theories, as well as in persons, success discloses faults and infirmities which failure might have concealed from observation. The notion, that the people have no need to limit their power over themselves, might seem axiomatic, when popular government was a thing only dreamed about, or read of as having existed at some distant period of the past. Neither was that notion necessarily disturbed by such temporary aberrations as those of the French Revolution, the worst of which were the work of an usurping few, and which, in any case, belonged, not to the permanent working of popular institutions, but to a sudden and convulsive outbreak against monarchical and aristocratic despotism. In time, however, a democratic republic came to occupy a large portion of the earth's surface, and made itself felt as one of the most powerful members of the community of nations; and elective and responsible government became subject to the observations and criticisms which wait upon a great existing fact. It was now perceived that such phrases as "self-government," and "the power of the people over themselves," do not express the true state of the case. The "people" who exercise the power are not always the same people with those over whom it is exercised; and the "self-government" spoken of is not the government of each by himself, but of each by all the rest. The will of the people, moreover, practically means the will of the most numerous or the most active *part* of the people; the majority, or those who succeed in making themselves accepted as the majority; the people, consequently, *may* desire to oppress a part of their number; and precautions are as much needed against this as against any other abuse of power. The limitation, therefore, of the power of government over individuals loses none of its importance when the holders of power are regularly accountable to the community, that is, to the strongest party therein. This view of things, recommending itself equally to the intelligence of thinkers and to the inclination of those important classes in European society to whose real or supposed interests democracy is adverse, has had no difficulty in establishing itself; and in political speculations "the tyranny of the majority" is now generally included among the evils against which society requires to be on its guard.

Like other tyrannies, the tyranny of the majority was at first, and is still vulgarly, held in dread, chiefly as operating through the acts of the public authorities. But reflecting persons perceived that when society is itself the tyrant—society collectively, over the separate individuals who compose it—its means of tyrannizing are not restricted to the acts which it may do by the hands of its political functionaries. Society can and does execute its own mandates: and if it issues wrong mandates instead of right, or any mandates at all in things with which it ought not to meddle, it practises a social tyranny more formidable than many kinds of political oppression, since, though not usually upheld by such extreme penalties, it leaves fewer means of escape, penetrating much more deeply into the details of life, and enslaving the soul itself. Protection, therefore, against the tyranny of the magistrate is not enough: there needs protection also against the tyranny of the prevailing opinion and feeling; against the tendency of society to impose, by other means than civil penalties, its own ideas and practices as rules of conduct on those who dissent from them; to fetter the development, and, if possible, prevent the formation, of any individuality not in harmony with its ways, and compel all characters to fashion themselves upon the model of its own. There is a limit to the legitimate interference of collective opinion with individual independence: and to find that limit, and maintain it against encroachment, is as indispensable to a good condition of human affairs, as protection against political despotism.

But though this proposition is not likely to be contested in general terms, the practical question, where to place the limit—how to make the fitting adjustment between individual independence and social control—is a subject on which nearly everything remains to be done. All that makes existence valuable to any one, depends on the enforcement of restraints upon the actions of other people. Some rules of conduct, therefore, must be imposed, by law in the first place, and by opinion on many things which are not fit subjects for the operation of law. What these rules should be, is the principal question in human affairs; but if we except a few of the most obvious cases, it is one of those which least progress has been made in resolving. No two ages, and scarcely any two countries, have decided it alike; and the decision of one age or country is a wonder to another. Yet the people of any given age and country no more suspect any difficulty in it, than if it were a subject on which mankind had always been agreed. The rules which obtain among themselves appear to them self-evident and self-justifying. This all but universal illusion is one of the examples of the magical influence of custom, which is not only, as the proverb says, a second nature, but is continually mistaken for the first. The effect of custom, in preventing any misgiving respecting the rules of conduct which mankind impose on one another, is all the more complete because the subject is one on which it is not generally considered necessary that reasons should be given, either by one person to others, or by each to himself. People are accustomed to believe, and have been encouraged in the belief by some who aspire to the character of philosophers, that their feelings, on subjects of this nature, are better than reasons, and render reasons unnecessary. The practical principle which guides them to their opinions on the regulation of human conduct, is the feeling in each person's mind that everybody should be required to act as he, and those with whom he sympathizes, would like them to act. No one, indeed, acknowledges to himself that his standard of judgement is his own liking; but an opinion on a point of conduct, not supported by reasons, can only count as one person's preference; and if the reasons, when given, are a mere appeal to a similar preference felt by other people, it is still only many people's liking instead of one. To an ordinary man, however, his own preference, thus supported, is not only a perfectly satisfactory reason, but the only one he generally has for any of his notions of morality, taste, or propriety, which are not expressly written in his religious creed; and his chief guide in the interpretation even of that. Men's opinions, accordingly, on what is laudable or blameable, are affected by all the multifarious causes which influence their wishes in regard to the conduct of others, and which are as numerous as those which determine their wishes on any other subject. Sometimes their reason—at other times their prejudices or superstitions: often their social affections, not seldom their anti-social ones, their envy or jealousy, their arrogance or contemptuousness: but most commonly, their desires or fears for themselves—their legitimate or illegitimate self-interest. Wherever there is an ascendant class, a large portion of the morality of the country emanates from its class interests, and its feelings of class superiority. The morality between Spartans and Helots, between planters and negroes, between princes and subjects, between nobles and roturiers, between men and women, has been for the most part the creation of these class interests and feelings: and the sentiments thus generated, react in turn upon the moral feelings of the members of the ascendant class, in their relations among themselves. Where, on the other hand, a class, formerly ascendant, has lost its ascendancy, or where its ascendancy is unpopular, the prevailing moral sentiments frequently bear the impress of an impatient dislike of superiority. Another grand determining principle of the rules of conduct, both in act and forbearance, which have been enforced by law or opinion, has been the servility of mankind towards the supposed preferences or aversions of their temporal masters, or of their gods. This servility, though essentially selfish, is not hypocrisy; it gives rise to perfectly genuine sentiments of abhorrence; it made men burn magicians and heretics. Among so many baser influences, the general and obvious interests of society have of course had a share, and a large one, in the direction of the moral sentiments: less, however, as a matter of reason, and on their own account, than as a consequence of the sympathies and antipathies which grew out of them: and sympathies and antipathies which had little or nothing to do with the interests of society, have made themselves felt in the establishment of moralities with quite as great force.

The likings and dislikings of society, or of some powerful portion of it, are thus the main thing which has practically determined the rules laid down for general observance, under the penalties of law or opinion. And in general, those who have been in advance of society in thought and feeling, have left this condition of things unassailed in principle, however they may have come into conflict with it in some of its details. They have occupied themselves rather in inquiring what things society ought to like or dislike, than in questioning whether its likings or dislikings should be a law to individuals. They preferred endeavouring to alter the feelings of mankind on the particular points on which they were themselves heretical, rather than make common cause in defence of freedom, with heretics generally. The only case in which the higher ground has been taken on principle and maintained with consistency, by any but an individual here and there, is that of religious belief: a case instructive in many ways, and not least so as forming a most striking instance of the fallibility of what is called the moral sense: for the *odium theologicum,* in a sincere bigot, is one of the most unequivocal cases of moral feeling. Those who first broke the yoke of what called itself the Universal Church, were in general as little willing to permit difference of religious opinion as that church itself. But when the heat of the conflict was over, without giving a complete victory to any party, and each church or sect was reduced to limit its hopes to retaining possession of the ground it already occupied; minorities, seeing that they had no chance of becoming majorities, were under the necessity of pleading to those whom they could not convert, for permission to differ. It is accordingly on this battlefield, almost solely, that the rights of the individual against society have been asserted on broad grounds of principle, and the claim of society to exercise authority over dissentients, openly controverted. The great writers to whom the world owes what religious liberty it possesses, have mostly asserted freedom of conscience as an indefeasible right, and denied absolutely that a human being is accountable to others for his religious belief. Yet so natural to mankind is intolerance in whatever they really care about, that religious freedom has hardly anywhere been practically realized, except where religious indifference, which dislikes to have its peace disturbed by theological quarrels, has added its weight to the scale. In the minds of almost all religious persons, even in the most tolerant countries, the duty of toleration is admitted with tacit reserves. One person will bear with dissent in matters of church government, but not of dogma; another can tolerate everybody, short of a Papist or a Unitarian; another, every one who believes in revealed religion; a few extend their charity a little further, but stop at the belief in a God and in a future state. Wherever the sentiment of the majority is still genuine and intense, it is found to have abated little of its claim to be obeyed.

In England, from the peculiar circumstances of our political history, though the yoke of opinion is perhaps heavier, that of law is lighter, than in most other countries of Europe; and there is considerable jealousy of direct interference, by the legislative or the executive power, with private conduct; not so much from any just regard for the independence of the individual, as from the still subsisting habit of looking on the government as representing an opposite interest to the public. The majority have not yet learnt to feel the power of the government their power, or its opinions their opinions. When they do so, individual liberty will probably be as much exposed to invasion from the government, as it already is from public opinion. But, as yet, there is a considerable amount of feeling ready to be called forth against any attempt of the law to control individuals in things in which they have not hitherto been accustomed to be controlled by it; and this with very little discrimination as to whether the matter is, or is not, within the legitimate sphere of legal control; insomuch that the feeling, highly salutary on the whole, is perhaps quite as often misplaced as well grounded in the particular instances of its application. There is, in fact, no recognized principle by which the propriety or impropriety of government interference is customarily tested. People decide according to their personal preferences. Some, whenever they see any good to be done, or evil to be remedied, would willingly instigate the government to undertake the business; while others prefer to bear almost any amount of social evil, rather than add one to the departments of human interests amenable to governmental control. And men range themselves on one or the other side in any particular case, according to this general direction of their sentiments; or according to the degree of interest which they feel in the particular thing which it is proposed that the government should do, or according to the belief they entertain that the government would, or would not, do it in the manner they prefer; but very rarely on account of any opinion to which they consistently adhere, as to what things are fit to be done by a government. And it seems to me that in consequence of this absence of rule or principle, one side is at present as often wrong as the other; the interference of government is, with about equal frequency, improperly invoked and improperly condemned.

The object of this Essay is to assert one very simple principle, as entitled to govern absolutely the dealings of society with the individual in the way of compulsion and control, whether the means used be physical force in the form of legal penalties, or the moral coercion of public opinion. That principle is, that the sole end for which mankind are warranted, individually or collectively, in interfering with the liberty of action of any of their number, is self-protection. That the only purpose for which power can be rightfully exercised over any member of a civilized community, against his will, is to prevent harm to others. His own good, either physical or moral, is not a sufficient warrant. He cannot rightfully be compelled to do or forbear because it will be better for him to do so, because it will make him happier, because, in the opinions of others, to do so would be wise, or even right. These are good reasons for remonstrating with him, or reasoning with him, or persuading him, or entreating him, but not for compelling him, or visiting him with any evil in case he do otherwise. To justify that, the conduct from which it is desired to deter him, must be calculated to produce evil to some one else. The only part of the conduct of any one, for which he is amenable to society, is that which concerns others. In the part which merely concerns himself, his independence is, of right, absolute. Over himself, over his own body and mind, the individual is sovereign.

It is, perhaps, hardly necessary to say that this doctrine is meant to apply only to human beings in the maturity of their faculties. We are not speaking of children, or of young persons below the age which the law may fix as that of manhood or womanhood. Those who are still in a state to require being taken care of by others, must be protected against their own actions as well as against external injury. For the same reason, we may leave out of consideration those backward states of society in which the race itself may be considered as in its nonage. The early difficulties in the way of spontaneous progress are so great, that there is seldom any choice of means for overcoming them; and a ruler full of the spirit of improvement is warranted in the use of any expedients that will attain an end, perhaps otherwise unattainable. Despotism is a legitimate mode of government in dealing with barbarians, provided the end be their improvement, and the means justified by actually effecting that end. Liberty, as a principle, has no application to any state of things anterior to the time when mankind have become capable of being improved by free and equal discussion. Until then, there is nothing for them but implicit obedience to an Akbar or a Charlemagne, if they are so fortunate as to find one. But as soon as mankind have attained the capacity of being guided to their own improvement by conviction or persuasion (a period long since reached in all nations with whom we need here concern ourselves), compulsion, either in the direct form or in that of pains and penalties for noncompliance, is no longer admissible as a means to their own good, and justifiable only for the security of others.

It is proper to state that I forgo any advantage which could be derived to my argument from the idea of abstract right, as a thing independent of utility. I regard utility as the ultimate appeal on all ethical questions; but it must be ulitity in the largest sense, grounded on the permanent interests of man as a progressive being. Those interests, I contend, authorize the subjection of individual spontaneity to external control, only in respect to those actions of each, which concern the interest of other people. If any one does an act hurtful to others, there is a prima facie case for punishing him, by law, or, where legal penalties are not safely applicable, by general disapprobation. There are also many positive acts for the benefit of others, which he may rightfully be compelled to perform; such as, to give evidence in a court of justice; to bear his fair share in the common defence, or in any other joint work necessary to the interest of the society of which he enjoys the protection; and to perform certain acts of individual beneficence, such as saving a fellow creature's life, or interposing to protect the defenceless against ill-usage, things which whenever it is obviously a man's duty to do, he may rightfully be made responsible to society for not doing. A person may cause evil to others not only by his actions but by his inaction, and in either case he is justly accountable to them for the injury. The latter case, it is true, requires a much more cautious exercise of compulsion than the former. To make any one answerable for doing evil to others, is the rule; to make him answerable for not preventing evil, is, comparatively speaking, the exception. Yet there are many cases clear enough and grave enough to justify that exception. In all things which regard the external relations of the individual, he is *de jure* amenable to those whose interests are concerned, and if need be, to society as their protector. There are often good reasons for not holding him to the responsibility; but these reasons must arise from the special expediencies of the case: either because it is a kind of case in which he is on the whole likely to act better, when left to his own discretion, than when controlled in any way in which society have it in their power to control him; or because the attempt to exercise control would produce other evils, greater than those which it would prevent. When such reasons as these preclude the enforcement of responsibility, the conscience of the agent himself should step into the vacant judgement-seat, and protect those interests of others which have no external protection; judging himself all the more rigidly, because the case does not admit of his being made accountable to the judgement of his fellow creatures.

But there is a sphere of action in which society, as distinguished from the individual, has, if any, only an indirect interest; comprehending all that portion of a person's life and conduct which affects only himself, or if it also affects others, only with their free, voluntary, and undeceived consent and participation. When I say only himself, I mean directly, and in the first instance: for whatever affects himself, may affect others through himself; and the objection which may be grounded on this contingency will receive consideration in the sequel. This, then, is the appropriate region of human liberty. It comprises, first, the inward domain of consciousness; demanding liberty of conscience, in the most comprehensive sense; liberty of thought and feeling; absolute freedom of opinion and sentiment on all subjects, practical or speculative, scientific, moral, or theological. The liberty of expressing and publishing opinions may seem to fall under a different principle, since it belongs to that part of the conduct of an individual which concerns other people; but, being almost of as much importance as the liberty of thought itself, and resting in great part on the same reasons, is practically inseparable from it. Secondly, the principle requires liberty of tastes and pursuits; of framing the plan of our life to suit our own character; of doing as we like, subject to such consequences as may follow: without impediment from our fellow creatures, so long as what we do does not harm them, even though they should think our conduct foolish, perverse, or wrong. Thirdly, from this liberty of each individual, follows the liberty, within the same limits, of combination among individuals; freedom to unite, for any purpose not involving harm to others: the persons combining being supposed to be of full age, and not forced or deceived.

No society in which these liberties are not, on the whole, respected, is free, whatever may be its form of government; and none is completely free in which they do not exist absolute and unqualified. The only freedom which deserves the name, is that of pursuing our own good in our own way, so long as we do not attempt to deprive others of theirs, or impede their efforts to obtain it. Each is the proper guardian of his own health, whether bodily, or mental and spiritual. Mankind are greater gainers by suffering each other to live as seems good to themselves, than by compelling each to live as seems good to the rest.

## Walter Pater

## Conclusion to

# STUDIES IN THE HISTORY
# OF THE RENAISSANCE

To regard all things and principles of things as inconstant modes or fashions has more and more become the tendency of modern thought. Let us begin with that which is without—our physical life. Fix upon it in one of its more exquisite intervals—the moment, for instance, of delicious recoil from the flood of water in summer heat. What is the whole physical life in that moment but a combination of natural elements to which science gives their names? But these elements, phosphorus and lime and delicate fibres, are present not in the human body alone: we detect them in places most remote from it. Our physical life is a perpetual motion of them—the passage of the blood, the wasting and repairing of the lenses of the eye, the modification of the tissues of the brain by every ray of light and sound—processes which science reduces to simpler and more elementary forces. Like the elements of which we are composed, the action of these forces extends beyond us; it rusts iron and ripens corn. Far out on every side of us those elements are broadcast, driven by many forces; and birth and gesture and death and the springing of violets from the grave are but a few out of ten thousand resultant combinations. That clear, perpetual outline of face and limb is but an image of ours, under which we group them—a design in a web, the actual threads of which pass out beyond it. This at least of flame-like our life has, that it is but the concurrence, renewed from moment to moment, of forces parting sooner or later on their ways.

Or if we begin with the inward whirl of thought and feeling, the whirlpool is still more rapid, the flame more eager and devouring. There it is no longer the gradual darkening of the eye and fading of colour from the wall—the movement of the shore-side, where the water flows down indeed, though in apparent rest—but the race of the mid-stream, a drift of momentary acts of sight and passion and thought. At first sight experience seems to bury us under a flood of

CONCLUSION TO *Studies in the History of the Renaissance* by Walter Pater: 1873.

external objects, pressing upon us with a sharp and importunate reality, calling us out of ourselves in a thousand forms of action. But when reflexion begins to act upon those objects they are dissipated under its influence; the cohesive force seems suspended like a trick of magic; each object is loosed into a group of impressions—colour, odour, texture—in the mind of the observer. And if we continue to dwell in thought on this world, not of objects in the solidity with which language invests them, but of impressions unstable, flickering, inconsistent, which burn and are extinguished with our consciousness of them, it contracts still further; the whole scope of observation is dwarfed to the narrow chamber of the individual mind. Experience, already reduced to a swarm of impressions, is ringed round for each one of us by that thick wall of personality through which no real voice has ever pierced on its way to us, or from us to that which we can only conjecture to be without. Every one of those impressions is the impression of the individual in his isolation, each mind keeping as a solitary prisoner its own dream of a world.

Analysis goes a step farther still, and assures us that those impressions of the individual mind to which, for each one of us, experience dwindles down, are in perpetual flight; that each of them is limited by time, and that as time is infinitely divisible, each of them is infinitely divisible also; all that is actual in it being a single moment, gone while we try to apprehend it, of which it may ever be more truly said that it has ceased to be than that it is. To such a tremulous wisp constantly reforming itself on the stream, to a single sharp impression, with a sense in it—a relic more or less fleeting—of such moments gone by, what is real in our life fines itself down. It is with this movement, with the passage and dissolution of impressions, images, sensations, that analysis leaves off—the continual vanishing away, that strange, perpetual weaving and unweaving of ourselves.

*Philosophiren,* says Novalis, *ist dephlegmatisiren, vivificiren.* The service of philosophy, of speculative culture, toward the human spirit is to rouse, to startle it into sharp and eager observation. Every moment some form grows perfect in hand or face; some tone on the hills or the sea is choicer than the rest; some mood of passion or insight or intellectual excitement is irresistibly real and attractive for us—but for the moment only. Not the fruit of experience, but experience itself, is the end. A counted number of pulses only is given to us of a variegated, dramatic life. How may we see in them all that is to be seen in them by the finest senses? How shall we pass most swiftly from point to point, and be present always at the focus where the greatest number of vital forces unite in their purest energy?

To burn always with this hard, gemlike flame, to maintain this ecstasy, is success in life. In a sense it might even be said that our failure is to form habits: for, after all, habit is relative to a stereotyped world, and meantime it is only the roughness of the eye that makes any two persons, things, situations, seem alike. While all melts under our feet, we may well catch at any exquisite passion, or any contribution to knowledge that seems by a lifted horizon to set the spirit free for a moment, or any stirring of the senses, strange dyes, strange colours, and curious odours, or work of the artist's hands, or the face of one's friend. Not to discriminate every moment some passionate attitude in those about us, and in the brilliancy of their gifts some tragic dividing of forces on their ways, is, on this short day of frost and sun, to sleep before evening. With this sense of the splendour of our experience and of its awful brevity, gathering all we are into one desperate effort to see and touch, we shall hardly have time to make theories about the things we see and touch. What we have to do is to be for ever curiously testing new opinions and courting new impressions, never acquiescing in a facile orthodoxy of Comte, or of Hegel, or of our own. Philosophical theories or ideas, as points of view, instruments of criticism, may help us to gather up what might otherwise pass unregarded by us. "Philosophy is the microscope of thought." The theory or idea or system which requires of us the sacrifice of any part of this experience, in consideration of some interest into which we cannot enter, or some abstract theory we have not identified with ourselves, or what is only conventional, has no real claim upon us.

One of the most beautiful passages in the writings of Rousseau is that in the sixth book of the *Confessions,* where he describes the awakening in him of the literary sense. An undefinable taint of death had always clung about him, and now in early manhood he believed himself smitten by mortal disease. He asked himself how he might make as much as possible of the interval that remained; and he was not biased by anything in his previous life when he decided that it must be by intellectual excitement, which he found just then in the clear, fresh writings of Voltaire. Well! we are all *condamnés,* as Victor Hugo says: we are all under sentence of death but with a sort of indefinite reprieve—*les hommes sont tous condamnés à mort avec les sursis indéfinis:* we have an interval, and then our place knows us no more. Some spend this interval in listlessness, some in high passions, the wisest—at least among "the children of this world"—in art and song. For our one chance lies in expanding that interval, in getting as many pulsations as possible into the given time. Great passions may give us this quickened sense of life, ecstasy and sorrow of love, the various forms of enthusiastic activity, disinterested or otherwise, which come naturally to many of us. Only be sure it is a passion—that it does yield you this fruit of a quickened, multiplied consciousness. Of this wisdom, the poetic passion, the desire of beauty, the love of art for art's sake, has most; for art comes to you professing frankly to give nothing but the highest quality to your moments as they pass, and simply for those moments' sake.

*Mark Twain*

# THE LOWEST ANIMAL*

In August, 1572, similar things were occurring in Paris and elsewhere in France. In this case it was Christian against Christian. The Roman Catholics, by previous concert, sprang a surprise upon the unprepared and unsuspecting Protestants, and butchered them by thousands—both sexes and all ages. This was the memorable St. Bartholomew's Day. At Rome the Pope and the Church gave public thanks to God when the happy news came.

During several centuries hundreds of heretics were burned at the stake every year because their religious opinions were not satisfactory to the Roman Church.

In all ages the savages of all lands have made the slaughtering of their neighboring brothers and the enslaving of their women and children the common business of their lives.

Hypocrisy, envy, malice, cruelty, vengefulness, seduction, rape, robbery, swindling, arson, bigamy, adultery, and the oppression and humiliation of the poor and the helpless in all ways have been and still are more or less common among both the civilized and uncivilized peoples of the earth.

For many centuries "the common brotherhood of man" has been urged—on Sundays—and "patriotism" on Sundays and weekdays

* This was to have been prefaced by newspaper clippings which, apparently, dealt with religious persecutions in Crete. The clippings have been lost.

THE LOWEST ANIMAL: From *Mark Twain, Letters from the Earth*, edited by Bernard DeVoto. Copyright © 1962 by The Mark Twain Company. Reprinted by permission of Harper & Row, Publishers, Inc.

both. Yet patriotism *contemplates the opposite of a common brother-hood.*

Woman's equality with man has never been conceded by any people, ancient or modern, civilized or savage.

I have been studying the traits and dispositions of the "lower animals" (so-called), and contrasting them with the traits and dispositions of man. I find the result humiliating to me. For it obliges me to renounce my allegiance to the Darwinian theory of the Ascent of Man from the Lower Animals; since it now seems plain to me that that theory ought to be vacated in favor of a new and truer one, this new and truer one to be named the *Des*cent of Man from the Higher Animals.

In proceeding toward this unpleasant conclusion I have not guessed or speculated or conjectured, but have used what is commonly called the scientific method. That is to say, I have subjected every postulate that presented itself to the crucial test of actual experiment, and have adopted it or rejected it according to the result. Thus I verified and established each step of my course in its turn before advancing to the next. These experiments were made in the London Zoological Gardens, and covered many months of painstaking and fatiguing work.

Before particularizing any of the experiments, I wish to state one or two things which seem to more properly belong in this place than further along. This in the interest of clearness. The massed experiments established to my satisfaction certain generalizations, to wit:

1. That the human race is of one distinct species. It exhibits slight variations—in color, stature, mental caliber, and so on—due to climate, environment, and so forth; but it is a species by itself, and not to be confounded with any other.

2. That the quadrupeds are a distinct family, also. This family exhibits variations—in color, size, food preferences, and so on; but it is a family by itself.

3. That the other families—the birds, the fishes, the insects, the reptiles, etc.—are more or less distinct, also. They are in the procession. They are links in the chain which stretches down from the higher animals to man at the bottom.

Some of my experiments were quite curious. In the course of my reading I had come across a case where, many years ago, some hunters on our Great Plains organized a buffalo hunt for the entertainment of an English earl—that, and to provide some fresh meat for his larder. They had charming sport. They killed seventy-two of those great animals; and ate part of one of them and left the seventy-one to rot. In order to determine the difference between an anaconda and an earl—if any—I caused seven young calves to be turned into the anaconda's cage. The grateful reptile immediately crushed one of them and swallowed it, then lay back satisfied. It showed no further interest in the calves, and no disposition to harm them. I tried this experiment with other anacondas; always with the same result. The fact stood proven that the difference between an earl and an anaconda is that the earl is cruel and the anaconda isn't; and that the earl wantonly destroys what he has no use for, but the anaconda doesn't. This seemed to suggest that the anaconda was not descended from the earl. It also seemed to suggest that the earl was descended from the anaconda, and had lost a good deal in the transition.

I was aware that many men who have accumulated more millions of money than they can ever use have shown a rabid hunger for more, and have not scrupled to cheat the ignorant and the helpless out of their poor servings in order to partially appease that appetite. I furnished a hundred different kinds of wild and tame animals the opportunity to accumulate vast stores of food, but none of them would do it. The squirrels and bees and certain birds made accumulations, but stopped when they had gathered a winter's supply, and could not be persuaded to add to it either honestly or by chicane. In order to bolster up a tottering reputation the ant pretended to store up supplies, but I was not deceived. I know the ant. These experiments convinced me that there is this difference between man and the higher animals: he is avaricious and miserly, they are not.

In the course of my experiments I convinced myself that among the animals man is the only one that harbors insults and injuries, broods over them, waits till a chance offers, then takes revenge. The passion of revenge is unknown to the higher animals.

Roosters keep harems, but it is by consent of their concubines; therefore no wrong is done. Men keep harems, but it is by brute force, privileged by atrocious laws which the other sex were allowed no hand in making. In this matter man occupies a far lower place than the rooster.

Cats are loose in their morals, but not consciously so. Man, in his descent from the cat, has brought the cat's looseness with him but has left the unconsciousness behind—the saving grace which excuses the cat. The cat is innocent, man is not.

Indecency, vulgarity, obscenity—these are strictly confined to man; he invented them. Among the higher animals there is no trace of them. They hide nothing; they are not ashamed. Man, with his soiled mind, covers himself. He will not even enter a drawing room with his breast and back naked, so alive are he and his mates to indecent suggestion. Man is "The Animal that Laughs." But so does the monkey, as Mr. Darwin pointed out; and so does the Australian bird that is called the laughing jackass. No—Man is the Animal that Blushes. He is the only one that does it—or has occasion to.

At the head of this article we see how "three monks were burnt to death" a few days ago, and a prior "put to death with atrocious cruelty." Do we inquire into the details? No; or we should find out that the prior was subjected to unprintable mutilations. Man—when he is a North American Indian—gouges out his prisoner's eyes; when he is King John, with a nephew to render untroublesome, he uses a red-hot iron; when he is a religious zealot dealing with heretics in the Middle Ages, he skins his captive alive and scatters salt on his back; in the first Richard's time he shuts up a multitude of Jew families in a tower and sets fire to it; in Columbus's time he captures a family of Spanish Jews and—but *that* is not printable; in our day in England a man is fined ten shillings for beating his mother nearly to death with a chair, and another man is fined forty shillings for having four pheasant eggs in his possession without being able to satisfactorily explain how he got them. Of all the animals, man is the only one that is cruel. He is the only one that inflicts pain for the pleasure of doing it. It is a trait that is not known to the higher animals. The cat plays with the frightened mouse; but she has this excuse, that she does not know that the mouse is suffering. The cat is moderate—unhumanly moderate: she only scares the mouse, she does not hurt it; she doesn't dig out its eyes, or tear off its skin, or drive splinters under its nails—man-fashion; when she is done playing with it she makes a sudden meal of it and puts it out of its trouble. Man is the Cruel Animal. He is alone in that distinction.

The higher animals engage in individual fights, but never in organized masses. Man is the only animal that deals in that atrocity of atrocities, War. He is the only one that gathers his brethren about him and goes forth in cold blood and with calm pulse to exterminate his kind. He is the only animal that for sordid wages will march out, as the Hessians did in our Revolution, and as the boyish Prince Napoleon did in the Zulu war, and help to slaughter strangers of his own species who have done him no harm and with whom he has no quarrel.

Man is the only animal that robs his helpless fellow of his country—takes possession of it and drives him out of it or destroys him.

Man has done this in all the ages. There is not an acre of ground on the globe that is in possession of its rightful owner, or that has not been taken away from owner after owner, cycle after cycle, by force and bloodshed.

Man is the only Slave. And he is the only animal who enslaves. He has always been a slave in one form or another, and has always held other slaves in bondage under him in one way or another. In our day he is always some man's slave for wages, and does that man's work; and this slave has other slaves under him for minor wages, and they do *his* work. The higher animals are the only ones who exclusively do their own work and provide their own living.

Man is the only Patriot. He sets himself apart in his own country, under his own flag, and sneers at the other nations, and keeps multitudinous uniformed assassins on hand at heavy expense to grab slices of other people's countries, and keep *them* from grabbing slices of *his*. And in the intervals between campaigns he washes the blood off his hands and works for "the universal brotherhood of man"— with his mouth.

Man is the Religious Animal. He is the only Religious Animal. He is the only animal that has the True Religion—several of them. He is the only animal that loves his neighbor as himself, and cuts his throat if his theology isn't straight. He has made a graveyard of the globe in trying his honest best to smooth his brother's path to happiness and heaven. He was at it in the time of the Caesars, he was at it in Mahomet's time, he was at it in the time of the Inquisition, he was at it in France a couple of centuries, he was at it in England in Mary's day, he has been at it ever since he first saw the light, he is at it today in Crete—as per the telegrams quoted above—he will be at it somewhere else tomorrow. The higher animals have no religion. And we are told that they are going to be left out, in the Hereafter. I wonder why? It seems questionable taste.

Man is the Reasoning Animal. Such is the claim. I think it is open to dispute. Indeed, my experiments have proven to me that he is the Unreasoning Animal. Note his history, as sketched above. It seems plain to me that whatever he is, he is *not* a reasoning animal. His record is the fantastic record of a maniac. I consider that the strongest count against his intelligence is the fact that with that record back of him he blandly sets himself up as the head animal of the lot: whereas by his own standards he is the bottom one.

In truth, man is incurably foolish. Simple things which the other animals easily learn, he is incapable of learning. Among my experiments was this. In an hour I taught a cat and a dog to be friends. I put them in a cage. In another hour I taught them to be friends with a rabbit. In the course of two days I was able to add a fox, a goose, a squirrel and some doves. Finally a monkey. They lived together in peace; even affectionately.

Next, in another cage I confined an Irish Catholic from Tipperary, and as soon as he seemed tame I added a Scotch Presbyterian from Aberdeen. Next a Turk from Constantinople; a Greek Christian from Crete; an Armenian; a Methodist from the wilds of Arkansas; a Buddhist from China; a Brahman from Benares. Finally, a Salvation Army Colonel from Wapping. Then I stayed away two whole days. When I came back to note results, the cage of Higher Animals was all right, but in the other there was but a chaos of gory odds and ends of turbans and fezzes and plaids and bones and flesh—not a specimen left alive. These Reasoning Animals had disagreed on a theological detail and carried the matter to a Higher Court.

One is obliged to concede that in true loftiness of character, Man cannot claim to approach even the meanest of the Higher Animals. It is plain that he is constitutionally incapable of approaching that altitude; that he is constitutionally afflicted with a Defect which must make such approach forever impossible, for it is manifest that this defect is permanent in him, indestructible, ineradicable.

I find this Defect to be the *Moral Sense*. He is the only animal that has it. It is the secret of his degradation. It is the quality *which enables him to do wrong*. It has no other office. It is incapable of performing any other function. It could never have been intended to perform any other. Without it, man could do no wrong. He would rise at once to the level of the Higher Animals.

Since the Moral Sense has but the one office, the one capacity—to enable man to do wrong—it is plainly without value to him. It is as valueless to him as is disease. In fact, it manifestly *is* a disease. *Rabies* is bad, but it is not so bad as this disease. Rabies enables a man to do a thing which he could not do when in a healthy state: kill his neighbor with a poisonous bite. No one is the better man for having rabies. The Moral Sense enables a man to do wrong. It enables him to do wrong in a thousand ways. Rabies is an innocent disease, compared to the Moral Sense. No one, then, can be the better man for having the Moral Sense. What, now, do we find the Primal Curse to have been? Plainly what it was in the beginning: the infliction upon man of the Moral Sense; the ability to distinguish good from evil; and with it, necessarily, the ability to *do* evil; for there can be no evil act without the presence of consciousness of it in the doer of it.

And so I find that we have descended and degenerated, from some far ancestor—some microscopic atom wandering at its pleasure between the mighty horizons of a drop of water perchance—insect by insect, animal by animal, reptile by reptile, down the long highway of smirchless innocence, till we have reached the bottom stage of development—namable as the Human Being. Below us—nothing. Nothing but the Frenchman.

There is only one possible stage below the Moral Sense; that is the Immoral Sense. The Frenchman has it. Man is but little lower than the angels. This definitely locates him. He is between the angels and the French.

Man seems to be a rickety poor sort of a thing, any way you take him; a kind of British Museum of infirmities and inferiorities. He is always undergoing repairs. A machine that was as unreliable as he is would have no market. On top of his specialty—the Moral Sense—are piled a multitude of minor infirmities; such a multitude, indeed, that one may broadly call them countless. The Higher Animals get their teeth without pain or inconvenience. Man gets his through months and months of cruel torture; and at a time of life when he is but ill able to bear it. As soon as he has got them they must all be pulled out again, for they were of no value in the first place, not worth the loss of a night's rest. The second set will answer for a while, by being reinforced occasionally with rubber or plugged up with gold; but he will never get a set which can really be depended on till a dentist makes him one. This set will be called "false" teeth—as if he had ever worn any other kind.

In a wild state—a natural state—the Higher Animals have a few diseases; diseases of little consequence; the main one is old age. But man starts in as a child and lives on diseases till the end, as a regular diet. He has mumps, measles, whooping cough, croup, tonsillitis, diphtheria, scarlet fever, almost as a matter of course. Afterward, as he goes along, his life continues to be threatened at every turn: by colds, coughs, asthma, bronchitis, itch, cholera, cancer, consumption, yellow fever, bilious fever, typhus fevers, hay fever, ague, chilblains, piles, inflammation of the entrails, indigestion, toothache, earache, deafness, dumbness, blindness, influenza, chicken pox, cowpox, smallpox, liver complaint, constipation, bloody flux, warts, pimples, boils, carbuncles, abscesses, bunions, corns, tumors, fistulas, pneumonia, softening of the brain, melancholia and fifteen other kinds of insanity; dysentery, jaundice, diseases of the heart, the bones, the skin, the scalp, the spleen, the kidneys, the nerves, the brain, the blood; scrofula, paralysis, leprosy, neuralgia, palsy, fits, headache, thirteen kinds of rheumatism, forty-six of gout, and a formidable supply of gross and unprintable disorders of one sort and another. Also—but why continue the list? The mere names of the agents appointed to keep this shackly machine out of repair would hide him from sight if printed on his body in the smallest type known to the founder's art. He is but a basket of pestilent corruption provided for the support and entertainment of swarming armies of bacilli—armies commissioned to rot him and destroy him, and each army equipped with a special detail of the work. The process of waylaying him, persecuting him, rotting him, killing him, begins with his first breath, and there is no mercy, no pity, no truce till he draws his last one.

Look at the workmanship of him, in certain of its particulars. What are his tonsils for? They perform no useful function; they have no value. They have no business there. They are but a trap. They have but the one office, the one industry: to provide tonsillitis and quinsy and such things for the possessor of them. And what is the vermiform appendix for? It has no value; it cannot perform any useful service. It is but an ambuscaded enemy whose sole interest in life is to lie in wait for stray grapeseeds and employ them to breed strangulated hernia. And what are the male's mammals for? For business, they are out of the question; as an ornament, they are a mistake. What is his beard for? It performs no useful function; it is a nuisance and a discomfort; all nations hate it; all nations persecute it with the razor. And because it is a nuisance and a discomfort, Nature never allows the supply of it to fall short, in any man's case, between puberty and the grave. You never see a man bald-headed on his chin. But his hair! It is a graceful ornament, it is a comfort, it is the best of all protections against certain perilous ailments, man prizes it above emeralds and rubies. And because of these things Nature puts it on, half the time, so that it won't stay. Man's sight, smell, hearing, sense of locality—how inferior they are. The condor sees a corpse at five miles; man has no telescope that can do it. The bloodhound follows a scent that is two days old. The robin hears the earthworm burrowing his course under the ground. The cat, deported in a closed basket, finds its way home again through twenty miles of country which it has never seen.

Certain functions lodged in the other sex perform in a lamentably inferior way as compared with the performance of the same functions in the Higher Animals. In the human being, menstruation, gestation and parturition are terms which stand for horrors. In the Higher Animals these things are hardly even inconveniences.

For style, look at the Bengal tiger—that ideal of grace, beauty, physical perfection, majesty. And then look at Man—that poor thing. He is the Animal of the Wig, the Trepanned Skull, the Ear Trumpet, the Glass Eye, the Pasteboard Nose, the Porcelain Teeth, the Silver Windpipe, the Wooden Leg—a creature that is mended and patched all over, from top to bottom. If he can't get renewals of his bric-a-brac in the next world, what will he look like?

He has just one stupendous superiority. In his intellect he is supreme. The Higher Animals cannot touch him there. It is curious, it is noteworthy, that no heaven has ever been offered him wherein his one sole superiority was provided with a chance to enjoy itself. Even when he himself has imagined a heaven, he has never made provision in it for intellectual joys. It is a striking omission. It seems a tacit confession that heavens are provided for the Higher Animals alone. This is matter for thought; and for serious thought. And it is full of a grim suggestion: that we are not as important, perhaps, as we had all along supposed we were.

*Henry James*

## Preface to

# THE SPOILS OF POYNTON

It was years ago, I remember, one Christmas Eve when I was dining with friends: a lady beside me made in the course of talk one of those allusions that I have always found myself recognising on the spot as "germs." The germ, wherever gathered, has ever been for me the germ of a "story," and most of the stories straining to shape under my hand have sprung from a single small seed, a seed as minute and wind-blown as that casual hint for "The Spoils of Poynton" dropped unwittingly by my neighbour, a mere floating particle in the stream of talk. What above all comes back to me with this reminiscence is the sense of the inveterate minuteness, on such happy occasions, of the precious particle—reduced, that is, to its mere fruitful essence. Such is the interesting truth about the stray suggestion, the wandering word, the vague echo, at touch of which the novelist's imagination winces as at the prick of some sharp point: its virtue is all in its needle-like quality, the power to penetrate as finely as possible. This fineness

PREFACE TO *The Spoils of Poynton:* A selection from that Preface. Reprinted from the New York Edition of *The Novels and Tales of Henry James* (Vol. X), Charles Scribner's Sons, 1908.

it is that communicates the virus of suggestion, anything more than the minimum of which spoils the operation. If one is given a hint at all designedly one is sure to be given too much; one's subject is in the merest grain, the speck of truth, of beauty, of reality, scarce visible to the common eye—since, I firmly hold, a good eye for a subject is anything but usual. Strange and attaching, certainly, the consistency with which the first thing to be done for the communicated and seized idea is to reduce almost to nought the form, the air as of a mere disjoined and lacerated lump of life, in which we may have happened to meet it. Life being all inclusion and confusion, and art being all discrimination  and selection, the latter, in search of the hard latent *value* with which alone it is concerned, sniffs round the mass as instinctively and unerringly as a dog suspicious of some buried bone. The difference here, however, is that, while the dog desires his bone but to destroy it, the artist finds in *his* tiny nugget, washed free of awkward accretions and hammered into a sacred hardness, the very stuff for a clear affirmation, the happiest chance for the indestructible. It at the same time amuses him again and again to note how, beyond the first step of the actual case, the case that constitutes for him his germ, his vital particle, his grain of gold, life persistently blunders and deviates, loses herself in the sand. The reason is of course that life has no direct sense whatever for the subject and is capable, luckily for us, of nothing but splendid waste. Hence the opportunity for the sublime economy of art, which rescues, which saves, and hoards and "banks," investing and reinvesting these fruits of toil in wondrous useful "works" and thus making up for us, desperate spendthrifts that we all naturally are, the most princely of incomes. It is the subtle secrets of that system, however, that are meanwhile the charming study, with an endless attraction, above all, in the question —endlessly baffling indeed—of the method at the heart of the madness; the madness, I mean, of a zeal, among the reflective sort, so disinterested. If life, presenting us the germ, and left merely to herself in such a business, gives the case away, almost always, before we can stop her, what are the signs for our guidance, what the primary laws for a saving selection, how do we know when and where to intervene, where do we place the beginnings of the wrong or the right deviation? Such would be the elements of an enquiry upon which, I hasten to say, it is quite forbidden me here to embark: I but glance at them in evidence of the rich pasture that at every turn surrounds the ruminant critic. The answer may be after all that mysteries here elude us, that general considerations fail or mislead, and that even the fondest of artists need ask no wider range than the logic of the particular case. The particular case, or in other words his relation to a given subject, once the relation is established, forms in itself a little world of exercise and agitation. Let him hold himself perhaps supremely fortunate if he can meet half the questions with which that air alone may swarm.

So it was, at any rate, that when my amiable friend, on the Christmas Eve, before the table that glowed safe and fair through the brown London night, spoke of such an odd matter as that a good lady in the north, always well looked on, was at daggers drawn with her only son, ever hitherto exemplary, over the ownership of the valuable furniture of a fine old house just accruing to the young man by his father's death, I instantly became aware, with my "sense for the subject," of the prick of inoculation; the *whole* of the virus, as I have called it, being infused by that single touch. There had been but ten words, yet I had recognised in them, as in a flash, all the possibilities of the little drama of my "Spoils," which glimmered then and there into life; so that when in the next breath I began to hear of action taken, on the beautiful ground, by our engaged adversaries, tipped each, from that instant, with the light of the highest distinction, I saw clumsy Life again at her stupid work. For the action taken, and on which my friend, as I knew she would, had already begun all complacently and benightedly further to report, I had absolutely, and could have, no scrap of use; one had been so perfectly qualified to say in advance: "It's the perfect little workable thing, but she'll strangle it in the cradle, even while she pretends, all so cheeringly, to rock it; wherefore I'll stay her hand while yet there's time." I didn't, of course, stay her hand—there never *is* in such cases "time"; and I had once more the full demonstration of the fatal futility of Fact. The turn taken by the excellent situation—excellent, for development, if arrested in the right place, that is in the germ—had the full measure of the classic ineptitude; to which with the full measure of the artistic irony one could once more, and for the thousandth time, but take off one's hat. It was not, however, that this in the least mattered, once the seed had been transplanted to richer soil; and I dwell on that almost inveterate redundancy of the wrong, as opposed to the ideal right, in any free flowering of the actual, by reason only of its approach to calculable regularity.

If there was nothing regular meanwhile, nothing more so than the habit of vigilance, in my quickly feeling where interest would really lie, so I could none the less acknowledge afresh that these small private cheers of recognition made the spirit easy and the temper bland for the confused whole. I "took" in fine, on the spot, to the rich bare little facts of the two related figures, embroiled perhaps all so sordidly; and for reasons of which I could most probably have given at the moment no decent account. Had I been asked why they were, in that stark nudity, to say nothing of that ugliness of attitude, "interesting," I fear I could have said nothing more to the point, even to my own questioning spirit, than "Well, you'll see!" By which of course I should have meant "Well, *I* shall see"—confident meanwhile (as against the appearance or the imputation of poor taste) that interest would spring as soon as one should begin really to see *anything*. That points, I think, to a large part of the very source of interest for the artist: it resides in the strong consciousness of his seeing all for himself. He has to borrow his motive, which is certainly half the battle; and this motive is his ground, his site and his foundation. But after that he only lends and gives, only builds and piles high, lays together the blocks quarried in the deeps of his imagination and on his personal premises. He thus remains all the while in intimate commerce with his motive, and can say to himself—what really more than anything else inflames and sustains him—that he alone has the *secret* of the particular case, he alone can measure the truth of the direction to be taken by his developed data. There can be for him, evidently, only one logic for these things; there can be for him only one truth and one direction—the quarter in which his subject most completely expresses itself. The careful ascertainment of how it shall do so, and the art of guiding it with consequent authority—since this sense of "authority" is for the master-builder the treasure of treasures, or at least the joy of joys—renews in the modern alchemist something like the old dream of the secret of life.

# E. M. Forster

## NOTES ON
## THE ENGLISH CHARACTER

*First Note.* I had better let the cat out of the bag at once and record my opinion that the character of the English is essentially middle-class. There is a sound historical reason for this, for, since

NOTES ON THE ENGLISH CHARACTER: From *Abinger Harvest*, copyright, 1936, 1964, by E. M. Forster. Reprinted by permission of Harcourt Brace Jovanovich, Inc.

the end of the eighteenth century, the middle classes have been the dominant force in our community. They gained wealth by the Industrial Revolution, political power by the Reform Bill of 1832; they are connected with the rise and organization of the British Empire; they are responsible for the literature of the nineteenth century. Solidity, caution, integrity, efficiency. Lack of imagination, hypocrisy. These qualities characterize the middle classes in every country, but in England they are national characteristics also, because only in England have the middle classes been in power for one hundred and fifty years. Napoleon, in his rude way, called us "a nation of shopkeepers." We prefer to call ourselves "a great commercial nation"—it sounds more dignified—but the two phrases amount to the same. Of course there are other classes: there is an aristocracy, there are the poor. But it is on the middle classes that the eye of the critic rests—just as it rests on the poor in Russia and on the aristocracy in Japan. Russia is symbolized by the peasant or by the factory worker; Japan by the samurai; the national figure of England is Mr. Bull with his top hat, his comfortable clothes, his substantial stomach, and his substantial balance at the bank. Saint George may caper on banners and in the speeches of politicians, but it is John Bull who delivers the goods. And even Saint George—if Gibbon is correct—wore a top hat once; he was an army contractor and supplied indifferent bacon. It all amounts to the same in the end.

*Second Note.* Just as the heart of England is the middle classes, so the heart of the middle classes is the public-school system. This extraordinary institution is local. It does not even exist all over the British Isles. It is unknown in Ireland, almost unknown in Scotland (countries excluded from my survey), and though it may inspire other great institutions—Aligarh, for example, and some of the schools in the United States—it remains unique, because it was created by the Anglo-Saxon middle classes, and can flourish only where they flourish. How perfectly it expresses their character—far better, for instance, than does the university, into which social and spiritual complexities have already entered. With its boarding-houses, its compulsory games, its system of prefects and fagging, its insistence on good form and on *esprit de corps,* it produces a type whose weight is out of all proportion to its numbers.

On leaving his school, the boy either sets to work at once—goes into the army or into business, or emigrates—or else proceeds to the university, and after three or four years there enters some other profession—becomes a barrister, doctor, civil servant, schoolmaster, or journalist. (If through some mishap he does not become a manual worker or an artist.) In all these careers his education, or the absence of it, influences him. Its memories influence him also. Many men look back on their school days as the happiest of their lives. They remember with regret that golden time when life, though hard, was not yet complex; when they all worked together and played together and thought together, so far as they thought at all; when they were taught that school is the world in miniature, and believed that no one can love his country who does not love his school. And they prolong that time as best they can by joining their Old Boys' society; indeed, some of them remain Old Boys and nothing else for the rest of their lives. They attribute all good to the school. They worship it. They quote the remark that "the battle of Waterloo was won on the playing-fields of Eton." It is nothing to them that the remark is inapplicable historically and was never made by the Duke of Wellington, and that the Duke of Wellington was an Irishman. They go on quoting it because it expresses their sentiments; they feel that if the Duke of Wellington didn't make it he ought to have, and if he wasn't an Englishman he ought to have been. And they go forth into a world that is not entirely composed of public-school men or even of Anglo-Saxons, but of men who are as various as the sands of the sea; into a world of whose richness and subtlety they have no conception. They go forth into it with well-developed bodies, fairly developed minds, and undeveloped hearts. And it is this undeveloped heart that is largely responsible for the difficulties of Englishmen abroad. An undeveloped heart—not a cold one. The difference is important, and on it my next note will be based.

For it is not that the Englishman can't feel—it is that he is afraid to feel. He has been taught at his public school that feeling is bad form. He must not express great joy or sorrow, or even open his mouth too wide when he talks—his pipe might fall out if he did. He must bottle up his emotions, or let them out only on a very special occasion.

Once upon a time (this is an anecdote) I went for a week's holiday on the Continent with an Indian friend. We both enjoyed ourselves and were sorry when the week was over, but on parting our behaviour was absolutely different. He was plunged in despair. He felt that because the holiday was over all happiness was over until the world ended. He could not express his sorrow too much. But in me the Englishman came out strong. I reflected that we should meet again in a month or two, and could write in the interval if we had anything to say; and under these circumstances I could not see what there was to make a fuss about. It wasn't as if we were parting forever or dying. "Buck up," I said, "do buck up." He refused to buck up, and I left him plunged in gloom.

The conclusion of the anecdote is even more instructive. For when we met the next month our conversation threw a good deal of light on the English character. I began by scolding my friend. I told him that he had been wrong to feel and display so much emotion upon so slight an occasion; that it was inappropriate. The word "inappropriate" roused him to fury. "What?" he cried. "Do you measure out your emotions as if they were potatoes?" I did not like the simile of the potatoes, but after a moment's reflection I said, "Yes, I do; and what's more, I think I ought to. A small occasion demands a little emotion, just as a large occasion demands a great one. I would like my emotions to be appropriate. This may be measuring them like potatoes, but it is better than slopping them about like water from a pail, which is what you did." He did not like the simile of the pail. "If those are your opinions, they part us forever," he cried, and left the room. Returning immediately, he added: "No— but your whole attitude toward emotion is wrong. Emotion has nothing to do with appropriateness. It matters only that it shall be sincere. I happened to feel deeply. I showed it. It doesn't matter whether I ought to have felt deeply or not."

This remark impressed me very much. Yet I could not agree with it, and said that I valued emotion as much as he did, but used it differently; if I poured it out on small occasions I was afraid of having none left for the great ones, and of being bankrupt at the crises of life. Note the word "bankrupt." I spoke as a member of a prudent middle-class nation, always anxious to meet my liabilities. But my friend spoke as an Oriental, and the Oriental has behind him a tradition, not of middle-class prudence, but of kingly munificence and splendour. He feels his resources are endless, just as John Bull feels his are finite. As regards material resources, the Oriental is clearly unwise. Money isn't endless. If we spend or give away all the money we have, we haven't any more, and must take the consequences, which are frequently unpleasant. But, as regards the resources of the spirit, he may be right. The emotions may be endless. The more we express them, the more we may have to express.

> True love in this differs from gold and clay,
> That to divide is not to take away,

says Shelley. Shelley, at all events, believes that the wealth of the spirit is endless; that we may express it copiously, passionately, and always; and that we can never feel sorrow or joy too acutely.

In the above anecdote, I have figured as a typical Englishman. I will now descend from that dizzy and somewhat unfamiliar height, and return to my business of note-taking. A note on the *slowness* of the English character. The Englishman appears to be cold and unemotional because he is really slow. When an event happens, he may understand it quickly enough with his mind, but he takes quite a while to feel it. Once upon a time a coach, containing some Englishmen and some Frenchmen, was driving over the Alps. The horses ran away, and as they were dashing across a bridge the coach caught on the stonework, tottered, and nearly fell into the ravine below. The Frenchmen were frantic with terror: they screamed and gesticulated and flung themselves about, as Frenchmen would. The Englishmen sat quite calm. An hour later the coach drew up at an inn to change horses, and by that time the situations were exactly reversed. The Frenchmen had forgotten all about the danger, and were chattering gaily; the Englishmen had just begun to feel it, and one had a nervous breakdown and was obliged to go to bed. We have here a clear physical difference between the two races—a difference that goes deep into character. The Frenchmen responded at once; the Englishmen responded in time. They were slow and they were also practical. Their instinct forbade them to throw themselves about in the coach, because it was more likely to tip over if they did. They had this extraordinary appreciation of *fact* that we shall notice again and again. When a disaster comes, the English instinct is to do what can be done first, and to postpone the feeling as long as possible. Hence they are splendid at emergencies. No doubt they are brave—no one will deny that—but bravery is partly an affair of the nerves, and the English nervous system is well equipped for meeting a physical emergency. It acts promptly and feels slowly. Such a combination is fruitful, and anyone who possesses it has gone a long way toward being brave. And when the action is over, then the Englishman can feel.

There is one more consideration—a most important one. If the English nature is cold, how is it that it has produced a great literature and a literature that is particularly great in poetry? Judged by its prose, English literature would not stand in the first rank. It is its poetry that raises it to the level of Greek, Persian, or French. And yet the English are supposed to be so unpoetical. How is this? The nation that produced the Elizabethan drama and the Lake Poets cannot be a cold, unpoetical nation. We can't get fire out of ice. Since literature always rests upon national character, there must be in the English nature hidden springs of fire to produce the fire we see. The warm sympathy, the romance, the imagination, that we look for in Englishmen whom we meet, and too often vainly look for, must exist in the nation as a whole, or we could not have this outburst of national song. An undeveloped heart—not a cold one.

The trouble is that the English nature is not at all easy to understand. It has a great air of simplicity, it advertises itself as simple, but the more we consider it, the greater the problems we shall encounter. People talk of the mysterious East, but the West also is mysterious. It has depths that do not reveal themselves at the first gaze. We know what the sea looks like from a distance: it is of one colour, and level, and obviously cannot contain such creatures as fish. But if we look into the sea over the edge of a boat, we see a dozen colours, and depth below depth, and fish swimming in them. That sea is the English character—apparently imperturbable and even. The depths and the colours are the English romanticism and the English sensitiveness—we do not expect to find such things, but they exist. And—to continue my metaphor—the fish are the English emotions, which are always trying to get up to the surface, but don't quite know how. For the most part we see them moving far below, distorted and obscure. Now and then they succeed and we exclaim, "Why, the Englishman has emotions! He actually can feel!" And occasionally we see that beautiful creature the flying fish, which rises out of the water altogether into the air and the sunlight. English literature is a flying fish. It is a sample of the life that goes on day after day beneath the surface; it is a proof that beauty and emotion exist in the salt, inhospitable sea.

And now let's get back to terra firma. The Englishman's attitude toward criticism will give us another starting-point. He is not annoyed by criticism. He listens or not as the case may be, smiles and passes on, saying, "Oh, the fellow's jealous"; "Oh, I'm used to Bernard Shaw; monkey tricks don't hurt me." It never occurs to him that the fellow may be accurate as well as jealous, and that he might do well to take the criticism to heart and profit by it. It never strikes him—except as a form of words—that he is capable of improvement; his self-complacency is abysmal. Other nations, both Oriental and European, have an uneasy feeling that they are not quite perfect. In consequence they resent criticism. It hurts them; and their snappy answers often mask a determination to improve themselves. Not so the Englishman. He has no uneasy feeling. Let the critics bark. And the "tolerant humorous attitude" with which he confronts them is not really tolerant, because it is insensitive, and not really humorous, because it is bounded by the titter and the guffaw.

Turn over the pages of *Punch*. There is neither wit, laughter, nor satire in our national jester—only the snigger of a suburban householder who can understand nothing that does not resemble himself. Week after week, under Mr. Punch's supervision, a man falls off his horse, or a colonel misses a golf ball, or a little girl makes a mistake in her prayers. Week after week ladies show not too much of their legs, foreigners are deprecated, originality condemned. Week after week a bricklayer does not do as much work as he ought and a futurist does more than he need. It is all supposed to be so good-tempered and clean; it is also supposed to be funny. It is actually an outstanding example of our attitude toward criticism: the middle-class Englishman, with a smile on his clean-shaven lips, is engaged in admiring himself and ignoring the rest of mankind. If, in those colourless pages, he came across anything that really was funny—a drawing by Max Beerbohm, for instance—his smile would disappear, and he would say to himself, "The fellow's a bit of a crank," and pass on.

This particular attitude reveals such insensitiveness as to suggest a more serious charge: is the Englishman altogether indifferent to the things of the spirit? Let us glance for a moment at his religion—not, indeed, at his theology, which would not merit inspection, but at the action on his daily life of his belief in the unseen. Here again his attitude is practical. But an innate decency comes out: he is thinking of others rather than of himself. Right conduct is his aim. He asks of his religion that it shall make him a better man in daily life; that he shall be more kind, more just, more merciful, more desirous to fight what is evil and to protect what is good. No one could call this a low conception. It is, as far as it goes, a spiritual one. Yet—and this seems to me typical of the race—it is only half the religious idea. Religion is more than an ethical code with a divine sanction. It is also a means through which man may get into direct connection with the divine, and, judging by history, few Englishmen have succeeded in doing this. We have produced no series of prophets, as has Judaism or Islam. We have not even produced a Joan of Arc, or a Savonarola. We have produced few saints. In Germany the Reformation was due to the passionate conviction of Luther. In England it was due to a palace intrigue. We can show a steady level of piety, a fixed determination to live decently according to our lights—little more.

Well, it is something. It clears us of the charge of being an unspiritual nation. That facile contrast between the spiritual East and the materialistic West can be pushed too far. The West also is spiritual. Only it expresses its belief, not in fasting and visions, not in prophetic

rapture, but in the daily round, the common task. An incomplete expression, if you like. I agree. But the argument underlying these scattered notes is that the Englishman is an incomplete person. Not a cold
or an unspiritual one. But undeveloped, incomplete.

The attitude of the average orthodox Englishman is often misunderstood. It is thought that he must know that a doctrine—say, like
that of the Trinity—is untrue. Moslems in particular feel that his faith
is a dishonest compromise between polytheism and monotheism. The
answer to this criticism is that the average orthodox Englishman is no
theologian. He regards the Trinity as a mystery that it is not his place
to solve. "I find difficulties enough in daily life," he will say. "I concern myself with those. As for the Trinity, it is a doctrine handed down
to me from my fathers, whom I respect, and I hope to hand it down
to my sons, and that they will respect me. No doubt it is true, or it
would not have been handed down. And no doubt the clergy could
explain it to me if I asked them; but, like myself, they are busy men,
and I will not take up their time."

In such an answer there is confusion of thought, if you like, but
no conscious deceit, which is alien to the English nature. The Englishman's deceit is generally unconscious.

For I have suggested earlier that the English are sometimes
hypocrites, and it is now my duty to develop this rather painful subject. Hypocrisy is the prime charge that is always brought against us.
The Germans are called brutal, the Spanish cruel, the Americans
superficial, and so on; but we are perfide Albion, the island of hypocrites, the people who have built up an Empire with a Bible in one
hand, a pistol in the other, and financial concessions in both pockets.
Is the charge true? I think it is; but while making it we must be quite
clear as to what we mean by hypocrisy. Do we mean *conscious* deceit?
Well, the English are comparatively guiltless of this; they have little
of the Renaissance villain about them. Do we mean *unconscious*
deceit? Muddle-headedness? Of this I believe them to be guilty. When
an Englishman has been led into a course of wrong action, he has
nearly always begun by muddling himself. A public-school education
does not make for mental clearness, and he possesses to a very high
degree the power of confusing his own mind. We have seen this
tendency at work in the domain of theology; how does it work in the
domain of conduct?

Jane Austen may seem an odd authority to cite, but Jane Austen
has, within her limits, a marvellous insight into the English mind.
Her range is limited, her characters never attempt any of the more
scarlet sins. But she has a merciless eye for questions of conduct, and

the classical example of two English people muddling themselves before they embark upon a wrong course of action is to be found in the opening chapters of *Sense and Sensibility*. Old Mr. Dashwood has just died. He has been twice married. By his first marriage he has a son, John; by his second marriage three daughters. The son is well off; the young ladies and their mother—for Mr. Dashwood's second wife survives him—are badly off. He has called his son to his death-bed and has solemnly adjured him to provide for the second family. Much moved, the young man promises, and mentally decides to give each of his sisters a thousand pounds; and then the comedy begins. For he announces his generous intention to his wife, and Mrs. John Dashwood by no means approves of depriving their own little boy of so large a sum. The thousand pounds are accordingly reduced to five hundred. But even this seems rather much. Might not an annuity to the stepmother be less of a wrench? Yes—but though less of a wrench it might be more of a drain, for "she is very stout and healthy, and scarcely forty." An occasional present of fifty pounds will be better, "and will, I think, be amply discharging my promise to my father." Or, better still, an occasional present of fish. And in the end nothing is done, nothing; the four impecunious ladies are not even helped in the moving of their furniture.

Well, are the John Dashwoods hypocrites? It depends upon our definition of hypocrisy. The young man could not see his evil impulses as they gathered force and gained on him. And even his wife, though a worse character, is also self-deceived. She reflects that old Mr. Dashwood may have been out of his mind at his death. She thinks of her own little boy—and surely a mother ought to think of her own child. She has muddled herself so completely that in one sentence she can refuse the ladies the income that would enable them to keep a carriage and in the next can say that they will not be keeping a carriage and so will have no expenses. No doubt men and women in other lands can muddle themselves, too, yet the state of mind of Mr. and Mrs. John Dashwood seems to me typical of England. They are slow —they take time even to do wrong; whereas people in other lands do wrong quickly.

There are national faults as there are national diseases, and perhaps one can draw a parallel between them. It has always impressed me that the national diseases of England should be cancer and consumption—slow, insidious, pretending to be something else; while the diseases proper to the South should be cholera and plague, which strike at a man when he is perfectly well and may leave him a corpse by evening. Mr. and Mrs. John Dashwood are moral consumptives.

They collapse gradually without realizing what the disease is. There is nothing dramatic or violent about their sin. You cannot call them villains.

Here is the place to glance at some of the other charges that have been brought against the English as a nation. They have, for instance, been accused of treachery, cruelty, and fanaticism. In these charges I have never been able to see the least point, because treachery and cruelty are conscious sins. The man knows he is doing wrong, and does it deliberately, like Tartuffe or Iago. He betrays his friend because he wishes to. He tortures his prisoners because he enjoys seeing the blood flow. He worships the Devil because he prefers evil to good. From villainies such as these the average Englishman is free. His character, which prevents his rising to certain heights, also prevents him from sinking to these depths. Because he doesn't produce mystics he doesn't produce villains either; he gives the world no prophets, but no anarchists, no fanatics—religious or political.

Of course there are cruel and treacherous people in England—one has only to look at the police courts—and examples of public infamy can be found, such as the Amritsar massacre. But one does not look at the police courts or the military mind to find the soul of any nation; and the more English people one meets the more convinced one becomes that the charges as a whole are untrue. Yet foreign critics often make them. Why? Partly because they fix their eyes on the criminal classes, partly because they are annoyed with certain genuine defects in the English character, and in their irritation throw in cruelty in order to make the problem simpler. Moral indignation is always agreeable, but nearly always misplaced. It is indulged in both by the English and by the critics of the English. They all find it great fun. The drawback is that while they are amusing themselves the world becomes neither wiser nor better.

The main point of these notes is that the English character is incomplete. No national character is complete. We have to look for some qualities in one part of the world and others in another. But the English character is incomplete in a way that is particularly annoying to the foreign observer. It has a bad surface—self-complacent, unsympathetic, and reserved. There is plenty of emotion further down, but it never gets used. There is plenty of brain power, but it is more often used to confirm prejudices than to dispel them. With such an equipment the Englishman cannot be popular. Only I would repeat: there is little vice in him and no real coldness. It is the machinery that is wrong.

I hope and believe myself that in the next twenty years we shall see a great change, and that the national character will alter into something that is less unique but more lovable. The supremacy of the middle classes is probably ending. What new element the working classes will introduce one cannot say, but at all events they will not have been educated at public schools. And whether these notes praise or blame the English character—that is only incidental. They are the notes of a student who is trying to get at the truth and would value the assistance of others. I believe myself that the truth is great and that it shall prevail. I have no faith in official caution and reticence. The cats are all out of their bags, and diplomacy cannot recall them. The nations *must* understand one another, and quickly; and without the interposition of their governments, for the shrinkage of the globe is throwing them into one another's arms. To that understanding these notes are a feeble contribution—notes on the English character as it has struck a novelist.

*William Carlos Williams*

## OF MEDICINE AND POETRY

When they ask me, as of late they frequently do, how I have for so many years continued an equal interest in medicine and the poem, I reply that they amount for me to nearly the same thing. Any worth-his-salt physician knows that no one is "cured." We recover from some somatic, some bodily "fever" where as observers we have seen various engagements between our battalions of cells playing at this or that lethal maneuver with other natural elements. It has been interesting. Various sewers or feed-mains have given way here or there under pressure: various new patterns have been thrown up for us upon the screen of our knowledge. But a cure is absurd, as absurd as calling these deployments "diseases." Sometimes the home team wins, sometimes the visitors. Great excitement. It is noteworthy that the sulfonamids, penicillin, came in about simultaneously with Ted Williams, Ralph Kiner, and the rubber ball. We want home runs, antibiotics to "cure" man with a single shot in the buttocks.

But after you've knocked the ball into the center-field bleachers

OF MEDICINE AND POETRY: William Carlos Williams, *The Autobiography.* Copyright 1951 by William Carlos Williams. Reprinted by permission of New Directions Publishing Corporation.

and won the game, you still have to go home to supper. So what? The ball park lies empty-eyed until the next game, the next season, the next bomb. Peanuts.

Medicine, as an art, never had much attraction for me, though it fascinated me, especially the physiology of the nervous system. That's something. Surgery always seemed to me particularly unsatisfying. What is there to cut off or out that will "cure" us? And to stand there for a lifetime sawing away! You'd better be a chef, if not a butcher. There is a joy in it, I realize, to know that you've really cut the cancer out and that the guy will come in to score, but I never wanted to be a surgeon. Marvelous men—I take off my hat to them. I knew one once who whenever he'd get into a malignant growth would take a hunk of it and rub it into his armpit afterward. Never knew why. It never hurt him, and he lived to a great old age. He had imagination, curiosity, and a sense of humor, I suppose.

The cured man, I want to say, is no different from any other. It is a trivial business unless you add the zest, whatever that is, to the picture. That's how I came to find writing such a necessity, to relieve me from such a dilemma. I found by practice, by trial and error, that to treat a man as something to which surgery, drugs, and hoodoo applied was an indifferent matter; to treat him as material for a work of art made him somehow come alive to me.

What I wanted to do with him (or her, or it) fascinated me. And it didn't make any difference, apparently, that he was in himself distinguished or otherwise. It wasn't that I wanted to save him because he was a good and useful member of society. Death had no respect for him for that reason, neither does the artist, neither did I. As far as I can tell that kind of "use" doesn't enter into it; I am myself curious as to what I do find. The attraction is bizarre.

Thus I have said "the mind." And the mind? I can't say that I have ever been interested in a completely mindless person. But I have known one or two that are close to mindless, certainly useless, even fatal to their families, or what remains of their families, whom yet I find far more interesting than plenty of others whom I serve.

These are the matters which obsess me so that I cannot stop writing. I can recall many from the past, boys and girls, bad pupils, renegades, dirty-minded and -fisted, that I miss keenly. When some old woman tells me of her daughter now happily married to a handicapper at the Garden City track, that she has two fine sons, I want to sing and dance. I am happy. I am stimulated. She is still alive. Why should I feel that way? She almost caused me to flunk out of grammar school. I almost ruined my young days over her.

But I didn't. I love her, ignorant, fulsome bit of flesh that she was, and some other really vicious bits of childhood who ruined the record of the whole class—dead of their excesses, most of them. They flatter my memory. The thing, the thing, of which I am in chase. The thing I cannot quite name was there then. My writing, the necessity for a continued assertion, the need for me to go on will not let me stop. To this day I am in pursuit of it, actually—not there, in the academies, nor even in the pursuit of a remote and difficult knowledge or skill.

They had no knowledge and no skill at all. They flunked out, got jailed, got "Mamie" with child, and fell away, if they survived, from their perfections.

There again, a word: their perfections. They were perfect, they seem to have been born perfect, to need nothing else. They were there, living before me, and I lived beside them, associated with them. Their very presence denied the need of "study," that is study by degrees to elucidate them. They were, living, the theme that all my life I have labored to elucidate, and when I could not elucidate them I have tried to put them down, to lay them upon the paper to record them: for to do that is, after all, a sort of elucidation.

It isn't because they fascinated me by their evildoings that they were "bad" boys or girls. Not at all. It was because they were there full of a perfection of the longest leap, the most unmitigated daring, the longest chances.

This immediacy, the thing, as I went on writing, living as I could, thinking a secret life I wanted to tell openly—if only I could—how it lives, secretly about us as much now as ever. It is the history, the anatomy of this, not subject to surgery, plumbing, or cures, that I wanted to tell. I don't know why. Why tell that which no one wants to hear? But I saw that when I was successful in portraying something, by accident, of that secret world of perfection, that they did want to listen. Definitely. And my "medicine" was the thing which gained me entrance to these secret gardens of the self. It lay there, another world, in the self. I was permitted by my medical badge to follow the poor, defeated body into those gulfs and grottos. And the astonishing thing is that at such times and in such places—foul as they may be with the stinking ischio-rectal abscesses of our comings and goings—just there, the thing, in all its greatest beauty, may for a moment be freed to fly for a moment guiltily about the room. In illness, in the permission I as a physician have had to be present at deaths and births, at the tormented battles between daughter and diabolic mother, shattered by a gone brain—just there—for a split second—from one side or the other, it has fluttered before me for a moment, a phrase which I quickly write down on anything at hand, any piece of paper I can grab.

It is an identifiable thing, and its characteristic, its chief character is that it is sure, all of a piece and, as I have said, instant and perfect: it comes, it is there, and it vanishes. But I have seen it, clearly. I have seen it. I know it because there it is. I have been possessed by it just as I was in the fifth grade—when she leaned over the back of the seat before me and greeted me with some obscene remarks—which I cannot repeat even if made by a child forty years ago, because no one would or could understand what I am saying that then, there, it had appeared.

The great world never much interested me (except at the back of my head) since its effects, from what I observed, were so disastrously trivial—other than in their bulk; smelled the same as most public places. As Bob McAlmon said after the well-dressed Spanish woman passed us in Juarez (I had said, Wow! there's perfume for you!):

"You mean that?" he said. "That's not perfume, I just call that whores."

## Louis Kronenberger

# A TASTE OF MONEY

Little in our time has been oftener quoted than Shaw's retort on Mr. Samuel Goldwyn when, in the course of their negotiations, the businessman stressed art and the artist, money. As a rebuke to the cant men use to disguise their venality, it was altogether fitting; but perhaps its deeper interest lay in Shaw's being as distinctly truthful as Mr. Goldwyn might seem disingenuous. I am also not sure that Shaw didn't know more about money than Mr. Goldwyn; or that he didn't care more. In any case, Shaw's steady insistence, as a great and very famous writer, on his due—his refusal to bate a sixpence from his royalties, or cut a line out of his plays—set a monumental ex-

A TASTE OF MONEY: Copyright © 1964 by Louis Kronenberger. Reprinted from *The Cart and the Horse*, by Louis Kronenberger by permission of Alfred A. Knopf, Inc.

ample which has doubtless fortified many writers since. Nor is it odd that it was Shaw who did it, for it was largely what was odd in Shaw that made him. He wanted money for no usual reasons. During his most affluent years, he had a rich wife and no children; did not drink, smoke, gamble, eat meat, have sex or live grandly. He wanted money for prideful or ironic reasons. Certainly it could help heal the hurts inflicted by his shabby-genteel background and his early London struggles. As a puritan again, Shaw—rather like the Quakers—found in money-making his prime worldly satisfaction. As a writer, it somehow gratified him to be a better businessman than the businessman. As a Socialist, it might amuse him to be a shrewder capitalist than the capitalist.

In any case, he remained our century's great example of a distinguished writer who made a large fortune—and by being as intransigent about his principles as about his payments. And yet, if it rejoiced the puritan in Shaw, it just a little jolts the puritan in us. Shaw, on money, got to be a trifle too insistent: however condign the rebuke to Mr. Goldwyn, it too much reassured all Mr. Goldwyn's scribbling minions. The minions might not live like Shaw—without meat, or cigars, or the rest—and might not write like him, either; but it helped them to know that in one very important respect they and he had something in common.

Untempted by the world's fleshpots, Shaw was also unmoved by its glitter. This was rarer than it may seem. In spite of the valid identification of artists with Bohemia, the two real truths in bohemianism are the artist's loathing of bourgeois morality and his frequent lack of good sense about money. But he is bohemian, not ascetic; dislikes Suburbia far more than society; is anti-Wall Street, not anti-wealth. At times indeed he can acquire very luxurious tastes, and be attracted by resplendent and seignorial backgrounds. Snobbery has never been given the serious attention it deserves, if only because few people have viewed it as a serious subject. But in various forms it can go very deep, and it frequently does so with writers. It is too bad that the word *snob* applies today equally to some one over-impressed by his own social position, and to some one over-impressed by other people's; the old distinction of *snob* (the aspiring outsider) and *nob* (the man of position) had real value. More often than we may suspect, the writer is an aspiring outsider. We need only think of the spell that the great world has exerted in all ages on literary men, whether Congreve or Pope, Swift or Sterne, Goethe or Balzac, Henry James or Proust, Scott Fitzgerald or Evelyn Waugh; and again, we need only think why. Being the most imaginative and memory-haunted of men, the writer may, to begin with, be a romantic —in love with a kind of patrician ideal, with a vision of breeding and elegance. His imagination may even make an ass of him; we need only remember, I think in Proust, some one's rapture at being asked to a very grand party and his boredom after he goes to it. And on just those terms imagination, in any perceptive writer, holds open the door while irony enters the room. But the memory-haunted writer may, in a most downright sense, remember slights and snubs that frayed his early life. Or, very simply, the writer could not bear the truth— Meredith, that his father had been in trade; Dickens, that his father had been in prison. Besides, there is even more snobbery about possessing money than about lacking it. By itself money is thought vulgar; it must be chaperoned by something socially acceptable.

And if there is a romantic reason for writers to climb, and a realistic reason as well, there is also a professional one—the interest that many writers have in "manners" and the social scene. Much of this plainly calls for first-hand knowledge. Beyond that, writers can have a desire for money and position thrust upon them—from their being given a taste of luxury that creates an appetite for it.

All these matters vary greatly, of course; and to a large number of writers they do not apply at all. But often one element or another does apply; and even where there is no social aspiration, there can be a cultural or purely economic one. The great point about writers and money today is their unprecedented opportunities for making it. It is all too easy to exaggerate the status of writers *as a whole*—for most of them the economic struggle is still painfully acute, which must be borne in mind with everything that follows. All the same, relatively many writers, often serious and good writers, have the sort of incomes today that a bare generation ago were confined to a handful of great names, or to authors of best-sellers and popular stage hits. In today's age of diversified literary rights, of bookclubs and paperbacks and digests, of serials and syndicates, of dramatizations and movie sales, of permissions and high-paying journalism, of radio, of TV for one's writings and TV for oneself, of lecturing and recordings, of grants and fellowships, of visiting professorships and residencies—an age in which one book can have nine lives and one fee can have six figures— a great many writers, despite high costs and high taxes, can live in the same world, indeed on the same street, as the rich and the prominent.

With this change in situation has come a decided change in attitude. The serious writer needn't think himself a name for the few, or Grub Street an address for the future. Nor need he see, between money and high standards, any necessary clash. Opportunity may not yet have knocked at his door, but it is assumed to know where he lives. Moreover, the moment Opportunity has knocked, all sorts of helpful other people will be writing and phoning and coming to call. Whoever invented the alphabet was clearly writer-conscious, putting the agent *and* the accountant *and* the analyst, at the very beginning. But even with so large a staff—or thanks to it—the writer can prosper. In his progress upward, he will use no executive elevators, and wherever he goes must still be Upper Bohemia. Upper Bohemia may picket Park Avenue; but it must often—by living on both sides of it— have to cross its own picket lines. And its children's schools, as it progresses, become less progressive; its views, as it advances, grow less advanced.

The point of all this is a quite concrete one: that there exist whole clusters of people in the arts who live *expensively*—at times through inherited wealth or moneyed marriages, but oftenest from what they earn. If we look for direct forebears on a *group* basis, we perhaps most readily find them in the Algonquin group of the 1920s. Here were people with citified interests and sophisticated tastes who, by way of Broadway and Hollywood, or of the light-touch writing that came to be centered in *The New Yorker,* made and spent a good deal of money. Witty and worldly, they were moderately concerned with culture and madly competitive about games; if they were light-weights, they effected—*The New Yorker* is the best proof—a kind of lightweight revolution. The most entertaining group of their time, and the deftest at group-promotion, they became in varying degrees the friends, the pets, the court jesters of the unstuffy rich, who wanted to be entertained. Even before the Algonquin set, of course, many individual writers had both the means and the desire to live hand-somely: yet even much later, scarcely any other literary circle had an aura of expensive living about it. It is noteworthy how many good writers went to places like Yaddo and the Macdowell Colony; or had guest cottages on rich men's estates; or, if flush, rented a place for the summer; or commonly—which fitted their tastes and their purses alike—contrived to live abroad.

Certainly, during this period, writers had their windfalls and fat years, and accordingly their sprees and splurges. But, even where their bank balances could support stylish living, their anti-bourgeois convictions often protested it. They did not, as so often today, live like rich people, or keep up their end with the rich people they went with. But the salient point is not that till recently writers seldom lived like rich men: it's that they didn't live like businessmen. They had agents to handle their work, and might seek out a "tax man" each year, from sheer ignorance of the tax laws. But few even very successful writers had agents in the sense they do today; indeed, they couldn't have had them in the sense they do today—as operating a vast, complex switchboard plugging in on all the sources of revenue I have already enumerated. And few writers a generation ago could have needed accountants and lawyers in the sense they do today. Today, just how they receive payment, and just when, bulks as large as how much payment they receive. Today, there is a labyrinth of technicalities to thread, of deductions to master; and perhaps such writers' biggest problems today involve real estate and the stock market, trust funds and self-incorporations. Many writers today are businessmen, not in the sense that they personally look after their own finances, but in the sense that they don't—that they employ experts. And the successful writer's day means, exactly like the businessman's, sessions with a secretary, all sorts of business letters and phone calls, an appointment at 10, a conference at 12, a business lunch at one, and very likely a cocktail or dinner date with a business side to it. If all these things on any one day are very unlikely, a day without several of them is even more so.

Thus far I am writing of those at the top. But, numerically, there are a good many writers at the top: if not many in proportion to the whole, far more than there have ever been before, and far faster in soaring upward. But—to move decidedly down—even in a world of notoriously inadequate incomes, the academic world, one finds many and diverse new sources of income. I don't mean salaries, which have generally risen at about the rate of living costs. It is rather how many teachers and professors are now editing textbooks and paperbacks; are now published in well-paying magazines, and appearing on radio and TV; are now lecturing extensively, and winning fellowships and grants. Nor does this apply only to big academic names, or to teachers with outside reputations. The door, now, opens and widens for quite young men, men who are creating a new breed of professor—men who lace their scholarship with sass, who can be at once academic and avant-garde, who go on cultural sight-seeing, and even slumming, tours. One particular field for them is the theatre; in the colleges themselves, "the theatre of the absurd," for example, has won many season bookings. Actually humor, satire, irony, wit appear more and more on the academic menu. Urbanity is not often on it, being still too big a problem for the chef; but the sense of change is noticeable, the degree of change enlivening.

The writer's new status—or, at any rate, new scope—constitutes a genuine gain. Many financial opportunities have opened for the better type of writer, often toward desirable ends. A serious article needs to be written on the pros and cons, the pluses and minuses, of superior writers who currently address large popular audiences in magazines, on TV, on the lecture platform. Certainly the mass audience is getting far better than its normal fare; and if not many in the audience are converted or even much stirred, that only stresses the glacier-like slowness of solving the problem. In any case, enough good writers today have such audiences as to constitute a kind of working minority. They are not going to win any one over from Yerby's level to Yeats's; indeed, their real value may lie less in making cultural recruits than in halting cultural deserters. A great American misfortune is the disintegration of the college graduate in the twenty years after he graduates—his loss of interest in what he had become acquainted with, his lack of interest in anything since. It is just such back-sliding readers (who have defaulted to the "wrong" magazines) that, by way of the finer voices in them, might be reclaimed.

In contributing to mass media, the writer himself may often have to simplify, but he need not falsify, and need sometimes not change a comma. To be sure, there may be a more than merely ironic disadvantage involved. The good writer's fringe benefits may be turning into his real financial stake, so that the poet makes money largely off permissions; the playwright counts most on that worst kind of audience, the "benefit" audience; the novelist most prospers on a hack stage version or film version of his novel. And if the tail, beyond wagging the dog, is making rather a lap-dog of it to boot, that in itself is no threat to the writer's *creative* career; it can possibly be the one way to ensure it. And certain fringe benefits are, for author and culture alike, true benefits—the serious paperback readers, the university lectures, the poetry readings and recordings at a high level.

The writer's changing financial status necessarily means a change in his psychology. One of the great cultural phenomena of our time is what the sociologist will eventually find a jargon phrase for, but what quite simply can be called the luxury hand-out. I mean all the forms of expense-account high living that many people earlier enjoyed only vicariously, via magazines and movies. Today even quite unimportant writers frequently share in them, and at a high level. The entertainment of fairly unimportant businessmen, however expensive, has seldom much style to it: it runs to the flashier "name" restaurants; to hit musicals, prize fights, World Series games, bars and night clubs. But, for the not very notable writer—who may well be a professor—magazine and publishing-house hospitality often means elegant restaurants, distinguished clubs, dinner with far better known people, besides literary lunch and cocktail parties. The same writer's lecturing involves luxury hotels and rich men's homes. All this becomes part of his professional life, and thus a conditioning factor of his own life. Moreover, along with the luxury hand-out, there now goes what might be called the swapped milieu. As the less stodgy bourgeois and professional world cultivates an artist-world informality, the artist tends toward more stylish and traditional living. The two groups share a penchant for a sort of *couleur-de-rose* peasant culture; the unstuffy rich eschew butlers and dinner jackets for buffet suppers and itinerant bartenders; the artist world fancies good wines and *cordon bleu* cooking, the very same bartenders and on occasion a caterer.

The fact that the two styles of living have grown largely interchangeable indicates something new for the writer, whether in terms of income or of inclination. Upper Bohemia, in one form or another, is an old tradition—but mostly with cultivated non-artists, with well-to-do people of "background" who want to keep what seems right with their world and slough off what seems oppressive. They want Bohemia's casualness without its messiness, they want traditionalism's well-bred comfort without its gentility. Something like this has also characterized *writers* of "background": one thinks of Bloomsbury or Gramercy Park. Their Upper Bohemias often acquire an academic air, or a snobbish and eventually stuffy one. Moreover, writers in such milieus can get to be rather dangerously lionized, or, even more dangerously, tamed. In general America's writers have lived a more careless life than this, whether from a lack of means, or of roots, or of desire. Certain writers might retain from their early life certain touchstones; but at least till well on in years they wanted something freer and unritualized. Or, if the Left Banks and the Provincetowns and the Majorcas were ritualized in their way, it was an anti-bourgeois way.

What the old bohemianism signified was not just a frequent lack of money but a fundamental unconcern for it. Some of its insouciance toward money may have been rationalization; or a prevailing radicalism; or a self-dramatizing romanticism. And certainly want of money could cause serious dislocations, could ruin lives and overturn careers. But there was yet a pretty deep-seated feeling that the terms of economic success, even the terms of bourgeois security, came too high. It was one thing for the Goldwyns to try to fatten their bank accounts by talking up "art"; that was an old, old dodge. But the artist himself —and beyond any romanticizing—had a recognition of his special role. He might at times be making a virtue of necessity, he might elevate into martyrdom the personal mess he had made of things. But the sense of vocation was not just highflown or self-congratulatory; there went with it an awareness of what it entailed—of the people it differed with, the conventions it quarreled with, the sanctities it defied.

To be sure, plenty of serious and gifted artists wanted to make money, wanted to make a lot of it; and a number of them did. Some, like Trollope, were entirely businesslike in their writing habits. Yet the fundamental attitude was different if only because the existing circumstances were. Opportunities were fewer; no book had nine lives. Moreover, bohemian living was not just a protest against bourgeois standards, it was a way of adjusting to economic ups and downs. Writers' lives were often makeshift and nomadic less from having no roots in a community than from having no stake in it. Owning a house meant sweating over a mortgage; possessions had, for a second home, the pawnshop; and banks were for borrowing money, not saving it.

Writing is the legatee, today, of what, whether or not it has reformed our culture, has in some sense revolutionized it. In spite (or because) of all the class-vs.-mass distinctions, and all the battles of the brows, a much widened market exists for capable writers.[1] Such writers can be had simultaneously, at every brow level—can be read in the same month in *Partisan Review, The New Yorker,* and *Look;* can be bought on the same day in a scholarly edition, a paperback abridgement, and a popular Digest; can be heard in the same week at Harvard, at The New School and on David Susskind. "Pop" culture, indeed, is acquiring much of the character of the old pop concerts. Just as, along with Strauss and Suppé, the concerts offered the more accessible works of Mozart and Beethoven, so today radio and TV provide great audiences with morsels, and sometimes tenderized meat, from the classics—and from today's avant-garde and "controversial" highbrows. Beyond that, on radio and TV there are all sorts of education and classroom programs; of talks by writers and critics; of poets' readings;[2] and of plays and music. What percentage of the total audience tune in on such things I don't know; but however small, it is huge compared with any pre-radio or TV audience. What percentage of the programs themselves would pass a cultural Pure-Food-and-Drug Act, I don't know either; but that they very much benefit living artists financially seems certain.

[1] Leonard Schechter, in the *New York Post,* described the symposium atmosphere of the first Patterson-Liston fight, with Budd Schulberg, Ben Hecht, A. J. Liebling, Gerald Kersh, Norman Mailer, and James Baldwin all covering it.
[2] Many poets today, I imagine, make more money from their readings than from their writings.

In that very certainty, there is for the have-not writers as well as the haves, for the beginner as well as the veteran, the sense that, with no taint of corruption, the pot of gold lies very close to hand. And already, in certain domains of art, the rewards are blazingly visible. A dozen years after Madison Avenue became a synonym for the big money in advertising and TV, it could as easily, through its art galleries, have become one for the big money in modern painting. In fact it is in painting and the theatre that the arts have most conspicuously become a business—and the artist a businessman in how he functions, a rich man in how he lives. On a very large small scale, there exists today an Upper Bohemia that in its standard of living is wholly top bracket. Its people have the same town and country places as the leisure class; the same kind of servants, of clothes and food and cars; the same architects and interior decorators, the same accommodations in the same ships and hotels. Nor can they be distinguished from Park Avenue on any basis of "bohemian" morality. Drinking, drug-taking, and every form of sexual freedom are as decided stigmata today of the rich man's world as of the artist's. No artist can any longer claim to be a bohemian or a rebel—or an artist—merely by invoking Priapus or Dionysius.

The theatre decidedly provides what is most comic and corrupting in the way of "creative" success. Part of what is both is inherent, from the theatre's own knack for being flashy and its need of being publicized. But part of it derives from Broadway's get-rich-quickness. The classic symbol of this, a generation ago, was Moss Hart, literally stepping out of his clothes to turn his bare back on his past and embark on a "gold-garter" period that, thirty years later, was simply a vast penthouse one. And the symbol has become something of a pattern. There are, for example, theatre people virtually never seen after dark out of evening clothes. One such, a man who first achieved notice celebrating a humbler side of the garment industry, once hailed me at an opening with "How d'you suppose I just *knew* I shouldn't dress tonight?" When, rather staggered, I said solemnly: "After all, it's a Monday night—and raining at that," "No, no, no," he answered. "We just *knew*—the X's aren't dressed either, and I assure you we didn't consult one another!"

What is peculiarly comic is that the splashiness, and the taking it seriously, seem most marked in Broadway comedy writers. Doubtless they have their own way of joking about it all, of being sure to get it said first. All the same, it is not for them a joke. More interestingly, not one of these elegantly fashionable comedy writers has written, with the faintest show of true elegance, a single drawing-room comedy.

Yet all this is but the anecdotal side of a great moneyed activity. The sovereignty of money is partly imposed on the playwright by the cost of the investment; is further imposed by the amount of box-office needed to keep the show alive; is finally imposed by the tactics, the pressures, the crises attending it all. There ensue all the legitimate differences of opinion and conflicts of interest, all the creative jitters and collaborating wrangling. And then, and far worse, the producer's itching palm may urge compromise; and then his whip hand decree it. The playwright, by now, has paid out so much in time and energy, in sleeplessness and exasperation, in controlling his temper and losing it, that creative satisfaction has vanished and the only reward is hard cash. The money, indeed, seems less a form of earnings than of damages.

In a quite different sense, the art world today seems too commercial and insidiously corrupting. To be sure, the art world has long contaminated people who worked in it in the precise sense that it refined them: it has provided a luxury life on rather a lackey basis. The luxury handout that is relatively new to the writers' world stretches back for centuries in the artists'. In every age the fashionable painter has been patronized and made a pet of by the rich, to inhabit a world of feasting and flattery. What, of course, makes the art world unique is the personal ownership of the artist's work. Composers, novelists, playwrights, poets offer their work to the public. But pictures and sculpture belong to individuals and institutions. And those who *sell* pictures and sculpture are often akin to those who sell tiaras and Rolls-Royces; and the art world, for all its cultivation, can have a voice quite as "full of money" as Scott Fitzgerald's Daisy Buchanan. It is a world that must not just allow for rich men's whims but that, like any courtier, must pander to them; and unobtrusively, like any guide or governess, correct their taste; and, like any interior decorator, minister to their pride of ownership and display.

The elegance of the art world's surroundings has tended to veil the frequent crassness of its motives. But the art world today is becoming more and more like the theatre world; today, too, there is less, almost, of the studio about it than of the stock exchange. And along with their Hollywood bidding and pricing, picture sales display a Hollywood garishness. Not only have the big auctions become plushier occasions than the grandest first nights; the sums involved make better "theatre." There is one sure way now in America to make what is artistic popular—the way of high finance. Thus dollars do make highbrows of us all: the sale-value of Gainsborough or Cézanne not only achieves headline prominence, it gains philistine respect. What decidedly helped give culture this new status was the $64,000 Question and all its TV siblings. The public saw culture and knowledge acquiring a big market value; and even after the quizzes were exposed as frauds, the taste they had fostered remained. The public is fascinated when millionaires—or museums—fight over pictures. Surely the museums must know that the gaudy prices they pay will set an unhealthful example. The doubtful wisdom of the Metropolitan paying over $2,000,000 for Rembrandt's *Aristotle Contemplating the Bust of Homer* seemed borne out by the crowds who flocked to see it. I watched them, and their "Ahs" were chiefly for the price and not the picture: they stood in vulgar awe as before a jeweler's window ablaze with huge diamonds. It was itself a spectacle of sorts, contemplating the public contemplating Aristotle contemplating Homer.

Without going into the artistic merits of Abstract Expressionism, surely the prices it has so quickly come to fetch make clear that involved are not just art lovers of Pollock and De Kooning as they might be of Ruysdael and De Hooch, but stockholders in Pollock and De Kooning as they might be of Pan Am and United Carbide. "Works of art" have great commodity value, are top status symbols. As a result, every one in the Big-Board art world is associated with the rich. And this touches those on the buying side as well as on the selling. Curators, like college presidents, are kept busy raising money and angling for bequests; and are to be found, oftener than college presidents, feeding at rich men's tables and imbibing the fumes of wealth.

I haven't traveled this road of art-and-finance hell-bent on achieving a destination. In itself the road runs through picturesque country, offering much that is new and revealing along the way. But the sense grows on one that it has become a heavily traveled road, and one that does reach a destination. Sensibly starting off, away from the genteel slums and messy bohemias of writers in the past, it yet winds up in exclusive residential subdivisions and a sort of conspicuous wasteland. The writer's position in all this may not be crucial; but his attitude *toward* his position, it would seem to me, is. Time out of mind, he has been fed high-sounding humbug, has heard that his slender means were not only a blessing, but a source of inspiration to boot. He has heard that what loftily set him apart from other men was his *not* striving for material success. Meanwhile, he whose great mission was to tell the truth had often, for a roof over his head, to curry favor. Well, all that has been exploded. My only wonder is whether, with the routing of the old familiar cant, a sort of reverse cant hasn't come to exist—a writer's cant, this time, in which he becomes his own victim. I have the sense that too often today *any* reservations about the artist's relation to money, any setting of limits to his concern for it, are thought arty, or outmoded, or just a new way to bilk him. I have a sense that it is today considered as much the artist's duty to regard himself as a businessman as it was formerly a businessman's dodge to segregate him as an artist.

This may be too glib an antithesis. But what strikes me as literal truth is that writers, as a whole, have been considerably more altered, and influenced, and infected by the life around them than they have themselves altered or influenced that life. And by writers I mean those with standards and values, those who would ruffle the shortcomings of society, not stroke them; who would protest, not comply. It strikes me that, though such writers don't feed pap to the public, they have begun to swallow the public's pap themselves, and that even as they attack America's materialism, in their own way they are succumbing to it. At any rate, it seems pertinent to determine how much of what they have become is mere surface accommodation to the life around them; how much is understandable adjustment to new forces and pressures; and how much, finally, seems a matter of choice and a subject for anxiety.

Certainly much today in the writer's way of life reflects the helpful side of a highly mechanized society. Whatever his other problems, surely it grows harder—on even a modest income—to suffer all the discomforts of home. Dishwashers prevail; diaper services abound; so do laundromats, and community nursery schools, and sitters, and time-saving appliances, and small summer cottages to be had by the month. All these are distinct benefits, and seldom at odds with a writer's chosen way of life. However varied their backgrounds, most writers, having gone to college, have acquired a similarity of surface behavior. Moreover, many writers today lecture and teach. Life, for most of them, grows what once might have been thought crushingly respectable. The party-going is more decorous; the domestic arrangements are more domestic. Writers' marriages may keep breaking up; but writers remarry today rather than live in sin, and their homes contain somebody's children. The children often go to rather orthodox schools. It all constitutes a much modified bohemia, less the result, I think, of changed ideas than of changing incomes.

Much of this is a matter of surfaces. But if writers conform more, in the sense that they placard their roles less, that is because their roles today gain general respect, and because their economic positions and professional prestige as often soothe their vanity as assault it. Where fundamentals are concerned, most writers worth their salt still live and think on their own terms. Writers haven't had their mouths stopped; and society, perhaps more than ever, is having its nose punched. What seems to me a danger has less to do with middle-classness than with materialism. Still untouched by the old shibboleths, writers are not nearly so immune to the new status symbols. Indeed, the danger may well lie in the actual by-passing of the kind of middle-class standard of living toward which all professional people move—by-passing it for the high-income scale of living which many writers already maintain.

They may still be relatively few, but they bulk large enough to provide an incentive. Moreover, they don't live expensively, in the gambler-style way that artists once did from hitting the jackpot; they do so with every assumption of permanence. Hence certain new factors have entered in. To begin with, when one lives expensively one starts going with others who do, and something embarrassed or self-conscious arises toward writers less affluent. As for the others who live expensively, they can be of many kinds—blueblooded country neighbors, or lion-hunters in town, or executives met on luxury liners. Mixing with them can be both instructive and enjoyable, but it can also foster dangerous identifications. The real danger is that the writer nowadays *can* often truly identify; and can, as seldom in the past, keep financially in step. Nowadays too, as seldom in the past, he may not be much out of step politically. There are few "dangerous radicals" in today's world of letters, while in its social world there are more and more liberals of a sort. A writer's morality may continue sound; but, rather than combat the world, it must often have to skirmish with his own way of life.

An ironical factor in his new approach to living is quite literally the business of the wife and kiddies. It need not even mean a very conservative or conventional wife; she may just be feminine and elegant. At any rate, it is usually she who enforces a more affluent standard once it is reached. Seldom is any of this blue-printed: it just works out that way. But to live so high the respectable writer must often work too hard—the more so, from refusing to prostitute himself. Or, simply from being frequently approached, he will take on too many assignments. And half-smudged creative work born of being too much in demand can prove as harmful as hackwork born of being too little. And what is dangerous, is that each material temptation involves no artistic misconduct, no conscious backsliding. But, after ten years, just where will it leave him?

Not too badly off, perhaps. At the end of ten years, he will still not be stuffy, or Babbitty, or reactionary. He will still eat and drink, and get up and go to bed, exactly as he pleases. He will hate bores, and not be one. He will be unintimidated by fashions in architecture or art or letters; make his own discoveries, reach his own conclusions; speak up for what he believes in and vote for the better man. The trouble is that all these virtues which still apply to him will apply equally to thousands of enlightened, self-governing businessmen.

*Robert Warshow*

# THE WESTERNER

The two most successful creations of American movies are the gangster and the Westerner: men with guns. Guns as physical objects, and the postures associated with their use, form the visual and emotional center of both types of films. I suppose this reflects the importance of guns in the fantasy life of Americans; but that is a less illuminating point than it appears to be.

The gangster movie, which no longer exists in its "classical" form, is a story of enterprise and success ending in precipitate failure. Success is conceived as an increasing power to work injury, it belongs to the city, and it is of course a form of evil (though the gangster's death, presented usually as "punishment," is perceived simply as defeat). The peculiarity of the gangster is his unceasing, nervous activity. The exact nature of his enterprises may remain vague, but his commitment to enterprise is always clear, and all the more clear because he operates outside the field of utility. He is without culture, without manners, without leisure, or at any rate his leisure is likely to be spent in debauchery so compulsively aggressive as to seem only another aspect of his "work." But he is graceful, moving like a dancer among the crowded dangers of the city.

Like other tycoons, the gangster is crude in conceiving his ends but by no means inarticulate; on the contrary, he is usually expansive and noisy (the introspective gangster is a fairly recent development), and can state definitely what he wants: to take over the North Side, to own a hundred suits, to be Number One. But new "frontiers" will

THE WESTERNER: From *The Immediate Experience* by Robert Warshow. Copyright 1954 by Doubleday & Co., Inc. Reprinted by permission of Paul Warshow.

present themselves infinitely, and by a rigid convention it is understood that as soon as he wishes to rest on his gains, he is on the way to destruction.

The gangster is lonely and melancholy, and can give the impression of a profound worldly wisdom. He appeals most to adolescents with their impatience and their feeling of being outsiders, but more generally he appeals to that side of all of us which refuses to believe in the "normal" possibilities of happiness and achievement; the gangster is the "no" to that great American "yes" which is stamped so big over our official culture and yet has so little to do with the way we really feel about our lives. But the gangster's loneliness and melancholy are not "authentic"; like everything else that belongs to him, they are not honestly come by: he is lonely and melancholy not because life ultimately demands such feelings but because he has put himself in a position where everybody wants to kill him and eventually somebody will. He is wide open and defenseless, incomplete because unable to accept any limits or come to terms with his own nature, fearful, loveless. And the story of his career is a nightmare inversion of the values of ambition and opportunity. From the window of Scarface's bullet-proof apartment can be seen an electric sign proclaiming: "The World Is Yours," and, if I remember, this sign is the last thing we see after Scarface lies dead in the street. In the end it is the gangster's weakness as much as his power and freedom that appeals to us; the world is not ours, but it is not his either, and in his death he "pays" for our fantasies, releasing us momentarily both from the concept of success, which he denies by caricaturing it, and from the need to succeed, which he shows to be dangerous.

The Western hero, by contrast, is a figure of repose. He resembles the gangster in being lonely and to some degree melancholy. But his melancholy comes from the "simple" recognition that life is unavoidably serious, not from the disproportions of his own temperament. And his loneliness is organic, not imposed on him by his situation but belonging to him intimately and testifying to his completeness. The gangster must reject others violently or draw them violently to him. The Westerner is not thus compelled to seek love; he is prepared to accept it, perhaps, but he never asks of it more than it can give, and we see him constantly in situations where love is at best an irrelevance. If there is a woman he loves, she is usually unable to understand his motives; she is against killing and being killed, and he finds it impossible to explain to her that there is no point in being "against" these things: they belong to his world.

Very often this woman is from the East and her failure to understand represents a clash of cultures. In the American mind, refinement, virtue, civilization, Christianity itself, are seen as feminine, and therefore women are often portrayed as possessing some kind of deeper wisdom, while the men, for all their apparent self-assurance, are fundamentally childish. But the West, lacking the graces of civilization, is the place "where men are men"; in Western movies, men have the deeper wisdom and the women are children. Those women in the Western movies who share the hero's understanding of life are prostitutes (or, as they are usually presented, bar-room entertainers) —women, that is, who have come to understand in the most practical way how love can be an irrelevance, and therefore "fallen" women. The gangster, too, associates with prostitutes, but for him the important things about a prostitute are her passive availability and her costliness: she is part of his winnings. In Western movies, the important thing about a prostitute is her quasi-masculine independence: nobody owns her, nothing has to be explained to her, and she is not, like a virtuous woman, a "value" that demands to be protected. When the Westerner leaves the prostitute for a virtuous woman—for love— he is in fact forsaking a way of life, though the point of the choice is often obscured by having the prostitute killed by getting into the line of fire.

The Westerner is *par excellence* a man of leisure. Even when he wears the badge of a marshal or, more rarely, owns a ranch, he appears to be unemployed. We see him standing at a bar, or playing poker—a game which expresses perfectly his talent for remaining relaxed in the midst of tension—or perhaps camping out on the plains on some extraordinary errand. If he does own a ranch, it is in the background; we are not actually aware that he owns anything except his horse, his guns, and the one worn suit of clothing which is likely to remain unchanged all through the movie. It comes as a surprise to see him take money from his pocket or an extra shirt from his saddlebags. As a rule we do not even know where he sleeps at night and don't think of asking. Yet it never occurs to us that he is a poor man; there is no poverty in Western movies, and really no wealth either: those great cattle domains and shipments of gold which figure so largely in the plots are moral and not material quantities, not the objects of contention but only its occasion. Possessions too are irrelevant.

Employment of some kind—usually unproductive—is always open to the Westerner, but when he accepts it, it is not because he needs to make a living, much less from any idea of "getting ahead." Where could he want to "get ahead" to? By the time we see him, he is already "there": he can ride a horse faultlessly, keep his countenance in the face of death, and draw his gun a little faster and shoot it a little straighter than anyone he is likely to meet. These are sharply defined acquirements, giving to the figure of the Westerner an apparent moral clarity which corresponds to the clarity of his physical image against his bare landscape; initially, at any rate, the Western movie presents itself as being without mystery, its whole universe comprehended in what we see on the screen.

Much of this apparent simplicity arises directly from those "cinematic" elements which have long been understood to give the Western theme its special appropriateness for the movies: the wide expanses of land, the free movement of men on horses. As guns constitute the visible moral center of the Western movie, suggesting continually the possibility of violence, so land and horses represent the movie's material basis, its sphere of action. But the land and the horses have also a moral significance: the physical freedom they represent belongs to the moral "openness" of the West—corresponding to the fact that guns are carried where they can be seen. (And, as we shall see, the character of land and horses changes as the Western film becomes more complex.)

The gangster's world is less open, and his arts not so easily identifiable as the Westerner's. Perhaps he too can keep his countenance, but the mask he wears is really no mask: its purpose is precisely to make evident the fact that he desperately wants to "get ahead" and will stop at nothing. Where the Westerner imposes himself by the appearance of unshakable control, the gangster's pre-eminence lies in the suggestion that he may at any moment lose control; his strength is not in being able to shoot faster or straighter than others, but in being more willing to shoot. "Do it first," says Scarface expounding his mode of operation, "and keep on doing it!" With the Westerner, it is a crucial point of honor *not* to "do it first"; his gun remains in its holster until the moment of combat.

There is no suggestion, however, that he draws the gun reluctantly. The Westerner could not fulfill himself if the moment did not finally come when he can shoot his enemy down. But because that moment is so thoroughly the expression of his being, it must be kept pure. He will not violate the accepted forms of combat though by doing so he could save a city. And he can wait. "When you call me that—smile!" the villain smiles weakly, soon he is laughing with horrible joviality, and the crisis is past. But it is allowed to pass because it must come again: sooner or later Trampas will "make his play," and the Virginian will be ready for him.

What does the Westerner fight for? We know he is on the side of justice and order, and of course it can be said he fights for these things. But such broad aims never correspond exactly to his real motives; they only offer him his opportunity. The Westerner himself, when an explanation is asked of him (usually by a woman), is likely to say that he does what he "has to do." If justice and order did not continually demand his protection, he would be without a calling. Indeed, we come upon him often in just that situation, as the reign of law settles over the West and he is forced to see that his day is over; those are the pictures which end with his death or with his departure for some more remote frontier. What he defends, at bottom, is the purity of his own image—in fact his honor. That is what makes him invulnerable. When the gangster is killed, his whole life is shown to have been a mistake, but the image the Westerner seeks to maintain can be presented as clearly in defeat as in victory: he fights not for advantage and not for the right, but to state what he is, and he must live in a world which permits that statement. The Westerner is the last gentleman, and the movies which over and over again tell his story are probably the last art form in which the concept of honor retains its strength.

Of course I do not mean to say that ideas of virtue and justice and courage have gone out of culture. Honor is more than these things: it is a style, concerned with harmonious appearances as much as with desirable consequences, and tending therefore toward the denial of life in favor of art. "Who hath it? he that died o' Wednesday." On the whole a world that leans to Falstaff's view is a more civilized and even, finally, a more graceful world. It is just the march of civilization that forces the Westerner to move on; and if we actually had to confront the question it might turn out that the woman who refuses to understand him is right as often as she is wrong. But we do not confront the question. Where the Westerner lives it is always about 1870—not the real 1870, either, or the real West—and he is killed or goes away when his position becomes problematical. The fact that he continues to hold our attention is evidence enough that, in his proper frame, he presents an image of personal nobility that is still real for us.

Clearly, this image easily becomes ridiculous: we need only look at William S. Hart or Tom Mix, who in the wooden absoluteness of their virtue represented little that an adult could take seriously; and doubtless such figures as Gene Autry or Roy Rogers are no better, though I confess I have seen none of their movies. Some film enthusiasts claim to find in the early, unsophisticated Westerns a "cinematic purity" that has since been lost; this idea is as valid, and finally as misleading, as T. S. Eliot's statement that *Everyman* is the only play in English that stays within the limitations of art. The truth is that the Westerner comes into the field of serious art only when his moral code, without ceasing to be compelling, is seen also to be imperfect. The Westerner at his best exhibits a moral ambiguity which darkens his image and saves him from absurdity; this ambiguity arises from the fact that, whatever his justifications, he is a killer of men.

In *The Virginian,* which is an archetypal Western movie as *Scarface* or *Little Caesar* are archetypal gangster movies, there is a lynching in which the hero (Gary Cooper), as leader of a posse, must supervise the hanging of his best friend for stealing cattle. With the growth of American "social consciousness," it is no longer possible to present a lynching in the movies unless the point is the illegality and injustice of the lynching itself; *The Ox-Bow Incident,* made in 1943, explicitly puts forward the newer point of view and can be regarded as a kind of "anti-Western." But in 1929, when *The Virginian* was made, the present inhibition about lynching was not yet in force; the justice, and therefore the necessity, of the hanging is never questioned —except by the schoolteacher from the East, whose refusal to understand serves as usual to set forth more sharply the deeper seriousness of the West. The Virginian is thus in a tragic dilemma where one moral absolute conflicts with another and the choice of either must leave a moral stain. If he had chosen to save his friend, he would have violated the image of himself that he had made essential to his existence, and the movie would have had to end with his death, for only by his death could the image have been restored. Having chosen instead to sacrifice his friend to the higher demands of the "code"— the only choice worthy of him, as even the friend understands—he is none the less stained by the killing, but what is needed now to set accounts straight is not his death but the death of the villain Trampas, the leader of the cattle thieves, who had escaped the posse and abandoned the Virginian's friend to his fate. Again the woman intervenes: Why must there be *more* killing? If the hero really loved her, he would leave town, refusing Trampas's challenge. What good will it be if Trampas should kill him? But the Virginian does once more what he "has to do," and in avenging his friend's death wipes out the stain on his own honor. Yet his victory cannot be complete: no death can be paid for and no stain truly wiped out; the movie is still a tragedy, for though the hero escapes with his life, he has been forced to confront the ultimate limits of his moral ideas.

This mature sense of limitation and unavoidable guilt is what gives the Westerner a "right" to his melancholy. It is true that the gangster's story is also a tragedy—in certain formal ways more clearly a tragedy than the Westerner's—but it is a romantic tragedy, based on a hero whose defeat springs with almost mechanical inevitability from the outrageous presumption of his demands: the gangster is *bound* to go on until he is killed. The Westerner is a more classical figure, self-contained and limited to begin with, seeking not to extend his dominion but only to assert his personal value, and his tragedy lies in the fact that even this circumscribed demand cannot be fully realized. Since the Westerner is not a murderer but (most of the time) a man of virtue, and since he is always prepared for defeat, he retains his inner invulnerability and his story need not end with his death (and usually does not); but what we finally respond to is not his victory but his defeat.

Up to a point, it is plain that the deeper seriousness of the good Western films comes from the introduction of a realism, both physical and psychological, that was missing with Tom Mix and William S. Hart. As lines of age have come into Gary Cooper's face since *The Virginian,* so the outlines of the Western movie in general have become less smooth, its background more drab. The sun still beats upon the town, but the camera is likely now to take advantage of this illumination to seek out more closely the shabbiness of buildings and furniture, the loose, worn hang of clothing, the wrinkles and dirt of the faces. Once it has been discovered that the true theme of the Western movie is not the freedom and expansiveness of frontier life, but its limitations, its material bareness, the pressures of obligation, then even the landscape itself ceases to be quite the arena of free movement it once was, but becomes instead a great empty waste, cutting down more often than it exaggerates the stature of the horseman who rides across it. We are more likely now to see the Westerner struggling against the obstacles of the physical world (as in the wonderful scenes on the desert and among the rocks in *The Last Posse*) than carelessly surmounting them. Even the horses, no longer the "friends" of man or the inspired chargers of knight-errantry, have lost much of the moral significance that once seemed to belong to them in their careering across the screen. It seems to me the horses grow tired and stumble more often than they did, and that we see them less frequently at the gallop.

In *The Gunfighter,* a remarkable film of a couple of years ago, the landscape has virtually disappeared. Most of the action takes place indoors, in a cheerless saloon where a tired "bad man" (Gregory Peck) contemplates the waste of his life, to be senselessly killed at the end by a vicious youngster setting off on the same futile path. The movie is done in cold, quiet tones of gray, and every object in it—faces, clothing, a table, the hero's heavy mustache—is given an air of uncompromising authenticity, suggesting those dim photographs of the nineteenth-century West in which Wyatt Earp, say, turns out to be a blank untidy figure posing awkwardly before some uninteresting building. This "authenticity," to be sure, is only aesthetic; the chief fact about nineteenth-century photographs, to my eyes at any rate, is how stonily they refuse to yield up the truth. But that limitation is just what is needed: by preserving some hint of the rigidity of archaic photography (only in tone and decor, never in composition), *The Gunfighter* can permit us to feel that we are looking at a more "real" West than the one the movies have accustomed us to—harder, duller, less "romantic"—and yet without forcing us outside the boundaries which give the Western movie its validity.

We come upon the hero of *The Gunfighter* at the end of a career in which he has never upheld justice and order, and has been at times, apparently, an actual criminal; in this case, it is clear that the hero has been wrong and the woman who has rejected his way of life has been right. He is thus without any of the larger justifications, and knows himself a ruined man. There can be no question of his "redeeming" himself in any socially constructive way. He is too much the victim of his own reputation to turn marshal as one of his old friends has done, and he is not offered the sentimental solution of a chance to give up his life for some good end; the whole point is that he exists outside the field of social value. Indeed, if we were once allowed to see him in the days of his "success," he might become a figure like the gangster, for his career has been aggressively "anti-social" and the practical problem he faces is the gangster's problem: there will always be somebody trying to kill him. Yet it is obviously absurd to speak of him as "anti-social," not only because we do not see him acting as a criminal, but more fundamentally because we do not see his milieu as a society. Of course it has its "social problems" and a kind of static history: civilization is always just at the point of driving out the old freedom; there are women and children to represent the possibility of a settled life; and there is the marshal, a bad man turned good, determined to keep at least his area of jurisdiction at peace. But these elements are not, in fact, a part of the film's "realism," even though they come out of the real history of the West; they belong to the conventions of the form, to that accepted framework which makes the film possible in the first place, and they exist not to provide a standard by which the gunfighter can be judged, but only to set him off. The true "civilization" of the Western movie is always embodied in an individual, good or bad is more a matter of personal bearing than of social consequences, and the conflict of good and bad is a duel between two men. Deeply troubled and obviously doomed, the gunfighter is the Western hero still, perhaps all the more because his value must express itself entirely in his own being—in his presence, the way he holds our eyes—and in contradiction to the facts. No matter what he has done, he *looks* right, and he remains invulnerable because, without acknowledging anyone else's right to judge him, he has judged his own failure and has already assimilated it, understanding—as no one else understands except the marshal and the bar-room girl—that he can do nothing but play out the drama of the gun fight again and again until the time comes when it will be he who gets killed. What "redeems" him is that he no longer believes in this drama and nevertheless will continue to play his role perfectly: the pattern is all.

The proper function of realism in the Western movie can only be to deepen the lines of that pattern. It is an art form for connoisseurs where the spectator derives his pleasure from the appreciation of minor variations within the working out of a pre-established order. One does not want too much novelty: it comes as a shock, for instance, when the hero is made to operate without a gun, as has been done in several pictures (e.g., *Destry Rides Again*), and our uneasiness is allayed only when he is finally compelled to put his "pacifism" aside. If the hero can be shown to be troubled, complex, fallible, even eccentric, or the villain given some psychological taint or, better, some evocative physical mannerism, to shade the colors of his villainy, that is all to the good. Indeed, that kind of variation is absolutely necessary to keep the type from becoming sterile; we do not want to see the same movie over and over again, only the same form. But when the impulse toward realism is extended into a "re-interpretation" of the West as a developed society, drawing our eyes away from the hero if only to the extent of showing him as the one dominant figure in a complex social order, then the pattern is broken and the West itself begins to be uninteresting. If the "social problems" of the frontier are to be the movie's chief concern, there is no longer any point in re-examining these problems twenty times a year; they have been solved, and the people for whom they once were real are dead. Moreover, the hero himself, still the film's central figure, now tends to become its one unassimilable element, since he is the most "unreal."

*The Ox-Bow Incident,* by denying the convention of the lynching, presents us with a modern "social drama" and evokes a corresponding response, but in doing so it almost makes the Western setting irrelevant, a mere backdrop of beautiful scenery. (It is significant that *The Ox-Bow Incident* has no hero; a hero would have to stop the lynching or be killed in trying to stop it, and then the "problem" of lynching would no longer be central.) Even in *The Gunfighter* the women and children are a little too much in evidence, threatening constantly to become a real focus of concern instead of simply part of the given framework; and the young tough who kills the hero has too much the air of juvenile criminality: the hero himself could never have been like that, and the idea of a cycle being repeated therefore loses its sharpness. But the most striking example of the confusion created by a too conscientious "social" realism is in the celebrated *High Noon*.

In *High Noon* we find Gary Cooper still the upholder of order that he was in *The Virginian*, but twenty-four years older, stooped, slower moving, awkward, his face lined, the flesh sagging, a less beautiful and weaker figure, but with the suggestion of greater depth that belongs almost automatically to age. Like the hero of *The Gunfighter*, he no longer has to assert his character and is no longer interested in the drama of combat; it is hard to imagine that he might once have been so youthful as to say, "When you call me that— smile!" In fact, when we come upon him he is hanging up his guns and his marshal's badge in order to begin a new, peaceful life with his bride, who is a Quaker. But then the news comes that a man he had sent to prison has been pardoned and will get to town on the noon train; three friends of this man have come to wait for him at the station, and when the freed convict arrives the four of them will come to kill the marshal. He is thus trapped; the bride will object, the hero himself will waver much more than he would have done twenty-four years ago, but in the end he will play out the drama because it is what he "has to do." All this belongs to the established form (there is even the "fallen woman" who understands the marshal's position as his wife does not). Leaving aside the crudity of building up suspense by means of the clock, the actual Western drama of *High Noon* is well handled and forms a good companion piece to *The Virginian*, showing in both conception and technique the ways in which the Western movie has naturally developed.

But there is a second drama along with the first. As the marshal sets out to find deputies to help him deal with the four gunmen, we are taken through the various social strata of the town, each group in turn refusing its assistance out of cowardice, malice, irresponsibility, or venality. With this we are in the field of "social drama"—of a very low order, incidentally, altogether unconvincing and displaying a vulgar anti-populism that has marred some other movies of Stanley Kramer's. But the falsity of the "social drama" is less important than the fact that it does not belong in the movie to begin with. The technical problem was to make it necessary for the marshal to face his enemies alone; to explain *why* the other townspeople are not at his side is to raise a question which does not exist in the proper frame of the Western movie, where the hero is "naturally" alone and it is only necessary to contrive the physical absence of those who might be his allies, if any contrivance is needed at all. In addition, though the hero of *High Noon* proves himself a better man than all around him the actual effect of this contrast is to lessen his stature; he becomes only a rejected man of virtue. In our final glimpse of him, as he rides away through the town where he has spent most of his life without really imposing himself on it, he is a pathetic rather than a tragic figure. And his departure has another meaning as well; the "social drama" has no place for him.

But there is also a different way of violating the Western form. This is to yield entirely to its static quality as legend and to the "cinematic" temptations of its landscape, the horses, the quiet men. John Ford's famous *Stagecoach* (1938) had much of this unhappy preoccupation with style, and the same director's *My Darling Clementine* (1946), a soft and beautiful movie about Wyatt Earp, goes further along the same path, offering indeed a superficial accuracy of historical reconstruction, but so loving in execution as to destroy the outlines of the Western legend, assimilating it to the more sentimental legend of rural America and making the hero a more dangerous Mr. Deeds. (*Powder River,* a recent "routine" Western shamelessly copied from *My Darling Clementine,* is in most ways a better film; lacking the benefit of a serious director, it is necessarily more concerned with drama than with style.)

The highest expression of this aestheticizing tendency is in George Stevens' *Shane,* where the legend of the West is virtually reduced to its essentials and then fixed in the dreamy clarity of a fairy tale. There never was so broad and bare and lovely a landscape as Stevens puts before us, or so unimaginably comfortless a "town" as the little group of buildings on the prairie to which the settlers must come for their supplies and to buy a drink. The mere physical progress of the film, following the style of *A Place in the Sun,* is so deliberately graceful that everything seems to be happening at the bottom of a clear lake. The hero (Alan Ladd) is hardly a man at all, but something like the Spirit of the West, beautiful in fringed buckskins. He emerges mysteriously from the plains, breathing sweetness and a melancholy which is no longer simply the Westerner's natural response to experience but has taken on spirituality; and when he has accomplished his mission, meeting and destroying in the black figure of Jack Palance a Spirit of Evil just as metaphysical as his own embodiment of virtue, he fades away again into the more distant West, a man whose "day is over," leaving behind the wondering little boy who might have imagined the whole story. The choice of Alan Ladd to play the leading role is alone an indication of this film's tendency. Actors like Gary Cooper or Gregory Peck are in themselves, as material objects, "realistic," seeming to bear in their bodies and their faces mortality, limitation, the knowledge of good and evil. Ladd is a more "aesthetic" object, with some of the "universality" of a piece of sculpture; his special quality is in his physical smoothness and serenity, unworldly and yet not innocent, but suggesting that no experience can really touch him. Stevens has tried to freeze the Western myth once and for all in the immobility of Alan Ladd's countenance. If *Shane* were "right," and fully successful, it might be possible to say there was no point in making any more Western movies; once the hero is apotheosized, variation and development are closed off.

*Shane* is not "right," but it is still true that the possibilities of fruitful variation in the Western movie are limited. The form can keep its freshness through endless repetitions only because of the special character of the film medium, where the physical difference between one object and another—above all, between one actor and another—is of such enormous importance, serving the function that is served by the variety of language in the perpetuation of literary types. In this sense, the "vocabulary" of films is much larger than that of literature and falls more readily into pleasing and significant arrangements. (That may explain why the middle levels of excellence are more easily reached in the movies than in literary forms, and perhaps also why the status of the movies as art is constantly being called into question.) But the advantage of this almost automatic particularity belongs to all films alike. Why does the Western movie especially have such a hold on our imagination?

Chiefly, I think, because it offers a serious orientation to the problem of violence such as can be found almost nowhere else in our culture. One of the well-known peculiarities of modern civilized opinion is its refusal to acknowledge the value of violence. This refusal is a virtue, but like many virtues it involves a certain willful blindness and it encourages hypocrisy. We train ourselves to be shocked or bored by cultural images of violence, and our very concept of heroism tends to be a passive one: we are less drawn to the brave young men who kill large numbers of our enemies than to the heroic prisoners who endure torture without capitulating. In art, though we may still be able to understand and participate in the values of the *Iliad,* a modern writer like Ernest Hemingway we find somewhat embarrassing; there is no doubt that he stirs us, but we cannot help recognizing also that he is a little childish. And in the criticism of popular culture, where the educated observer is usually under the illusion that he has nothing at stake, the presence of images of violence is often assumed to be in itself a sufficient ground for condemnation.

These attitudes, however, have not reduced the element of violence in our culture but, if anything, have helped to free it from moral control by letting it take on the aura of "emancipation." The celebration of acts of violence is left more and more to the irresponsible: on the higher cultural levels to writers like Céline, and lower down to Mickey Spillane or Horace McCoy, or to the comic books, television, and the movies. The gangster movie, with its numerous variations, belongs to this cultural "underground" which sets forth the attractions of violence in the face of all our higher social attitudes. It is a more "modern" genre than the Western, perhaps even more profound, because it confronts industrial society on its own ground— the city—and because, like much of our advanced art, it gains its effects by a gross insistence on its own narrow logic. But it is antisocial, resting on fantasies of irresponsible freedom. If we are brought finally to acquiesce in the denial of the fantasies, it is only because they have been shown to be dangerous, not because they have given way to a better vision of behavior.[1]

In war movies, to be sure, it is possible to present the uses of violence within a framework of responsibility. But there is the disadvantage that modern war is a co-operative enterprise; its violence is largely impersonal, and heroism belongs to the group more than to the individual. The hero of a war movie is most often simply a leader, and his superiority is likely to be expressed in a denial of the heroic: you are not supposed to be brave, you are supposed to get the job done and stay alive (this too, of course, is a kind of heroic

[1] I am not concerned here with the actual social consequences of gangster movies, though I suspect they could not have been so pernicious as they were thought to be. Some of the compromises introduced to avoid the supposed bad effects of the old gangster movies may be, if anything, more dangerous, for the sadistic violence that once belonged only to the gangster is now commonly enlisted on the side of the law and thus goes undefeated, allowing us (if we wish) to find in the movies a sort of "confirmation" of our fantasies.

posture, but a new—and "practical"—one). At its best, the war movie may represent a more civilized point of view than the Western, and if it were not continually marred by ideological sentimentality we might hope to find it developing into a higher form of drama. But it cannot supply the values we seek in the Western.

Those values are in the image of a single man who wears a gun on his thigh. The gun tells us that he lives in a world of violence, and even that he "believes in violence." But the drama is one of self-restraint: the moment of violence must come in its own time and according to its special laws, or else it is valueless. There is little cruelty in Western movies, and little sentimentality; our eyes are not focused on the sufferings of the defeated but on the deportment of the hero. Really, it is not violence at all which is the "point" of the Western movie, but a certain image of man, a style, which expresses itself most clearly in violence. Watch a child with his toy guns and you will see: what most interests him is not (as we so much fear) the fantasy of hurting others, but to work out how a man might look when he shoots or is shot. A hero is one who looks like a hero.

Whatever the limitations of such an idea in experience, it has always been valid in art, and has a special validity in an art where appearances are everything. The Western hero is necessarily an archaic figure; we do not really believe in him and would not have him step out of his rigidly conventionalized background. But his archaicism does not take away from his power; on the contrary, it adds to it by keeping him just a little beyond the reach of common sense and of absolutized emotion, the two usual impulses of our art. And he has, after all, his own kind of relevance. He is there to remind us of the possibility of style in an age which has put on itself the burden of pretending that style has no meaning, and, in the midst of our anxieties over the problem of violence, to suggest that even in killing or being killed we are not freed from the necessity of establishing satisfactory modes of behavior. Above all, the movies in which the Westerner plays out his role preserve for us the pleasure of a complete and self-contained drama—and one which still effortlessly crosses the boundaries which divide our culture—in a time when other, more consciously serious art forms are increasingly complex, uncertain, and ill-defined.

*Pauline Kael*

# NOTES ON HEART AND MIND

Is anyone surprised that the critics and journalists who only a few weeks ago were acclaiming the new creative freedom of young American moviemakers are now climbing aboard the new sentimentality? The press may use the term "romance" for this deliberately fabricated regression in recent movies, but in Hollywood the businessmen talk more crassly. They say, "We're going back to heart." The back-to-heart movement is accompanied by strong pressures on reviewers, who are informed that they have lost touch with the public. Reviewers are supposed to show *their* heart by puckering up for every big movie.

As part of the Pop impulse of the sixties, movies have been elevated to a central position among the arts—a dominant, almost overwhelming position. Those who grew up during this period have been so sold on Pop and so saturated with it that they appear to have lost their bearings in the arts. And so when they discover that, of course, Pop isn't enough, and they want some depth and meaning from movies, they head right for the slick synthetic. Those who have abandoned interest in literature except for the à-la-mode mixture of Pop and sticky, such as Vonnegut, Hesse, Tolkien, Brautigan, and a little I Ching, are likely to have comparably fashionable tastes in movies. To the children of "Blow-Up," movies that are literary in the worst way—movies that superficially resemble head books and art films—can seem profound and suggestive. Every few months, there is a new spate of secondhand lyrical tricks. Robert Redford is impaled, like a poor butterfly, in frozen frames at the end of picture after picture. Directors have become so fond of telescopic lenses that any actor crossing a street in a movie may linger in transit for a hazy eternity—the movie equivalent of a series of dots. The audience accepts this sort of thing in movies that not only are without the vitality of Pop but are enervated and tenuous—like the worst of what earlier generations of college students fled from when they went to the movies. If you don't have that sense of the range of possibilities and pleasures which is developed from reading, from an interest in drama and the other arts, or even from a longer span of movie-going,

NOTES ON HEART AND MIND: Reprinted by permission; © 1971 The New Yorker Magazine, Inc.

it's easy to overrate the fancy, novelettish alienation of a "Five Easy Pieces." But while it's perfectly understandable that those without much to compare such a movie to may think it's great—just as a child's judgment of a movie may be ingenuous and droll because he has so few previous experiences to relate it to—this inexperience provides the opening for the media-hype. There is probably more insensate praise in movie reviews now than in any other field, including writing on rock. The new tendency is to write appreciatively at the highest possible pitch, as if the reviewer had no scale of values but only a hearsay knowledge of the peaks. And everything he likes becomes a new peak.

If one opens a newspaper to the movie pages and reads the quotes, one is confronted with a choice of masterpieces, but I didn't write a column last week because the new movies defeated me—I couldn't think of anything worth saying about them. You come out of a movie like "There's a Girl in My Soup" or "I Love My Wife" feeling that your pocket has been picked and your mind has been stunted.

Movie critics have always had to become acrobats, jumping from level to level, trying not to attack the timid amateurs the way we attack the successful hacks. The danger in this act is that one may fall into the trap of condescension. This used to take the form of that horrible debonair style which was once the gentleman-critics' specialty. They were so superior to the subject that they never dealt with it. Now it more frequently takes the form of a wisecracking put-down. And that's the bottom of the trap, because, as all critics know, the worst danger of the profession is that one may sink to the level of what one is reviewing. What sustains a critic from falling to the level of an "I Love My Wife" and making shrivelling bad jokes about its shrivelling bad jokes? Last week, I couldn't find anything sustaining; rage isn't condescending, but one wears oneself down, and these films weren't worth it.

Though sinking to the level of the work is a danger to the critic, to movies the more serious danger, of course, is that critics may not *rise* to the level of what they're reviewing. And, even with movies as bad as they are now, I think this is often the case, because those who stoop to review become insensitive.

I don't trust critics who say they care only for the highest and the best; it's an inhuman position, and I don't believe them. I think it's simply their method of exalting themselves. It's not always easy to analyze what is going wrong in movies, what is going right—even if only in small ways—and why. One might think this an exercise in futility, but, ideally, the regular reviewer provides a touchstone for movie lovers—so that they have a basis for checking themselves out—and for all those actively involved in movies. The regular reviewer knows he will not effect a radical transformation of movies, but he may be able to help us keep our bearings. Movies, far more than the traditional arts, are tied to big money. Without a few independent critics, there's nothing between the public and the advertisers.

Movie executives often say critics should be the same age as the average moviegoer; sometimes they say reviewers shouldn't go on for more than three years or they won't have the same enthusiasm as the audience. The executives don't understand what criticism is; they want it to be an extension of their advertising departments. They want moviegoers to be uninformed and without memory, so they can be happy consumers.

In most cases, the conglomerates that make the movies partly own the magazines and radio stations and TV channels, or, if they don't own them, advertise in them or have some interlocking connection with them. That accounts for a lot of the praise that is showered on movies. Then, too, many critics, knowing that the young dig movies, are afraid of being left behind. Besides, the critics don't get quoted in the ads unless they rhapsodize over a picture (or are willing to accept being misquoted and distorted), and each time they get quoted, their bosses are happy and their names become better known. There are critics whose reviews hardly anybody ever sees but who are widely known for their ecstatic quotes. The radio and TV boys get the point: their reviews *are* quotes.

A reviewer delivering quickie reviews at the end of a radio or television news program typically reacts to a picture "strictly on its own merits"; that is, he tells the theme, he praises or pans the structure, he says a few words about the acting, the photography, etc. He reviews a movie in a cheerful vacuum, and he is generally perfectly sincere when he tells you that he says exactly what he thinks.

To be the movie critic for a network, no training or background is necessary; "too much" interest in movies may be a disqualification. Novices are thought to speak to the public on the public's own terms. They age, but, like the critic on your hometown paper, they remain novices in criticism, because there is no need for them to learn; they understand that their job is dependent on keeping everybody happy, and they are generally not the kind of people who learn anyway. They can say "what they think" with more sincerity if they're the kind of people who don't realize they can say what they think because they don't think.

It is often said that it doesn't matter how bad a reviewer is as long as he stays in the job, because people learn how to read him. It's true they may learn how to interpret his enthusiasms, but what about the young practitioners of an art form? Bad notices—or being ignored—are death to them. In this mass medium, in which big-budget productions are hugely advertised—they're like epidemics spreading over the media—a new artist or a young artist working on a small budget doesn't stand a chance unless he gets the help of the press. A writer or a painter can generally keep going even if he fails to reach an audience; even a dramatist may be able to keep going, though he is creatively crippled if his plays aren't staged. But if a movie director fails to reach an audience, he simply can't get the money to go on making pictures.

The industry and many established actors on talk shows love the idea that the public doesn't need the critics; the young filmmaker knows different. Most of the new pictures that try to break the molds risk confusing audiences, and just about all the pictures that express new social impulses or that are critical or rebellious are small-budget pictures. If a few critics don't go all the way for them, the public doesn't hear about them in time to keep the directors working and to keep the art of film alive. It cannot be kept alive by pictures like "The Odd Couple," "Cactus Flower," or "Airport"; those are the ones that don't require the help of the press (though they often get it). The audience finds its way to them with the help of the advertising.

The casual moviegoer is often drawn to new versions of what he used to enjoy—the TV watcher to "Airport," the aging art-house patron to the latest Chabrol. One can't quarrel with his enjoyment of them, only with his evaluation of them. A critic's point of view is likely to be somewhat different from the casual moviegoer's. The successful second-rate will probably anger him more than the fifth-rate, because it represents the triumph of aesthetic senility.

Since a critic may cost his publication advertising revenue—and no longer just from the loss of movie advertising but from records and whatever else the conglomerate is into—independent, disinterested criticism becomes rarer than ever just at the time when, because of the central importance of movies, it is needed most. The pressure is so strong on reviewers to do what is wanted of them that many of them give in and reserve their fire for pathetic little sex pictures—cheap porny pix—which they can safely attack because there's no big advertising money behind them. That way, the reviewer can keep his paper happy and at the same time get credit for high-mindedness in his community. Most of the people who give him credit never go to the movies anyway. Middle-aged people, particularly women, often use pornography as a self-congratulatory excuse for not reading and for not going to the movies. It becomes a righteous form of abstention for those who prefer "Hee Haw" or "The Beverly Hillbillies."

In some ways, last week's movies probably aren't worse than movies of a decade or two or three ago, but there is something dead and nerveless about them; they don't know how to connect with the audience, and they have lost the simplicity and the narrative strength that used to pull one through bad movies. TV has destroyed the narrative qualities of older movies, but the restlessness one feels while watching a chopped-up movie on TV is mitigated by the fact that one isn't necessarily paying much attention. In a movie theater, with nothing else to do, one is likely to become depressed. We've been told for some years now that visual excitement is what matters, but even the rare movie that is extraordinary to look at may be demoralizing. When it's obvious that the picture is going nowhere, there's an awful letdown of expectations, and for most people there seems to be nothing left but dumb submission; walking out may be too positive an act for the depressed state one falls into.

Yet even those who go enough to know how awful movies have been this year say, "But what else is there? Bad as they are, movies are better than the theater." However, the thing that has happened to the theater in the past decade is happening now to movies. On the average, Americans go to only seven movies a year. And as there were scarcely seven halfway good American movies for them to go to last year (and few from abroad), chances are they'll go to even fewer in 1971. "There's a Girl in My Soup" reminds you of why you stopped going to Broadway comedies. One never even knows what the principal characters are meant to be; it's not merely that this movie has no connection with any people who ever lived but that it doesn't sustain its own artifices. It's like going to see "Swan Lake" and finding that no one knew the dancers should be trained to get on their points.

When movies were bad a decade ago, it wasn't such a serious matter; despite the greatness of some films, movies in general weren't expected to be more than casual, light entertainment. You weren't expected to get your ideas of artistic possibilities from movies. I remember seeing "To Have and Have Not" the night it opened, in 1944, and I remember how everyone loved it, but if anyone I knew had said that it was a masterpiece comparable to the greatest works of literature or drama, he would have been laughed at as a fool who obviously didn't know literature or drama. Now, by and large, even the college-educated moviegoer isn't expected to, and the media constantly apply superlatives to works that lack even the spirit and energy of a "To Have and Have Not."

What must it be like for those who know and love only movies, and not literature as well? Even if they don't consciously miss it, surely the loss of the imaginative ranging over experience is irreparable.

There's been almost no fight for it. Fiction has been abandoned casually and quickly. There haven't even been journalists to defend it. On TV talk shows, the hosts have generally given up even the pretense of having read the books that are being plugged. There are several cooking celebrities on TV but no TV personality who discusses books. If you ask college students to name half a dozen movie critics, they have no trouble supplying names. If you ask them to name three book critics, they flounder, and finally one of them may triumphantly recall the name of a critic who abandoned regular reviewing before they were born.

If a movie is a bowdlerization of a book and the movie's director is acclaimed for his artistry, surely something has gone askew. In some cases, directors add virtually nothing, and diminish and cheapen what was in the original, and yet the fraction of the original they manage to reproduce is sufficient to make their reputations.

Film theorists often say that film art is, "by its nature," closest to painting and music, but all these years movie companies haven't been buying paintings and symphonies to adapt, they've been buying plays and novels. And although the movies based on those plays and novels have visual and rhythmic qualities, their basic material has nevertheless come from the theater and from books.

When a movie based on a book goes wrong but one isn't sure exactly how or why, one of the best ways to find out is to go to the book. The changes that have been made in the course of the adaptation frequently upset the structure, the characterizations, and the theme itself.

Generally speaking, when people become angry if you refer to the original novel or play while you're discussing a movie, it means they haven't read it. Twenty years ago, they hadn't always, either, but they didn't feel they didn't need to. McLuhanism and the media have broken the back of the book business; they've freed people from the shame of not reading. They've rationalized becoming stupid and watching television.

And television has become the principal advertising medium for movies. Even the few talk shows that held out against the show-biz personalities for a while are now loaded with movie people plugging away and often inflicting pain and embarrassment by trying to sing. Talk shows are becoming amateur hours for professionals.

Although good movies have often been made from inferior books, in the last few years I've been embarrassed to discover that even when movies have been made from books that aren't especially worth reading, the books are still often superior. That is to say, even our second- and third-string writers have more complex sensibilities than the movies that cannibalize them. A very minor novel like Ken Kolb's "Getting Straight" is a case in point. And I think reading Thomas Berger's "Little Big Man"—which is almost a major novel—is probably stronger than the movie even as a visual experience. American fiction seems to have reached a fairly high plateau at the very time when college students were deciding movies were more interesting. They didn't make that decision without encouragement from the media. Would they have made it without encouragement? I don't know. But the new dominance of Pop is the culmination of processes that have been at work in the mass media for many years. Gradually, as the things people used to fear would happen happened, ways were found to refer to the changes positively instead of negatively, and so "the herd instinct" that mass culture was expected to lead to became "the new tribalism."

If some people would rather see the movie than read the book, this may be a fact of life that we must allow for, but let's not pretend that people get the same things out of both, or that nothing is lost. The media-hype encourages the sacrifice of literature.

Movies are good at action; they're not good at reflective thought or conceptual thinking. They're good for immediate stimulus, but they're not a good means of involving people in the other arts or in learning about a subject. The film techniques themselves seem to stand in the way of the development of curiosity.

Movies don't help you to develop independence of mind. They don't give you much to mull over, and they don't give you the data you need in order to consider the issues they raise.

A young film critic recently told me that he needed to read more books than he did before he got the job—that he felt empty after seeing films daily. I don't have any doubts about movies' being a great art form, and what makes film criticism so peculiarly absorbing is observing—and becoming involved in—the ongoing battle of art and commerce. But movies alone are not enough: a steady diet of mass culture is a form of deprivation. Most movies are shaped by calculations about what will sell; the question they're asking about new projects in Hollywood is, "In what way is it like 'Love Story'?"

A teacher writes that "literate students are getting into the terms of film and the history of film in the same way that they have always got into the terms of literature, for example, and the history and evolution of that art form." If movies had become what they might be, this would make sense, but to study mass culture in the same terms as traditional art forms is to accept the shallowness of mass culture. It could mean that the schools are beginning to accept the advertisers' evaluations; the teachers don't want to be left behind, either.

The Faulkner who collaborated on the screenplay for "To Have and Have Not" is not commensurate with the Faulkner of the novels. Faulkner's work for hire is fun, but it's not his major work (though, as things are going, he and many other writers may remain known only for the hackwork they did to support the work they cared about). Yet until writers as well as directors can bring their full powers to American movies, American movies are not going to be the works of imagination and daring that the media claim they are already.

Writers who go to Hollywood still follow the classic pattern: either you get disgusted by "them" and you leave or you want the money and you become them.

Allowing for exceptions, there is still one basic difference between the traditional arts and the mass-media arts: in the traditional arts, the artist grows; in a mass medium, the artist decays profitably.

From indications in the press, the new line will be that the moviemakers have had too much freedom; the unstated corollary is that the businessmen know what's best. Moviemakers need more freedom, not less, or they'll never work through the transitional stage that American movies are in. If Hollywood tries to return to its childhood via romantic slop, movies will just get worse and worse. But if the advertisers and the media can blur the distinction between movies that are made in freedom as collaborative forms of expression and movies that are packaged, how many moviemakers will be strong enough to fight against success?

The film medium is too expensive for the kind of soft, sweet college students who want to work in it. Some of the most talented are lovely innocents; they will be the first to fall.

The great men of the screen have had to be tough; perhaps because of this, the great men of the screen have been crazy men. Jean Renoir is the only proof that it is possible to be great and sane in movies, and he hasn't worked often in recent years.

# Abraham Kaplan

## THE AESTHETICS OF
## THE POPULAR ARTS

Aesthetics is so largely occupied with the good in art that it has little to say about what is merely better or worse, and especially about what is worse. Unremitting talk about the good, however, is not only boring but usually inconsequential as well. Aesthetic theory that is preoccupied with artistic virtue is largely irrelevant both to artistic experience and to critical practice, confronted as they are with so much vice. The study of *dis*-values may have much to offer both aesthetics and criticsm for the same reasons that the physiologist looks to disease and the priest becomes learned in sin. Artistic taste and understanding might better be served by a museum of horribilia, presented as such, than by the unvarying display of perfection, whose natural habitat comes to be confined to the museum. It is from this standpoint that I invite attention to the aesthetics of the popular arts.

Most aestheticians, I think, are Platonists at least in this respect: they analyze the realm of value by looking chiefly to its ideal embodiments. Disvalues are left to implicit negation: if artistic excellence is *this,* what is not this specifies the inferior product. The vulgar and tasteless, the derivative and academic, brummagem, borax, and kitsch —such as these are left to purely tacit and inferential analysis. Are there, after all, Ideas of hair, mud, and dirt? The time will come, says Parmenides, when philosophy will not despise even the meanest things, even those of which the mention may provoke a smile.

By the popular arts I do not mean what has recently come to be known as pop art. This, like junk art and some of the theater of the absurd, is the present generation's version of dada. In some measure, no doubt, it serves as a device for enlarging the range of artistic possibilities, exploring the beauty in what is conventionally dismissed as meaningless and ugly, as well as the ugliness in what is conventionally extolled as beautiful. Basically, it is a revolt against the artistic establishment, a reaction against the oppressiveness of the academic and familiar. As such, it is derivative, as though to say, "You call *this*

THE AESTHETICS OF THE POPULAR ARTS: © 1967 by Abraham Kaplan. Reprinted by permission of The American Society for Aesthetics and the author.

junk?" If it is lacking in artistic virtue, its vice is like that of watching a voyeur—the sins of another are presupposed. It is what pop art presupposes that I am calling *popular art.*

Second, I do not mean simply *bad art,* neither the downright failures nor those that fall just short of some set of critical requirements. It is a question of *how* they fail and, even more, to what sort of success they aspire. Maxwell Anderson's verse dramas and Dali's *Last Supper* are not very good, but they are not popular art in the sense I intend it. Popular art may be bad art, but the converse is not necessarily true. It is a particular species of the unaesthetic that I want to isolate.

Similarly, I set aside what may be deprecated as merely minor art. Its products are likely to be more popular, in the straightforward sense, than those which have greatness. The *Rubaiyat* may be more widely read than *De rerum natura,* and *The Hound of the Baskervilles* more than *Crime and Punishment,* but each is excellent after its own kind. A work of minor art is not necessarily a minor work. Greatness, that is to say, is a distinctive aesthetic attribute—a matter of scope or depth and so forth; the word is not just a designation for the highest degree of artistic value. The lack of greatness may be a necessary condition for popular art, but most surely it is not a sufficient condition.

Neither is popular art to be confused with folk art, though it is by no means always easy to differentiate them in specific cases. Folk art is popular in the special sense of being produced by "the people"—that is to say, anonymously, without self-consciousness, and not in an explicitly aesthetic context. Yet this is, strictly speaking, a matter of accident rather than essence. What is involved is again a distinctive aesthetic attribute, which need not be produced only in that way. Some folk art has been created deliberately to be just that, and by identifiable and even contemporary artists—Carl Sandburg, Stephen Vincent Benét, and many others in other media. *The Song of Songs,* Byzantine icons, and perhaps Gothic cathedrals are products of folk art, but none of them is in the least representative of what I intend by the popular arts.

We come closer with the category of mass art, what is mass-produced or reproduced, and is responded to by vast numbers of people. Yet here, too, qualifications must be made. The specification of origin and destination does not of itself determine just what it is that is being produced and responded to. There is no fixed a priori relation between quantity and quality, and especially not between quantity and certain specific qualities as distinguished from worth in general. Vulgarity after all, in spite of its etymology, is not *constituted* by being popular. Spinoza's dictum that all things excellent are as difficult as they are rare has much merit, but it is the difficulty that I want to track down; rarity may be the mark of what is difficult, but it is not, surely, the substance of the difficulty.

The *kind* of taste that the popular arts satisfy, and not how widespread that taste is, is what distinguishes them. On this basis, I provisionally identify my subject as *midbrow art,* to be contrasted with what appeals to either highbrow or lowbrow tastes. Popular art is what is found neither in the literary reviews nor in the pulp magazines, but in the slicks; neither in gallery paintings nor on calendars, but on Christmas cards and billboards; neither in serious music nor in jazz, but in Tin Pan Alley. The popular arts may very well appeal to a mass audience, but they have characteristics that distinguish them from other varieties of mass art, and distinctive contexts and patterns of presentation. A work of popular art may be a best seller, but it is not assigned in freshman English nor reprinted as a comic. It may win an Academy Award, but it will be shown neither at the local Art Cinema nor on the late, late show.

Many social scientists think that these symptoms—for they are no more than that—provide an etiology of the disease. Midbrow art, they say, is more properly designated *middle-class art*. It is a product of the characteristic features of modern society: capitalism, democracy, and technology. Capitalism has made art a commodity, and provided the means to satisfy the ever widening demands for the refinements of life that earlier periods reserved to a small elite. Democracy, with its apotheosis of majorities and of public opinion, has inevitably reduced the level of taste to that of the lowest common denominator. The technology of the mass media precludes the care and craftsmanship that alone can create works of art. For a time it was fashionable to lay these charges particularly at American doors, to view the popular arts as the distinctive feature of American culture; but by now, I think, most of those who take this line see popular art more generally, if not more generously, as only "the sickness of the age."

I have no doubt that a good case can be made for this point of view. The trouble with such an explanation, however, is that it explains too much, and none of it with the illumination hoped for. Sidney Morgenbesser once pointedly suggested as an examination question for a course in the history of civilization, "Name two important events since 1600 *not* connected with the rise of the middle class." To be sure, this rise is one of the most significant determinants of modern culture, its effects as far-reaching as they are profound. But what are we saying about the culture when we characterize it as middle-class? The social forms and institutions to which reference is being made provide the possibility of satisfying popular taste, and perhaps also explain why society tries to satisfy it. But they do not explain what that taste is, what interests its satisfaction serves, nor how these interests relate to those satisfied in genuinely aesthetic experience.

My thesis is this: that popular art is not the degradation of taste but its immaturity, not the product of external social forces but produced by a dynamic intrinsic to the aesthetic experience itself. Modern society, like all others, has its own style, and leaves its imprint on all it embraces. But this is only to say that our popular art is *ours,* not that it is our sole possession. Popular art is usually said to stem from about the beginning of the eighteenth century, but in its essence it is not, I think, a particularity of our time and place. It is as universal as art itself.

We might characterize popular art first, as is most often done, with respect to its *form.* Popular art is said to be simple and unsophisticated, aesthetically deficient because of its artlessness. It lacks quality because it makes no qualifications to its flat statement. Everything is straightforward, with no place for complications. And it is standardized as well as simplified: one product is much like another. It is lifeless, Bergson would say, because it is only a succession of mechanical repetitions, while what is vital in art is endlessly variable. But it is just the deadly routine that is so popular. Confronted with that, we know just where we are, know what we are being offered, and what is expected of us in return. It is less unsettling to deal with machines than with people, who have lives of their own to lead. For we can then respond with mechanical routines ourselves, and what could be simpler and more reliably satisfying?

Yet this account of the matter is itself too simple to be satisfactory. For why should simplicity be unaesthetic? Art always strips away what is unessential, and purity has always been recognized as a virtue. Put the adjective *classic* before it and simplicity becomes a term of high regard. What is simple is not therefore simple-minded. Art always concentrates, indeed it owes its force to the power of interests that have been secured against distraction and dissipation. Art, we may say, does away with unnecessary complications. We can condemn popular art for treating as expendable the *necessary* complications, but nothing has been added to our aesthetic understanding till we have been given some specification of what complexity is necessary and what is not.

There is a similar lack in the condemnation of popular art as being standardized. If the term is to have more than a persuasive definition, its meaning must be distinguished from the *stylizations* that unite the works of a particular culture, period, school, or individual artist. One Egyptian statue is much like another, after all, just as there are marked resemblances among Elizabethan tragedies or among Italian operas. Such works are not for that reason assigned the status of popular art. The standardization of popular art does not mean that forms are stylized but that they are *stereotyped*. The failing does not lie in the recurrence of the forms but in deficiencies even in the first occurrence. The characters and situations of the usual movie, words and music of popular songs, the scenes and sentiments of magazine illustrations are all very much of a piece, each after its own kind. (There was a time in my youth when every great man of history talked and looked like either George Arliss or Paul Muni.) It would be more accurate to say that the fault of these stereotypes—what makes them stereotypes—is not that each instance of the type so closely resembles all the others, but that the type as a whole so little resembles anything outside it.

The stereotype presents us with the blueprint of a form, rather than the form itself. Where the simplifications of great art show us human nature in its nakedness, the stereotypes of popular art strip away even the flesh, and the still, sad music of humanity is reduced to the rattle of dry bones. It is not simplification but schematization that is achieved; what is put before us is not the substance of the text but a reader's digest. All art selects what is significant and suppresses the trivial. But for popular art the criteria of significance are fixed by the needs of the standardization, by the editor of the digest and not by the Author of the reality to be grasped. Popular art is never a discovery, only a reaffirmation. Both producer and consumer of popular art confine themselves to what fits into their own schemes, rather than omitting only what is unnecessary to the grasp of the scheme of things. The world of popular art is bounded by the limited horizons of what we think we know already; it is two-dimensional because we are determined to view it without budging a step from where we stand.

The simplification characteristic of popular art amounts to this, that we restrict ourselves to what *already* comes within our grasp. Every stereotype is the crystallization of a prejudice—that is, a prejudgment, a reduction of the empirical to the a priori. This is reflected in the ease with which popular art lends itself to the categorization of genres; even the inanimate materials of its medium have been typecast.

Popular art is dominated throughout by the star system, not only in its actors but in all its elements, whatever the medium. Every work of art, to be sure, has its dominant elements, to which the rest are subordinate. But in popular art it is the dominant ones alone that are the objects of interest, the ground of its satisfaction. Everything else is an unnecessary complication, only blunting the point to be made. By contrast, great art is in this sense pointless; everything in it is significant, everything makes its own contribution to the aesthetic substance. The domain of popular art is, paradoxically, an aristocracy, as it were: some few elements are singled out as the carriers of whatever meaning the work has while the rest are merged into an anonymous mass. The life of the country is reduced to the mannered gestures of its king. It is this that gives the effect of simplification and standardization. The elements of the schema, of course, need not be characters in the strict sense; action, color, texture, melody, or rhythm may all be simplified and standardized in just this way.

What popular art schematizes it also abstracts from a fully aesthetic context. Such an abstraction is what we call a *formula;* in formula art the schema is called upon to do the work of the full-bodied original, as though a newspaper consisted entirely of headlines. The abstraction can always be made, as is implied in the very concept of style, and of specific stylistic traits. We can always apply formulas to art; the point is that popular art gives us the formula but nothing to apply it to. Popular art uses formulas, not for analysis but for the experience itself. Such substance as it has is only the disordered residue of other more or less aesthetic experiences, themselves well on the way towards schematization. Popular art is thus doubly derivative: art first becomes academic and then it becomes popular; as art achieves style it provides the seeds of its own destruction.

This whole line of analysis might be summarized in the statement that popular art simply lacks form—not that it is in the literal sense formless, that is, chaotic, but that form in the aesthetic sense has no useful application to it, is irrelevant to its status and function as popular art. The order exhibited by any organized whole I call *shape;* it is an attribute of the objects of popular art as of any other objects. But *form* attaches to the work of art rather than the art product, to use Dewey's terms. Form is a displacement onto the object of the structure of our experience of the object; it is this experience that is the primary locus of aesthetic quality. What we say about form refers at bottom to the pull of the perceptual and psychodynamic forces at work when the art object is experienced in an ideal context.

In denying form to popular art, I am saying that no such work of structuring is involved in it. In the usual idiom, popular art is pre-digested: whatever work needs to be done has already been done beforehand. To recognize that how much you get out of an art experience depends on how much you put into it is not moralistic but strictly aesthetic. Popular art provides no purchase for any significant effort to make it out. What it presents may arouse curiosity but it does not create suspense. Our interest is focused on outcomes (as in the well-named "whodunit"), but not on the unfolding of events. If we are caught up at all, it is only with the plot, in a generic sense in which plot applies to painting and music as well as to literature. But so long as we only want to know how it all comes out, it comes out just as it does with no effort on our part, and we have only traced a shape rather than experienced a form.

In an important respect it might be said that we have had no experience at all. I mean more than is conveyed by Dewey's insight that *an* experience is constituted by form. I mean that the interests aroused by popular art are such as to be capable of satisfaction by knowledge *about* their object rather than acquaintance with it. Or rather, acquaintance, in the colloquial sense, is all that is called for or even possible; it does not grow into intimate friendship, which presupposes that we have given something of ourselves. Direct experience is replaced by second-hand apprehension, and all we know about the object is as superficial as its hold on us. The paradigm of our enjoyment of popular art is provided by the story of the writers' club that has listed and numbered all possible jokes, which are accordingly never told but only called out by number. "And why is *he* laughing so hard?" "O, he never heard it before!"

Thus popular art may be marked by a great emphasis on its newness—it is first-run, the latest thing. Prior exposure diminishes whatever satisfactions it can provide. Alternatively, it may be endlessly repeated: familiarity gives the illusion of intimacy. Most often, popular art is characterized by a combination of novelty and repetition: the same beloved star appears in what can be described as a new role. The novelty whips up a flagging interest. At the same time the repetition minimizes the demands made on us: we can see at a glance what is going on, and we know already how it will all turn out. Curiosity is easily satisfied, but suspense may be intolerable if we must join in the work of its resoluton. Here, as Theodore Adorno has pointed out, the infantile need for protection makes itself felt; we are safe on the old, familiar ground. Popular art tosses baby in the air a very little way, and quickly catches him again.

In sum, what is unaesthetic about popular art is its formlessness.

It does not invite or even permit the sustained effort necessary to the creation of an artistic form. But it provides us with an illusion of achievement while in fact we remain passive.

More specifically, there is work undone on both perceptual and psychodynamic levels.

As to the first, aesthetic *perception* is replaced by mere *recognition*. Perceptual discrimination is cut off, as in most nonaesthetic contexts, at the point where we have seen enough to know what we are looking at. Moreover, the perception is faithful, not to the perceptual materials actually presented, but to the stereotyped expectations that are operative. In popular art, Kant's Copernican revolution reaches its furthest bounds: the object conforms wholly to the knower. And recognition means also that perception is the locus of no inherent value; it is only instrumental to making our way, and the road is laid out wide and smooth before us. We perceive popular art only so as to recognize it for what it is, and the object of perception consists of no more than its marks of recognition. This is what is conveyed by the designation *kitsch:* an object is kitsch when it bears the label *Art* (with a capital "A"), so disposed that we see and respond only to the label.

On the psychodynamic level, the aesthetic *response* is replaced by a mere *reaction*. The difference between them is this: a reaction, in the sense I intend it, is almost wholly determined by the initial stimulus, antecedently and externally fixed, while a response follows a course that is not laid out beforehand but is significantly shaped by a process of self-stimulation occurring then and there. Spontaneity and imagination come into play; in the aesthetic experience we do not simply react to signals but engage in a creative interpretation of symbols. The response to an art object shares in the work of its creation, and only thereby is a work of art produced. But in popular art everything has already been done. As Dwight Macdonald put it, the spectator's reactions are included in what is presented to him; there is nothing that calls upon him to make his own responses. Thus the background music for the popular movie signalizes the birth of love with melodious strings and the approach of death by chords on the organ; contrast these signals with the demanding substance of, say, Prokofieff's music for Eisenstein's *Alexander Nevsky*. To vary the metaphor, popular art is a dictatorship forever organizing spontaneous demonstrations and forever congratulating itself on its freedoms.

In the taste for popular art there is a marked intolerance of ambiguity. It is not just that we shrink from doing that much work—the work, that is, of creative interpretation. At bottom, aesthetic ambiguity is frightening. That is why the newest art is always either funny or infuriating: we laugh at what we cannot understand so as to discharge the tension of the fear it arouses, and what is perceived as a threat may also provoke anger. But art is always a challenge; the artist assumes responsibility only for marking out the scope of our own responsible effort. Art is a confrontation with our freedom to create, plunging us into an inchoate world with the awesome words "Let there be . . . !" forming on our own lips. Popular art is a device for remaining in the same old world and assuring ourselves that we like it, because we are afraid to change it. The paradigmatic expression of popular taste is J. Alfred Prufrock's, "Do I dare disturb the universe?" But the artist dares, and dares his audience to share his daring, and the art depends upon the disturbance.

At best, popular art replaces ambiguity by some degree of complexity. This is most clearly demonstrated by the so-called *adult Western,* which has moved beyond the infantilism of "good guys" and "bad guys," by assigning virtues and vices to both heroes and villains. But the moral qualities themselves remain unambiguous in both sign and substance. The genre, for the most part, is still far from the insight into the nature of good and evil invited, say, by Melville's Captain Ahab or, even more, by his Billy Budd. Yet, *High Noon* is undeniably a far cry from *The Lone Ranger.*

In short, popular art is simple basically in the sense of easy. It contrasts with art in the markedly lesser demands that it makes for creative endeavor on the part of its audience. An artistic form, like a life form, is a creation, and like the living thing again, one which demands a co-optive effort, in this case between artist and audience. We cannot look to popular art for a fresh vision, turn to it for new directions out of the constraints of convention. Unexplored meanings call for their own language, which must be fashioned by a community with the courage and energy of pioneers. But for a new language there must be something new to say; what the pioneer can never do without is—a frontier.

Quite another approach to the analysis of popular art is by way of feeling rather than form. Popular art may be characterized by the kinds of emotions involved in it, or by its means of evoking or expressing them.

Thus there is a common view that popular art is merely *entertainment,* in a pejorative sense. It does not instruct, does not answer to any interests other than those aroused then and there; it is just interesting in itself. Popular art offers us something with which to fill our empty lives; we turn to it always in quiet desperation. It is a specific against boredom, and is thus an inevitable concomitant of the industrial civilization that simultaneously gives us leisure and alienates us from anything that might make our leisure meaningful.

Whatever merits this view may have as sociology, as aesthetics I do not find it very helpful. That the interests satisfied by popular art are self-contained is hardly distinctive of the type. All art has inherent value, independent of its direct contributions to extra-aesthetic concerns. And all art has a certain intrinsic value, affording delight in the form and color of the aesthetic surface, independent of depth meaning. That something is entertaining, that it gives joy to the beholder without regard to more serious interests, so-called, is scarcely a reason, therefore, for refusing it artistic status. It is surely no more than snobbery or a perverted puritanism to disparage entertainment value, or to deny it to art. That art must be boring is a prejudice of popular taste; the aesthetician may have been subtly influenced by the same prejudice when he identifies popular art as entertainment. His logic might be compared to that pseudo-Kantianism which infers that we are moral only when we help those we hate, for only then can we be sure that we are actuated by duty and not by mere inclination.

In any case, the question still remains, What makes popular art entertaining? To invoke a contrast with boredom is not of much help, for that is a descriptive category, not an explanatory one; as well say that work is an antidote to laziness. Indeed, I think the claim might be more defensible that popular art, far from countering boredom, perpetuates and intensifies it.

We are entertained, in the primary sense, when we are housed and fed, and not merely amused; popular art only makes us guests in our own home. This is to say that popular art is not, as is often supposed, a *diversion,* redirecting our interests, diverting them to other and more satisfying objects of interest. It does not arouse new interests but reinforces old ones. Such satisfaction as it affords stems from the evocation in memory of past satisfactions, or even from remembered fantasies of fulfillment. What we enjoy is not the work of popular art but what it brings to mind. There is a nostalgia characteristic of the experience of popular art, not because the work as a form is familiar but because its very substance is familiarity.

The skill of the artist is not in providing an experience but in providing occasions for reliving one. The emotions that come into being are not *expressed* by his materials but are *associated* with them. They are not embodied in the object but are conveyed by it, transmitted. The object is only an intermediary between past and present; emotional investment and even attention are withdrawn from it as soon as it has delivered its message. In the experience of popular art we lose ourselves, not in a work of art but in the pools of memory stirred up. Poetry becomes a congeries of poetic symbols which now only signalize feeling, as in the lyrics of popular songs; drama presents dramatic materials but does not dramatize them—brain surgery, or landing the crippled airliner; painting becomes illustration or didactic narrative from Jean Greuze to Norman Rockwell.

Conventions are, to be sure, at work; the associations aroused are not wholly adventitious and idiosyncratic. But *convention* is one thing and *style* is another. One is extrinsic to the materials, giving them shape; the other is the very substance of their form. The difference is like that between a railroad track and a satellite's orbit: convention is laid down beforehand, guiding reactions along a fixed path, while style has no existence antecedent to and independent of the ongoing response itself. For this reason popular art so easily becomes dated, as society changes its conventional associations; seen today, *A Father's Curse* surely evokes laughter rather than pity or fear. On the other hand, a work of art may become popular as its expressive substance is replaced by associations—Whistler's *"Mother"* is a case in point.

Rather than saying, then, that popular art provides us with *substitute* gratifications, I think it would be less misleading to credit it with giving us the *same* gratifications, such as they are, all over again. It is not even quite right to say that at least a symbolic object replaces the real one—the feelings evoked by the painting are after all directed towards the viewer's mother, not Whistler's. If there is in some sense a substitution, there can be no question, at any rate, of a sublimation. There is little empirical evidence supporting the view that popular art provides catharsis, in the operational sense that exposure, say, to stories of violence makes us less violent in behavior, or that if we can look lustfully we are content with committing adultery only in our hearts. For that matter, there is even less evidence that popular art, on the contrary, *produces* corresponding behavior, as alarmist guardians of public morals so loudly proclaim. The point is that popular art leaves our feelings essentially unchanged, and therefore also leaves unchanged their relation to action. It neither transforms nor fulfills our desires but only reminds us of them. Its gratifications are those of touching an aching tooth.

Popular art wallows in emotion while art transcends it, giving us understanding and thereby mastery of our feelings. For popular art, feelings themselves are the ultimate subject matter; they are not present as a quality of the experience of something objectified, but are only stimulated by the object. The addiction to such stimuli is like the frenzied and forever frustrated pursuit of happiness by those lost souls who have never learned that happiness accrues only when the object of pursuit has its own substance. Popular art ministers to this misery, panders to it, we may say. What popular art has in common with prostitution is not that it is commercialized; art also claims its price, and the price is often a high one. The point is that here we are being offered consummations without fulfillment, invited to perform the gestures of love on condition that they remain without meaning. We are not drawn out of ourselves but are driven deeper into loneliness. The vestments of our passions are very much in evidence in popular art; what could throb more with human feeling than our soap operas and bedroom sonatas? Yet it is all "but a paltry thing, a tattered coat upon a stick"—there is no life within. Emotion is not a monopoly of popular art, as Dickens, Tschaikovsky, or Turner might testify; but these artists do not traffic in emotion. Popular art, on the contrary, deals in nothing else. That is why it is so commonly judged by its impact. To say truly that it is sensational would be high praise; what we usually get is an anaesthetic.

There is yet another reason for questioning whether popular art provides relief from boredom, bringing color into gray lives. The popular audience may be chronically bored, but this is not to say that it is without feeling. On the contrary, it is feeling above all that the audience contributes to the aesthetic situation and that the popular artist then exploits. Popular art does not supply a missing ingredient in our lives, but cooks up a savory mess from the ingredients at hand. For that matter, art is never engaged in the importation of feeling. The stuff of aesthetic experience, so far as emotions are involved in it, is universal. There is no man—this side of downright pathology, at any rate—for whom affect is a rare and strange delight, and for which he must turn to art. What *is* true is that feelings are commonly undergone without awareness, experienced without perspective, blurred both in their own detail and in the interconnections that give them significance. In a word, they are usually lacking in *depth,* whatever their intensity. Popular art is correspondingly shallow.

In a fully aesthetic experience, feeling is deepened, given new content and meaning. Till then, we did not know what it was we felt; one could say that the feeling was not truly ours. It is in this sense that art provides us with feeling: it makes us aware of something that comes to be only in the intense and structured experience of the awareness. We become selves as we come to self-consciousness, no longer unthinking creatures of feeling but men whose emotions are meaningful to us. But popular art provides no such mirror of the mind, or if we do find our feelings dimly reflected in it, we cannot pass through the looking glass to confront our hidden selves. We are caught up on the surface, and our feelings remain superficial and deficient, as unreal as their reflections. The shades with which the world of popular art is peopled seem to us substantial when we ourselves are still only fictitious characters.

Superficial, affected, spurious—this is the dictionary meaning of *sentimental*. So far as feeling goes, it is sentimentality that is most distinctive of popular art. There is a sense, I suppose, in which we could say that all feeling starts as sentiment: however deep down you go you must begin at the surface. The point is that popular art leaves our feelings as it finds them, formless and immature. The objects of sentiment are of genuine worth—cynicism has its own immaturity. But the feelings called forth spring up too quickly and easily to acquire substance and depth. They are so lightly triggered that there is no chance to build up a significant emotional discharge.

Dewey has criticized sentimentality as being disjoined from action, but it is only action within the experience itself that is relevant here. Maintaining a certain psychic distance is essential to the aesthetic attitude. In another connection William James tells of the Russian aristocrat who weeps at the tragedy on the stage while her waiting coachman is freezing to death outside the theater. What makes her tears sentimental is not that she does not hurry to his relief, but that she is incapable of more than the very beginnings of pity even at the play: her eyes are dry within. She is not experiencing a catharsis, for there is scarcely anything there to be purged. She does not participate in the action of the drama but only reacts to it, that is, reenacts feelings she has not made truly her own. The tears are real enough, but they have no reason—only a cause.

In the eighteenth century a "sentiment" meant a moralistic apothegm (as in *The School for Scandal*). The words are full of feeling, but the speaker is not. The object of the sentiment so well defines the feelings called for that the definition itself is mistaken for the feeling. The true man of sentiment is far from being a hypocrite; his feeling is sincere enough as far as it goes, but it goes nowhere. Sentimentality is a mark always of a certain deficiency of feeling; it is always just words, a promise that scarcely begins to move toward fulfillment.

Yet, paradoxically, there is also something excessive about sentimentality. Stephen Pepper has characterized it as a violation of "emotional decorum," an abandonment of proper restraint. But it is easy for us to beg the question of how much is excessive. There are no a priori limits to the intensity of feeling that art can encompass. There is boundless depth in David's cry, "O my son Absalom, my son, my son Absalom! Would I had died instead of you, O Absalom, my son, my son!" No doubt there are those who would find it excessive; undeniably it does not express an Anglo-Saxon attitude, but it is also undeniably free from sentimentality. Cultures may differ in their tolerance for sentimentality, or even proclivity towards it, but the quality itself is not wholly a cultural variable.

It is only an excess of a special kind that is in question here. We must distinguish sentimentality from sensibility, that is, a ready responsiveness to demands on our feelings. Art has no purchase at all on insensibility. Unless a man is capable of being moved, and moved deeply, in circumstances where his antecedent interests are not engaged, art has nothing for him. Of such a man we may well ask, "What's Hecuba to him or he to Hecuba, that he should weep for her?" Sensibility becomes sentimental when there is some disproportion between the response and its object, when the response is indiscriminate and uncontrolled. Emotion, Beethoven once said, is for women, and I think we all understand him; but we are to keep in mind the difference between such women as Elizabeth Bennet and her mother.

It is this difference that we want to get at. Dewey comes very near the mark, I believe, in characterizing sentimentality as "excess of receptivity without perception of meaning." It is this lack of meaning, and not intensity of feeling, that makes the receptivity excessive. Popular art is not sentimental because it evokes so much feeling, but because it calls for so much more feeling than either its artist or audience can handle. The trouble is not too much feeling but too little understanding; there is too little to be understood. The tearjerker provides an occasion for the tears it invites, but *why* we weep lies outside the occasion and beyond our perception. In art, apprehensions are enlarged; we feel in more detail and in broader perspective. It is in this sense that there is a catharsis: emotions are transcended as we move along the dimension of their meaning from a subjective state to the objective forms in which feeling has become patterned.

The sentimentalist makes himself the standard of proportionality of feeling; the only meaning that matters to him is what he has stored up within. As R. H. Blythe has beautifully said (in his treatise on *haiku,* I think), sentimentality is loving something more than God does. It is viewing things in their significance only for the viewer; his emotions are decisive, and they are their own justification.

There is a systematic rationalization of this "subjectivist madness"—romanticism. The metaphysics of romanticism first reads the ego into the cosmos, then triumphantly produces an ontological basis for its self-centeredness. To be is to be felt—by me; and my own being is defined by the depth of my feeling. Reality is perceived by the romantic only as the locus and ground of his emotional response; his sentimentality is rationalized by the defense-mechanism of projection. It is noteworthy that the style of popular art—in so far as it achieves style—tends always toward the romantic: that is the best that it can do with its sentimentality.

Here at last we may have come upon an underlying connection between popular art and the organization of modern society. The connection is not by way of democratization and the technology of mass production. It is, rather, by way of the ideological import of the bourgeois revolution, from which Huizinga, Hauser, and many others date the rise of popular art. For in this ideology, social reality is defined for each individual by himself. It is a world of his own choosing, not a feudal order externally fixed; it is constituted by free contract rather than imposed status. The sober bourgeois becomes a hero of romance, as in Shaw's *Arms and the Man.* The rationalizations of the entrepreneur are refined into the metaphysics of romanticism and vulgarized into popular art. Midbrow art may be really middle class after all.

Sentimentality, then, moves in a closed circle around the self. The emotions released by a stimulus to sentiment satisfy a proprietary interest, and one which is directed inward. The important thing is that they are *my* feelings, and what is more, feelings about *me.* The prototype of sentimentality is self-pity. Popular art provides subjects and situations that make it easy to see ourselves in its materials. We await only a signal to rush into identification. All art invites the self, but it does so in a way that draws us out of ourselves. Art enlarges and transforms the self that has been brought to the aesthetic encounter. The aesthetic experience begins with empathy: we must give ourselves to it. But in the consummation art repays our willing identification by giving us an identity. We do not see ourselves in art but truly *find* ourselves there, become what before was only a bare potentiality. Popular art accepts and discharges the obligation on our own recognizance. It takes us at face value, but leaves us to contemplate our own empty features. Narcissus, W. H. Auden conjectured, was probably a hydrocephalic idiot, who stared into the pool and concluded, "On me it looks good!" The self-centeredness of popular art is the measure of our own diminishing.

Perhaps the most common characterization of popular art is that it is *escapist*. There is no doubt that it can produce a kind of narcosis, a state of insensibility arresting thought and feeling as well as action— in a word, a trance. We do not look at popular art, we stare into it, as we would into flames or moving waters. I think it not accidental that the most popular media, movies and television, are viewed in the dark; as the nightingale trills her commercial we may well ask with Keats, Do I wake or sleep? The medium itself is such stuff as dreams are made on.

If there is any responsiveness, it is focused largely on sensory values. What we are fed is not only predigested but also attractively packaged. Technicolor and vistavision, all that Aristotle called "spectacle," make up for shortcomings in character and action. A source of delight itself is sweetness of sound, shape, and color. Indeed, this is what is popularly known as beauty, and what art recurrently has revolted against. (It is not only modern art that has cultivated the ugly, though the academy makes of the cultivation a cult.) For such beauty is indeed only skin-deep. A truly aesthetic surface does not preclude depth meanings but shows them forth, embodying them in the materials presented to sense. A face with character is not necessarily much to look at.

Popular art seeks to escape ugliness, not to transform it. There is nothing like a pretty face to help you forget your troubles, and popular art can prettify everything, even—and perhaps especially— the face of death. It provides an escape first, therefore, by shutting out the reality, glossing over it.

But popular art is said to do more; it seems to provide an escape not only *from* something but also *to* something else, shuts out the real world by opening the door to another. We do not just forget our troubles but are reminded of them to enjoy the fantasy of overcoming them. I once met a man whose occupation was driving truckloads of explosives; his recreation was reading adventure stories— *they* all end happily. Popular art is as likely to relieve anxiety as boredom.

The world of popular art is unreal not just in the sense that it consists of symbols rather than realities—"it's only a movie." Science, too, replaces things by abstract representations of them, but it is not for that reason derogated as an escape from reality. It may serve as such for some scientists: they may turn to symbols because they cannot relate happily to people and things. But what makes it science, after all, is that it is capable of bringing us back to the realities, however far from them it detours in its abstractions. Whether symbols are essentially an escape depends at bottom on what they symbolize. Popular art is unreal, not as being sign rather than substance, but because what it signifies is unreal. All art is illusion, inducing us as we experience it to take art for life. But some of it is true to life, illusory without being deceptive. Popular art is a tissue of falsehoods.

Popular art depicts the world, not as it is, nor even as it might be, but as we would have it. In that world we are neither strangers nor afraid, for it is of our own making. Everything in it is selected and placed in our interest. It is a world exhausted in a single perspective—our own—and it is peopled by cardboard figures that disappear when viewed edgewise. Art opens to us a landscape over which we may roam freely, unfolds events that can be seen through the eyes of even the least of their participants. Popular art limits our identifications, and restricts our movements. We are not to ask whether the rescued maiden can cook, nor do we see the gallant knight through the eyes of the dragon, who is after all only wondering where his next meal will come from. In real drama, said Friedrich Hebbel, all the characters must be in the right. That is how God sees them, which is to say, how they are. Art, like science, raises us up to divine objectivity; popular art is all too human.

Hebbel's own work has been characterized as "a raw facing of unvarnished things." In popular art all things are varnished—glossy and slick. They must be beautified and their defects polished, lest they evoke a disturbing pity and fear rather than a soothing sentimentality. In the romanticist perversion of Kant the object is not apprehended till it has been transformed, not by the categories of understanding but by the stereotypes of feeling. Where art presents to immediate experience the values in facts, popular art only gives assurance that the facts support our prejudged values. Don Quixote sees himself as a victim of enchantment, but when he is brought home caged as a madman it is our own sanity that we reassess. The triumph of art is to make of the barber's basin a shining helmet after all, but the triumph is in the achievement, not the presupposition.

It must be admitted that popular art is more sophisticated today than it was a generation or so ago. But often its realism is only another romantic pose. Psychiatrists speak of a comparable "flight into health": the neurosis protects itself by hiding behind the symptoms of rationality. In popular art, it is a matter of taking over the shapes of realism but not the forms. Melodrama is converted to tragedy by the simple expedient of having the principals die at the end, and by choosing repugnant subjects—drug addiction, sadism, psychosis. And the modern hero of popular art is given a generous admixture of human failings; but no one is really fooled—he is only superman in disguise. Indeed, the disguise is so transparent that it can be discarded: we have come full circle from Nick Carter through Sam Spade to James Bond.

Yet, is not all art fantasy, not the symbolic replication of reality but the fulfillment of a wish? To be sure! But what is wish-fulfilling is the art itself, and not the world it depicts. Who would wish to endure the events of a Greek tragedy, walk the agonized gardens of El Greco, or embrace Picasso's ladies of Avignon? There is an art of the ideal, but the world that art depicts is by no means always idealized. Aesthetic pleasure does not demand that the real world be replaced by an ideal one but that the reality be transformed: it is in the form that we find fulfillment. The subject matter must be satisfying in itself only when there has been no transformation of represented subject to expressive substance.

For this reason popular art could as well be said to suffer from too little fantasy as too much: it does not do enough with its materials. Its imagination is reproductive rather than creative. When it comes to breaking out of the constraints of reality, what better examples are there than *Midsummer Night's Dream* and *The Tempest,* the paintings of Hieronymous Bosch, or the sculpture of the Hindu pantheon? But popular art is so bound to reality it gives us nowhere to escape *to,* save deeper within a self that is already painfully constricted. The eighteenth century usefully distinguished between fancy and imagination, according to whether fantasy has worked far enough to confer reality on its own products. Popular art is all fancy. If it sees the world as a prison, it contents itself with painting on the walls an open door. The mind of popular art is its own place, and in itself makes a heaven of hell; but this is Satan speaking, living out his damnation. If popular art gives us dominion, we are thereby condemned to live in the unimaginative worlds of our own creation.

Though all art is fantasy, there is a mature as well as an infantile process. Art looks out on the world with the delight and wonder of a child, but the regression, as Ernst Kris has put it, is in the service of the ego, not the id. Reality is transformed only the better to lay hold on it, just as in the working of the scientific imagination. We do not escape from the reality but from the constrictions of our unimaginative experience of it. Art may be produced for children—Lewis Carroll and Robert Louis Stevenson—or with a childlike quality—Paul Klee and Joan Miro—but it is not therefore childish. It is this childishness, however, that characterizes popular art: the fairy tale is retold for adult consumption, but stripped of just those qualities of creative imagination in which lies the artistry of the original.

In mature fantasy both the reality principle and the pleasure principle are at work. Popular art is concerned only with the pleasure, and for just this reason it can provide only immature satisfactions. Where art makes manifest such significance in the reality as gives pleasure in its apprehension, popular art gives pleasure only in encouraging the pretence that we have been pleased. The circle is closed within: we ourselves have the desires and we ourselves satisfy them. The difference is that between masturbation and a mature love that reaches outside the self. In responding to popular art we do not escape from reality—we have not yet attained to the reality. Beneath the pleasure in popular art is the pathos of the note lying outside the orphanage wall: "Whoever finds this, I love you!"

What popular art does, Ernest Vandenhaag points out, is to blur the line between fantasy and reality. It is not a question of escaping, for we do not even know where we are. Plato's attack on all art has unmistakable force when applied to popular art—*that* is a dream within a dream. The aesthetic experience calls for—and contributes to—a certain maturity, a capacity for enough distance to give perspective, and enough wisdom to see oneself in perspective. It is only in such objectification that both self and world attain reality. The magic of art may have its genesis in infantile delusions of omnipotence, but these delusions persist just in so far as self and world, fantasy and reality, remain undifferentiated. Art does not feed the delusion that we can do anything, but on the contrary shows forth the limits of our powers. The magic is that we transcend those limits in our aesthetically structured awareness of them. Popular art is escapist only in so far as it turns its back on a world it has never known.

Now, what are the social functions of popular art? What, after all, makes popular art so popular? The usual reply follows the account that conceives of popular art in terms of distinctive features of modern society. The major premise is the alienation and deracination of modern man; the minor premise is that popular art serves to counter these forces, providing a basis for at least an ersatz community. Popular art reaches out to the lowest common denominator of society; it provides the touch of nature that makes all men kin, or, at least, all men who share the conventions of a common culture.

Unfortunately, empirical data to support this conclusion are lacking; on the contrary, such evidence as we have tends to refute it. Popular art does *not,* as is so commonly supposed, leave out whatever might offend anyone. Its mass appeal seems to derive from "a distinctive 'majority taste' rather than widespread satisfaction of a polyglot of tastes." Popular art does not answer to the mean of our tastes but to the mode, in the sense both of statistics and of fashion. It is art that might better be said to appeal to a common denominator; this is what we call the universality of art. If the appeal is not universally responded to, it is because the art is not understood, and because we do not understand ourselves well enough to know what is in us.

In so far as the function of popular art today is to be explained in terms of social conditions rather than psychic processes, the situation seems to me to be the reverse of what the previous account relies on. It is not man who is alienated and uprooted, but art. In our time art has become increasingly dissociated from the cultural concerns with which it has been so intimately involved throughout most of its history—religion, love, war, politics, and the struggle for subsistence. Art today is, in Dewey's brilliant phrase, "the beauty-parlor of civilization." Popular art at least pretends to a social relevance, and is not only willing but eager to find a place for itself outside the museum.

But I hope that nothing I have said is heard as a cry of despair over the decadence of the times. On the contrary, I believe that popular art today is neither worse nor more common than it always has been. There is a wider audience today for art of every kind: the mass of the Athenian population were slaves, and not much more than that in Renaissance Italy or Elizabethan England. There may be more poor stuff produced today because there are more people to consume it, but this is even more true, proportionately, for the superior product. Nor do I sympathize with the view that ours is an age of barbarism to be defined, according to Ortega y Gasset, as "the absence of standards to which appeal can be made." What is absent, to my mind, is only a cultural elite that sets forth and enforces the standards; and I say, so much the better! It is ironic that popular art is taken as a sign of barbarism; every real development in the history of art, and not only the modern movement, was first greeted as a repudiation of aesthetic standards. My objection to popular art is just the contrary, that it is too rigidly bound to the standards of the academy. Kitsch is the homage paid by popular art to those standards: Oscar and Emmy are avatars of the muse.

Art is too often talked about with a breathless solemnity, and viewed with a kind of religious awe; if high art needs its high priests, I hope that aesthetics will leave that office to the critics. To put it plainly, there is much snobbery in the aesthetic domain, and especially in the contempt for popular art on no other basis than its popularity. We speak of popular art in terms of its media (paperbacks, movies, television) as though to say, "Can any good come out of Nazareth?"; or else by the popular genres (western, mystery, love story, science fiction) as though they can be condemned wholesale. For audiences, art is more of a status symbol than ever; its appearance in the mass media is marked by a flourish of trumpets, as befits its status; the sponsor may even go so far as to omit his commercials. I am saying that even where popular art vulgarizes yesterday's art, it might anticipate tomorrow's—baroque once meant something like kitsch. I am willing to prophesy that even television has art in its future.

But if not, what then? Aesthetic judgment is one thing and personal taste another. The values of art, like all else aesthetic, can only be analyzed contextually. There is a time and a place even for popular art. Champagne and Napoleon brandy are admittedly the best of beverages; but on a Sunday afternoon in the ballpark we want a coke, or maybe a glass of beer. "Even if we have all the virtues," Zarathustra reminds us, "there is still one thing needful: to send the virtues themselves to sleep at the right time." If popular art gives us pleasant dreams, we can only be grateful—when we have wakened.

# BIOGRAPHICAL NOTES

*Francis Bacon* (1561–1626), English statesman and writer, was the author of many philosophical, literary, and legal works. Of these the best known are *The Advancement of Learning* (1605), the *Novum Organum* (1620), and the *New Atlantis* (1627). Perhaps the most popular of his works were his *Essays* (1597, 1612, 1625), from which "Of Studies" is taken.

*Russell Baker* (b. 1925) was seven years with the Baltimore *Sun* and eight years with the Washington bureau of the New York *Times*. Since 1962 he has been a columnist and editorial writer for the New York *Times*. Among his writings are *An American in Washington* (1961), *No Cause for Panic* (1964), and *All Things Considered* (1965).

*James Baldwin* (b. 1924), American novelist and essayist, has written four novels: *Go Tell It on the Mountain* (1953), *Giovanni's Room* (1956), *Another Country* (1961), and *Tell Me How Long the Train's Been Gone* (1968). As an essayist, he has been a brilliant and effective spokesman for American Negroes; his essays are collected in three volumes: *Notes of a Native Son* (1955), *Nobody Knows My Name: More Notes of a Native Son* (1961), and *The Fire Next Time* (1963).

*Daniel Bell* (b. 1919) is a professor of sociology at Harvard and a Research Associate to the Program on Technology and Society. He has been an editor of *Common Sense, The New Leader,* and *Fortune.* He is the author of *The End of Ideology* (1959) and editor of *The Radical Right* (1963).

*David Bronsen* (b. 1926), who took degrees at the University of Paris and the University of Vienna, is a professor of German at Washington University in St. Louis, Missouri. His interests in German baroque literature, twentieth-century German literature, and humanism and reformation have frequently been turned into articles for German quarterlies.

*Willa Cather* (1873–1947), American novelist and short-story writer, made her first impression on the literary world with *O Pioneers!* (1913). Among her subsequent works were *The Song of the Lark* (1915), *My Ántonia* (1918), *The Professor's House* (1925), *Death Comes for the*

*Archbishop* (1927), and *Shadows on the Rock* (1931). Few Americans have written so well about pioneers in Nebraska and the Southwest.

*John Ciardi* (b. 1916), American poet, educator, editor, and critic, has published a number of volumes of poetry, including *Homeward to America* (1940), and has received many honors for his work. He taught at Harvard and Rutgers and has been staff lecturer in poetry and director of the Bread Loaf Writers' Conference. Ciardi edited *Mid-Century American Poets* (1950) and is now poetry editor for the *Saturday Review*. The first two volumes of his translation of Dante's *Divine Comedy* appeared in 1954 and 1961.

*Benjamin DeMott* (b. 1924), a professor at Amherst College, has been a visiting professor of humanities at Massachusetts Institute of Technology. He was awarded a Guggenheim fellowship in 1963. Among Professor DeMott's writings are *The Body's Cage* (a novel, 1959), *Hells and Benefits* (essays, 1962), and *Surviving the Seventies* (1971).

*Thomas De Quincey* (1785–1859), English writer and critic, is best known for *Confessions of an English Opium-Eater* (1822) and for essays on the work of such writers as Wordsworth, Coleridge, Lamb, Shakespeare, and Pope.

*Alan Devoe* (1909–1955), American naturalist and writer, for years was the author of the monthly department "Down to Earth" in the *American Mercury*. He was an associate editor of the *Writer* and a contributing editor of *Audubon Magazine*. He wrote many articles and several books on nature, including *Lives Around Us* (1942) and *This Fascinating Animal World* (1951).

*Joan Didion* (b. 1934), journalist and novelist, has been editor of *Vogue*, a contributing editor of the *National Review*, and the writer of articles and features for *Mademoiselle* and other magazines. Her books include *Run River* (1963) and *Slouching Towards Bethlehem* (1968).

*Paul R. Ehrlich* (b. 1932) is a professor in the department of biological sciences at Stanford University. A leading authority in the field of ecology, he is especially interested in population biology. The essay reprinted here particularly expresses his interest. Among his recent books is *The Population Bomb* (1968).

*Loren Eiseley* (b. 1907) is University Professor of Anthropology and History of Science in the Graduate School of Arts and Sciences of the University of Pennsylvania. He has been a prolific contributor to scientific journals and national magazines, and his books include *The Immense Journey* (1957), *Darwin's Century* (1958), *The Mind as Nature* (1962), and *The Night Country* (1971). He has received many honors and awards, including a Guggenheim fellowship (1964–65) and more than ten honorary degrees from American universities.

*Ralph Ellison* (b. 1914) achieved fame in 1952 with the publication of *Invisible Man*, winner of a National Book Award. He also edited *Negro Quarterly* and participated in the Federal Writers Project. He has lectured and taught at a number of institutions, including the Salzburg Seminar in Austria, Bard College, where he was an instructor in Russian and American literature from 1958 to 1961, and Yale, where he was Visiting Fellow in American Studies in 1964. *Shadow and Act*, a collection of his essays, appeared in 1964.

*William Faulkner* (1897–1962), one of America's Nobel Prize winners in literature, is internationally known for such novels as *The Sound and the Fury* (1929), *Light in August* (1932), and *A Fable* (1954). Shortly before his death he published *The Reivers*, another novel about the people of his imaginary Southern locale, Yoknapatawpha County. Recognition of his stature came slowly, but Faulkner's artistic reputation is now firmly established.

*F. Scott Fitzgerald* (1896–1940) published his first novel, *This Side of Paradise* (1920), and immediately became one of the most popular and successful writers of the "jazz age." His second novel, *The Beautiful and the Damned* (1922), and his finest work, *The Great Gatsby* (1925), established his reputation. Although he suffered both personal and professional reverses during the last years of his life, his *Tender Is the Night* (1934) and *The Last Tycoon* (an unfinished novel published posthumously in 1941) were impressive.

*Edward Morgan Forster* (1879–1970), English novelist and lecturer, was perhaps best known for his novels *Howards End* (1910) and *A Passage to India* (1924) and for his lectures in criticism, *Aspects of the Novel* (1927). Many of his essays were reprinted in *Abinger Harvest* (1936) and *Two Cheers for Democracy* (1951). He also collaborated on the libretto for Benjamin Britten's opera *Billy Budd*. His novel *Maurice* was published posthumously in 1971.

*Herbert Gold* (b. 1924), American essayist and novelist, has taught literature at four major universities. Among his novels are *Birth of a Hero* (1951), *The Man Who Was Not with It* (1956), and *Therefore Be Bold* (1961). Many of his essays, including the one reprinted in this book, deal with the insensitivity and alienation of men in modern society.

*John Burdon Saunderson Haldane* (1892–1964), English man of science, wrote such works as *Animal Biology* (1927, with Julian Huxley), *The Biochemistry of Genetics* (1954, based on lectures given at University College, London), and *Adventures of a Biologist* (1940, published in England under the title *Keeping Cool and Other Essays*).

*Ernest Hemingway* (1899–1961), one of America's Nobel Prize winners in literature, was one of the world's renowned stylistic innovators. His early novels—*The Sun Also Rises* (1926) and *A Farewell to Arms* (1929) —were followed by what was perhaps his most popular novel, *For Whom the Bell Tolls* (1940). *A Moveable Feast* (1964), from which "Scott Fitzgerald" is reprinted, contains Hemingway's recollections of Paris in the 1920s. *Islands in the Stream* was posthumously published in 1970.

*Hermann Hesse* (1877–1962), German novelist and poet, lived most of his life in Switzerland. Best known in America for novels like *Demian* (1919), *Steppenwolf* (1927), and *Magister Ludi* (translated 1949), Hesse was awarded the Goethe prize in 1946 and the Nobel Prize in 1947. Much of his writing was concerned with the struggle against loneliness and alienation in twentieth-century society.

*Thomas Hobbes* (1588–1679), English philosopher, lived through the most turbulent years of the seventeenth century in England, and during his long life he knew Francis Bacon, Ben Jonson, Galileo, and Descartes. His greatest work was *The Leviathan* (1651), a treatise on political economy, from which a short selection is reprinted here.

*Eric Hoffer* (b. 1902), a laborer and a longshoreman in San Francisco, educated himself by wide reading. For *The True Believer* (1951) he received the Commonwealth Club of California Gold Medal. He later wrote *The Passionate State of Mind* (1955), *The Ordeal of Change* (1963), and *First Things, Last Things* (1971).

*Julian Huxley* (b. 1887), English biologist and writer, has served as professor of zoology and as honorary lecturer at King's College, University of London. He was knighted for his services to science and to the British government and was director general of UNESCO from 1947 to 1948. His publications include articles, reports, books, television programs, film commentaries, and lectures. Two of his recent books are *Essays of a Humanist* (1964) and *The Human Crisis* (1964). He has been biology editor of the *Encyclopædia Britannica*.

*Thomas Henry Huxley* (1825–1895), English biologist and writer, became famous by 1850 through the publication of his scientific papers. His crowning honor came in 1883 with his election to the presidency of the Royal Society. Among his many published volumes are *On the Origin of Species* (1863), *Lay Sermons* (1870), *American Addresses* (1877), and *Evolution and Ethics* (1893).

*Henry James* (1843–1916), novelist and critic, was born in New York City but lived most of his life in England and became a British subject in 1915. *The Spoils of Poynton,* one of his many novels analyzing American, British, and Continental character, was published in 1897. The preface was written later for the New York Edition of the novel (1908). Among James' best-known novels are *The American* (1877), *Portrait of a Lady* (1881), *The Wings of the Dove* (1902), and *The Ambassadors* (1903). His elder brother was the philosopher and psychologist William James.

*Randall Jarrell* (1914–1965), American poet, critic, and teacher, taught at Kenyon, the University of Texas, Sarah Lawrence, and the Women's College of the University of North Carolina. He published many volumes of poetry, including *Selected Poems* (1955). He also published a volume of criticism, *Poetry and the Age* (1953), and a novel, *Pictures from an Institution* (1954).

*Pauline Kael* (b. 1919), appointed a Guggenheim fellow in 1964, is one of America's most prominent movie critics. She served as movie critic for *The New Republic* in 1966–67, and since that time she has been the movie critic for *The New Yorker*. Her books include *I Lost It at the Movies* (1965) and *Kiss Kiss Bang Bang* (1968).

*Abraham Kaplan* (b. 1918), a Russian-born philosopher, teaches at the University of Michigan. He is co-author of *Power and Society* (1950) and author of *The New World of Philosophy* (1961) and *The Conduct of Inquiry: Methodology for Behavioral Science* (1964). Professor Kaplan uses his wide knowledge of philosophy to look at the "disvalues" in art. He was appointed a Guggenheim fellow in 1945.

*Alfred Kazin* (b. 1915) is the author of *On Native Grounds* (1942), a critical survey of American literature; *A Walker in the City* (1951), a sensitive and evocative reminiscence of his New York childhood; and *The Inmost Leaf* (1955), a collection of essays. More recently he has published *Contemporaries* (1962) and *Starting Out in the Thirties* (1965). He is also the editor of several books, including *The Portable William Blake* (1946), and is a contributor to a number of periodicals.

*Yrjö Kokko* (b. 1903) is a distinguished Finnish writer whose book *The Way of the Four Winds* received the Grand Literary Prize of the Finnish State and has been widely acclaimed throughout Scandinavia. In the opinion of Peter Freuchen, Danish writer and explorer, the book has already become a classic.

*Louis Kronenberger* (b. 1904), American novelist and critic, has been an editor of *Time* and *Fortune*. He has lectured at Oxford, and he has held professorships at Columbia and at Brandeis, where he is professor of theater arts. Among his many books are *Kings and Desperate Men* (1941) and *A Month of Sundays* (1961); he recently published (with W. H. Auden) *A Book of Aphorisms*.

*David Herbert Lawrence* (1885–1930), British novelist, poet, essayist, and playwright, is perhaps best known for his novels *Sons and Lovers* (1913), *The Plumed Serpent* (1926), and *Lady Chatterley's Lover* (1928). A collected edition of his poems was published in 1928. One of Lawrence's major themes, the relationships between the sexes, appears in the present essay.

*Harry Levin* (b. 1912) is Irving Babbitt Professor of Comparative Literature at Harvard. Some of his interpretations of literature appear in *James Joyce: A Critical Introduction* (1941), *Symbolism and Fiction* (1956), *The Question of Hamlet* (1959), and *The Gates of Horn: A Study of Five French Realists* (1963). In 1962 he received an LL.D. from St. Andrews University, Scotland.

*Mary McCarthy* (b. 1912), novelist, short-story writer, and critic, was graduated from Vassar in 1933 and became a book reviewer for *Nation* and *The New Republic* and a drama critic for the *Partisan Review*. She later taught at Bard and Sarah Lawrence. Among her novels are *The Company She Keeps* (1942), *The Groves of Academe* (1952), *A Charmed Life* (1955), *The Group* (1963), and *Birds of America* (1971). Two of her other books are brilliant descriptions of cities: *Venice Observed* (1956) and *The Stones of Florence* (1959). A collection of her articles, *On the Contrary*, was published in 1961.

*Norman Mailer* (b. 1923), American novelist and journalist, is the author of many books of fiction, essays, poetry, and social comment. Among his best-known novels are *The Naked and the Dead* (1948), *The Deer Park* (1955), and *An American Dream* (1965). He has contributed to a variety of newspapers and periodicals, and among his books of contemporary social history are *Armies of the Night* (1968), *Miami and the Siege of Chicago* (1968), and *Of a Fire on the Moon* (1970), here excerpted.

*John Stuart Mill* (1806–1873), English philosopher and political economist, was the author of *A System of Logic* (1843), *Principles of Political Economy* (1848), and an essay, *On Liberty* (1859). A portion of the introduction to *On Liberty* is reprinted here.

*Arthur Miller* (b. 1915), now an internationally known American dramatist, achieved his first success in 1945 with *Focus*, a novel. But it is such plays as *All My Sons*, *The Crucible*, and especially *Death of a Salesman*, the Pulitzer Prize play for 1949, which have established him as a major writer. His more recent plays include *After the Fall* (1963) and *Incident at Vichy* (1964).

*Lawrence E. Mintz* is completing his doctoral work in American Studies at Michigan State University. He has been a Woodrow Wilson fellow.

*Robert A. Nisbet* (b. 1913), trained as a sociologist, became interested in the status and future of higher education in America. From 1950 to 1963 he was Dean of Arts and Sciences and Vice Chancellor of the University of California, Riverside. In 1963 he was appointed a Guggenheim fellow. Professor Nisbet's books include *The Quest for Community* (1953), *The Sociological Tradition* (1966), *Social Change and History* (1969), and *The Social Bond* (1970).

*David J. O'Brien* (b. 1938), who has been a professor of history at Loyola College (Quebec) and Holy Cross College in Massachusetts, is particularly interested in American Catholic intellectual and ecclesiastical history and in American and European church history. Much of his writing has been concerned with the American Catholic and social reform and organized labor.

*George Orwell* is the pseudonym of Eric Blair (1903–1950), British novelist and essayist who served with the Indian Imperial Police in Burma from 1922 to 1927. His best-known books are his satirical fantasies *Animal Farm* (1945) and *Nineteen Eighty-Four* (1949).

*Walter Pater* (1839–1894), British writer and critic of art and literature, achieved a great reputation with the publication of *Studies in the History of the Renaissance* (1873). He withheld the conclusion from publication in the first edition because he feared it might be misinterpreted as advocacy of license and hedonism. Other works by Pater include *Marius the Epicurean* (1885) and *Appreciations* (1889).

*Maxwell Perkins* (1884–1947), American editor and publisher, began his career in 1907 as a reporter for the New York *Times*. In 1910 he joined the publishing firm of Charles Scribner's Sons, where he remained until his death. Through helping young American novelists, Perkins became one of the twentieth century's most famous editors; his book *Editor to Author* (1960), a collection of letters selected and edited with commentary and an introduction by John Hall Wheelock, gives a remarkable insight into editor-author relationships.

*Alexander Petrunkevitch* (1875–1964), a Russian-born geologist, taught at both Harvard and Yale and served as a visiting professor at the University of Indiana and the University of Puerto Rico. He was one of the world's authorities on spiders, his first important book, *Index Catalogue of Spiders of North, Central, and South America,* having been published in 1911. He has also translated English poetry into Russian and Russian poetry into English.

*Norman Podhoretz* (b. 1930) graduated from Columbia and took further degrees from the Jewish Theological Seminary and Cambridge. In addition to being the editor of *Commentary,* he contributes to many periodicals and has published *Doings and Undoings: The 50's and After in American Writing* (1964) and *Making It* (1967).

*Richard Poirier* (b. 1925), a Ph.D. from Harvard and a professor of English at the State University, New Brunswick, N.J., has written on Henry James, has contributed to a collection of criticism on William Faulkner, and is the author of *The Performing Self* (1971). His avocational interests are American painting, travel, films, and food.

*James Harvey Robinson* (1863–1936), American historian and university professor, received his Ph.D. in 1890 from the University of Freiburg for a thesis on "The Original and Derived Features of the Constitution of the United States." Subsequently he published such works as *Introduction to the History of Western Europe* (1903) and *The Mind in the Making* (1921); in 1919–21 he helped found the New School for Social Research in New York City.

*Peter Schrag* (b. 1931) has been a contributor to many national magazines including *The New Republic, Commonweal, Progressive,* and the *College Board Review.* He has been both a writer and editor for *Saturday Review.* His books include *Voices in the Classroom* (1965) and (as editor) *The European Mind and the Discovery of a New World* (1965).

*Eric Sevareid* (b. 1912) is a well-known television correspondent and commentator. He is also an author, and his published work includes *Not So Wild a Dream* (1946), *Small Sounds in the Night* (1956), and *This Is Eric Sevareid* (1964).

*Grahame J. C. Smith* (b. 1942), an ecologist who teaches at Brown University in the Division of Biomedical Science, is interested in the behavior of insect parasitoids on different host species.

*Jonathan Swift* (1667–1745), Irish-born satirist and poet, was the author of *The Battle of the Books* (1704), *The Tale of a Tub* (1704), and *Gulliver's Travels* (1726). His "Modest Proposal," which is reprinted here, was one of a number of pamphlets he wrote to protest England's treatment of Ireland.

*Dylan Thomas* (1914–1953), born in South Wales, was a newspaper reporter, a documentary-film script writer, and a novelist; but above all he was a lyric poet, considered by many to be the greatest of his generation. His early death brought to an end a distinguished and colorful career. *Collected Poems* (1953), *Adventures in the Skin Trade* (1955, a fragment of a novel), and *Under Milk Wood* (a play for voices) are among his best-known works.

*Henry David Thoreau* (1817–1862), American author and naturalist, is best known for *Walden; or, Life in the Woods* (1854), his record of his sojourn alone in a small hut on the shore of Walden Pond. An independent individualist, he expressed in *Walden* much of the philosophy more explicitly stated in his famous essay *On the Duty of Civil Disobedience* (1849).

*Calvin Trillin* (b. 1935), a frequent contributor to *The New Yorker,* is known for his book *An Education in Georgia: The Integration of Charlayne Hunter and Hamilton Holmes* (1964), the first twelve chapters of which were published in *The New Yorker.* The book brings into focus a "confused story of Civil Rights."

*Diana Trilling* (b. 1905) is the author of *Claremont Essays* (1964) and many other essays and articles on literary, political, and social subjects. She edited *The Portable D. H. Lawrence* (1947) and *Selected Letters of D. H. Lawrence* (1958) and was the recipient of a Guggenheim fellowship.

*Lionel Trilling* (b. 1905), George Edward Woodberry Professor of Literature and Criticism at Columbia, has also been George Eastman Visiting Professor at Oxford. Two of his best-known books are *The Middle of the Journey* (1947) and *The Liberal Imagination: Essays on Literature and Society* (1950). He has contributed to many periodicals and has served on the advisory board of *Partisan Review.*

*Mark Twain* (1835–1910), born in Florida, Missouri, and reared in Hannibal, became a printer, a steamboat pilot, a novelist, and a journalist. The pseudonym Mark Twain (his name was Samuel Langhorne Clemens) was adopted in 1862. The best-known of his American classics is *The Adventures of Huckleberry Finn* (1884).

*Kurt Vonnegut, Jr.* (b. 1922), is a novelist, short-story writer, and dramatist who has written for many popular magazines as well as for television and the off-Broadway stage. Long a writer of science fiction, Vonnegut achieved both critical acclaim and widespread popularity with the publication of *Cat's Cradle* (1963) and *God Bless You, Mr. Rosewater* (1965). With *Slaughterhouse-Five* (1969) he became what some critics have called a "cult hero."

*George Wald* (b. 1906) is a professor of biology at Harvard University. His brilliant research in biochemistry and physiology of vision has been reported in many scientific journals, and he has been honored by a Nobel Prize for medicine (1967) as well as by many honorary degrees from European and American universities. He is the co-author of *General Education in a Free Society* (1962).

*Robert Warshow* (1917–1955), American writer and critic, contributed articles to many periodicals, including *Commentary,* of which he was an editor for nine years. Before his untimely death he had already won widespread recognition for his original criticism of literature and films and for his mastery of prose style.

*William Carlos Williams* (1883–1963), an outstanding writer and famous physician, was one of America's half dozen great poets of the twentieth century. In addition to spending a lifetime as a pediatrician, he wrote poetry, essays, novels, and an autobiography. Among his many awards were the National Book Award, Bollinger Prize, Levinson Prize, and Pulitzer Prize. He is probably best remembered for his long poem *Paterson.*

# AUTHOR–TITLE INDEX

D 4 5
E 6
F 7
G 8
H 9
I 0
J 1